Modern Philosophy

Modern Philosophy

This is a remix by Marcus Adams and is based on the work of Walter Ott and Alex Dunn

WALTER OTT AND ALEX DUNN AND MARCUS ADAMS

This book was produced using Pressbooks.com, and PDF rendering was done by PrinceXML.

Cover image by Andy Feliciotti. Located at https://unsplash.com/photos/m3oLLB7w3Xg.

Published by SUNY OER Services
Milne Library
State University of New York at Geneseo
Geneseo, NY 14454

Distributed by State University of New York Press

ISBN: 978-1-64176-041-6

Contents

1. Preface

This book combines readings from primary sources with two pedagogical tools. Paragraphs in italics introduce figures and texts, or draw connections among the readings. Numbered study questions sometimes ask you to reconstruct an argument from the text, using numbered premises. Some of the premises or the conclusion are usually given. You might need more or fewer lines to state the argument; you might also choose to start your reconstruction with different premises than those provided. The sections added by Adams (Hobbes and Cavendish) do not yet include these pedagogical tools, but Adams plans to incorporate these in a future edition.

Only excerpts of the major works are included. Descartes's *Meditations*, Hume's *Enquiry* and Kant's *Prolegomena* are largely unabridged. Minor stylistic changes have been made to the original texts; in particular, many more paragraph breaks have been added.

The introductory chapter, (Minilogic and Glossary), is designed to introduce the basic tools of philosophy and sketch some basic principles and positions.

Authors and Acknowledgements

Modern Philosophy was created by Walter Ott. Other contributors include Antonia LoLordo and Lydia Patton.

The creation of *Modern Philosophy* was made possible by the Virginia Tech Philosophy Department and a Virginia Tech CIDER grant.

This modified version of the text was written in Markdown (with pandoc-exclusive extensions) by Alexander Dunn. Using the free utility pandoc, this version can be easily converted to HTML, PDF, EPUB, and many other formats. This version is hosted on GitHub; please copy and edit it, and feel free to submit your changes to the public repository.

The present version, which adds readings from Thomas Hobbes and Margaret Cavendish, was remixed by Marcus Adams using Pressbooks.

Sources

Unless otherwise noted, all texts are in the public domain. All other material is the author's and is licensed under the Creative Commons Attribution-NonCommercial-ShareAlike 3.0 Unported License.

1. Background
    1. Aristotle
        a. *Categories*–Translated by E.M. Edghill
        b. *Physics*–Translated by R. P. Hardie and R. K. Gaye
        c. *Posterior Analytics*–Translated by E.S. Bouchier
    2. Aquinas
        a. *On the Eternity of the World*–Translated by Robert T. Miller (copyright 1991, 1997)

  b. *Summa Contra Gentiles*–Translated by Joseph Rickaby

  c. *Summa Theologicae*–Translated by Fathers of the English Dominican Province (Part 1, Volume 1 and Volume 2, Part 2, Part 3)

2. Descartes

  1. *The Principles of Philosophy*–Translated by John Veitch

  2. *Discourse on Method*–Translated by John Veitch

  3. *Meditations on First Philosophy*–Translated by John Veitch

  4. *Objections and Replies*–Translated by Jonathan Bennett, (copyright 2010–2015)

3. Spinoza

  1. *The Ethics*–Translated by R.H.M. Elwes

4. Hobbes

  1. *Leviathan*, Chapters I-XVII (1651)

5. Cavendish

  1. *Philosophical Letters*, Section I, Letters I-XXIX (1664)

6. Locke

  1. *An Essay Concerning Human Understanding*–Second edition, 1690 (Part 1, Part 2)

7. Berkeley

  1. *A Treatise Concerning the Principles of Human Knowledge*

  2. *De Motu (On Motion)*–edited by A.C. Fraser, 1871

8. Hume

  1. *An Enquiry Concerning Human Understanding*

  2. *A Treatise of Human Nature*

9. Kant

  1. *Prolegomena to Any Future Metaphysics*–Translated by P. Carus

  2. *The Critique of Pure Reason*–Translated by J. Meiklejohn

2. René Descartes (1596–1650)

- Descartes' *Discourse on Method*, Part Five (1637)
- Descartes' *The Principles of Philosophy* (1644)
  - Part One, Section Fifty-one: What substance is, and that the term is not applicable to God and the creatures in the same sense
  - Part One, Section Fifty-two: That the term is applicable univocally to the mind and the body, and how substance itself is known
  - Part One, Section Sixty: Of distinctions; and first of the real
  - Part One, Section Sixty-one: Of the modal distinction
  - Part One, Section Sixty-two: Of the distinction of reason (conceptual distinction)
  - Part One, Section Sixty-three: How thought and extension may be distinctly known, as constituting, the one the nature of mind, the other that of body
  - Part One, Section Sixty-four: How these may likewise be distinctly conceived as modes of substance
  - Part Two, Section Four: That the nature of body consists not in weight hardness, colour and the like, but in extension alone
  - Part Two, Section Eleven: How space is not in reality different from corporeal substance
  - Part Two, Section Twelve: How space differs from body in our mode of conceiving it
  - Part Two, Section Twenty-four: What motion is, taking the term in its common use
  - Part Two, Section Twenty-five: What motion is properly so called
- Descartes' *Meditations on First Philosophy* (1641)
  - Synopsis of the Six Following Meditations
  - First Meditation: Of the Things on Which We May Doubt
  - Second Meditation: Of the Nature of the Human Mind; and that It is More Easily Known than the Body
  - Third Meditation: Of God: That He Exists
  - Fourth Meditation: Of Truth and Error
  - Fifth Meditation: Of the Essence of Material Things; and, Again, of God; That He Exists
  - Sixth Meditation: Of the Existence of Material Things, and of the Real Distinction Between the Mind and Body of Man
  - Objections and Replies to the Meditations
    - Antoine Arnauld's objection to the argument for the real distinction and Descartes's reply
    - Arnauld's circularity objection and Descartes's reply

It is important to keep in mind that Descartes's strictly philosophical works are but a tiny portion of his overall output. Desmond Clarke's insistence that Descartes was a 'practicing scientist who, somewhat unfortunately, wrote a few short and relatively unimportant philosophical essays' is a useful corrective, although it's not quite true.

One of Descartes's earliest works (1629-33) is The World (also known as the Treatise on Light). Descartes decided not to publish it in light of Galileo's run-in with the church over the Copernican hypothesis. In 1637, Descartes published the Discourse on Method, which includes a summary of parts of this early work.

Descartes published the Meditations in Latin in 1641; a French translation soon followed. Some of Descartes's friends circulated the manuscript and collected objections to the work, to which Descartes replied.

In 1644, Descartes published his Principles of Philosophy, a work he hoped would replace the standard scholastic textbooks then in use. Our selection sets out the basic categories of his metaphysics and should be read alongside the Meditations.

(Textual note: the standard translation is The Philosophical Writings of Descartes, edited by J. Cottingham, R. Stoothoff, and D. Murdoch ('CSM'). The original texts are Ouevres de Descartes, edited by P. Adam and C. Tannery ('AT'). If you are writing a paper on Descartes, you will want to consult the CSM, which is on reserve at Newman. Other editions—those of Roger Ariew, or Haldane and Ross—can be used as well. Many of Descartes's works are available on the web.)

We begin with an excerpt from the Discourse on Method, in which Descartes summarizes some of his conclusions in The World. This introduces Descartes's mechanical conception of nature, a conception that extends to animals, human and otherwise. This is followed by selections from the Principles, the Meditations, and the Objections and Replies.

In these selections, it is important to keep in mind Descartes's overall project: sweeping away the Aristotelian world of forms and animal and vegetative souls and replacing it with a world of machines.

Descartes' *Discourse on Method*, Part Five (1637)

Descartes has been recapitulating his discussion of the nature of matter from The World. On this view, matter is extension—a bit of matter is nothing over and above a region of space. (See the Principles above). He then moves on to apply this conception to animals.

And, in the last place, what above all is here worthy of observation, is the generation of the animal spirits, which are like a very subtle wind, or rather a very pure and vivid flame which, continually ascending in great abundance from the heart to the brain, thence penetrates through the nerves into the muscles, and gives motion to all the members; so that to account for other parts of the blood which, as most agitated and penetrating, are the fittest to compose these spirits, proceeding towards the brain, it is not necessary to suppose any other cause, than simply, that the arteries which carry them thither proceed from the heart in the most direct lines, and that, according to the rules of mechanics which are the same with those of nature, when many objects tend at once to the same point where there is not sufficient room for all (as is the case with the parts of the blood which flow forth from the left cavity of the heart and tend towards the brain), the weaker and less agitated parts must necessarily be driven aside from that point by the stronger which alone in this way reach it.

I had expounded all these matters with sufficient minuteness in the Treatise which I formerly thought of publishing. And after these, I had shown what must be the fabric of the nerves and muscles of the human body to give the animal spirits contained in it the power to move the members, as when we see heads shortly after they have been struck off still move and bite the earth, although no longer animated; what changes must take place in the brain to produce waking, sleep, and dreams; how light, sounds, odors, tastes, heat, and all the other qualities of external objects impress it with different ideas by means of the senses; how hunger, thirst, and the other internal affections can likewise impress upon it divers ideas; what must be understood by the common sense (*sensus communis*) in which these ideas are received, by the memory which retains them, by the fantasy which can change them in various ways, and out of them compose new ideas, and which, by the same means, distributing the animal spirits through the muscles, can cause the members of such a body to move in as many different ways, and in a manner as suited, whether to the objects that are presented to its senses or to its internal affections, as can take place in our own case apart from the guidance of the will.

Nor will this appear at all strange to those who are acquainted with the variety of movements performed by the different automata, or moving machines fabricated by human industry, and that with help of but few pieces compared with the great multitude of bones, muscles, nerves, arteries, veins, and other parts that are found in the body of each animal. Such persons will look upon this body as a machine made by the hands of God, which is incomparably better arranged, and adequate to movements more admirable than is any machine of human invention. And here I specially stayed to show that, were there such machines exactly resembling organs and outward form an ape or any other irrational animal, we could have no means of knowing that they were in any respect of a different nature from these animals; but if there were machines bearing the image of our bodies, and capable of imitating our actions as far as it is morally possible, there would still remain two most certain tests whereby to know that they were not therefore really men.

1. [These machines] could never use words or other signs arranged in such a manner as is competent to us in order to declare our thoughts to others: for we may easily conceive a machine to be so constructed that it emits vocables, and even that it emits some correspondent to the action upon it of external objects which cause a change in its organs; for example, if touched in a particular place it may demand what we wish to say to it; if in another it may cry out that it is hurt, and such like; but not that it should arrange them variously so as appositely to reply to what is said in its presence, as men of the lowest grade of intellect can do.
2. Although such machines might execute many things with equal or perhaps greater perfection than any of us, they would, without doubt, fail in certain others from which it could be discovered that they did not act from knowledge, but solely from the disposition of their organs: for while Reason is an universal instrument that is alike available on every occasion, these organs, on the contrary, need a particular arrangement for each particular action; whence it must be morally impossible that there should exist in any machine a diversity of organs sufficient to enable it to act in all the occurrences of life, in the way in which our reason enables us to act.

Again, by means of these two tests we may likewise know the difference between men and brutes. For it is highly deserving of remark, that there are no men so dull and stupid, not even idiots, as to be incapable of joining together different words, and thereby constructing a declaration by which to make their thoughts understood; and that on the other hand, there is no other animal, however perfect or happily circumstanced, which can do the like. ...

And this proves not only that the brutes have less Reason than man, but that they have none at all: for we see that very little is required to enable a person to speak; and since a certain inequality of capacity is observable among animals of the same species, as well as among men, and since some are more capable of being instructed than others, it is incredible that the most perfect ape or parrot of its species, should not in this be equal to the most stupid infant of its kind or at least to one that was crack-brained, unless the soul of brutes were of a nature wholly different from ours. And we ought not to confound speech with the natural movements which indicate the passions, and can be imitated by machines as well as manifested by animals; nor must it be thought with certain of the ancients, that the brutes speak, although we do not understand their language. For if such were the case, since they are endowed with many organs analogous to ours, they could as easily communicate their thoughts to us as to their fellows. ...

I had after this described the Reasonable Soul, and shown that it could by no means be educed from the power of matter, as the other things of which I had spoken, but that it must be expressly created; and that it is not sufficient that it be lodged in the human body exactly like a pilot in a ship, unless perhaps to move its members, but that it is necessary for it to be joined and united more closely to the body, in order to have sensations and appetites similar to ours, and thus constitute a real man. I here entered, in conclusion, upon the subject of the soul at considerable length, because it is of the greatest moment: for after the error of those who deny the existence of God, an error which I think I have already sufficiently refuted, there is none that is more powerful in leading feeble minds astray from the straight path of virtue than the supposition that the soul of the brutes is of the same nature with our own; and consequently that after this life we have nothing to hope for or fear, more than flies and ants. But when we know how far they differ, we much better comprehend the reasons that establish that the soul is of a nature wholly independent of the body, and that consequently it is not liable to die with the latter and, finally, because no other causes are observed capable of destroying it, we are naturally led thence to judge that it is immortal.

Descartes' *The Principles of Philosophy* (1644)

Part One, Section Fifty-one: What substance is, and that the term is not applicable to God and the creatures in the same sense

...By 'substance' we can conceive nothing else than a thing which exists in such a way as to stand in need of nothing beyond itself in order to its existence. And, in truth, there can be conceived but one substance which is absolutely independent, and that is God. We perceive that all other things can exist only by help of the concourse of God. And, accordingly, the term substance does not apply to God and the creatures **univocally**, to adopt a term familiar in the schools; that is, no signification of this word can be distinctly understood which is common to God and them.

Part One, Section Fifty-two: That the term is applicable univocally to the mind and the body, and how substance itself is known

Created substances, however, whether corporeal or thinking, may be conceived under this common concept; for these are things which, in order to their existence, stand in need of nothing but the concourse of God. But yet substance cannot be first discovered merely from its being a thing which exists independently, for existence by itself is not observed by us. We easily, however, discover substance itself from any attribute of it, by this common notion, that of nothing there are no attributes, properties, or qualities: for, from perceiving that some attribute is present, we infer that some existing thing or substance to which it may be attributed is also of necessity present.

Part One, Section Sixty: Of distinctions; and first of the real

[The distinctions between things are] threefold, viz., real, modal, and of reason. The real properly subsists between two or more substances; and it is sufficient to assure us that two substances are really mutually distinct, if only we are able clearly and distinctly to conceive the one of them without the other. For the knowledge we have of God renders it certain that he can effect all that of which we have a distinct idea. Thus, for example, since we have now the idea of an extended and corporeal substance, though we as yet do not know with certainty whether any such thing is really existent, nevertheless, merely because we have the idea of it, we may be assured that such a thing may exist; and, if it really exists, that every part which we can determine by thought must be really distinct from the other parts of the same substance. In the same way, since every one is conscious that he thinks, and that he in thought can exclude from himself every other substance, whether thinking or extended, it is certain that each of us thus considered is really distinct from every other thinking and corporeal substance. And although we suppose that God united a body to a soul so closely that it was impossible to form a more intimate union, and thus made a composite whole, the two substances would remain really distinct, notwithstanding this union; for with whatever tie God connected them, he was not able to rid himself of the power he possessed of separating them, or of conserving the one apart from the other, and the things which God can separate or conserve separately are really distinct.

Part One, Section Sixty-one: Of the modal distinction

There are two kinds of modal distinctions, viz., that between the mode properly so-called and the substance of which it is a mode, and that between two modes of the same substance. Of the former we have an example in this, that we can clearly apprehend substance apart from the mode which we say differs from it; while, on the other hand, we cannot conceive this mode without conceiving the substance itself.

There is, for example, a modal distinction between figure or motion and corporeal substance in which both exist; there is a similar distinction between affirmation or recollection and the mind. Of the latter kind we have an illustration in our ability to recognise the one of two modes apart from the other, as figure apart from motion, and motion apart from figure; though we cannot think of either the one or the other without thinking of the common substance in which they adhere. ...

Part One, Section Sixty-two: Of the distinction of reason (conceptual distinction)

Finally, the distinction of reason is that between a substance and some one of its attributes, without which it is impossible for us to distinctly conceive the substance itself; or between two such attributes of a common substance, the one of which we try to think without the other. This distinction is manifest from our inability to form a clear and distinct idea of such a substance, if we separate from it such attribute; or to have a clear perception of the one of two such attributes if we separate it from the other. For example, because any substance which ceases to endure ceases also to exist, duration is not distinct from substance except in thought (*ratione*); and in general all the modes of thinking which we consider as in objects differ only in thought, as well from the objects of which they are thought as from each other in a common object. ...

Part One, Section Sixty-three: How thought and extension may be distinctly known, as constituting, the one the nature of mind, the other that of body

Thought and extension may be regarded as constituting the natures of intelligent and corporeal substance; and then they must not be otherwise conceived than as the thinking and extended substances themselves, that is, as mind and body, which in this way are conceived with the greatest clearness and distinctness. Moreover, we more easily conceive extended or thinking substance than substance by itself, or with the omission of its thinking or extension. For there is some difficulty in abstracting the notion of substance from the notions of thinking and extension, which, in truth, are only diverse in thought itself (i.e., conceptually different) ...

Part One, Section Sixty-four: How these may likewise be distinctly conceived as modes of substance

Thought and extension may be also considered as modes of substance; in as far, namely, as the same mind may have many different thoughts, and the same body, with its size unchanged, may be extended in several diverse ways, at one time more in length and less in breadth or depth, and at another time more in breadth and less in length; and then they are modally distinguished from substance, and can be conceived not less clearly and distinctly, provided they be not regarded as substances or things separated from others, but simply as modes of things. For by regarding them as in the substances of which they are the modes, we distinguish them from these substances, and take them for what in truth they are: whereas, on the other hand, if we wish to consider them apart from the substances in which they are, we should by this itself regard them as self-subsisting things, and thus confound the ideas of mode and substance.

Part Two, Section Four: That the nature of body consists not in weight hardness, colour and the like, but in extension alone

In this way we will discern that the nature of matter or body, considered in general, does not consist in its being hard, or ponderous, or coloured, or that which affects our senses in any other way, but simply in its being a substance extended in length, breadth, and depth. For with respect to hardness, we know nothing of it by sense farther than that the parts of hard bodies resist the motion of our hands on coming into contact with them; but if every time our hands moved towards any part, all the bodies in that place receded as quickly as our hands approached, we should never feel hardness; and yet we have no reason to believe that bodies which might thus recede would on this account lose that which makes them bodies. The nature of body does not, therefore, consist in hardness. In the same way, it may be shown that weight, colour, and all the other qualities of this sort, which are perceived in corporeal matter, may be taken from it, while it remains complete: it thus follows that the nature of body depends on none of these.

Part Two, Section Eleven: How space is not in reality different from corporeal substance

And indeed it will be easy to discern that it is the same extension which constitutes the nature of body as of space, and that these two things are mutually diverse only as the nature of the genus and species differs from that of the individual, provided we reflect on the idea we have of any body, taking a stone for example, and reject all that is not essential to the nature of body. In the first place, then, hardness may be rejected, because if the stone were liquefied or reduced to powder, it would no longer possess hardness, and yet would not cease to be a body; colour also may be thrown out of account, because we have frequently seen stones so transparent as to have no colour; again, we may reject weight, because we have the case of fire, which, though very light, is still a body; and, finally, we may reject cold, heat, and all the other qualities of this sort, either because they are not considered as in the stone, or because, with the change of these qualities, the stone is not supposed to have lost the nature of body. After this examination we will find that nothing remains in the idea of body, except that it is something extended in length, breadth, and depth; and this something is comprised in our idea of space, not only of that which is full of body, but even of what is called void space.

Part Two, Section Twelve: How space differs from body in our mode of conceiving it

There is, however, some difference between them in the mode of conception; for if we remove a stone from the space or place in which it was, we conceive that its extension also is taken away, because we regard this as particular, and inseparable from the stone itself; but meanwhile we suppose that the same extension of place in which this stone was remains, although the place of the stone be occupied by wood, water, air, or by any other body, or be even supposed vacant, because we now consider extension in general, and think that the same is common to stones, wood, water, air, and other bodies, and even to a vacuum itself, if there is any such thing, provided it be of the same magnitude and figure as before, and preserve the same situation among the external bodies which determine this space.

In the following two sections, Descartes is confronting the problem of transference: how can one body produce motion in another? (See Aquinas's treatment of this in his Chapter Sixty-nine, Section Seven.) Is the answer Descartes gives here compatible with occasionalism? How might he react to Aquinas's answer?

Part Two, Section Twenty-four: What motion is, taking the term in its common use

But motion ... in the ordinary sense of the term, is nothing more than **the action by which a body passes from one place to another.** And just as we have remarked above that the same thing may be said to change and not to change place at the same time, so also we may say that the same thing is at the same time moved and not moved. Thus, for example, a person seated in a vessel which is setting sail, thinks he is in motion if he look to the shore that he has left, and consider it as fixed; but not if he regard the ship itself, among the parts of which he preserves always the same situation. Moreover, because we are accustomed to suppose that there is no motion without action, and that in rest there is the cessation of action, the person thus seated is more properly said to be at rest than in motion, seeing he is not conscious of being in action.

Part Two, Section Twenty-five: What motion is properly *so* called

But if, instead of occupying ourselves with that which has no foundation, unless in ordinary usage, we desire to know what ought to be understood by motion according to the truth of the thing, we may say, in order to give it a determinate nature, that it is **the transporting of one part of matter or of one body from the vicinity of those bodies that are in immediate contact with it, or which we regard as at rest,** to the vicinity of other bodies. By a body as a part of matter, I understand all that which is transferred together, although it be perhaps composed of several parts, which in themselves have other motions; and I say that it is the transporting and not the force or action which transports, with the view of showing that motion is always in the movable thing, not in that which moves; for it seems to me that we are not accustomed to distinguish these two things with sufficient accuracy. Farther, I understand that it is a mode of the movable thing, and not a substance, just as figure is a property of the thing figured, and repose of that which is at rest.

---

1. *When are two things are really distinct? How can we know that they are distinct?*
2. *What kind of distinction holds between a substance and its essence—real, conceptual (a distinction of reason), or modal?*
3. *Aristotle gave several criteria for substance-hood. What criterion does Descartes give? Is it the same as Aristotle's?*

Descartes' *Meditations on First Philosophy* (1641)

The Meditations are among the most frequently misread works of the modern period. Descartes is often seen as primarily concerned with epistemology and in particular the problem of skepticism. But remember that the title of the work is Meditations on First Philosophy, and 'first philosophy' always refers to metaphysics, not epistemology. And Descartes himself refers to the work in correspondence as his 'metaphysics'. Skepticism is merely a tool Descartes exploits; it is not an independently important or interesting subject.

Failure to see this stems from the failure to see the work's polemical purpose. Descartes's target audience here is the scholastics; while Descartes and his adversaries agree on some key doctrines—that God exists, for example, and that the soul is immortal—they disagree on nearly everything else. Rather than arguing against their views directly, Descartes chooses a literary form that allows him to subvert their views—particularly empiricism, existentialism, and their belief in a multitude of natural kinds.

The meditator is not Descartes himself, but instead a literary character. (For confirmation of this, see the last paragraph of his Synopsis below.) As you read the first two meditations, keep this in mind. Look for clues to the meditator's true identity: what kinds of views does she hold, as she begins her reflections?

The synopsis that follows is helpful, but you might want to read it after having read the work as a whole.

Synopsis of the Six Following Meditations

In the First Meditation I expound the grounds on which we may doubt in general of all things, and especially of material objects, so long at least, as we have no other foundations for the sciences than those we have hitherto possessed. Now, although the utility of a doubt so general may not be manifest at first sight, it is nevertheless of the greatest, since it delivers us from all prejudice, and affords the easiest pathway by which the mind may withdraw itself from the senses; and finally makes it impossible for us to doubt wherever we afterward discover truth.

In the Second, the mind which, in the exercise of the freedom peculiar to itself, supposes that no object is, of the existence of which it has even the slightest doubt, finds that, meanwhile, it must itself exist. And this point is likewise of the highest moment, for the mind is thus enabled easily to distinguish what pertains to itself, that is, to the intellectual nature, from what is to be referred to the body. But since some, perhaps, will expect, at this stage of our progress, a statement of the reasons which establish the doctrine of the immortality of the soul, I think it proper here to make such aware, that it was my aim to write nothing of which I could not give exact demonstration, and that I therefore felt myself obliged to adopt an order similar to that in use among the geometers, viz., to premise all upon which the proposition in question depends, before coming to any conclusion respecting it. Now, the first and chief prerequisite for the knowledge of the immortality of the soul is our being able to form the clearest possible conception (*conceptus*−concept) of the soul itself, and such as shall be absolutely distinct from all our notions of body; and how this is to be accomplished is there shown. There is required, besides this, the assurance that all objects which we clearly and distinctly think are true (really exist) in that very mode in which we think them; and this could not be established previously to the Fourth Meditation.

Farther, it is necessary, for the same purpose, that we possess a distinct conception of corporeal nature, which is given partly in the Second and partly in the Fifth and Sixth Meditations. And, finally, on these grounds, we are necessitated to conclude, that all those objects which are clearly and distinctly conceived to be diverse substances, as mind and body, are substances really reciprocally distinct; and this inference is made in the Sixth Meditation. The absolute distinction of mind and body is, besides, confirmed in this Second Meditation, by showing that we cannot conceive body unless as divisible; while, on the other hand, mind cannot be conceived unless as indivisible. For we are not able to conceive the half of a mind, as we can of any body, however small, so that the natures of these two substances are to be held, not only as diverse, but even in some measure as contraries.

I have not, however, pursued this discussion further in the present treatise, as well for the reason that these considerations are sufficient to show that the destruction of the mind does not follow from the corruption of the body, and thus to afford to men the hope of a future life, as also because the premises from which it is competent for us to infer the immortality of the soul, involve an explication of the whole principles of Physics: in order to establish, in the first place, that generally all substances, that is, all things which can exist only in consequence of having been created by God, are in their own nature incorruptible, and can never cease to be, unless God himself, by refusing his concurrence to them, reduce them to nothing; and, in the second place, that body, taken generally, is a substance, and therefore can never perish, but that the human body, in as far as it differs from other bodies, is constituted only by a certain configuration of members, and by other accidents of this sort, while the human mind is not made up of accidents, but is a pure substance. For although all the accidents of the mind be changed−although, for example, it think certain things, will others, and perceive others, the mind itself does not vary with these changes; while, on the contrary, the human body is no longer the same if a change take place in the form of any of its parts: from which it follows that the body may, indeed, without difficulty perish, but that the mind is in its own nature immortal.

In the Third Meditation, I have unfolded at sufficient length, as appears to me, my chief argument for the existence of God. But yet, since I was there desirous to avoid the use of comparisons taken from material objects, that I might withdraw, as far as possible, the minds of my readers from the senses, numerous obscurities perhaps remain, which, however, will, I trust, be afterward entirely removed in the *Replies to the Objections*: thus among other things, it may be difficult to understand how the idea of a being absolutely perfect, which is found in our minds, possesses so much objective reality (i.e., participates by representation in so many degrees of being and perfection) that it must be held to arise from a cause absolutely perfect. This is illustrated in the Replies by the comparison of a highly perfect machine, the idea of which exists in the mind of some workman; for as the objective (i.e., representative) perfection of this idea must have some cause, viz., either the science of the workman, or of some other person from whom he has received the idea, in the same way the idea of God, which is found in us, demands God himself for its cause.

In the Fourth, it is shown that all which we clearly and distinctly perceive (apprehend) is true; and, at the same time, is explained wherein consists the nature of error; points that require to be known as well for confirming the preceding truths, as for the better understanding of those that are to follow. But, meanwhile, it must be observed, that I do not at all there treat of Sin, that is, of error committed in the pursuit of good and evil, but of that sort alone which arises in the determination of the true and the false. Nor do I refer to matters of faith, or to the conduct of life, but only to what regards speculative truths, and such as are known by means of the natural light alone.

In the Fifth, besides the illustration of corporeal nature, taken genetically, a new demonstration is given of the existence of God, not free, perhaps, any more than the former, from certain difficulties, but of these the solution will be found in the *Replies to the Objections*. I further show, in what sense it is true that the certitude of geometrical demonstrations themselves is dependent on the knowledge of God.

Finally, in the Sixth, the act of the understanding (*intellectio*) is distinguished from that of the imagination (*imaginatio*); the marks of this distinction are described; the human mind is shown to be really distinct from the body, and, nevertheless, to be so closely conjoined therewith, as together to form, as it were, a unity. The whole of the errors which arise from the senses are brought under review, while the means of avoiding them are pointed out; and, finally, all the grounds are adduced from which the existence of material objects may be inferred; not, however, because I deemed them of great utility in establishing what they prove, viz., that there is in reality a world, that men are possessed of bodies, and the like, the truth of which no one of sound mind ever seriously doubted; but because, from a close consideration of them, it is perceived that they are neither so strong nor clear as the reasonings which conduct us to the knowledge of our mind and of God; so that the latter are, of all which come under human knowledge, the most certain and manifest—a conclusion which it was my single aim in these *Meditations* to establish; on which account I here omit mention of the various other questions which, in the course of the discussion, I had occasion likewise to consider.

First Meditation: Of the Things on Which We May Doubt

Several years have now elapsed since I first became aware that I had accepted, even from my youth, many false opinions for true, and that consequently what I afterward based on such principles was highly doubtful; and from that time I was convinced of the necessity of undertaking once in my life to rid myself of all the opinions I had adopted, and of commencing anew the work of building from the foundation, if I desired to establish a firm and abiding superstructure in the sciences. But as this enterprise appeared to me to be one of great magnitude, I waited until I had attained an age so mature as to leave me no hope that at any stage of life more advanced I should be better able to execute my design. On this account, I have delayed so long that I should henceforth consider I was doing wrong were I still to consume in deliberation any of the time that now remains for action.

Today, then, since I have opportunely freed my mind from all cares (and am happily disturbed by no passions), and since I am in the secure possession of leisure in a peaceable retirement, I will at length apply myself earnestly and freely to the general overthrow of all my former opinions. But, to this end, it will not be necessary for me to show that the whole of these are false—a point, perhaps, which I shall never reach; but as even now my reason convinces me that I ought not the less carefully to withhold belief from what is not entirely certain and indubitable, than from what is manifestly false, it will be sufficient to justify the rejection of the whole if I shall find in each some ground for doubt. Nor for this purpose will it be necessary even to deal with each belief individually, which would be truly an endless labor; but, as the removal from below of the foundation necessarily involves the downfall of the whole edifice, I will at once approach the criticism of the principles on which all my former beliefs rested.

All that I have, up to this moment, accepted as possessed of the highest truth and certainty, I received either from or through the senses. I observed, however, that these sometimes misled us; and it is the part of prudence not to place absolute confidence in that by which we have even once been deceived.

But it may be said that, although the senses occasionally mislead us respecting minute objects, and such as are so far removed from us as to be beyond the reach of close observation, there are yet many other of their informations (presentations), of the truth of which it is manifestly impossible to doubt; as for example, that I am in this place, seated by the fire, clothed in a winter dressing gown, that I hold in my hands this piece of paper, with other intimations of the same nature. But how could I deny that I possess these hands and this body, and withal escape being classed with persons in a state of insanity, whose brains are so disordered and clouded by dark bilious vapors as to cause them pertinaciously to assert that they are monarchs when they are in the greatest poverty; or clothed in gold and purple when destitute of any covering; or that their head is made of clay, their body of glass, or that they are gourds? I should certainly be not less insane than they, were I to regulate my procedure according to examples so extravagant.

Though this be true, I must nevertheless here consider that I am a man, and that, consequently, I am in the habit of sleeping, and representing to myself in dreams those same things, or even sometimes others less probable, which the insane think are presented to them in their waking moments. How often have I dreamt that I was in these familiar circumstances, that I was dressed, and occupied this place by the fire, when I was lying undressed in bed? At the present moment, however, I certainly look upon this paper with eyes wide awake; the head which I now move is not asleep; I extend this hand consciously and with express purpose, and I perceive it; the occurrences in sleep are not so distinct as I all this. But I cannot forget that, at other times I have been deceived in sleep by similar illusions; and, attentively considering those cases, I perceive so clearly that there exist no certain marks by which the state of waking can ever be distinguished from sleep, that I feel greatly astonished; and in amazement I almost persuade myself that I am now dreaming.

Let us suppose, then, that we are dreaming, and that all these particulars—namely, the opening of the eyes, the motion of the head, the forth-putting of the hands—are merely illusions; and even that we really possess neither an entire body nor hands such as we see. Nevertheless it must be admitted at least that the objects which appear to us in sleep are, as it were, painted representations which could not have been formed unless in the likeness of realities; and, therefore, that those general objects, at all events, namely, eyes, a head, hands, and an entire body, are not simply imaginary, but really existent. For, in truth, painters themselves, even when they study to represent sirens and satyrs by forms the most fantastic and extraordinary, cannot bestow upon them natures absolutely new, but can only make a certain medley of the members of different animals; or if they chance to imagine something so novel that nothing at all similar has ever been seen before, and such as is, therefore, purely fictitious and absolutely false, it is at least certain that the colors of which this is composed are real.

And on the same principle, although these general objects, viz., a body, eyes, a head, hands, and the like, be imaginary, we are nevertheless absolutely necessitated to admit the reality at least of some other objects still more simple and universal than these, of which, just as of certain real colors, all those images of things, whether true and real, or false and fantastic, that are found in our consciousness (*cogitatio*), are formed.

To this class of objects seem to belong corporeal nature in general and its extension; the figure of extended things, their quantity or magnitude, and their number, as also the place in, and the time during, which they exist, and other things of the same sort. We will not, therefore, perhaps reason illegitimately if we conclude from this that Physics, Astronomy, Medicine, and all the other sciences that have for their end the consideration of composite objects, are indeed of a doubtful character; but that Arithmetic, Geometry, and the other sciences of the same class, which regard merely the simplest and most general objects, and scarcely inquire whether or not these are really existent, contain somewhat that is certain and indubitable: for whether I am awake or dreaming, it remains true that two and three make five, and that a square has but four sides; nor does it seem possible that truths so apparent can ever fall under a suspicion of falsity.

Nevertheless, the belief that there is a God who is all powerful, and who created me, such as I am, has, for a long time, obtained steady possession of my mind. How, then, do I know that he has not arranged that there should be neither earth, nor sky, nor any extended thing, nor figure, nor magnitude, nor place, providing at the same time, however, for the rise in me of the perceptions of all these objects, and the persuasion that these do not exist otherwise than as I perceive them? And further, as I sometimes think that others are in error respecting matters of which they believe themselves to possess a perfect knowledge, how do I know that I am not also deceived each time I add together two and three, or number the sides of a square, or form some judgment still more simple, if more simple indeed can be imagined? But perhaps God has not been willing that I should be thus deceived, for he is said to be supremely good. If, however, it were repugnant to the goodness of God to have created me subject to constant deception, it would seem likewise to be contrary to his goodness to allow me to be occasionally deceived; and yet it is clear that this is permitted. Some, indeed, might perhaps be found who would be disposed rather to deny the existence of a Being so powerful than to believe that there is nothing certain. But let us for the present refrain from opposing this opinion, and grant that all which is here said of God is fabulous: nevertheless, in whatever way it be supposed that I reach the state in which I exist, whether by fate, or chance, or by an endless series of antecedents and consequents, or by any other means, it is clear (since to be deceived and to err is a certain defect) that the probability of my being so imperfect as to be the constant victim of deception, will be increased exactly in proportion as the power possessed by the cause, to which they assign my origin, is lessened. To these reasonings I have assuredly nothing to reply, but am constrained at last to avow that there is nothing of all that I formerly believed to be true of which it is impossible to doubt, and that not through thoughtlessness or levity, but from cogent and maturely considered reasons; so that henceforward, if I desire to discover anything certain, I ought not the less carefully to refrain from assenting to those same opinions than to what might be shown to be manifestly false.

But it is not sufficient to have made these observations; care must be taken likewise to keep them in remembrance. For those old and customary opinions perpetually recur–long and familiar usage giving them the right of occupying my mind, even almost against my will, and subduing my belief; nor will I lose the habit of deferring to them and confiding in them so long as I shall consider them to be what in truth they are, viz., opinions to some extent doubtful, as I have already shown, but still highly probable, and such as it is much more reasonable to believe than deny. It is for this reason I am persuaded that I shall not be doing wrong, if, taking an opposite judgment of deliberate design, I become my own deceiver, by supposing, for a time, that all those opinions are entirely false and imaginary, until at length, having thus balanced my old by my new prejudices, my judgment shall no longer be turned aside by perverted usage from the path that may conduct to the perception of truth. For I am assured that, meanwhile, there will arise neither peril nor error from this course, and that I cannot for the present yield too much to distrust, since the end I now seek is not action but knowledge.

I will suppose, then, not that God, who is sovereignly good and the fountain of truth, but that some malignant demon, who is at once exceedingly potent and deceitful, has employed all his artifice to deceive me; I will suppose that the sky, the air, the earth, colors, figures, sounds, and all external things, are nothing better than the illusions of dreams, by means of which this being has laid snares for my credulity; I will consider myself as without hands, eyes, flesh, blood, or any of the senses, and as falsely believing that I am possessed of these; I will continue resolutely fixed in this belief, and if indeed by this means it be not in my power to arrive at the knowledge of truth, I shall at least do what is in my power, viz., suspend my judgment, and guard with settled purpose against giving my assent to what is false, and being imposed upon by this deceiver, whatever be his power and artifice.

But this undertaking is arduous, and a certain indolence insensibly leads me back to my ordinary course of life; and just as the captive, who, perchance, was enjoying in his dreams an imaginary liberty, when he begins to suspect that it is but a vision, dreads awakening, and conspires with the agreeable illusions that the deception may be prolonged; so I, of my own accord, fall back into the train of my former beliefs, and fear to arouse myself from my slumber, lest the time of laborious wakefulness that would succeed this quiet rest, in place of bringing any light of day, should prove inadequate to dispel the darkness that will arise from the difficulties that have now been raised.

---

1. *In this meditation, Descartes presents three skeptical arguments. There is a common pattern: in each case, rather than reacting directly to the skeptical argument and trying to overthrow it, the meditator retreats to some apparently more solid ground, until, at the end of the meditation, _____.*
2. *What are the skeptical arguments? How effective are they?*

    1. *Premise:* Sometimes the senses deceive us.*Conclusion:* The senses should never be trusted.

    What is wrong with this argument? Is there a way to grant the premise while denying the conclusion?

    1. *Premise:* Sometimes, while dreaming, ___.*Conclusion:* Therefore, right now I cannot tell ___.

    This is what we might call the 'literal' dream argument. Can you think of any way to respond? (You might want to come back to this after having read the Sixth Meditation. But there's a more threatening version of this argument—the 'metaphorical dream argument':

    1. *Premise (Alternate):* Dreaming shows that we can have sensory experiences even when they do not correspond to anything in the world.*Conclusion (Alternate):* I have no reason to think that my entire experience isn't like a dream, in that it corresponds to nothing outside of me.
    2. *Premise:* There might be an omnipotent being, capable of making all my inferences _____, even when I think _____.*Conclusion:* I cannot trust my own powers of _____.

    Which of these arguments is most important? Which of the three 'areas of retreat' does it threaten?

To think about while reading the following Meditations: What is the purpose of the skeptical doubts introduced here?

After all, they were hardly new, even in the seventeenth century. Rather snottily, Thomas Hobbes points out that they can be found in ancient writers like Plato: 'I would have preferred the author, so very distinguished in the realm of new speculations, not to have published these old things.' Descartes responds that he included them partly to show how firm the truths he later arrives at really are, and partly to 'prepare the minds of the readers for the consideration of matters geared to the understanding and for distinguishing them from corporeal things, goals for which these arguments seem wholly necessary.' How do you think the doubt accomplishes these goals?

Second Meditation: Of the Nature of the Human Mind; and that It is More Easily Known than the Body

In the Second Meditation, Descartes is concerned to show the primacy of the intellect over the senses. The point of the skeptical arguments is to call the senses into question; here we'll see not only that the senses don't tell us that anything exists, they don't tell us anything about the nature of what exists.

The most puzzling feature of this meditation is the long discussion of the piece of wax. What on earth is it doing here? What is it supposed to accomplish? (Hint: recall the scholastic doctrine of existentialism. Does Descartes endorse it, or not? If not, how must the Meditator proceed, if she ultimately wants to prove that the external world exists?)

The meditation of yesterday has filled my mind with so many doubts, that it is no longer in my power to forget them. Nor do I see, meanwhile, any principle on which they can be resolved; and, just as if I had fallen all of a sudden into very deep water, I am so greatly disconcerted as to be unable either to plant my feet firmly on the bottom or sustain myself by swimming on the surface. I will, nevertheless, make an effort, and try anew the same path on which I had entered yesterday, that is, proceed by casting aside all that admits of the slightest doubt, not less than if I had discovered it to be absolutely false; and I will continue always in this track until I shall find something that is certain, or at least, if I can do nothing more, until I shall know with certainty that there is nothing certain. Archimedes, that he might transport the entire globe from the place it occupied to another, demanded only a point that was firm and immovable; so, also, I shall be entitled to entertain the highest expectations, if I am fortunate enough to discover only one thing that is certain and indubitable.

I suppose, accordingly, that all the things which I see are false (fictitious); I believe that none of those objects which my fallacious memory represents ever existed; I suppose that I possess no senses; I believe that body, figure, extension, motion, and place are merely fictions of my mind. What is there, then, that can be esteemed true? Perhaps this only, that there is absolutely nothing certain.

But how do I know that there is not something different altogether from the objects I have now enumerated, of which it is impossible to entertain the slightest doubt? Is there not a God, or some being, by whatever name I may designate him, who causes these thoughts, to arise in my mind? But why suppose such a being, for it may be I myself am capable of producing them? Am I, then, at least not something? But I before denied that I possessed senses or a body; I hesitate, however, for what follows from that? Am I so dependent on the body and the senses that without these I cannot exist? But I had the persuasion that there was absolutely nothing in the world, that there was no sky and no earth, neither minds nor bodies; was I not, therefore, at the same time, persuaded that I did not exist? Far from it; I assuredly existed, since I was persuaded. But there is I know not what being, who is possessed at once of the highest power and the deepest cunning, who is constantly employing all his ingenuity in deceiving me. Doubtless, then, I exist, since I am deceived; and, let him deceive me as he may, he can never bring it about that I am nothing, so long as I shall be conscious that I am something. So that it must, in fine, be maintained, all things being maturely and carefully considered, that this proposition 'I am, I exist', is necessarily true each time it is expressed by me, or conceived in my mind.

But I do not yet know with sufficient clearness what I am, though assured that I am; and hence, in the next place, I must take care, lest perchance I inconsiderately substitute some other object in room of what is properly myself, and thus wander from truth, even in that knowledge (cognition) which I hold to be of all others the most certain and evident. For this reason, I will now consider anew what I formerly believed myself to be, before I entered on the present train of thought; and of my previous opinion I will retrench all that can in the least be invalidated by the grounds of doubt I have adduced, in order that there may at length remain nothing but what is certain and indubitable. What then did I formerly think I was? Undoubtedly I judged that I was a man. But what is a man? Shall I say a rational animal? Assuredly not; for it would be necessary forthwith to inquire into what is meant by animal, and what by rational, and thus, from a single question, I should insensibly glide into others, and these more difficult than the first; nor do I now possess enough of leisure to warrant me in wasting my time amid subtleties of this sort. I prefer here to attend to the thoughts that sprung up of themselves in my mind, and were inspired by my own nature alone, when I applied myself to the consideration of what I was.

In the first place, then, I thought that I possessed a countenance, hands, arms, and all the fabric of members that appears in a corpse, and which I called by the name of body. It further occurred to me that I was nourished, that I walked, perceived, and thought, and all those actions I referred to the soul; but what the soul itself was I either did not stay to consider, or, if I did, I imagined that it was something extremely rare and subtile, like wind, or flame, or ether, spread through my grosser parts. As regarded the body, I did not even doubt of its nature, but thought I distinctly knew it, and if I had wished to describe it according to the notions I then entertained, I should have explained myself in this manner: By body I understand all that can be terminated by a certain figure; that can be comprised in a certain place, and so fill a certain spice as therefrom to exclude every other body; that can be perceived either by touch, sight, hearing, taste, or smell; that can be moved in different ways, not indeed of itself, but by something foreign to it by which it is touched and from which it receives the impression; for the power of self-motion, as likewise that of perceiving and thinking, I held as by no means pertaining to the nature of body; on the contrary, I was somewhat astonished to find such faculties existing in some bodies.

But as to myself, what can I now say that I am, since I suppose there exists an extremely powerful, and, if I may so speak, malignant being, whose whole endeavors are directed toward deceiving me? Can I affirm that I possess any one of all those attributes of which I have lately spoken as belonging to the nature of body? After attentively considering them in my own mind, I find none of them that can properly be said to belong to myself. To recount them were idle and tedious. Let us pass, then, to the attributes of the soul. The first mentioned were the powers of nutrition and walking; but, if it be true that I have no body, it is true likewise that I am capable neither of walking nor of being nourished. Perception is another attribute of the soul; but perception too is impossible without the body; besides, I have frequently, during sleep, believed that I perceived objects which I afterward observed I did not in reality perceive. Thinking is another attribute of the soul; and here I discover what properly belongs to myself. This alone is inseparable from me. I am—I exist: this is certain; but how often? As often as I think; for perhaps it would even happen, if I should wholly cease to think, that I should at the same time altogether cease to be. I now admit nothing that is not necessarily true. I am therefore, precisely speaking, only a thinking thing, that is, a mind (*mens sive animus*), understanding, or reason, terms whose signification was before unknown to me. I am, however, a real thing, and really existent; but what thing? The answer was, a thinking thing. The question now arises, am I anything besides? I will stimulate my imagination with a view to discover whether I am not still something more than a thinking being. Now it in plain I am not the assemblage of members called the human body; I am not a thin and penetrating air diffused through all these members, or wind, or flame, or vapor, or breath, or any of all the things I can imagine; *for* I supposed that all these were not, and, without changing the supposition, I find that I still feel assured of my existence.

But it is true, perhaps, that those very things which I suppose to be non-existent, because they are unknown to me, are not in troth different from myself whom I know. This is a point I cannot determine, and do not now enter into any dispute regarding it. I can only judge of things that are known to me: I am conscious that I exist, and I who know that I exist inquire into what I am. It is, however, perfectly certain that the knowledge of my existence, thus precisely taken, is not dependent on things, the existence of which is as yet unknown to me: and consequently it is not dependent on any of the things I can feign in imagination. Moreover, the phrase itself, I frame an image (*effingo*), reminds me of my error; for I should in truth frame one if I were to imagine myself to be anything, since to imagine is nothing more than to contemplate the figure or image of a corporeal thing; but I already know that I exist, and that it is possible at the same time that all those images, and in general all that relates to the nature of body, are merely dreams or chimeras. From this I discover that it is not more reasonable to say, 'I will excite my imagination that I may know more distinctly what I am', than to express myself as follows: 'I am now awake, and perceive something real; but because my perception is not sufficiently clear, I will of express purpose go to sleep that my dreams may represent to me the object of my perception with more truth and clearness'. And, therefore, I know that nothing of all that I can embrace in imagination belongs to the knowledge which I have of myself, and that there is need to recall with the utmost care the mind from this mode of thinking, that it may be able to know its own nature with perfect distinctness.

But what, then, am I? A thinking thing, it has been said. But what is a thinking thing? It is a thing that doubts, understands, conceives, affirms, denies, wills, refuses; that imagines also, and perceives. Assuredly it is not little, if all these properties belong to my nature. But why should they not belong to it? Am I not that very being who now doubts of almost everything; who, for all that, understands and conceives certain things; who affirms one alone as true, and denies the others; who desires to know more of them, and does not wish to be deceived; who imagines many things, sometimes even despite his will; and is likewise percipient of many, as if through the medium of the senses. Is there nothing of all this as true as that I am, even although I should be always dreaming, and although he who gave me being employed all his ingenuity to deceive me? Is there also any one of these attributes that can be properly distinguished from my thought, or that can be said to be separate from myself? For it is of itself so evident that it is I who doubt, I who understand, and I who desire, that it is here unnecessary to add anything by way of rendering it more clear. And I am as certainly the same being who imagines; for although it maybe (as I before supposed) that nothing I imagine is true, still the power of imagination does not cease really to exist in me and to form part of my thought. In fine, I am the same being who perceives, that is, who apprehends certain objects as by the organs of sense, since, in truth, I see light, hear a noise, and feel heat. But it will be said that these presentations are false, and that I am dreaming. Let it be so. At all events it is certain that I seem to see light, hear a noise, and feel heat; this cannot be false, and this is what in me is properly called perceiving (*sentire*), which is nothing else than thinking. From this I begin to know what I am with somewhat greater clearness and distinctness than heretofore.

But, nevertheless, it still seems to me, and I cannot help believing, that corporeal things, whose images are formed by thought, and are examined by the same, are known with much greater distinctness than that I know not what part of myself which is not imaginable; although, in truth, it may seem strange to say that I know and comprehend with greater distinctness things whose existence appears to me doubtful, that are unknown, and do not belong to me, than others of whose reality I am persuaded, that are known to me, and appertain to my proper nature; in a word, than myself. But I see clearly what is the state of the case. My mind is apt to wander, and will not yet submit to be restrained within the limits of truth. Let us therefore leave the mind to itself once more, and, according to it every kind of liberty, permit it to consider the objects that appear to it from without, in order that, having afterward withdrawn it from these gently and opportunely, and fixed it on the consideration of its being and the properties it finds in itself, it may then be the more easily controlled.

Let us now accordingly consider the objects that are commonly thought to be the most easily, and likewise the most distinctly known, viz., the bodies we touch and see; not, indeed, bodies in general, for these general notions are usually somewhat more confused, but one body in particular. Take, for example, this piece of wax; it is quite fresh, having been but recently taken from the beehive; it has not yet lost the sweetness of the honey it contained; it still retains somewhat of the odor of the flowers from which it was gathered; its color, figure, size, are apparent (to the sight); it is hard, cold, easily handled; and sounds when struck upon with the finger. In fine, all that contributes to make a body as distinctly known as possible, is found in the one before us. But, while I am speaking, let it be placed near the fire—what remained of the taste exhales, the smell evaporates, the color changes, its figure is destroyed, its size increases, it becomes liquid, it grows hot, it can hardly be handled, and, although struck upon, it emits no sound. Does the same wax still remain after this change? It must be admitted that it does remain; no one doubts it, or judges otherwise. What, then, was it I knew with so much distinctness in the piece of wax? Assuredly, it could be nothing of all that I observed by means of the senses, since all the things that fell under taste, smell, sight, touch, and hearing are changed, and yet the same wax remains. It was perhaps what I now think, viz., that this wax was neither the sweetness of honey, the pleasant odor of flowers, the whiteness, the figure, nor the sound, but only a body that a little before appeared to me conspicuous under these forms, and which is now perceived under others. But, to speak precisely, what is it that I imagine when I think of it in this way? Let it be attentively considered, and, retrenching all that does not belong to the wax, let us see what remains.

There certainly remains nothing, except something extended, flexible, and movable. But what is meant by flexible and movable? Is it not that I imagine that the piece of wax, being round, is capable of becoming square, or of passing from a square into a triangular figure? Assuredly such is not the case, because I conceive that it admits of an infinity of similar changes; and I am, moreover, unable to compass this infinity by imagination, and consequently this conception which I have of the wax is not the product of the faculty of imagination. But what now is this extension? Is it not also unknown? for it becomes greater when the wax is melted, greater when it is boiled, and greater still when the heat increases; and I should not conceive clearly and according to truth, the wax as it is, if I did not suppose that the piece we are considering admitted even of a wider variety of extension than I ever imagined. I must, therefore, admit that I cannot even comprehend by imagination what the piece of wax is, and that it is the mind alone which perceives it. I speak of one piece in particular; for as to wax in general, this is still more evident. But what is the piece of wax that can be perceived only by the understanding or mind? It is certainly the same which I see, touch, imagine; and, in fine, it is the same which, from the beginning, I believed it to be. But (and this it is of moment to observe) the perception of it is neither an act of sight, of touch, nor of imagination, and never was either of these, though it might formerly seem so, but is simply an intuition (*inspectio*) of the mind, which may be imperfect and confused, as it formerly was, or very clear and distinct, as it is at present, according as the attention is more or less directed to the elements which it contains, and of which it is composed.

But, meanwhile, I feel greatly astonished when I observe the weakness of my mind, and its proneness to error. For although, without at all giving expression to what I think, I consider all this in my own mind, words yet occasionally impede my progress, and I am almost led into error by the terms of ordinary language. We say, for example, that we see the same wax when it is before us, and not that we judge it to be the same from its retaining the same color and figure: whence I should forthwith be disposed to conclude that the wax is known by the act of sight, and not by the intuition of the mind alone, were it not for the analogous instance of human beings passing on in the street below, as observed from a window. In this case I do not fail to say that I see the men themselves, just as I say that I see the wax; and yet what do I see from the window beyond hats and cloaks that might cover artificial machines, whose motions might be determined by springs? But I judge that there are human beings from these appearances, and thus I comprehend, by the faculty of judgment alone which is in the mind, what I believed I saw with my eyes.

The man who makes it his aim to rise to knowledge superior to the common, ought to be ashamed to seek occasions of doubting from the vulgar forms of speech: instead, therefore, of doing this, I shall proceed with the matter in hand, and inquire whether I had a clearer and more perfect perception of the piece of wax when I first saw it, and when I thought I knew it by means of the external sense itself, or, at all events, by the common sense (*sensus communis*), as it is called, that is, by the imaginative faculty; or whether I rather apprehend it more clearly at present, after having examined with greater care, both what it is, and in what way it can be known. It would certainly be ridiculous to entertain any doubt on this point. For what, in that first perception, was there distinct? What did I perceive which any animal might not have perceived? But when I distinguish the wax from its exterior forms, and when, as if I had stripped it of its vestments, I consider it quite naked, it is certain, although some error may still be found in my judgment, that I cannot, nevertheless, thus apprehend it without possessing a human mind.

But, finally, what shall I say of the mind itself, that is, of myself? for as yet I do not admit that I am anything but mind. What, then! I who seem to possess so distinct an apprehension of the piece of wax, do I not know myself, both with greater truth and certitude, and also much more distinctly and clearly? For if I judge that the wax exists because I see it, it assuredly follows, much more evidently, that I myself am or exist, for the same reason: for it is possible that what I see may not in truth be wax, and that I do not even possess eyes with which to see anything; but it cannot be that when I see, or, which comes to the same thing, when I think I see, I myself who think am nothing. So likewise, if I judge that the wax exists because I touch it, it will still also follow that I am; and if I determine that my imagination, or any other cause, whatever it be, persuades me of the existence of the wax, I will still draw the same conclusion. And what is here remarked of the piece of wax, is applicable to all the other things that are external to me. And further, if the notion or perception of wax appeared to me more precise and distinct, after that not only sight and touch, but many other causes besides, rendered it manifest to my apprehension, with how much greater distinctness must I now know myself, since all the reasons that contribute to the knowledge of the nature of wax, or of any body whatever, manifest still better the nature of my mind? And there are besides so many other things in the mind itself that contribute to the illustration of its nature, that those dependent on the body, to which I have here referred, scarcely merit to be taken into account.

But, in conclusion, I find I have insensibly reverted to the point I desired; for, since it is now manifest to me that bodies themselves are not properly perceived by the senses nor by the faculty of imagination, but by the intellect alone; and since they are not perceived because they are seen and touched, but only because they are understood or rightly comprehended by thought, I readily discover that there is nothing more easily or clearly apprehended than my own mind. But because it is difficult to rid one's self so promptly of an opinion to which one has been long accustomed, it will be desirable to tarry for some time at this stage, that, by long continued meditation, I may more deeply impress upon my memory this new knowledge.

---

1. *Who is the meditator? What kinds of views does she hold, as she begins her meditations?*
2. *Descartes thinks that many of the beliefs and thoughts we attribute merely to the senses depend on the intellect. How does the example of the automata ('artificial machines') show this?*
3. *What would Descartes make of the scholastic doctrine of existentialism?*
4. *What is the essence of the wax? What would a scholastic make of Descartes's conclusion?*
5. *How does the wax argument work? (Look back at the 'stone' argument from the* Principles.*) Try to reconstruct the wax argument below.*

   Premise 1: At a given time—call it 5pm—the wax has a set of determinate properties, including determinate size, shape, taste, color, and so on.
   Premise 2: At a later time—say, 5:05 pm, the wax _____
   Conclusion: The essence of the wax—and of all material things—is nothing but _____.

Third Meditation: Of God: That He Exists

1. *In this meditation, Descartes continues to use his own view of the order of knowledge, which the skeptical arguments help to establish: contra existentialism, Cartesian essentialism holds that one cannot know that something exists without first _____. Descartes uses some scholastic jargon in this Meditation, which can be very misleading. Watch out for these phrases; they mean roughly the opposite of what it sounds like they should mean.* The 'formal reality' of a thing is just its reality or existence. Descartes thinks there is a hierarchy of reality: as he explains to Hobbes (in the Replies to the third Objections), God is at the top, followed by created substances, and finally their modes. God exists more fully than anything else does, simply because created substances depend for their existence on _____, and modes depend on _____.
2. *Formal reality is to be contrasted with 'objective reality,' the reality or being a thing has in virtue of what it represents. All ideas are modes of the mind; so they all have the same degree of formal reality. But they can differ in objective reality, because they can represent _____.* What else, besides ideas, has objective reality?

But this doesn't mean that Descartes is an idealist, someone who thinks that only ideas exist. God, created substances, and their modes, all have some degree of ____ reality.

I will now close my eyes, I will stop my ears, I will turn away my senses from their objects, I will even efface from my consciousness all the images of corporeal things; or at least, because this can hardly be accomplished, I will consider them as empty and false; and thus, holding converse only with myself, and closely examining my nature, I will endeavor to obtain by degrees a more intimate and familiar knowledge of myself. I am a thinking (conscious) thing, that is, a being who doubts, affirms, denies, knows a few objects, and is ignorant of many—who loves, hates, wills, refuses, who imagines likewise, and perceives; for, as I before remarked, although the things which I perceive or imagine are perhaps nothing at all apart from me and in themselves, I am nevertheless assured that those modes of consciousness which I call perceptions and imaginations, in as far only as they are modes of consciousness, exist in me. And in the little I have said I think I have summed up all that I really know, or at least all that up to this time I was aware I knew.

Now, as I am endeavoring to extend my knowledge more widely, I will use circumspection, and consider with care whether I can still discover in myself anything further which I have not yet hitherto observed. I am certain that I am a thinking thing; but do I not therefore likewise know what is required to render me certain of a truth? In this first knowledge, doubtless, there is nothing that gives me assurance of its truth except the clear and distinct perception of what I affirm, which would not indeed be sufficient to give me the assurance that what I say is true, if it could ever happen that anything I thus clearly and distinctly perceived should prove false; and accordingly it seems to me that I may now take as a general rule, that all that is very clearly and distinctly apprehended (conceived) is true.

Nevertheless I before received and admitted many things as wholly certain and manifest, which yet I afterward found to be doubtful. What, then, were those? They were the earth, the sky, the stars, and all the other objects which I was in the habit of perceiving by the senses. But what was it that I clearly and distinctly perceived in them? Nothing more than that the ideas and the thoughts of those objects were presented to my mind. And even now I do not deny that these ideas are found in my mind. But there was yet another thing which I affirmed, and which, from having been accustomed to believe it, I thought I clearly perceived, although, in truth, I did not perceive it at all; I mean the existence of objects external to me, from which those ideas proceeded, and to which they had a perfect resemblance; and it was here I was mistaken, or if I judged correctly, this assuredly was not to be traced to any knowledge I possessed.

But when I considered any matter in arithmetic and geometry, that was very simple and easy, as, for example, that two and three added together make five, and things of this sort, did I not view them with at least sufficient clearness to warrant me in affirming their truth? Indeed, if I afterward judged that we ought to doubt of these things, it was for no other reason than because it occurred to me that a God might perhaps have given me such a nature as that I should be deceived, even respecting the matters that appeared to me the most evidently true. But as often as this preconceived opinion of the sovereign power of a God presents itself to my mind, I am constrained to admit that it is easy for him, if he wishes it, to cause me to err even in matters where I think I possess the highest evidence; and, on the other hand, as often as I direct my attention to things which I think I apprehend with great clearness, I am so persuaded of their truth that I naturally break out into expressions such as these: 'Deceive me who may, no one will yet ever be able to bring it about that I am not, so long as I shall be conscious that I am, or at any future time cause it to be true that I have never been, it being now true that I am, or make two and three more or less than five, in supposing which, and other like absurdities, I discover a manifest contradiction.'

And in truth, as I have no ground for believing that God is deceitful, and as, indeed, I have not even considered the reasons by which the existence of a God of any kind is established, the ground of doubt that rests only on this supposition is very slight, and, so to speak, metaphysical. But, that I may be able wholly to remove it, I must inquire whether there is a God, as soon as an opportunity of doing so shall present itself; and if I find that there is a God, I must examine likewise whether he can be a deceiver; for, without the knowledge of these two truths, I do not see that I can ever be certain of anything. And that I may be enabled to examine this without interrupting the order of meditation I have proposed to myself (which is, to pass by degrees from the notions that I shall find first in my mind to those I shall afterward discover in it), it is necessary at this stage to divide all my thoughts into certain classes, and to consider in which of these classes truth and error are, strictly speaking, to be found.

Of my thoughts some are, as it were, images of things, and to these alone properly belongs the name **idea**; as when I think of, or represent to my mind, a man, a chimera, the sky, an angel or God. Others, again, have certain other forms; as when I will, fear, affirm, or deny, I always, indeed, apprehend something as the object of my thought, but I also embrace in thought something more than the representation of the object; and of this class of thoughts some are called volitions or affections, and others judgments.

Now, with respect to ideas, if these are considered only in themselves, and are not referred to any object beyond them, they cannot, properly speaking, be false; for, whether I imagine a goat or chimera, it is not less true that I imagine the one than the other. Nor need we fear that falsity may exist in the will or affections; for, although I may desire objects that are wrong, and even that never existed, it is still true that I desire them. There thus only remain our judgments, in which we must take diligent heed that we be not deceived. But the chief and most ordinary error that arises in them consists in judging that the ideas which are in us are like or conformed to the things that are external to us; for assuredly, if we but considered the ideas themselves as certain modes of our thought (consciousness), without referring them to anything beyond, they would hardly afford any occasion of error.

But among these ideas, some appear to me to be *innate*, others *adventitious*, and others to be made by myself (*factitious*); for, as I have the power of conceiving what is called a thing, or a truth, or a thought, it seems to me that I hold this power from no other source than my own nature; but if I now hear a noise, if I see the sun, or if I feel heat, I have all along judged that these sensations proceeded from certain objects existing out of myself; and, in fine, it appears to me that sirens, hippogryphs, and the like, are inventions of my own mind. But I may even perhaps come to be of opinion that all my ideas are of the class which I call adventitious, or that they are all innate, or that they are all factitious; for I have not yet clearly discovered their true origin; and what I have here principally to do is to consider, with reference to those that appear to come from certain objects without me, what grounds there are for thinking them like these objects.

The **first** of these grounds is that it seems to me I am so taught by nature; and the **second** that I am conscious that those ideas are not dependent on my will, and therefore not on myself, for they are frequently presented to me against my will, as at present, whether I will or not, I feel heat; and I am thus persuaded that this sensation or idea (*sensum vel ideam*) of heat is produced in me by something different from myself, viz., by the heat of the fire by which I sit. And it is very reasonable to suppose that this object impresses me with its own likeness rather than any other thing.

But I must consider whether these reasons are sufficiently strong and convincing. When I speak of being taught by nature in this matter, I understand by the word 'nature' only a certain spontaneous impetus that impels me to believe in a resemblance between ideas and their objects, and not a natural light that affords a knowledge of its truth. But these two things are widely different; for what the natural light shows to be true can be in no degree doubtful, as, for example, that I am because I doubt, and other truths of the like kind; inasmuch as I possess no other faculty whereby to distinguish truth from error, which can teach me the falsity of what the natural light declares to be true, and which is equally trustworthy; but with respect to seemingly natural impulses, I have observed, when the question related to the choice of right or wrong in action, that they frequently led me to take the worse part; nor do I see that I have any better ground for following them in what relates to truth and error. Then, with respect to the other reason, which is that because these ideas do not depend on my will, they must arise from objects existing without me, I do not find it more convincing than the former; for just as those natural impulses, of which I have lately spoken, are found in me, notwithstanding that they are not always in harmony with my will, so likewise it may be that I possess some power not sufficiently known to myself capable of producing ideas without the aid of external objects, and, indeed, it has always hitherto appeared to me that they are formed during sleep, by some power of this nature, without the aid of anything external.

And, in fine, although I should grant that they proceeded from those objects, it is not a necessary consequence that they must be like them. On the contrary, I have observed, in a number of instances, that there was a great difference between the object and its idea. Thus, for example, I find in my mind two wholly diverse ideas of the sun; the one, by which it appears to me extremely small draws its origin from the senses, and should be placed in the class of adventitious ideas; the other, by which it seems to be many times larger than the whole earth, is taken up on astronomical grounds, that is, elicited from certain notions born with me, or is framed by myself in some other manner. These two ideas cannot certainly both resemble the same sun; and reason teaches me that the one which seems to have immediately emanated from it is the most unlike. And these things sufficiently prove that hitherto it has not been from a certain and deliberate judgment, but only from a sort of blind impulse, that I believed in the existence of certain things different from myself, which, by the organs of sense, or by whatever other means it might be,, conveyed their ideas or images into my mind and impressed it with their likenesses.

But there is still another way of inquiring whether, of the objects whose ideas are in my mind, there are any that exist out of me. If ideas are taken in so far only as they are certain modes of consciousness, I do not remark any difference or inequality among them, and all seem, in the same manner, to proceed from myself; but, considering them as images, of which one represents one thing and another a different, it is evident that a great diversity obtains among them. For, without doubt, those that represent substances are something more, and contain in themselves, so to speak, more objective reality, than those that represent only modes or accidents; and again, the idea by which I conceive a God—sovereign, eternal, infinite, immutable, all-knowing, all-powerful, and the creator of all things that are out of himself—this, I say, has certainly in it more objective reality than those ideas by which finite substances are represented.

Now, it is manifest by the natural light that there must at least be as much reality in the efficient and total cause as in its effect; for whence can the effect draw its reality if not from its cause? And how could the cause communicate to it this reality unless it possessed it in itself? And hence it follows, not only that what is cannot be produced by what is not, but likewise that the more perfect, in other words, that which contains in itself more reality, cannot be the effect of the less perfect; and this is not only evidently true of those effects, whose reality is actual or formal, but likewise of ideas, whose reality is only considered as objective. Thus, for example, the stone that is not yet in existence, cannot now commence to be, unless it be produced by that which possesses in itself, formally or eminently, all that enters into its composition (in other words, by that which contains in itself the same properties that are in the stone, or others superior to them); and heat can only be produced in a subject that was before devoid of it, by a cause that is of an order, degree, or kind, at least as perfect as heat; and so of the others.

But further, even the idea of the heat, or of the stone, cannot exist in me unless it be put there by a cause that contains, at least, as much reality as I conceive existent in the heat or in the stone: for although that cause may not transmit into my idea anything of its actual or formal reality, we ought not on this account to imagine that it is less real; but we ought to consider that, as every idea is a work of the mind, its nature is such as of itself to demand no other formal reality than that which it borrows from our consciousness, of which it is but a mode (that is, a manner or way of thinking). But in order that an idea may contain this objective reality rather than that, it must doubtless derive it from some cause in which is found at least as much formal reality as the idea contains of objective; for, if we suppose that there is found in an idea anything which was not in its cause, it must of course derive this from nothing. But, however imperfect may be the mode of existence by which a thing is, objectively or by representation, in the understanding by its idea, we certainly cannot, for all that, allege that this mode of existence is nothing, nor, consequently, that the idea owes its origin to nothing. Nor must it be imagined that, since the reality which is considered in these ideas is only objective, the same reality need not be formally (actually) in the causes of these ideas, but only objectively: for, just as the mode of existing objectively belongs to ideas by their peculiar nature, so likewise the mode of existing formally appertains to the causes of these ideas (at least to the first and principal), by their peculiar nature. And although an idea may give rise to another idea, this regress cannot, nevertheless, be infinite; we must in the end reach a first idea, the cause of which is, as it were, the archetype in which all the reality or perfection that is found, objectively or by representation, in these ideas is contained formally and in act. I am thus clearly taught by the natural light that ideas exist in me as pictures or images, which may, in truth, readily fall short of the perfection of the objects from which they are taken, but can never contain anything greater or more perfect.

And in proportion to the time and care with which I examine all those matters, the conviction of their truth brightens and becomes distinct. But, to sum up, what conclusion shall I draw from it all? It is this: if the objective reality or perfection of any one of my ideas be such as clearly to convince me, that this same reality exists in me neither formally nor eminently, and if, as follows from this, I myself cannot be the cause of it, it is a necessary consequence that I am not alone in the world, but that there is besides myself some other being who exists as the cause of that idea; while, on the contrary, if no such idea be found in my mind, I shall have no sufficient ground of assurance of the existence of any other being besides myself; for, after a most careful search, I have, up to this moment, been unable to discover any other ground.

But, among these my ideas, besides that which represents myself, respecting which there can be here no difficulty, there is one that represents a God; others that represent corporeal and inanimate things; others angels; others animals; and, finally, there are some that represent men like myself. But with respect to the ideas that represent other men, or animals, or angels, I can easily suppose that they were formed by the mingling and composition of the other ideas which I have of myself, of corporeal things, and of God, although they were, apart from myself, neither men, animals, nor angels. And with regard to the ideas of corporeal objects, I never discovered in them anything so great or excellent which I myself did not appear capable of originating; for, by considering these ideas closely and scrutinizing them individually, in the same way that I yesterday examined the idea of wax, I find that there is but little in them that is clearly and distinctly perceived. As belonging to the class of things that are clearly apprehended, I recognize the following, viz., magnitude or extension in length, breadth, and depth; figure, which results from the termination of extension; situation, which bodies of diverse figures preserve with reference to each other; and motion or the change of situation; to which may be added substance, duration, and number.

But with regard to light, colors, sounds, odors, tastes, heat, cold, and the other tactile qualities, they are thought with so much obscurity and confusion, that I cannot determine even whether they are true or false; in other words, whether or not the ideas I have of these qualities are in truth the ideas of real objects. For although I before remarked that it is only in judgments that formal falsity, or falsity properly so called, can be met with, there may nevertheless be found in ideas a certain material falsity, which arises when they represent what is nothing as if it were something. Thus, for example, the ideas I have of cold and heat are so far from being clear and distinct, that I am unable from them to discover whether cold is only the privation of heat, or heat the privation of cold; or whether they are or are not real qualities: and since, ideas being as it were images there can be none that does not seem to us to represent some object, the idea which represents cold as something real and positive will not improperly be called false, if it be correct to say that cold is nothing but a privation of heat; and so in other cases. To ideas of this kind, indeed, it is not necessary that I should assign any author besides myself: for if they are false, that is, represent objects that are unreal, the natural light teaches me that they proceed from nothing; in other words, that they are in me only because something is wanting to the perfection of my nature; but if these ideas are true, yet because they exhibit to me so little reality that I cannot even distinguish the object represented from non-being, I do not see why I should not be the author of them.

With reference to those ideas of corporeal things that are clear and distinct, there are some which, as appears to me, might have been taken from the idea I have of myself, as those of substance, duration, number, and the like. For when I think that a stone is a substance, or a thing capable of existing of itself, and that I am likewise a substance, although I conceive that I am a thinking and non-extended thing, and that the stone, on the contrary, is extended and unconscious, there being thus the greatest diversity between the two concepts, yet these two ideas seem to have this in common that they both represent substances. In the same way, when I think of myself as now existing, and recollect besides that I existed some time ago, and when I am conscious of various thoughts whose number I know, I then acquire the ideas of duration and number, which I can afterward transfer to as many objects as I please. With respect to the other qualities that go to make up the ideas of corporeal objects, viz., extension, figure, situation, and motion, it is true that they are not formally in me, since I am merely a thinking being; but because they are only certain modes of substance, and because I myself am a substance, it seems possible that they may be contained in me eminently.

There only remains, therefore, the idea of God, in which I must consider whether there is anything that cannot be supposed to originate with myself. By the name God, I understand a substance infinite, eternal, immutable, independent, all-knowing, all-powerful, and by which I myself, and every other thing that exists, if any such there be, were created. But these properties are so great and excellent, that the more attentively I consider them the less I feel persuaded that the idea I have of them owes its origin to myself alone. And thus it is absolutely necessary to conclude, from all that I have before said, that God exists: for though the idea of substance be in my mind owing to this, that I myself am a substance, I should not, however, have the idea of an infinite substance, seeing I am a finite being, unless it were given me by some substance in reality infinite.

And I must not imagine that I do not apprehend the infinite by a true idea, but only by the negation of the finite, in the same way that I comprehend repose and darkness by the negation of motion and light: since, on the contrary, I clearly perceive that there is more reality in the infinite substance than in the finite, and therefore that in some way I possess the perception (notion) of the infinite before that of the finite, that is, the perception of God before that of myself, for how could I know that I doubt, desire, or that something is wanting to me, and that I am not wholly perfect, if I possessed no idea of a being more perfect than myself, by comparison of which I knew the deficiencies of my nature?

And it cannot be said that this idea of God is perhaps materially false, and consequently that it may have arisen from nothing (in other words, that it may exist in me from my imperfection), as I before said of the ideas of heat and cold, and the like: for, on the contrary, as this idea is very clear and distinct, and contains in itself more objective reality than any other, there can be no one of itself more true, or less open to the suspicion of falsity.

The idea, I say, of a being supremely perfect, and infinite, is in the highest degree true; for although, perhaps, we may imagine that such a being does not exist, we cannot, nevertheless, suppose that his idea represents nothing real, as I have already said of the idea of cold. It is likewise clear and distinct in the highest degree, since whatever the mind clearly and distinctly conceives as real or true, and as implying any perfection, is contained entire in this idea. And this is true, nevertheless, although I do not comprehend the infinite, and although there may be in God an infinity of things that I cannot comprehend, nor perhaps even compass by thought in any way; for it is of the nature of the infinite that it should not be comprehended by the finite; and it is enough that I rightly understand this, and judge that all which I clearly perceive, and in which I know there is some perfection, and perhaps also an infinity of properties of which I am ignorant, are formally or eminently in God, in order that the idea I have of him may become the most true, clear, and distinct of all the ideas in my mind.

But perhaps I am something more than I suppose myself to be, and it may be that all those perfections which I attribute to God, in some way exist potentially in me, although they do not yet show themselves, and are not reduced to act. Indeed, I am already conscious that my knowledge is being increased and perfected by degrees; and I see nothing to prevent it from thus gradually increasing to infinity, nor any reason why, after such increase and perfection, I should not be able thereby to acquire all the other perfections of the divine nature; nor, in fine, why the power I possess of acquiring those perfections, if it really now exist in me, should not be sufficient to produce the ideas of them. Yet, on looking more closely into the matter, I discover that this cannot be; for, in the first place, although it were true that my knowledge daily acquired new degrees of perfection, and although there were potentially in my nature much that was not as yet actually in it, still all these excellences make not the slightest approach to the idea I have of God, in whom there is no perfection merely potentially (but rather all actually) existent; for it is even an unmistakable token of imperfection in my knowledge, that it is augmented by degrees.

Further, although my knowledge increase more and more, nevertheless I am not, therefore, induced to think that it will ever be actually infinite, since it can never reach that point beyond which it shall be incapable of further increase. But I conceive God as actually infinite, so that nothing can be added to his perfection. And, in fine, I readily perceive that the objective being of an idea cannot be produced by a being that is merely potentially existent, which, properly speaking, is nothing, but only by a being existing formally or actually.

And, truly, I see nothing in all that I have now said which it is not easy for any one, who shall carefully consider it, to discern by the natural light; but when I allow my attention in some degree to relax, the vision of my mind being obscured, and, as it were, blinded by the images of sensible objects, I do not readily remember the reason why the idea of a being more perfect than myself, must of necessity have proceeded from a being in reality more perfect. On this account I am here desirous to inquire further, whether I, who possess this idea of God, could exist supposing there were no God. And I ask, from whom could I, in that case, derive my existence? Perhaps from myself, or from my parents, or from some other causes less perfect than God; for anything more perfect, or even equal to God, cannot be thought or imagined. But if I were independent of every other existence, and were myself the author of my being, I should doubt of nothing, I should desire nothing, and, in fine, no perfection would be lacking to me; for I should have bestowed upon myself every perfection of which I possess the idea, and I should thus be God.

And it must not be imagined that what is now wanting to me is perhaps of more difficult acquisition than that of which I am already possessed; for, on the contrary, it is quite manifest that it was a matter of much higher difficulty that I, a thinking being, should arise from nothing, than it would be for me to acquire the knowledge of many things of which I am ignorant, and which are merely the accidents of a thinking substance; and certainly, if I possessed of myself the greater perfection of which I have now spoken—in other words, if I were the author of my own existence—I would not at least have denied to myself things that may be more easily obtained (as that infinite variety of knowledge of which I am at present destitute). I could not, indeed, have denied to myself any property which I perceive is contained in the idea of God, because there is none of these that seems to me to be more difficult to make or acquire; and if there were any that should happen to be more difficult to acquire, they would certainly appear so to me (supposing that I myself were the source of the other things I possess), because I should discover in them a limit to my power. And though I were to suppose that I always was as I now am, I should not, on this ground, escape the force of these reasonings, since it would not follow, even on this supposition, that no author of my existence needed to be sought after. For the whole time of my life may be divided into an infinity of parts, each of which is in no way dependent on any other; and, accordingly, because I was in existence a short time ago, it does not follow that I must now exist, unless in this moment some cause create me anew as it were, that is, conserve me. In truth, it is perfectly clear and evident to all who will attentively consider the nature of duration, that the conservation of a substance, in each moment of its duration, requires the same power and act that would be necessary to create it, supposing it were not yet in existence; so that it is manifestly a dictate of the natural light that conservation and creation differ merely in respect of our mode of thinking and not in reality. All that is here required, therefore, is that I interrogate myself to discover whether I possess any power by means of which I can bring it about that I, who now am, shall exist a moment afterward: for, since I am merely a thinking thing (or since, at least, the precise question, in the meantime, is only of that part of myself), if such a power resided in me, I should, without doubt, be conscious of it; but I am conscious of no such power, and thereby I manifestly know that I am dependent upon some being different from myself.

But perhaps the being upon whom I am dependent is not God, and I have been produced either by my parents, or by some causes less perfect than God. This cannot be: for, as I before said, it is perfectly evident that there must at least be as much reality in the cause as in its effect; and accordingly, since I am a thinking thing and possess in myself an idea of God, whatever in the end be the cause of my existence, it must of necessity be admitted that it is likewise a thinking being, and that it possesses in itself the idea and all the perfections I attribute to God. Then it may again be inquired whether this cause owes its origin and existence to itself, or to some other cause. For if it be self-existent, it follows, from what I have before laid down, that this cause is God; for, since it possesses the perfection of self-existence, it must likewise, without doubt, have the power of actually possessing every perfection of which it has the idea—in other words, all the perfections I conceive to belong to God. But if it owe its existence to another cause than, itself, we demand again, for a similar reason, whether this second cause exists of itself or through some other, until, from stage to stage, we at length arrive at an ultimate cause, which will be God. And it is quite manifest that in this matter there can be no infinite regress of causes, seeing that the question raised respects not so much the cause which once produced me, as that by which I am at this present moment conserved.

Nor can it be supposed that several causes concurred in my production, and that from one I received the idea of one of the perfections I attribute to God, and from another the idea of some other, and thus that all those perfections are indeed found somewhere in the universe, but do not all exist together in a single being who is God; for, on the contrary, the unity, the simplicity, or inseparability of all the properties of God, is one of the chief perfections I conceive him to possess; and the idea of this unity of all the perfections of God could certainly not be put into my mind by any cause from which I did not likewise receive the ideas of all the other perfections; for no power could enable me to embrace them in an inseparable unity, without at the same time giving me the knowledge of what they were and of their existence in a particular mode.

Finally, with regard to my parents (from whom it appears I sprung), although all that I believed respecting them be true, it does not, nevertheless, follow that I am conserved by them, or even that I was produced by them, in so far as I am a thinking being. All that, at the most, they contributed to my origin was the giving of certain dispositions (modifications) to the matter in which I have hitherto judged that I or my mind, which is what alone I now consider to be myself, is inclosed; and thus there can here be no difficulty with respect to them, and it is absolutely necessary to conclude from this alone that I am, and possess the idea of a being absolutely perfect, that is, of God, that his existence is most clearly demonstrated.

There remains only the inquiry as to the way in which I received this idea from God; for I have not drawn it from the senses, nor is it even presented to me unexpectedly, as is usual with the ideas of sensible objects, when these are presented or appear to be presented to the external organs of the senses; it is not even a pure production or fiction of my mind, for it is not in my power to take from or add to it; and consequently there but remains the alternative that it is innate, in the same way as is the idea of myself. And, in truth, it is not to be wondered at that God, at my creation, implanted this idea in me, that it might serve, as it were, for the mark of the workman impressed on his work; and it is not also necessary that the mark should be something different from the work itself; but considering only that God is my creator, it is highly probable that he in some way fashioned me after his own image and likeness, and that I perceive this likeness, in which is contained the idea of God, by the same faculty by which I apprehend myself, in other words, when I make myself the object of reflection, I not only find that I am an incomplete, imperfect, and dependent being, and one who unceasingly aspires after something better and greater than he is; but, at the same time, I am assured likewise that he upon whom I am dependent possesses in himself all the goods after which I aspire (and the ideas of which I find in my mind), and that not merely indefinitely and potentially, but infinitely and actually, and that he is thus God. And the whole force of the argument of which I have here availed myself to establish the existence of God, consists in this, that I perceive I could not possibly be of such a nature as I am, and yet have in my mind the idea of a God, if God did not in reality exist—this same God, I say, whose idea is in my mind—that is, a being who possesses all those lofty perfections, of which the mind may have some slight conception, without, however, being able fully to comprehend them, and who is wholly superior to all defect and has nothing that marks imperfection: whence it is sufficiently manifest that he cannot be a deceiver, since it is a dictate of the natural light that all fraud and deception spring from some defect.

But before I examine this with more attention, and pass on to the consideration of other truths that may be evolved out of it, I think it proper to remain here for some time in the contemplation of God himself—that I may ponder at leisure his marvelous attributes—and behold, admire, and adore the beauty of this light so unspeakably great, as far, at least, as the strength of my mind, which is to some degree dazzled by the sight, will permit. For just as we learn by faith that the supreme felicity of another life consists in the contemplation of the divine majesty alone, so even now we learn from experience that a like meditation, though incomparably less perfect, is the source of the highest satisfaction of which we are susceptible in this life.

1. What are the three classes of ideas the meditator speaks of? Some ideas at least seem to be innate; others seem to be _____ or _____.
2. The main argument here shows that at least one idea has to fall into one of the three classes above. Which idea is it, and what class does it fall into?
3. Descartes uses a causal principle here: the cause must have at least as much reality as the effect. What's the justification for this?
4. Applied to ideas, the principle says that there must be at least as much _____ reality in the cause of an idea as there is _____ in the idea itself. (See the synopsis of this meditation for an example.)Given this principle, what can we say about the idea of God?
5. Descartes gives a second argument for God's existence, based on the nature of time and his existence at this moment. How is Descartes's argument different from a traditional cosmological argument? Finally, do you think this is really an independent argument, or does it in some way rely on the argument from the idea of God?

Fourth Meditation: Of Truth and Error

In the Third Meditation, the Meditator tried to prove what we might call the Epistemic Principle (EP):

Epistemic Principle

Everything (that is, every proposition) I clearly and distinctly perceive (that is, believe and thoroughly understand) is true.

The Meditator's overall argument for EP works roughly like this:

Premise 1: I exist.
  Premise 2: God exists.
  Premise 3: God is not a _____.
  Conclusion: The Epistemic Principle is true.

This strategy creates a problem for the Meditator, though: how can I ever make a mistake? This is just a special case of the problem of evil: if God is all powerful and all good, how can bad things happen to good people? The Fourth Meditation is devoted to answering this special case.

I have been habituated these bygone days to detach my mind from the senses, and I have accurately observed that there is exceedingly little which is known with certainty respecting corporeal objects, that we know much more of the human mind, and still more of God himself. I am thus able now without difficulty to abstract my mind from the contemplation of sensible or imaginable objects, and apply it to those which, as disengaged from all matter, are purely intelligible. And certainly the idea I have of the human mind in so far as it is a thinking thing, and not extended in length, breadth, and depth, and participating in none of the properties of body, is incomparably more distinct than the idea of any corporeal object; and when I consider that I doubt, in other words, that I am an incomplete and dependent being, the idea of a complete and independent being, that is to say of God, occurs to my mind with so much clearness and distinctness, and from the fact alone that this idea is found in me, or that I who possess it exist, the conclusions that

God exists, and that my own existence, each moment of its continuance, is absolutely dependent upon him, are so manifest, as to lead me to believe it impossible that the human mind can know anything with more clearness and certitude. And now I seem to discover a path that will conduct us from the contemplation of the true God, in whom are contained all the treasures of science and wisdom, to the knowledge of the other things in the universe.

For, in the first place, I discover that it is impossible for him ever to deceive me, for in all fraud and deceit there is a certain imperfection: and although it may seem that the ability to deceive is a mark of subtlety or power, yet the will testifies without doubt of malice and weakness; and such, accordingly, cannot be found in God. In the next place, I am conscious that I possess a certain faculty of judging (or of discerning truth from error), which I doubtless received from God, along with whatever else is mine; and since it is impossible that he should will to deceive me, if is likewise certain that he has not given me a faculty that will ever lead me into error, provided I use it aright.

And there would remain no doubt on this head, did it not seem to follow from this, that I can never therefore be deceived; for if all I possess be from God, and if he planted in me no faculty that is deceitful, it seems to follow that I can never fall into error. Accordingly, it is true that when I think only of God, and turn wholly to him, I discover in myself no cause of error or falsity: but immediately thereafter, recurring to myself, experience assures me that I am nevertheless subject to innumerable errors. When I come to inquire into the cause of these, I observe that there is not only present to my consciousness a real and positive idea of God, or of a being supremely perfect, but also, so to speak, a certain negative idea of nothing, in other words, of that which is at an infinite distance from every sort of perfection, and that I am, as it were, a mean between God and nothing, or placed in such a way between absolute existence and non-existence, that there is in truth nothing in me to lead me into error, in so far as an absolute being is my creator; but that, on the other hand, as I thus likewise participate in some degree of nothing or of nonbeing, in other words, as I am not myself the supreme Being, and as I am wanting in many perfections, it is not surprising I should fall into error. And I hence discern that error, so far as error is not something real, which depends for its existence on God, but is simply defect; and therefore that, in order to fall into it, it is not necessary God should have given me a faculty expressly for this end, but that my being deceived arises from the circumstance that the power which God has given me of discerning truth from error is not infinite.

Nevertheless this is not yet quite satisfactory; for error is not a pure negation (in other words, it is not the simple deficiency or want of some knowledge which is not due), but the privation or want of some knowledge which it would seem I ought to possess. But, on considering the nature of God, it seems impossible that he should have planted in his creature any faculty not perfect in its kind, that is, wanting in some perfection due to it: for if it be true, that in proportion to the skill of the maker the perfection of his work is greater, what thing can have been produced by the supreme Creator of the universe that is not absolutely perfect in all its parts? And assuredly there is no doubt that God could have created me such as that I should never be deceived; it is certain, likewise, that he always wills what is best: is it better, then, that I should be capable of being deceived than that I should not?

Considering this more attentively, the first thing that occurs to me is the reflection that I must not be surprised if I am not always capable of comprehending the reasons why God acts as he does; nor must I doubt of his existence because I find, perhaps, that there are several other things besides the present respecting which I understand neither why nor how they were created by him; for, knowing already that my nature is extremely weak and limited, and that the nature of God, on the other hand, is immense, incomprehensible, and infinite, I have no longer any difficulty in discerning that there is an infinity of things in his power whose causes transcend the grasp of my mind: and this consideration alone is sufficient to convince me, that the whole class of final causes is of no avail in physical or natural things; for it appears to me that I cannot, without exposing myself to the charge of temerity, seek to discover the impenetrable ends of God.

It further occurs to me that we must not consider only one creature apart from the others, if we wish to determine the perfection of the works of God, but generally all his creatures together; for the same object that might perhaps, with some show of reason, be deemed highly imperfect if it were alone in the world, may for all that be the most perfect possible, considered as forming part of the whole universe: and although, as it was my purpose to doubt of everything, I only as yet know with certainty my own existence and that of God, nevertheless, after having remarked the infinite power of God, I cannot deny that we may have produced many other objects, or at least that he is able to produce them, so that I may occupy a place in the relation of a part to the great whole of his creatures.

Whereupon, regarding myself more closely, and considering what my errors are (which alone testify to the existence of imperfection in me), I observe that these depend on the concurrence of two causes, viz., the faculty of cognition, which I possess, and that of election or the power of free choice—in other words, the understanding and the will. For by the understanding alone, I neither affirm nor deny anything but merely apprehend the ideas regarding which I may form a judgment; nor is any error, properly so called, found in it thus accurately taken. And although there are perhaps innumerable objects in the world of which I have no idea in my understanding, it cannot, on that account be said that I am deprived of those ideas (as of something that is due to my nature), but simply that I do not possess them, because, in truth, there is no ground to prove that Deity ought to have endowed me with a larger faculty of cognition than he has actually bestowed upon me; and however skillful a workman I suppose him to be, I have no reason, on that account, to think that it was obligatory on him to give to each of his works all the perfections he is able to bestow upon some. Nor, moreover, can I complain that God has not given me freedom of choice, or a will sufficiently ample and perfect, since, in truth, I am conscious of will so ample and extended as to be superior to all limits. And what appears to me here to be highly remarkable is that, of all the other properties I possess, there is none so great and perfect as that I do not clearly discern it could be still greater and more perfect.

For, to take an example, if I consider the faculty of understanding which I possess, I find that it is of very small extent, and greatly limited, and at the same time I form the idea of another faculty of the same nature, much more ample and even infinite, and seeing that I can frame the idea of it, I discover, from this circumstance alone, that it pertains to the nature of God. In the same way, if I examine the faculty of memory or imagination, or any other faculty I possess, I find none that is not small and circumscribed, and in God immense and infinite. It is the faculty of will only, or freedom of choice, which I experience to be so great that I am unable to conceive the idea of another that shall be more ample and extended; so that it is chiefly my will which leads me to discern that I bear a certain image and similitude of God. For although the faculty of will is incomparably greater in God than in myself, as well in respect of the knowledge and power that are conjoined with it, and that render it stronger and more efficacious, as in respect of the object, since in him it extends to a greater number of things, it does not, nevertheless, appear to me greater, considered in itself formally and precisely: for the power of will consists only in this, that we are able to do or not to do the same thing (that is, to affirm or deny, to pursue or shun it), or rather in this alone, that in affirming or denying, pursuing or shunning, what is proposed to us by the understanding, we so act that we are not conscious of being determined to a particular action by any external force. For, to the possession of freedom, it is not necessary that I be alike indifferent toward each of two contraries; but, on the contrary, the more I am inclined toward the one, whether because I clearly know that in it there is the reason of truth and goodness, or because God thus internally disposes my thought, the more freely do I choose and embrace it; and assuredly divine grace and natural knowledge, very far from diminishing liberty, rather augment and fortify it. But the indifference of which I am conscious when I am not impelled to one side rather than to another for want of a reason, is the lowest grade of liberty, and manifests defect or negation of knowledge rather than perfection of will; for if I always clearly knew what was true and good, I should never have any difficulty in determining what judgment I ought to come to, and what choice I ought to make, and I should thus be entirely free without ever being indifferent.

From all this I discover, however, that neither the power of willing, which I have received from God, is of itself the source of my errors, for it is exceedingly ample and perfect in its kind; nor even the power of understanding, for as I conceive no object unless by means of the faculty that God bestowed upon me, all that I conceive is doubtless rightly conceived by me, and it is impossible for me to be deceived in it.

Whence, then, spring my errors? They arise from this cause alone, that I do not restrain the will, which is of much wider range than the understanding, within the same limits, but extend it even to things I do not understand, and as the will is of itself indifferent to such, it readily falls into error and sin by choosing the false in room of the true, and evil instead of good.

For example, when I lately considered whether anything really existed in the world, and found that because I considered this question, it very manifestly followed that I myself existed, I could not but judge that what I so clearly conceived was true, not that I was forced to this judgment by any external cause, but simply because great clearness of the understanding was succeeded by strong inclination in the will; and I believed this the more freely and spontaneously in proportion as I was less indifferent with respect to it. But now I not only know that I exist, insofar as I am a thinking being, but there is likewise presented to my mind a certain idea of corporeal nature; hence I am in doubt as to whether the thinking nature which is in me, or rather which I myself am, is different from that corporeal nature, or whether both are merely one and the same thing, and I here suppose that I am as yet ignorant of any reason that would determine me to adopt the one belief in preference to the other; whence it happens that it is a matter of perfect indifference to me which of the two suppositions I affirm or deny, or whether I form any judgment at all in the matter.

This indifference, moreover, extends not only to things of which the understanding has no knowledge at all, but in general also to all those which it does not discover with perfect clearness at the moment the will is deliberating upon them; for, however probable the conjectures may be that dispose me to form a judgment in a particular matter, the simple knowledge that these are merely conjectures, and not certain and indubitable reasons, is sufficient to lead me to form one that is directly the opposite. Of this I lately had abundant experience, when I laid aside as false all that I had before held for true, on the single ground that I could in some degree doubt of it. But if I abstain from judging of a thing when I do not conceive it with sufficient clearness and distinctness, it is plain that I act rightly, and am not deceived; but if I resolve to deny or affirm, I then do not make a right use of my free will; and if I affirm what is false, it is evident that I am deceived; moreover, even although I judge according to truth, I stumble upon it by chance, and do not therefore escape the imputation of a wrong use of my freedom; for it is a dictate of the natural light, that the knowledge of the understanding ought always to precede the determination of the will.

And it is this wrong use of the freedom of the will in which is found the privation that constitutes the form of error. Privation, I say, is found in the act, in so far as it proceeds from myself, but it does not exist in the faculty which I received from God, nor even in the act, in so far as it depends on him; for I have assuredly no reason to complain that God has not given me a greater power of intelligence or more perfect natural light than he has actually bestowed, since it is of the nature of a finite understanding not to comprehend many things, and of the nature of a created understanding to be finite; on the contrary, I have every reason to render thanks to God, who owed me nothing, for having given me all the perfections I possess, and I should be far from thinking that he has unjustly deprived me of, or kept back, the other perfections which he has not bestowed upon me.

I have no reason, moreover, to complain because he has given me a will more ample than my understanding, since, as the will consists only of a single element, and that indivisible, it would appear that this faculty is of such a nature that nothing could be taken from it without destroying it; and certainly, the more extensive it is, the more cause I have to thank the goodness of him who bestowed it upon me.

And, finally, I ought not also to complain that God concurs with me in forming the acts of this will, or the judgments in which I am deceived, because those acts are wholly true and good, in so far as they depend on God; and the ability to form them is a higher degree of perfection in my nature than the want of it would be. With regard to privation, in which alone consists the formal reason of error and sin, this does not require the concurrence of God, because it is not a thing (or an existence), and if it be referred to God as to its cause, it ought not to be called 'privation', but 'negation', according to the signification of these words in the schools. For in truth it is no imperfection in God that he has accorded to me the power of giving or withholding my assent from certain things of which he has not put a clear and distinct knowledge in my understanding; but it is doubtless an imperfection in me that I do not use my freedom aright, and readily give my judgment on matters which I only obscurely and confusedly conceive.

I perceive, nevertheless, that it was easy for God so to have constituted me as that I should never be deceived, although I still remained free and possessed of a limited knowledge, viz., by implanting in my understanding a clear and distinct knowledge of all the objects respecting which I should ever have to deliberate; or simply by so deeply engraving on my memory the resolution to judge of nothing without previously possessing a clear and distinct conception of it, that I should never forget it. And I easily understand that, in so far as I consider myself as a single whole, without reference to any other being in the universe, I should have been much more perfect than I now am, had God created me superior to error; but I cannot therefore deny that it is not somehow a greater perfection in the universe, that certain of its parts are not exempt from defect, as others are, than if they were all perfectly alike.

And I have no right to complain because God, who placed me in the world, was not willing that I should sustain that character which of all others is the chief and most perfect; I have even good reason to remain satisfied on the ground that, if he has not given me the perfection of being superior to error by the first means I have pointed out above, which depends on a clear and evident knowledge of all the matters regarding which I can deliberate, he has at least left in my power the other means, which is, firmly to retain the resolution never to judge where the truth is not clearly known to me: for, although I am conscious of the weakness of not being able to keep my mind continually fixed on the same thought, I can nevertheless, by attentive and oft-repeated meditation, impress it so strongly on my memory that I shall never fail to recollect it as often as I require it, and I can acquire in this way the habitude of not erring; and since it is in being superior to error that the highest and chief perfection of man consists, I deem that I have not gained little by this day's meditation, in having discovered the source of error and falsity.

And certainly this can be no other than what I have now explained: for as often as I so restrain my will within the limits of my knowledge, that it forms no judgment except regarding objects which are clearly and distinctly represented to it by the understanding, I can never be deceived; because every clear and distinct conception is doubtless something, and as such cannot owe its origin to nothing, but must of necessity have

God for its author—God, I say, who, as supremely perfect, cannot, without a contradiction, be the cause of any error; and consequently it is necessary to conclude that every such conception or judgment is true. Nor have I merely learned today what I must avoid to escape error, but also what I must do to arrive at the knowledge of truth; for I will assuredly reach truth if I only fix my attention sufficiently on all the things I conceive perfectly, and separate these from others which I conceive more confusedly and obscurely; to which for the future I shall give diligent heed.

---

1. *What is the main problem the Meditator must answer here?*
2. *How does she answer it?*
3. *How can we avoid error?*

Fifth Meditation: Of the Essence of Material Things; and, Again, of God; That He Exists

According to Descartes's essentialism, before we can close the book on skepticism about the external world, we have to know clearly and distinctly _____. So that's what we'll achieve in this Meditation; we'll also get a clearer understanding of the relationship between substance and essence, and another argument that God exists.

Several other questions remain for consideration respecting the attributes of God and my own nature or mind. I will, however, on some other occasion perhaps resume the investigation of these. Meanwhile, as I have discovered what must be done and what avoided to arrive at the knowledge of truth, what I have chiefly to do is to essay to emerge from the state of doubt in which I have for some time been, and to discover whether anything can be known with certainty regarding material objects. But before considering whether such objects as I conceive exist without me, I must examine their ideas in so far as these are to be found in my consciousness, and discover which of them are distinct and which confused.

In the first place, I distinctly imagine that quantity which the philosophers commonly call 'continuous', or the extension in length, breadth, and depth that is in this quantity, or rather in the object to which it is attributed. Further, I can enumerate in it many diverse parts, and attribute to each of these all sorts of sizes, figures, situations, and local motions; and, in fine, I can assign to each of these motions all degrees of duration. And I not only distinctly know these things when I thus consider them in general; but besides, by a little attention, I discover innumerable particulars respecting figures, numbers, motion, and the like, which are so evidently true, and so accordant with my nature, that when I now discover them I do not so much appear to learn anything new, as to call to remembrance what I before knew, or for the first time to remark what was before in my mind, but to which I had not hitherto directed my attention. And what I here find of most importance is, that I discover in my mind innumerable ideas of certain objects, which cannot be esteemed pure negations, although perhaps they possess no reality beyond my thought, and which are not framed by me though it may be in my power to think, or not to think them, but possess true and immutable natures of their own. As, for example, when I imagine a triangle, although there is not perhaps and never was in any place in the universe apart from my thought one such figure, it remains true nevertheless that this figure possesses a certain determinate nature, form, or essence, which is immutable and eternal, and not framed by me, nor in any degree dependent on my thought; as appears from the circumstance, that diverse properties of the triangle may be demonstrated, viz., that its three angles are equal to two right, that its greatest side is subtended by its greatest angle, and the like, which, whether I will or not, I now clearly discern to belong to it, although before I did not at all think of them, when, for the first time, I imagined a triangle, and which accordingly cannot be said to have been invented by me.

Nor is it a valid objection to allege, that perhaps this idea of a triangle came into my mind by the medium of the senses, through my having seen bodies of a triangular figure; for I am able to form in thought an innumerable variety of figures with regard to which it cannot be supposed that they were ever objects of sense, and I can nevertheless demonstrate diverse properties of their nature no less than of the triangle, all of which are assuredly true since I clearly conceive them: and they are therefore something, and not mere negations; for it is highly evident that all that is true is something (truth being identical with existence); and I have already fully shown the truth of the principle, that whatever is clearly and distinctly known is true. And although this had not been demonstrated, yet the nature of my mind is such as to compel me to assert to what I clearly conceive while I so conceive it; and I recollect that even when I still strongly adhered to the objects of sense, I reckoned among the number of the most certain truths those I clearly conceived relating to figures, numbers, and other matters that pertain to arithmetic and geometry, and in general to the pure mathematics.

But now if because I can draw from my thought the idea of an object, it follows that all I clearly and distinctly apprehend to pertain to this object, does in truth belong to it, may I not from this derive an argument for the existence of God? It is certain that I no less find the idea of a God in my consciousness, that is the idea of a being supremely perfect, than that of any figure or number whatever: and I know with not less clearness and distinctness that an actual and eternal existence pertains to his nature than that all which is demonstrable of any figure or number really belongs to the nature of that figure or number; and, therefore, although all the conclusions of the preceding meditations were false, the existence of God would pass with me for a truth at least as certain as I ever judged any truth of mathematics to be, although indeed such a doctrine may at first sight appear to contain more sophistry than truth. For, as I have been accustomed in every other matter to distinguish between existence and essence, I easily believe that the existence can be separated from the essence of God, and that thus God may be conceived as not actually existing. But, nevertheless, when I think of it more attentively, it appears that the existence can no more be separated from the essence of God, than the idea of a mountain from that of a valley, or the equality of its three angles to two right angles, from the essence of a rectilineal triangle; so that it is not less impossible to conceive a God, that is, a being supremely perfect, to whom existence is wanting, or who is devoid of a certain perfection, than to conceive a mountain without a valley.

But though, in truth, I cannot conceive a God unless as existing, any more than I can a mountain without a valley, yet, just as it does not follow that there is any mountain in the world merely because I conceive a mountain with a valley, so likewise, though I conceive God as existing, it does not seem to follow on that account that God exists; for my thought imposes no necessity on things; and as I may imagine a winged horse, though there be none such, so I could perhaps attribute existence to God, though no God existed. But the cases are not analogous, and a fallacy lurks under the semblance of this objection: for because I cannot conceive a mountain without a valley, it does not follow that there is any mountain or valley in existence, but simply that the mountain or valley, whether they do or do not exist, are inseparable from each other; whereas, on the other hand, because I cannot conceive God unless as existing, it follows that existence is inseparable from him, and therefore that he really exists: not that this is brought about by my thought, or that it imposes any necessity on things, but, on the contrary, the necessity which lies in the thing itself, that is, the necessity of the existence of God, determines me to think in this way: for it is not in my power to conceive a God without existence, that is, a being supremely perfect, and yet devoid of an absolute perfection, as I am free to imagine a horse with or without wings.

Nor must it be alleged here as an objection, that it is in truth necessary to admit that God exists, after having supposed him to possess all perfections, since existence is one of them, but that my original supposition was not necessary; just as it is not necessary to think that all quadrilateral figures can be inscribed in the circle, since, if I supposed this, I should be constrained to admit that the rhombus, being a figure of four sides, can be therein inscribed, which, however, is manifestly false. This objection is, I say, incompetent; for although it may not be necessary that I shall at any time entertain the notion of God, yet each time I happen to think of a first and sovereign being, and to draw, so to speak, the idea of him from the storehouse of the mind, I am necessitated to attribute to him all kinds of perfections, though I may not then enumerate them all, nor think of each of them in particular. And this necessity is sufficient, as soon as I discover that existence is a perfection, to cause me to infer the existence of this first and sovereign being; just as it is not necessary that I should ever imagine any triangle, but whenever I am desirous of considering a rectilineal figure composed of only three angles, it is absolutely necessary to attribute those properties to it from which it is correctly inferred that its three angles are not greater than two right angles, although perhaps I may not then advert to this relation in particular. But when I consider what figures are capable of being inscribed in the circle, it is by no means necessary to hold that all quadrilateral figures are of this number; on the contrary, I cannot even imagine such to be the case, so long as I shall be unwilling to accept in thought anything that I do not clearly and distinctly conceive; and consequently there is a vast difference between false suppositions, as is the one in question, and the true ideas that were born with me, the first and chief of which is the idea of God. For indeed I discern on many grounds that this idea is not factitious depending simply on my thought, but that it is the representation of a true and immutable nature: in the first place because I can conceive no other being, except God, to whose essence existence necessarily pertains; in the second, because it is impossible to conceive two or more gods of this kind; and it being supposed that one such God exists, I clearly see that he must have existed from all eternity, and will exist to all eternity; and finally, because I apprehend many other properties in God, none of which I can either diminish or change.

But, indeed, whatever mode of proof I in the end adopt, it always returns to this, that it is only the things I clearly and distinctly conceive which have the power of completely persuading me. And although, of the objects I conceive in this manner, some, indeed, are obvious to every one, while others are only discovered after close and careful investigation; nevertheless after they are once discovered, the latter are not esteemed less certain than the former. Thus, for example, to take the case of a right-angled triangle, although it is not so manifest at first that the square of the base is equal to the squares of the other two sides, as that the base is opposite to the greatest angle; nevertheless, after it is once apprehended, we are as firmly persuaded of the truth of the former as of the latter. And, with respect to God, if I were not pre-occupied by prejudices, and my thought beset on all sides by the continual presence of the images of sensible objects, I should know nothing sooner or more easily than the fact of his being. For is there any truth more clear than the existence of a Supreme Being, or of God, seeing it is to his essence alone that necessary and eternal existence pertains? And although the right conception of this truth has cost me much close thinking, nevertheless at present I feel not only as assured of it as of what I deem most certain, but

I remark further that the certitude of all other truths is so absolutely dependent on it, that without this knowledge it is impossible ever to know anything perfectly.

For although I am of such a nature as to be unable, while I possess a very clear and distinct apprehension of a matter, to resist the conviction of its truth, yet because my constitution is also such as to incapacitate me from keeping my mind continually fixed on the same object, and as I frequently recollect a past judgment without at the same time being able to recall the grounds of it, it may happen meanwhile that other reasons are presented to me which would readily cause me to change my opinion, if I did not know that God existed; and thus I should possess no true and certain knowledge, but merely vague and vacillating opinions. Thus, for example, when I consider the nature of the [rectilineal] triangle, it most clearly appears to me, who have been instructed in the principles of geometry, that its three angles are equal to two right angles, and I find it impossible to believe otherwise, while I apply my mind to the demonstration; but as soon as I cease from attending to the process of proof, although I still remember that I had a clear comprehension of it, yet I may readily come to doubt of the truth demonstrated, if I do not know that there is a God: for I may persuade myself that I have been so constituted by nature as to be sometimes deceived, even in matters which I think I apprehend with the greatest evidence and certitude, especially when I recollect that I frequently considered many things to be true and certain which other reasons afterward constrained me to reckon as wholly false.

But after I have discovered that God exists, seeing I also at the same time observed that all things depend on him, and that he is no deceiver, and thence inferred that all which I clearly and distinctly perceive is of necessity true: although I no longer attend to the grounds of a judgment, no opposite reason can be alleged sufficient to lead me to doubt of its truth, provided only I remember that I once possessed a clear and distinct comprehension of it. My knowledge of it thus becomes true and certain. And this same knowledge extends likewise to whatever I remember to have formerly demonstrated, as the truths of geometry and the like: for what can be alleged against them to lead me to doubt of them? Will it be that my nature is such that I may be frequently deceived? But I already know that I cannot be deceived in judgments of the grounds of which I possess a clear knowledge. Will it be that I formerly deemed things to be true and certain which I afterward discovered to be false? But I had no clear and distinct knowledge of any of those things, and, being as yet ignorant of the rule by which I am assured of the truth of a judgment, I was led to give my assent to them on grounds which I afterward discovered were less strong than at the time I imagined them to be. What further objection, then, is there? Will it be said that perhaps I am dreaming (an objection I lately myself raised), or that all the thoughts of which I am now conscious have no more truth than the reveries of my dreams? But although, in truth, I should be dreaming, the rule still holds that all which is clearly presented to my intellect is indisputably true.

And thus I very clearly see that the certitude and truth of all science depends on the knowledge alone of the true God, insomuch that, before I knew him, I could have no perfect knowledge of any other thing. And now that I know him, I possess the means of acquiring a perfect knowledge respecting innumerable matters, as well relative to God himself and other intellectual objects as to corporeal nature, in so far as it is the object of pure mathematics (which do not consider whether it exists or not).

---

1. *What is Descartes's second argument for the existence of God?*
2. *What advantages does it have over* a posteriori *arguments?*
3. *Why couldn't the Meditator give an* a posteriori *argument, like the argument for design?*

4. *What key presupposition(s) does the ontological argument make?*

Sixth Meditation: Of the Existence of Material Things, and of the Real Distinction Between the Mind and Body of Man

There now only remains the inquiry as to whether material things exist. With regard to this question, I at least know with certainty that such things may exist, in as far as they constitute the object of the pure mathematics, since, regarding them in this aspect, I can conceive them clearly and distinctly. For there can be no doubt that God possesses the power of producing all the objects I am able distinctly to conceive, and I never considered anything impossible to him, unless when I experienced a contradiction in the attempt to conceive it aright. Further, the faculty of imagination which I possess, and of which I am conscious that I make use when I apply myself to the consideration of material things, is sufficient to persuade me of their existence: for, when I attentively consider what imagination is, I find that it is simply a certain application of the cognitive faculty (*facultas cognoscitiva*) to a body which is immediately present to it, and which therefore exists.

And to render this quite clear, I remark, in the first place, the difference that subsists between imagination and pure intellection (or conception). For example, when I imagine a triangle I not only conceive that it is a figure comprehended by three lines, but at the same time also I look upon these three lines as present by the power and internal application of my mind, and this is what I call imagining. But if I desire to think of a chiliogon, I indeed rightly conceive that it is a figure composed of a thousand sides, as easily as I conceive that a triangle is a figure composed of only three sides; but I cannot imagine the thousand sides of a chiliogon as I do the three sides of a triangle, nor, so to speak, view them as present. And although, in accordance with the habit I have of always imagining something when I think of corporeal things, it may happen that, in conceiving a chiliogon, I confusedly represent some figure to myself, yet it is quite evident that this is not a chiliogon, since it in no wise differs from that which I would represent to myself, if I were to think of a myriogon, or any other figure of many sides; nor would this representation be of any use in discovering and unfolding the properties that constitute the difference between a chiliogon and other polygons. But if the question turns on a pentagon, it is quite true that I can conceive its figure, as well as that of a chiliogon, without the aid of imagination; but I can likewise imagine it by applying the attention of my mind to its five sides, and at the same time to the area which they contain. Thus I observe that a special effort of mind is necessary to the act of imagination, which is not required to conceiving or understanding; and this special exertion of mind clearly shows the difference between imagination and pure intellection. I remark, besides, that this power of imagination which I possess, in as far as it differs from the power of conceiving, is in no way necessary to my nature or essence, that is, to the essence of my mind; for although I did not possess it, I should still remain the same that I now am, from which it seems we may conclude that it depends on something different from the mind.

And I easily understand that, if some body exists, with which my mind is so conjoined and united as to be able, as it were, to consider it when it chooses, it may thus imagine corporeal objects; so that this mode of thinking differs from pure intellection only in this respect, that the mind in conceiving turns in some way upon itself, and considers some one of the ideas it possesses within itself; but in imagining it turns toward the body, and contemplates in it some object conformed to the idea which it either of itself conceived or apprehended by sense. I easily understand, I say, that imagination may be thus formed, if it is true that there are bodies; and because I find no other obvious mode of explaining it, I thence, with probability, conjecture that they exist, but only with probability; and although I carefully examine all things, nevertheless I do not find that, from the distinct idea of corporeal nature I have in my imagination, I can necessarily infer the existence of any body.

But I am accustomed to imagine many other objects besides that corporeal nature which is the object of the pure mathematics, as, for example, colors, sounds, tastes, pain, and the like, although with less distinctness; and, inasmuch as I perceive these objects much better by the senses, through the medium of which and of memory, they seem to have reached the imagination, I believe that, in order the more advantageously to examine them, it is proper I should at the same time examine what sense-perception is, and inquire whether from those ideas that are apprehended by this mode of thinking [consciousness], I cannot obtain a certain proof of the existence of corporeal objects.

And, in the **first** place, I will recall to my mind the things I have hitherto held as true, because perceived by the senses, and the foundations upon which my belief in their truth rested; I will, in the **second** place, examine the reasons that afterward constrained me to doubt of them; and, finally, I will consider what of them I ought now to believe.

First, then, I perceived that I had a head, hands, feet, and other members composing that body which I considered as part, or perhaps even as the whole, of myself. I perceived further, that that body was placed among many others, by which it was capable of being affected in diverse ways, both beneficial and hurtful; and what was beneficial I remarked by a certain sensation of pleasure, and what was hurtful by a sensation of pain. And besides this pleasure and pain, I was likewise conscious of hunger, thirst, and other appetites, as well as certain corporeal inclinations toward joy, sadness, anger, and similar passions. And, out of myself, besides the extension, figure, and motions of bodies, I likewise perceived in them hardness, heat, and the other tactile qualities, and, in addition, light, colors, odors, tastes, and sounds, the variety of which gave me the means of distinguishing the sky, the earth, the sea, and generally all the other bodies, from one another.

And certainly, considering the ideas of all these qualities, which were presented to my mind, and which alone I properly and immediately perceived, it was not without reason that I thought I perceived certain objects wholly different from my thought, namely, bodies from which those ideas proceeded; for I was conscious that the ideas were presented to me without my consent being required, so that I could not perceive any object, however desirous I might be, unless it were present to the organ of sense; and it was wholly out of my power not to perceive it when it was thus present.

And because the ideas I perceived by the senses were much more lively and clear, and even, in their own way, more distinct than any of those I could of myself frame by meditation, or which I found impressed on my memory, it seemed that they could not have proceeded from myself, and must therefore have been caused in me by some other objects; and as of those objects I had no knowledge beyond what the ideas themselves gave me, nothing was so likely to occur to my mind as the supposition that the objects were similar to the ideas which they caused.

And because I recollected also that I had formerly trusted to the senses, rather than to reason, and that the ideas which I myself formed were not so clear as those I perceived by sense, and that they were even for the most part composed of parts of the latter, I was readily persuaded that I had no idea in my intellect which had not formerly passed through the senses.

Nor was I altogether wrong in likewise believing that that body which, by a special right, I called my own, pertained to me more properly and strictly than any of the others; for in truth, I could never be separated from it as from other bodies; I felt in it and on account of it all my appetites and affections, and in fine I was affected in its parts by pain and the titillation of pleasure, and not in the parts of the other bodies that were separated from it.

But when I inquired into the reason why, from this I know not what sensation of pain, sadness of mind should follow, and why from the sensation of pleasure, joy should arise, or why this indescribable twitching of the stomach, which I call hunger, should put me in mind of taking food, and the parchedness of the throat of drink, and so in other cases, I was unable to give any explanation, unless that I was so taught by nature; for there is assuredly no affinity, at least none that I am able to comprehend, between this irritation of the stomach and the desire of food, any more than between the perception of an object that causes pain and the consciousness of sadness which springs from the perception. And in the same way it seemed to me that all the other judgments I had formed regarding the objects of sense, were dictates of nature; because I remarked that those judgments were formed in me, before I had leisure to weigh and consider the reasons that might constrain me to form them.

But, afterward, a wide experience by degrees sapped the faith I had reposed in my senses; for I frequently observed that towers, which at a distance seemed round, appeared square, when more closely viewed, and that colossal figures, raised on the summits of these towers, looked like small statues, when viewed from the bottom of them; and, in other instances without number, I also discovered error in judgments founded on the external senses; and not only in those founded on the external, but even in those that rested on the internal senses; for is there anything more internal than pain? And yet I have sometimes been informed by parties whose arm or leg had been amputated, that they still occasionally seemed to feel pain in that part of the body which they had lost—a circumstance that led me to think that I could not be quite certain even that any one of my members was affected when I felt pain in it.

And to these grounds of doubt I shortly afterward also added two others of very wide generality: the *first* of them was that I believed I never perceived anything when awake which I could not occasionally think I also perceived when asleep, and as I do not believe that the ideas I seem to perceive in my sleep proceed from objects external to me, I did not any more observe any ground for believing this of such as I seem to perceive when awake; the *second* was that since I was as yet ignorant of the author of my being or at least supposed myself to be so, I saw nothing to prevent my having been so constituted by nature as that I should be deceived even in matters that appeared to me to possess the greatest truth.

And, with respect to the grounds on which I had before been persuaded of the existence of sensible objects, I had no great difficulty in finding suitable answers to them; for as nature seemed to incline me to many things from which reason made me averse, I thought that I ought not to confide much in its teachings. And although the perceptions of the senses were not dependent on my will, I did not think that I ought on that ground to conclude that they proceeded from things different from myself, since perhaps there might be found in me some faculty, though hitherto unknown to me, which produced them.

But now that I begin to know myself better, and to discover more clearly the author of my being, I do not, indeed, think that I ought rashly to admit all which the senses seem to teach, nor, on the other hand, is it my conviction that I ought to doubt in general of their teachings.

And, first, because I know that all which I clearly and distinctly conceive can be produced by God exactly as I conceive it, it is sufficient that I am able clearly and distinctly to conceive one thing apart from another, in order to be certain that the one is different from the other, seeing they may at least be made to exist separately, by the omnipotence of God; and it matters not by what power this separation is made, in order to be compelled to judge them different; and, therefore, merely because I know with certitude that I exist, and because, in the meantime, I do not observe that anything necessarily belongs to my nature or essence beyond my being a thinking thing, I rightly conclude that my essence consists only in my being a thinking thing (a substance whose whole essence or nature is merely thinking).

And although I may—or rather, as I will shortly say, although I certainly do—possess a body with which I am very closely conjoined; nevertheless, because, on the one hand, I have a clear and distinct idea of myself, in as far as I am only a thinking and unextended thing, and as, on the other hand, I possess a distinct idea of body, in as far as it is only an extended and unthinking thing, it is certain that I am entirely and truly distinct from my body, and may exist without it.

Moreover, I find in myself diverse faculties of thinking that have each their special mode: for example, I find I possess the faculties of imagining and perceiving, without which I can indeed clearly and distinctly conceive myself as entire, but I cannot reciprocally conceive them without conceiving myself, that is to say, without an intelligent substance in which they reside, for (in the notion we have of them, or to use the terms of the schools) in their formal concept, they comprise some sort of intellection; whence I perceive that they are distinct from myself as modes are from things. I remark likewise certain other faculties, as the power of changing place, of assuming diverse figures, and the like, that cannot be conceived and cannot therefore exist, any more than the preceding, apart from a substance in which they inhere. It is very evident, however, that these faculties, if they really exist, must belong to some corporeal or extended substance, since in their clear and distinct concept there is contained some sort of extension, but no intellection at all. Further, I cannot doubt but that there is in me a certain passive faculty of perception, that is, of receiving and taking knowledge of the ideas of sensible things; but this would be useless to me, if there did not also exist in me, or in some other thing, another active faculty capable of forming and producing those ideas. But this active faculty cannot be in me, in as far as I am but a thinking thing, seeing that it does not presuppose thought, and also that those ideas are frequently produced in my mind without my contributing to it in any way, and even frequently contrary to my will. This faculty must therefore exist in some substance different from me, in which all the objective reality of the ideas that are produced by this faculty, is contained formally or eminently, as I before remarked: and this substance is either a body, that is to say, a corporeal nature in which is contained formally (and in effect) all that is, objectively and by representation, in those ideas; or it is God himself, or some other creature, of a rank superior to body, in which the same is contained eminently.

But as God is no deceiver, it is manifest that he does not of himself and immediately communicate those ideas to me, nor even by the intervention of any creature in which their objective reality is not formally, but only eminently, contained. For as he has given me no faculty whereby I can discover this to be the case, but, on the contrary, a very strong inclination to believe that those ideas arise from corporeal objects, I do not see how he could be vindicated from the charge of deceit, if in truth they proceeded from any other source, or were produced by other causes than corporeal things: and accordingly it must be concluded, that corporeal objects exist. Nevertheless, they are not perhaps exactly such as we perceive by the senses, for their comprehension by the senses is, in many instances, very obscure and confused; but it is at least necessary to admit that all which I clearly and distinctly conceive as in them, that is, generally speaking, all that is comprehended in the object of speculative geometry, really exists external to me.

But with respect to other things which are either only particular, as, for example, that the sun is of such a size and figure, etc., or are conceived with less clearness and distinctness, as light, sound, pain, and the like, although they are highly dubious and uncertain, nevertheless on the ground alone that God is no deceiver, and that consequently he has permitted no falsity in my opinions which he has not likewise given me a faculty of correcting, I think I may with safety conclude that I possess in myself the means of arriving at the truth. And, in the first place, it cannot be doubted that in each of the dictates of nature there is some truth: for by nature, considered in general, I now understand nothing more than God himself, or the order and disposition established by God in created things; and by my nature in particular I understand the assemblage of all that God has given me.

But there is nothing which that nature teaches me more expressly or more sensibly than that I have a body which is ill affected when I feel pain, and stands in need of food and drink when I experience the sensations of hunger and thirst, etc. And therefore I ought not to doubt but that there is some truth in these informations.

Nature likewise teaches me by these sensations of pain, hunger, thirst, etc., that I am not only lodged in my body as a pilot in a vessel, but that I am besides so intimately conjoined, and as it were intermixed with it, that my mind and body compose a certain unity. For if this were not the case, I should not feel pain when my body is hurt, seeing I am merely a thinking thing, but should perceive the wound by the understanding alone, just as a pilot perceives by sight when any part of his vessel is damaged; and when my body has need of food or drink, I should have a clear knowledge of this, and not be made aware of it by the confused sensations of hunger and thirst: for, in truth, all these sensations of hunger, thirst, pain, etc., are nothing more than certain confused modes of thinking, arising from the union and apparent fusion of mind and body.

Besides this, nature teaches me that my own body is surrounded by many other bodies, some of which I have to seek after, and others to shun. And indeed, as I perceive different sorts of colors, sounds, odors, tastes, heat, hardness, etc., I safely conclude that there are in the bodies from which the diverse perceptions of the senses proceed, certain varieties corresponding to them, although, perhaps, not in reality like them; and since, among these diverse perceptions of the senses, some are agreeable, and others disagreeable, there can be no doubt that my body, or rather my entire self, in as far as I am composed of body and mind, may be variously affected, both beneficially and hurtfully, by surrounding bodies.

But there are many other beliefs which though seemingly the teaching of nature, are not in reality so, but which obtained a place in my mind through a habit of judging inconsiderately of things. It may thus easily happen that such judgments shall contain error: thus, for example, the opinion I have that all space in which there is nothing to affect my senses is void; that in a hot body there is something in every respect similar to the idea of heat in my mind; that in a white or green body there is the same whiteness or greenness which I perceive; that in a bitter or sweet body there is the same taste, and so in other instances; that the stars, towers, and all distant bodies, are of the same size and figure as they appear to our eyes, etc.

But that I may avoid everything like indistinctness of conception, I must accurately define what I properly understand by 'being taught by nature'. For 'nature' is here taken in a narrower sense than when it signifies the sum of all the things which God has given me; seeing that in that meaning the notion comprehends much that belongs only to the mind (to which I am not here to be understood as referring when I use the term 'nature'); as, for example, the notion I have of the truth, that what is done cannot be undone, and all the other truths I discern by the natural light without the aid of the body; and seeing that it comprehends likewise much besides that belongs only to body, and is not here any more contained under the name nature, as the quality of heaviness, and the like, of which I do not speak, the term being reserved exclusively to designate the things which God has given to me as a being composed of mind and body.

But nature, taking the term in the sense explained, teaches me to shun what causes in me the sensation of pain, and to pursue what affords me the sensation of pleasure, and other things of this sort; but I do not discover that it teaches me, in addition to this, from these diverse perceptions of the senses, to draw any conclusions respecting external objects without a previous careful and mature consideration of them by the mind: for it is, as appears to me, the office of the mind alone, and not of the composite whole of mind and body, to discern the truth in those matters. Thus, although the impression a star makes on my eye is not larger than that from the flame of a candle, I do not, nevertheless, experience any real or positive impulse determining me to believe that the star is not greater than the flame; the true account of the matter being merely that I have so judged from my youth without any rational ground. And, though on approaching the fire I feel heat, and even pain on approaching it too closely, I have, however, from this no ground for holding that something resembling the heat I feel is in the fire, any more than that there is something similar to the pain; all that I have ground for believing is, that there is something in it, whatever it may be, which excites in me those sensations of heat or pain. So also, although there are spaces in which I find nothing to excite and affect my senses, I must not therefore conclude that those spaces contain in them no body; for I see that in this, as in many other similar matters, I have been accustomed to pervert the order of nature, because these perceptions of the senses, although given me by nature merely to signify to my mind what things are beneficial and hurtful to the composite whole of which it is a part, and being sufficiently clear and distinct for that purpose, are nevertheless used by me as infallible rules by which to determine immediately the essence of the bodies that exist out of me, of which they can of course afford me only the most obscure and confused knowledge. ...

It is quite manifest that, notwithstanding the sovereign goodness of God, the nature of man, in so far as it is composed of mind and body, cannot but be sometimes misleading. For, if there is any cause which excites, not in the foot, but in some one of the parts of the nerves that stretch from the foot to the brain, or even in the brain itself, the same movement that is ordinarily created when the foot is ill affected, pain will be felt, as it were, in the foot, and the senses will thus be naturally deceived; for as the same movement in the brain can but impress the mind with the same sensation, and as this sensation is much more frequently excited by a cause which hurts the foot than by one acting in a different quarter, it is reasonable that it should lead the mind to feel pain in the foot rather than in any other part of the body. And if it sometimes happens that the parchedness of the throat does not arise, as is usual, from drink being necessary for the health of the body, but from quite the opposite cause, as is the case with the dropsical, yet it is much better that it should be deceitful in that instance, than if, on the contrary, it were continually fallacious when the body is well-disposed; and the same holds true in other cases.

And certainly this consideration is of great service, not only in enabling me to recognize the errors to which my nature is liable, but likewise in rendering it more easy to avoid or correct them: for, knowing that all my senses more usually indicate to me what is true than what is false, in matters relating to the advantage of the body, and being able almost always to make use of more than a single sense in examining the same object, and besides this, being able to use my memory in connecting present with past knowledge, and my understanding which has already discovered all the causes of my errors, I ought no longer to fear that falsity may be met with in what is daily presented to me by the senses. And I ought to reject all the doubts of those bygone days, as hyperbolical and ridiculous, especially the general uncertainty respecting sleep, which I could not distinguish from the waking state: for I now find a very marked difference between the two states, in respect that our memory can never connect our dreams with each other and with the course of life, in the way it is in the habit of doing with events that occur when we are awake. And, in truth, if some one, when I am awake, appeared to me all of a sudden and as suddenly disappeared, as do the images I see in sleep, so that I could not observe either whence he came or whither he went, I should not without reason esteem it either a specter or phantom formed in my brain, rather than a real man. But when I perceive objects with regard to which I can distinctly determine both the place whence they come, and that in which they are, and the time at which they appear to me, and when, without interruption, I can connect the perception I have of them with the whole of the other parts of my life, I am perfectly sure that what I thus perceive occurs while I am awake and not during sleep. And I ought not in the least degree to doubt of the truth of these presentations, if, after having called together all my senses, my memory, and my understanding for the purpose of examining them, no deliverance is given by any one of these faculties which is repugnant to that of any other: for since God is no deceiver, it necessarily follows that I am not herein deceived. But because the necessities of action frequently oblige us to come to a determination before we have had leisure for so careful an examination, it must be confessed that the life of man is frequently obnoxious to error with respect to individual objects; and we must, in conclusion, acknowledge the weakness of our nature.

---

1. Descartes believes that, in addition to sensation and imagination, minds have an intellect, which does not depend on these other faculties. What is his argument for this?
2. In this meditation, Descartes gives his famous modal argument for the real distinction between mind and body. (It's in the paragraph that starts 'And, firstly, because I know that all which I clearly and distinctly conceive.') First, have a look at the selections from the Principles above. What is a real distinction? A and B are really distinct when and only when _____. So the conclusion of Descartes's argument is not that mind and body do exist separately, but only that _____. (Similarly, water and dirt are really distinct, even when they combine to form mud.) Reconstruct Descartes's argument:

   Premise 1: Everything I clearly and distinctly conceive is _____.
   Premise 2: I can clearly and distinctly conceive of _____ and _____.
   Conclusion: Mind and body are really distinct substances; that is, _____.
3. The Meditator has finally gotten her world back—she now has an argument to prove that there is an external world. To which of the skeptical arguments in Meditation One is this a reply? Reconstruct the argument in your own way.

Objections and Replies to the Meditations

Antoine Arnauld's objection to the argument for the real distinction and Descartes's reply

Antoine Arnauld

I can't see anywhere in the entire work an argument that could serve to prove this claim, apart from what is laid down at the start [this isn't an exact quotation from the Meditations]:'I can deny that any body exists, or that anything is extended, but while I am thus denying, or thinking, it goes on being certain to me that I exist. Thus, I am a thinking thing, not a body, and body doesn't come into the knowledge I have of myself.'

But so far as I can see, all that follows from this is that I can obtain some knowledge of myself without knowledge of the body. But it isn't clear to me that this knowledge is complete and adequate, enabling me to be certain that I'm not mistaken in excluding body from my essence. I'll explain through an example.

   Suppose someone knows for certain that the angle in a semicircle is a right angle, and thus that this angle and the diameter of the circle form a right-angled triangle. In spite of knowing this, he may doubt, or not yet have grasped for certain, that the square on the hypotenuse equals the sum of the squares on the other two sides;

indeed he may even deny this if he has been misled by some fallacy. (For brevity's sake, I'll express this as 'the triangle's having the property P'.) But now, if he argues in the same way that Descartes does, he may appear to have confirmation of his false belief, as follows: 'I vividly and clearly perceive that the triangle is right-angled; but I doubt that it has the property P; therefore it doesn't belong to the essence of the triangle that it has the property P.'

Again, even if I deny that the square on the hypotenuse equals the sum of the squares on the other two sides, I still remain sure that the triangle is right-angled—my mind retains the vivid and clear knowledge that one of its angles is a right angle. And given that this is so, not even God could bring it about that the triangle is not right-angled. Therefore, I might argue, the property P that I can doubt—or indeed that I can remove—while leaving my idea of the triangle intact doesn't belong to the essence of the triangle. Now look again at what Descartes says:

'I know that if I have a vivid and clear thought of something, God could have created it in a way that exactly corresponds to my thought. So the fact that I can vividly and clearly think of one thing apart from another assures me that the two things are distinct from one another, since they can be separated by God.'

I vividly and clearly understand that this triangle is right-angled, without understanding that the triangle has the property P. It follows, on Descartes's pattern of reasoning, that God at least could create a right-angled triangle with the square on its hypotenuse not equal to the sum of the squares on the other sides!

The only possible reply to this that I can see is to say that the man in this example doesn't vividly and clearly perceive that the triangle is right-angled. But how is my perception of the nature of my mind any clearer than his perception of the nature of the triangle?

Now although the man in the example vividly and clearly knows that the triangle is right-angled, he is wrong in thinking that property P doesn't belong to the nature or essence of the triangle. Similarly, although I vividly and clearly know my nature to be something that thinks, mightn't I also be wrong in thinking that nothing else belongs to my nature apart from my being a thinking thing? Perhaps my being an extended thing also belongs to my nature.

---

1. Which premise of the Sixth Meditation argument for the real distinction does Arnauld challenge? What is the problem with it?

Descartes

Although we can vividly and clearly understand that a triangle in a semicircle is right-angled without being aware of its having property P, we cannot have a clear understanding of a triangle's having property P without at the same time taking in that it is right-angled. In contrast with that, we can vividly and clearly perceive the mind without the body and the body without the mind.And although it is possible to have a concept of triangle inscribed in a semicircle that doesn't include the triangle's having property P, i.e., equality between the square on the hypotenuse and the sum of the squares on the other sides, it is not possible to have a concept of triangle inscribed in a semicircle that does include there being no ratio at all between the square on the hypotenuse and the squares on the other sides. Hence, though we may be unaware of what the ratio is, we can't rule out any candidate unless we clearly understand that it is wrong for the triangle; and we can't clearly understand this for the ratio equality, because it is right for the triangle. So the concept in question must, in an indirect and oblique way, involve the property P: it must involve a thought of 'some ratio or other' which could take the value equality. In contrast with this, the concept of body doesn't include–or even indirectly and obliquely involve–anything at all that belongs to the mind, and the concept of mind doesn't include–or even indirectly and obliquely involve–anything at all that belongs to the body.

Arnauld's circularity objection and Descartes's reply

Arnauld

I have one further worry, namely how Descartes avoids reasoning in a circle when he says that it's only because we know that God exists that we are sure that whatever we vividly and clearly perceive is true.But we can be sure that God exists only because we vividly and clearly perceive this; so before we can be sure that God exists we need to be able to be sure that whatever we perceive clearly and evidently is true.

Descartes clearly argues for the Epistemic Principle (everything I clearly and distinctly perceive is true), which is not to be confused with the Conceivability Principle (everything I clearly and distinctly conceive is possible). Arnauld's argument is that he cannot use the existence of God to prove the EP, since he must rely on the EP to prove _____.

Descartes

Lastly, as to my not being guilty of circularity when I said that our only reason for being sure that what we vividly and clearly perceive is true is the fact that we know for sure that God exists, and that we are sure that God exists only because we perceive this clearly: I have already given an adequate explanation of this point [in the Second Reply], where I distinguished perceiving something clearly from remembering having perceived it clearly at an earlier time.At first we are sure that God exists because we are attending to the arguments that prove this; but afterwards all we need to be certain that God exists is our memory that we did earlier perceive this clearly. This memory wouldn't be sufficient if we didn't know that God exists and isn't a deceiver.

---

1. One of the most controversial areas of Descartes scholarship concerns this 'Cartesian circle'. What exactly do you think Descartes is saying in his reply to Arnauld? Why does Descartes think he is not guilty of committing himself to a vicious circle?

3. Thomas Hobbes (1588–1679)

Thomas Hobbes's *Leviathan* (1651)

Excerpt includes Chapters 1-17. The basis for this text was the CC0 1.0 Public Domain edition available on the EEBO-TCP website hosted at https://quod.lib.umich.edu/e/eebogroup/ Light changes to modernize spellings have been made throughout by Marcus Adams. Terms in Greek have been transliterated. Capitalization from the 1651 edition has been retained.

Introduction

NATURE (the Art whereby God has made and governs the World) is by the Art of man, as in many other things, so in this also imitated, that it can make an Artificial Animal. For seeing life is but a motion of Limbs, the beginning whereof is in some principal part within; why may we not say, that all Automata (i.e., engines that move themselves by springs and wheels as doth a watch) have an artificial life? For what is the Heart, but a Spring; and the Nerves, but so many Strings; and the joints, but so many Wheels, giving motion to the whole Body, such as was intended by the Artificer? Art goes yet further, imitating that Rational and most excellent work of Nature, Man. For by Art is created that great LEVIATHAN called a COMMONWEALTH, or STATE, (in Latin CIVITAS) which is but an Artificial Man; though of greater stature and strength than the Natural, for whose protection and defense it was intended; and in which, the Sovereignty is an Artificial Soul, as giving life and motion to the whole body; The Magistrates, and other Officers of Judicature and Execution, artificial Joints; Reward and Punishment (by which fastened to the seat of the Sovereignty, every joint and member is moved to perform his duty) are the Nerves, that do the same in the Body Natural; The Wealth and Riches of all the particular members, are the Strength; *Salus Populi* (the people's safety) its Business; Counselors, by whom all things needful for it to know, are suggested unto it, are the Memory; Equity and Laws, an artificial Reason and Will; Concord, Health; Sedition, Sickness; and Civil war, Death. Lastly, the Pacts and Covenants, by which the parts of this Body Politic were at first made, set together, and united, resemble that Fiat, or the Let us make man, pronounced by God in the Creation.

To describe the Nature of this Artificial man, I will consider

- First, the Matter thereof, and the Artificer; both which is Man.
- Secondly, How, and by what Covenants it is made; what are the Rights and just Power or Authority of a Sovereign; and what it is that preserves and dissolves it.
- Thirdly, what is a Christian Commonwealth.
- Lastly, what is the Kingdom of Darkness.

Concerning the first, there is a saying much usurped of late, That Wisdom is acquired, not by reading of Books, but of Men. Consequently whereunto, those persons, that for the most part can give no other proof of being wise, take great delight to shew what they think they have read in men, by uncharitable censures of one another behind their backs. But there is another saying not of late understood, by which they might learn truly to read one another, if they would take the pains; and that is, *nosce teipsum*, Read thy self: which was not meant, as it is now used, to countenance, either the barbarous state of men in power, towards their inferiors; or to encourage men of low degree, to a saucy behavior towards their betters; But to teach us, that for the similitude of the thoughts, and Passions of one man, to the thoughts, and Passions of another, whosoever looks into himself, and considers what he doth, when he does think, opine, reason, hope, fear, &c, and upon what grounds; he shall thereby read and know, what are the thoughts, and Passions of all other men, upon the like occasions. I say the similitude of Passions, which are the same in all men, desire, fear, hope, &c; not the similitude of the objects of the Passions, which are the things desired, feared, hoped, &c: for these the constitution individual, and particular education do so vary, and they are so easy to be kept from our knowledge, that the characters of man's heart, blotted and confounded as they are, with dissembling, lying, counterfeiting, and erroneous doctrines, are legible only to him that searches hearts. And though by men's actions we do discover their design sometimes; yet to do it without comparing them with our own, and distinguishing all circumstances, by which the case may come to be altered, is to decipher without a key, and be for the most part deceived, by too much trust, or by too much diffidence; as he that reads, is himself a good or evil man.

But let one man read another by his actions never so perfectly, it serves him only with his acquaintance, which are but few. He that is to govern a whole Nation, must read in himself, not this, or that particular man; but Mankind: which though it be hard to do, harder than to learn any Language, or Science; yet, when I shall have set down my own reading orderly, and perspicuously, the pains left another, will be only to consider, if he also find not the same in himself. For this kind of Doctrine, admits no other Demonstration.

Concerning the Thoughts of man, I will consider them first Singly, and afterwards in Train, or dependence upon one another. Singly, they are every one a Representation or Appearance, of some quality, or other Accident of a body without us; which is commonly called an Object. Which Object works on the Eyes, Ears, and other parts of man's body; and by diversity of working, produces diversity of Appearances.

The Original of them all, is that which we call SENSE; (For there is no conception in a man's mind, which has not at first, totally, or by parts, been begotten upon the organs of Sense.) The rest are derived from that original.

To know the natural cause of Sense, is not very necessary to the business now in hand; and I have elsewhere written of the same at large. Nevertheless, to fill each part of my present method, I will briefly deliver the same in this place.

The cause of Sense, is the External Body, or Object, which presses the organ proper to each Sense, either immediately, as in the Taste and Touch; or mediately, as in Seeing, Hearing, and Smelling: which pressure, by the mediation of Nerves, and other strings, and membranes of the body, continued inwards to the Brain, and Heart, causes there a resistance, or counter-pressure, or endeavor of the heart, to deliver itself: which endeavor because Outward, seems to be some matter without. And this seeming, or fancy, is that which men call Sense; and consists, as to the Eye, in a Light, or Color figured; To the Ear, in a Sound; To the Nostril, in an Odor; To the Tongue and Palate, in a Savor; And to the rest of the body, in Heat, Cold, Hardness, Softness, and such other qualities, as we discern by Feeling. All which qualities called Sensible, are in the object that causes them, but so many several motions of the matter, by which it presses our organs diversely. Neither in us that are pressed, are they anything else, but divers motions; (for motion, produces nothing but motion.) But their appearance to us is Fancy, the same waking, that dreaming. And as pressing, rubbing, or striking the Eye, makes us fancy a light; and pressing the Ear, produces a din; so do the bodies also we see, or hear, produce the same by their strong, though unobserved action. For if those Colors, and Sounds, were in the Bodies, or Objects that cause them, they could not be severed from them, as by glasses, and in Echoes by reflection, we see they are; where we know the thing we see, is in one place; the appearance, in another. And though at some certain distance, the real, and very object seem invested with the fancy it begets in us; Yet still the object is one thing, the image or fancy is another. So that Sense in all cases, is nothing else but original fancy, caused (as I have said) by the pressure, that is, by the motion, of external things upon our Eyes, Ears, and other organs thereunto ordained.

But the Philosophy Schools, through all the Universities of Christendom, grounded upon certain Texts of Aristotle, teach another doctrine; and say, For the cause of Vision, that the thing seen, sends forth on every side a visible species (in English) a visible show, apparition, or aspect, or a being seen; the receiving whereof into the Eye, is Seeing. And for the cause of Hearing, that the thing heard, sends forth an Audible species, that is, an Audible aspect, or Audible being seen; which entering at the Ear, makes Hearing. Nay for the cause of Understanding also, they say the thing Understood sends forth intelligible species, that is, an intelligible being seen; which coming into the Understanding, makes us Understand. I say not this, as disapproving the use of Universities: but because I am to speak hereafter of their office in a Commonwealth, I must let you see on all occasions by the way, what things would be amended in them; among which the frequency of insignificant Speech is one.

Chapter 2 Of Imagination

That when a thing lies still, unless somewhat else stir it, it will lie still forever, is a truth that no man doubts of. But that when a thing is in motion, it will eternally be in motion, unless somewhat else stay it, though the reason be the same, (namely, that nothing can change itself,) is not so easily assented to. For men measure, not only other men, but all other things, by themselves: and because they find themselves subject after motion to pain, and lassitude, think every thing else grows weary of motion, and seeks repose of its own accord; little considering, whether it be not some other motion, wherein that desire of rest they find in themselves, consists. From hence it is, that the Schools say, Heavy bodies fall downwards, out of an appetite to rest, and to conserve their nature in that place which is most proper for them; ascribing appetite, and Knowledge of what is good for their conservation, (which is more than man has) to things inanimate, absurdly.

When a Body is once in motion, it moves (unless something else hinder it) eternally; and whatsoever hinders it, cannot in an instant, but in time, and by degrees quite extinguish it: And as we see in the water, though the wind cease, the waves give not over rolling for a long time after; so also it happens in that motion, which is made in the internal parts of a man, then, when he Sees, Dreams, &c. For after the object is removed, or the eye shut, we still retain an image of the thing seen, though more obscure than when we see it. And this is it, the Latins call Imagination, from the image made in seeing; and apply the same, though improperly, to all the other senses. But the Greeks call it Fancy; which signifies appearance, and is as proper to one sense, as to another. IMAGINATION therefore is nothing but decaying sense; and is found in men, and many other living Creatures, as well sleeping, as waking.

The decay of Sense in men waking, is not the decay of the motion made in sense; but an obscuring of it, in such manner, as the light of the Sun obscures the light of the Stars; which stars do no less exercise their virtue by which they are visible, in the day, than in the night. But because among many strokes, which our eyes, ears, and other organs receive from external bodies, the predominant only is sensible; therefore the light of the Sun being predominant, we are not affected with the action of the stars. And any object being removed from our eyes, though the impression it made in us remain; yet other objects more present succeeding, and working on us, the Imagination of the past is obscured, and made weak; as the voice of a man is in the noise of the day. From whence it follows, that the longer the time is, after the sight, or Sense of any object, the weaker is the Imagination. For the continual change of man's body, destroys in time the parts which in sense were moved: So that distance of time, and of place, has one and the same effect in us. For as at a great distance of place, that which we look at, appears dim, and without distinction of the smaller parts; and as Voices grow weak, and inarticulate: so also after great distance of time, our imagination of the Past is weak; and we lose (for example) of Cities we have seen, many particular Streets; and of Actions, many particular Circumstances. This decaying sense, when we would express the thing itself, (I mean fancy itself,) we call Imagination; as I said before: But when we would express the decay, and signify that the Sense is fading, old, and past, it is called Memory. So that Imagination and Memory, are but one thing, which for divers considerations have divers names.

Much memory, or memory of many things, is called Experience. Again, Imagination being only of those things which have been formerly perceived by Sense, either all at once, or by parts at several times; The former, (which is the imagining the whole object, as it was presented to the sense) is simple Imagination; as when one imagines a man, or horse, which he has seen before. The other is Compounded; as when from the sight of a man at one time, and of a horse at another, we conceive in our mind a Centaur. So when a man compounds the image of his own person, with the image of the actions of another man; as when a man imagines himself a Hercules, or an Alexander, (which happens often to them that are much taken with reading of Romances) it is a compound imagination, and properly but a Fiction of the mind. There be also other Imaginations that rise in men, (though waking) from the great impression made in sense: As from gazing upon the Sun, the impression leaves an image of the Sun before our eyes a long time after; and from being long and vehemently attend upon Geometrical Figures, a man shall in the dark, (though awake) have the Images of Lines, and Angles before his eyes: which kind of Fancy has no particular name; as being a thing that doth not commonly fall into men's discourse.

The imaginations of them that sleep, are those we call Dreams. And these also (as all other Imaginations) have been before, either totally, or by parcels in the Sense. And because in sense, the Brain, and Nerves, which are the necessary Organs of sense, are so benumbed in sleep, as not easily to be moved by the action of External Objects, there can happen in sleep, no Imagination; and therefore no Dream, but what proceeds from the agitation of the inward parts of man's body; which inward parts, for the connection they have with the Brain, and other Organs, when they be distempered, do keep the same in motion; whereby the Imaginations there formerly made, appear as if a man were waking; saving that the Organs of Sense being now benumbed, so as there is no new object, which can master and obscure them with a more vigorous impression, a Dream must needs be more clear, in this silence of sense, than are our waking thoughts. And hence it comes to pass, that it is a hard matter, and by many thought impossible to distinguish exactly between Sense and Dreaming. For my part, when I consider, that in Dreams, I do not often, nor constantly think of the same Persons, Places, Objects, and Actions that I do waking; nor remember so long a train of coherent thoughts, Dreaming, as at other times; And because waking I often observe the absurdity of Dreams, but never dream of the absurdities of my waking Thoughts; I am well satisfied, that being awake, I know I dream not; though when I dream, I think my self awake.

And seeing dreams are caused by the distemper of some of the inward parts of the Body; divers distempers must needs cause different Dreams. And hence it is, that lying cold breeds Dreams of Fear, and raises the thought and Image of some fearful object (the motion from the brain to the inner parts, and from the inner parts to the Brain being reciprocal:) And that as Anger causes heat in some parts of the Body, when we are awake; so when we sleep, the over heating of the same parts causes Anger, and raises up in the brain the Imagination of an Enemy. In the same manner; as natural kindness, when we are awake causes desire; and desire makes heat in certain other parts of the body; so also, too much heat in those parts, while we sleep, raises in the brain an imagination of some kindness shown. In sum, our Dreams are the reverse of our waking Imaginations; The motion when we are awake, beginning at one end; and when we Dream, at another.

The most difficult discerning of a man's Dream, from his waking thoughts, is then, when by some accident we observe not that we have slept: which is easy to happen to a man full of fearful thoughts; and whose conscience is much troubled; and that sleeps, without the circumstances, of going to bed, or putting off his clothes, as one that nods in a chair. For he that takes pains, and industriously lays himself to sleep, in case any uncouth and exorbitant fancy come unto him, cannot easily think it other than a Dream. We read of Marcus Brutus, (one that had his life given him by Julius Caesar, and was also his favorite, and notwithstanding murdered him,) how at Philippi, the night before he gave battle to Augustus Caesar, he saw a fearful apparition, which is commonly related by Historians as a Vision: but considering the circumstances, one may easily judge to have been but a short Dream. For sitting in his tent, pensive and troubled with the horror of his rash act, it was not hard for him, slumbering in the cold, to dream of that which most frightened him; which fear, as by degrees it made him wake; so also it must needs make the Apparition by degrees to vanish: And having no assurance that he slept, he could have no cause to think it a Dream, or anything but a Vision. And this is no very rare Accident: for even they that be perfectly awake, if they be timorous, and superstitious, possessed with fearful tales, and alone in the dark, are subject to the like fancies; and believe they see spirits and dead men's Ghosts walking in Churchyards; whereas it is either their Fancy only, or else the knavery of such persons, as make use of such superstitious fear, to pass disguised in the night, to places they would not be known to haunt.

From this ignorance of how to distinguish Dreams, and other strong Fancies, from Vision and Sense, did arise the greatest part of the Religion of the Gentiles in time past, that worshiped Satyrs, Fawns, Nymphs, and the like; and nowadays the opinion that rude people have of Fairies, Ghosts, and Goblins; and of the power of Witches. For as for Witches, I think not that their witchcraft is any real power; but yet that they are justly punished, for the false belief they have, that they can do such mischief, joined with their purpose to do it if they can: their trade being nearer to a new Religion, than to a Craft or Science. And for Fairies, and walking Ghosts, the opinion of them has I think been on purpose, either taught, or not confuted, to keep in credit the use of Exorcism, of Crosses, of holy Water, and other such inventions of Ghostly men. Nevertheless, there is no doubt, but God can make unnatural Apparitions: But that he does it so often, as men need to fear such things, more than they fear the stay, or change, of the course of Nature, which he also can stay, and change, is no point of Christian faith. But evil men under pretext that God can do anything, are so bold as to say anything when it serves their turn, though they think it untrue; It is the part of a wise man, to believe them no further, than right reason makes that which they say, appear credible. If this superstitious fear of Spirits were taken away, and with it, Prognostiques from Dreams, false Prophecies, and many other things depending thereon, by which, crafty ambitious persons abuse the simple people, men would be much more fitted than they are for civil Obedience.

And this ought to be the work of the Schools: but they rather nourish such doctrine. For (not knowing what Imagination, or the Senses are), what they receive, they reach: some saying, that Imaginations rise of themselves, and have no cause: Others that they rise most commonly from the Will; and that Good thoughts are blown (inspired) into a man, by God; and Evil thoughts by the Devil: or that Good thoughts are powered (infused) into a man, by God, and Evil ones by the Devil. Some say the Senses receive the Species of things, and deliver them to the Common-sense; and the Common Sense delivers them over to the Fancy, and the Fancy to the Memory, and the Memory to the Judgement, like handing of things from one to another, with many words making nothing understood.

The Imagination that is raised in man (or any other creature indued with the faculty of imagining) by words, or other voluntary signs, is that we generally call Understanding; and is common to Man and Beast. For a dog by custom will understand the call, or the rating of his Master; and so will many other Beasts. That Understanding which is peculiar to man, is the Understanding not only his will; but his conceptions and thoughts, by the sequel and contexture of the names of things into Affirmations, Negations, and other forms of Speech: And of this kind of Understanding I shall speak hereafter.

By Consequence, or Train of Thoughts, I understand that succession of one Thought to another, which is called (to distinguish it from Discourse in words) Mental Discourse.

When a man thinks on anything whatsoever, His next Thought after, is not altogether so casual as it seems to be. Not every Thought to every Thought succeeds indifferently. But as we have no Imagination, whereof we have not formerly had Sense, in whole, or in parts; so we have no Transition from one Imagination to another, whereof we never had the like before in our Senses. The reason whereof is this. All Fancies are Motions within us, relics of those made in the Sense: And those motions that immediately succeeded one another in the sense, continue also together after Sense: In so much as the former coming again to take place, and be predominant, the later follows, by coherence of the matter moved, in such manner, as water upon a plain Table is drawn which way any one part of it is guided by the finger. But because in sense, to one and the same thing perceived, sometimes one thing, sometimes another succeeds, it comes to pass in time, that in the Imagining of anything, there is no certainty what we shall Imagine next; Only this is certain, it shall be something that succeeded the same before, at one time or another.

This Train of Thoughts, or Mental Discourse, is of two sorts. The first is Unguided, without Design, and inconstant; Wherein there is no Passionate Thought, to govern and direct those that follow, to itself, as the end and scope of some desire, or other passion: In which case the thoughts are said to wander, and seem impertinent one to another, as in a Dream. Such are Commonly the thoughts of men, that are not only without company, but also without care of anything; though even then their Thoughts are as busy as at other times, but without harmony; as the sound which a Lute out of tune would yield to any man; or in tune, to one that could not play. And yet in this wild ranging of the mind, a man may oftentimes perceive the way of it, and the dependence of one thought upon another. For in a Discourse of our present civil war, what could seem more impertinent, than to ask (as one did) what was the value of a Roman Penny? Yet the Coherence to me was manifest enough. For the Thought of the war, introduced the Thought of the delivering up the King to his Enemies; The Thought of that, brought in the Thought of the delivering up of Christ; and that again the Thought of the 30 pence, which was the price of that treason: and thence easily followed that malicious question; and all this in a moment of time; for Thought is quick.

The second is more constant; as being regulated by some desire, and design. For the impression made by such things as we desire, or fear, is strong, and permanent, or, (if it cease for a time,) of quick return: so strong it is sometimes, as to hinder and break our sleep. From Desire, arises the Thought of some means we have seen produce the like of that which we aim at; and from the thought of that, the thought of means to that mean; and so continually, till we come to some beginning within our own power. And because the End, by the greatness of the impression, comes often to mind, in case our thoughts begin to wander, they are quickly again reduced into the way: which observed by one of the seven wise men, made him give men this precept, which is now worn out, *respice finem*; that is to say, in all your actions, look often upon what you would have, as the thing that directs all your thoughts in the way to attain it.

The train of regulated Thoughts is of two kinds; One, when of an effect imagined, we seek the causes, or means that produce it: and this is common to Man and Beast. The other is, when imagining anything whatsoever, we seek all the possible effects, that can by it be produced; that is to say, we imagine what we can do with it, when we have it. Of which I have not at any time seen any sign, but in man only; for this is a curiosity hardly incident to the nature of any living creature that has no other Passion but sensual, such as are hunger, thirst, lust, and anger. In sum, the Discourse of the Mind, when it is governed by design, is nothing but Seeking, or the faculty of Invention, which the Latins call *Sagacitas*, and *Solertia*; a hunting out of the causes, of some effect, present or past; or of the effects, of some present or past cause. Sometimes a man seeks what he has lost; and from that place, and time, wherein he misses it, his mind runs back, from place to place, and time to time, to find where, and when he had it; that is to say, to find some certain, and limited time and place, in which to begin a method of seeking. Again, from thence, his thoughts run over the same places and times, to find what action, or other occasion might make him lose it. This we call Remembrance, or Calling to mind: the Latins call it *Reminiscentia*, as it were a Re-conning of our former actions.

Sometimes a man knows a place determinate, within the compass whereof he is to seek; and then his thoughts run over all the parts thereof, in the same manner, as one would sweep a room, to find a jewel; or as a Spaniel ranges the field, till he find a sent; or as a man should run over the Alphabet, to start a rhyme.

Sometime a man desires to know the event of an action; and then he thinks of some like action past, and the events thereof one after another; supposing like events will follow like actions. As he that foresees what will become of a Criminal, re-cons what he has seen follow on the like Crime before; having this order of thoughts, The Crime, the Officer, the Prison, the Judge, and the Gallows. Which kind of thoughts, is called Foresight, and Prudence, or Providence; and sometimes Wisdom; though such conjecture, through the difficulty of observing all circumstances, be very fallacious. But this is certain; by how much one man has more experience of things past, than another; by so much also he is more Prudent, and his expectations will less seldom fail him. The Present only has a being in Nature; things Past have a being in the Memory only, but things to come have no being at all; the Future being but a fiction of the mind, applying the sequels of actions Past, to the actions that are Present; which with most certainty is done by him that has most Experience; but not with certainty enough. And though it be called Prudence, when the Event answers our Expectation; yet in its own nature, it is but Presumption. For the foresight of things to come, which is Providence, belongs only to him by whose will they are to come. From him only, and supernaturally, proceeds Prophecy. The best Prophet naturally is the best guesser; and the best guesser, he that is most versed and studied in the matters he guesses at: for he has most Signs to guess by.

A Sign, is the Event Antecedent, of the Consequent; and contrarily, the Consequent of the Antecedent, when the like Consequences have been observed, before: And the more often they have been observed, the less uncertain is the Sign. And therefore he that has most experience in any kind of business, has most Signs, whereby to guess at the Future time; and consequently is the most prudent: And so much more prudent than he that is new in that kind of business, as not to be equaled by any advantage of natural and extemporary wit: though perhaps many young men think the contrary.

Nevertheless it is not Prudence that distinguishes man from beast. There be beasts, that at a year old observe more, and pursue that which is for their good, more prudently, than a child can do at ten.

As Prudence is a Presumption of the Future, contracted from the Experience of time Past, So there is a Presumption of things Past taken from other things (not future but) past also. For he that has seen by what courses and degrees, a flourishing State has first come into civil war, and then to ruin; upon the sight of the ruins of any other State, will guess, the like war, and the like courses have been there also. But this conjecture, has the same uncertainty almost with the conjecture of the Future; both being grounded only upon Experience.

There is no other act of man's mind, that I can remember, naturally planted in him, so, as to need no other thing, to the exercise of it, but to be born a man, and live with the use of his five Senses. Those other Faculties, of which I shall speak by and by, and which seem proper to man only, are acquired, and increased by study and industry; and of most men learned by instruction, and discipline; and proceed all from the invention of Words, and Speech. For besides Sense, and Thoughts, and the Train of thoughts, the mind of man has no other motion; though by the help of Speech, and Method, the same Faculties may be improved to such a height, as to distinguish men from all other living Creatures.

Whatsoever we imagine, is Finite. Therefore there is no Idea, or conception of anything we call Infinite. No man can have in his mind an Image of infinite magnitude; nor conceive infinite swiftness, infinite time, or infinite force, or infinite power. When we say anything is infinite, we signify only, that we are not able to conceive the ends, and bounds of the thing named; having no Conception of the thing, but of our own inability. And therefore the Name of God is used, not to make us conceive him; (for he is Incomprehensible; and his greatness, and power are inconceivable;) but that we may honor him. Also because whatsoever (as I said before,) we conceive, has been perceived first by sense, either all at once, or by parts; a man can have no thought, representing anything, not subject to sense. No man therefore can conceive anything, but he must conceive it in some place; and indued with some determinate magnitude; and which may be divided into parts; nor that anything is all in this place, and all in another place at the same time; nor that two, or more things can be in one, and the same place at once: For none of these things ever have, or can be incident to Sense; but are absurd speeches, taken upon credit (without any signification at all,) from deceived Philosophers, and deceived, or deceiving Schoolmen.

Chapter 4 Of Speech

The Invention of Printing, though ingenious, compared with the invention of Letters, is no great matter. But who was the first that found the use of Letters, is not known. He that first brought them into Greece, men say was Cadmus, the sonne of Agenor, King of Phaenicia. A profitable Invention for continuing the memory of time past, and the conjunction of mankind, dispersed into so many, and distant regions of the Earth; and with all difficult, as proceeding from a watchful observation of the divers motions of the Tongue, Palate, Lips, and other organs of Speech; whereby to make as many differences of characters, to remember them. But the most noble and profitable invention of all other, was that of SPEECH, consisting of Names or Appellations, and their Connection; whereby men register their Thoughts; recall them when they are past; and also declare them one to another for mutual utility and conversation; without which, there had been among men, neither Commonwealth, nor Society, nor Contract, nor Peace, no more than among Lions, Bears, and Wolves. The first author of Speech was God himself, that instructed Adam how to name such creatures as he presented to his sight; For the Scripture goes no further in this matter. But this was sufficient to direct him to add more names, as the experience and use of the creatures should give him occasion; and to join them in such manner by degrees, as to make himself understood; and so by succession of time, so much language might be gotten, as he had found use for; though not so copious, as an Orator or Philosopher has need of. For I do not find anything in the Scripture, out of which, directly or by consequence can be gathered, that Adam was taught the names of all Figures, Numbers, Measures, Colors, Sounds, Fancies, Relations; much less the names of Words and Speech, as General, Special, Affirmative, Negative, Interrogative, Optative, Infinitive, all which are useful; and least of all, of Entity, Intentionality, Quiddity, and other insignificant words of the School.

But all this language gotten, and augmented by Adam and his posterity, was again lost at the tower of Babel, when by the hand of God, every man was stricken for his rebellion, with an oblivion of his former language. And being hereby forced to disperse themselves into several parts of the world, it must needs be, that the diversity of Tongues that now is, proceeded by degrees from them, in such manner, as need (the mother of all inventions) taught them; and in tract of time grew every where more copious.

The general use of Speech, is to transfer our Mental Discourse, into Verbal; or the Train of our Thoughts, into a Train of Words; and that for two commodities; whereof one is, the Registering of the Consequences of our Thoughts; which being apt to slip out of our memory, and put us to a new labor, may again be recalled, by such words as they were marked by. So that the first use of names, is to serve for Marks, or Notes of remembrance. Another is, when many use the same words, to signify (by their connection and order,) one to another, what they conceive, or think of each matter; and also what they desire, fear, or have any other passion for. And for this use they are called Signs. Special uses of Speech are these; First, to Register, what by cogitation, we find to be the cause of anything, present or past; and what we find things present or past may produce, or effect: which in sum, is acquiring of Arts. Secondly, to shew to others that knowledge which we have attained; which is, to Counsel, and Teach one another. Thirdly, to make known to others our wills, and purposes, that we may have the mutual help of one another. Fourthly, to please and delight our selves, and others, by playing with our words, for pleasure or ornament, innocently.

To these Uses, there are also four correspondent Abuses. First, when men register their thoughts wrong, by the inconstancy of the signification of their words; by which they register for their conceptions, that which they never conceived; and so deceive themselves. Secondly, when they use words metaphorically; that is, in other sense than that they are ordained for; and thereby deceive others. Thirdly, when by words they declare that to be their will, which is not. Fourthly, when they use them to grieve one another: for seeing nature has armed living creatures, some with teeth, some with horns, and some with hands, to grieve an enemy, it is but an abuse of Speech, to grieve him with the tongue, unless it be one whom we are obliged to govern; and then it is not to grieve, but to correct and amend.

The manner how Speech serves to the remembrance of the consequence of causes and effects, consists in the imposing of Names, and the Connection of them.

Of Names, some are Proper, and singular to one only thing; as Peter, John, This man, this Tree: and some are Common to many things; as Man, Horse, Tree; every of which though but one Name, is nevertheless the name of divers particular things; in respect of all which together, it is called an Universal; there being nothing in the world Universal but Names; for the things named, are every one of them Individual and Singular.

One Universal name is imposed on many things, for their similitude in some quality, or other accident: And whereas a Proper Name brings to mind one thing only; Universals recall any one of those many.

And of Names Universal, some are of more, and some of less extent; the larger comprehending the less large: and some again of equal extent, comprehending each other reciprocally. As for example, the Name Body is of larger signification than the word Man, and comprehends it; and the names Man and Rational, are of equal extent, comprehending mutually one another. But here we must take notice, that by a Name is not always understood, as in Grammar, one only Word; but sometimes by circumlocution many words together. For all these words, He that in his actions observes the Laws of his Country, make but one Name, equivalent to this one word, Just.

By this imposition of Names, some of larger, some of stricter signification, we turn the reckoning of the consequences of things imagined in the mind, into a reckoning of the consequences of Appellations. For example, a man that has no use of Speech at all, (such, as is born and remains perfectly deaf and dumb,) if he set before his eyes a triangle, and by it two right angles, (such as are the corners of a square figure,) he may by meditation compare and find, that the three angles of that triangle, are equal to those two right angles that stand by it. But if another triangle be shown him different in shape from the former, he cannot know without a new labor, whether the three angles of that also be equal to the same. But he that has the use of words, when he observes, that such equality was consequent, not to the length of the sides, nor to any other particular thing in his triangle; but only to this, that the sides were straight, and the angles three; and that that was all, for which he named it a Triangle; will boldly conclude Universally, that such equality of angles is in all triangles whatsoever; and register his invention in these general terms, Every triangle has its three angles equal to two right angles. And thus the consequence found in one particular, comes to be registered and remembered, as an Universal rule; and discharges our mental reckoning, of time and place; and delivers us from all labor of the mind, saving the first; and makes that which was found true here, and now, to be true in all times and places.

But the use of words in registering our thoughts, is in nothing so evident as in Numbering. A natural fool that could never learn by heart the order of numeral words, as one, two, and three, may observe every stroke of the Clock, and nod to it, or say one, one, one; but can never know what hour it strikes. And it seems, there was a time when those names of number were not in use; and men were fain to apply their fingers of one or both hands, to those things they desired to keep account of; and that thence it proceeded, that now our numeral words are but ten, in any Nation, and in some but five, and then they begin again. And he that can tell ten, if he recite them out of order, will lose himself, and not know when he has done: Much less will he be able to add, and subtract, and perform all other operations of Arithmetic. So that without words, there is no possibility of reckoning of Numbers; much less of Magnitudes, of Swiftness, of Force, and other things, the reckonings whereof are necessary to the being, or well-being of mankind.

When two Names are joined together into a Consequence, or Affirmation; as thus, A man is a living creature; or thus, if he be a man, he is a living creature, If the later name Living creature, signify all that the former name Man signifies, then the affirmation, or consequence is true; otherwise false. For True and False are attributes of Speech, not of Things. And where Speech is not, there is neither Truth nor Falsehood. Error there may be, as when we expect that which shall not be; or suspect what has not been: but in neither case can a man be charged with Untruth.

Seeing then that truth consists in the right ordering of names in our affirmations, a man that seeks precise truth, had need to remember what every name he uses stands for; and to place it accordingly; or else he will find himself entangled in words, as a bird in lime twigs; the more he struggles, the more belimed. And therefore in Geometry, (which is the only Science that it has pleased God hitherto to bestow on mankind,) men begin at settling the significations of their words; which settling of significations, they call Definitions; and place them in the beginning of their reckoning.

By this it appears how necessary it is for any man that aspires to true Knowledge, to examine the Definitions of former Authors; and either to correct them, where they are negligently set down; or to make them himself. For the errors of Definitions multiply themselves, according as the reckoning proceeds; and lead men into absurdities, which at last they see, but cannot avoid, without reckoning anew from the beginning; in which lies the foundation of their errors. From whence it happens, that they which trust to books, do as they that cast up many little sums into a greater, without considering whether those little sums were rightly cast up or not; and at last finding the error visible, and not mistrusting their first grounds, know not which way to clear themselves; but spend time in fluttering over their books; as birds that entering by the chimney, and finding themselves enclosed in a chamber, flutter at the false light of a glass window, for want of wit to consider which way they came in. So that in the right Definition of Names, lies the first use of Speech; which is the Acquisition of Science: And in wrong, or no Definitions, lies the first abuse; from which proceed all false and senseless Tenets; which make those men that take their instruction from the authority of books, and not from their own meditation, to be as much below the condition of ignorant men, as men endued with true Science are above it. For between true Science, and erroneous doctrines, Ignorance is in the middle. Natural sense and imagination, are not subject to absurdity. Nature itself cannot err: and as men abound in copiousness of language; so they become more wise, or more mad than ordinary. Nor is it possible without Letters for any man to become either excellently wise, or (unless his memory be hurt by disease, or ill constitution of organs) excellently foolish. For words are wise men's counters, they do but reckon by them: but they are the money of fools, that value them by the authority of an Aristotle, a Cicero, or a Thomas, or any other Doctor whatsoever, if but a man.

Subject to Names, is whatsoever can enter into, or be considered in an account; and be added one to another to make a sum; or subtracted one from another, and leave a remainder. The Latins called Accounts of money *Rationes*, and accounting, *Ratiocinatio*: and that which we in bills or books of account call Items, they called *Nomina*; that is, Names: and thence it seems to proceed, that they extended the word *Ratio*, to the faculty of Reckoning in all other things. The Greeks have but one word *Logos*, for both Speech and Reason; not that they thought there was no Speech without Reason; but no Reasoning without Speech: And the act of reasoning they called Syllogism; which signifies summing up of the consequences of one saying to another. And because the same things may enter into account for divers accidents; their names are (to shew that diversity) diversely wrested, and diversified. This diversity of names may be reduced to four general heads.

First, a thing may enter into account for Matter, or Body; as living, sensible, rational, hot, cold, moved, quiet; with all which names the word Matter, or Body is understood; all such, being names of Matter.

Secondly, it may enter into account, or be considered, for some accident or quality, which we conceive to be in it; as for being moved, for being so long, for being hot, &c; and then, of the name of the thing itself, by a little change or wresting, we make a name for that accident, which we consider; and for living put into the account life; for moved, motion; for hot, heat; for long, length, and the like: And all such Names, are the names of the accidents and properties, by which one Matter, and Body is distinguished from another. These are called names Abstract; because severed (not from Matter, but) from the account of Matter.

Thirdly, we bring into account, the Properties of our own bodies, whereby we make such distinction: as when anything is Seen by us, we reckon not the thing itself; but the sight, the Color, the Idea of it in the fancy: and when anything is heard, we reckon it not; but the hearing, or sound only, which is our fancy or conception of it by the Ear: and such are names of fancies.

Fourthly, we bring into account, consider, and give names, to Names themselves, and to Speeches: For, general, universal, special, equivocal, are names of Names. And Affirmation, Interrogation, Commandment, Narration, Syllogism, Sermon, Oration, and many other such, are names of Speeches. And this is all the variety of Names Positive; which are put to mark somewhat which is in Nature, or may be feigned by the mind of man, as Bodies that are, or may be conceived to be; or of bodies, the Properties that are, or may be feigned to be; or Words and Speech.

There be also other Names, called Negative; which are notes to signify that a word is not the name of the thing in question; as these words Nothing, no man, infinite, indocible, three want four, and the like; which are nevertheless of use in reckoning, or in correcting of reckoning; and call to mind our past cogitations, though they be not names of any thing; because they make us refuse to admit of Names not rightly used.

All other Names, are but insignificant sounds; and those of two sorts. One, when they are new, and yet their meaning not explained by Definition; whereof there have been abundance coined by School-men, and puzzled Philosophers.

Another, when men make a name of two Names, whose significations are contradictory and inconsistent; as this name, an incorporeall body, or (which is all one) an incorporeal substance, and a great number more. For whensoever any affirmation is false, the two names of which it is composed, put together and made one, signify nothing at all. For example, if it be a false affirmation to say a quadrangle is round, the word round quadrangle signifies nothing; but is a mere sound. So likewise if it be false, to say that virtue can be poured, or blown up and down; the words In-Poured virtue, In-blown virtue, are as absurd and insignificant, as a round quadrangle. And therefore you shall hardly meet with a senseless and insignificant word, that is not made up of some Latin or Greek names. A Frenchman seldom hears our Savior called by the name of *Parole*, but by the name of *Verbe* often; yet *Verbe* and *Parole* differ no more, but that one is Latin, the other French.

When a man upon the hearing of any Speech, has those thoughts which the words of that Speech, and their connection, were ordained and constituted to signify; Then he is said to understand it: Understanding being nothing else, but conception caused by Speech. And therefore if Speech be peculiar to man (as for ought I know it is,) then is Understanding peculiar to him also. And therefore of absurd and false affirmations, in case they be universal, there can be no Understanding; though many think they understand, then, when they do but repeat the words softly, or con them in their mind.

What kinds of Speeches signify the Appetites, Aversions, and Passions of man's mind; and of their use and abuse, I shall speak when I have spoken of the Passions.

The names of such things as affect us, that is, which please, and displease us, because all men be not alike affected with the same thing, nor the same man at all times, are in the common discourses of men, of inconstant signification. For seeing all names are imposed to signify our conceptions; and all our affections are but conceptions; when we conceive the same things differently, we can hardly avoid different naming of them. For though the nature of that we conceive, be the same; yet the diversity of our reception of it, in respect of different constitutions of body, and prejudices of opinion, gives every thing a tincture of our different passions. And therefore in reasoning, a man must take heed of words; which besides the signification of what we imagine of their nature, have a signification also of the nature, disposition, and interest of the speaker; such as are the names of Virtues, and Vices; For one man calls Wisdom, what another calls fear; and one cruelty, what another justice; one prodigality, what another magnanimity; and one gravity, what another stupidity, &c. And therefore such names can never be true grounds of any ratiocination. No more can Metaphors, and Tropes of speech: but these are less dangerous, because they profess their inconstancy; which the other do not.

Chapter 5 Of Reason, and Science

When a man Reasons, he does nothing else but conceive a sum total, from Addition of parcels; or conceive a Remainder; from Subtraction of one sum from another: which (if it be done by Words,) is conceiving of the consequence of the names of all the parts, to the name of the whole; or from the names of the whole and one part, to the name of the other part. And though in some things, (as in numbers,) besides Adding and Subtracting, men name other operations, as Multiplying and Dividing; yet they are the same; for Multiplication, is but Adding together of things equal; and Division, but Subtracting of one thing, as often as we can. These operations are not incident to Numbers only, but to all manner of things that can be added together, and taken one out of another. For as Arithmeticians teach to add and subtract in numbers;

so the Geometricians teach the same in lines, figures (solid and superficial,) angles, proportions, times, degrees of swiftness, force, power, and the like; The Logicians teach the same in Consequences of words; adding together two Names, to make an Affirmation; and two Affirmations, to make a Syllogism; and many Syllogisms to make a Demonstration; and from the sum, or Conclusion of a Syllogism, they subtract one Proposition, to find the other. Writers of Politics, add together Pactions, to find men's duties; and Lawyers, Laws, and facts, to find what is right and wrong in the actions of private men. In sum, in what matter soever there is place for addition and subtraction, there also is place for Reason; and where these have no place, there Reason has nothing at all to do.

Out of all which we may define, (that is to say determine,) what that is, which is meant by this word Reason, when we reckon it among the Faculties of the mind. For REASON, in this sense, is nothing but Reckoning (that is, Adding and Subtracting) of the Consequences of general names agreed upon, for the marking and signifying of our thoughts; I say marking them, when we reckon by our selves; and signifying, when we demonstrate, or approve our reckonings to other men.

And as in Arithmetic, unpracticed men must, and Professors themselves may often err, and cast up false; so also in any other subject of Reasoning, the ablest, most attentive, and most practiced men, may deceive themselves, and infer false Conclusions; Not but that Reason itself is always Right Reason, as well as Arithmetic is a certain and infallible Art: But no one man's Reason, nor the Reason of any one number of men, makes the certainty; no more than an account is therefore well cast up, because a great many men have unanimously approved it. And therefore, as when there is a controversy in an account, the parties must by their own accord, set up for right Reason, the Reason of some Arbitrator, or Judge, to whose sentence they will both stand, or their controversy must either come to blows, or be undecided, for want of a right Reason constituted by Nature; so is it also in all debates of what kind soever: And when men that think themselves wiser than all others, clamor and demand right Reason for judge; yet seek no more, but that things should be determined, by no other men's reason but their own, it is as intolerable in the society of men, as it is in play after trump is turned, to use for trump on every occasion, that suite whereof they have most in their hand. For they do nothing else, that will have every of their passions, as it comes to bear sway in them, to be taken for right Reason, and that in their own controversies: bewraying their want of right Reason, by the claim they lay to it.

The Use and End of Reason, is not the finding of the sum, and truth of one, or a few consequences, remote from the first definitions, and settled significations of names; but to begin at these; and proceed from one consequence to another. For there can be no certainty of the last Conclusion, without a certainty of all those Affirmations and Negations, on which it was grounded, and inferred. As when a master of a family, in taking an account, casts up the sums of all the bills of expense, into one sum; and not regarding how each bill is summed up, by those that give them in account; nor what it is he pays for; he advantages himself no more, than if he allowed the account in gross, trusting to every of the accountants skill and honesty: so also in Reasoning of all other things, he that takes up conclusions on the trust of Authors, and doth not fetch them from the first Items in every Reckoning, (which are the significations of names settled by definitions), loses his labor; and does not know anything; but only believes.

When a man reckons without the use of words, which may be done in particular things, (as when upon the sight of any one thing, we conjecture what was likely to have preceded, or is likely to follow upon it;) if that which he thought likely to follow, follows not; or that which he thought likely to have preceded it, has not preceded it, this is called ERROR; to which even the most prudent men are subject. But when we Reason in Words of general signification, and fall upon a general inference which is false; though it be commonly called Error, it is indeed an ABSURDITY, or senseless Speech. For Error is but a deception, in presuming that somewhat is past, or to come; of which, though it were not past, or not to come; yet there was no impossibility discoverable. But when we make a general assertion, unless it be a true one, the possibility of it is inconceivable. And words whereby we conceive nothing but the sound, are those we call Absurd, Insignificant, and Non-sense. And therefore if a man should talk to me of a round Quadrangle; or accidents of Bread in Cheese; or Immaterial Substances; or of A free Subject; A free-will; or any Free, but free from being hindered by opposition, I should not say he were in an Error; but that his words were without meaning; that is to say, Absurd. I have said before, (in the second chapter,) that a Man did excel all other Animals in this faculty, that when he conceived anything whatsoever, he was apt to inquire the consequences of it, and what effects he could do with it. And now I add this other degree of the same excellence, that he can by words reduce the consequences he finds to general Rules, called Theorems, or Aphorisms; that is, he can Reason, or reckon, not only in number; but in all other things, whereof one may be added unto, or subtracted from another.

But this privilege, is allayed by another; and that is, by the privilege of Absurdity; to which no living creature is subject, but man only. And of men, those are of all most subject to it, that profess Philosophy. For it is most true that Cicero says of them somewhere; that there can be nothing so absurd, but may be found in the books of Philosophers. And the reason is manifest. For there is not one of them that begins his ratiocination from the Definitions, or Explications of the names they are to use; which is a method that has been used only in Geometry; whose Conclusions have thereby been made indisputable.

The first cause of Absurd conclusions I ascribe to the want of Method; in that they begin not their Ratiocination from Definitions; that is, from settled significations of their words: as if they could cast account, without knowing the value of the numeral words, one, two, and three.

And whereas all bodies enter into account upon divers considerations, (which I have mentioned in the precedent chapter;) these considerations being diversely named, divers absurdities proceed from the confusion, and unfit connection of their names into assertions. And therefore

The second cause of Absurd assertions, I ascribe to the giving of names of bodies, to accidents; or of accidents, to bodies; As they do, that say, Faith is infused, or inspired; when nothing can be poured, or breathed into anything, but body; and that, extension is body; that phantasms are spirits, &c.

The third I ascribe to the giving of the names of the accidents of bodies without us, to the accidents of our own bodies; as they do that say, the color is in the body; the sound is in the air, &c.

The fourth, to the giving of the names of bodies, to names, or speeches; as they do that say, that there be things universal; that a living creature is Genus, or a general thing, &c.

The fifth, to the giving of the names of accidents, to names and speeches; as they do that say, the nature of a thing is its definition; a man's command is his will; and the like.

The sixth, to the use of Metaphors, Tropes, and other Rhetorical figures, in stead of words proper. For though it be lawful to say, (for example) in common speech, the way goes, or leads hither, or thither, The Proverb says this or that (whereas ways cannot go, nor Proverbs speak;) yet in reckoning, and seeking of truth, such speeches are not to be admitted.

The seventh, to names that signify nothing; but are taken up, and learned by rote from the Schools, as hypostatical, transubstantiate, consubstantiate, eternal-Now, and the like canting of School-men.

To him that can avoid these things, it is not easy to fall into any absurdity, unless it be by the length of an account; wherein he may perhaps forget what went before. For all men by nature reason alike, and well, when they have good principles. For who is so stupid, as both to mistake in Geometry, and also to persist in it, when another detects his error to him?

By this it appears that Reason is not as Sense, and Memory, borne with us; nor gotten by Experience only, as Prudence is; but attained by Industry; first in apt imposing of Names; and secondly by getting a good and orderly Method in proceeding from the Elements, which are Names, to Assertions made by Connection of one of them to another; and so to Syllogisms, which are the Connections of one Assertion to another, till we come to a knowledge of all the Consequences of names appertaining to the subject in hand; and that is it, men call SCIENCE. And whereas Sense and Memory are but knowledge of Fact, which is a thing past, and irrevocable; Science is the knowledge of Consequences, and dependence of one fact upon another: by which, out of that we can presently do, we know how to do something else when we will, or the like, another time: Because when we see how anything comes about, upon what causes, and by what manner; when the like causes come into our power, we see how to make it produce the like effects.

Children therefore are not endued with Reason at all, till they have attained the use of Speech: but are called Reasonable Creatures, for the possibility apparent of having the use of Reason in time to come. And the most part of men, though they have the use of Reasoning a little way, as in numbering to some degree; yet it serves them to little use in common life; in which they govern themselves, some better, some worse, according to their differences of experience, quickness of memory, and inclinations to several ends; but specially according to good or evil fortune, and the errors of one another. For as for Science, or certain rules of their actions, they are so far from it, that they know not what it is. Geometry they have thought Conjuring: But for other Sciences, they who have not been taught the beginnings, and some progress in them, that they may see how they be acquired and generated, are in this point like children, that having no thought of generation, are made believe by the women, that their brothers and sisters are not born, but found in the garden.

But yet they that have no Science, are in better, and nobler condition with their natural Prudence; than men, that by mis-reasoning, or by trusting them that reason wrong, fall upon false and absurd general rules. For ignorance of causes, and of rules, does not set men so far out of their way, as relying on false rules, and taking for causes of what they aspire to, those that are not so, but rather causes of the contrary.

To conclude, The Light of humane minds is Perspicuous Words, but by exact definitions first snuffed, and purged from ambiguity; Reason is the pace; Increase of Science, the way; and the Benefit of mankind, the end. And on the contrary, Metaphors, and senseless and ambiguous words, are like *ignes fatui*; and reasoning upon them, is wandering among innumerable absurdities; and their end, contention, and sedition, or contempt.

As, much Experience, is Prudence; so, is much Science, Sapience. For though we usually have one name of Wisdom for them both; yet the Latins did always distinguish between *Prudentia* and *Sapientia*; ascribing the former to Experience, the later to Science. But to make their difference appear more clearly, let us suppose one man endued with an excellent natural use, and dexterity in handling his arms; and another to have added to that dexterity, an acquired Science, of where he can offend, or be offended by his adversary, in every possible posture, or guard: The ability of the former, would be to the ability of the later, as Prudence to Sapience; both useful, but the later infallible. But they that trusting only to the authority of books, follow the blind blindly, are like him that trusting to the false rules of a master of Fence, ventures presumptuously upon an adversary, that either kills, or disgraces him.

The signs of Science, are some, certain and infallible; some, uncertain. Certain, when he that pretends the Science of anything, can teach the same; that is to say, demonstrate the truth thereof perspicuously to another: Uncertain, when only some particular events answer to his pretense, and upon many occasions prove so as he says they must. Signs of prudence are all uncertain; because to observe by experience, and remember all circumstances that may alter the success, is impossible. But in any business, whereof a man has not infallible Science to proceed by; to forsake his own natural judgement, and be guided by general sentences read in Authors, and subject to many exceptions, is a sign of folly, and generally scorned by the name of Pedantry. And even of those men themselves, that in Councils of the Commonwealth, love to shew their reading of Politics and History, very few do it in their domestic affairs, where their particular interest is concerned; having Prudence enough for their private affairs: but in public they study more the reputation of their own wit, than the success of another's business.

Chapter 6 Of the Interiour Beginnings of Voluntary Motions; commonly called the PASSIONS. And the Speeches by which they are expressed

There be in Animals, two sorts of Motions peculiar to them: One called Vital; begun in generation, and continued without interruption through their whole life; such as are the course of the Blood, the Pulse, the Breathing, the Concoction, Nutrition, Excretion, &c; to which Motions there needs no help of Imagination: The other is Animal motion, otherwise called Voluntary motion; as to go, to speak, to move any of our limbs, in such manner as is first fancied in our minds. That Sense, is Motion in the organs and interior parts of man's body, caused by the action of the things we See, Hear, &c; And that Fancy is but the Relics of the same Motion, remaining after Sense, has been already said in the first and second Chapters. And because going, speaking, and the like Voluntary motions, depend always upon a precedent thought of whither, which way, and what; it is evident, that the Imagination is the first internal beginning of all Voluntary Motion. And although unstudied men, doe not conceive any motion at all to be there, where the thing moved is invisible; or the space it is moved in, is (for the shortness of it) insensible; yet that doth not hinder, but that such Motions are. For let a space be never so little, that which is moved over a greater space, whereof that little one is part, must first be moved over that. These small beginnings of Motion, within the body of Man, before they appear in walking, speaking, striking, and other visible actions, are commonly called ENDEAVOR.

This Endeavor, when it is toward something which causes it, is called APPETITE, or DESIRE; the later, being the general name; and the other, often-times restrained to signify the Desire of Food, namely Hunger and Thirst. And when the Endeavor is fromward something, it is generally called AVERSION. These words Appetite, and Aversion we have from the Latins; and they both of them signify the motions, one of approaching, the other of retiring. So also do the Greek words for the same, which are *horme*, and *aphorme*. For Nature itself does often press upon men those truths, which afterwards, when they look for somewhat beyond Nature, they stumble at. For the Schools find in mere Appetite to go, or move, no actual Motion at all: but because some Motion they must acknowledge, they call it Metaphorical Motion; which is but an absurd speech: for though Words may be called metaphorical; Bodies, and Motions cannot.

That which men Desire, they are also said to LOVE: and to HATE those things, for which they have Aversion. So that Desire, and Love, are the same thing; save that by Desire, we always signify the Absence of the Object; by Love, most commonly the Presence of the same. So also by Aversion, we signify the Absence; and by Hate, the Presence of the Object.

Of Appetites, and Aversions, some are born with men; as Appetite of food, Appetite of excretion, and exoneration, (which may also and more properly be called Aversions, from somewhat they feel in their Bodies;) and some other Appetites, not many. The rest, which are Appetites of particular things, proceed from Experience, and trial of their effects upon themselves, or other men. For of things we know not at all, or believe not to be, we can have no further Desire, than to taste and try. But Aversion we have for things, not only which we know have hurt us; but also that we do not know whether they will hurt us, or not.

Those things which we neither Desire, nor Hate, we are said to Contemne: CONTEMPT being nothing else but an immobility, or contumacy of the Heart, in resisting the action of certain things; and proceeding from that the Heart is already moved otherwise, by other more potent objects; or from want of experience of them.

And because the constitution of a man's Body, is in continual mutation; it is impossible that all the same things should always cause in him the same Appetites, and Aversions: much less can all men consent, in the Desire of almost any one and the same Object.

But whatsoever is the object of any man's Appetite or Desire; that is it, which he for his part calls Good: And the object of his Hate, and Aversion, Evil; And of his Contempt, Vile, and Inconsiderable. For these words of Good, Evil, and Contemptible, are ever used with relation to the person that uses them: There being nothing simply and absolutely so; nor any common Rule of Good and Evil, to be taken from the nature of the objects themselves; but from the Person of the man (where there is no Commonwealth;) or, (in a Commonwealth,) from the Person that represents it; or from an Arbitrator or Judge, whom men disagreeing shall by consent set up, and make his sentence the Rule thereof.

The Latin Tongue has two words, whose significations approach to those of Good and Evil; but are not precisely the same; And those are *Pulchrum* and *Turpe*. Whereof the former signifies that, which by some apparent signs promises Good; and the later, that, which promises Evil. But in our Tongue we have not so general names to express them by. But for *Pulchrum*, we say in some things, Fair; in others Beautiful, or Handsome, or Gallant, or Honorable, or Comely, or Amiable; and for *Turpe*, Foul, Deformed, Ugly, Base, Nauseous, and the like, as the subject shall require; All which words, in their proper places signify nothing else, but the Mine, or Countenance, that promises Good and Evil. So that of Good there be three kinds; Good in the Promise, that is *Pulchrum*; Good in Effect, as the end desired, which is called *Jucundum*, Delightful; and Good as the Means, which is called *Utile*, Profitable; and as many of Evil: For Evil, in Promise, is that they call *Turpe*; Evil in Effect, and End, is *Molestum*, Unpleasant, Troublesome; and Evil in the Means, *Inutile*, Unprofitable, Hurtful.

As, in Sense, that which is really within us, is (as I have said before) only Motion, caused by the action of external objects, but in appearance; to the Sight, Light and Color; to the Ear, Sound; to the Nostril, Odor, &c: so, when the action of the same object is continued from the Eyes, Ears, and other organs to the Heart; the real effect there is nothing but Motion, or Endeavor; which consists in Appetite, or Aversion, to, or from the object moving. But the apparence, or sense of that motion, is that we either call DELIGHT, or TROUBLE OF MIND.

This Motion, which is called Appetite, and for the appearance of it Delight, and Pleasure, seems to be, a corroboration of Vital motion, and a help thereunto; and therefore such things as caused Delight, were not improperly called *Jucunda*, (*à Juvando*,) from helping or fortifying; and the contrary, *Molesta*, Offensive, from hindering, and troubling the motion vital.

Pleasure therefore, (or Delight,) is the appearance, or sense of Good; and Molestation or Displeasure, the appearance, or sense of Evil. And consequently all Appetite, Desire, and Love, is accompanied with some Delight more or less; and all Hatred, and Aversion, with more or less Displeasure and Offence.

Of Pleasures, or Delights, some arise from the sense of an object Present; And those may be called Pleasures of Sense, (The word sensual, as it is used by those only that condemn them, having no place till there be Laws.) Of this kind are all Onerations and Exonerations of the body; as also all that is pleasant, in the Sight, Hearing, Smell, Taste, or Touch; Others arise from the Expectation, that proceeds from foresight of the End, or Consequence of things; whether those things in the Sense Please or Displease: And these are Pleasures of the Mind of him that draws those consequences; and are generally called JOY. In the like manner, Displeasures, are some in the Sense, and called PAIN; others, in the Expectation of consequences, and are called GRIEF.

These simple Passions called Appetite, Desire, Love, Aversion, Hate, Joy, and Grief, have their names for divers considerations diversified. As first, when they one succeed another, they are diversely called from the opinion men have of the likelihood of attaining what they desire. Secondly, from the object loved or hated. Thirdly, from the consideration of many of them together. Fourthly, from the Alteration or succession itself.

For Appetite with an opinion of attaining, is called HOPE.

The same, without such opinion, DESPAIR.

Aversion, with opinion of Hurt from the object, FEAR.

The same, with hope of avoiding that Hurt by resistance, COURAGE.

Sudden Courage, ANGER.

Constant Hope, CONFIDENCE of our selves.

Constant Despair, DIFFIDENCE of our selves.

Anger for great hurt done to another, when we conceive the same to be done by Injury, INDIGNATION.

Desire of good to another, BENEVOLENCE, GOOD WILL, CHARITY. If to man generally, GOOD NATURE.

Desire of Riches, COVETOUSNESS: a name used always in signification of blame; because men contending for them, are displeased with one another's attaining them; though the desire in itself, be to be blamed, or allowed, according to the means by which those Riches are sought.

Desire of Office; or precedence, AMBITION: a name used also in the worse sense, for the reason before mentioned.

Desire of things that conduce but a little to our ends; And fear of things that are but of little hindrance, PUSILLANIMITY.

Contempt of little helps, and hindrances, MAGNANIMITY.

Magnanimity, in danger of Death, or Wounds, VALOR, FORTITUDE.

Magnanimity, in the use of Riches, LIBERALITY.

Pusillanimity, in the same WRETCHEDNESS, MISERABLENESS; or PARSIMONY; as it is liked, or disliked.

Love of Persons for society, KINDNESS.

Love of Persons for Pleasing the sense only, NATURAL LUST.

Love of the same, acquired from Rumination, that is, Imagination of Pleasure past, LUXURY.

Love of one singularly, with desire to be singularly beloved, THE PASSION OF LOVE. The same, with fear that the love is not mutual, JEALOUSY.

Desire, by doing hurt to another, to make him condemn some fact of his own, REVENGEFULNESS.

Desire, to know why, and how, CURIOSITY; such as is in no living creature but Man: so that Man is distinguished, not only by his Reason; but also by this singular Passion from other Animals; in whom the appetite of food, and other pleasures of Sense, by predominance, take away the care of knowing causes; which is a Lust of the mind, that by a perseverance of delight in the continual and indefatigable generation of Knowledge, exceeds the short vehemence of any carnal Pleasure.

Fear of power invisible, feigned by the mind, or imagined from tales publicly allowed, RELIGION; not allowed, SUPERSTITION. And when the power imagined, is truly such as we imagine, TRUE RELIGION.

Fear, without the apprehension of why, or what, PANIC TERROR; called so from the Fables, that make Pan the author of them; whereas in truth, there is always in him that so fears, first, some apprehension of the cause, though the rest run away by Example; every one supposing his fellow to know why. And therefore this Passion happens to none but in a throng, or multitude of people.

Joy, from apprehension of novelty, ADMIRATION; proper to Man, because it excites the appetite of knowing the cause.

Joy, arising from imagination of a man's own power and ability, is that exultation of the mind which is called GLORIFYING: which if grounded upon the experience of his own former actions, is the same with Confidence: but if grounded on the flattery of others; or only supposed by himself, for delight in the consequences of it, is called VAIN-GLORY: which name is properly given; because a well-grounded Confidence begets Attempt; whereas the supposing of power does not, and is therefore rightly called Vain.

Grief, from opinion of want of power, is called DEJECTION of mind.

The vain-glory which consists in the feigning or supposing of abilities in our selves, which we know are not, is most incident to young men, and nourished by the Histories, or Fictions of Gallant Persons, and is corrected oftentimes by Age, and Employment.

Sudden Glory, is the passion which makes those Grimaces called LAUGHTER; and is caused either by some sudden act of their own, that pleases them; or by the apprehension of some deformed thing in another, by comparison whereof they suddenly applaud themselves. And it is incident most to them, that are conscious of the fewest abilities in themselves, who are forced to keep themselves in their own favor, by observing the imperfections of other men. And therefore much Laughter at the defects of others, is a sign of Pusillanimity. For of great minds, one of the proper works is, to help and free others from scorn; and compare themselves only with the most able.

On the contrary, Sudden Dejection, is the passion that causes WEEPING; and is caused by such accidents, as suddenly take away some vehement hope, or some prop of their power: And they are most subject to it, that rely principally on helps external, such as are Women, and Children. Therefore some Weep for the loss of Friends, Others for their unkindness; others for the sudden stop made to their thoughts of revenge, by Reconciliation. But in all cases, both Laughter, and Weeping, are sudden motions; Custom taking them both away. For no man Laughs at old jests, or Weeps for an old calamity.

Grief, for the discovery of some defect of ability, is SHAME, or the passion that discovers itself in BLUSHING; and consists in the apprehension of some thing dishonorable; and in young men, is a sign of the love of good reputation; and commendable: In old men it is a sign of the same, but because it comes too late, not commendable.

The Contempt of good Reputation is called IMPUDENCE.

Grief, for the Calamity of another, is PITY; and arises from the imagination that the like calamity may befall himself; and therefore is called also COMPASSION, and in the phrase of this present time a FELLOW-FEELING: And therefore for Calamity arriving from great wickedness, the best men have the least Pity; and for the same Calamity, those have least Pity, that think themselves least obnoxious to the same.

Contempt, or little sense of the calamity of others, is that which men call CRUELTY; proceeding from Security of their own fortune. For, that any man should take pleasure in other men's great harms, without other end of his own, I do not conceive it possible.

Grief, for the success of a Competitor in wealth, honor, or other good, if it be joined with Endeavor to enforce our own abilities to equal or exceed him, is called EMULATION: But joined with Endeavor to supplant, or hinder a Competitor, ENVY.

When in the mind of man, Appetites, and Aversions, Hopes, and Fears, concerning one and the same thing, arise alternately; and divers good and evil consequences of the doing, or omitting the thing propounded, come successively into our thoughts; so that sometimes we have an Appetite to it; sometimes an Aversion from it; sometimes Hope to be able to do it; sometimes Despair, or Fear to attempt it; the whole sum of Desires, Aversions, Hopes and Fears, continued till the thing be either done, or thought impossible, is that we call DELIBERATION.

Therefore of things past, there is no Deliberation; because manifestly impossible to be changed: nor of things known to be impossible, or thought so; because men know, or think such Deliberation vain. But of things impossible, which we think possible, we may Deliberate; not knowing it is in vain. And it is called Deliberation; because it is a putting an end to the Liberty we had of doing, or omitting, according to our own Appetite, or Aversion.

This alternate Succession of Appetites, Aversions, Hopes and Fears, is no less in other living Creatures then in Man: and therefore Beasts also Deliberate.

Every Deliberation is then said to End, when that whereof they Deliberate, is either done, or thought impossible; because till then we retain the liberty of doing, or omitting, according to our Appetite, or Aversion.

In Deliberation, the last Appetite, or Aversion, immediately adhering to the action, or to the omission thereof, is that we call the WILL; the Act, (not the faculty,) of Willing. And Beasts that have Deliberation, must necessarily also have Will. The Definition of the Will, given commonly by the Schools, that it is a Rational Appetite, is not good. For if it were, then could there be no Voluntary Act against Reason. For a Voluntary Act is that, which proceeds from the Will, and no other. But if in stead of a Rational Appetite, we shall say an Appetite resulting from a precedent Deliberation, then the Definition is the same that I have given here. Will therefore is the last Appetite in Deliberating. And though we say in common Discourse, a man had a Will once to do a thing, that nevertheless he forbore to do; yet that is properly but an Inclination, which makes no Action Voluntary; because the action depends not of it, but of the last Inclination, or Appetite. For if the intervening Appetites, make any action Voluntary; then by the same Reason all intervening Aversions, should make the same action Involuntary; and so one and the same action, should be both Voluntary & Involuntary.

By this it is manifest, that not only actions that have their beginning from Covetousness, Ambition, Lust, or other Appetites to the thing propounded; but also those that have their beginning from Aversion, or Fear of those consequences that follow the omission, are voluntary actions.

The forms of Speech by which the Passions are expressed, are partly the same, and partly different from those, by which we express our Thoughts. And first, generally all Passions may be expressed Indicatively; as I love, I fear, I joy, I deliberate, I will, I command: but some of them have particular expressions by themselves, which nevertheless are not affirmations, unless it be when they serve to make other inferences, besides that of the Passion they proceed from. Deliberation is expressed Subjunctively; which is a speech proper to signify suppositions, with their consequences; as, If this be done, then this will follow; and differs not from the language of Reasoning, save that Reasoning is in general words; but Deliberation for the most part is of Particulars. The language of Desire, and Aversion, is Imperative; as Do this, forbear that; which when the party is obliged to do, or forbear, is Command; otherwise Prayer; or else Counsel. The language of Vain-Glory, of Indignation, Pity and Revengefulness, Optative: But of the Desire to know, there is a peculiar expression, called Interrogative; as, What is it, when shall it, how is it done, and why so? other language of the Passions I find none: For Cursing, Swearing, Reviling, and the like, do not signify as Speech; but as the actions of a tongue accustomed.

These forms of Speech, I say, are expressions, or voluntary significations of our Passions: but certain signs they be not; because they may be used arbitrarily, whether they that use them, have such Passions or not. The best signs of Passions present, are either in the countenance, motions of the body, actions, and ends, or aims, which we otherwise know the man to have.

And because in Deliberation, the Appetites, and Aversions are raised by foresight of the good and evil consequences, and sequels of the action whereof we Deliberate; the good or evils effect thereof depends on the foresight of a long chain of consequences, of which very seldom any man is able to see to the end. But for so far as a man sees, if the Good in those consequences, be greater than the Evil, the whole chain is that which Writers call Apparent, or Seeming Good. And contrarily, when the Evil exceeds the Good, the whole is Apparent, or Seeming Evil: so that he who has by Experience, or Reason, the greatest and surest prospect of Consequences, Deliberates best himself; and is able when he will, to give the best counsel unto others,

Continual success in obtaining those things which a man from time to time desires, that is to say, continual prospering, is that men call FELICITY; I mean the Felicity of this life. For there is no such thing as perpetual Tranquility of mind, while we live here; because Life itself is but Motion, and can never be without Desire, nor without Fear, no more than without Sense. What kind of Felicity God has ordained to them that devoutly honor him, a man shall no sooner know, than enjoy; being joys, that now are as incomprehensible, as the word of School-men Beatifical Vision is unintelligible.

The form of Speech whereby men signify their opinion of the Goodness of anything, is PRAISE. That whereby they signify the power and greatness of anything, is MAGNIFYING. And that whereby they signify the opinion they have of a man's Felicity, is by the Greeks called *makarismos*, for which we have no name in our tongue. And thus much is sufficient for the present purpose, to have been said of the PASSIONS.

Chapter 7 Of the Ends, or Resolutions of DISCOURSE

OF all Discourse, governed by desire of Knowledge, there is at last an End, either by attaining, or by giving over. And in the chain of Discourse, wheresoever it be interrupted, there is an End for that time.

If the Discourse be merely Mental, it consists of thoughts that the thing will be, and will not be or that it has been, and has not been, alternately. So that wheresoever you break off the chain of a man's Discourse, you leave him in a Presumption of it will be, or, it will not be; or it has been, or, has not been. All which is Opinion. And that which is alternate Appetite, in Deliberating concerning Good and Evil; the same is alternate Opinion, in the Inquiry of the truth of Past, and Future. And as the last Appetite in Deliberation, is called the Will; so the last Opinion in search of the truth of Past, and Future, is called the JUDGEMENT, or Resolute and Final Sentence of him that discourses. And as the whole chain of Appetites alternate, in the question of Good, or Bad, is called Deliberation; so the whole chain of Opinions alternate, in the question of True, or False, is called DOUBT.

No Discourse whatsoever, can End in absolute knowledge of Fact, past, or to come. For, as for the knowledge of Fact, it is originally, Sense; and ever after, Memory. And for the knowledge of Consequence, which I have said before is called Science, it is not Absolute, but Conditional. No man can know by Discourse, that this, or that, is, has been, or will be; which is to know absolutely: but only, that if This be, That is; if This has been, That has been; if This shall be, That shall be: which is to know conditionally; and that not the consequence of one thing to another; but of one name of a thing, to another name of the same thing.

And therefore, when the Discourse is put into Speech, and begins with the Definitions of Words, and proceeds by Connection of the same into general Affirmations, and of these again into Syllogisms; the End or last sum is called the Conclusion; and the thought of the mind by it signified, is that conditional Knowledge, or Knowledge of the consequence of words, which is commonly called SCIENCE. But if the first ground of such Discourse, be not Definitions; or if the Definitions be not rightly joined together into Syllogisms, then the End or Conclusion, is again OPINION, namely of the truth of somewhat said, though sometimes in absurd and senseless words, without possibility of being understood. When two, or more men, know of one and the same fact, they are said to be CONSCIOUS of it one to another; which is as much as to know it together. And because such are fittest witnesses of the facts of one another, or of a third; it was, and ever will be reputed a very Evil act, for any man to speak against his Conscience: or to corrupt or force another so to do: Insomuch that the plea of Conscience, has been always hearkened unto very diligently in all times. Afterwards, men made use of the same word metaphorically, for the knowledge of their own secret facts, and secret thoughts; and therefore it is Rhetorically said, that the Conscience is a thousand witnesses. And last of all, men, vehemently in love with their own new opinions, (though never so absurd,) and obstinately bent to maintain them, gave those their opinions also that reverenced name of Conscience, as if they would have it seem unlawful, to change or speak against them; and so pretend to know they are true, when they know at most, but that they think so.

When a man's Discourse begins not at Definitions, it begins either at some other contemplation of his own, and then it is still called Opinion; Or it begins at some saying of another, of whose ability to know the truth, and of whose honesty in not deceiving, he doubts not; and then the Discourse is not so much concerning the Thing, as the Person; And the Resolution is called BELIEF, and FAITH: Faith, in the man; Belief, both of the man, and of the truth of what he says. So that in Belief are two opinions; one of the saying of the man; the other of his virtue. To have faith in, or trust to, or believe a man, signify the same thing; namely, an opinion of the veracity of the man: But to believe what is said, signifies only an opinion of the truth of the saying. But we are to observe that this Phrase, I believe in; as also the Latin, *Credo in*; and the Greek, *pisteuo auto*: are never used but in the writings of Divines. In stead of them, in other writings are put, I believe him; I trust him; I have faith in him; I rely on him: and in Latin, *Credo illi*; *fido illi*: and in Greek, *pisteuo auto*: and that this singularity of the Ecclesiastic use of the word has raised many disputes about the right object of the Christian Faith.

But by Believing in, as it is in the Creed, is meant, not trust in the Person; but Confession and acknowledgement of the Doctrine. For not only Christians, but all manner of men do so believe in God, as to hold all for truth they hear him say, whether they understand it, or not; which is all the Faith and trust can possibly be had in any person whatsoever: But they do not all believe the Doctrine of the Creed.

From whence we may infer, that when we believe any saying whatsoever it be, to be true, from arguments taken, not from the thing itself, or from the principles of natural Reason, but from the Authority, and good opinion we have, of him that has said it; then is the speaker, or person we believe in, or trust in, and whose word we take, the object of our Faith; and the Honor done in Believing, is done to him only. And consequently, when we Believe that the Scriptures are the word of God, having no immediate revelation from God himself, our Belief, Faith, and Trust is in the Church; whose word we take, and acquiesce therein. And they that believe that which a Prophet relates unto them in the name of God, take the word of the Prophet, do honor to him, and in him trust, and believe, touching the truth of what he relates, whether he be a true, or a false Prophet. And so it is also with all other History. For if I should not believe all that is written by Historians, of the glorious acts of Alexander, or Caesar; I do not think the Ghost of Alexander, or Caesar, had any just cause to be offended; or any body else, but the Historian. If Livy say the Gods made once a Cow speak, and we believe it not; we distrust not God therein, but Livy. So that it is evident, that whatsoever we believe, upon no other reason, then what is drawn from authority of men only, and their writings; whether they be sent from God or not, is Faith in men only.

Chapter 8 Of the VIRTUES commonly called INTELLECTUAL; and their contrary DEFECTS

VIRTUE generally, in all sorts of subjects, is somewhat that is valued for eminence; and consists in comparison. For if all things were equally in all men, nothing would be prized. And by Virtues INTELLECTUAL, are always understood such abilities of the mind, as men praise, value, and desire should be in themselves; and go commonly under the name of a good wit; though the same word Wit, be used also, to distinguish one certain ability from the rest.

These Virtues are of two sorts; Natural, and Acquired. By Natural, I mean not, that which a man has from his Birth: for that is nothing else but Sense; wherein men differ so little one from another, and from brute Beasts, as it is not to be reckoned among Virtues. But I mean, that Wit, which is gotten by Use only, and Experience; without Method, Culture, or Instruction. This NATURAL WIT, consists principally in two things; Celerity of Imagining, (that is, swift succession of one thought to another;) and steady direction to some approved end. On the Contrary a slow Imagination, makes that Defect, or fault of the mind, which is commonly called DULLNESS, Stupidity, and sometimes by other names that signify slowness of motion, or difficulty to be moved.

And this difference of quickness, is caused by the difference of men's passions; that love and dislike, some one thing, some another: and therefore some men's thoughts run one way, some another; and are held to, and observe differently the things that pass through their imagination. And whereas in this succession of men's thoughts, there is nothing to observe in the things they think on, but either in what they be like one another, or in what they be unlike, or what they serve for, or how they serve to such a purpose; Those that observe their similitudes, in case they be such as are but rarely observed by others, are said to have a Good Wit; by which, in this occasion, is meant a Good Fancy. But they that observe their differences, and dissimilitudes; which is called Distinguishing, and Discerning, and Judging between thing and thing; in case, such discerning be not easy, are said to have a good Judgement: and particularly in matter of conversation and business; wherein, times, places, and persons are to be discerned, this Virtue is called DISCRETION. The former, that is, Fancy, without the help of Judgement, is not commended as a Virtue: but the later which is Judgement, and Discretion, is commended for itself, without the help of Fancy. Besides the Discretion of times, places, and persons, necessary to a good Fancy, there is required also an often application of his thoughts to their End; that is to say, to some use to be made of them. This done; he that has this Virtue, will be easily fitted with similitudes, that will please, not only by illustration of his discourse, and adorning it with new and apt metaphors; but also, by the rarity of their invention. But without Steadiness, and Direction to some End, a great Fancy is one kind of Madness; such as they have, that entering into any discourse, are snatched from their purpose, by every thing that comes in their thought, into so many, and so long digressions, and Parentheses, that they utterly lose themselves: Which kind of folly, I know no particular name for: but the cause of it is, sometimes want of experience; whereby that seems to a man new and rare, which doth not so to others: sometimes Pusillanimity; by which that seems great to him, which other men think a trifle: and whatsoever is new, or great, and therefore thought fit to be told, withdraws a man by degrees from the intended way of his discourse.

In a good Poem, whether it be Epic, or Dramatic; as also in Sonnets, Epigrams, and other Pieces, both

Judgement and Fancy are required: But the Fancy must be more eminent; because they please for the Extravagancy; but ought not to displease by Indiscretion.

In a good History, the Judgement must be eminent; because the goodness consists, in the Method, in the Truth, and in the Choice of the actions that are most profitable to be known. Fancy has no place, but only in adorning the stile.

In Orations of Praise, and in Invectives, the Fancy is predominant; because the design is not truth, but to Honor or Dishonor; which is done by noble, or by vile comparisons. The Judgement does but suggest what circumstances make an action laudable, or culpable.

In Hortatives, and Pleadings, as Truth, or Disguise serves best to the Design in hand; so is the Judgement, or the Fancy most required.

In Demonstration, in Counsel, and all rigorous search of Truth, Judgement does all; except sometimes the understanding have need to be opened by some apt similitude; and then there is so much use of Fancy. But for Metaphors, they are in this case utterly excluded. For seeing they openly profess deceit; to admit them into Counsel, or Reasoning, were manifest folly.

And in any Discourse whatsoever, if the defect of Discretion be apparent, how extravagant soever the Fancy be, the whole discourse will be taken for a sign of want of wit, and so will it never when the Discretion is manifest, though the Fancy be never so ordinary.

The secret thoughts of a man run over all things, holy, profane, clean, obscene grave, and light, without shame, or blame; which verbal discourse cannot do, farther than the Judgement shall approve of the Time, Place, and Persons. An Anatomist, or a Physician may speak, or write his judgement of unclean things; because it is not to please, but profit: but for another man to write his extravagant, and pleasant fancies of the same, is as if a man, from being tumbled into the dirt, should come and present himself before good company. And 'tis the want of Discretion that makes the difference. Again, in professed remissness of mind, and familiar company, a man may play with the sounds, and equivocal significations of words; and that many times with encounters of extraordinary Fancy: but in a Sermon, or in public, or before persons unknown, or whom we ought to reverence, there is no gingling of words that will not be accounted folly: and the difference is only in the want of Discretion. So that where Wit is wanting, it is not Fancy that is wanting, but Discretion. Judgement therefore without Fancy is Wit, but Fancy without Judgement not.

When the thoughts of a man, that has a design in hand, running over a multitude of things, observes how they conduce to that design; or what design they may conduce unto; if his observations be such as are not easy, or usual, This wit of his is called PRUDENCE; and depends on much Experience, and Memory of the like things, and their consequences heretofore. In which there is not so much difference of Men, as there is in their Fancies and Judgement; Because the Experience of men equal in age, is not much unequal, as to the quantity; but lies in different occasions; every one having his private designs. To govern well a family, and a kingdom, are not different degrees of Prudence; but different sorts of business; no more then to draw a picture in little, or as great, or greater then the life, are different degrees of Art. A plain husband-man is more Prudent in affairs of his own house, then a Privy Counselor in the affairs of another man.

To Prudence, if you add the use of unjust, or dishonest means, such as usually are prompted to men by Fear, or Want; you have that Crooked Wisdom, which is called CRAFT; which is a sign of Pusillanimity. For Magnanimity is contempt of unjust, or dishonest helps. And that which the Latins call *Versutia*, (translated into English, Shifting,) and is a putting off of a present danger or incommodity, by engaging into a greater; as when a man robs one to pay another, is but a shorter sighted Craft, called *Versutia*, from *Versura*, which signifies taking money at usury, for the present payment of interest.

As for acquired Wit, (I mean acquired by method and instruction,) there is none but Reason; which is grounded on the right use of Speech; and produces the Sciences. But of Reason and Science, I have already spoken in the fifth and sixth Chapters.

The causes of this difference of Wits, are in the Passions: and the difference of Passions, proceeds partly from the different Constitution of the body, and partly from different Education. For if the difference proceeded from the temper of the brain, and the organs of Sense, either exterior or interior, there would be no less difference of men in their Sight, Hearing, or other Senses, than in their Fancies, and Discretions. It proceeds therefore from the Passions; which are different, not only from the difference of men's complexions; but also from their difference of customs, and education.

The Passions that most of all cause the differences of Wit, are principally, the more or less Desire of Power, of Riches, of Knowledge, and of Honor. All which may be reduced to the first, that is Desire of Power. For Riches, Knowledge and Honor are but several sorts of Power.

And therefore, a man who has no great Passion for any of these things; but is as men term it indifferent; though he may be so far a good man, as to be free from giving offence; yet he cannot possibly have either a great Fancy, or much Judgement. For the Thoughts, are to the Desires, as Scouts, and Spies, to range abroad, and find the way to the things Desired: All Steadiness of the mind's motion, and all quickness of the same, proceeding from thence. For as to have no Desire, is to be Dead: so to have weak Passions, is Dullness; and to have Passions indifferently for every thing, GIDDINESS, and Distraction, and to have stronger, and more vehement Passions for anything, than is ordinarily seen in others, is that which men call MADNESS.

Whereof there be almost as many kinds, as of the Passions themselves. Sometimes the extraordinary and extravagant Passion, proceeds from the evil constitution of the organs of the Body, or harm done them; and sometimes the hurt, and indisposition of the Organs, is caused by the vehemence, or long continuance of the Passion. But in both cases the Madness is of one and the same nature.

The Passion, whose violence, or continuance makes Madness, is either great vain-Glory; which is commonly called Pride, and self-conceit; or great Dejection of mind.

Pride, subjects a man to Anger, the excess whereof, is the Madness called RAGE, and FURY. And thus it comes to pass that excessive desire of Revenge, when it becomes habitual, hurts the organs, and becomes Rage: That excessive love, with jealousy, becomes also Rage: Excessive opinion of a man's own self, for divine inspiration, for wisdom, learning, form, and the like, becomes Distraction, and Giddiness: The same, joined with Envy, Rage: Vehement opinion of the truth of anything, contradicted by others, Rage.

Dejection, subjects a man to causeless fears; which is a Madness commonly called MELANCHOLY, apparent also in divers manners; as in haunting of solitudes, and graves; in superstitious behavior; and in fearing some one, some another particular thing. In sum, all Passions that produce strange and unusual behavior, are called by the general name of Madness. But of the several kinds of Madness, he that would take the pains, might enroll a legion. And if the Excesses be madness, there is no doubt but the Passions themselves, when they tend to Evil, are degrees of the same.

For example, though the effect of folly, in them that are possessed of an opinion of being inspired, be not visible always in one man, by any very extravagant action, that proceeds from such Passion; yet when many of them conspire together, the Rage of the whole multitude is visible enough. For what argument of Madness can there be greater, than to clamor, strike, and throw stones at our best friends? Yet this is somewhat less than such a multitude will do. For they will clamor, fight against, and destroy those, by whom all their life-time before, they have been protected, and secured from injury. And if this be Madness in the multitude, it is the same in every particular man. For as in the midst of the sea, though a man perceive no sound of that part of the water next him; yet he is well assured, that part contributes as much, to the Roaring of the Sea, as any other part, of the same quantity: so also, though we perceive no great unquietness, in one, or two men; yet we may be well assured, that their singular Passions, are parts of the Seditious roaring of a troubled Nation. And if there were nothing else that bewrayed their madness; yet that very arrogating such inspiration to themselves, is argument enough. If some man in Bedlam should entertain you with sober discourse; and you desire in taking leave, to know what he were, that you might another time requite his civility; and he should tell you, he were God the Father; I think you need expect no extravagant action for argument of his Madness.

This opinion of Inspiration, called commonly, Private Spirit, begins very often, from some lucky finding of an Error generally held by others; and not knowing, or not remembering, by what conduct of reason, they came to so singular a truth, (as they think it, though it be many times an untruth they light on,) they presently admire themselves; as being in the special grace of God Almighty, who has revealed the same to them supernaturally, by his Spirit.

Again, that Madness is nothing else, but too much appearing Passion, may be gathered out of the effects of Wine, which are the same with those of the evil disposition of the organs. For the variety of behavior in men that have drunk too much, is the same with that of Mad-men: some of them Raging, others Loving, others Laughing, all extravagantly, but according to their several domineering Passions: For the effect of the wine, does but remove Dissimulation; and take from them the sight of the deformity of their Passions. For, (I believe) the most sober men, when they walk alone without care and employment of the mind, would be unwilling the vanity and Extravagance of their thoughts at that time should be publicly seen: which is a confession, that Passions unguided, are for the most part mere Madness.

The opinions of the world, both in ancient and later ages, concerning the cause of madness, have been two. Some, deriving them from the Passions; some, from Daemons, or Spirits, either good, or bad, which they thought might enter into a man, possess him, and move his organs in such strange, and uncouth manner, as mad-men use to do. The former sort therefore, called such men, Mad-men: but the Later, called them sometimes Daemonics, (that is, possessed with spirits;) sometimes *Energumeni*, (that is, agitated, or moved with spirits;) and now in Italy they are called not only *Pazzi*, Madmen; but also *Spiritati*, men possessed.

There was once a great conflux of people in Abdera, a City of the Greeks, at the acting of the Tragedy of Andromeda, upon an extreme hot day: whereupon, a great many of the spectators falling into Fevers, had this accident from the heat, and from the Tragedy together, that they did nothing but pronounce Iambiques, with the names of Perseus and Andromeda; which together with the Fever, was cured, by the coming on of Winter: And this madness was thought to proceed from the Passion imprinted by the Tragedy. Likewise there reigned a fit of madness in another Grecian City, which seized only the young Maidens; and caused many of them to hang themselves. This was by most then thought an act of the Devil. But one that suspected, that contempt of life in them, might proceed from some Passion of the mind, and supposing they did not contemne also their honor, gave counsel to the Magistrates, to strip such as so hang'd themselves, and let them hang out naked. This the story says cured that madness. But on the other side, the same Grecian, did often ascribe madness, to the operation of the Eumenides, or Furys; and sometimes of Ceres, Phoebus, and other Gods: so much did men attribute to Phantasmes, as to think them aëreal living bodies; and generally to call them Spirits. And as the Romans in this, held the same opinion with the Greeks: so also did the Jews; For they called mad-men Prophets, or (according as they thought the spirits good or bad) Daemonics; and some of them called both Prophets, and Daemonics, mad-men; and some called the same man both Daemonics, and mad-man. But for the Gentiles, 'tis no wonder; because Diseases, and Health; Vices, and Virtues; and many natural accidents, were with them termed, and worshiped as Daemons. So that a man was to understand by Daemon, as well (sometimes) an Ague, as a Devil. But for the Jews to have such opinion, is somewhat strange. For neither Moses, nor Abraham pretended to Prophecy by possession of a Spirit; but from the voice of God; or by a Vision or Dream: Nor is there anything in his Law, Moral, or Ceremonial, by which they were taught, there was any such Enthusiasm; or any Possession. When God is sad, Numb. 11. 25. to take from the Spirit that was in Moses, and give to the 70. Elders, the Spirit of God (taking it for the substance of God) is not divided. The Scriptures by the Spirit of God in man, mean a man's spirit, inclined to Godliness. And where it is said Exod. 28. 3. Whom I have filled with the spirit of wisdom to make garments for Aaron, is not meant a spirit put into them, that can make garments; but the wisdom of their own spirits in that kind of work. In the like sense, the spirit of man, when it produces unclean actions, is ordinarily called an unclean spirit; and so other spirits, though not always, yet as often as the virtue or vice so styled, is extraordinary, and Eminent. Neither did the other Prophets of the old Testament pretend Enthusiasm; or, that God spake in them; but to them by Voice, Vision, or Dream; and the Burden of the Lord was not Possession, but Command. How then could the Jews fall into this opinion of possession? I can imagine no reason, but that which is common to all men; namely, the want of curiosity to search natural causes; and their placing Felicity, in the acquisition of the gross pleasures of the Senses, and the things that most immediately conduce thereto. For they that see any strange, and unusual ability, or defect in a man's mind; unless they see withal, from what cause it may probably proceed, can hardly think it natural; and if not natural, they must needs think it supernatural; and then what can it be, but that either God, or the Devil is in him? And hence it came to pass, when our Savior Mark 3. 21.) was compassed about with the multitude, those of the house doubted he was mad, and went out to hold him: but the Scribes said he had Beelzebub, and that was it, by which he cast out devils; as if the greater mad-man had awed the lesser. And that (John 10. 20.) some said, He has a Devil, and is mad; whereas others holding him for a Prophet, said, These are not the words of one that has a Devil. So in the old Testament he that came to anoint Jehu, 2 Kings 9. 11. was a Prophet; but some of the company asked Jehu, What came that mad-man for? So that in sum, it is manifest, that whosoever behaved himself in extraordinary manner, was thought by the Jews to be possessed either with a good, or evil spirit; except by the Sadducees, who erred so far on the other hand, as not to believe there were at all any spirits, (which is very near to direct Atheism;) and thereby perhaps the more provoked others, to term such men Daemonics, rather than mad-men.

But why then does our Savior proceed in the curing of them, as if they were possessed; and not as if they were mad? To which I can give no other kind of answer, but that which is given to those that urge the Scripture in like manner against the opinion of the motion of the Earth. The Scripture was written to shew unto men the kingdom of God, and to prepare their minds to become his obedient subjects; leaving the world, and the Philosophy thereof, to the disputation of men, for the exercising of their natural Reason. Whether the Earths, or Suns motion make the day, and night; or whether the Exorbitant actions of men, proceed from Passion, or from the Devil, (so we worship him not) it is all one, as to our obedience, and subjection to God Almighty; which is the thing for which the Scripture was written. As for that our Savior speaks to the disease, as to a person; it is the usual phrase of all that cure by words only, as Christ did, (and Enchanters pretend to do, whether they speak to a Devil or not.) For is not Christ also said (Math. 8. 26.) to have rebuked the winds? Is not he said also (Luk. 4. 39.) to rebuke a Fever? Yet this does not argue that a Fever is a Devil. And whereas many of those Devils are said to confess Christ; it is not necessary to interpret those places otherwise, than that those mad-men confessed him. And whereas our Savior (Math. 12. 43.) speaks of an unclean Spirit, that having gone out of a man, wanders through dry places, seeking rest, and finding none; and returning into the same man, with seven other spirits worse than himself; It is manifestly a Parable, alluding to a man, that after a little endeavor to quit his lusts, is vanquished by the strength of them; and becomes seven times worse than he was. So that I see nothing at all in the Scripture, that requires a belief, that Daemonics were any other thing but Mad-men.

There is yet another fault in the Discourses of some men; which may also be numbered among the sorts of Madness; namely, that abuse of words, whereof I have spoken before in the fifth chapter, by the Name of Absurdity. And that is, when men speak such words, as put together, have in them no signification at all; but are fallen upon by some, through misunderstanding of the words they have received, and repeat by rote; by others, from intention to deceive by obscurity. And this is incident to none but those, that converse in questions of matters incomprehensible, as the School-men; or in questions of abstruse Philosophy. The common sort of men seldom speak Insignificantly, and are therefore, by those other Egregious persons counted Idiots. But to be assured their words are without anything correspondent to them in the mind, there would need some Examples; which if any man require, let him take a School-man into his hands, and see if he can translate any one chapter concerning any difficult point; as the Trinity; the Deity; the nature of Christ; Transubstantiation; Free-will, &c. into any of the modern tongues, so as to make the same intelligible; or into any tolerable Latin, such as they were acquainted withal, that lived when the Latin tongue was Vulgar. What is the meaning of these words. The first cause does not necessarily inflow anything into the second, by force of the Essential subordination of the second causes, by Which it may help it to work? They are the Translation of the Title of the sixth chapter of Suarez first Book, Of the Concourse, Motion, and Help of God. When men write whole volumes of such stuff, are they not Mad, or intend to make others so? And particularly, in the question of Transubstantiation; where after certain words spoken, they that say, the Whiteness, Roundness, Magnitude, Quality, Corruptibility, all which are incorporeal, &c. go out of the Wafer, into the Body of our blessed Savior, do they not make those "-nesses", "-tudes", and "-ties", to be so many spirits possessing his body? For by Spirits, they mean always things, that being incorporeal, are nevertheless moveable from one place to another. So that this kind of Absurdity, may rightly be numbered among the many sorts of Madness; and all the time that guided by clear Thoughts of their worldly lust, they forbear disputing, or writing thus, but lucid intervals. And thus much of the Virtues and Defects Intellectual.

Chapter 9 Of the Severall SUBJECTS of KNOWLEDGE

There are of KNOWLEDGE two kinds; whereof one is Knowledge of Fact: the other Knowledge of the Consequence of one Affirmation to another. The former is nothing else, but Sense and Memory, and is Absolute Knowledge; as when we see a Fact doing, or remember it done: And this is the Knowledge required in a Witness. The later is called Science; and is Conditional; as when we know, that, If the figure shown be a Circle, then any straight line through the Center shall divide it into two equal parts. And this is the Knowledge required in a Philosopher; that is to say, of him that pretends to Reasoning.

The Register of Knowledge of Fact is called History. Whereof there be two sorts: one called Natural History; which is the History of such Facts, or Effects of Nature, as have no Dependence on Man's Will; Such as are the Histories of Metals, Plants, Animals, Regions, and the like. The other, is Civil History; which is the History of the Voluntary Actions of men in Commonwealths.

The Registers of Science, are such Books as contain the Demonstrations of Consequences of one Affirmation, to another; and are commonly called Books of Philosophy; whereof the sorts are many, according to the diversity of the Matter; And may be divided in such manner as I have divided them in the following Table.

- SCIENCE, that is, Knowledge of Consequences; which is called also PHILOSOPHY.
  - Consequences from the Accidents of Bodies Natural; which is called NATURAL PHILOSOPHY.
    - Consequences from the Accidents common to all Bodies Natural; which are Quantity, and Motion.
      - Consequences from Quantity, and Motion indeterminate; which being the Principles, or first foundation of Philosophy, is called Philosophia Prima.
        - PHILOSOPHIA PRIMA.
      - Consequences from Motion, and Quantity determined.
        - Consequences from Quantity, and Motion determined
          - By Figure, ...
            - Mathematics,
              - GEOMETRY
              - ARITHMETIC
          - By Number,. . . .
            - Mathematics,
              - GEOMETRY.
              - ARITHMETIC
        - Consequences from the Motion, and Quantity of Bodies in special.
          - Consequences from the Motion, and Quantity of the great parts of the World, as the Earth and Stars,
            - Cosmography,
              - ASTRONOMY.
              - GEOGRAPHY.
          - Consequences from the Motion of Special kinds, and Figures of Body,
            - Mechanics,
              - Science of ENGINEERS.
              - ARCHITECTURE
              - NAVIGATION.
            - Doctrine of Weight,
    - PHYSIQUES, or Consequences for Qualities.
      - Consequences from the Qualities of Bodies Transient, such as sometimes appear, sometimes vanish, ... METEOROLOGY
      - Consequences from the Qualities of Bodies Permanent.
        - Consequences from the Qualities of the Stars.
          - Consequences from the Light of the Stars. Out of this, and the Motion of the Sun, is made the Science of . . . . SCIOGRAPHY.
          - Consequences from the Influence of the Stars, ... ASTROLOGY.

- Consequences of the Qualities from Liquid Bodies that fill the space between the Stars; such as are the Air, or substance ethereal.
- Consequences from the Qualities of Bodies Terrestrial.
  - Consequences from the parts of the Earth, that are without Sense,
    - Consequences from the Qualities of Minerals, as Stones, Metals, &c.
    - Consequences from the Qualities of Vegetables.
  - Consequences from the Qualities of Animals.
    - Consequences from the Qualities of Animals in general
      - Consequences from Vision, ... OPTICS.
      - Consequences from Sounds, ... MUSIC.
      - Consequences from the rest of the Senses.
    - Consequences from the Qualities of Men in special
      - Consequences from the Passions of Men, ... ETHICS.
      - Consequences from Speech,
        - In Magnifying, Vilifying, &c. POETRY.
        - In Persuading, . . RHETHORIC
        - In Reasoning, . . . LOGIC.
        - In Contracting, . . The Science of JUST and UNJUST.
- Consequences from the Accidents of Politic Bodies; which is called POLITICS, and CIVIL PHILOSOPHY.
  - 1. Of Consequences from the Institution of COMMONWEALTHS, to the Rights, and Duties of the Body Politic, or Sovereign
  - 2. Of Consequences from the same, to the Duty, and Right of the Subjects.

Chapter 10 Of POWER, WORTH, DIGNITY, HONOUR, and WORTHINESSE

The POWER of a Man, (to take it Universally,) is his present means, to obtain some future apparent Good. And is either Original, or Instrumental.

Natural Power, is the eminence of the Faculties of Body, or Mind: as extraordinary Strength, Form, Prudence, Arts, Eloquence, Liberality, Nobility. Instrumental are those Powers, which acquired by these, or by fortune, are means and Instruments to acquire more: as Riches, Reputation, Friends, and the secret working of God, which men call Good Luck. For the nature of Power, is in this point, like to Fame, increasing as it proceeds; or like the motion of heavy bodies, which the further they go, make still the more hast.

The Greatest of humane Powers, is that which is compounded of the Powers of most men, united by consent, in one person, Natural, or Civil, that has the use of all their Powers depending on his will; such as is the Power of a Commonwealth: Or depending on the wills of each particular; such as is the Power of a Faction, or of divers factions leagued. Therefore to have servants, is Power; To have friends, is Power: for they are strengths united.

Also Riches joined with liberality, is Power; because it procures friends, and servants: Without liberality, not so; because in this case they defend not; but expose men to Envy, as a Prey.

Reputation of power, is Power; because it draws with it the adherence of those that need protection.

So is Reputation of love of a man's Country, (called Popularity,) for the same Reason.

Also, what quality soever makes a man beloved, or feared of many; or the reputation of such quality, is Power; because it is a means to have the assistance, and service of many.

Good success is Power; because it makes reputation of Wisdom, or good fortune; which makes men either fear him, or rely on him.

Affability of men already in power, is increase of Power; because it gains love.

Reputation of Prudence in the conduct of Peace or War, is Power; because to prudent men, we commit the government of our selves, more willingly than to others.

Nobility is Power, not in all places, but only in those Commonwealths, where it has Privileges: for in such privileges consists their Power.

Eloquence is power; because it is seeming Prudence.

Form is Power; because being a promise of Good, it recommends men to the favor of women and strangers.

The Sciences, are small Power; because not eminent; and therefore, not acknowledged in any man; nor are at all, but in a few; and in them, but of a few things. For Science is of that nature, as none can understand it to be, but such as in a good measure have attained it.

Arts of public use, as Fortification, making of Engines, and other Instruments of War; because they confer to Defense, and Victory, are Power: And though the true Mother of them, be Science, namely the Mathematics; yet, because they are brought into the Light, by the hand of the Artificer, they be esteemed (the Midwife passing with the vulgar for the Mother,) as his issue.

The Value, or WORTH of a man, is as of all other things, his Price; that is to say, so much as would be given for the use of his Power: and therefore is not absolute; but a thing dependent on the need and judgement of another. An able conductor of Soldiers, is of great Price in time of War present, or imminent; but in Peace not so. A learned and uncorrupt Judge, is much Worth in time of Peace; but not so much in War. And as in other things, so in men, not the seller, but the buyer determines the Price. For let a man (as most men do,) rate themselves at the highest Value they can; yet their true Value is no more than it is esteemed by others.

The manifestation of the Value we set on one another, is that which is commonly called Honoring, and Dishonoring. To Value a man at a high rate, is to Honor him; at a low rate, is to Dishonor him. But high, and low, in this case, is to be understood by comparison to the rate that each man sets on himself.

The public worth of a man, which is the Value set on him by the Commonwealth, is that which men commonly call DIGNITY. And this Value of him by the Commonwealth, is understood, by offices of Command, Judicature, public Employment; or by Names and Titles, introduced for distinction of such Value.

To pray to another, for aide of any kind, is to HONOR; because a sign we have an opinion he has power to help; and the more difficult the aid is, the more is the Honor.

To obey, is to Honor; because no man obeys them, whom they think have no power to help, or hurt them. And consequently to disobey, is to Dishonor.

To give great gifts to a man, is to Honor him; because 'tis buying of Protection, and acknowledging of Power. To give little gifts, is to Dishonor; because it is but Alms, and signifies an opinion of the need of small helps.

To be sedulous in promoting another's good; also to flatter, is to Honor; as a sign we seek his protection or aid. To neglect, is to Dishonor.

To give way, or place to another, in any Commodity, is to Honor; being a confession of greater power. To arrogate, is to Dishonor.

To show any sign of love, or fear of another, is to Honor; for both to love, and to fear, is to value. To contemn, or less to love or fear, then he expects, is to Dishonor; for 'tis undervaluing.

To praise, magnify, or call happy, is to Honor; because nothing but goodness, power, and felicity is valued. To revile, mock, or pity, is to Dishonor.

To speak to another with consideration, to appear before him with decency, and humility, is to Honor him; as signs of fear to offend. To speak to him rashly, to do anything before him obscenely, slovenly, impudently, is to Dishonor.

To believe, to trust, to rely on another, is to Honor him; sign of opinion of his virtue and power. To distrust, or not believe, is to Dishonor,

To hearken to a man's counsel, or discourse of what kind soever, is to Honor; as a sign we think him wise, or eloquent, or witty. To sleep, or go forth, or talk the while, is to Dishonor.

To do those things to another, which he takes for signs of Honor, or which the Law or Custom makes so, is to Honor; because in approving the Honor done by others, he acknowledges the power which others acknowledge. To refuse to do them, is to Dishonor.

To agree with in opinion, is to Honor; as being a sign of approving his judgement, and wisdom. To dissent, is Dishonor, and an upbraiding of error; and (if the dissent be in many things) of folly.

To imitate, is to Honor; for it is vehemently to approve. To imitate ones Enemy, is to Dishonor.

To honor those another honors, is to Honor him; as a sign of approbation of his judgement. To honor his Enemies, is to Dishonor him.

To employ in counsel, or in actions of difficulty, is to Honor; as a sign of opinion of his wisdom, or other power. To deny employment in the same cases, to those that seek it, is to Dishonor.

All these ways of Honoring, are natural; and as well within, as without Commonwealths. But in Commonwealths, where he, or they that have the supreme Authority, can make whatsoever they please, to stand for signs of Honor, there be other Honors.

A Sovereign Honors a Subject, with whatsoever Title, or Office, or Employment, or Action, that he himself will have taken for a sign of his will to Honor him.

The King of Persia, Honored Mordecai, when he appointed he should be conducted through the streets in the Kings Garment, upon one of the Kings Horses, with a Crown on his head, and a Prince before him, proclaiming, Thus shall it be done to him that the King will honor. And yet another King of Persia, or the same another time, to one that demanded for some great service, to wear one of the Kings robes, gave him leave so to do; but with this addition, that he should wear it as the Kings fool; and then it was Dishonor. So that of Civil Honor, the Fountain is in the person of the Commonwealth, and depends on the Will of the Sovereign; and is therefore temporary, and called Civil Honor; such as are Magistracy, Offices, Titles; and in some places Coats, and Scutcheons painted: and men Honor such as have them, as having so many signs of favor in the Commonwealth; which favor is Power.

Honorable is whatsoever possession, action, or quality, is an argument and sign of Power.

And therefore To be Honored, loved, or feared of many, is Honorable; as arguments of Power. To be Honored of few or none, Dishonorable.

Dominion, and Victory is Honorable; because acquired by Power; and Servitude, for need, or fear, is Dishonorable.

Good fortune (if lasting,) Honorable; as a sign of the favor of God. Ill fortune, and losses, Dishonorable. Riches, are Honorable; for they are Power. Poverty, Dishonorable. Magnanimity, Liberality, Hope, Courage, Confidence, are Honorable; for they proceed from the conscience of Power. Pusillanimity, Parsimony, Fear, Diffidence, are Dishonorable.

Timely Resolution, or determination of what a man is to do, is Honorable; as being the contempt of small difficulties, and dangers. And Irresolution, Dishonorable; as a sign of too much valuing of little impediments, and little advantages: For when a man has weighed things as long as the time permits, and resolves not, the difference of weight is but little; and therefore if he resolve not, he overvalues little things, which is Pusillanimity.

All Actions, and Speeches, that proceed, or seem to proceed from much Experience, Science, Discretion, or Wit, are Honorable; For all these are Powers. Actions, or Words that proceed from Error, Ignorance, or Folly, Dishonorable.

Gravity, as far forth as it seems to proceed from a mind employed on some thing else, is Honorable; because employment is a sign of Power. But if it seem to proceed from a purpose to appear grave, it is Dishonorable. For the gravity of the former, is like the steadiness of a Ship laden with Merchandise; but of the later, like the steadiness of a Ship ballasted with Sand, and other trash.

To be Conspicuous, that is to say, to be known, for Wealth, Office, great Actions, or any eminent Good, is Honorable; as a sign of the power for which he is conspicuous. On the contrary, Obscurity, is Dishonorable.

To be descended from conspicuous Parents, is Honorable; because they the more easily attain the aids, and friends of their Ancestors. On the contrary, to be descended from obscure Parentage, is Dishonorable.

Actions proceeding from Equity, joined with loss, are Honorable; as signs of Magnanimity: for Magnanimity is a sign of Power. On the contrary, Craft, Shifting, neglect of Equity, is Dishonorable.

Covetousness of great Riches, and ambition of great Honors, are Honorable; as signs of power to obtain them. Covetousness, and ambition, of little gains, or preferments, is Dishonorable.

Nor does it alter the case of Honor, whether an action (so it be great and difficult, and consequently a sign of much power,) be just or unjust: for Honor consists only in the opinion of Power. Therefore the ancient Heathen did not think they Dishonored, but greatly Honored the Gods, when they introduced them in their Poems, committing Rapes, Thefts, and other great, but unjust, or unclean acts: In so much as nothing is so much celebrated in Jupiter, as his Adulteries; nor in Mercury, as his Frauds, and Thefts: of whose praises, in a hymn of Homer, the greatest is this, that being born in the morning, he had invented Music at noon, and before night, stolen away the Cattle of Apollo, from his Herdsmen.

Also among men, till there were constituted great Commonwealths, it was thought no dishonor to be a Pirate, or a Highway Thief; but rather a lawful Trade, not only among the Greeks, but also among all other Nations; as is manifest by the Histories of ancient time. And at this day, in this part of the world, private Duels are, and always will be Honorable, though unlawful, till such time as there shall be Honor ordained for them that refuse, and Ignominy for them that make the Challenge. For Duels also are many times effects of Courage; and the ground of Courage is always Strength or Skill, which are Power; though for the most part they be effects of rash speaking, and of the fear of Dishonor, in one, or both the Combatants; who engaged by rashness, are driven into the Lists to avoid disgrace.

Scutcheons, and Coats of Arms hereditary, where they have any eminent Privileges, are Honorable; otherwise not: for their Power consists either in such Privileges, or in Riches, or some such thing as is equally honored in other men. This kind of Honor, commonly called Gentry, has been derived from the Ancient Germans. For there never was any such thing known, where the German Customs were unknown. Nor is it now any where in use, where the Germans have not inhabited. The ancient Greek Commanders, when they went to war, had their Shields painted with such Devises as they pleased; insomuch as an unpainted Buckler was a sign of Poverty, and of a common Soldier: but they transmitted not the Inheritance of them. The Romans transmitted the Marks of their Families: but they were the Images, not the Devises of their Ancestors. Among the people of Asia, Africa, and America, there is not, nor was ever, any such thing. The Germans only had that custom; from whom it has been derived into England, France, Spain and Italy, when in great numbers they either aided the Romans, or made their own Conquests in these Western parts of the world.

For Germany, being anciently, as all other Countries, in their beginnings, divided among an infinite number of little Lords, or Masters of Families, that continually had wars one with another; those Masters, or Lords, principally to the end they might, when they were Covered with Arms, be known by their followers; and partly for ornament, both painted their Armor, or their Scutcheon, or Coat, with the picture of some Beast, or other thing; and also put some eminent and visible mark upon the Crest of their Helmets. And this ornament both of the Arms, and Crest, descended by inheritance to their Children; to the eldest pure, and to the rest with some note of diversity, such as the Old master, that is to say in Dutch, the *Here-alt* thought fit. But when many such Families, joined together, made a greater Monarchy, this duty of the Hereault, to distinguish Scutcheons, was made a private Office a part. And the issue of these Lords, is the great and ancient Gentry; which for the most part bear living creatures, noted for courage, and rapine; or Castles, Battlements, Belts, Weapons, Bars, Palisadoes, and other notes of War; nothing being then in honor, but virtue military. Afterwards, not only Kings, but popular Commonwealths, gave divers manners of Scutcheons, to such as went forth to the War, or returned from it, for encouragement, or recompense to their service. All which, by an observing Reader, may be found in such ancient Histories, Greek and Latin, as make mention of the German Nation, and Manners, in their times.

Titles of Honor, such as are Duke, Count, Marquis, and Baron, are Honorable; as signifying the value set upon them by the Sovereign Power of the Commonwealth: Which Titles, were in old time titles of Office, and Command, derived some from the Romans, some from the Germans, and French. Dukes, in Latin *Duces*, being Generals in War: Counts, Comites, such as bare the General company out of friendship; and were left to govern and defend places conquered, and pacified: Marquises, Marchiones, were Counts that governed the Marches, or bounds of the Empire. Which titles of Duke, Count, and Marquis, came into the Empire, about the time of Constantine the Great, from the customs of the German Militia. But Baron, seems to have been a Title of the Gauls, and signifies a Great man; such as were the Kings, or Princes men, whom they employed in war about their persons; and seems to be derived from *Vir*, to *Ber*, and *Bar*, that signified the same in the Language of the Gauls, that *Vir* in Latin; and thence to *Bero*, and *Baro*: so that such men were called *Berones*, and after *Barones*; and (in Spanish) *Varones*. But he that would know more particularly the original of Titles of Honor, may find it, as I have done this, in Mr. Selden's most excellent Treatise of that subject. In process of time these offices of Honor, by occasion of trouble, and for reasons of good and peaceable government, were turned into mere Titles; serving for the most part, to distinguish the precedence, place, and order of subjects in the Commonwealth: and men were made Dukes, Counts, Marquises, and Barons of Places, wherein they had neither possession, nor command: and other Titles also, were devised to the same end.

WORTHINESS, is a thing different from the worth, or value of a man; and also from his merit, or desert;

and consists in a particular power, or ability for that, whereof he is said to be worthy: which particular ability, is usually named FITNESS, or Aptitude.

For he is Worthiest to be a Commander, to be a Judge, or to have any other charge, that is best fitted, with the qualities required to the well discharging of it; and Worthiest of Riches, that has the qualities most requisite for the well using of them: any of which qualities being absent, one may nevertheless be a Worthy man, and valuable for some thing else. Again, a man may be Worthy of Riches, Office, and Employment, that nevertheless, can plead no right to have it before another; and therefore cannot be said to merit or deserve it. For Merit, presupposes a right, and that the thing deserved is due by promise: Of which I shall say more hereafter, when I shall speak of Contracts.

Chapter 11 Of the difference of MANNERS

BY MANNERS, I mean not here, Decency of behavior; as how one man should salute another, or how a man should wash his mouth, or pick his teeth before company, and such other points of the Small Morals; But those qualities of mankind, that concern their living together in Peace, and Unity. To which end we are to consider, that the Felicity of this life, consists not in the repose of a mind satisfied. For there is no such *Finis ultimus*, (utmost aim,) nor *Summum Bonum*, (greatest Good,) as is spoken of in the Books of the old Moral Philosophers. Nor can a man any more live, whose Desires are at an end, than he, whose Senses and Imaginations are at a stand. Felicity is a continual progress of the desire, from one object to another; the attaining of the former, being still but the way to the later. The cause whereof is, That the Object of man's desire, is not to enjoy once only, and for one instant of time; but to assure forever, the way of his future desire. And therefore the voluntary actions and inclinations of all men, tend, not only to the procuring, but also to the assuring of a contented life; and differ only in the way: which arises partly from the diversity of passions, in divers men; and partly from the difference of the knowledge, or opinion each one has of the causes, which produce the effect desired.

So that in the first place, I put for a general inclination of all mankind, a perpetual and restless desire of Power after power, that ceases only in Death. And the cause of this, is not always that a man hopes for a more intensive delight, than he has already attained to; or that he cannot be content with a moderate power: but because he cannot assure the power and means to live well, which he has present, without the acquisition of more. And from hence it is, that Kings, whose power is greatest, turn their endeavors to the assuring it at home by Laws, or abroad by Wars: and when that is done, there succeeds a new desire; in some, of Fame from new Conquest; in others, of ease and sensual pleasure; in others, of admiration, or being flattered for excellence in some art, or other ability of the mind.

Competition of Riches, Honor, Command, or other power, inclines to Contention, Enmity, and War: Because the way of one Competitor, to the attaining of his desire, is to kill, subdue, supplant, or repel the other. Particularly, competition of praise, inclines to a reverence of Antiquity. For men contend with the living, not with the dead; to these ascribing more than due, that they may obscure the glory of the other.

Desire of Ease, and sensual Delight, disposes men to obey a common Power: Because by such Desires, a man doth abandon the protection might be hoped for from his own Industry, and labor. Fear of Death, and Wounds, disposes to the same; and for the same reason. On the contrary, needy men, and hardy, not contented with their present condition; as also, all men that are ambitious of Military command, are inclined to continue the causes of war; and to stir up trouble and sedition: for there is no honor Military but by war; nor any such hope to mend an ill game, as by causing a new shuffle.

Desire of Knowledge, and Arts of Peace, inclines men to obey a common Power: For such Desire, contains a desire of leisure; and consequently protection from some other Power than their own.

Desire of Praise, disposes to laudable actions, such as please them whose judgement they value; for of those men whom we contemn, we contemn also the Praises. Desire of Fame after death does the same. And though after death, there be no sense of the praise given us on Earth, as being joys, that are either swallowed up in the unspeakable joys of Heaven, or extinguished in the extreme torments of Hell: yet is not such Fame vain; because men have a present delight therein, from the foresight of it, and of the benefit that may redound thereby to their posterity: which though they now see not, yet they imagine; and anything that is pleasure in the sense, the same also is pleasure in the imagination.

To have received from one, to whom we think our selves equal, greater benefits than there is hope to Requite, disposes to counterfeit love; but really secret hatred; and puts a man into the estate of a desperate debtor, that in declining the sight of his creditor, tacitly wishes him there, where he might never see him more. For benefits oblige; and obligation is thralldom; and unrequitable obligation, perpetual thralldom; which is to one's equal, hateful. But to have received benefits from one, whom we acknowledge for superior, inclines to love; because the obligation is no new depression: and cheerful acceptation, (which men call Gratitude,) is such an honor done to the obliger, as is taken generally for retribution. Also to receive benefits, though from an equal, or inferior, as long as there is hope of requital, disposes to love: for in the intention of the receiver, the obligation is of aid, and service mutual; from whence proceeds an Emulation of who shall exceed in benefiting; the most noble and profitable contention possible; wherein the victor is pleased with his victory, and the other revenged by confessing it.

To have done more hurt to a man, than he can, or is willing to expiate, inclines the doer to hate the sufferer. For he must expect revenge, or forgiveness; both which are hateful.

Fear of oppression, disposes a man to anticipate, or to seek aid by society: for there is no other way by which a man can secure his life and liberty.

Men that distrust their own subtlety, are in tumult, and sedition, better disposed for victory, than they that suppose themselves wife, or crafty. For these love to consult, the other (fearing to be circumvented,) to strike first. And in sedition, men being always in the precincts of battle, to hold together, and use all advantages of force, is a better stratagem, than any that can proceed from subtlety of Wit.

Vain-glorious men, such as without being conscious to themselves of great sufficiency, delight in supposing themselves gallant men, are inclined only to ostentation; but not to attempt: Because when danger or difficulty appears, they look for nothing but to have their insufficiency discovered.

Vain-glorious men, such as estimate their sufficiency by the flattery of other men, or the fortune of some precedent action, without assured ground of hope from the true knowledge of themselves, are inclined to rash engaging; and in the approach of danger, or difficulty, to retire if they can: because not seeing the way of safety, they will rather hazard their honor, which may be salved with an excuse; than their lives, for which no salve is sufficient.

Men that have a strong opinion of their own wisdom in matter of government, are disposed to Ambition. Because without public Employment in counsel or magistracy, the honor of their wisdom is lost. And therefore Eloquent speakers are inclined to Ambition; for Eloquence seems wisdom, both to themselves and others.

Pusillanimity disposes men to Irresolution, and consequently to lose the occasions, and fittest opportunities of action. For after men have been in deliberation till the time of action approach, if it be not then manifest what is best to be done, 'tis a sign, the difference of Motives, the one way and the other, are not great: Therefore not to resolve then, is to lose the occasion by weighing of trifles; which is Pusillanimity.

Frugality, (though in poor men a Virtue,) makes a man inapt to achieve such actions, as require the strength of many men at once: For it weakens their Endeavor, which is to be nourished and kept in vigor by Reward.

Eloquence, with flattery, disposes men to confide in them that have it; because the former is seeming Wisdom, the later seeming Kindness. Add to them Military reputation, and it disposes men to adhere, and subject themselves to those men that have them. The two former, having given them caution against danger from him; the later gives them caution against danger from others.

Want of Science, that is, Ignorance of causes, disposes, or rather constrains a man to rely on the advise, and authority of others. For all men whom the truth concerns, if they rely not on their own, must rely on the opinion of some other, whom they think wiser than themselves, and see not why he should deceive them.

Ignorance of the signification of words; which is, want of understanding, disposes men to take on trust, not only the truth they know not; but also the errors; and which is more, the non-sense of them they trust: For neither Error, nor non-sense, can without a perfect understanding of words, be detected.

From the same it proceeds, that men give different names, to one and the same thing, from the difference of their own passions: As they that approve a private opinion, call it Opinion; but they that dislike it, Heresy: and yet heresy signifies no more than private opinion; but has only a greater tincture of choler.

From the same also it proceeds, that men cannot distinguish, without study and great understanding, between one action of many men, and many actions of one multitude; as for example, between the one action of all the Senators of Rome in killing Catiline, and the many actions of a number of Senators in killing Caesar; and therefore are disposed to take for the action of the people, that which is a multitude of actions done by a multitude of men, led perhaps by the persuasion of one.

Ignorance of the causes, and original constitution of Right, Equity, Law, and Justice, disposes a man to make Custom and Example the rule of his actions; in such manner, as to think that Unjust which it has been the custom to punish; and that Just, of the impunity and approbation whereof they can produce an Example, or (as the Lawyers which only use this false measure of Justice barbarously call it) a Precedent; like little children, that have no other rule of good and evil manners, but the correction they receive from their Parents, and Masters; save that children are constant to their rule, whereas men are not so; because grown strong, and stubborn, they appeal from custom to reason, and from reason to custom, as it serves their turn; receding from custom when their interest requires it, and setting themselves against reason, as often as reason is against them: Which is the cause, that the doctrine of Right and Wrong, is perpetually disputed, both by the Pen and the Sword: Whereas the doctrine of Lines, and Figures, is not so; because men care not, in that subject what be truth, as a thing that crosses no man's ambition, profit, or lust. For I doubt not, but if it had been a thing contrary to any man's right of dominion, or to the interest of men that have dominion, That the three Angles of a Triangle, should be equal to two Angles of a Square; that doctrine should have been, if not disputed, yet by the burning of all books of Geometry, suppressed, as far as he whom it concerned was able.

Ignorance of remote causes, disposes men to attribute all events, to the causes immediate, and Instrumental: For these are all the causes they perceive. And hence it comes to pass, that in all places, men that are grieved with payments to the Public, discharge their anger upon the Publicans, that is to say, Farmers, Collectors, and other Officers of the public Revenue; and adhere to such as find fault with the public Government; and thereby, when they have engaged themselves beyond hope of justification, fall also upon the Supreme Authority, for fear of punishment, or shame of receiving pardon.

Ignorance of natural causes disposes a man to Credulity, so as to believe many times impossibilities: For such know nothing to the contrary, but that they may be true; being unable to detect the Impossibility. And Credulity, because men love to be hearkened unto in company, disposes them to lying: so that Ignorance itself without Malice, is able to make a man both to believe lies, and tell them; and sometimes also to invent them.

Anxiety for the future time, disposes men to inquire into the causes of things: because the knowledge of them, makes men the better able to order the present to their best advantage.

Curiosity, or love of the knowledge of causes, draws a man from consideration of the effect, to seek the cause; and again, the cause of that cause; till of necessity he must come to this thought at last, that there is some cause, whereof there is no former cause, but is eternal; which is it men call God. So that it is impossible to make any profound inquiry into natural causes, without being inclined thereby to believe there is one God Eternal; though they cannot have any Idea of him in their mind, answerable to his nature. For as a man that is born blind, hearing men talk of warming themselves by the fire, and being brought to warm himself by the same, may easily conceive, and assure himself, there is somewhat there, which men call Fire, and is the cause of the heat he feels; but cannot imagine what it is like; nor have an Idea of it in his mind, such as they have that see it: so also, by the visible things of this world, and their admirable order, a man may conceive there is a cause of them, which men call God; and yet not have an Idea, or Image of him in his mind.

And they that make little, or no inquiry into the natural causes of things, yet from the fear that proceeds from the ignorance itself, of what it is that has the power to do them much good or harm, are inclined to suppose, and feign unto themselves, several kinds of Powers Invisible; and to stand in awe of their own imaginations; and in time of distress to invoke them; as also in the time of an expected good success, to give them thanks; making the creatures of their own fancy, their Gods. By which means it has come to pass, that from the innumerable variety of Fancy, men have created in the world innumerable sorts of Gods. And this Fear of things invisible, is the natural Seed of that, which every one in himself calls Religion; and in them that worship, or fear that Power otherwise than they do, Superstition.

And this seed of Religion, having been observed by many; some of those that have observed it, have been inclined thereby to nourish, dress, and form it into Laws; and to add to it of their own invention, any opinion of the causes of future events, by which they thought they should best be able to govern others, and make unto themselves the greatest use of their Powers.

Chapter 12 Of RELIGION

Seeing there are no signs, nor fruit of Religion, but in Man only; there is no cause to doubt, but that the seed of Religion, is also only in Man; and consists in some peculiar quality, or at least in some eminent degree thereof, not to be found in other Living creatures.

And first, it is peculiar to the nature of Man, to be inquisitive into the Causes of the Events they see, some more, some less; but all men so much, as to be curious in the search of the causes of their own good and evil fortune.

Secondly, upon the sight of anything that ha a Beginning, to think also it had a cause, which determined the same to begin, then when it did, rather than sooner or later.

Thirdly, whereas there is no other Felicity of Beasts, but the enjoying of their quotidian Food, Ease, and

Lusts; as having little, or no foresight of the time to come, for want of observation, and memory of the order, consequence, and dependence of the things they see; Man observes how one Event has been produced by another; and remembers in them Antecedence and Consequence; And when he cannot assure himself of the true causes of things, (for the causes of good and evil fortune for the most part are invisible,) he supposes causes of them, either such as his own fancy suggests; or trusts to the Authority of other men, such as he thinks to be his friends, and wiser than himself.

The two first, make Anxiety. For being assured that there be causes of all things that have arrived hitherto, or shall arrive hereafter; it is impossible for a man, who continually endeavors to secure himself against the evil he fears, and procure the good he desires, not to be in a perpetual solicitude of the time to come; So that every man, especially those that are over provident, are in an estate like to that of Prometheus. For as Prometheus, (which interpreted, is, The prudent man,) was bound to the hill Caucasus, a place of large prospect, where, an Eagle feeding on his liver, devoured in the day, as much as was repaired in the night: So that man, which looks too far before him, in the care of future time, has his heart all the day long, gnawed on by fear of death, poverty, or other calamity; and has no repose, nor pause of his anxiety, but in sleep.

This perpetual fear, always accompanying mankind in the ignorance of causes, as it were in the Dark, must needs have for object something. And therefore when there is nothing to be seen, there is nothing to accuse, either of their good, or evil fortune, but some Power, or Agent Invisible: In which sense perhaps it was, that some of the old Poets said, that the Gods were at first created by humane Fear: which spoken of the Gods, (that is to say, of the many Gods of the Gentiles) is very true. But the acknowledging of one God Eternal, Infinite, and Omnipotent, may more easily be derived, from the desire men have to know the causes of natural bodies, and their several virtues, and operations; than from the fear of what was to be fall them in time to come. For he that from any effect he sees come to pass, should reason to the next and immediate cause thereof, and from thence to the cause of that cause, and plunge himself profoundly in the pursuit of causes; shall at last come to this, that there must be (as even the Heathen Philosophers confessed) one First Mover; that is, a First, and an Eternal cause of all things; which is that which men mean by the name of God: And all this without thought of their fortune; the solicitude whereof, both inclines to fear, and hinders them from the search of the causes of other things; and thereby gives occasion of feigning of as many Gods, as there be men that feign them.

And for the matter, or substance of the Invisible Agents, so fancied; they could not by natural cogitation, fall upon any other conceit, but that it was the same with that of the Soul of man; and that the Soul of man, was of the same substance, with that which appears in a Dream, to one that sleeps; or in a Looking-glass, to one that is awake; which, men not knowing that such apparitions are nothing else but creatures of the Fancy, think to be real, and external Substances; and therefore call them Ghosts; as the Latins called them *Imagines*, and *Umbrae*; and thought them Spirits, that is, thin aëreall bodies; and those Invisible Agents, which they feared, to bee like them; save that they appear, and vanish when they please. But the opinion that such Spirits were Incorporeal, or Immaterial, could never enter into the mind of any man by nature; because, though men may put together words of contradictory signification, as Spirit, and Incorporeal; yet they can never have the imagination of any thing answering to them: And therefore, men that by their own meditation, arrive to the acknowledgement of one Infinite, Omnipotent, and Eternal God, choose rather to confess he is Incomprehensible, and above their understanding; than to define his Nature by Spirit Incorporeal, and then confess their definition to be unintelligible: or if they give him such a title, it is not Dogmatically, with intention to make the Divine Nature understood; but Piously, to honor him with attributes, of significations, as remote as they can from the grossness of Bodies Visible.

Then, for the way by which they think these Invisible Agents wrought their effects; that is to say, what immediate causes they used, in bringing things to pass, men that know not what it is that we call causing, (that is, almost all men) have no other rule to guess by, but by observing, and remembering what they have seen to precede the like effect at some other time, or times before, without seeing between the antecedent and subsequent Event, any dependence or connection at all: And therefore from the like things past, they expect the like things to come; and hope for good or evil luck, superstitiously, from things that have no part at all in the causing of it: As the Athenians did for their war at Lepanto, demand another Phormio; The Pompeian faction for their war in Africa, another Scipio; and others have done in divers other occasions since. In like manner they attribute their fortune to a stander by, to a lucky or unlucky place, to words spoken, especially if the name of God be among them; as Charming, and Conjuring (the Liturgy of Witches;) insomuch as to believe, they have power to turn a stone into bread, bread into a man, or any thing, into any thing.

Thirdly, for the worship which naturally men exhibit to Powers invisible, it can be no other, but such expressions of their reverence, as they would use towards men; Gifts, Petitions, Thanks, Submission of Body, Considerate Addresses, sober Behavior, premeditated Words, Swearing (that is, assuring one another of their promises,) by invoking them. Beyond that reason suggests nothing; but leaves them either to rest there; or for further ceremonies, to rely on those they believe to be wiser than themselves.

Lastly, concerning how these Invisible Powers declare to men the things which shall hereafter come to pass, especially concerning their good or evil fortune in general, or good or ill success in any particular undertaking, men are naturally at a stand; save that using to conjecture of the time to come, by the time past, they are very apt, not only to take casual things, after one or two encounters, for Prognostics of the like encounter ever after, but also to believe the like Prognostics from other men, of whom they have once conceived a good opinion.

And in these four things, Opinion of Ghosts, Ignorance of second causes, Devotion towards what men fear, and Taking of things Casual for Prognostics, consists the Natural seed of Religion; which by reason of the different Fancies, Judgments, and Passions of several men, has grown up into ceremonies so different, that those which are used by one man, are for the most part ridiculous to another.

For these seeds have received culture from two sorts of men. One sort have been they, that have nourished, and ordered them, according to their own invention. The other, have done it, by Gods commandment, and direction: but both sorts have done it, with a purpose to make those men that relied on them, the more apt to Obedience, Laws, Peace, Charity, and civil Society. So that the Religion of the former sort, is a part of humane Politics; and teaches part of the duty which Earthly Kings require of their Subjects. And the Religion of the later sort is Divine Politics; and contains Precepts to those that have yielded themselves subjects in the Kingdom of God. Of the former sort, were all the founders of Commonwealths, and the Law-givers of the Gentiles: Of the later sort, were Abraham, Moses, and our Blessed Savior; by whom have been derived unto us the Laws of the Kingdom of God.

And for that part of Religion, which consists in opinions concerning the nature of Powers Invisible, there is almost nothing that has a name, that has not been esteemed among the Gentiles, in one place or another, a God, or Devil; or by their Poets feigned to be inanimated, inhabited, or possessed by some Spirit or other.

The unformed matter of the World, was a God, by the name of Chaos.

The Heaven, the Ocean, the Planets, the Fire, the Earth, the Winds, were so many Gods.

Men, Women, a Bird, a Crocodile, a Calf, a Dog, a Snake, an Onion, a Leek, Deified. Besides, that they filled almost all places, with spirits called Daemons: the plains, with Pan, and Panises, or Satyrs; the Woods, with

Fawns, and Nymphs; the Sea, with Tritons, and other Nymphs; every River, and Fountain, with a Ghost of his name, and with Nymphs; every house, with its Lares, or Familiars; every man, with his Genius; Hell, with Ghosts, and spiritual Officers, as Charon, Cerberus, and the Furies; and in the night time, all places with Larvae, Lemures, Ghosts of men deceased, and a whole kingdom of Fairies, and Bugbears. They have also ascribed Divinity, and built Temples to mere Accidents, and Qualities; such as are Time, Night, Day, Peace, Concord, Love, Contention, Virtue, Honor, Health, Rust, Fever, and the like; which when they prayed for, or against, they prayed to, as if there were Ghosts of those names hanging over their heads, and letting fall, or withholding that Good, or Evil, for, or against which they prayed. They invoked also their own Wit, by the name of Muses; their own Ignorance, by the name of Fortune; their own Lust, by the name of Cupid; their own Rage, by the name Furies; their own privy members by the name of Priapus; and attributed their pollutions, to Incubi, and Succubae: insomuch as there was nothing, which a Poet could introduce as a person in his Poem, which they did not make either a God, or a Devil.

The same authors of the Religion of the Gentiles, observing the second ground for Religion, which is men's Ignorance of causes; and thereby their aptness to attribute their fortune to causes, on which there was no dependence at all apparent, took occasion to obtrude on their ignorance, in stead of second causes, a kind of second and ministerial Gods; ascribing the cause of Fecundity, to Venus; the cause of Arts, to Apollo; of Subtlety and Craft, to Mercury; of Tempests and storms, to Aeolus; and of other effects, to other Gods: insomuch as there was among the Heathen almost as great variety of Gods, as of business.

And to the Worship, which naturally men conceived fit to be used towards their Gods, namely Oblations, Prayers, Thanks, and the rest formerly named; the same Legislators of the Gentiles have added their Images, both in Picture, and Sculpture; that the more ignorant sort, (that is to say, the most part, or generality of the people,) thinking the Gods for whose representation they were made, were really included, and as it were housed within them, might so much the more stand in fear of them: And endowed them with lands, and houses, and officers, and revenues, set apart from all other humane uses; that is, consecrated, and made holy to those their Idols; as Caverns, Groves, Woods, Mountains, and whole Islands; and have attributed to them, not only the shapes, some of Men, some of Beasts, some of Monsters; but also the Faculties, and Passions of men and beasts; as Sense, Speech, Sex, Lust, Generation, (and this not only by mixing one with another, to propagate the kind of Gods; but also by mixing with men, and women, to beget mongrel Gods, and but inmates of Heaven, as Bacchus, Hercules, and others;) besides, Anger. Revenge, and other passions of living creatures, and the actions proceeding from them, as Fraud, Theft, Adultery, Sodomy, and any vice that may be taken for an effect of Power, or a cause of Pleasure; and all such Vices, as among men are taken to be against Law, rather than against Honor.

Lastly, to the Prognostics of time to come; which are naturally, but Conjectures upon the Experience of time past; and supernaturally, divine Revelation; the same authors of the Religion of the Gentiles, partly upon pretended Experience, partly upon pretended Revelation, have added innumerable other superstitious ways of Divination; and made men believe they should find their fortunes, sometimes in the ambiguous or senseless answers of the Priests at Delphi, Delos, Ammon, and other famous Oracles; which answers, were made ambiguous by design, to own the event both ways; or absurd, by the intoxicating vapor of the place, which is very frequent in sulfurous Caverns: Sometimes in the leaves of the Sybils; of whose Prophecies (like those perhaps of Nostradamus; for the fragments now extant seem to be the invention of later times) there were some books in reputation in the time of the Roman Republics Sometimes in the insignificant Speeches of Madmen, supposed to be possessed with a divine Spirit; which Possession they called Enthusiasm; and these kinds of foretelling events, were accounted Theomancy, or Prophecy:

Sometimes in the aspect of the Stars at their Nativity; which was called Horoscopy, and esteemed a part of judiciary Astrology: Sometimes in their own hopes and fears, called Thumomancy, or Presage: Sometimes in the Prediction of Witches, that pretended conference with the dead; which is called Necromancy, Conjuring, and Witchcraft; and is but juggling and confederate knavery: Sometimes in the Casual flight, or feeding of birds; called Augury: Sometimes in the Entrails of a sacrificed beast; which was *Aruspicina*: Sometimes in Dreams: Sometimes in Croaking of Ravens, or chattering of Birds: Sometimes in the Lineaments of the face; which was called Metoposcopy; or by Palmistry in the lines of the hand; in casual words, called *Omina*: Sometimes in Monsters, or unusual accidents; as Eclipses, Comets, rare Meteors, Earthquakes, Inundations, uncouth Births, and the like, which they called *Portenta*, and *Ostenta*, because they thought them to portend, or foreshow some great Calamity to come: Sometimes, in mere Lottery, as Cross and Pile; counting holes in a sieve; dipping of Verses in Homer, and Virgil; and innumerable other such vain conceits. So easy are men to be drawn to believe anything, from such men as have gotten credit with them; and can with gentleness, and dexterity, take hold of their fear, and ignorance.

And therefore the first Founders, and Legislators of Commonwealths among the Gentiles, whose ends were only to keep the people in obedience, and peace, have in all places taken care; First, to imprint in their minds a belief, that those precepts which they gave concerning Religion, might not be thought to proceed from their own device, but from the dictates of some God, or other Spirit; or else that they themselves were of a higher nature than mere mortals, that their Laws might the more easily be received: So Numa Pompilius pretended to receive the Ceremonies he instituted among the Romans, from the Nymph Egeria: and the first King and founder of the Kingdom of Peru, pretended himself and his wife to be the children of the Sun: and Mahomet, to set up his new Religion, pretended to have conferences with the Holy Ghost, in form of a Dove. Secondly, they have had a care, to make it believed, that the same things were displeasing to the Gods, which were forbidden by the Laws. Thirdly, to prescribe Ceremonies, Supplications, Sacrifices, and Festivals, by which they were to believe, the anger of the Gods might be appeased; and that ill success in War, great contagions of Sickness, Earthquakes, and each man's private Misery, came from the Anger of the Gods; and their Anger from the Neglect of their Worship, or the forgetting, or mistaking some point of the Ceremonies required. And though among the ancient Romans, men were not forbidden to deny, that which in the Poets is written of the pains, and pleasures after this life; which divers of great authority, and gravity in that state have in their Harangues openly derided; yet that belief was always more cherished, than the contrary.

And by these, and such other Institutions, they obtained in order to their end, (which was the peace of the Commonwealth,) that the common people in their misfortunes, laying the fault on neglect, or error in their Ceremonies, or on their own disobedience to the laws, were the less apt to mutiny against their Governors. And being entertained with the pomp, and pastime of Festivals, and public Games, made in honor of the Gods, needed nothing else but bread, to keep them from discontent, murmuring, and commotion against the State. And therefore the Romans, that had conquered the greatest part of the then known World, made no scruple of tolerating any Religion whatsoever in the City of Rome itself; unless it had something in it, that could not consist with their Civil Government; nor do we read, that any Religion was there forbidden, but that of the Jews; who (being the peculiar Kingdom of God) thought it unlawful to acknowledge subjection to any mortal King or State whatsoever. And thus you see how the Religion of the Gentiles was a part of their Policy.

But where God himself, by supernatural Revelation, planted Religion; there he also made to himself a peculiar Kingdom; and gave Laws, not only of behavior towards himself; but also towards one another; and thereby in the Kingdom of God, the Policy, and laws Civil, are a part of Religion; and therefore the distinction of Temporal, and Spiritual Domination, has there no place. It is true, that God is King of all the Earth: Yet may he be King of a peculiar, and chosen Nation. For there is no more incongruity therein, than that he that has the general command of the whole Army, should have withal a peculiar Regiment, or Company of his own. God is King of all the Earth by his Power: but of his chosen people, he is King by Covenant. But to speak more largely of the Kingdom of God, both by Nature, and Covenant, I have in the following discourse assigned another place.

From the propagation of Religion, it is not hard to understand the causes of the resolution of the same into its first seeds, or principles; which are only an opinion of a Deity, and Powers invisible, and supernatural; that can never be so abolished out of humane nature, but that new Religions may again be made to spring out of them, by the culture of such men, as for such purpose are in reputation.

For seeing all formed Religion, is founded at first, upon the faith which a multitude has in some one person, whom they believe not only to be a wise man, and to labor to procure their happiness, but also to be a holy man, to whom God himself vouchsafe to declare his will supernaturally; It follows necessarily, when they that have the Government of Religion, shall come to have either the wisdom of those men, their sincerity, or their love suspected; or that they shall be unable to shew any probable token of Divine Revelation; that the Religion which they desire to uphold, must be suspected likewise; and (without the fear of the Civil Sword) contradicted and rejected.

That which takes away the reputation of Wisdom, in him that forms a Religion, or adds to it when it is already formed, is the enjoining of a belief of contradictories: For both parts of a contradiction cannot possibly be true: and therefore to enjoin the belief of them, is an argument of ignorance; which detects the Author in that; and discredits him in all things else he shall propound as from revelation supernatural: which revelation a man may indeed have of many things above, but of nothing against natural reason.

That which takes away the reputation of Sincerity, is the doing, or saying of such things, as appear to be signs, that what they require other men to believe, is not believed by themselves; all which doings, or sayings are therefore called Scandalous, because they be stumbling blocks, that make men to fall in the way of Religion: as Injustice, Cruelty, Profaneness, Avarice, and Luxury. For who can believe, that he that doth ordinarily such actions, as proceed from any of these roots, believes there is any such Invisible Power to be feared, as he affrights other men withal, for lesser faults?

That which takes away the reputation of Love, is the being detected of private ends: as when the belief they require of others, conduces or seems to conduce to the acquiring of Dominion, Riches, Dignity, or secure Pleasure, to themselves only, or specially. For that which men reap benefit by to themselves, they are thought to do for their own sake, and not for love of others.

Lastly, the testimony that men can render of divine Calling, can be no other, than the operation of Miracles; or true Prophecy, (which also is a Miracle;) or extraordinary Felicity. And therefore, to those points of Religion, which have been received from them that did such Miracles; those that are added by such, as approve not their Calling by some Miracle, obtain no greater belief, than what the Custom, and Laws of the places, in which they be educated, have wrought into them. For as in natural things, men of judgement require natural signs, and arguments; so in supernatural things, they require signs supernatural, (which are Miracles,) before they consent inwardly, and from their hearts.

All which causes of the weakening of men's faith, do manifestly appear in the Examples following. First, we have the Example of the children of Israel; who when Moses, that had approved his Calling to them by Miracles, and by the happy conduct of them out of Egypt, was absent but 40 days, revolted from the worship of the true God, recommended to them by him; and setting up a Golden Calf for their God, relapsed into the Idolatry of the Egyptians; from whom they had been so lately delivered. And again, after Moses, Aaron, Joshua, and that generation which had seen the great works of God in Israel, were dead; another generation arose, and served Baal. So that Miracles failing, Faith also failed.

Again, when the sons of Samuel, being constituted by their father Judges in Bersabee, received bribes, and judged unjustly, the people of Israel refused any more to have God to be their King, in other manner than he was King of other people; and therefore cried out to Samuel, to choose them a King after the manner of the Nations. So that Justice failing, Faith also failed: Insomuch, as they deposed their God, from reigning over them.

And whereas in the planting of Christian Religion, the Oracles ceased in all parts of the Roman Empire, and the number of Christians increased wonderfully every day, and in every place, by the preaching of the Apostles, and Evangelists; a great part of that success, may reasonably be attributed, to the contempt, into which the Priests of the Gentiles of that time, had brought themselves, by their uncleannesse, avarice, and juggling between Princes. Also the Religion of the Church of Rome, was partly, for the same cause abolished in England, and many other parts of Christendom; insomuch, as the failing of Virtue in the Pastors, makes Faith fail in the People: and partly from bringing of the Philosophy, and doctrine of Aristotle into Religion, by the School-men; from whence there arose so many contradictions, and absurdities, as brought the Clergy into a reputation both of Ignorance, and of Fraudulent intention; and inclined people to revolt from them, either against the will of their own Princes, as in France, and Holland; or with their will, as in England.

Lastly, among the points by the Church of Rome declared necessary for Salvation, there be so many, manifestly to the advantage of the Pope, and of his spiritual subjects, residing in the territories of other Christian Princes, that were it not for the mutual emulation of those Princes, they might without war, or trouble, exclude all foreign Authority, as easily as it has been excluded in England. For who is there that does not see, to whose benefit it conduces, to have it believed, that a King has not his Authority from Christ, unless a Bishop crown him? That a King, if he be a Priest, cannot Marry? That whether a Prince be born in lawful Marriage, or not, must be judged by Authority from Rome? That Subjects may be freed from their Allegiance, if by the Court of Rome, the King be judged an Heretic? That a King (as Chilperic of France) may be deposed by a Pope (as Pope Zachary,) for no cause; and his Kingdom given to one of his Subjects? That the Clergy, and Regulars, in what Country soever, shall be exempt from the Jurisdiction of their King, in cases criminal? Or who does not see, to whose profit redound the Fees of private Masses, and Vales of Purgatory; with other signs of private interest, enough to mortify the most lively Faith, if (as I said) the civil Magistrate, and Custom did not more sustain it, than any opinion they have of the Sanctity, Wisdom, or Probity of their Teachers? So that I may attribute all the changes of Religion in the world, to one and the same cause; and that is, unpleasing Priests; and those not only among Catholics, but even in that Church that has presumed most of Reformation.

Chapter 13 Of the NATURAL CONDITION of Mankind, as concerning their Felicity, and Misery

Nature has made men so equal, in the faculties of body, and mind; as that though there be found one man sometimes manifestly stronger in body, or of quicker mind then another; yet when all is reckoned together, the difference between man, and man, is not so considerable, as that one man can thereupon claim to himself any benefit, to which another may not pretend, as well as he. For as to the strength of body, the weakest has strength enough to kill the strongest, either by secret machination, or by confederacy with others, that are in the fame danger with himself.

And as to the faculties of the mind, (setting aside the arts grounded upon words, and especially that skill of proceeding upon general, and infallible rules, called Science; which very few have, and but in few things; as being not a native faculty, born with us; nor attained, (as Prudence,) while we look after somewhat else,) I find yet a greater equality among men, than that of strength. For Prudence, is but Experience; which equal time, equally bestows on all men, in those things they equally apply themselves unto. That which may perhaps make such equality incredible, is but a vain conceit of one's own wisdom, which almost all men think they have in a greater degree, than the Vulgar; that is, than all men but themselves, and a few others, whom by Fame, or for concurring with themselves, they approve. For such is the nature of men, that howsoever they may acknowledge many others to be more witty, or more eloquent, or more learned; Yet they will hardly believe there be many so wise as themselves: For they see their own wit at hand, and other men's at a distance. But this proves rather that men are in that point equal, than unequal. For there is not ordinarily a greater sign of the equal distribution of anything, than that every man is contented with his share.

From this equality of ability, arises equality of hope in the attaining of our Ends. And therefore if any two men desire the same thing, which nevertheless they cannot both enjoy, they become enemies; and in the way to their End, (which is principally their own conservation, and sometimes their delectation only,) endeavor to destroy, or subdue one another. And from hence it comes to pass, that where an Invader has no more to fear, than another man's single power; if one plant, sow, build, or possess a convenient Seat, others may probably be expected to come prepared with forces united, to dispossess, and deprive him, not only of the fruit of his labor, but also of his life, or liberty. And the Invader again is in the like danger of another.

And from this diffidence of one another, there is no way for any man to secure himself, so reasonable, as Anticipation; that is, by force, or wiles, to master the persons of all men he can, so long, till he see no other power great enough to endanger him: And this is no more than his own conservation requires, and is generally allowed. Also because there be some, that taking pleasure in contemplating their own power in the acts of conquest, which they pursue farther than their security requires; if others, that otherwise would be glad to be at ease within modest bounds, should not by invasion increase their power, they would not be able, long time, by standing only on their defense, to subsist. And by consequence, such augmentation of dominion over men, being necessary to a man's conservation, it ought to be allowed him.

Again, men have no pleasure, (but on the contrary a great deal of grief) in keeping company, where there is no power able to over-awe them all. For every man looks that his companion should value him, at the same rate he sets upon himself: And upon all signs of contempt, or undervaluing, naturally endeavors, as far as he dares (which among them that have no common power to keep them in quiet, is far enough to make them destroy each other,) to extort a greater value from his contemners, by dommage; and from others, by the example.

So that in the nature of man, we find three principal causes of quarrel. First, Competition; Secondly, Diffidence; Thirdly, Glory.

The first, makes men invade for Gain; the second, for Safety; and the third, for Reputation. The first use Violence, to make themselves Masters of other men's persons, wives, children, and cattle; the second, to defend them; the third, for trifles, as a word, a smile, a different opinion, and any other sign of undervalue, either direct in their Persons, or by reflection in their Kindred, their Friends, their Nation, their Profession, or their Name.

Hereby it is manifest, that during the time men live without a common Power to keep them all in awe, they are in that condition which is called War; and such a war, as is of every man, against every man. For WAR, consists not in Battle only, or the act of fighting; but in a tract of time, wherein the Will to contend by

Battle is sufficiently known: and therefore the notion of Time, is to be considered in the nature of War; as it is in the nature of Weather. For as the nature of Foul weather, lies not in a shower or two of rain; but in an inclination thereto of many days together: So the nature of War, consists not in actual fighting; but in the known disposition thereto, during all the time there is no assurance to the contrary. All other time is PEACE.

Whatsoever therefore is consequent to a time of War, where every man is Enemy to every man; the same is consequent to the time, wherein men live without other security, than what their own strength, and their own invention shall furnish them withal. In such condition, there is no place for Industry; because the fruit thereof is uncertain: and consequently no Culture of the Earth; no Navigation, nor use of the commodities that may be imported by Sea; no commodious Building; no Instruments of moving, and removing such things as require much force; no Knowledge of the face of the Earth; no account of Time; no Arts; no Letters; no Society; and which is worst of all, continual fear, and danger of violent death; And the life of man, solitary, poor, nasty, brutish, and short.

It may seem strange to some man, that has not well weighed these things; that Nature should thus dissociate, and render men apt to invade, and destroy one another: and he may therefore, not trusting to this Inference, made from the Passions, desire perhaps to have the same confirmed by Experience. Let him therefore consider with himself, when taking a journey, he arms himself, and seeks to go well accompanied; when going to sleep, he locks his doors; when even in his house he locks his chests; and this when he knows there be Laws, and public Officers, armed, to revenge all injuries shall be done him; what opinion he has of his fellow subjects, when he rides armed; of his fellow Citizens, when he locks his doors; and of his children, and servants, when he locks his chests. Does he not there as much accuse mankind by his actions, as I do by my words? But neither of us accuse man's nature in it. The Desires, and other Passions of man, are in themselves no Sin. No more are the Actions, that proceed from those Passions, till they know a Law that forbids them: which till Laws be made they cannot know: nor can any Law be made, till they have agreed upon the Person that shall make it.

It may peradventure be thought, there was never such a time, nor condition of war as this; and I believe it was never generally so, over all the world: but there are many places, where they live so now. For the savage people in many places of America, except the government of small Families, the concord whereof depends on natural lust, have no government at all; and live at this day in that brutish manner, as I said before. Howsoever, it may be perceived what manner of life there would be, where there were no common Power to fear; by the manner of life, which men that have formerly lived under a peaceful government, use to degenerate into, in a civil War.

But though there had never been any time, wherein particular men were in a condition of war one against another; yet in all times, Kings, and Persons of Sovereign authority, because of their Independency, are in continual jealousies, and in the state and posture of Gladiators; having their weapons pointing, and their eyes fixed on one another; that is, their Forts, Garrisons, and Guns upon the Frontiers of their Kingdoms; and continual Spies upon their neighbors; which is a posture of War. But because they uphold thereby, the Industry of their Subjects; there does not follow from it, that misery, which accompanies the Liberty of particular men.

To this war of every man against every man, this also is consequent; that nothing can be Unjust. The notions of Right and Wrong, Justice and Injustice have there no place. Where there is no common Power, there is no Law: where no Law, no Injustice. Force, and Fraud, are in war the two Cardinal virtues. Justice, and Injustice are none of the Faculties neither of the Body, nor Mind. If they were, they might be in a man that were alone in the world, as well as his Senses, and Passions. They are Qualities, that relate to men in

Society, not in Solitude. It is consequent also to the same condition, that there be no Propriety, no Dominion, no Mine and Thine distinct; but only that to be every man's, that he can get; and for so long, as he can keep it. And thus much for the ill condition, which man by mere Nature is actually placed in; though with a possibility to come out of it, consisting partly in the Passions, partly in his Reason.

The Passions that incline men to Peace, are Fear of Death; Desire of such things as are necessary to commodious living; and a Hope by their Industry to obtain them. And Reason suggests convenient Articles of Peace, upon which men may be drawn to agreement. These Articles, are they, which otherwise are called the Laws of Nature: whereof I shall speak more particularly, in the two following Chapters.

Chapter 14 Of the first and second NATURALL LAWES, and of CONTRACTS

Te RIGHT OF NATURE, which Writers commonly call *Jus Naturale*, is the Liberty each man has, to use his own power, as he will himself, for the preservation of his own Nature; that is to say, of his own Life; and consequently, of doing anything, which in his own Judgement, and Reason, he shall conceive to be the aptest means thereunto.

By LIBERTY, is understood, according to the proper signification of the word, the absence of external Impediments: which Impediments, may often take away part of a man's power to do what he would; but cannot hinder him from using the power left him, according as his judgement, and reason shall dictate to him.

A LAW OF NATURE, (*Lex Naturalis*,) is a Precept, or general Rule, found out by Reason, by which a man is forbidden to do, that, which is destructive of his life, or takes away the means of preserving the same; and to omit, that, by which he thinks it may be best preserved. For though they that speak of this subject, use to confound *Jus*, and *Lex*, Right and Law; yet they ought to be distinguished; because RIGHT, consists in liberty to do, or to forbear; Whereas LAW, determines, and binds to one of them: so that Law, and Right, differ as much, as Obligation, and Liberty; which in one and the same matter are inconsistent.

And because the condition of Man, (as has been declared in the precedent Chapter) is a condition of War of every one against every one; in which case every one is governed by his own Reason; and there is nothing he can make use of, that may not be a help unto him, in preserving his life against his enemies; It follows, that in such a condition, every man has a Right to every thing; even to one another's body. And therefore, as long as this natural Right of every man to every thing endures, there can be no security to any man, (how strong or wise soever he be,) of living out the time, which Nature ordinarily allows men to live. And consequently it is a precept, or general rule of Reason, That every man, ought to endeavor Peace, as far as he has hope of obtaining it; and when he cannot obtain it, that he may seek, and use, all helps, and advantages of War. The first branch of which Rule, contains the first, and Fundamental Law of Nature; which is, to seek Peace, and follow it. The Second, the sum of the Right of Nature; which is, By all means we can, to defend our selves.

From this Fundamental Law of Nature, by which men are commanded to endeavor Peace, is derived this second Law; That a man be willing, when others are so too, as far-forth, as for Peace, and defense of himself he shall think it necessary, to lay down this right to all things; and be contented with so much liberty against other men, as he would allow other men against himself. For as long as every man holds this Right, of doing anything he likes; so long are all men in the condition of War. But if other men will not lay down their Right, as well as he; then there is no Reason for any one, to divest himself of his: For that were to expose himself to Prey, (which no man is bound to) rather than to dispose himself to Peace. This is that Law of the Gospel;

Whatsoever you require that others should do to you, that do ye to them. And that Law of all men, *Quod tibi fieri non vis, alteri ne feceris.*

To lay down a man's Right to anything, is to divest himself of the Liberty, of hindering another of the benefit of his own Right to the same. For he that renounces, or passes away his Right, gives not to any other man a Right which he had not before; because there is nothing to which every man had not Right by Nature: but only stands out of his way, that he may enjoy his own original Right, without hindrance from him; not without hindrance from another. So that the effect which redounds to one man, by another man's defect of Right, is but so much diminution of impediments to the use of his own Right original.

Right is laid aside, either by simply Renouncing it; or by Transferring it to another. By Simply RENOUNCING; when he cares not to whom the benefit thereof redounds. By TRANSFERRING; when he intends the benefit thereof to some certain person, or persons. And when a man has in either manner abandoned, or granted away his Right; then is he said to be OBLIGED, or BOUND, not to hinder those, to whom such Right is granted, or abandoned, from the benefit of it: and that he Ought, and it is his DUTY, not to make void that voluntary act of his own: and that such hindrance is INJUSTICE, and INJURY, as being *Sine Jure*; the Right being before renounced, or transferred. So that Injury, or Injustice, in the controversies of the world, is somewhat like to that, which in the disputations of Scholars is called Absurdity. For as it is there called an Absurdity, to contradict what one maintained in the Beginning: so in the world, it is called Injustice, and Injury, voluntarily to undo that, which from the beginning he had voluntarily done. The way by which a man either simply Renounces, or Transfers his Right, is a Declaration, or Signification, by some voluntary and sufficient sign, or signs, that he doth so Renounce, or Transfer; or has so Renounced, or Transferred the same, to him that accepts it. And these Signs are either Words only, or Actions only; or (as it happens most often) both Words, and Actions. And the same are the BONDS, by which men are bound, and obliged: Bonds, that have their strength, not from their own Nature, (for nothing is more easily broken then a man's word,) but from Fear of some evil consequence upon the rupture.

Whensoever a man Transfers his Right, or Renounces it; it is either in consideration of some Right reciprocally transferred to himself; or for some other good he hopes for thereby. For it is a voluntary act: and of the voluntary acts of every man, the object is some Good to himself. And therefore there be some Rights, which no man can be understood by any words, or other signs, to have abandoned; or transferred. As first a man cannot lay down the right of resisting them, that assault him by force, to take away his life; because he cannot be understood to aim thereby, at any Good to himself. The same may be said of Wounds; and Chains, and Imprisonment; both because there is no benefit consequent to such patience; as there is to the patience of suffering another to be wounded, or imprisoned: as also because a man cannot tell, when he sees men proceed against him by violence, whether they intend his death or not. And lastly the motive, and end for which this renouncing, and transferring of Right is introduced, is nothing else but the security of a man's person, in his life, and in the means of so preserving life, as not to be weary of it. And therefore if a man by words, or other signs, seem to despoil himself of the End, for which those signs were intended; he is not to be understood as if he meant it, or that it was his will; but that he was ignorant of how such words and actions were to be interpreted.

The mutual transferring of Right, is that which men call CONTRACT.

There is difference, between transferring of Right to the Thing; and transferring, or tradition, that is, delivery of the Thing itself. For the Thing may be delivered together with the Translation of the Right; as in buying and selling with ready money; or exchange of goods, or lands: and it may be delivered some time after.

Again, one of the Contractors, may deliver the Thing contracted for on his part, and leave the other to perform his part at some determinate time after, and in the mean time be trusted; and then the Contract on his part, is called PACT, or COVENANT: Or both parts may contract now, to perform hereafter: in which cases, he that is to perform in time to come, being trusted, his performance is called Keeping of Promise, or Faith; and the failing of performance (if it be voluntary) Violation of Faith.

When the transferring of Right, is not mutual; but one of the parties transfers, in hope to gain thereby friendship, or service from another, or from his friends; or in hope to gain the reputation of Charity, or Magnanimity; or to deliver his mind from the pain of compassion; or in hope of reward in heaven; This is not Contract, but GIFT, FREE-GIFT, GRACE: which words signify one and the same thing.

Signs of Contract, are either Express, or by Inference. Express, are words spoken with understanding of what they signify: And such words are either of the time Present, or Past; as, I Give, I Grant, I have Given, I have Granted, I will that this be yours: Or of the future; as, I will Give, I will Grant: which words of the future, are called PROMISE.

Signs by Inference, are sometimes the consequence of Words; sometimes the consequence of Silence; sometimes the consequence of Actions; sometimes the consequence of Forbearing an Action: and generally a sign by Inference, of any Contract, is whatsoever sufficiently argues the will of the Contractor.

Words alone, if they be of the time to come, and contain a bare promise, are an insufficient sign of a Free-gift and therefore not obligatory. For if they be of the time to Come, as, Tomorrow I will Give, they are a sign I have not given yet, and consequently that my right is not transferred, but remains till I transfer it by some other Act. But if the words be of the time Present, or Past, as, I have given, or do give to be delivered tomorrow, then is my tomorrow's Right given away to day; and that by the virtue of the words, though there were no other argument of my will. And there is a great difference in the signification of these words; *Volo hoc tuum esse cras*, and *Cras dabo*; that is, between I will that this be thine tomorrow, and, I will give it thee tomorrow: For the word I will, in the former manner of speech, signifies an act of the will Present; but in the later, it signifies a promise of an act of the will to Come: and therefore the former words, being of the Present, transfer a future right; the later, that be of the Future, transfer nothing. But if there be other signs of the Will to transfer a Right, besides Words; then, though the gift be Free, yet may the Right be understood to pass by words of the future: as if a man propound a Prize to him that comes first to the end of a race, The gift is Free; and though the words be of the Future, yet the Right passes: for if he would not have his words so be understood, he should not have let them run.

In Contracts, the right passes, not only where the words are of the time Present, or Past; but also where they are of the Future: because all Contract is mutual translation, or change of Right; and therefore he that promises only, because he has already received the benefit for which he promises, is to be understood as if he intended the Right should pass: for unless he had been content to have his words so understood, the other would not have performed his part first. And for that cause, in buying, and selling, and other acts of Contract, a Promise is equivalent to a Covenant; and therefore obligatory.

He that performs first in the case of a Contract, is said to MERIT that which he is to receive by the performance of the other; and he has it as Due. Also when a Prize is propounded to many, which is to be given to him only that wins; or money is thrown among many, to be enjoyed by them that catch it; though this be a Free gift; yet so to Win, or so to Catch, is to Merit, and to have it as DUE. For the Right is transferred in the Propounding of the Prize, and in throwing down the money; though it be not determined to whom, but by the Event of the contention. But there is between these two sorts of Merit, this difference, that In Contract, I Merit by virtue of my own power, and the Contractors need; but in this case of Free gift, I am enabled to Merit only by the benignity of the Giver: In Contract, I merit at the Contractors hand that he should depart with his right; In this case of Gift, I Merit not that the giver should part with his right; but that when he has parted with it, it should be mine, rather than another's. And this I think to be the meaning of that distinction of the Schools, between *Meritum congrui*, and *Meritum condigni*. For God Almighty, having promised Paradise to those men (hoodwinked with carnal desires,) that can walk through this world according to the Precepts, and Limits prescribed by him; they say, he that shall so walk, shall Merit Paradise *ex congruo*. But because no man can demand a right to it, by his own Righteousness, or any other power in himself, but by the Free Grace of God only; they say, no man can Merit Paradise *ex condigno*. This I say, I think is the meaning of that distinction; but because Disputers do not agree upon the signification of their own terms of Art, longer than it serves their turn; I will not affirm anything of their meaning: only this I say; when a gift is given indefinitely, as a prize to be contended for, he that wins Merits, and may claim the Prize as Due.

If a Covenant be made, wherein neither of the parties perform presently, but trust one another; in the condition of mere Nature, (which is a condition of War of every man against every man,) upon any reasonable suspicion, it is Void: But if there be a common Power set over them both, with right and force sufficient to compel performance; it is not Void. For he that performs first, has no assurance the other will perform after; because the bonds of words are too weak to bridle men's ambition, avarice, anger, and other Passions, without the fear of some coercive Power; which in the condition of mere Nature, where all men are equal, and judges of the justness of their own fears, cannot possibly be supposed. And therefore he which performs first, does but betray himself to his enemy; contrary to the Right (he can never abandon) of defending his life, and means of living.

But in a civil estate, where there is a Power set up to constrain those that would otherwise violate their faith, that fear is no more reasonable; and for that cause, he which by the Covenant is to perform first, is obliged so to do.

The cause of fear, which makes such a Covenant invalid, must be always something arising after the Covenant made; as some new fact, or other sign of the Will not to perform: else it cannot make the Covenant void. For that which could not hinder a man from promising, ought not to be admitted as a hindrance of performing.

He that transfers any Right, transfers the Means of enjoying it, as far as lies in his power. As he that sells Land, is understood to transfers the Herbage, and whatsoever grows upon it; Nor can he that sells a Mill turn away the Stream that drives it. And they that give to a man the Right of government in Sovereignty, are understood to give him the right of levying money to maintain Soldiers; and of appointing Magistrates for the administration of Justice.

To make Covenants with bruit Beasts, is impossible; because not understanding our speech, they understand not, nor accept of any translation of Right; nor can translate any Right to another: and without mutual acceptation, there is no Covenant.

To make Covenant with God, is impossible, but by Mediation of such as God speaks to, either by Revelation supernatural, or by his Lieutenants that govern under him, and in his Name: For otherwise we know not whether our Covenants be accepted, or not. And therefore they that Vow anything contrary to any law of Nature, Vow in vain; as being a thing unjust to pay such Vow. And if it be a thing commanded by the Law of Nature, it is not the Vow, but the Law that binds them.

The matter, or subject of a Covenant, is always something that falls under deliberation; (For to Covenant, is an act of the Will; that is to say an act, and the last act, of deliberation;) and is therefore always understood to be something to come; and which is judged Possible for him that Covenants, to perform.

And therefore, to promise that which is known to be Impossible, is no Covenant. But if that prove impossible afterwards, which before was thought possible, the Covenant is valid, and binds, (though not to the thing itself,) yet to the value; or, if that also be impossible, to the unfeigned endeavor of performing as much as is possible: for to more no man can be obliged.

Men are freed of their Covenants two ways; by Performing; or by being Forgiven. For Performance, is the natural end of obligation; and Forgiveness, the restitution of liberty; as being a re-transferring of that Right, in which the obligation consisted.

Covenants entered into by fear, in the condition of mere Nature, are obligatory. For example, if I Covenant to pay a ransom, or service for my life, to an enemy; I am bound by it. For it is a Contract, wherein one receives the benefit of life; the other is to receive money, or service for it; and consequently, where no other Law (as in the condition, of mere Nature) forbids the performance, the Covenant is valid. Therefore Prisoners of war, if trusted with the payment of their Ransom, are obliged to pay it: And if a weaker Prince, make a disadvantageous peace with a stronger, for fear; he is bound to keep it; unless (as has been said before) there arises some new, and just cause of fear, to renew the war. And even in Commonwealths, if I be forced to redeem myself from a Thief by promising him money, I am bound to pay it, till the Civil Law discharge me. For whatsoever I may lawfully do without Obligation, the same I may lawfully Covenant to do through fear: and what I lawfully Covenant, I cannot lawfully break.

A former Covenant, makes void a later. For a man that has passed away his Right to one man to day, has it not to pass tomorrow to another: and therefore the later promise passes no Right, but is null.

A Covenant not to defend myself from force, by force, is always void. For (as I have shewed before) no man can transfer, or lay down his Right to save himself from Death, Wounds, and Imprisonment, (the avoiding whereof is the only End of laying down any Right, and therefore the promise of not resisting force, in no Covenant transfers any right; nor is obliging. For though a man may Covenant thus, Unless I do so, or so, kill me; he cannot Covenant thus, Unless I do so, or so, I will not resist you, when you come to kill me. For man by nature chooses the lesser evil, which is danger of death in resisting; rather than the greater, which is certain and present death in not resisting. And this is granted to be true by all men, in that they lead Criminals to Execution, and Prison, with armed men, notwithstanding that such Criminals have consented to the Law, by which they are condemned.

A Covenant to accuse oneself, without assurance of pardon, is likewise invalid. For in the condition of Nature, where every man is Judge, there is no place for Accusation: and in the Civil State, the Accusation is followed with Punishment; which being Force, a man is not obliged not to resist. The same is also true, of the Accusation of those, by whose Condemnation a man falls into misery; as of a Father, Wife, or Benefactor. For the Testimony of such an Accuser, if it be not willingly given, is presumed to be corrupted by Nature; and therefore not to be received: and where a man's Testimony is not to be credited, he is not bound to give it. Also Accusations upon Torture, are not to be reputed as Testimonies. For Torture is to be used but as means of conjecture, and light, in the further examination, and search of truth: and what is in that case confessed, tends to the ease of him that is Tortured; not to the informing of the Torturers: and therefore ought not to have the credit of a sufficient Testimony: for whether he deliver himself by true, or false Accusation, he does it by the Right of preserving his own life.

The force of Words, being (as I have formerly noted) too weak to hold men to the performance of their Covenants; there are in man's nature, but two imaginable helps to strengthen it. And those are either a Fear of the consequence of breaking their word; or a Glory, or Pride in appearing not to need to break it. This later is a Generosity too rarely found to be presumed on, especially in the pursuers of Wealth, Command, or sensual Pleasure; which are the greatest part of Mankind. The Passion to be reckoned upon, is Fear; whereof there be two very general Objects: one, The Power of Spirits Invisible; the other, The Power of those men they shall therein Offend. Of these two, though the former be the greater Power, yet the fear of the later is commonly the greater Fear. The Fear of the former is in every man, his own Religion: which has place in the nature of man before Civil Society. The later has not so; at least not place enough, to keep men to their promises; because in the condition of mere Nature, the inequality of Power is not discerned, but by the event of Battle. So that before the time of Civil Society, or in the interruption thereof by War, there is nothing can strengthen a Covenant of Peace agreed on, against the temptations of Avarice, Ambition, Lust, or other strong desire, but the fear of that Invisible Power, which they every one Worship as God; and Fear as a Revenger of their perfidy. All therefore that can be done between two men not subject to Civil Power, is to put one another to swear by the God he fears: Which Swearing, or OATH, is a Form of Speech, added to a Promise; by which he that promises, signifies, that unless he perform, he renounces the mercy of his God, or calls to him for vengeance on himself. Such was the Heathen Form, Let Jupiter kill me else, as I kill this Beast. So is our Form, I shall do thus, and thus, so help me God. And this, with the Rites and Ceremonies, which every one uses in his own Religion, that the fear of breaking faith might be the greater.

By this it appears, that an Oath taken according to any other Form, or Rite, then his, that swears, is in vain; and no Oath: And that there is no Swearing by anything which the Swearer thinks not God. For though men have sometimes used to swear by their Kings, for fear, or flattery; yet they would have it thereby understood, they attributed to them Divine honor. And that Swearing unnecessarily by God, is but profaning of his name: and Swearing by other things, as men do in common discourse, is not Swearing, but an impious Custom, gotten by too much vehemence of talking.

It appears also, that the Oath adds nothing to the Obligation. For a Covenant, if lawful, binds in the sight of God, without the Oath, as much as with it: if unlawful, binds not at all; though it be confirmed with an Oath.

Chapter 15 Of other Lawes of Nature

Fom that law of Nature, by which we are obliged to transfer to another, such Rights, as being retained, hinder the peace of Mankind, there follows a Third; which is this, That men perform their Covenants made: without which, Covenants are in vain, and but Empty words; and the Right of all men to all things remaining, wee are still in the condition of War.

And in this law of Nature, consists the Fountain and Original of JUSTICE. For where no Covenant has preceded, there has no Right been transferred, and every man has right to every thing; and consequently, no action can be Unjust. But when a Covenant is made, then to break it is Unjust: And the definition of INJUSTICE, is no other than the not Performance of Covenant. And whatsoever is not Unjust, is Just.

But because Covenants of mutual trust, where there is a fear of not performance on either part, (as has been said in the former Chapter,) are invalid; though the Original of Justice be the making of Covenants; yet Injustice actually there can be none, till the cause of such fear be taken away; which while men are in the natural condition of War, cannot be done. Therefore before the names of Just, and Unjust can have place, there must be some coercive Power, to compel men equally to the performance of their Covenants, by the terror of some punishment, greater than the benefit they expect by the breach of their Covenant; and to make good that Propriety, which by mutual Contract men acquire, in recompense of the universal Right they abandon: and such power there is none before the erection of a Commonwealth. And this is also to be gathered out of the ordinary definition of Justice in the Schools: For they say, that Justice is the constant Will of giving to every man his own. And therefore where there is no Own, that is, no Propriety, there is no Injustice; and where there is no coercive Power erected, that is, where there is no Commonwealth, there is no Propriety; all men having Right to all things: Therefore where there is no Commonwealth, there nothing is Unjust. So that the nature of Justice, consists in keeping of valid Covenants: but the Validity of Covenants begins not but with the Constitution of a Civil Power, sufficient to compel men to keep them: And then it is also that Propriety begins.

The Fool has said in his heart, there is no such thing as Justice; and sometimes also with his tongue; seriously alleging, that every man's conservation, and contentment, being committed to his own care, there could be no reason, why every man might not do what he thought conduced thereunto: and therefore also to make, or not make; keep, or not keep Covenants, was not against Reason, when it conduced to ones benefit. He does not therein deny, that there be Covenants; and that they are sometimes broken, sometimes kept; and that such breach of them may be called Injustice, and the observance of them Justice: but he questions, whether Injustice, taking away the fear of God, (for the same Fool has said in his heart there is no God,) may not sometimes stand with that Reason, which dictates to every man his own good; and particularly then, when it conduces to such a benefit, as shall put a man in a condition, to neglect not only the dispraise, and revilings, but also the power of other men. The Kingdom of God is gotten by violence: but what if it could be gotten by unjust violence? were it against Reason so to get it, when it is impossible to receive hurt by it? and if it be not against Reason, it is not against Justice: or else Justice is not to be approved for good. From such reasoning as this, Successful wickedness has obtained the name of Virtue: and some that in all other things have disallowed the violation of Faith; yet have allowed it, when it is for the getting of a Kingdom. And the Heathen that believed, that Saturn was deposed by his son Jupiter, believed nevertheless the same Jupiter to be the avenger of Injustice: Somewhat like to a piece of Law in Coke's *Commentaries on Littleton*; where he says, If the right Heir of the Crown be attainted of Treason; yet the Crown shall descend to him, and *eo instante* the Attainder be void: From which instances a man will be very prone to infer; that when the Heir apparent of a Kingdom, shall kill him that is in possession, though his father; you may call it Injustice, or by what other name you will; yet it can never be against Reason, seeing all the voluntary actions of men tend to the benefit of themselves; and those actions are most Reasonable, that conduce most to their ends. This specious reasoning is nevertheless false.

For the question is not of promises mutual, where there is no security of performance on either side; as when there is no Civil Power erected over the parties promising; for such promises are no Covenants: But either where one of the parties has performed already; or where there is a Power to make him perform; there is the question whether it be against reason, that is, against the benefit of the other to perform, or not. And I say it is not against reason. For the manifestation whereof, we are to consider; First, that when a man doth a thing, which notwithstanding anything can be foreseen, and reckoned on, tends to his own destruction, howsoever some accident which he could not expect, arriving may turn it to his benefit; yet such events do not make it reasonably or wisely done. Secondly, that in a condition of War, wherein every man to every man, for want of a common Power to keep them all in awe, is an Enemy, there is no man can hope by his own strength, or wit, to defend himself from destruction, without the help of Confederates; where every one expects the same defense by the Confederation, that any one else does: and therefore he which declares he thinks it reason to deceive those that help him, can in reason expect no other means of safety, than what can be had from his own single Power. He therefore that breaks his Covenant, and consequently declares that he thinks he may with reason do so, cannot be received into any Society, that unite themselves for Peace and Defense, but by the error of them that receive him; nor when he is received, be retained in it, without seeing the danger of their error; which errors a man cannot reasonably reckon upon as the means of his security: and therefore if he be left, or cast out of Society, he perishs; and if he live in Society, it is by the errors of other men, which he could not foresee, nor reckon upon; and consequently against the reason of his preservation; and so, as all men that contribute not to his destruction, forbear him only out of ignorance of what is good for themselves.

As for the Instance of gaining the secure and perpetual felicity of Heaven, by any way; it is frivolous: there being but one way imaginable; and that is not breaking, but keeping of Covenant.

And for the other Instance of attaining Sovereignty by Rebellion; it is manifest, that though the event follow, yet because it cannot reasonably be expected, but rather the contrary; and because by gaining it so, others are taught to gain the same in like manner, the attempt thereof is against reason. Justice therefore, that is to say, Keeping of Covenant, is a Rule of Reason, by which we are forbidden to do anything destructive to our life; and consequently a Law of Nature.

There be some that proceed further; and will not have the Law of Nature, to be those Rules which conduce to the preservation of man's life on earth; but to the attaining of an eternal felicity after death; to which they think the breach of Covenant may conduce; and consequently be just and reasonable; (such are they that think it a work of merit to kill, or depose, or rebel against, the Sovereign Power constituted over them by their own consent.) But because there is no natural knowledge of man's estate after death; much less of the reward that is then to be given to breach of Faith; but only a belief grounded upon other men's saying, that they know it supernaturally, or that they know those, that knew them, that knew others, that knew it supernaturally; Breach of Faith cannot be called a Precept of Reason, or Nature.

Others, that allow for a Law of Nature, the keeping of Faith, do nevertheless make exception of certain persons; as Heretics, and such as use not to perform their Covenant to others: And this also is against reason. For if any fault of a man, be sufficient to discharge our Covenant made; the same ought in reason to have been sufficient to have hindered the making of it.

The names of Just, and Injust, when they are attributed to Men, signify one thing; and when they are attributed to Actions, another. When they are attributed to Men, they signify Conformity, or Inconformity of Manners, to Reason. But when they are attributed to Actions, they signify the Conformity, or Inconformity to Reason, not of Manners, or manner of life, but of particular Actions. A Just man therefore, is he that takes all the care he can, that his Actions may be all Just: and an Unjust man, is he that neglects it. And such men are more often in our Language styled by the names of Righteous, and Unrighteous; then Just, and Unjust; though the meaning be the same. Therefore a Righteous man, does not lose that Title, by one, or a few unjust Actions, that proceed from sudden Passion, or mistake of Things, or Persons: nor does an Unrighteous man, lose his character, for such Actions, as he does, or forbears to do, for fear: because his Will is not framed by the Justice, but by the apparent benefit of what he is to do. That which gives to humane Actions the relish of Justice, is a certain Nobleness or Gallantness of courage, (rarely found,) by which a man scorns to be beholding for the contentment of his life, to fraud, or breach of promise. This Justice of the Manners, is that which is meant, where Justice is called a Virtue; and Injustice a Vice.

But the Justice of Actions denominates men, not Just, but Guiltless: and the Injustice of the same, (which is also called Injury,) gives them but the name of Guilty.

Again, the Injustice of Manners, is the disposition, or aptitude to do Injury; and is Injustice before it proceed to Act; and without supposing any individual person injured. But the Injustice of an Action, (that is to say Injury,) supposes an individual person Injured; namely him, to whom the Covenant was made: And therefore many times the injury is received by one man, when the damage redounds to another. As when the Master commands his servant to give money to a stranger; if it be not done, the Injury is done to the Master, whom he had before Covenanted to obey; but the damage redounds to the stranger, to whom he had no Obligation; and therefore could not Injure him. And so also in Commonwealths, private men may remit to one another their debts; but not robberies or other violences, whereby they are damaged; because the detaining of Debt, is an Injury to themselves; but Robbery and Violence, are Injuries to the Person of the Commonwealth.

Whatsoever is done to a man, conformable to his own Will signified to the doer, is no Injury to him. For if he that does it, has not passed away his original right to do what he please, by some Antecedent Covenant, there is no breach of Covenant; and therefore no Injury done him. And if he have; then his Will to have it done being signified, is a release of that Covenant: and so again there is no Injury done him.

Justice of Actions, is by Writers divided into Commutative, and Distributive: and the former they say consists in proportion Arithmetical; the later in proportion Geometrical. Commutative therefore, they place in the equality of value of the things contracted for; And Distributive, in the distribution of equal benefit, to men of equal merit. As if it were Injustice to sell dearer than we buy; or to give more to a man than he merits. The value of all things contracted for, is measured by the Appetite of the Contractors: and therefore the just value, is that which they be contented to give. And Merit (besides that which is by Covenant, where the performance on one part, merits the performance of the other part, and falls under Justice Commutative, not Distributive,) is not due by Justice; but is rewarded of Grace only. And therefore this distinction, in the sense wherein it uses to be expounded, is not right. To speak properly, Commutative Justice, is the Justice of a Contractor; that is, a Performance of Covenant, in Buying, and Selling; Hiring, and Letting to Hire; Lending, and Borrowing; Exchanging, Bartering, and other acts of Contract.

And Distributive Justice, the Justice of an Arbitrator; that is to say, the act of defining what is Just. Wherein, (being trusted by them that make him Arbitrator,) if he perform his Trust, he is said to distribute to every man his own: and this is indeed Just Distribution, and may be called (though improperly) Distributive Justice; but more properly Equity; which also is a Law of Nature, as shall be shown in due place.

As Justice depends on Antecedent Covenant; so does GRATITUDE depend on Antecedent Grace; that is to say, Antecedent Free-gift: and is the fourth Law of Nature; which may be conceived in this Form, That a man which receives Benefit from another of mere Grace, Endeavor that he which gives it, have no reasonable cause to repent him of his good will. For no man gives, but with intention of Good to himself; because Gift is Voluntary; and of all Voluntary Acts, the Object is to every man his own Good; of which if men see they shall be frustrated, there will be no beginning of benevolence, or trust; nor consequently of mutual help; nor of reconciliation of one man to another; and therefore they are to remain still in the condition of War; which is contrary to the first and Fundamental Law of Nature, which commands men to Seek Peace. The breach of this Law, is called Ingratitude; and has the same relation to Grace, that Injustice has to Obligation by Covenant,

A fifth Law of Nature, is COMPLAISANCE; that is to say, That every man strive to accommodate himself to the rest. For the understanding whereof, we may consider, that there is in men's aptness to Society; a diversity of Nature, rising from their diversity of Affections; not unlike to that we see in stones brought together for building of an Edifice. For as that stone which by the asperity, and irregularity of Figure, takes more room from others, than itself fills; and for the hardness, cannot be easily made plain, and thereby hinders the building, is by the builders cast away as unprofitable, and troublesome: so also, a man that by asperity of Nature, will strive to retain those things which to himself are superfluous, and to others necessary; and for the stubbornness of his Passions, cannot be corrected, is to be left, or cast out of Society, as cumbersome thereunto. For seeing every man, not only by Right, but also by necessity of Nature, is supposed to endeavor all he can, to obtain that which is necessary for his conservation; He that shall oppose himself against it, for things superfluous, is guilty of the war that thereupon is to follow; and therefore doth that, which is contrary to the fundamental Law of Nature, which commands to seek Peace. The observers of this Law, may be called SOCIABLE, (the Latins call them *Commodi*? The contrary, Stubborn, Insociable, Froward, Intractable.

A sixth Law of Nature, is this, That upon caution of the Future time, a man ought to pardon the offences past of them that repenting, desire it. For PARDON, is nothing but granting of Peace; which though granted to them that persevere in their hostility, be not Peace, but Fear; yet not granted to them that give caution of the Future time, is sign of an aversion to Peace; and therefore contrary to the Law of Nature.

A seventh is, That in Revenges, (that is, retribution of Evil for Evil,) Men look not at the greatness of the evil past, but the greatness of the good to follow. Whereby we are forbidden to inflict punishment with any other design, than for correction of the offender, or direction of others. For this Law is consequent to the next before it, that commands Pardon, upon security of the Future time. Besides, Revenge without respect to the Example, and profit to come, is a triumph, or glorying in the hurt of another, tending to no end; (for the End is always somewhat to Come;) and glorying to no end, is vain-glory, and contrary to reason; and to hurt without reason, tends to the introduction of War; which is against the Law of Nature; and is commonly styled by the name of Cruelty.

And because all signs of hatred, or contempt, provoke to fight; insomuch as most men choose rather to hazard their life, than not to be revenged; we may in the eighth place, for a Law of Nature, set down this Precept, That no man by deed, word, countenance, or gesture, declare Hatred, or Contempt of another. The breach of which Law, is commonly called Contumely.

The question who is the better man, has no place in the condition of mere Nature; where, (as has been shown before,) all men are equal. The inequality that now is, has bin introduced by the Laws civil. I know that Aristotle in the first book of his *Politics*, for a foundation of his doctrine, makes men by Nature, some more worthy to Command, meaning the wiser sort (such as he thought himself to be for his Philosophy;) others to Serve, (meaning those that had strong bodies, but were not Philosophers as he;) as if Master and Servant were not introduced by consent of men, but by difference of Wit: which is not only against reason; but also against experience. For there are very few so foolish, that had not rather govern themselves, than be governed by others: Nor when the wise in their own conceit, contend by force, with them who distrust their own wisdom, do they always, or often, or almost at any time, get the Victory. If Nature therefore have made men equal, that equality is to be acknowledged: or if Nature have made men unequal; yet because men that think themselves equal, will not enter into conditions of Peace, but upon Equal terms, such equality must be admitted. And therefore for the ninth law of Nature, I put this, 'That every man acknowledge other for his Equal by Nature. The breach of this Precept is Pride.

On this law, depends another, That at the entrance into conditions of Peace, no man require to reserve to himself any Right, which he is not content should be reserved to every one of the rest. As it is necessary for all men that seek peace, to lay down certain Rights of Nature; that is to say, not to have liberty to do all they list: so is it necessary for man's life, to retain some; as right to govern their own bodies; enjoy air, water, motion, ways to go from place to place; and all things else without which a man cannot live, or not live well. If in this case, at the making of Peace, men require for themselves, that which they would not have to be granted to others, they do contrary to the precedent law, that commands the acknowledgment of natural equality, and therefore also against the law of Nature. The observers of this law, are those we call Modest, and the breakers Arrogant men. The Greeks call the violation of this law *pleonexia*; that is, a desire of more than their share.

Also if a man be trusted to judge between man and man, it is a precept of the Law of Nature, that he deal Equally between them. For without that, the Controversies of men cannot be determined but by War. He therefore that is partial in judgment, does what in him lies, to deter men from the use of Judges, and Arbitrators; and consequently, (against the fundamental Law of Nature) is the cause of War.

The observance of this law, from the equal distribution to each man, of that which in reason belongs to him, is called EQUITY, and (as I have said before) distributive Justice: the violation, Acception of persons, *prosopolepsia*.

And from this follows another law, That such things as cannot be divided, be enjoyed in Common, if it can be; and if the quantity of the thing permit, without Stint; otherwise Proportionably to the number of them that have Right. For otherwise the distribution is Unequal, and contrary to Equity.

But some things there be, that can neither be divided, nor enjoyed in common. Then, The Law of Nature, which prescribes Equity, requires, That the Entire Right; or else, (making the use alternate,) the First Possession, be determined by Lot. For equal distribution, is of the Law of Nature; and other means of equal distribution cannot be imagined.

Of Lots there be two sorts, Arbitrary, and Natural. Arbitrary, is that which is agreed on by the Competitors: Natural, is either Primogeniture, (which the Greek calls *kleronomia*, which signifies, Given by Lot; or First Seizure.

And therefore those things which cannot be enjoyed in common, nor divided, ought to be adjudged to the First Possessor; and in some cases to the First-Borne, as acquired by Lot.

It is also a Law of Nature, That all men that mediate Peace, be allowed safe Conduct. For the Law that commands Peace, as the End, commands Intercession, as the Means; and to Intercession the Means is safe Conduct.

And because, though men be never so willing to observe these Laws, there may nevertheless arise questions concerning a man's action; First, whether it were done, or not done; Secondly (if done) whether against the Law, or not against the Law; the former whereof, is called a question Of Fact; the later a question Of Right; therefore unless the parties to the question, Covenant mutually to stand to the sentence of another, they are as far from Peace as ever. This other, to whose Sentence they submit, is called an ARBITRATOR. And therefore it is of the Law of Nature, That they that are at controversy, submit their Right to the judgement of an Arbitrator.

And seeing every man is presumed to do all things in order to his own benefit, no man is a fit Arbitrator in his own cause: and if he were never so fit; yet Equity allowing to each party equal benefit, if one be admitted to be Judge, the other is to be admitted also; & so the controversy, that is, the cause of War, remains, against the Law of Nature.

For the same reason no man in any Cause ought to be received for Arbitrator, to whom greater profit, or honor, or pleasure apparently arises out of the victory of one party, than of the other: for he has taken (though an unavoidable bribe, yet) a bribe; and no man can be obliged to trust him. And thus also the controversy, and the condition of War remains, contrary to the Law of Nature.

And in a controversy of Fact, the Judge being to give no more credit to one, than to the other, (if there be no other Arguments) must give credit to a third; or to a third and fourth; or more: For else the question is undecided, and left to force, contrary to the Law of Nature.

These are the Laws of Nature, dictating Peace, for a means of the conservation of men in multitudes; and which only concern the doctrine of Civil Society. There be other things tending to the destruction of particular men; as Drunkenness, and all other parts of Intemperance; which may therefore also be reckoned among those things which the Law of Nature has forbidden; but are not necessary to be mentioned, nor are pertinent enough to this place.

And though this may seem too subtle a deduction of the Laws of Nature, to be taken notice of by all men; whereof the most part are too busy in getting food, and the rest too negligent to understand; yet to leave all men inexcusable, they have been contracted into one easy sum, intelligible, even to the meanest capacity; and that is, Do not that to another, which you would not have done to yourself; which shows him, that he has no more to do in learning the Laws of Nature, but, when weighing the actions of other men with his own, they seem too heavy, to put them into the other part of the balance, and his own into their place, that his own passions, and self-love, may add nothing to the weight; and then there is none of these Laws of Nature that will not appear unto him very reasonable.

The Laws of Nature oblige *in foro interno*; that is to say, they bind to a desire they should take place: but *in foro externo*; that is, to the putting them in act, not always. For he that should be modest, and tractable, and perform all he promises, in such time, and place, where no man else should do so, should but make himself a prey to others, and procure his own certain ruin, contrary to the ground of all Laws of Nature, which tend to Natures preservation. And again, he that having sufficient Security, that others shall observe the same Laws towards him, observes them not himself, seeks not Peace, but War; & consequently the destruction of his Nature by Violence.

And whatsoever Laws bind *in foro interno*, may be broken, not only by a fact contrary to the Law, but also by a fact according to it, in case a man think it contrary. For though his Action in this case, be according to the Law; yet his Purpose was against the Law; which where the Obligation is *in foro interno*, is a breach.

The Laws of Nature are Immutable and Eternal; For Injustice, Ingratitude, Arrogance, Pride, Iniquity, Acception of persons, and the rest, can never be made lawful. For it can never be that War shall preserve life, and Peace destroy it.

The sames Laws, because they oblige only to a desire, and endeavor, I mean an unfeigned and constant endeavor, are easy to be observed. For in that they require nothing but endeavor; he that endeavors their performance, fulfills them; and he that fulfills the Law, is Just.

And the Science of them, is the true and only Moral Philosophy. For Moral Philosophy is nothing else but the Science of what is Good, and Evil, in the conversation, and Society of mankind. Good, and Evil, are names that signify our Appetites, and Aversions; which in different tempers, customs, and doctrines of men, are different: And divers men, differ not only in their Judgement, on the senses of what is pleasant, and unpleasant to the taste, smell, hearing, touch, and sight; but also of what is conformable, or disagreeable to Reason, in the actions of common life. Nay, the same man, in divers times, differs from himself; and one time praises, that is, calls Good, what another time he dispraises, and calls Evil: From whence arise Disputes, Controversies, and at last War. And therefore so long a man is in the condition of mere Nature, (which is a condition of War,) as private Appetite is the measure of Good, and Evil: And consequently all men agree on this, that Peace is Good, and therefore also the way, or means of Peace, which (as I have shewed before) are Justice, Gratitude, Modesty, Equity, Mercy, & the rest of the Laws of Nature, are good; that is to say, Moral Virtues; and their contrary Vices, Evil. Now the science of Virtue and Vice, is Moral Philosophy; and therefore the true Doctrine of the Laws of Nature, is the true Moral Philosophy. But the Writers of Moral Philosophy, though they acknowledge the same Virtues and Vices; Yet not seeing wherein consisted their Goodness; nor that they come to be praised, as the means of peaceable, sociable, and comfortable living; place them in a mediocrity of passions: as if not the Cause, but the Degree of daring, made Fortitude; or not the Cause, but the Quantity of a gift, made Liberality.

These dictates of Reason, men use to call by the name of Laws, but improperly: for they are but Conclusions, or Theorems concerning what conduces to the conservation and defense of themselves; whereas Law, properly is the word of him, that by right has command over others. But yet if we consider the same Theorems, as delivered in the word of God, that by right commands all things; then are they properly called Laws.

Chapter 16 Of PERSONS, AUTHORS, and things Personated

A PERSON, is he, whose words or actions are considered, either as his own, or as representing the words or actions of another man, or of any other thing to whom they are attributed, whether Truly or by Fiction.

When they are considered as his own, then is he called a Natural Person: And when they are considered as representing the words and actions of another, then is he a Feigned or Artificial person.

The word Person is Latin: instead whereof the Greeks have *prosopon*, which signifies the Face, as *Persona* in Latin signifies the disguise, or outward appearance of a man, counterfeited on the Stage; and sometimes more particularly that part of it, which disguises the face, as a Mask or Vizard: And from the Stage, has been translated to any Representer of speech and action, as well in Tribunals, as Theaters. So that a Person, is the same that an Actor is, both on the Stage and in common Conversation; and to Personate, is to Act, or Represent himself, or another; and he that acts another, is said to bear his Person, or act in his name; (in which sense Cicero uses it where he says, *Unus sustineo tres Personas; Mei, Adversarii, & Judicis*, I bear three Persons; my own, my Adversaries, and the Judges;) and is called in diverse occasions, diversely; as a Representer, or Representative, a Lieutenant, a Vicar, an Attorney, a Deputy, a Procurator, an Actor, and the like.

Of Persons Artificial, some have their words and actions Owned by those whom they represent. And then the Person is the Actor; and he that owns his words and actions, is the AUTHOR: In which case the Actor acts by Authority. For that which in speaking of goods and possessions, is called an Owner, and in Latin *Dominus*, in Greek *kurios*; speaking of Actions, is called Author. And as the Right of possession, is called Dominion; so the Right of doing any Action, is called AUTHORITY. So that by Authority, is always understood a Right of doing any act: and done by Authority, done by Commission, or Licence from him whose right it is.

From hence it follows, that when the Actor makes a Covenant by Authority, he binds thereby the Author, no less than if he had made it himself; and no less subjects him to all the consequences of the same. And therefore all that has been said formerly, (Chap. 14.) of the nature of Covenants between man and man in their natural capacity, is true also when they are made by their Actors, Representers, or Procurators, that have authority from them, so far-forth as is in their Commission, but no farther.

And therefore he that makes a Covenant with the Actor, or Representer, not knowing the Authority he has, doth it at his own peril. For no man is obliged by a Covenant, whereof he is not Author; nor consequently by a Covenant made against, or beside the Authority he gave.

When the Actor doth anything against the Law of Nature by command of the Author, if he be obliged by former Covenant to obey him, not he, but the Author breaks the Law of Nature: for though the Action be against the Law of Nature; yet it is not his: but contrarily, to refuse to do it, is against the Law of Nature, that forbids breach of Covenant.

And he that makes a Covenant with the Author, by mediation of the Actor, not knowing what Authority he has, but only takes his word; in case such Authority be not made manifest unto him upon demand, is no longer obliged: For the Covenant made with the Author, is not valid, without his Counter-assurance. But if he that so Covenants, knew before hand he was to expect no other assurance, than the Actors word; then is the Covenant valid; because the Actor in this case makes himself the Author. And therefore, as when the Authority is evident, the Covenant obliges the Author, not the Actor; so when the Authority is feigned, it obliges the Actor only; there being no Author but himself.

There are few things, that are incapable of being represented by Fiction. Inanimate things, as a Church, an Hospital, a Bridge, may be Personated by a Rector, Master, or Overseer. But things Inanimate, cannot be Authors, nor therefore give Authority to their Actors: Yet the Actors may have Authority to procure their maintenance, given them by those that are Owners, or Governors of those things. And therefore, such things cannot be Personated, before there be some state of Civil Government.

Likewise Children, Fools, and Mad-men that have no use of Reason, may be Personated by Guardians, or Curators; but can be no Authors (during that time) of any action done by them, longer then (when they shall recover the use of Reason) they shall judge the same reasonable. Yet during the Folly, he that has right of governing them, may give Authority to the Guardian. But this again has no place but in a State Civill, because before such estate, there is no Dominion of Persons.

An Idol, or mere Figment of the brain, may be Personated; as were the Gods of the Heathen; which by such Officers as the State appointed, were Personated, and held Possessions, and other Goods, and Rights, which men from time to time dedicated, and consecrated unto them. But Idols cannot be Authors: for an Idol is nothing. The Authority proceeded from the State: and therefore before introduction of Civil Government, the Gods of the Heathen could not be Personated.

The true God may be Personated. As he was; first, by Moses; who governed the Israelites, (that were not his, but God's people,) not in his own name, with *Hoc dicit Moses*; but in God's Name, with *Hoc dicit Dominus*. Secondly by the Son of man, his own Son, our Blessed Savior Jesus Christ, that came to reduce the Jews, and induce all Nations into the Kingdom of his Father; not as of himself, but as sent from his Father. And thirdly, by the Holy Ghost, or Comforter, speaking, and working in the Apostles: which Holy Ghost, was a Comforter that came not of himself; but was sent, and proceeded from them both.

A Multitude of men, are made One Person, when they are by one man, or one Person, Represented; so that it be done with the consent of every one of that Multitude in particular. For it is the Unity of the Representer, not the Unity of the Represented, that makes the Person One. And it is the Representer that bears the Person, and but one Person: And Unity, cannot otherwise be understood in Multitude.

And because the Multitude naturally is not One, but Many; they cannot be understood for one; but many Authors, of every thing their Representative saith, or doth in their name; Every man giving their common Representer, Authority from himself in particular; and owning all the actions the Representer doth, in case they give him Authority without stint: Otherwise, when they limit him in what, and how far he shall represent them, none of them owns more, than they gave him commission to Act.

And if the Representative consist of many men, the voice of the greater number, must be considered as the voice of them all. For if the lesser number pronounce (for example) in the Affirmative, and the greater in the Negative, there will be Negatives more than enough to destroy the Affirmatives; and thereby the excess of Negatives, standing un-contradicted, are the only voice the Representative has.

And a Representative of even number, especially when the number is not great, whereby the contradictory voices are oftentimes equal, is therefore oftentimes mute, and incapable of Action. Yet in some cases contradictory voices equal in number, may determine a question; as in condemning, or absolving, equality of votes, even in that they condemn not, do absolve; but not on the contrary condemn, in that they absolve not. For when a Cause is heard; not to condemn, is to absolve: but on the contrary, to say that not absolving, is condemning, is not true. The like it is in a deliberation of executing presently, or deferring till another time: For when the voices are equal, the not decreeing Execution, is a decree of Dilation.

Or if the number be odd, as three, or more, (men, or assemblies;) whereof every one has by a Negative Voice, authority to take away the effect of all the Affirmative Voices of the rest, This number is no Representative; because by the diversity of Opinions, and Interests of men, it becomes oftentimes, and in cases of the greatest consequence, a mute Person, and inapt, as for many things else, so for the government of a Multitude, especially in time of War.

Of Authors there be two sorts. The first simply so called; which I have before defined to be him, that owns the Action of another simply. The second is he, that owns an Action, or Covenant of another conditionally; that is to say, he undertakes to do it, if the other doth it not, at, or before a certain time. And these Authors conditional, are generally called SURETIES, in Latin *Fidejussores*, and *Sponsores*; and particularly for Debt, *Praedes*; and for Appearance before a Judge, or Magistrate, *Vades*.

Chapter 17 Of the Causes, Generation, and Definition of a COMMONWEALTH

The final Cause, End, or Design of men, (who naturally love Liberty, and Dominion over others,) in the introduction of that restraint upon themselves, (in which wee see them live in Commonwealths,) is the foresight of their own preservation, and of a more contented life thereby; that is to say, of getting themselves out from that miserable condition of War, which is necessarily consequent (as has been shown) to the natural Passions of men, when there is no visible Power to keep them in awe, and tie them by fear of punishment to the performance of their Covenants, and observation of those Laws of Nature set down in the fourteenth and fifteenth Chapters.

For the Laws of Nature (as Justice, Equity, Modesty, Mercy, and (in sum) doing to others, as wee would be done to,) of themselves, without the terror of some Power, to cause them to be observed, are contrary to our natural Passions, that carry us to Partiality, Pride, Revenge, and the like. And Covenants, without the Sword, are but Words, and of no strength to secure a man at all. Therefore notwithstanding the Laws of Nature, (which every one has then kept, when he has the will to keep them, when he can do it safely,) if there be no Power erected, or not great enough for our security; every man will, and may lawfully rely on his own strength and art, for caution against all other men. And in all places, where men have lived by small Families, to rob and spoil one another, has been a Trade, and so far from being reputed against the Law of Nature, that the greater spoils they gained, the greater was their honor; and men observed no other Laws therein, but the Laws of Honor; that is, to abstain from cruelty, leaving to men their lives, and instruments of husbandry. And as small Families did then; so now do Cities and Kingdoms which are but greater Families (for their own security) enlarge their Dominions, upon all pretenses of danger, and fear of Invasion, or assistance that may be given to Invaders, endeavor as much as they can, to subdue, or weaken their neighbors, by open force, and secret arts, for want of other Caution, justly; and are remembered for it in after ages with honor.

Nor is it the joining together of a small number of men, that gives them this security; because in small numbers, small additions on the one side or the other, make the advantage of strength so great, as is sufficient to carry the Victory; and therefore gives encouragement to an Invasion. The Multitude sufficient to confide in for our Security, is not determined by any certain number, but by comparison with the Enemy we fear; and is then sufficient, when the odds of the Enemy is not of so visible and conspicuous moment, to determine the event of war, as to move him to attempt.

And be there never so great a Multitude; yet if their actions be directed according to their particular judgments, and particular appetites, they can expect thereby no defense, nor protection, neither against a Common enemy, nor against the injuries of one another. For being distracted in opinions concerning the best use and application of their strength, they do not help, but hinder one another; and reduce their strength by mutual opposition to nothing: whereby they are easily, not only subdued by a very few that agree together; but also when there is no common enemy, they make war upon each other, for their particular interests. For if we could suppose a great Multitude of men to consent in the observation of Justice, and other Laws of Nature, without a common Power to keep them all in awe; we might as well suppose all Mankind to do the same; and then there neither would be, nor need to be any Civil Government, or Commonwealth at all; because there would be Peace without subjection.

Nor is it enough for the security, which men desire should last all the time of their life, that they be governed, and directed by one judgement, for a limited time; as in one Battle, or one War. For though they obtain a Victory by their unanimous endeavor against a foreign enemy; yet afterwards, when either they have no common enemy, or he that by one part is held for an enemy, is by another part held for a friend, they must needs by the difference of their interests dissolve, and fall again into a War among themselves.

It is true, that certain living creatures, as Bees, and Ants, live sociably one with another, (which are therefore by Aristotle numbered among Political creatures;) and yet have no other direction, than their particular judgments and appetites; nor speech, whereby one of them can signify to another, what he thinks expedient for the common benefit: and therefore some man may perhaps desire to know, why Mankind cannot do the same. To which I answer,

First, that men are continually in competition for Honor and Dignity, which these creatures are not; and consequently among men there arises on that ground, Envy and Hatred, and finally War; but among these not so.

Secondly, that among these creatures, the Common good differs not from the Private; and being by nature inclined to their private, they procure thereby the common benefit. But man, whose Joy consists in comparing himself with other men, can relish nothing but what is eminent.

Thirdly, that these creatures, having not (as man) the use of reason, do not see, nor think they see any fault, in the administration of their common business: whereas among men, there are very many, that think themselves wiser, and abler to govern the Public, better than the rest; and these strive to reform and innovate, one this way, another that way; and thereby bring it into Distraction and Civil war.

Fourthly, that these creatures, though they have some use of voice, in making known to one another their desires, and other affections; yet they want that art of words, by which some men can represent to others, that which is Good, in the likeness of Evil; and Evil, in the likeness of Good; and augment, or diminish the apparent greatness of Good and Evil; discontenting men, and troubling their Peace at their pleasure.

Fifthly, irrational creatures cannot distinguish between Injury, and Damage; and therefore as long as they be at ease, they are not offended with their fellows: whereas Man is then most troublesome, when he is most at ease: for then it is that he loves to shew his Wisdom, and control the Actions of them that govern the Commonwealth.

Lastly, the agreement of these creatures is Natural; that of men, is by Covenant only, which is Artificial: and therefore it is no wonder if there be somewhat else required (besides Covenant) to make their Agreement constant and lasting; which is a Common Power, to keep them in awe, and to direct their actions to the Common Benefit.

The only way to erect such a Common Power, as may be able to defend them from the invasion of Foreigners, and the injuries of one another, and thereby to secure them in such sort, as that by their own industry, and by the fruit of the Earth, they may nourish themselves and live contentedly; is, to confer all their power and strength upon one Man, or upon one Assembly of men, that may reduce all their Wills, by plurality of voices, unto one Will: which is as much as to say, to appoint one Man, or Assembly of men, to bear their Person; and every one to own, and acknowledge himself to be Author of whatsoever he that so bears their Person, shall Act, or cause to be Acted, in those things which concern the Common Peace and Safety; and therein to submit their Wills, every one to his Will, and their Judgments, to his Judgment. This is more than Consent, or Concord; it is a real Unity of them all, in one and the same Person, made by Covenant of every man with every man, in such manner, as if every man should say to every man, I Authorize and give up my Right of Governing myself, to this Man, or to this Assembly of men, on this condition, that thou give up thy Right to him, and Authorize all his Actions in like manner. This done, the Multitude so united in one Person, is called a COMMONWEALTH, in Latin CIVITAS. This is the Generation of that great LEVIATHAN, or rather (to speak more reverently) of that Mortal God, to which wee owe under the Immortal God, our peace and defense. For by this Authority, given him by every particular man in the Commonwealth, he has the use of so much Power and Strength conferred on him, that by terror thereof, he is enabled to perform the wills of them all, to Peace at home, and mutual aid against their enemies abroad. And in him consists the Essence of the Commonwealth; which (to define it,) is One Person, of whose Acts a great Multitude, by mutual Covenants one with another, have made themselves every one the Author, to the end he may use the strength and means of them all, as he shall think expedient, for their Peace and Common Defense.

And he that carries this Person, is called SOVEREIGN, and said to have Sovereign Power; and every one besides, his SUBJECT.

The attaining to this Sovereign Power, is by two ways. One, by Natural force; as when a man makes his children, to submit themselves, and their children to his government, as being able to destroy them if they refuse; or by War subdues his enemies to his will, giving them their lives on that condition. The other, is when men agree among themselves, to submit to some Man, or Assembly of men, voluntarily, on confidence to be protected by him against all others. This later, may be called a Political Commonwealth, or Commonwealth by Institution; and the former, a Commonwealth by Acquisition. And first, I shall speak of a Commonwealth by Institution.

4. Margaret Cavendish (1623-1673)

Philosophical Letters: Or, Modest Reflections Upon Some Opinions in Natural Philosophy, Maintained By Several Famous and Learned Authors of this Age, Expressed by way of Letters (1664)

Excerpt includes Letters I-XXIX from Section I. The basis for this text was the CC0 1.0 Public Domain available on the EEBO-TCP website hosted at https://quod.lib.umich.edu/e/eebogroup/ Light changes to modernize spellings and paragraph breaks have been made throughout by Marcus Adams. The goal has been to preserve the structure of phrasings, with minor spelling changes to make the text more accessible for students. Capitalization from the 1664 edition has been retained.

- A Preface to the Reader
- Letter I
- Letter II
- Letter III
- Letter IV
- Letter V
- Letter VI
- Letter VII
- Letter VIII
- Letter IX
- Letter X
- Letter XI
- Letter XII
- Letter XIII
- Letter XIV
- Letter XV
- Letter XVI
- Letter XVII
- Letter XVIII
- Letter XIX
- Letter XX
- Letter XXI
- Letter XXII
- Letter XXIII
- Letter XXIV
- Letter XXV
- Letter XXVI

A Preface to the Reader

Worthy Readers,

I did not write this Book out of delight, love or humor to contradiction; for I would rather praise, than contradict any Person or Persons that are ingenious; but by reason Opinion is free, and may pass without a pass-port, I took the liberty to declare my own opinions as other Philosophers do, and to that purpose I have here set down several famous and learned Author's opinions, and my answers to them in the form of Letters, which was the easiest way for me to write; and by so doing, I have done that, which I would have bone unto me; for I am as willing to have my opinions contradicted, as I do contradict others: for I love Reason so well, that whosoever can bring most rational and probable arguments, shall have my vote, although against my own opinion. But you may say, If contradictions were frequent, there would be no agreement among Mankind. I answer; It is very true: Wherefore Contradictions are better in general Books, than in particular Families, and in Schools better than in Public States, and better in Philosophy than in Divinity. All which considered, I shun, as much as I can, not to discourse or write of either Church or State. But I desire so much favor, or rather Justice of you, Worthy Readers, as not to interpret my objections or answers any other ways than against several opinions in Philosophy; for I am confident there is not any body, that does esteem, respect and honor learned and ingenious Persons more than I do: Wherefore judge me neither to be of a contradicting humor, nor of a vain-glorious mind for dissenting from other men's opinions, but rather that it is done out of love to Truth, and to make my own opinions the more intelligible, which cannot better be done than by arguing and comparing other men's opinions with them.

The Authors whose opinions I mention, I have read, as I found them printed, in my native Language, except Descartes, who being in Latin, I had some few places translated to me out of his works; and I must confess, that since I have read the works of these learned men, I understand the names and terms of Art a little better than I did before; but it is not so much as to make me a Scholar, nor yet so little, but that, had I read more before I did begin to write my other Book called *Philosophical Opinions*, they would have been more intelligible; for my error was, I began to write so early, that I had not lived so long as to be able to read many Authors; I cannot say, I divulged my opinions as soon as I had conceived them, but yet I divulged them too soon to have them artificial and methodical, But since what is past, cannot be recalled, I must desire you to excuse those faults, which were committed for want of experience and learning. As for School-learning, had I applied myself to it, yet I am confident I should never have arrived to any; for I am so incapable of Learning, that I could never attain to the knowledge of any other Language but my native, especially by the Rules of Art: wherefore I do not repent that I spent not my time in Learning, for I consider, it is better to write wittily than learnedly; nevertheless, I love and esteem Learning, although I am not capable of it. But you may say, I have expressed neither Wit nor Learning in my Writings: Truly, if not, I am the more sorry for it; but self-conceit, which is natural to mankind, especially to our Sex, did flatter and secretly persuade me that my Writings had Sense and Reason, Wit and Variety; but Judgment being not called to Counsel, I yielded to Self-conceits flattery, and so put out my Writings to be Printed as fast as I could, without being reviewed or corrected: Neither did I fear any censure, for Self-conceit had persuaded me, I should be highly applauded; wherefore I made such haste, that I had three or four Books printed presently after each other.

But to return to this present Work, I must desire you, worthy Readers, to read first my Book called *Philosophical and Physical Opinions*, before you censure this, for this Book is but an explanation of the former, wherein is contained the Ground of my *Opinions*, and those that will judge well of a Building, must first consider the Foundation; to which purpose I will repeat some few Heads and Principles of my *Opinions*, which are these following: First, That Nature is Infinite, and the Eternal Servant of God: Next, That she is Corporeal, and partly self-moving, dividable and composable; that all and every particular Creature, as also all perception and variety in Nature, is made by corporeal self-motion, which I name sensitive and rational matter, which is life and knowledge, sense and reason.

Again, That these sensitive and rational parts of matter are the purest and subtlest parts of Nature, as the active parts, the knowing, understanding and prudent parts, the designing, architectonical and working parts, nay, the Life and Soul of Nature, and that there is not any Creature or part of nature without this Life and Soul; and that not only Animals, but also Vegetables, Minerals and Elements, and what more is in Nature, are endued with this Life and Soul, Sense and Reason: and because this Life and Soul is a corporeal Substance, it is both dividable and composable; for it divides and removes parts from parts, as also composes and joins parts to parts, and works in a perpetual motion without rest; by which actions not any Creature can challenge a particular Life and Soul to itself, but every Creature may have by the dividing and composing nature of this self-moving matter more or fewer natural souls and lives.

These and the like actions of corporeal Nature or natural Matter you may find more at large described in my aforementioned Book of *Philosophical Opinions*, and more clearly repeated and explained in this present.

'Tis true, the way of arguing I use, is common, but the Principles, Heads and Grounds of my Opinions are my own, not borrowed or stolen in the least from any; and the first time I divulged them, was in the year 1653, since which time I have reviewed, reformed and reprinted them twice; for at first, as my Conceptions were new and my own, so my Judgment was young, and my Experience little, so that I had not so much knowledge as to declare them artificially and methodically; for as I mentioned before, I was always inapt to learn by the Rules of Art. But although they may be defective for want of Terms of Art, and artificial expressions, yet I am sure they are not defective for want of Sense and Reason: And if any one can bring more Sense and Reason to disprove these my opinions, I shall not repine or grieve, but either acknowledge my error, if I find myself in any, or defend them as rationally as I can, if it be but done justly and honestly, without deceit, spite, or malice; for I cannot choose but acquaint you, Noble Readers, I have been informed, that if I should be answered in my Writings, it would be done rather under the name and cover of a Woman, than of a Man, the reason is, because no man dare or will set his name to the contradiction of a Lady; and to confirm you the better herein, there has one Chapter of my Book called *The Worlds Olio*, treating of a Monastical Life, been answer'd already in a little Pamphlet, under the name of a woman, although she did little towards it; wherefore it being a Hermaphroditical Book, I judged it not worthy taking notice of. The like shall I do to any other that will answer this present work of mine, or contradict my opinions indirectly with fraud and deceit.

But I cannot conceive why it should be a disgrace to any man to maintain his own or other's opinions against a woman, so it be done with respect and civility; but to become a cheat by dissembling, and quit the Breeches for a Petticoat, merely out of spite and malice, is base, and not fit for the honor of a man, or the masculine sex. Besides, it will easily be known; for a Philosopher or Philosopheress is not produced on a sudden.

Wherefore, although I do not care, nor fear contradiction, yet I desire it may be done without fraud or deceit, spite and malice; and then I shall be ready to defend my opinions the best I can, while I live, and after

I am dead, I hope those that are just and honorable will also defend me from all sophistry, malice, spite and envy, for which Heaven will bless them. In the mean time, Worthy Readers, I should rejoice to see that my Works are acceptable to you, for if you be not partial, you will easily pardon those faults you find, when you do consider both my sex and breeding; for which favor and justice, I shall always remain,

Your most obliged Servant,

M. N.

Letter I

MADAM,

You have been pleased to send me the Works of four Famous and Learned Authors, to wit, of two most Famous Philosophers of our Age, Descartes, and Hobbes, and of that Learned Philosopher and Divine Dr. More, as also of that Famous Physician and Chymist Van Helmont. Which Works you have sent me not only to peruse, but also to give my judgment of them, and to send you word by the usual way of our Correspondence, which is by Letters, how far, and wherein I do dissent from these Famous Authors, their Opinions in Natural Philosophy. To tell you truly, Madam, your Commands did at first much affright me, for it did appear, as if you had commanded me to get upon a high Rock, and fling myself into the Sea, where neither a Ship, nor a Plank, nor any kind of help was near to rescue me, and save my life; but that I was forced to sink, by reason I cannot swim: So I having no Learning nor Art to assist me in this dangerous undertaking, thought, I must of necessity perish under the rough censures of my Readers, and be not only accounted a fool for my labor, but a vain and presumptuous person, to undertake things surpassing the ability of my performance; but on the other side I considered first, that those Worthy Authors, were they my censurers, would not deny me the same liberty they take themselves; which is, that I may dissent from their Opinions, as well as they dissent from others, and from among themselves: And if I should express more Vanity than Wit, more Ignorance than Knowledge, more Folly than Discretion, it being according to the Nature of our Sex, I hoped that my Masculine Readers would civilly excuse me, and my Female Readers could not justly condemn me.

Next I considered with myself, that it would be a great advantage for my Book called *Philosophical Opinions*, as to make it more perspicuous and intelligible by the opposition of other Opinions, since two opposite things placed near each other, are the better discerned; for I must confess, that when I did put forth my Philosophical Work at first, I was not so well skilled in the Terms or Expressions usual in Natural Philosophy; and therefore for want of their knowledge, I could not declare my meaning so plainly and clearly as I ought to have done, which may be a sufficient argument to my Readers, that I have not read heretofore any Natural Philosophers, and taken some Light from them; but that my Opinions did merely issue from the Fountain of my own Brain, without any other help or assistance.

Wherefore since for want of proper Expressions, my named Book of Philosophy was accused of obscurity and intricacy, I thought your Commands would be a means to explain and clear it the better, although not by an Artificial way, as by Logical Arguments or Mathematical Demonstrations, yet by expressing my Sense and Meaning more properly and clearly than I have done heretofore: But the chief reason of all was, the Authority of your Command, which did work so powerfully with me, that I could not resist, although it were to the disgrace of my own judgment and wit; and therefore I am fully resolved now to go on as far, and as well as the Natural strength of my Reason will reach: but since neither the strength of my Body, nor of my understanding, or wit, is able to mark every line, or every word of their works, and to argue upon them, I shall only pick out the ground Opinions of the aforementioned Authors, and those which do directly dissent from mine, upon which I intend to make some few Reflections, according to the ability of my Reason; and I shall merely go upon the bare Ground of Natural Philosophy, and not mix Divinity with it, as many Philosophers use to do, except it be in those places, where I am forced by the Authors' Arguments to reflect upon it, which yet shall be rather with an expression of my ignorance, than a positive declaration of my opinion or judgment thereof; for I think it not only an absurdity, but an injury to the holy Profession of Divinity to draw her to the Proofs in Natural Philosophy; wherefore I shall strictly follow the Guidance of Natural Reason, and keep to my own ground and Principles as much as I can; which that I may perform the better, I humbly desire the help and assistance of your Favor, that according to that real and entire Affection you bear to me, you would be pleased to tell me unfeignedly, if I should chance to err or contradict but the least probability of truth in any thing; for I honor Truth so much, as I bow down to its shadow with the greatest respect and reverence; and I esteem those persons most, that love and honor Truth with the same zeal and fervor, whether they be Ancient or Modern Writers.

Thus, Madam, although I am destitute of the help of Arts, yet being supported by your Favor and wise Directions, I shall not fear any smiles of scorn, or words of reproach; for I am confident you will defend me against all the mischievous and poisonous Teeth of malicious detractors. I shall besides, implore the assistance of the Sacred Church, and the Learned Schools, to take me into their Protection, and shelter my weak endeavors: For though I am but an ignorant and simple Woman, yet I am their devoted and honest Servant, who shall never quit the respect and honor due to them, but live and die theirs, as also,

MADAM,

Your Ladyship's humble and faithful Servant.

Letter II

MADAM,

Before I begin my Reflections upon the Opinions of those Authors you sent me, I will answer first your Objection concerning the Ground of my Philosophy, which is Infinite Matter: For you were pleased to mention, That you could not well apprehend, how it was possible, that many Infinites could be contained in one Infinite, since one Infinite takes up all Place Imaginary, leaving no room for any other; Also, if one Infinite should be contained in another Infinite, that which contains, must of necessity be bigger than that which is contained, whereby the Nature of Infinite would be lost; as having no bigger nor less, but being of an Infinite quantity.

First of all, Madam, there is no such thing as All in Infinite, nor any such thing as All the Place, for Infinite is not circumscribed nor limited: Next, as for that one Infinite cannot be in another Infinite, I answer, as well as one Finite can be in another Finite; for one Creature is not only composed of Parts, but one Part lies within another, and one Figure within another, and one Motion within another. As for example, Animal Kind, have they not Internal and External Parts, and so Internal and External Motions? And are not Animals, Vegetables and Minerals enclosed in the Elements?

But as for Infinites, you must know, Madam, that there are several kinds of Infinites. For there is first Infinite in quantity or bulk, that is such a big and great Corporeal substance, which exceeds all bounds and limits of measure, and may be called Infinite in Magnitude. Next there is Infinite in Number, which exceeds all numeration and account, and may be termed Infinite in Multitude; Again there is Infinite in Quality; as for example, Infinite degrees of softness, hardness, thickness, thinness, heat and cold, &c. also Infinite degrees of Motion, and so Infinite Creations, Infinite Compositions, Dissolutions, Contractions, Dilations, Digestions, Expulsions; also Infinite degrees of Strength, Knowledge, Power, &c. Besides there is Infinite in Time, which is properly named Eternal.

Now, when I say, that there is but one Infinite, and that Infinite is the Only Matter, I mean infinite in bulk and quantity. And this Onely matter, because it is Infinite in bulk, must of necessity be divisible into infinite Parts, that is, infinite in number, not in bulk or quantity; for though Infinite Parts in number make up one infinite in quantity, yet they considered in themselves, cannot be said Infinite, because every Part is of a certain limited and circumscribed Figure, Quantity and Proportion, whereas Infinite has no limits nor bounds: besides it is against the nature of a single Part to be Infinite, or else there would be no difference between the Part and the whole, the nature of a Part requiring that it must be less than its whole, but all what is less has a determined quantity, and so becomes finite. Therefore it is no absurdity to say, that an Infinite may have both Finite and Infinite Parts, Finite in Quantity, Infinite in Number.

But those that say, if there were an Infinite Body, that each of its Parts must of necessity be Infinite too, are much mistaken; for it is a contradiction in the same Terms to say One Infinite Part, for the very Name of a Part includes a Finiteness, but take all parts of an Infinite Body together, then you may rightly say they are infinite. Nay Reason will inform you plainly, for example: Imagine an Infinite number of grains of Corn in one heap, surely if the number of Grains be Infinite, you must grant of necessity the bulk or body, which contains this infinite number of grains, to be Infinite too; to wit, Infinite in quantity, and yet you will find each Grain in itself to be Finite. But you will say, an Infinite Body cannot have parts, for if it be Infinite, it must be Infinite in Quantity, and therefore of one bulk, and one continued quantity, but Infinite parts in number make a discrete quantity.

I answer it is all one; for a Body of a continued quantity may be divided and severed into so many Parts either actually, or mentally in our Conceptions or thoughts; besides nature is one continued Body, for there is no such Vacuum in Nature, as if her Parts did hang together like a linked Chain; nor can any of her Parts subsist single and by itself, but all the Parts of Infinite Nature, although they are in one continued Piece, yet are they several and discerned from each other by their several Figures. And by this, I hope, you will understand my meaning, when I say, that several Infinites may be included or comprehended in one Infinite; for by the one Infinite, I understand Infinite in Quantity, which includes Infinite in Number, that is Infinite Parts; then Infinite in Quality, as Infinite degrees of Rarity, Density, Swiftness, Slowness, Hardness, Softness, &c. Infinite degrees of Motions, Infinite Creations, Dissolutions, Contractions, Dilations, Alterations, &c. Infinite degrees of Wisdom, Strength, Power, &c. and lastly Infinite in Time or Duration, which is Eternity, for Infinite and Eternal are inseparable; All which Infinites are contained in the Onely Matter as many Letters are contained in one Word, many Words in one Line, many Lines in one Book.

But you will say perhaps, if I attribute an Infinite Wisdom, Strength, Power, Knowledge, &c. to Nature; then Nature is in all coequal with God, for God has the same Attributes: I answer, Not at all; for I desire you to understand me rightly, when I speak of Infinite Nature, and when I speak of the Infinite Deity, for there is great difference between them, for it is one thing a Deitical or Divine Infinite, and another a Natural Infinite; You know, that God is a Spirit, and not a bodily substance, again that Nature is a Body, and not a Spirit, and therefore none of these Infinites can obstruct or hinder each other, as being different in their kinds, for a Spirit being no Body, requires no place, Place being an attribute which only belongs to a Body, and therefore when I call Nature Infinite, I mean an Infinite extension of Body, containing an Infinite number of Parts; but what does an Infinite extension of Body hinder the Infiniteness of God, as an Immaterial Spiritual being?

Next, when I do attribute an Infinite Power, Wisdom, Knowledge, &c. to Nature, I do not understand a

Divine, but a Natural Infinite Wisdom and Power, that is, such as properly belongs to Nature, and not a supernatural, as is in god; For Nature having Infinite parts of Infinite degrees, must also have an Infinite natural wisdom to order her natural Infinite parts and actions, and consequently an Infinite natural power to put her wisdom into act; and so of the rest of her attributes, which are all natural: But God's Attributes being supernatural, transcend much these natural infinite attributes; for God, being the God of Nature, has not only Nature's Infinite Wisdom and Power, but besides, a Supernatural and Incomprehensible Infinite Wisdom and Power; which in no ways do hinder each other, but may very well subsist together. Neither does God's Infinite Justice and his Infinite Mercy hinder each other; for God's Attributes, though they be all several Infinites, yet they make but one Infinite.

But you will say, If Nature's Wisdom and Power extends no further than to natural things, it is not Infinite, but limited and restrained. I answer, That does not take away the Infiniteness of Nature; for there may be several kinds of Infinites, as I related before, and one may be as perfect an Infinite as the other in its kind. For example: Suppose a Line to be extended infinitely in length, you will call this Line Infinite, although it have not an Infinite breadth: Also, if an infinite length and breadth join together, you will call it, an Infinite Superficies, although it wants an infinite depth; and yet every Infinite, in its kinde, is a Perfect Infinite, if I may call it so: Why then shall not Nature also be said to have an Infinite Natural Wisdom and Power, although she has not a Divine Wisdom and Power? Can we say, Man has not a free Will, because he has not an absolute free Will, as God has? Wherefore, a Natural Infinite, and the Infinite God, may well stand together, without any opposition or hindrance, or without any detracting or derogating from the Omnipotency and Glory of God; for God remains still the God of Nature, and is an Infinite Immaterial Purity, when as Nature is an Infinite Corporeal Substance; and Immaterial and Material cannot obstruct each other. And though an Infinite Corporeal cannot make an Infinite Immaterial, yet an Infinite Immaterial can make an Infinite Corporeal, by reason there is as much difference in the Power as in the Purity: And the disparity between the Natural and Divine Infinite is such, as they cannot join, mix, and work together, unless you do believe that Divine Actions can have allay.

But you may say, Purity belongs only to natural things, and none but natural bodies can be said purified, but God exceeds all Purity. 'Tis true: But if there were infinite degrees of Purity in Matter, Matter might at last become Immaterial, and so from an Infinite Material turn to an Infinite Immaterial, and from Nature to be God: A great, but an impossible Change. For I do verily believe, that there can be but one Omnipotent God, and he cannot admit of addition, or diminution; and that which is Material cannot be Immaterial, and what is Immaterial cannot become Material, I mean, so, as to change their natures; for Nature is what God was pleased she should be; and will be what she was, until God be pleased to make her otherwise.

Wherefore there can be no new Creation of matter, motion, or figure; nor any annihilation of any matter, motion, or figure in Nature, unless God do create a new Nature: For the changing of Matter into several particular Figures, does not prove an annihilation of particular Figures; nor the cessation of particular Motions an annihilation of them: Neither does the variation of the Onely Matter produce an annihilation of any part of Matter, nor the variation of figures and motions of Matter cause an alteration in the nature of Onely Matter: Wherefore there cannot be new Lives, Souls or Bodies in Nature; for, could there be any thing new in Nature, or any thing annihilated, there would not be any stability in Nature, as a continuance of every kind and sort of Creatures, but there would be a confusion between the new and old matter, motions, and figures, as between old and new Nature.

In truth, it would be like new Wine in old Vessels, by which all would break into disorder. Neither can supernatural and natural effects be mixed together, no more than material and immaterial things or beings:

Therefore it is probable, God has ordained Nature to work in herself by his Leave, Will, and Free Gift. But there have been, and are still strange and erroneous Opinions, and great differences among Natural Philosophers, concerning the Principles of Natural things; some will have them Atoms, others will have the first Principles to be Salt, Sulfur and Mercury; some will have them to be the four Elements, as Fire, Air, Water, and Earth; and others will have but one of these Elements; also some will have Gas and Blas, Ferments, Idea's, and the like; but what they believe to be Principles and Causes of natural things, are only Effects; for in all Probability it appears to humane sense and reason, that the cause of every particular material Creature is the onely and Infinite Matter, which has Motions and Figures inseparably united; for Matter, Motion and Figure, are but one thing, indivisible in its Nature. And as for Immaterial Spirits, there is surely no such thing in Infinite Nature, to wit, so as to be Parts of Nature; for Nature is altogether Material, but this opinion proceeds from the separation or abstraction of Motion form Matter, viz. that man thinks matter and motion to be dividable from each other, and believes motion to be a thing by itself, naming it an Immaterial thing, which has a being, but not a bodily substance.

But various and different effects do not prove a different Matter or Cause, neither do they prove an unsettled Cause, only the variety of Effects has obscured the Cause from the several parts, which makes Particular Creatures partly Ignorant, and partly knowing. But in my opinion, Nature is material, and not any thing in Nature, what belongs to her, is immaterial; but whatsoever is Immaterial, is Supernatural, Therefore Motions, Forms, Thoughts, Ideas, Conceptions, Sympathies, Antipathies, Accidents, Qualities, as also Natural Life, and Soul, are all Material: And as for Colors, Scents, Light, Sound, Heat, Cold, and the like, those that believe them not to be substances or material things, surely their brain or heart (take what place you will for the forming of Conceptions) moves very Irregularly, and they might as well say, Our sensitive Organs are not material; for what Objects soever, that are subject to our senses, cannot in sense be denied to be Corporeal, when as those things that are not subject to our senses, can be conceived in reason to be Immaterial? But some Philosophers striving to express their wit, obstruct reason; and drawing Divinity to prove Sense and Reason, weaken Faith so, as their mixed Divine Philosophy becomes mere Poetical Fictions, and Romantical expressions, making material Bodies immaterial Spirits, and immaterial Spirits material Bodies; and some have conceived some things neither to be Material nor Immaterial, but between both.

Truly, Madam, I wish their Wits had been less, and their Judgments more, as not to jumble Natural and Supernatural things together, but to distinguish either clearly, for such Mixtures are neither Natural nor Divine; But as I said, the Confusion comes from their too nice abstractions, and from the separation of Figure and Motion from Matter, as not conceiving them indivisible; but if God, and his servant Nature were as Intricate and Confuse in their Works, as Men in their Understandings and Words, the Universe and Production of all Creatures would soon be without Order and Government, so as there would be a horrid and Eternal War both in Heaven, and in the World, and so pitying their troubled Brains, and wishing them the Light of Reason, that they may clearly perceive the Truth, I rest

MADAM,

Your real Friend and faithful Servant.

Letter III

MADAM,

It seems you are offended at my Opinion, that Nature is Eternal without beginning, which, you say, is to make her God, or at least coequal with God; But, if you apprehend my meaning rightly, you will say, I do not: For first, God is an Immaterial and Spiritual Infinite Being, which Propriety God cannot give away to any Creature, nor make another God in Essence like to him, for God's Attributes are not communicable to any Creature; Yet this does not hinder, that God should not make Infinite and Eternal Matter, for that is as easy to him, as to make a Finite Creature, Infinite Matter being quite of another Nature than God is, to wit, Corporeal, when God is Incorporeal, the difference whereof I have declared in my former Letter. But as for Nature, that it cannot be Eternal without beginning, because God is the Creator and Cause of it, and that the Creator must be before the Creature, as the Cause before the Effect, so, that it is impossible for Nature to be without a beginning; if you will speak naturally, as human reason guides you, and bring an Argument concluding from the Priority of the Cause before the Effect, give me leave to tell you, that God is not tied to Natural Rules, but that he can do beyond our Understanding, and therefore he is neither bound up to time, as to be before, for if we will do this, we must not allow, that the Eternal Son of God is Co-eternal with the Father, because nature requires a Father to exist before the Son, but in God is no time, but all Eternity; and if you allow, that God has made some Creatures, as Supernatural Spirits, to live Eternally, why should he not as well have made a Creature from all Eternity? For God's making is not our making, he needs no Priority of Time.

But you may say, the Comparison of the Eternal Generation of the Son of God is Mystical and Divine, and not to be applied to natural things: I answer, The action by which God created the World or made Nature, was it natural of supernatural? surely you will say it was a Supernatural and God-like action, why then will you apply Natural Rules to a God-like and Supernatural Action? for what Man knows, how and when God created Nature?

You will say, the Scripture does teach us that, for it is not Six thousand years, when God created this World. I answer, the holy Scripture informs us only of the Creation of this Visible World, but not of Nature and natural Matter; for I firmly believe according to the Word of God, that this World has been Created, as is described by Moses, but what is that to natural Matter? There may have been worlds before, as many are of the opinion that there have been men before Adam, and many among Divines do believe, that after the destruction of this World God will Create a new World again, as a new Heaven, and a new Earth; and if this be probable, or at least may be believed without any prejudice to the holy Scripture, why may it not be probably believed that there have been other worlds before this visible World? for nothing is impossible with God; and all this does derogate nothing from the Honor and Glory of God, but rather increases his Divine Power. But as for the Creation of this present World, it is related, that there was first a rude and indigested Heap, or Chaos, without form, void and dark; and God said, Let it be light; Let there be a Firmament in the midst of the Waters, and let the Waters under the Heaven be gathered together, and let the dry Land appear; Let the Earth bring forth Grass, the Herb yielding seed, and the Fruit-tree yielding Fruit after its own kind; and let there be Lights in the Firmament, the one to rule the Day, and the other the Night; and let the Waters bring forth abundantly the moving Creature that has life; and let the Earth bring forth living Creatures after its kind; and at last God said, Let us make Man, and all what was made, God saw it was good. Thus all was made by God's Command, and who executed his Command but the Material servant of God, Nature? which ordered her self-moving matter into such several Figures as God commanded, and God approved of them.

And thus, Madam, I verily believe the Creation of the World, and that God is the Sole and omnipotent Creator of Heaven and Earth, and of all Creatures therein; nay, although I believe Nature to have been from Eternity, yet I believe also that God is the God and Author of Nature, and has made Nature and natural Matter in a way and manner proper to his Omnipotence and Incomprehensible by us: I will pass by natural Arguments and Proofs, as not belonging to such an Omnipotent Action; as for example, how the nature of relative terms requires, that they must both exist at one point of Time, viz. a Master and his Servant, and a King and his Subjects; for one bearing relation to the other, can in no ways be considered as different from one another in formiliness or later-ness of Time; but as I said, these being merely natural things, I will nor cannot apply them to Supernatural and Divine Actions.

But if you ask me, how it is possible that Nature, the Effect and Creature of God, can be Eternal without beginning? I will desire you to answer me first, how a Creature can be Eternal without end, as, for example, Supernatural Spirits are, and then I will answer you, how a Creature can be Eternal without beginning; For Eternity consists herein, that it has neither beginning nor end; and if it be easy for God to make a Being without end, it is not difficult for Him to make a Being without beginning. One thing more I will add, which is, That if Nature has not been made by God from all Eternity, then the Title of God, as being a Creator, which is a Title and action, upon which our Faith is grounded, (for it is the first Article in our Creed) has been accessory to God, as I said, not full Six thousand years ago; but there is not anything accessory to God, he being the Perfection himself.

But, Madam, all what I speak, is under the liberty of Natural Philosophy, and by the Light of Reason only, not of Revelation; and my Reason being not infallible, I will not declare my Opinions for an infallible Truth: Neither do I think, that they are offensive either to Church or State, for I submit to the Laws of One, and believe the Doctrine of the Other, so much, that if it were for the advantage of either, I should be willing to sacrifice my Life, especially for the Church; yea, had I millions of Lives, and every Life was either to suffer torment or to live in ease, I would prefer torment for the benefit of the Church; and therefore, if I knew that my Opinions should give any offence to the Church, I should be ready every minute to alter them: And as much as I am bound in all duty to the obedience of the Church, as much am I particularly bound to your Ladyship, for your entire love and sincere affection towards me, for which I shall live and die,

MADAM,

Your most faithful Friend, and humble Servant.

Letter IV

MADAM,

I have chosen, in the first place, the Work of that famous Philosopher Hobbes, called *Leviathan*, wherein I find he says, That the cause of sense or sensitive perception is the external body or Object, which presses the Organ proper to each Sense. To which I answer, according to the ground of my own *Philosophical Opinions*, That all things, and therefore outward objects as well as sensitive organs, have both Sense and Reason, yet neither the objects nor the organs are the cause of them; for Perception is but the effect of the Sensitive and rational Motions, and not the Motions of the Perception; neither does the pressure of parts upon parts make Perception; for although Matter by the power of self-motion is as much composable as dividable, and parts do join to parts, yet that does not make perception; nay, the several parts, betwixt which the Perception is made, may be at such a distance, as not capable to press.

As for example, Two men may see or hear each other at a distance, and yet there may be other bodies between them, that do not move to those perceptions, so that no pressure can be made, for all pressures are by some constraint and force; wherefore, according to my Opinion, the Sensitive and Rational free Motions, do pattern out each others object, as Figure and Voice in each others Eye and Ear; for Life and Knowledge, which I name Rational and Sensitive Matter, are in every Creature, and in all parts of every Creature, and make all perceptions in Nature, because they are the self-moving parts of Nature, and according as those

Corporeal, Rational, and Sensitive Motions move, such or such perceptions are made: But these self-moving parts being of different degrees (for the Rational matter is purer than the Sensitive) it causes a double perception in all Creatures, whereof one is made by the Rational corporeal motions, and the other by the Sensitive; and though both perceptions are in all the body, and in every part of the body of a Creature, yet the sensitive corporeal motions having their proper organs, as Work-houses, in which they work some sorts of perceptions, those perceptions are most commonly made in those organs, and are double again; for the sensitive motions work either on the inside or on the outside of those organs, on the inside in Dreams, on the out-side awake; and although both the Rational and the Sensitive matter are inseparably joined and mixed together, yet do they not always work together, for oftentimes the Rational works without any sensitive patterns, and the sensitive again without any rational patterns.

But mistake me not, Madam, for I do not absolutely confine the sensitive perception to the Organs, nor the rational to the Brain, but as they are both in the whole body, so they may work in the whole body according to their own motions. Neither do I say, that there is no other perception in the Eye but sight, in the Ear but hearing, and so forth, but the sensitive organs have other perceptions besides these; and if the sensitive and rational motions be irregular in those parts, between which the perception is made, as for example, in the two aforementioned men, that see and hear each other, then they both neither see nor hear each other perfectly; and if one's motions be perfect, but the other's irregular and erroneous, then one sees and hears better than the other; or if the Sensitive and Rational motions move more regularly and make perfecter patterns in the Eye than in the Ear, then they see better than they hear; and if more regularly and perfectly in the Ear than in the Eye, they hear better than they see: And so it may be said of each man singly, for one man may see the other better and more perfectly, than the other may see him; and this man may hear the other better and more perfectly, than the other may hear him; whereas, if perception were made by pressure, there would not be any such mistakes; besides the hard pressure of objects, in my opinion, would rather annoy and obscure, than inform. But as soon as the object is removed, the Perception of it, made by the sensitive motions in the Organs, ceases, by reason the sensitive Motions cease from patterning, but yet the Rational Motions do not always cease so suddenly, because the sensitive corporeal Motions work with the Inanimate Matter, and therefore cannot retain particular figures long, whereas the Rational Matter does only move in its own substance and parts of matter, and upon none other, as my Book of *Philosophical Opinions* will inform you better.

And thus Perception, in my opinion, is not made by Pressure, nor by Species, nor by matter going either from the Organ to the Object, or from the Object into the Organ. By this it is also manifest, that Understanding comes not from Exterior Objects, or from the Exterior sensitive Organs; for as Exterior Objects do not make Perception, so they do neither make Understanding, but it is the rational matter that does it, for Understanding may be without exterior objects and sensitive organs; And this in short is the opinion of

MADAM,

Your faithful Friend and Servant.

Letter V

MADAM,

Your Author's opinion is, that when a thing lies still, unless somewhat else stir it, it will lie still for ever; but when a thing is in motion, it will eternally be in motion, unless somewhat else stay it; the reason is, saith he, because nothing can change itself; To tell you truly, Madam, I am not of his opinion, for if Matter moves itself, as certainly it does, then the least part of Matter, were it so small as to seem Indivisible, will move itself.

'Tis true, it could not desist from motion, as being its nature to move, and no thing can change its Nature; for God himself, who hath more power than self-moving Matter, cannot change himself from being God; but that Motion should proceed from another exterior Body, joining with, or touching that body which it moves, is in my opinion not probable; for though Nature is all Corporeal, and her actions are Corporeal Motions, yet that does not prove, that the Motion of particular Creatures or Parts is caused by the joining, touching or pressing of parts upon parts; for it is not the several parts that make motion, but motion makes them; and yet Motion is not the cause of Matter, but Matter is the cause of Motion, for Matter might subsist without Motion, but not Motion without Matter, only there could be no perception without Motion, nor no Variety, if Matter were not self-moving; but Matter, if it were all Inanimate and void of Motion, would lie as a dull, dead and senseless heap; But that all Motion comes by joining or pressing of other parts, I deny, for if sensitive and rational perceptions, which are sensitive and rational motions, in the body, and in the mind, were made by the pressure of outward objects, pressing the sensitive organs, and so the brain or interior parts of the Body, they would cause such dents and holes therein, as to make them sore and patched in a short time.

Besides, what was represented in this manner, would always remain, or at least not so soon be dissolved, and then those pressures would make a strange and horrid confusion of Figures, for not any figure would be distinct; Wherefore my opinion is, that the sensitive and rational Matter does make or pattern out the figures of several Objects, and does dissolve them in a moment of time; as for example, when the eye sees the object first of a Man, then of a Horse, then of another Creature, the sensitive motions in the eye move first into the figure of the Man, then straight into the figure of the Horse, so that the Man's figure is dissolved and altered into the figure of the Horse, and so forth; but if the eye sees many figures at once, then so many several figures are made by the sensitive Corporeal Motions, and as many by the Rational Motions, which are Sight and Memory, at once: But in sleep both the sensitive and rational Motions make the figures without patterns, that is, exterior objects, which is the cause that they are often erroneous, whereas, if it were the former Impression of the Objects, there could not possibly be imperfect Dreams or Remembrances, for fading of Figures requires as much motion, as impression, and impression and fading are very different and opposite motions; nay, if Perception was made by Impression, there could not possibly be a fading or decay of the figures printed either in the Mind or Body, whereas yet, as there is alteration of Motions in self-moving Matter, so there is also an alteration of figures made by these motions.

But you will say, it does not follow, if Perception be made by Impression, that it must needs continue and not decay; for if you touch and move a string, the motion does not continue for ever, but ceases by degrees; I answer, There is great difference between Prime self-motion, and forced or Artificial Motions; for Artificial Motions are only an Imitation of Natural Motions, and not the same, but caused by Natural Motions; for although there is no Art that is not made by Nature, yet Nature is not made by Art; Wherefore we cannot rationally judge of Perception by comparing it to the motion of a string, and its alteration to the ceasing of that motion, for Nature moves not by force, but freely.

'Tis true, 'tis the freedom in Nature for one man to give another a box on the Ear, or to trip up his heels, or for one or more men to fight with each other; yet these actions are not like the actions of loving Embraces and Kissing each other; neither are the actions one and the same, when a man strikes himself, and when he strikes another; and so is likewise the action of impression, and the action of self-figuring not one and the same, but different; for the action of impression is forced, and the action of self-figuring is free; Wherefore the comparison of the forced motions of a string, rope, watch, or the like, can have no place here; for though the rope, made of flax or hemp, may have the perception of a Vegetable, yet not of the hand, or the like, that touched or struck it; and although the hand does occasion the rope to move in such a manner, yet it is not the motion of the hand, by which it moves, and when it ceases, its natural and inherent power to move is not lessened; like as a man, that hath left off carving or painting, hath no less skill than he had before, neither is that skill lost when he plays upon the Lute or Virginals, or plows, plants, and the like, but he hath only altered his action, as from carving to painting, or from painting to playing, and so to plowing and planting, which is not through disability but choice.

But you will say, it is nevertheless a cessation of such a motion. I grant it: but the ceasing of such a motion is not the ceasing of self-moving matter from all motions, neither is cessation as much as annihilation, for the motion lies in the power of the matter to repeat it, as oft it will, if it be not overpowered, for more parts, or more strength, or more motions may over-power the less; Wherefore forced, or artificial and free Natural motions are different in their effects, although they have but one Cause, which is the self-moving matter, and though Matter is but active and passive, yet there is great Variety, and so great difference in force and liberty, objects and perceptions, sense and reason, and the like. But to conclude, perception is not made by the pressure of objects, no more than hemp is made by the Rope-maker, or metal by the Bell-founder or Ringer, and yet neither the rope nor the metal is without sense and reason, but the natural motions of the metal, and the artificial motions of the Ringer are different; wherefore a natural effect in truth cannot be produced from an artificial cause, neither can the ceasing of particular forced or artificial motions be a proof for the ceasing of general, natural, free motions, as that matter itself should cease to move; for there is no such thing as rest in Nature, but there is an alteration of motions and figures in self-moving matter, which alteration causes variety as well in opinions, as in every thing else.

Wherefore in my opinion, though sense alters, yet it does not decay, for the rational and sensitive part of matter is as lasting as matter itself, but that which is named decay of sense, is only the alteration of motions, and not an obscurity of motions, like as the motions of memory and forgetfulness, and the repetition of the same motions is called remembrance. And thus much of this subject for the present, to which I add no more but rest

MADAM,

Your faithful Friend and Servant.

Letter VI

MADAM,

Your Author discoursing of Imagination, saith, That as soon as any object is removed from our Eyes, though the Impression that is made in us, remain, yet other objects more present succeeding and working on us, the Imagination of the past is obscured and made weak. To which I answer, first, that he conceives Sense and Imagination to be all one, for he says, Imagination is nothing else, but a fading or decaying sense; whereas in my opinion they are different, not only their matter, but their motions also being distinct and different; for Imagination is a rational perception, and sense a sensitive perception; wherefore as much as the rational matter differs from the sensitive, as much does Imagination differ from Sense.

Next I say, that Impressions do not remain in the body of sensitive matter, but it is in its power to make or repeat the like figures; Neither is Imagination less, when the object is absent, than when present, but the figure patterned out in the sensitive organs, being altered, and remaining only in the Rational part of matter, is not so perspicuous and clear, as when it was both in the Sense and in the Mind: And to prove that Imagination of things past does not grow weaker by distance of time, as your Author says, many a man in his old age, will have as perfect an Imagination of what is past in his younger years, as if he saw it present. And as for your Author's opinion, that Imagination and Memory are one and the same, I grant, that they are made of one kind of Matter; but although the Matter is one and the same, yet several motions in the several parts make Imagination and Memory several things: As for Example, a Man may Imagine that which never came into his Senses, wherefore Imagination is not one and the same thing with Memory.

But your Author seems to make all Sense, as it were, one Motion, but not all Motion Sense, whereas surely there is no Motion, but is either Sensitive or Rational; for Reason is but a pure and refined Sense, and Sense a grosser Reason. Yet all sensitive and rational Motions are not one and the same; for forced or Artificial Motions, though they proceed from sensitive matter, yet are they so different from the free and Prime Natural Motions, that they seem, as it were, quite of another nature: And this distinction neglected is the Cause, that many make Appetites and Passions, Perceptions and Objects, and the like, as one, without any or but little difference. But having discoursed of the difference of these Motions in my former Letter, I will not be tedious to you, with repeating it again, but remain,

MADAM,

Your faithful Friend and Servant.

Letter VII

MADAM,

Your Author's opinion, concerning Dreams, seems to me in some part very rational and probable, in some part not; For when he says, that Dreams are only Imaginations of them that sleep, which imaginations have been before either totally or by parcels in the Sense; and that the organs of Sense, as the Brain and the Nerves, being benumb'd in sleep, as not easily to be moved by external objects, those Imaginations proceed only from the agitation of the inward parts of man's body, which for the connection they have with the Brain, and other organs, when they be distemper'd, do keep the same in motion, whereby the Imaginations there formerly made, appear as if a man were waking.

This seems to my Reason not very probable. For, first, Dreams are not absolutely Imaginations, except we do call all Motions and Actions of the Sensitive and Rational Matter, Imaginations. Neither is it necessary, that all Imaginations must have been before either totally or by parcels in the Sense; neither is there any benumbing of the organs of Sense in sleep. But Dreams, according to my opinion, are made by the Sensitive and Rational Corporeal Motions, by figuring several objects, as awake; only the difference is, that the Sensitive motions in Dreams work by rote and on the inside of the Sensitive organs, when as awake they work according to the patterns of outward objects, and exteriously or on the outside of the sensitive Organs, so that sleep or dreams are nothing else but an alteration of motions, from moving exteriously to move interiously, and from working after a Pattern to work by rote: I do not say that the body is without all exterior motions, when asleep, as breathing and beating of the Pulse (although these motions are rather interior than exterior,) but that only the sensitive organs are outwardly shut, so as not to receive the patterns of outward Objects, nevertheless the sensitive Motions do not cease from moving inwardly, or on the inside of the sensitive Organs; But the rational matter does often, as awake, so asleep or in dreams, make such figures, as the sensitive did never make either from outward objects, or of its own accord; for the sensitive has sometimes liberty to work without Objects, but the Rational much more, which is not bound either to the patterns of Exterior objects, or of the sensitive voluntary Figures.

Wherefore it is not divers distempers, as your Author says, that cause different Dreams, or Cold, or Heat; neither are Dreams the reverse of our waking Imaginations, nor all the Figures in Dreams are not made with their heels up, and their heads downwards, though some are; but this error or irregularity proceeds from want of exterior Objects or Patterns, and by reason the sensitive Motions work by rote; neither are the Motions reverse, because they work inwardly asleep, and outwardly awake, for Mad-men awake see several Figures without Objects. In short, sleeping and waking is somewhat after that manner, when men are called either out of their doors, or stay within their houses; or like a Ship, where the Mariners work all under hatches, whereof you will find more in my *Philosophical Opinions*; and so taking my leave, I rest

MADAM,

Your faithful Friend and Servant.

Letter VIII

MADAM,

Your Author going on in his discourse of Imagination, says, That, as we have no Imagination, whereof we have not formerly had sense, in whole or in parts; so we have not Transition from one Imagination to another, whereof we never had the like before in our senses. To which my answer is in short, that the Rational part of Matter in one composed figure, as in Man, or the like Creature, may make such figures, as the senses did never make in that composed Figure or Creature; And though your Author reproves those that say, be Imaginations rise of themselves; yet, if the self-moving part of Matter, which I call Rational, makes Imaginations, they must needs rise of themselves; for the Rational part of matter being free and self-moving, depends upon nothing, neither Sense nor Object, I mean, so, as not to be able to work without them. Next, when your Author, defining Understanding, says that it is nothing else, but can Imagination raised by words or other voluntary signs.

My Answer is, that Understanding, and so Words and Signs are made by self-moving Matter, that is, Sense and Reason, and not Sense and Reason by Words and Signs; wherefore Thoughts are not like Water upon a plain Table, which is drawn and guided by the finger this or that way, for every Part of self-moving matter is not always forced, persuaded or directed, for if all the Parts of Sense and Reason were ruled by force or persuasion, not any wounded Creature would fail to be healed, or any disease to be cured by outward Applications, for outward Applications to Wounds and Diseases might have more force, than any Object to the Eye: But though there is great affinity and sympathy between parts, yet there is also great difference and antipathy betwixt them, which is the cause that many objects cannot with all their endeavors work such effects upon the Interior parts, although they are closely press'd, for Impressions of objects do not always affect those parts they press.

Wherefore, I am not of your Author's opinion, that all Parts of Matter press one another; It is true, Madam, there cannot be any part single, but yet this does not prove, that parts must needs press each other: And as for his Train of Thoughts, I must confess, that Thoughts for the most part are made orderly, but yet they do not follow each other like Geese, for surely, man has sometimes very different thoughts; as for Example, a man sometime is very sad for the death of his Friend, and thinks of his own death, and immediately thinks of a wanton Mistress, which later thought, surely, the thought of Death did not draw in; wherefore, though some thought may be the Ring-leader of others, yet many are made without leaders.

Again, your Author in his description of the Mind says, that the discourse of the mind, when it it is govern'd by design, is nothing but seeking, or the Faculty of Invention; a hunting out of the Causes of some Effects, present or past; or of the Effects of some present or past Cause. Sometimes a man seeks what he has lost, and from that Place and Time wherein he misses it, his mind runs back from place to place, and time to time, to find where and when he had it, that is to say, to find some certain and limited Time and Place, in which to begin a method of Seeking. And from thence his thoughts run over the same places and times to find what action or other occasion might make him lose it. This we call Remembrance or calling to mind. Sometimes a man knows a place determinate, within the compass whereof he is to seek, and then his thoughts run over all the Parts thereof in the same manner as one would sweep a room to find a Jewel, or as a Spaniel ranges the field till he find a sent; or as a Man should run over the Alphabet to start a Rime.

Thus far your Author: In which discourse I do not perceive that he defines what the Mind is, but I say, that if, according to his opinion, nothing moves itself, but one thing moves another, then the Mind must do nothing, but move backward and forward, nay, only forward, and if all actions were thrusting or pressing of parts, it would be like a crowd of People, and there would be but little or no motion, for the crowd would make a stoppage, like water in a glass, the mouth of the Glass being turned downwards, no water can pass out, by reason the numerous drops are so closely press'd, as they cannot move exteriously.

Next, I cannot conceive how the Mind can run back either to Time or Place, for as for Place, the mind is enclosed in the body, and the running about in the parts of the body or brain will not inform it of an Exterior place or object; besides, objects being the cause of the minds motion, it must return to its Cause, and so move until it come to the object, that moved it first, so that the mind must run out of the body to that object, which moved it to such a Thought, although that object were removed out of the World (as the phrase is:) But for the mind to move backward, to Time past, is more than it can do; Wherefore in my opinion, Remembrance, or the like, is only a repetition of such Figures as were like to the Objects; and for Thoughts in Particular, they are several figures, made by the mind, which is the Rational Part of matter, in its own substance, either voluntarily, or by imitation, whereof you may see more in my Book of *Philosophical Opinions.*

Hence I conclude, that Prudence is nothing else, but a comparing of Figures to Figures, and of the several actions of those Figures, as repeating former Figures, and comparing them to others of the like nature, qualities, proprieties, as also chances, fortunes, &c. Which figuring and repeating is done actually, in and by the Rational Matter, so that all the observation of the mind on outward Objects is only an actual repetition of the mind, as moving in such or such figures and actions; and when the mind makes voluntary Figures with those repeated Figures, and compares them together, this comparing is Examination; and when several Figures agree and join, it is Conclusion or Judgment: likewise does Experience proceed from repeating and comparing of several Figures in the Mind, and the more several Figures are repeated and compared, the greater the experience is.

One thing more there is in the same Chapter, which I cannot let pass without examination; Your Author says, That things Present only have a being in Nature, things Past only a being in the Memory, but things to come have no being at all; Which how it possibly can be, I am not able to conceive; for certainly, if nothing in nature is lost or annihilated, what is past, and what is to come, has as well a being, as what is present; and, if that which is now, had its being before, why may it not also have its being hereafter? It might as well be said, that what is once forgot, cannot be remembered; for whatsoever is in Nature, has as much a being as the Mind, and there is not any action, or motion, or figure, in Nature, but may be repeated, that is, may return to its former Figure, when it is altered and dissolved; But by reason Nature delights in variety, repetitions are not so frequently made, especially of those things or creatures, which are composed by the sensitive corporeal motions in the inanimate part of Matter, because they are not so easily wrought, as the Rational matter can work upon its own parts, being more pliant in itself, than the Inanimate matter is; And this is the reason, that there are so many repetitions of one and the same Figure in the Rational matter, which is the Mind, but seldom any in the Gross and inanimate part of Matter, for Nature loves ease and freedom.

But to conclude, Madam, I perceive your Author confines Sense only to Animal-kind, and Reason only to Mankind: Truly, it is out of self-love, when one Creature prefers his own Excellency before another, for nature being endued with self-love, all Creatures have self-love too, because they are all Parts of Nature; and when Parts agree or disagree, it is out of Interest and Self-love; but Man herein exceeds all the rest, as having a supernatural Soul, whose actions also are supernatural, To which I leave him, and rest,

MADAM,

Your faithful Friend and Servant.

Letter IX

MADAM,

When your Author discourses of the use of Speech or Words and Names, he is pleas'd to say, That their use is to serve for marks and notes of Remembrance; Whereof to give you my opinion, I say, That Speech is natural to the shape of Man; and though sometimes it serves for marks or notes of remembrance, yet it does not always, for all other Animals have Memory without the help of Speech, and so have deaf and dumb men, nay more than those that hear and speak: Wherefore, though Words are useful to the mind, and so to the memory, yet both can be without them, whereas Words cannot be without Memory; for take a Bird and teach him to speak, if he had not Memory, before he heard the words, he could never learn them.

You will ask me, Madam, What then, is Memory the Cause of Speech? I answer, Life and Knowledge, which is Sense and Reason, as it creates and makes all sorts of Creatures, so also among the rest it makes Words: And as I said before, that Memory may be without the help of Speech or Words, so I say also, that there is a possibility of reckoning of numbers, as also of magnitudes, of swiftness, of force, and other things without words, although your Author denies it: But some men are so much for Art, as they endeavor to make Art, which is only a Drudgery-maid of Nature, the chief Mistress, and Nature her Servant, which is as much as to prefer Effects before the Cause, Nature before God, Discord before Unity and Concord.

Again, your Author, in his Chapter of Reason, defines Reason to be nothing else but Reckoning: I answer, That in my opinion Reckoning is not Reason itself, but only an effect or action of Reason; for Reason, as it is the chiefest and purest degree of animate matter, works variously and in divers motions, by which it produces various and divers effects, which are several Perceptions, as Conception, Imagination, Fancy, Memory, Remembrance, Understanding, Judgment, Knowledge, and all the Passions, with many more: Wherefore this Reason is not in one undivided part, nor bound to one motion, for it is in every Creature more or less, and moves in its own parts variously; and in some Creatures, as for example, in some men, it moves more variously than in others, which is the cause that some men are more dull and stupid, than others; neither does Reason always move in one Creature regularly, which is the cause, that some men are mad or foolish: And though all men are made by the direction of Reason, and endued with Reason, from the first time of their birth, yet all have not the like Capacities, Understandings, Imaginations, Wits, Fancies, Passions, &c. but some more, some less, and some regular, some irregular, according to the motions of Reason or Rational part of animate matter; and though some rational parts may make use of other rational Parts, as one man of another man's Conceptions, yet all these parts cannot associate together; as for example, all the Material parts of several objects, no not their species, cannot enter or touch the eye without danger of hurting or loosing it, nevertheless the eye makes use of the objects by patterning them out, and so does the rational matter; by taking patterns from the sensitive.

And thus knowledge or perception of objects, both sensitive and rational, is taken without the pressure of any other parts; for though parts join to parts, (for no part can be single) yet this joining does not necessarily infer the pressure of objects upon the sensitive organs; Whereof I have already discoursed sufficiently heretofore, to which I refer you, and rest

MADAM,

Your faithful Friend and Servant.

Letter X

Understanding, says your Author, is nothing else but Conception caused by speech, and therefore, if speech be peculiar to man, (as, for ought I know, it is) then is understanding peculiar to him also. Where he confines Understanding only to speech and to Mankind; But, by his leave, Madam, I surely believe, that there is more understanding in Nature, than that, which is in speech, for if there were not, I cannot conceive, how all the exact forms in Generations could be produced, or how there could be such distinct degrees of several sorts and kinds of Creatures, or distinctions of times and seasons, and so many exact motions and figures in Nature.

Considering all this, my reason persuades me, that all Understanding, which is a part of Knowledge, is not caused by speech, for all the motions of the Celestial Orbs are not made by speech, neither is the knowledge or understanding which a man has, when sick, as to know or understand he is sick, made by speech, nor by outward objects, especially in a disease he never heard, nor saw, nor smelt, nor tasted, nor touched; Wherefore all Perception, Sensation, Memory, Imagination, Appetite, Understanding, and the like, are not made nor caused by outward objects, nor by speech. And as for names of things, they are but different postures of the figures in our mind or thoughts, made by the Rational matter; But Reasoning is a comparing of the several figures with their several postures and actions in the Mind, which joined with the several words, made by the sensitive motions, inform another distinct and separate part, as another man, of their minds conceptions, understanding, opinions, and the like.

Concerning Addition and Subtraction, wherein your Author says Reasoning consists, I grant, that it is an act of Reasoning, yet it does not make Sense or Reason, which is Life and Knowledge, but Sense and Reason which is self-motion, makes addition and subtraction of several Parts of matter; for had matter not self-motion, it could not divide nor compose, nor make such varieties, without great and lingering retardants, if not confusion. Wherefore all, what is made in Nature, is made by self-moving matter, which self-moving matter does not at all times move regularly, but often irregularly, which causes false Logic, false Arithmetic, and the like; and if there be not a certainty in these self-motions or actions of Nature, much less in Art, which is but a secondary action; and therefore, neither speech, words, nor exterior objects cause Understanding or Reason.

And although many parts of the Rational and Sensitive Matter joined into one, may be stronger by their association, and over-power other parts that are not so well knit and united, yet these are not the less pure; only these Parts and Motions being not equal in several Creatures, make their Knowledge and Reason more or less: For, when a man has more Rational Matter well regulated, and so more Wisdom than another, that same man may chance to overpower the other, whose Rational Matter is more irregular, but yet not so much by strength of the united Parts, as by their subtlety; for the Rational Matter moving regularly, is more strong with subtlety, than the sensitive with force; so that Wisdom is stronger than Life, being more pure, and so more active; for in my opinion, there is a degree of difference between Life and Knowledge, as my Book of *Philosophical Opinions* will inform you.

Again, your Author says, That Man does excel all other Animals in this faculty, that when he conceives any thing whatsoever, he is apt to inquire the Consequences of it, and what effects he can do with it: Besides this (says he) Man has another degree of Excellence, that he can by Words reduce the Consequences he finds to General Rules called Theorems or Aphorisms, that is, he can reason or reckon not only in Number, but in all other things, whereof one may be added unto, or subtracted from another.

To which I answer, That according to my Reason I cannot perceive, but that all Creatures may do as much; but by reason they do it not after the same manner or way as Man, Man denies, they can do it at all; which is very hard; for what man knows, whether Fish do not Know more of the nature of Water, and ebbing and flowing, and the saltiness of the Sea? or whether Birds do not know more of the nature and degrees of Air, or the cause of Tempests? or whether Worms do not know more of the nature of Earth, and how Plants are produced? or Bees of the several sorts of juices of Flowers, than Men? And whether they do not make there Aphorisms and Theorems by their manner of Intelligence? For, though they have not the speech of Man, yet thence does not follow, that they have no Intelligence at all. But the Ignorance of Men concerning other Creatures is the cause of despising other Creatures, imagining themselves as petty God's in Nature, when as Nature is not capable to make one God, much less so many as Mankind; and were it not for Man's supernatural Soul, Man would not be more Supreme, than other Creatures in Nature, But (says your Author) this Privilege in Man is allay'd by another, which is, No living Creature is subject to absurdity, but only Man.

Certainly, Madam, I believe the contrary, to wit, that all other Creatures do as often commit mistakes and absurdities as Man, and if it were not to avoid tediousness, I could present sufficient proofs to you: Wherefore I think, not only Man but also other Creatures may be Philosophers and subject to absurdities as aptly as Men; for Man does, nor cannot truly know the Faculties, and Abilities or Actions of all other Creatures, no not of his own Kind as Man-Kind, for if he do measure all men by himself he will be very much mistaken, for what he conceives to be true or wise, another may conceive to be false and foolish.

But Man may have one way of Knowledge in Philosophy and other Arts; and other Creatures another way, and yet other Creatures manner or way may be as Intelligible and Instructive to each other as Man's, I mean, in those things which are Natural. Wherefore I cannot consent to what your Author says, That Children are not endued with Reason at all, till they have attained to the use of Speech; for Reason is in those Creatures which have not Speech, witness Horses, especially those which are taught in the manage, and many other Animals. And as for the weak understanding in Children, I have discoursed thereof in my Book of Philosophy; The rest of this discourse, lest I tire you too much at once, I shall reserve for the next, resting in the mean time,

MADAM,

Your faithful Friend and Servant.

Letter XI

MADAM,

I sent you word in my last, that your Author's opinion is, That Children are not endued with Reason at all, until they have attained to the use of Speech, in the same Chapter he speaks to the same purpose thus: Reason is not as Sense and Memory born with us, nor gotten by experience only, as Prudence is, but attained by industry. To which I reply only this, That it might as well be said, a Child when new born has not flesh and blood, because by taking in nourishment or food, the Child grows to have more flesh and blood; or, that a Child is not born with two legs, because he cannot go, or with two arms and hands, because he cannot help himself; or that he is not born with a tongue, because he cannot speak: For although Reason does not move in a Child as in a Man, in Infancy as in Youth, in Youth as in Age, yet that does not prove that Children are without Reason, because they cannot run and prate: I grant, some other Creatures appear to have more Knowledge when new born than others; as for example, a young Foal has more knowledge than a young Child, because a Child cannot run and play; besides a Foal knows his own Dam, and can tell where to take his food, as to run and suck his Dam, when as an Infant cannot do so, nor all beasts, though most of them can, but yet this does not prove, that a Child has no reason at all.

Neither can I perceive that man is a Monopolizer of all Reason, or Animals of all Sense, but that Sense and Reason are in other Creatures as well as in Man and Animals; for example, Drugs, as Vegetables and Minerals, although they cannot slice, pound or infuse, as man can, yet they can work upon man more subtly, wisely, and as sensibly either by purging, vomiting, spitting, or any other way, as man by mincing, pounding and infusing them, and Vegetables will as wisely nourish Men, as Men can nourish Vegetables; Also some Vegetables are as malicious and mischievous to Man, as Man is to one another, witness Hemlock, Nightshade, and many more; and a little Poppy will as soon, nay sooner cause a Man to sleep, though silently, than a Nurse a Child with singing and rocking; But because they do not act in such manner or way as Man, Man judges them to be without sense and reason; and because they do not prate and talk as Man, Man believes they have not so much wit as he has; and because they cannot run and go, Man thinks they are not industrious; the like for Infants concerning Reason.

But certainly, it is not local motion or speech that makes sense and reason, but sense and reason makes them; neither is sense and reason bound only to the actions of Man, but it is free to the actions, forms, figures and proprieties of all Creatures; for if none but Man had reason, and none but Animals sense, the World could not be so exact, and so well in order as it is: but Nature is wiser than Man with all his Arts, for these are only produced through the variety of Natures actions, and disputes through the superfluous varieties of Man's follies or ignorance, not knowing Nature's powerful life and knowledge: But I wonder, Madam, your Author says in this place, That Reason is not born with Man, when as in another place, he says, That every man brought Philosophy, that is Natural reason with him into the World; Which how it agree, I will leave to others to judge, and to him to reconcile it, remaining in the mean time,

MADAM,

Your Constant Friend and Faithful Servant.

Letter XII

MADAM,

Two sorts of motions, I find your Author does attribute to Animals, viz. Vital and Animal, the Vital motions, says he, are begun in Generation, and continued without Interruption through their whole life, and those are the Course of the Blood, the Pulse, the Breathing, Conviction, Nutrition, Excretion, &c. to which motions there needs no help of Imaginations; But the animal Motions, otherwise called voluntary Motions, are to go, to speak, to move any of our limbs, in such manner as is first fancied in our minds: And because going, speaking, and the like voluntary motions, depend always upon a precedent thought of whither, which way, and what, it is evident, that the Imagination is the first Internal beginning of all voluntary Motion. Thus far your Author.

Whereof in short I give you my opinion, first concerning Vital Motions, that it appears improbable if not impossible to me, that Generation should be the cause and beginning of Life, because Life must of necessity be the cause of Generation, life being the Generator of all things, for without life motion could not be, and without motion not any thing could be begun, increased, perfected, or dissolved. Next, that Imagination is not necessary to Vital Motions, it is probable it may not, but yet there is required Knowledge, which I name Reason; for if there were not Knowledge in all Generations or Productions, there could not any distinct Creature be made or produced, for then all Generations would be confusedly mixed, neither would there be any distinct kinds or sorts of Creatures, nor no different Faculties, Proprieties, and the like. Thirdly, concerning Animal Motions, which your Author names Voluntary Motions, as to go, to speak, to move any of our limbs, in such manner as is first fancied in our minds, and that they depend upon a precedent thought of whither, which way, and what, and that Imagination is the first Internal beginning of them; I think, by your Author's leave, it does imply a contradiction, to call them Voluntary Motions, and yet to say they are caused and depend upon our Imagination; for if the Imagination draws them this way, or that way, how can they be voluntary motions, being in a manner forced and necessitated to move according to Fancy or Imagination? But when he goes on in the same place and treats of Endeavor, Appetite, Desire, Hunger, Thirst, Aversion, Love, Hate, and the like, he derives one from the other, and treats well as a Moral Philosopher; but whether it be according to the truth or probability of Natural Philosophy, I will leave to others to judge, for in my opinion Passions and Appetites are very different, Appetites being made by the motions of the sensitive Life, and Passions, as also Imagination, Memory, &c. by the motions of the rational Life, which is the cause that Appetites belong more to the actions of the Body than the Mind.

'Tis true, the Sensitive and Rational self-moving matter does so much resemble each other in their actions, as it is difficult to distinguish them. But having treated hereof at large in my other Philosophical Work, to cut off repetitions, I will refer you to that, and desire you to compare our opinions together: But certainly there is so much variety in one and the same sort of Passions, and so of Appetites, as it cannot be easily express'd.

To conclude, I do not perceive that your Author tells or expresses what the cause is of such or such actions, only he mentions their dependence, which is, as if a man should converse with a Nobleman's Friend or Servant, and not know the Lord himself. But leaving him for this time, it is sufficient to me, that I know your Ladyship, and your Ladyship knows me, that I am,

MADAM,

Your faithful Friend and humble Servant.

Letter XIII

MADAM,

Having obey'd your Commands in giving you my opinion of the First Part of the Book of that famous and learned Author you sent me, I would go on; but seeing he treats in his following Parts of the Politics, I was forced to stay my Pen, because of these following Reasons.

First, That a Woman is not employed in State Affairs, unless an absolute Queen. Next, That to study the Politics, is but loss of Time, unless a man were sure to be a Favorite to an absolute Prince. Thirdly, That it is but a deceiving Profession, and requires more Craft than Wisdom. All which considered, I did not read that part of your Author.

But as for his Natural Philosophy, I will send you my opinion so far as I understand it: For what belongs to Art, as to Geometry, being no Scholar, I shall not trouble myself withal. And so I'll take my leave of you, when I have in two or three words answered the Question you sent me last, which was, Whether Nature be the Art of God, Man the Art of Nature, and a Politic Government the Art of Man? To which I answer, 'Tis probable it may be so; only I add this, That Nature does not rule God, nor Man Nature, nor Politic Government Man; for the Effect cannot rule the Cause, but the Cause does rule the Effect: Wherefore if men do not naturally agree, Art cannot make unity among them, or associate them into one Politic Body and so rule them; But man thinks he governs, when as it is Nature that does it, for as nature does unite or divide parts regularly or irregularly, and moves the several minds of men and the several parts of men's bodies, so war is made or peace kept: Thus it is not the artificial form that governs men in a Politic Government, but a natural power, for though natural motion can make artificial things, yet artificial things cannot make natural power; and we might as well say, nature is governed by the art of nature, as to say man is ruled by the art and invention of men. The truth is, Man rules an artificial Government, and not the Government Man, just like as a Watch-maker rules his Watch, and not the Watch the Watch-maker. And thus I conclude and rest,

MADAM,

Your faithful Friend and Servant.

Letter XIV

MADAM,

Concerning the other Book of that learned Author Hobbes you sent me, called *Elements of Philosophy*, I shall likewise according to your desire, give you my judgment and opinion of it as I have done of the former, not that I intend to prejudice him any ways thereby, but only to mark those places wherein I seem to dissent from his opinions, which liberty, I hope, he will not deny me; And in order to this, I have read over the first Chapter of the mentioned Book, treating of Philosophy in General, wherein among the rest, discoursing of the Utility of Natural Philosophy, and relating the commodities and benefits which proceed from so many arts and sciences, he is pleased to say, that they are enjoyed almost by all people of Europe, Asia, and some of Africa, only the Americans, and those that live near the Poles do want them: But why, says he, have they sharper wits than these? Have not all men one kind of soul, and the same faculties of mind?

To which, give me leave, Madam, to add, That my opinion is, that there is a difference between the Divine and the Natural soul of man, and though the natural mind or soul is of one kind, yet being made of rational matter, it is dividable and composable, by which division and composition, men may have more or less wit, or quicker and slower wit; the like for Judgments, Imaginations, Fancies, Opinions, &c. For were the natural rational mind indivisible, all men would have the like degree of wit or understanding, all men would be Philosophers or fools, which by reason they are not, it proves the natural rational mind is dividable and composable, making variations of its own several parts by self-motion; for it is not the several outward objects, or foreign instructions, that make the variety of the mind; neither is wit or ingenuity alike in all men; for some are natural Poets, Philosophers, and the like, without learning, and some are far more ingenious than others, although their breeding is obscure and mean, Neither will learning make all men Scholars, for some will continue Dunces all their life time; Neither does much experience make all men wise, for some are not any ways advanced in their wisdom by much and long experiences; And as for Poetry, it is according to the common Proverb, a Poet is born, not made; Indeed learning does rather hurt Fancy, for great Scholars are not always good Poets, nor all States-men Natural Philosophers, nor all Experienced Men Wise Men, nor all Judges Just, nor all Divines Pious, nor all Pleaders or Preachers Eloquent, nor all Moral Philosophers Virtuous; But all this is occasioned by the various Motions of the rational self-moving matter, which is the Natural Mind. And thus much for the present of the difference of wits and faculties of the mind; I add no more, but rest,

MADAM,

Your faithful Friend and Servant.

Letter XV

MADAM,

My Discourse for the present shall be of Infinite, and the question shall be first Whether several Finite parts, how many soever there be, can make an Infinite. Your Author says, that several Finite parts when they are all put together make a whole Finite; which, if his meaning be of a certain determinate number, how big soever, of finite parts, I do willingly grant, for all what is determinate and limited, is not Infinite but Finite; neither is there any such thing, as Whole or All in Infinite; but if his meaning be, that no Infinite can be made of finite parts, though infinite in number, I deny it.

Next he says there can be no such thing as One in Infinite, because No thing can be said One, except there be another to compare it withal; which in my opinion does not follow, for there is but One God, who is Infinite, and has none other to be compared withal, and so there may be but one Onely Infinite in Nature, which is Matter. But when he says, there cannot be an Infinite and Eternal Division, is very true, viz, in this sense, that one single part cannot be actually infinitely divided, for the Compositions hinder the Divisions in Nature, and the Divisions the Compositions, so that Nature, being Matter, cannot be composed so, as not to have parts, nor divided so, as that her parts should not be composed, but there are nevertheless infinite divided parts in Nature, and in this sense there may also be infinite divisions, as I have declared in my Book of Philosophy. And thus there are Infinite divisions of Infinite parts in Nature, but not Infinite actual divisions of one single part; But though Infinite is without end, yet my discourse of it shall be but short and end here, though not my affection, which shall last and continue with the life of

MADAM,

Your Faithful Friend and Humble Servant.

Letter XVI

MADAM,

An Accident, says your Author, is nothing else, but the manner of our Conception of body, or that Faculty of any body, by which it works in us a Conception of itself; To which I willingly consent; but yet I say, that these qualities cannot be separated from the body, for as impossible it is that the essence of Nature should be separable from Nature, as impossible is it that the various modes or alterations, either of Figures or Motions, should be separable from matter or body; Wherefore when he goes on, and says, An accident is not a body, but in a body, yet not so, as if any thing were contained therein, as it for example, redness were in blood in the same manner as blood is in a bloody cloth; but as magnitude is in that which is great, rest in that which rests, motion in that which is moved.

I answer, that in my opinion, not any thing in Nature can be without a body, and that redness is as well in blood, as blood is in a bloody cloth, or any other color in any thing else; for there is no color without a body, but every color has as well a body as any thing else, and if Color be a separable accident, I would fain know, how it can be separated from a subject, being bodiless, for that which is no body is nothing, and nothing cannot be taken away from any thing; Wherefore as for natural Color it cannot be taken away from any creature, without the parts of its substance or body; and as for artificial Colors, when they are taken away, it is a separation of two bodies, which joined together; and if Color, or Hardness, or Softness do change, it is nothing else but an alteration of motions and not an annihilation, for all changes and alterations remain in the power of Corporeal motions, as I have said in other places; for we might as well say, life does not remain in nature, when a body turns from an animal to some other figure, as believe that those, they name accidents, do not remain in Corporeal Motions.

Wherefore I am not of your Author's mind, when he says, that when a White thing is made black, the whiteness perishes; for it cannot perish, although it is altered from white to black, being in the power of the same matter, to turn it again from black to white, so as it may make infinite Repetitions of the same thing; but by reason nature takes delight in variety, she seldom uses such repetitions; nevertheless that does not take away the Power of self-moving matter, for it does not; and it cannot, are two several things, and the latter does not necessarily follow upon the former; Wherefore not any, the least thing, can perish in Nature, for if this were possible, the whole body of nature might perish also, for if so many. Figures and Creatures should be annihilated and perish without any supply or new Creation, Nature would grow less, and at last become nothing; besides it is as difficult for Nature to turn something into nothing, as to Create something out of nothing; Wherefore as there is no annihilation or perishing in Nature, so there is neither any new Creation in Nature.

But your Author makes a difference between bodies and accidents, saying, that bodies are things and not Generated, but accidents are Generated and not things, Truly, Madam, these accidents seem to me to be like Van Helmont's Lights, Gases, Blazes and Ideas; and Dr More's Immaterial Substances or Daemons, only in this Dr More has the better, that his Immaterial Substances, are beings, which subsist of themselves, whereas accidents do not, but their existence is in other bodies; But what they call Accidents, are in my opinion nothing else but Corporeal Motions, and if these accidents be generated, they must needs be bodies, for how nothing can be Generated in nature, is not conceivable, and yet your Author denies, a that Accidents are something, namely some part of a natural thing; But as for Generations, they are only various actions of self-moving matter, or a variety of Corporeal Motions, and so are all Accidents whatsoever, so that there is not any thing in nature, that can be made new, or destroyed, for whatsoever was and shall be, is in nature, though not always in act, yet in power, as in the nature and power of Corporeal motions, which is self-moving matter, And as there is no new Generation of Accidents, so there is neither a new Generation of Motions.

Wherefore when your Author says, be That, when the hand, being moved, moves the pen, the motion does not go out of the hand into the pen, for so the writing might be continued, though the hand stood still, but a new motion is generated in the pen, and is the pens motion: I am of his opinion, that the motion does not go out of the hand into the pen, and that the motion of the pen, is the pens own motion; but I deny, that after holding the hand a little while still, and beginning to write again, a new motion of the pen is generated; for it is only a repetition, and not a new generation, for the Hand, Pen and Ink, repeat but the same motion or action of writing: Besides, Generation is made by Connection or Conjunction of parts, moving by consent to such or such Figures, but the motion of the Hand or the Pen is always one and the same; wherefore it is but the variation and repetition in and of the same motion of the Hand, or Pen, which may be continued in that manner infinitely, just as the same Corporeal Motions can make infinite variations and repetitions of one and the same Figure, repeating it as oft as they please, as also making Copy of Copy.

And although I do not deny, but there are Generations in Nature, yet not annihilations or perishings, for if any one motion or figure should perish, the matter must perish also; and if any one part of matter can perish, all the matter in nature may perish also; and if there can any new thing be made or created in nature, which has not been before, there may also be a new Nature, and so by perishings and new Creations, this World would not have continued an age; But surely whatsoever is in Nature, has been existent always. Wherefore to conclude, it is not the generation and perishing of an Accident that makes its subject to be changed, but the production and alteration of the Form, makes it said to be generated or destroyed, for matter will change its motions and figures without perishing or annihilating; and whether there were words or not, there would be such causes and effects; But having not the art of Logic to dispute with artificial words, nor the art of Geometry to demonstrate my opinions by Mathematical Figures, I fear they will not be so well received by the Learned; However, I leave them to any man's unprejudiced Reason and Judgment, and devote myself to your service, as becomes,

MADAM,

Your Ladyship's humble and faithful Servant.

Letter XVII

MADAM,

Your Author concerning Place and Magnitude says, that Place is nothing out of the mind, nor Magnitude any thing within it; for Place is a mere Phantasm of a body of such quantity and figure, and Magnitude a peculiar accident of the body; But this does not well agree with my reason, for I believe that Place, Magnitude and Body are but one thing, and that Place is as true an extension as Magnitude, and not a feigned one; Neither am I of his opinion, that Place is Immovable, but that place moves, according as the body moves, for not any body wants place, because place and body is but one thing, and wheresoever is body, there is also place, and wheresoever is place, there is body, as being one and the same; Wherefore Motion cannot be a relinquishing of one place and acquiring another, for there is no such thing as place different from body, but what is called change of place, is nothing but change of corporeal motions; for, say an house stands in such a place, if the house be gone, the place is gone also, as being impossible that the place of the house should remain, when the house is taken away; like as a man when he is gone out of his chamber, his place is gone too.

'Tis true, if the ground or foundation do yet remain, one may say, there stood such an house heretofore, but yet the place of the house is not there really at that present, unless the same house be built up again as it was before, and then it has its place as before; Nevertheless the house being not there, it cannot be said that either place or house are annihilated, viz, when the materials are dissolved, no not when transformed into millions of several other figures, for the house remains still in the power of all those several parts of matter; and as for space, it is only a distance betwixt some parts or bodies; But an Empty place signifies to my opinion Nothing, for if place and body are one and the same, and empty is as much as nothing, then certainly these two words cannot consist together, but are destructive to one another.

Concerning, that your Author says; Two bodies cannot be together in the same place, nor one body in two places at the same time, is very true, for there are no more places than bodies, nor more bodies than places, and this is to be understood as well of the grosser, as the purest parts of nature, of the mind as well as of the body, of the rational and sensitive animate matter as well as of the inanimate, for there is no matter, how pure and subtle soever, but is embodied, and all that has body has place. Likewise I am of his opinion, That one body has always one and the same magnitude; for, in my opinion, magnitude, place and body do not differ, and as place, so magnitude can never be separated from body. But when he speaks of Rest, I cannot believe there is any such thing truly in Nature, for it is impossible to prove, that any thing is without Motion, either consistent, or composing, or dissolving, or transforming motions, or the like, although not altogether perceptible by our senses, for all the Matter is either moving or moved, and although the moved parts are not capable to receive the nature of self-motion from the self-moving parts, yet these self-moving parts, being joined and mixed with all other parts of the moved matter, do always move the same; for the Moved or Inanimate part of Matter, although it is a Part of itself, yet it is so intermixed with the self-moving Animate Matter, as they make but one Body; and though some parts of the Inanimate may be as pure as the Sensitive Animate Matter, yet they are never so subtle as to be self-moving.

Wherefore the Sensitive moves in the Inanimate, and the Rational in the Sensitive, but often the Rational moves in itself. And, although there is no rest in nature, nevertheless Matter could have been without Motion, when as it is impossible that Matter could be without place or magnitude, no more than Variety can be without motion; And thus much at this present: I conclude, and rest,

MADAM,
Your Faithful Friend and Servant.

Letter XVIII

MADAM,
Passing by those Chapters of your Author, that treat of Power and Act, Identity and Difference, Analogism, Angle and Figure, Figures deficient, dimension of Circles, and several others, most of which belong to art, as to Geometry, and the like; I am come to that wherein he discourses of Sense and Animal Motion, saying, That some Natural bodies have in themselves the patterns almost of all things, and others of none at all.

Whereof my opinion is, that the sensitive and rational parts of Matter are the living and knowing parts of Nature, and no part of nature can challenge them only to itself, nor no creature can be sure, that sense is only in Animal-kind, and reason in Man-kind; for can any one think or believe that Nature is ignorant and dead in all her other parts besides Animals? Truly this is a very unreasonable opinion; for no man, as wise as he thinks himself, nay were all Mankind joined into one body, yet they are not able to know it, unless there were no variety of parts in nature, but only one whole and indivisible body, for other Creatures may know and perceive as much as Animals, although they have not the same Sensitive Organs, nor the same manner or way of Perception.

Next your Author says, The cause of Sense or Perception consists herein, that the first organ of sense is touched and pressed; For when the uttermost part of the organ is pressed, it no sooner yields, but the part next within it is pressed also, and in this manner the pressure or motion is propagated through all the parts of the organ to the innermost. And thus also the pressure of the uttermost part proceeds from the pressure of some more remote body, and so continually, till we come to that, from which, as from its fountain, we derive the Phantasm or Idea, that is made in us by our sense: And this, whatsoever it be, is that we commonly call the object; Sense therefore is some Internal motion in the Sentient, Generated by some Internal motion of the Parts of the object, and propagated through all the media to the innermost part of the organ. Moreover there being a resistance or reaction in the organ, by reason of its internal motion against the motion propagated from the object, there is also an endeavor in the organ opposite to the endeavor proceeding from the object, and when that endeavor inwards is the last action in the act of sense, then from the reaction a Phantasm or Idea has its being. This is your Author's opinion, which if it were so, perception could not be effected so suddenly, nay I think the sentient by so many pressures in so many perceptions, would at last be pressed to death, besides the organs would take a great deal of hurt, nay totally be removed out of their places, so as the eye would in time be pressed into the center of the brain; And if there were any Resistance, Reaction or Endeavor in the organ, opposite to the Endeavor of the object, there would, in my opinion, be always a war between the animal senses and the objects, the endeavor of the objects pressing one way, and the senses pressing the other way, and if equal in their strengths, they would make a stop, and the sensitive organs would be very much pained; Truly, Madam, in my opinion, it would be like that Custom which formerly has been used at Newcastle, when a man was married, the guests divided themselves, behind and before the Bridegroom; the one party driving him back, the other forwards, so that one time a Bridegroom was killed in this fashion.

But certainly Nature has a more quick and easy way of giving intelligence and knowledge to her Creatures, and does not use such constraint and force in her actions; Neither is sense or sensitive perception a mere Phantasm or Idea, but a Corporeal action of the sensitive and rational matter, and according to the variation of the objects or patterns, and the sensitive and rational motions, the perception also is various, produced not by external pressure, but by internal self-motion, as I have declared heretofore; and to prove, that the sensitive and rational corporeal motions are the only cause of perception; I say, if those motions in an animal move in another way, and not to such perceptions, then that animal can neither hear, see, taste, smell, nor touch, although all his sensitive organs be perfect, as is evident in a man falling into a swoon, where all the time he is in a swoon, the pressure of the objects is made without any effect; Wherefore, as the sensitive and rational corporeal motions make all that is in nature, so likewise they make perception, as being perception itself, for all self-motion is perception, but all perception is not animal perception, or after an animal way; and therefore sense cannot decay nor die; but what is called a decay or death, is nothing else but a change or alteration of those Motions.

But you will say, Madam, it may be, that one body, as an object, leaves the print of its figure, in the next adjoining body, until it comes to the organ of sense, I answer that then soft bodies only must be pressed, and the object must be so hard as to make a print, and as for rare parts of matter, they are not able to retain a print without self-motion; Wherefore it is not probable that the parts of air should receive a print, and print the same again upon the adjoining part, until the last part of the air print it upon the eye; and that the exterior parts of the organ should print upon the interior, till it come to the center of the Brain, without self-motion.

Wherefore in my opinion, Perception is not caused either by the printing of objects, nor by pressures, for pressures would make a general stop of all natural motions, especially if there were any reaction or resistance of sense; but according to my reason, the sensitive and rational corporeal motions in one body, pattern out the Figure of another body, as of an exterior object, which may be done easily without any pressure or reaction; I will not say, that there is no pressure or reaction in Nature, but pressure and reaction does not make perception, for the sensitive and rational parts of matter make all perception and variety of motion, being the most subtil parts of Nature, as self-moving, as also dividable, and composable, and alterable in their figurative motions, for this Perceptive matter can change its substance into any figure whatsoever in nature, as being not bound to one constant figure. But having treated hereof before, and being to say more of it hereafter, this shall suffice for the present, remaining always,

MADAM,

Your constant Friend and faithful Servant.

Letter XIX

MADAM,

To discourse of the World and Stars, is more than I am able to do, wanting the art of Astronomy and Geometry; wherefore passing by that Chapter of your Author, I am come to that wherein he treats of Light, Heat and Colors; and to give you my opinion of Light, I say, it is not the light of the Sun, that makes an Animal see, for we can see inwardly in Dreams without the Sun's light, but it is the sensitive and rational Motions in the Eye and Brain that make such a figure as Light; For if Light did press upon the Eye, according to your Author's opinion, it might put the Eye into as much pain as Fire does, when it sticks its points into our skin or flesh.

The same may be said of Colors, for the sensitive motions make such a figure, which is such a Color, and such a Figure, which is such a Color; Wherefore Light, Heat and Color, are not bare and bodiless qualities; but such figures made by corporeal self-motions, and are as well real and corporeal objects as other figures are; and when these figures change or alter, it is onely that their motions alter, which may alter and change heat into cold, and light into darkness, and black color into white. But by reason the motions of the Sun are so constant, as the motions of any other kind of Creatures, it is no more subject to be altered than all the World, unless Nature did it by the command of God; for though the Parts of self-moving Matter be alterable, yet all are not altered; and this is the reason, that the figure of Light in our eye and brain is altered, as well as it is alterable, but not the real figure of the Sun, neither does the Sun enter our eyes; and as the Light of the Sun is made or patterned in the eye, so is the light of Glow-worms-tails, and Cats-eyes, that shine in the dark, made not by the Sun's, but their own motions in their own parts; The like when we dream of Light, the sensitive corporeal motions working inwardly, make the figure of light on the inside of the eye, as they did pattern out the figure of light on the out side of the eye when awake, and the objects before them; for the sensitive motions of the eye pattern out the figure of the object in the eye, and the rational motions make the same figure in their own substance.

But there is some difference between those figures that perceive light, and those that are light themselves; for when we sleep, there is made the figure of light, but not from a copy; but when the eye sees light, that figure is made from a copy of the real figure of the Sun; but those lights which are inherent, as in Glow-worms-tails, are original lights, in which is as much difference as between a Man and his Picture; and as for the swiftness of the Motions of light, and the violence of the Motions of fire, it is very probable they are so, but they are a certain particular kind or sort of swift and violent motions; neither will all sorts of swift and violent motions make fire or light, as for example the swift and violent Circular motion of a Whirlwind neither makes light nor fire; Neither is all fire light, nor all light fire, for there is a sort of dead fire, as in Spices, Spirits, Oils, and the like; and several sorts of lights, which are not hot, as the light which is made in Dreams, as also the inherent lights in Glow-worms, Cats-eyes, Fish-bones, and the like; all which several fires and lights are made by the self-moving matter and motions distinguishable by their figures, for those Motions make such a figure for the Suns light, such a figure for Glow-worms light, such a figure for Cats-eyes light, and so some alteration in every sort of light; The same for Fire, only Fire-light is a mixed figure, as partly of the figure of Fire, and partly of the figure of Light: Also Colors are made after the like manner, viz. so many several Colors, so many several Figures; and as these Figures are less or more different, so are the Colors.

Thus, Madam, whosoever will study Nature, must consider the Figures of every Creature, as well as their Motions, and must not make abstractions of Motion and Figure from Matter, nor of Matter from Motion and Figure, for they are inseparable, as being but one thing, viz. Corporeal Figurative Motions; and whosoever conceives any of them as abstract, will, in my opinion, very much err; but men are apt to make more difficulties and enforcements in nature than nature ever knew.

But to return to Light: There is no better argument to prove that all objects of sight are figured in the Eye, by the sensitive, voluntary or self-motions, without the pressure of objects, but that not only the pressure of light would hurt the tender Eye, but that the eye does not see all objects according to their Magnitude, but sometimes bigger, sometimes less: as for example, when the eye looks through a small passage, as a Prospective-glass, by reason of the difficulty of seeing a body through a small hole, and the double figure of the glass being convex and concave, the corporeal motions use more force, by which the object is enlarged, like as a spark of fire by force is dilated into a great fire, and a drop of water by blowing into a bubble; so the corporeal motions do double and treble their strength, making the Image of the object exceeding large in the eye; for though the eye be contracted, yet the Image in the eye is enlarged to a great extension; for the sensitive and rational matter is extremely subtle, by reason it is extremely pure, by which it has more means and ways of magnifying than the Perspective-glass. But I intend to write more of this subject in my next, and so I break off here, resting,

MADAM,

Your Faithful Friend and Servant.

Letter XX

MADAM,

Some perhaps will question the truth or probability of my saying, that Light is a Body, objecting that if light were a body, when the Sun is absent or retires under our Horizon, its light would leave an empty place, or if there were no empty place but all full, the light of the Sun at its return would not have room to display itself, especially in so great a compass as it does, for two bodies cannot be in one place at one time. I answer, all bodies carry their places along with them, for body and place go together and are inseparable, and when the light of the Sun is gone, darkness succeeds, and when darkness is gone, light succeeds, so that it is with light and darkness as with all Creatures else; For you cannot believe, that if the whole World were removed, there would be a place of the world left, for there cannot be an empty nothing, no more than there can be an empty something; but if the world were annihilated, the place would be annihilated too, place and body being one and the same thing; and therefore in my opinion, there be no more places than there are bodies, nor no more bodies than there are places.

Secondly, They will think it absurd that I say, the eye can see without light; but in my opinion it seems not absurd, but very rational, for we may see in dreams, and some do see in the dark, not in their fancy or imagination, but really; and as for dreams, the sensitive corporeal motions make a light on the inside of the organ of sight really, as I have declared in my former Letter. But that we do not see ordinarily without exterior Light, the reason is, that the sensitive Motions cannot find the outward objects to pattern out without exterior light, but all perception does not proceed from light, for all other perception besides animal sight requires not light.

Neither in my opinion, does the Perception of sight in all Creatures but Animals, but yet Animals do often see in the dark, and in sleep: I will not say but that the animate matter which by self-motion does make the Perception of light with other perceptive Figures, and so animal perceptive light may be the presenter or ground perceptive figure of sight; yet the sensitive corporeal motions can make other figures without the help of light, and such as light did never present: But when the eye patterns out an exterior object presented by light, it patterns also out the object of light; for the sensitive motions can make many figures by one act, not only in several organs, but in one organ; as for example, there is presented to sight a piece of Embroidery, wherein is silk, silver and gold upon Satin in several forms or figures, as several flowers, the sensitive motions straight by one and the same act, pattern out all those several figures of flowers, as also the figures of Silk, Silver, Gold and Satin, without any pressure of these objects, or motions in the medium, for if they all should press, the eye would no more see the exterior objects, than the nose, being stopped, could smell a presented perfume;

Thirdly, They may ask me, if sight be made in the eye, and proceeds not from the outward object, what is the reason that we do not see inwardly, but outwardly as from us? I answer, when we see objects outwardly, as from us, then the sensitive motions work on the outside of the organ, which organ being outwardly convex, causes us to see outwardly, as from us, but in dreams we see inwardly; also the sensitive motions do pattern out the distance together with the object: But you will say, the body of the distance, as the air, cannot be perceived, and yet we can perceive the distance.

I answer, you could not perceive the distance, but by such or such an object as is subject to your sight; for you do not see the distance more than the air, or the like rare body, that is between grosser objects; for if there were no stars, nor planets, nor clouds, nor earth, nor water, but only air, you would not see any space or distance; but light being a more visible body than air, you might figure the body of air by light, but so, as in an extensive or dilating way; for when the mind or the rational matter conceives any thing that has not such an exact figure, or is not so perceptible by our senses; then the mind uses art, and makes such figures, which stand like to that; as for example, to express infinite to itself, it dilates it parts without alteration, and without limitation or circumference; Likewise, when it will conceive a constant succession of Time, it draws out its parts into the figure of a line; and if eternity, it figures a line without beginning and end. But as for Immaterial, no mind can conceive that, for it cannot put itself into nothing, although it can dilate and rarefy itself to an higher degree, but must stay within the circle of natural bodies, as I within the circle of your Commands, to express myself,

MADAM,

Your faithful Friend and obedient Servant.

Letter XXI

MADAM,

Heat and Cold, according to your Author's opinion, are made by Dilation and Contraction: for says he, When the Motion of the ambient ethereal substance makes the spirits and fluid parts of our bodies tend outwards, we acknowledge heat, but by the endeavor inwards of the same spirits and humors we feel cold: so that to cool is to make the exterior parts of the body endeavor inwards, by a motion contrary to that of calefaction, by which the internal parts are called outwards. He therefore that would know the cause of Cold, must find by what motion the exterior parts of any body endeavor to retire inwards.

But I desire you to consider, Madam, that there be moist Colds, and dry Heats, as well as dry Colds, and moist Heats; wherefore all sorts of Cold are not made by the retiring of parts inwards, which is contraction or attraction; neither are all sorts of Heat made by parts tending outwards, which is dilation or rarefaction; for a moist cold is made by dilation, and a dry heat by contraction, as well as a moist heat is made by dilation, and a dry cold by contraction: But your Author makes not this difference, but only a difference between a dilated heat, and a contracted cold; but because a cold wind is made by breath blown through pinched or contracted lips, and an hot wind by breath through opened and extended lips, should we judge that all heat and cold must be made after one manner or way? The contracted mouth makes Wind as well as the dilated, but yet Wind is not made that way, as heat and cold; for it may be, that only the air pressed together makes wind, or it may be that the corporeal motions in the air may change air into wind, as they change water into vapor, and vapor into air; or it may be something else that is invisible and rare, as air; and there may be several sorts of wind, air, heat, cold, as of all other Creatures, more than man is capable to know. As for your Author's opinion concerning the congealing of Water, and how Ice is made, I will not contradict it, only I think nature has an easier way to effect it, than he describes. Wherefore my opinion is, that it is done by altering motions; as for example, the corporeal motions making the figure of water by dilation in a Circle figure, only alter from such a dilating circular figure into a contracted square, which is Ice, or into such a contracted triangle, as is snow: And thus water and vapor may be changed with ease, without any forcing, pressing, raking, or the like.

The same may be said of hard and bent bodies; and of restitution, as also of air, thunder and lightning, which are all done by an easy change of motion, and changing into such or such a figure is not the motion of Generation, which is to build a new house with old materials, but only a Transformation; I say a new house with old materials; not that I mean there is any new Creation in nature, of any thing that was not before in nature; for nature is not God, to make new beings out of nothing, but any thing may be called new, when it is altered from one figure into another. I add no more at this time, but rest,

MADAM,

Your faithful Friend and Servant.

Letter XXII

MADAM,

The Generation of sound, according to your worthy Author's opinion, is as follows: As Vision, says he, so hearing is Generated by the medium, but but not in the same manner; for sight is from pressure, that is, from an endeavor, in which there is no perceptible progression of any of the parts of the medium, but one part urging or thrusting on another, propagates that action successively to any distance whatsoever; where as the motion of the medium, by which sound is made, is a stroke; for when we hear, the drum of the Ear, which is the first organ of hearing, is struck, and the drum being stricken, the *Pia Mater* is also shaken, and with it the arteries inserted into it, by which the action propagated to the heart itself, by the reaction of the heart a Phantasm is made which we call Sound.

Thus far your Author: To which give me leave to reply, that I fear, if the Ear was bound to hear any loud Music, or another sound a good while, it would soundly be beaten, and grow sore and bruised with so many strokes; but since a pleasant sound would be rendered very unpleasant in this manner, my opinion is, that like as in the Eye, so in the Ear the corporeal sensitive motions do pattern out as many several figures, as sounds are presented to them; but if these motions be irregular, then the figure of the sound in the ear is not perfect according to the original; for if it be, that the motions are tired with figuring, or the object of sound be too far distant from the sensitive organ, then they move slowly and weakly, not that they are tired or weak in strength, but with working and repeating one and the same object, and so through love to variety, change from working regularly to move irregularly, so as not to pattern outward objects as they ought, and then there are no such patterns made at all, which we call to be deaf; and sometimes the sensitive motions do not so readily perceive a soft sound near, as a stronger farther off. But to prove it is not the outward object of sound with its striking or pressing motion, nor the medium, that causes this perception of sense, if there be a great solid body, as a wall, or any other partition betwixt two rooms, parting the object and the sensitive organ, so, as the sound is not able to press it, nevertheless the perception will be made.

And as for pipes to convey sounds, the perception is more fixed and perfecter in united than in dilated or extended bodies, and then the sensitive motions can make perfecter patterns; for the stronger the objects are, the more perfect are the figures and patterns of the objects, and the more perfect is the perception. But when the sound is quite out of the ear, then the sensitive motions have altered the patterning of such figures to some other action; and when the sound fades by degrees, then the figure or pattern alters by degrees; but for the most part the sensitive corporeal motions alter according as the objects are presented, or the perception patterns out. Neither do they usually make figures of outward objects, if not perceived by the senses, unless through Irregularities as in Mad men, which see such and such things, when as these things are not near, and then the sensitive motions work by rote, or after their own voluntary invention. As for Reflection, it is a double perception, and so a double figure of one object; like as many pictures of one man, where some are more perfect than others, for a copy of a copy is not so perfect as a copy of an original. But the recoiling of sound is, that the sensitive motions in the ear begin a new pattern, before they dissolved the former, so as there is no perfect alteration or change, from making to dissolving, but pattern is made upon pattern, which causes a confusion of figures, the one being neither perfectly finished, nor the other perfectly made. But it is to be observed, that not always the sensitive motions in the organs take their pattern from the original, but from copies; as for example, the sensitive motions in the eye, pattern out the figure of an eye in a glass, and so do not take a pattern from the original itself, but by another pattern, representing the figure of the eye in a Looking-glass; The same does the Ear, by patterning out Echoes, which is but a pattern of a pattern; But when as a man hears himself speak or make a sound, then the corporeal sensitive motions in the Ear, pattern out the object or figure made by the motions of the tongue and the throat, which is voice; By which we may observe, that there may be many figures made by several motions from one original; as for example, the figure of a word is made in a man's mouth, then the copy of that figure is made in the ear, then in the brain, and then in the memory, and all this in one Man.

Also a word being made in a man's mouth, the air takes a copy or many copies thereof; but the Ear patterns them both out, first the original coming from the mouth, and then the copy made in the air, which is called an Echo, and yet not any strikes or touches each others parts, only perceives and patterns out each others figure. Neither are their substances the same, although the figures be alike; for the figure of a man may be carved in wood, then cut in brass, then in stone, and so forth, where the figure may be always the same, although the substances which do pattern out the figure are several, viz. Wood, Brass, Stone, &c. and so likewise may the figure of a stone be figured in the fleshy substance of the Eye, or the figure of light or color, and yet the substance of the Eye remains still the same; neither does the substantial figure of a stone, or tree, patterned out by the sensitive corporeal motions, in the flesh of an animal eye, change from being a vegetable or mineral, to an animal, and if this cannot be done by nature, much less by art; for if the figure of an animal be carved in wood or stone, it does not give the wood or stone any animal knowledge, nor an animal substance, as flesh, bones, blood, &c. no more does the patterning or figuring of a Tree give a vegetable knowledge, or the substance of wood to the eye, for the figure of an outward object does not alter the substance that patterns it out or figures it, but the patterning substance does pattern out the figure, in itself, or in its own substance, so as the figure which is pattern'd, has the same life and knowledge with the substance by and in which it is figured or pattern'd, and the inherent motions of the same substance; and according as the sensitive and rational self-moving matter moves, so figures are made; and thus we see, that lives, knowledges, motions and figures are all material, and all Creatures are endued with life, knowledge, motion and figure, but not all alike or after the same manner. But to conclude this discourse of perception of Sound, the Ear may take the object of sound afar off, as well as at a near distance; not only if many figures of the same sound be made from that great distance, but if the interposing parts be not so thick, close, or many as to hinder or obscure the object from the animal Perception in the sensitive organ; for if a man lays his Ear near to the Ground, the Ear may hear at a far distance, as well as the Eye can see, for it may hear the noise of a troop afar off, perception being very subtle and active.

Also there may several Copies be made from the Original, and from the last Copy nearest to the Ear, the Ear may take a pattern, and so pattern out the noise in the organ, without any strokes to the Ear, for the subtle matter in all Creatures does inform and perceive. But this is well to be observed, that the figures of objects are as soon made, as perceived by the sensitive motions in their work of patterning. And this is my Opinion concerning the Perception of Sound, which together with the rest I leave to your Ladyships and others wiser Judgment, and rest,

MADAM,

Your faithful Friend and Servant.

Letter XXIII

MADAM,

I perceive by your last, that you cannot well apprehend my meaning, when I say that the print or figure of a Body Printed or Carved, is not made by the motions of the body Printing or Carving it, but by the motions of the body or substance Printed or Carved; for say you, Does a piece of Wood carve itself, or a black Patch of a Lady cut its own figure by its own motions? Before I answer you, Madam, give me leave to ask you this question, whether it be the motion of the hand, or the Instrument, or both, that print or carve such or such a body? Perchance you will say, that the motion of the hand moves the Instrument, and the Instrument moves the Wood which is to be carved: Then I ask, whether the motion that moves the Instrument, be the Instruments, or the Hands? Perchance you will say the Hands; but I answer, how can it be the Hands motion, if it be in the Instrument?

You will say, perhaps, the motion of the hand is transferred out of the hand into the instrument, and so from the instrument into the carved figure; but give me leave to ask you, was this motion of the hand, that was transferred, Corporeal or Incorporeal? If you say, Corporeal, then the hand must become less and weak, but if Incorporeal, I ask you, how a bodiless motion can have force and strength to carve and cut? But put an Impossible proposition, as that there is an Immaterial motion, and that this Incorporeal motion could be transferred out of one body into another; then I ask you, when the hand and instrument cease to move, what is become of the motion? Perhaps you will say, the motion perishes or is annihilated, and when the hand

and the instrument do move again, to the carving or cutting of the figure, then a new Incorporeal Motion is created.

Truly then there will be a perpetual creation and annihilation of Incorporeal motions, that is, of that which naturally is nothing; for an Incorporeal being is as much as a natural No-thing, for Natural reason cannot know nor have naturally any perception or Idea of an Incorporeal being: besides, if the motion be Incorporeal, then it must needs be a supernatural Spirit, for there is not any thing else Immaterial but they, and then it will be either an Angel or a Devil, or the Immortal Soul of man; but if you say it is the supernatural Soul, truly I cannot be persuaded that the supernatural Soul should not have any other employment than to carve or cut prints, or figures, or move in the hands, or heels, or legs, or arms of a Man; for other animals have the same kind of Motions, and then they might have a Supernatural Soul as well as Man, which moves in them. But if you say, that these transferable motions are material, then every action whereby the hand moves to the making or moving of some other body, would lessen the number of the motions in the hand, and weaken it, so that in the writing of one letter, the hand would not be able to write a second letter, at least not a third. But I pray, Madam, consider rationally, that though the Artificer or Workman be the occasion of the motions of the carved body, yet the motions of the body that is carved, are they which put themselves into such or such a figure, or give themselves such or such a print as the Artificer intended; for a Watch, although the Artist or Watch-maker be the occasional cause that the Watch moves in such or such an artificial figure, as the figure of a Watch, yet it is the Watches own motion by which it moves; for when you carry the Watch about you, certainly the Watch-maker's hand is not then with it as to move it; or if the motion of the Watch-makers hand be transferred into the Watch, then certainly the Watch-maker cannot make another Watch, unless there be a new creation of new motions made in his hands; so that God and Nature would be as much troubled and concerned in the making of Watches, as in the making of a new World; for God created this World in six days, and rested the seventh day, but this would be a perpetual Creation.

Wherefore I say that some things may be Occasional causes of other things, but not the Prime or Principal causes; and this distinction is very well to be considered, for there are no frequenter mistakes than to confound these two different causes, which make so many confusions in natural Philosophy; and this is the Opinion of,

MADAM,

Your Faithful Friend and Servant.

Letter XXIV

MADAM,

In answer to your question, What makes Echo, I say, it is that which makes all the effects of Nature, viz. self-moving matter; I know, the common opinion is, that Echo is made like as the figure of a Face, or the like, in a Looking-glass, and that the Reverberation of sound is like the Reflection of sight in a Looking-glass; But I am not of that opinion, for both Echo, and that which is called the Reflection in a Looking-glass, are made by the self-moving matter, by way of patterning and copying out. But then you will ask me, whether the glass takes the copy of the face, or the face prints its copy on the glass, or whether it be the medium of light and air that makes it?

I answer, although many Learned men say, that as all perception, so also the seeing of ones face in a Looking-glass, and Echo, are made by impression and reaction; yet I cannot in my simplicity conceive it, how bodies that come not near, or touch each other, can make a figure by impression and reaction: They say it proceeds from the motions of the Medium of light, or air, or both, viz. that the Medium is like a long stick with two ends, whereof one touches the object, the other the organ of sense, and that one end of it moving, the other moves also at the same point of Time, by which motions it may make many several figures; But I cannot conceive, how this motion of pressing forward and backward should make so many figures, wherein there is so much variety and curiosity.

But, say light and air are as one figure, and like as a seal do print another body; I answer, if any thing could print, yet it is not probable, that so soft and rare bodies as light and air, could print such solid bodies as glass, nor could air by reverberation make such a sound as Echo. But mistake me not, for, I do not say, that the Corporeal motions of light or air, cannot, or do not pencil, copy, or pattern out any figure, for both light and air are very active in such sorts of Motions, but I say, they cannot do it on any other bodies but their own. But to cut off tedious and unnecessary disputes, I return to the expressing of my own opinion, and believe, that the glass in its own substance does figure out the copy of the face, or the like, and from that copy the sensitive motions in the eyes take another copy, and so the rational from the sensitive; and in this manner is made both rational and sensitive perception, sight and knowledge. The same with Echoes; for the air patterns out the copy of the sound, and then the sensitive corporeal motions in the ear pattern again this copy from the air, and so do make the perception and sense of hearing.

You may ask me, Madam, if it be so, that the glass and the air copy out the figure of the face and of sound, whether the Glass may be said to see and the Air to speak? I answer, I cannot tell that; for though I say, that the air repeats the words, and the glass represents the face, yet I cannot guess what their perceptions are, only this I may say, that the air has an elemental, and the glass a mineral, but not an animal perception. But if these figures were made by the pressures of several objects or parts, and by reaction, there could not be such variety as there is, for they could but act by one sort of motion: Likewise is it improbable, that sounds, words or voices, should like a company of Wild-Geese fly in the air, and so enter into the ears of the hearers, as they into their nests: Neither can I conceive, how in this manner a word can enter so many ears, that is, be divided into every ear, and yet strike every ear with an undivided vocal sound.

You will say, as a small fire does heat and warm all those that stand by; for the heat issues from the fire, as the light from the Sun. I answer, all what issues and has motion, has a Body, and yet most learned men deny that sound, light and heat have bodies: But if they grand of light that it has a body, they say it moves and presses the air, and the air the eye, and so of heat; which if so, then the air must not move to any other motion but light, and only to one sort of light, as the Suns light; for if it did move in any other motion, it would disturb the light; for if a Bird did but fly in the air, it would give all the region of air another motion, and so put out, or alter the light, or at least disturb it; and wind would make a great disturbance in it. Besides, if one body did give another body motion, it must needs give it also substance, for motion is either something or nothing, body or no body, substance or no substance; if nothing, it cannot enter into another body; if something, it must lessen the bulk of the body it quits, and increase the bulk of the body it enters, and so the Sun and Fire with giving light and heat, would become less, for they cannot both give and keep at once, for this is as impossible, as for a man to give to another creature his human Nature, and yet to keep it still.

Wherefore my opinion is for heat, that when many men stand round about a fire, and are heated and warmed by it, the fire does not give them any thing, nor do they receive something from the fire, but the sensitive motions in their bodies pattern out the object of the fires heat, and so they become more or less hot according as their patterns are numerous or perfect; And as for air, it patterns out the light of the Sun, and the sensitive motions in the eyes of animals pattern out the light in the air. The like for Echoes, or any other sound, and for the figures which are presented in a Looking-glass. And thus millions of parts or creatures may make patterns of one or more objects, and the objects neither give nor loose any thing. And this I repeat here, that my meaning of Perception may be the better understood, which is the desire of,

MADAM,

Your faithful Friend and Servant.

Letter XXV

MADAM,

I perceive you are not fully satisfied with my former Letter concerning Echo, and a figure presented in a Looking-glass; for you say, how is it possible, if Echo consists in the ears patterning out of a voice or sound, but that it will make a confusion in all the parts of the air? My answer is, that I doe not say that Echo is only made by the patterning out of the voice or sound, but by repeating the same voice or sound, which repetition is named an Echo, for millions of ears in animals may pattern out a voice or words, and yet never repeat them, and so may millions of parts of the air; wherefore Echo does not consist in the bare patterning out, but in the repetition of the same sound or words, which are pattern'd out; and so some parts of the air may at one and the same time pattern out a sound and not repeat it, and some may both pattern out, and repeat it, but some may neither pattern out, nor repeat it, and therefore the Repetition, not the bare Patterning out is called Echo: Just as when two or more men do answer or mock each other, and repeat each others words, it is not necessary, if there were a thousand standers by, that they should all do the same.

And as for the figure presented in a Looking-glass, I cannot conceive it to be made by pressure and reaction; for although there is both pressure and reaction in nature, and those very frequent among natures Parts, yet they do neither make perception nor production. although both pressure and reaction are made by corporeal self-motions; Wherefore the figure presented in a Looking-glass, or any other smooth glassy body, is, in my opinion, only made by the motions of the Looking-glass, which do both pattern out; and present the figure of an external object in the Glass.

But you will say, why do not the motions of other bodies pattern out, and present the figures of external objects, as well as smooth glassy bodies do? I answer, they may pattern out external objects, for any thing I know; but the reason that their figures are not presented to our eyes, lies partly in the presenting subject itself, partly in our sight; for it is observed, that two things are chiefly required in a subject that will present the figure of an external object; first it must be smooth, even and glassy, next it must not be transparent: the first is manifest by experience; for the subject being rough and uneven, will never be able to present such a figure; as for example, A piece of steel rough and unpolished, although it may perhaps pattern out the figure of an external object, yet it will never present its figure, but as soon as it is polished, and made smooth and glassy, the figure is presently perceived. But this is to be observed, that smooth and glassy bodies do not always pattern out exterior objects exactly, but some better, some worse; like as Painters have not all the same ingenuity; neither do all eyes pattern out all objects exactly; which proves that the perception of sight is not made by pressure and reaction, otherwise there would be no difference, but all eyes would see alike, Next I say, it is observed, that the subject which will present the figure of an external object, must not be transparent; the reason is, that the figure of Light being a substance of a piercing and penetrating quality, has more force on transparent, than on other solid dark bodies, and so disturbs the figure of an external object pattern'd out in a transparent body, and quite over-masters it.

But you will say, you have found by experience, that if you hold a burning Candle before a Transparent glass, although it be in an open Sun-light, yet the figure of light and flame of the Candle will clearly be seen in the Glass. I answer, that it is another thing with the figure of Candle-light, than of a dusk-ish or dark body; for a Candlelight, though it is not of the same sort as the Suns light, yet it is of the same nature and quality, and therefore the Candle-light does resist and oppose the light of the Sun, so that it cannot have so much power over it, as over the figures of other bodies patterned out and presented in Transparent-glass. Lastly, I say, that the fault often-times lies in the perceptive motions of our sight, which is evident by a plain and Concave-glass; for in a plain Looking-glass, the further you go from it, the more your figure presented in the glass seems to draw backward; and in a Concave-glass, the nearer you go to it, the more seems your figure to come forth: which effects are like as an house or tree appears to a Traveler; for, as the man moves from the house or tree, so the house or tree seems to move from the man; or like one that sails upon a Ship, who imagines that the Ship stands still, and the Land moves; when as yet it is the Man and the Ship that moves, and not the House, or Tree, or the Land: so when a Man turns round in a quick motion, or when his head is dizzy, he imagines the room or place, where he is, turns round. Wherefore it is the Inherent Perceptive motions in the Eye, and not the motions in the Looking-glass, which cause these effects. And as for several figures that are presented in one glass, it is absurd to imagine that so many several figures made by so many several motions should touch the eye; certainly this would make such a disturbance, if all figures were to enter or but to touch the eye, as the eye would not perceive any of them, at least not distinctly; Wherefore it is most probable that the glass patterns out those figures, and the sensitive corporeal motions in the eye take again a pattern from those figures patterned out by the glass, and so make copies of copies; but the reason why several figures are presented in one glass in several places, is, that two perfect figures cannot be in one point, nor made by one motion, but by several corporeal motions.

Concerning a Looking-glass, made in the form or shape of a Cylinder, why it represents the figure of an external object in another shape and posture than the object is, the cause is the shape and form of the Glass, and not the patterning motions in the Glass. But this discourse belongs properly to the Optics, wherefore I will leave it to those that are versed in that Art, to inquire and search more after the rational truth thereof. In the mean time, my opinion is, that though the object is the occasion of the figure presented in a Looking-glass, yet the figure is made by the motions of the glass or body that presents it, and that the figure of the glass perhaps may be patterned out as much by the motions of the object in its own substance, as the figure of the object is patterned out and presented by the motions of the glass in its own body or substance. And thus I conclude and rest,

MADAM,

Your Faithful Friend and Servant.

Letter XXVI

MADAM,

Since I mentioned in my last that Light did disturb the figures of External objects presented in Transparent bodies; you were pleased to ask, Whether light does penetrate transparent bodies? I answer, for any thing I know, it may; for when I consider the subtle, piercing and penetrating nature of light, I believe it does; but again, when I consider that light is presented to our sight by transparent bodies only, and not by dusk-ish and dark bodies, and yet that those dusk-ish bodies are more porous than the transparent bodies, so that the light has more passage to pass through them, than through transparent bodies; but that on the contrary, those dark bodies, as Wood, and the like, do quite obscure the light, when as transparent bodies, as Glass, &c. transmit it, I am half persuaded that the transparent bodies, as Glass, rather present the Light by patterning it out, than by giving it passage: Also I am of a mind, that the air in a room may pattern out the Light from the Glass, for the Light in a room does not appear so clear as in the Glass; also if the Glass be any way defective, it does not present the Light so perfectly, whereas, if it were the penetration of light through the glass, the light would pass through all sorts of glass alike, which it does not, but is more clearly seen through some, and more obscurely through others, according to the goodness or purity of the glass.

But you may say, that the light divulges the imperfection or goodness of the glass; I answer, so it does of any other objects perceived by our sight; for light is the presenter of objects to the sense and perception of sight, and for any thing I know, the corporeal optic motions make the figure of light, the ground figure of all other figures patterned out by the corporeal optic motions, as in dreams, or when as some do see in the dark, that is, without the help of exterior light. But you may say, That if the glass and the air in a room did pattern out the figure of light, those patterns of light would remain when light is absent: I answer, That is not usual in nature; for when the object removes, the Pattern alters; I will not say but that the corporeal optic motions may work by rote without objects, but that is irregular, as in some distempers. And thus, Madam, I have given you my opinion also to this your question; if you have any more scruples, I pray let me know of them, and assure your self that I shall be ready upon all occasions to express myself,

MADAM,

Your humble and faithful Servant.

Letter XXVII

MADAM,

Your desire is to know, why sound is louder in a Vault, and in a large Room than in a less? I answer, A Vault or arched Figure is the freest from obstruction, as being without corners and points, so as the sensitive and rational corporeal motions of the Ear can have a better perception; like as the Eye can see farthest from a hill than being upon a level ground, because the prospect is freer from the hill, as without obstruction, unless it be so cloudy that the clouds do hinder the perception; And as the eye can have a better prospect upon a hill, so the ear a stronger perception in a Vault; And as for sound, that it is better perceived in a large, than in a little close room or place, it is somewhat like the perception of sent, for the more the odorous parts are bruised, the stronger is that perception of sent, as being repeated double or treble, which makes the perception stronger, like as a thick body is stronger than a thin one.

So likewise the perception of sound in the air; for though not all the parts of the air make repetitions, yet some or many make patterns of the sound; the truth is, Air is as industrious to divulge or present a found, by patterns to the Ear, as light does objects to the Eye. But then you may ask me, Why a long hollow pipe does convey a voice to the ear more readily, than any large and open place? My answer is, That the Parts of the air in a long pipe are more Composed and not at liberty to wander, so that upon necessity they must move only to the patterning out of the sound, having no choice, which makes the sound much stronger, and the perception of the Ear perfecter; But as for Pipes, Vaults, Prospects, as also figures presented in a room through a little hole, inverted, and many the like, belongs more to Artists than to my study, for though Natural Philosophy gives or points out the Ground, and shews the reason, yet it is the Artist that Works; Besides it is more proper for Mathematicians to discourse of, which study I am not versed in; and so leaving it to them, I rest,

MADAM,
Your faithful Friend and Servant.

Letter XXVIII

MADAM,

From Sound I am come to Scent, in the discourse whereof, your Author is pleased to set down these following propositions: 1. That smelling is hindered by cold and helped by heat; 2. That when the Wind blows from the object, the smell is the stronger, and when it blows from the sentient towards the object, the weaker, which by experience is found in dogs, that follow the track of beasts by the Scent; 3. That such bodies as are least pervious to the fluid medium, yield less smell than such as are more pervious: 4. That such bodies as are of their own nature odorous, become yet more odorous, when they are bruised: 5. That when the breath is stopped (at least in man) nothing can be smelt: 6. That the Sense of smelling is also taken away by the stopping of the Nostrils, though the mouth be left open.

To begin from the last, I say, that the nose is like the other sensitive organs, which if they be stopped, the corporeal sensitive motions cannot take copies of the exterior objects, and therefore must alter their action of patterning to some other, for when the eye is shut and cannot perceive outward objects then it works to the Sense of Touch, or on the inside of the organ to some phantasms; and so do the rest of the Senses. As for the stopping of breath, why it hinders the Scent, the cause is, that the nostrils and the mouth are the chief organs, to receive air and to let out breath: but though they be common passages for air and breath, yet taste is only made in the mouth and tongue, and scent in the nose; not by the pressure of meat, and the odoriferous object, but by patterning out the several figures or objects of scent and taste, for the nose and the mouth will smell and taste one, nay several things at the same time, like as the eye will see light, color, and other objects at once, which I think can hardly be done by pressures; and the reason is, that the sensitive motions in the sensitive organs make patterns of several objects at one time, which is the cause, that when flowers, and such like odoriferous bodies are bruised, there are as many figures made as there are parts bruised or divided, and by reason of so many figures the sensitive knowledge is stronger; but that stones, minerals, and the like, seem not so strong to our smell, the reason is, that their parts being close and united, the sensitive motions in the organ cannot so readily perceive and pattern them out, as those bodies which are more porous and divided. But as for the wind blowing the scent either to or from the sentient, it is like a window or door that by the motion of opening and shutting, hinders or disturbs the sight; for bodies coming between the object and the organ, make a stop of that perception.

And as for the Dogs smelling out the track of Beasts, the cause is, that the earth or ground has taken a copy of that scent, which copy the sensitive motions in the nose of the Dog do pattern out, and so long as that figure or copy lasts, the Dog perceives the scent, but if he does not follow or hunt readily, then there is either no perfect copy made by the ground, or otherwise he cannot find it, which causes him to seek and smell about until he has it; and thus smell is not made by the motion of the air, but by the figuring motions in the nose: Where it is also to be observed, that not only the motions in one, but in millions of noses, may pattern out one little object at one time, and therefore it is not, that the object of scent fills a room by sending out the scent from its substance, but that so many figures are made of that object of scent by so many several sensitive motions, which pattern the same out; and so the air, or ground, or any other creature, whose sensitive motions pattern out the object of scent, may perceive the same, although their sensitive organs are not like to those of animal creatures; for if there be but such sensitive motions and perceptions, it is no matter for such organs.

Lastly, it is to be observed, That all Creatures have not the same strength of smelling, but some smell stronger, some weaker, according to the disposition of their sensitive motions: Also there be other parts in the body, which pattern out the object of scent, besides the nose, but those are interior parts, and take their patterns from the nose as the organ properly designed for it; neither is their resentment the same, because their motions are not alike, for the stomach may perceive and pattern out a scent with aversion, when the nose may pattern it out with pleasure. And thus much also of Scent; I conclude and rest,

MADAM,

Your faithful Friend and Servant.

Letter XXIX

MADAM,

Concerning your Learned Author's discourse of Density and Rarity, he defines Thick to be that, which takes up more parts of a space given; and thin, which contains fewer parts of the same magnitude: not that there is more matter in one place than in another equal place, but a greater quantity of some named body; wherefore the multitude and paucity of the parts contained within the same space do constitute density and rarity.

Where of my opinion is, That there is no more nor less space or place than body according to its dilation or contraction, and that space and place are dilated and contracted with the body, according to the magnitude of the body, for body, place and magnitude are the same thing, only place is in regard of the several parts of the body, and there is as well space betwixt things distant a hairs breadth from one another, as betwixt things distant a million of miles, but yet this space is nothing from the body; but it makes, that that body has not the same place with this body, that is, that this body is not that body, and that this bodies place is not that bodies place. Next your Author says, He has already clearly enough demonstrated, that there can be no beginning of motion, but from an external and moved body, and that heavy bodies being once cast upwards cannot be cast down again, but by external motion. Truly, Madam, I will not speak of your Author's demonstrations, for it is done most by art, which I have no knowledge in, but I think I have probably declared, that all the actions of nature are not forced by one part, driving, pressing, or shoving another, as a man does a wheel-barrow, or a whip a horse; nor by reactions, as if men were at foot-ball or cuffs, or as men with carts meeting each other in a narrow lane.

But to prove there is no self-motion in nature, he goes on and says; To attribute to created bodies the power to move themselves, what is it else, than to say that there be creatures which have no dependence upon the Creator? To which I answer, That if man, (who is but a single part of nature) has given him by God the power and a free will of moving himself, why should not God give it to Nature? Neither can I see, how it can take off the dependence upon God, more than Eternity; for if there be an Eternal Creator, there is also an Eternal Creature, and if an Eternal Master, an Eternal Servant, which is Nature; and yet Nature is subject to God's Command, and depends upon him; and if all God's Attributes be Infinite, then his Bounty is Infinite also, which cannot be exercised but by an Infinite Gift, but a Gift does not cause a less dependence. I do not say, That man has an absolute Free-will, or power to move, according to his desire; for it is not conceived, that a part can have an absolute power: nevertheless his motion both of body and mind is a free and self-motion, and such a self-motion has every thing in Nature according to its figure or shape; for motion and figure, being inherent in matter, matter moves figuratively. Yet do I not say, That there is no hindrance, obstruction and opposition in nature; but as there is no particular Creature, that has an absolute power of self-moving; so that Creature which has the advantage of strength, subtlety, or policy, shape, or figure, and the like, may oppose and over-power another which is inferior to it, in all this; yet this hindrance and opposition does not take away self-motion.

But I perceive your Author is much for necessitation, and against free-will, which I leave to Moral Philosophers and Divines. And as for the ascending of light, and descending of heavy bodies, there may be many causes, but these four are perceivable by our senses, as bulk, or quantity of body, grossness of substance, density, and shape or figure, which make heavy bodies descend: But little quantity, purity of substance, rarity, and figure or shape make light bodies ascend. Wherefore I cannot believe, that there are certain little bodies as atoms, and by reason of their smallness, invisible, differing from one another in consistence, figure, motion and magnitude, intermingled with the air, which should be the cause of the descending of heavy bodies. And concerning air, whether it be subject to our senses or not, I say, that if air be neither hot, nor cold, it is not subject; but if it be, the sensitive motions will soon pattern it out, and declare it. I'll conclude with your Author's question, What the cause is, that a man does not feel the weight of Water in Water? and answer, it is the dilating nature of Water. But of this question and of Water I shall treat more fully hereafter, and so I rest,

MADAM,

Your faithful Friend and Servant.

5. John Locke's (1632–1704) Essay Concerning Human Understanding (1689)

- The Project of the *Essay*
- *Against Innate Knowledge*
- Ideas and their Origin
- Simple ideas
- Primary and Secondary Qualities
- Complex Ideas
- Substance/substratum
- Natural kinds
- Body
- Mind
- Personal Identity
- The Limits of Knowledge
- God

As Locke admits, his Essay is something of a mess, from an editorial point of view. What follows are what I take to be some of the most important passages from the book, grouped under topical headings in an attempt to make a coherent and systematic whole. Parts and headings are given in bold and are purely my invention. Section headings are given in italics, and are Locke's. Otherwise, all material in italics is mine, not Locke's. '...' indicates an omission.

The Essay is organized into Books, Chapters, and Sections. The start of each section cites book.chapter.section. For example, 'I.i.5' means Book I, chapter i, section 5.

(Textual note: the standard edition of the Essay is that of P.H. Nidditch (Oxford, 1975); but Roger Woolhouse's Penguin edition is superior in some respects.)

<!–The headings are as follows:

A. The Project

B. Against Innate Knowledge

C. Ideas and their Origin

D. Simple Ideas

E. Primary and Secondary Qualities

F. Complex Ideas

G. Substance/substratum

H. Natural Kinds

I. Body

J. Mind

K. Personal Identity

L. The Limits of Knowledge

M. God–>

(From *The Epistle to the Reader*) Were it fit to trouble thee with the history of this Essay, I should tell thee, that five or six friends meeting at my chamber, and discoursing on a subject very remote from this, found themselves quickly at a stand, by the difficulties that rose on every side. After we had awhile puzzled ourselves, without coming any nearer a resolution of those doubts which perplexed us, it came into my thoughts that we took a wrong course; and that before we set ourselves upon inquiries of that nature, it was necessary to examine our own abilities, and see what **objects** our understandings were, or were not, fitted to deal with. ...

The commonwealth of learning is not at this time without master-builders, whose mighty designs, in advancing the sciences, will leave lasting monuments to the admiration of posterity: but every one must not hope to be a Boyle or a Sydenham; and in an age that produces such masters as the great Huygenius and the incomparable Mr. Newton, with some others of that strain, it is ambition enough to be employed as an under-labourer in clearing the ground a little, and removing some of the rubbish that lies in the way to knowledge ...

(From I.i.1—*An Inquiry into the Understanding pleasant and useful*) Since it is the **understanding** that sets man above the rest of sensible beings, and gives him all the advantage and dominion which he has over them; it is certainly a subject, even for its nobleness, worth our labour to inquire into. The understanding, like the eye, whilst it makes us see and perceive all other things, takes no notice of itself; and it requires and art and pains to set it at a distance and make it its own object. ...

(From I.i.2—*Design*) This, therefore, being my purpose—to inquire into the original, certainty, and extent of **human knowledge**, together with the grounds and degrees of **belief**, **opinion**, and **assent** ...

(From I.i.3—*Method*) It is therefore worth while to search out the bounds between opinion and knowledge; and examine by what measures, in things whereof we have no certain knowledge, we ought to regulate our assent and moderate our persuasion. In order whereunto I shall pursue this following method: First, I shall inquire into the original of those ideas, notions, or whatever else you please to call them, which a man observes, and is conscious to himself he has in his mind; and the ways whereby the understanding comes to be furnished with them. Secondly, I shall endeavour to show what knowledge the understanding hath by those ideas; and the certainty, evidence, and extent of it. Thirdly, I shall make some inquiry into the nature and grounds of **faith** or **opinion**: whereby I mean that assent which we give to any proposition as true, of whose truth yet we have no certain knowledge. And here we shall have occasion to examine the reasons and degrees of **assent**.

(From I.i.4—*Useful to know the Extent of our Comprehension*) If we can find out how far the understanding can extend its view; how far it has faculties to attain certainty; and in what cases it can only judge and guess, we may learn to content ourselves with what is attainable by us in this state.

(From I.i.5—*Our Capacity suited to our State and Concerns*) It will be no excuse to an idle and untoward servant, who would not attend his business by candle light, to plead that he had not broad sunshine. The Candle that is set up in us shines bright enough for all our purposes.

(From I.i.6—*Knowledge of our Capacity a Cure of Scepticism and Idleness*) When we know our own strength, we shall the better know what to undertake with hopes of success; and when we have well surveyed the **powers** of our own minds, and made some estimate what we may expect from them, we shall not be inclined either to sit still, and not set our thoughts on work at all, in despair of knowing anything; nor on the other side, question everything, and disclaim all knowledge, because some things are not to be understood. It is of great use to the sailor to know the length of his line, though he cannot with it fathom all the depths of the ocean. It is well he knows that it is long enough to reach the bottom, at such places as are necessary to direct his voyage, and caution him against running upon shoals that may ruin him. Our business here is not to know all things, but those which concern our conduct. If we can find out those measures, whereby a rational creature, put in that state in which man is in this world, may and ought to govern his opinions, and actions depending thereon, we need not to be troubled that some other things escape our knowledge.

---

1. *What is Locke's main project in the Essay?*
2. *What's the point of pursuing it? What advantages does he expect to obtain from it?*
3. *What is distinctive about Locke's project? What would Locke think of the method of, say, Spinoza?*

Against Innate Knowledge

Given Locke's project, it makes sense that he begins by attacking the doctrine of innate knowledge. This attack was partly responsible for the Essay's being banned at Oxford in 1704. Can you think why these thoughts might sound dangerous, and why Locke's project begins where it does?

(From I.ii.5–*Not on Mind naturally imprinted, because not known to Children, Idiots, &c.*) For, first, it is evident, that all children and idiots have not the least apprehension or thought of them. And the want of that is enough to destroy that universal assent which must needs be the necessary concomitant of all innate truths: it seeming to me near a contradiction to say, that there are truths imprinted on the soul, which it perceives or understands not: imprinting, if it signify anything, being nothing else but the making certain truths to be perceived. For to imprint anything on the mind without the mind's perceiving it, seems to me hardly intelligible. If therefore children and idiots have souls, have minds, with those impressions upon them, *they* must unavoidably perceive them ...

[I]f the capacity of knowing be the natural impression contended for, all the truths a man ever comes to know will, by this account, be every one of them innate; and this great point will amount to no more, but only to a very improper way of speaking; which, whilst it pretends to assert the contrary, says nothing different from those who deny innate principles. For nobody, I think, ever denied that the mind was capable of knowing several truths.

(From I.ii.15–*The Steps by which the Mind attains several Truths*) The senses at first let in **particular** ideas, and furnish the yet empty cabinet, and the mind by degrees growing familiar with some of them, they are lodged in the memory, and names got to them. Afterwards, the mind proceeding further, abstracts them, and by degrees learns the use of general names. In this manner the mind comes to be furnished with ideas and language, the **materials** about which to exercise its discursive faculty. And the use of reason becomes daily more visible, as these materials that give it employment increase. But though the having of general ideas and the use of general words and reason usually grow together, yet I see not how this any way proves them innate.

(From I.iv.20–*No innate Ideas in the Memory*) To which let me add: if there be any innate ideas, any ideas in the mind which the mind does not actually think on, they must be lodged in the memory; and from thence must be brought into view by remembrance; i.e., must be known, when they are remembered, to have been perceptions in the mind before; unless remembrance can be without remembrance. For, to remember is to perceive anything with memory, or with a consciousness that it was perceived or known before. Without this, whatever idea comes into the mind is new, and not remembered; this consciousness of its having been in the mind before, being that which distinguishes remembering from all other ways of thinking.

Whatever idea was never **perceived** by the mind was never in the mind. Whatever idea is in the mind, is, either an actual perception, or else, having been an actual perception, is so in the mind that, by the memory, it can be made an actual perception again. Whenever there is the actual perception of any idea without memory, the idea appears perfectly new and unknown before to the understanding. Whenever the memory brings any idea into actual view, it is with a consciousness that it had been there before, and was not wholly a stranger to the mind. Whether this be not so, I appeal to every one's observation. And then I desire an instance of an idea, pretended to be innate, which (before any impression of it by ways hereafter to be mentioned) any one could revive and remember, as an idea he had formerly known; without which consciousness of a former perception there is no remembrance; and whatever idea comes into the mind without *that* consciousness is not remembered, or comes not out of the memory, nor can be said to be in the mind before that appearance. For what is not either actually in view or in the memory, is in the mind no way at all, and is all one as if it had never been there. ...

[W]hatever idea, being not actually in view, is in the mind, is there only by being in the memory; and if it be not in the memory, it is not in the mind; and if it be in the memory, it cannot by the memory be brought into actual view without a perception that it comes out of the memory; which is this, that it had been known before, and is now remembered. If therefore there be any innate ideas, they must be in the memory, or else nowhere in the mind; and if they be in the memory, they can be revived without any impression from without; and whenever they are brought into the mind they are remembered, i. E. They bring with them a perception of their not being wholly new to it. ...

By this it may be tried whether there be any innate ideas in the mind before impression from sensation or reflection. I would fain meet with the man who, when he came to the use of reason, or at any other time, remembered any of them; and to whom, after he was born, they were never new. If any one will say, there are ideas in the mind that are *not* in the memory, I desire him to explain himself, and make what he says intelligible.

---

1. *Why is Locke concerned to deny the doctrine of innate principles? Can you connect this with Locke's project?*
2. *Can you extract an argument from these texts that might apply to innate ideas (as opposed to principles)? There seem to be three possible ways to cash out what it means to say that an idea is innate. It might be innate as a capacity; it might always be present to the mind; or it might be lodged in the memory. What does Locke think is wrong with this last option (memory)? (See esp. Chapter 4, Section 20 above—hint: Locke seems to think there's something contradictory about innateness.)*

Premise 1: An innate idea is in the memory.
Premise 2: Any idea in the memory, when recovered, brings with it...

It's one thing to attack the doctrines of innate knowledge and innate ideas; it's another to come up with a replacement for them. Locke must explain how all our ideas are generated solely out of the materials given to us in experience, and how experience alone can justify our knowledge claims.

(From I.1.8–*What Idea stands for*) Thus much I thought necessary to say concerning the occasion of this inquiry into human understanding. But, before I proceed on to what I have thought on this subject, I must here in the entrance beg pardon of my reader for the frequent use of the word **idea**, which he will find in the following treatise. It being that term which, I think, serves best to stand for whatsoever is the **object** of the understanding when a man thinks, I have used it to express whatever is meant by **phantasm, notion, species**, or **whatever** it is **which the mind can** be **employed about** in **thinking**; and I could not avoid frequently using it. I presume it will be easily granted me, that there are such **ideas** in men's minds: every one is conscious of them in himself; and men's words and actions will satisfy him that they are in others.

(From IV.xxi.4) [S]ince the things the mind contemplates are none of them, besides itself, present to the understanding, it is necessary that something else, as a sign or representation of the thing it considers, should be present to it: and these are **ideas**.

(From II.i.2–*All Ideas come from Sensation or Reflection*) Let us then suppose the mind to be, as we say, white paper, void of all characters, without any ideas: how comes it to be furnished? ... To this I answer, in one word, from **experience**. In that all our knowledge is founded; and from that it ultimately derives itself. Our observation employed either, about external sensible objects, or about the internal operations of our minds perceived and reflected on by ourselves, is that which supplies our understandings with all the **materials** of thinking. These two are the fountains of knowledge, from whence all the ideas we have, or can naturally have, do spring.

(From II.i.3–*The Objects of Sensation one Source of Ideas*) First, our senses, conversant about particular sensible objects, do convey into the mind several distinct perceptions of things, according to those various ways wherein those objects do affect them. And thus we come by those **ideas** we have of yellow, white, heat, cold, soft, hard, bitter, sweet, and all those which we call sensible qualities ...

(From II.i.4–*The Operations of our Minds, the other Source of them*) Secondly, the other fountain from which experience furnisheth the understanding with ideas is, the perception of the operations of our own mind within us, as it is employed about the ideas it has got. ... And such are perception, thinking, doubting, believing, reasoning, knowing, willing, and all the different actings of our own minds ...

(From II.i.5–*All our Ideas are of the one or of the other of these*) ... These, when we have taken a full survey of them, and their several modes, and the compositions made out of them we shall find to contain all our whole stock of ideas; and that we have nothing in our minds which did not come in one of these two ways. Let any one examine his own thoughts, and thoroughly search into his understanding; and then let him tell me, whether all the original ideas he has there, are any other than of the objects of his senses, or of the operations of his mind, considered as objects of his reflection.

Locke thinks that sensation and reflection are our only sources of ideas. We should now look at his response to Descartes's argument for a third source of ideas, namely, the intellect (see the second paragraph of the Sixth Meditation.

(From II.xxix.13–*Complex ideas may be distinct in one part, and confused in another*) Our complex ideas, being made up of collections, and so variety of simple ones, may accordingly be very clear and distinct in one part, and very obscure and confused in another. In a man who speaks of a chiliaedron, or a body of a thousand sides, the ideas of the figure may be very confused, though that of the number be very distinct; so that he being able to discourse and demonstrate concerning that part of his complex idea which depends upon the number of thousand, he is apt to think he has a distinct idea of a chiliaedron; though it be plain he has no precise idea of its figure, so as to distinguish it, by that, from one that has but 999 sides: the not observing whereof causes no small error in men's thoughts, and confusion in their discourses.

---

1. *How does Locke respond to Descartes's argument for the distinction between the intellect and the imagination? Who is right?*

Simple ideas

(From II.i.1–*Uncompounded Appearances*) The better to understand the nature, manner, and extent of our knowledge, one thing is carefully to be observed concerning the ideas we have; and that is, that some of them, are **simple** and some **complex**.

   Though the qualities that affect our senses are, in the things themselves, so united and blended, that there is no separation, no distance between them; yet it is plain, the ideas they produce in the mind enter by the senses simple; and unmixed. For, though the sight and touch often take in from the same object, at the same time, different ideas;–as a man sees at once motion and colour; the hand feels softness and warmth in the same piece of wax: yet the simple ideas thus united in the same subject, are as perfectly distinct as those that come in by different senses.

   (From II.iii.1–*Division of simple ideas*) The better to conceive the ideas we receive from sensation, it may not be amiss for us to consider them, in reference to the different ways whereby they make their approaches to our minds, and make themselves perceivable by us. **First**, then, there are some which come into our minds by **one sense only. Secondly**, there are others that convey themselves into the mind by **more senses than one. Thirdly**, others that are had from **reflection only. Fourthly**, there are some that make themselves way, and are suggested to the mind by **all the ways of sensation and reflection.**

---

1. *Classify these ideas, according to the above system (II.iii.1):*

    1. the idea of blue _____

    2. the idea of square _____

3. the idea of hoping _____
4. the idea of straight _____

As we'll see, some ideas turn out to be ideas of powers rather than of qualities. So we'll need a story about how we get our idea of power as a building block, before we can move on to the primary/secondary quality distinction.

(From II.xxi.1–*This Idea [of power] how got*) The mind being every day informed, by the senses, of the alteration of those simple ideas it observes in things without; and taking notice how one comes to an end, and ceases to be, and another begins to exist which was not before; reflecting also on what passes within itself, and observing a constant change of its ideas, sometimes by the impression of outward objects on the senses, and sometimes by the determination of its own choice; and concluding from what it has so constantly observed to have been, that the like changes will for the future be made in the same things, by like agents, and by the like ways, considers in one thing the possibility of having any of its simple ideas changed, and in another the possibility of making that change; and so comes by that idea which we call **power**. Thus we say, fire has a power to melt gold, i.e., to destroy the consistency of its insensible parts, and consequently its hardness, and make it fluid ... In which, and the like cases, the power we consider is in reference to the change of perceivable ideas. For we cannot observe any alteration to be made in, or operation upon anything, but by the observable change of its sensible ideas; nor conceive any alteration to be made, but by conceiving a change of some of its ideas.

(From II.xxi.2–*Power, active and passive*) Power thus considered is two-fold, viz. As able to make, or able to receive any change. The one may be called **active**, and the other **passive** power. Whether matter be not wholly destitute of active power, as its author, God, is truly above all passive power; and whether the intermediate state of created spirits be not that alone which is capable of both active and passive power, may be worth consideration. I shall not now enter into that inquiry, my present business being not to search into the original of power, but how we come by the **idea** of it. But since active powers make so great a part of our complex ideas of natural substances, (as we shall see hereafter,) and I mention them as such, according to common apprehension; yet they being not, perhaps, so truly **active** powers as our hasty thoughts are apt to represent them, I judge it not amiss, by this intimation, to direct our minds to the consideration of god and spirits, for the clearest idea of **active** power.

(From II.xxi.3–*Power includes Relation*) I confess power includes in it some kind of **relation** (a relation to action or change,) as indeed which of our ideas of what kind soever, when attentively considered, does not. For, our ideas of extension, duration, and number, do they not all contain in them a secret relation of the parts? figure and motion have something relative in them much more visibly. ... Our idea therefore of power, I think, may well have a place amongst other **simple ideas**, and be considered as one of them; being one of those that make a principal ingredient in our complex ideas of substances, as we shall hereafter have occasion to observe.

(From II.xxi.4–*The clearest Idea of active Power had from Spirit*) [I]f we will consider it attentively, bodies, by our senses, do not afford us so clear and distinct an idea of active power, as we have from reflection on the operations of our minds. For all power relating to action, and there being but two sorts of action whereof we have an idea, viz. Thinking and motion, let us consider whence we have the clearest ideas of the powers which produce these actions.

1. Of thinking, body affords us no idea at all; it is only from reflection that we have that.

2. Neither have we from body any idea of the beginning of motion. A body at rest affords us no idea of any active power to move; and when it is set in motion itself, that motion is rather a passion than an action in it. For, when the ball obeys the motion of a billiard-stick, it is not any action of the ball, but bare passion. Also when by impulse it sets another ball in motion that lay in its way, it only communicates the motion it had received from another, and loses in itself so much as the other received: which gives us but a very obscure idea of an **active** power of moving in body, whilst we observe it only to **transfer**, but not **produce** any motion.

---

1. *Is the idea of power a simple idea or not? What turns on this?*
2. *How does the mind form an idea of power?*
3. *Why does sensation not give us an idea of active power?*

Primary and Secondary Qualities

II.viii is intended as a further discussion of simple ideas. Locke draws what should by now be a familiar distinction. Can you reconstruct Locke's argument?

(From II.viii.7–*Ideas in the Mind, Qualities in Bodies*) To discover the nature of our **ideas** the better, and to, discourse of them intelligibly, it will be convenient to distinguish them as **they are ideas** or **perceptions in our minds**; and as **they are modifications of matter** in **the bodies that cause such perceptions** in us ...

(From II.viii.8–*Our Ideas and the Qualities of Bodies*) Whatsoever the mind perceives **in itself**, or is the immediate object of perception, thought, or understanding, that I call **idea**; and the power to produce any idea in our mind, I call **quality** of the subject wherein that power is. Thus a snowball having the power to produce in us the ideas of white, cold, and round–the power to produce those ideas in us, as they are in the snowball, I call qualities; and as they are sensations or perceptions in our understandings, I call them ideas; which **ideas**, if I speak of sometimes as in the things themselves, I would be understood to mean those qualities in the objects which produce them in us.

(From II.viii.9–*Primary Qualities of Bodies*) Concerning these qualities, we, I think, observe these primary ones in bodies that produce simple ideas in us, viz. **solidity, extension, motion** or **rest, nubmer** or **figure**. These, which I call **original** or **primary** qualities of body, are wholly inseparable from it; and such as in all the alterations and changes it suffers, all the force can be used upon it, it constantly keeps; and such as sense constantly finds in every particle of matter which has bulk enough to be perceived; and the mind finds inseparable from every particle of matter, though less than to make itself singly be perceived by our senses: e.g., take a grain of wheat, divide it into two parts; each part has still solidity, extension, figure, and mobility: divide it again, and it retains still the same qualities ...

(From II.viii.11–*How Bodies produce Ideas in us*) The next thing to be considered is, how bodies operate one upon another; and that is manifestly by impulse, and nothing else. It being impossible to conceive that body should operate on **what** it **does not touch** (which is all one as to imagine it can operate where it is not), or when it does touch, operate any other way than by motion.

(From II.viii.13—*How secondary Qualities produce their ideas*) After the same manner that the ideas of these original qualities are produced in us, we may conceive that the ideas of **secondary** qualities are also produced, viz. By the operation of insensible particles on our senses. ... [L]et us suppose at present that, the different motions and figures, bulk and number, of such particles, affecting the several organs of our senses, produce in us those different sensations which we have from the colours and smells of bodies ... It being no more impossible to conceive that god should annex such ideas to such motions, with which they have no similitude, than that he should annex the idea of pain to the motion of a piece of steel dividing our flesh, with which that idea hath no resemblance.

(From II.viii.14—*They depend on the primary Qualities*) What I have said concerning colours and smells may be understood also of tastes and sounds, and other the like sensible qualities; which, whatever reality we by mistake attribute to them, are in truth nothing in the objects themselves, but powers to produce various sensations in us; and depend on those primary qualities, viz. Bulk, figure, texture, and motion of parts and therefore I call them **secondary qualities**.

(From II.viii.15—*Ideas of primary Qualities are Resemblances; of secondary, not*) From whence I think it easy to draw this observation, that the ideas of primary qualities of bodies are resemblances of them, and their patterns do really exist in the bodies themselves, but the ideas produced in us by these secondary qualities have no resemblance of them at all. There is nothing like our ideas, existing in the bodies themselves. They are, in the bodies we denominate from them, only a power to produce those sensations in us ...

(From II.viii.17—*The ideas of the Primary alone really exist*) The particular bulk, number, figure, and motion of the parts of fire or snow are really in them, whether any one's senses perceive them or no: and therefore they may be called **real** qualities, because they really exist in those bodies. But light, heat, whiteness, or coldness, are no more really in them than sickness or pain is in manna. Take away the sensation of them; let not the eyes see light or colours, nor the can hear sounds; let the palate not taste, nor the nose smell, and all colours, tastes, odours, and sounds, as **they are such particular ideas**, vanish and cease, and are reduced to their causes, i.e., bulk, figure, and motion of parts.

(From II.viii.19—*Examples*) Let us consider the red and white colours in porphyry. Hinder light from striking on it, and its colours vanish; it no longer produces any such ideas in us: upon the return of light it produces these appearances on us again. Can any one think any real alterations are made in the porphyry by the presence or absence of light; and that those ideas of whiteness and redness are really in porphyry in the light, when it is plain it **has no colour in the dark**? It has, indeed, such a configuration of particles, both night and day, as are apt, by the rays of light rebounding from some parts of that hard stone, to produce in us the idea of redness, and from others the idea of whiteness; but whiteness or redness are not in it at any time, but such a texture that hath the power to produce such a sensation in us.

(From II.viii.20) Pound an almond, and the clear white colour will be altered into a dirty one, and the sweet taste into an oily one. What real alteration can the beating of the pestle make in an body, but an alteration of the texture of it?

(From II.viii.21—*Explains how water felt as cold by one hand may be warm to the other*) Ideas being thus distinguished and understood, we may be able to give an account how the same water, at the same time, may produce the idea of cold by one hand and of heat by the other: whereas it is impossible that the same water, if those ideas were really in it, should at the same time be both hot and cold. For, if we imagine **warmth**, as it is in our hands, to be nothing but a certain sort and degree of motion in the minute particles of our nerves or animal spirits, we may understand how it is possible that the same water may, at the same time, produce the sensations of heat in one hand and cold in the other; which yet **figure** never does, that never producing the idea of a square by one hand which has produced the idea of a globe by another.

Locke argues for three theses in this chapter:

1. Ideas of secondary qualities do not resemble anything in the objects that 'have' them
2. Secondary qualities depend on primary
3. Secondary qualities are nothing but powers in objects to produce certain ideas in us

If there were no observers or perceivers, what would the world be like, according to Locke? That is, what qualities does a physical object have in itself?

How does Locke argue for his three theses? Let's start with (i): ideas of secondary qualities resemble nothing in the objects.

Recall Aquinas's picture of (bodily) causation: one object (e.g., fire) produces in another the same kind of quality it has in itself (e.g., heat). Why does Locke think that there isn't really any heat in the first object? Let's take a case where fire produces a sensation of heat in a person. If our sensation of heat resembled any quality in the object, that quality would have to be the cause of the heat that it produces.

1. *Why does Locke reject this? (see especially II.viii.11 above).*
2. *Locke argues for a further thesis:*

1. Secondary qualities depend on primary

   Why think that the color of an object (i.e., the color ideas it produces in us) depends on its primary qualities? (Hint: use II.viii.20)

   Finally, what about thesis (iii): secondary qualities are nothing but powers in objects to produce certain ideas in us? Well, this is just to combine (i) and (ii). If they're not resemblances, and they depend on the primary qualities, then to say that a body has a particular color is just to say that its parts are so arranged as to produce a given idea in us. (Note that primary qualities are powers and genuine qualities in objects; secondary are merely powers.)

   But as Locke points out, ideas of secondary qualities depend not just on the objects; they also depend on the perceivers.

1. *Think of as many different ways to change the color of this room as you can.*

Complex Ideas

So far, we've dealt only with simple ideas. But our experience doesn't seem to come to us packaged in simple, discrete elements. So Locke needs to deal with how we generate experiences (and thoughts) of ordinary objects—what he calls 'substances'– out of simple ideas.

(From II.xii.1—*Made by the Mind out of simple Ones*) We have hitherto considered those ideas, in the reception whereof the mind is only passive, which are those simple ones received from sensation and reflection before mentioned, whereof the mind cannot make one to itself, nor have any idea which does not wholly consist of them. ... Ideas thus made up of several simple ones put together, I call **complex**.

(From II.xii.2—*Made voluntarily*) In this faculty of repeating and joining together its ideas, the mind has great power in varying and multiplying the objects of its thoughts, infinitely beyond what sensation or reflection furnished it with: but all this still confined to those simple ideas which it received from those two sources, and which are the ultimate materials of all its compositions.

(From II.xii.3—*Complex ideas are either of Modes, Substances, or Relations*)

(From II.xxiii.1—*Ideas of substances, how made*) The mind being, as I have declared, furnished with a great number of the simple ideas, conveyed in by the senses as they are found in exterior things, or by reflection on its own operations, takes notice also that a certain number of these simple ideas go constantly together; which being presumed to belong to one thing, and words being suited to common apprehensions, and made use of for quick dispatch are called, so united in one subject, by one name; which, by inadvertency, we are apt afterward to talk of and consider as one simple idea, which indeed is a complication of many ideas together: because, as I have said, not imagining how these simple ideas **can** subsist by themselves, we accustom ourselves to suppose some **substratum** wherein they do subsist, and from which they do result, which therefore we call **substance**.

---

1. *List the ideas necessary to construct an idea of a substance like Helga (a dog).*

Substance/substratum

Our simple ideas represent qualities; to think of a substance like a dog, however, we need to think of these qualities as inhering in or being unified by some underlying substratum (which he sometimes also calls 'pure substance in general'). What is Locke's attitude toward this substratum, and our knowledge of it?

(From II.xiii.19—*Substance and accidents of little use in Philosophy*) They who first ran into the notion of **accidents**, as a sort of real beings that needed something to inhere in, were forced to find out the word **substance** to support them. Had the poor Indian philosopher (who imagined that the earth also wanted something to bear it up) but thought of this word substance, he needed not to have been at the trouble to find an elephant to support it, and a tortoise to support his elephant: the word substance would have done it effectually. And he that inquired might have taken it for as good an answer from an Indian philosopher—that substance, without knowing what it is, is that which supports the earth, as take it for a sufficient answer and good doctrine from our european philosophers—that substance, without knowing what it is, is that which supports accidents. So that of substance, we have no idea of what it is, but only a confused obscure one of what it does.

(From II.xiii.20—*Sticking on and under-propping*) Whatever a learned man may do here, an intelligent american, who inquired into the nature of things, would scarce take it for a satisfactory account, if, desiring to learn our architecture, he should be told that a pillar is a thing supported by a basis, and a basis something that supported a pillar. Would he not think himself mocked, instead of taught, with such an account as this? ... Were the latin words, *inhaerentia* and *substantio*, put into the plain english ones that answer them, and were called **sticking** on and **under-propping**, they would better discover to us the very great clearness there is in the doctrine of substance and accidents, and show of what use they are in deciding of questions in philosophy.

(From II.xxiii.23—*Our obscure Idea of Substance in general*) So that if any one will examine himself concerning his notion of pure substance in general, he will find he has no other idea of it at all, but only a supposition of he knows not what **support** of such qualities which are capable of producing simple ideas in us; which qualities are commonly called accidents. If any one should be asked, what is the subject wherein colour or weight inheres, he would have nothing to say, but the solid extended parts; and if he were demanded, what is it that solidity and extension adhere in, he would not be in a much better case than the Indian before mentioned who, saying that the world was supported by a great elephant, was asked what the elephant rested on; to which his answer was—a great tortoise: but being again pressed to know what gave support to the broad-backed tortoise, replied—**something, he knew not what**.

---

1. *It's vital to see that by 'substance' Locke means here 'substratum': that in which properties inhere. This notion is akin to Aristotle's notion of prime matter. Why might one say that Locke has a love/hate relationship with substratum?*

Natural kinds

Now that we know how we think about individual substances (e.g., an elephant), we need to know how we can think about kinds or sorts of things. I'm not limited to thinking (or talking) about individual substances; I can make claims that apply to groups or sorts of substances. Locke's abstraction is the mechanism by which we move from purely determinate ideas to general ones.

Keep in mind that Locke has two kinds of fish to fry in this context: the Cartesians, who think that the essence of body is just extension, and the Aristotelians, who think that the world presents itself to us as if it were 'carved at the joints' into innumerable distinct natural kinds. In this context, Locke's role as an 'under-labourer' to science is most in evidence.

(From III.ii.6—*How general Words are made*) ... Words become general by being made the signs of general ideas: and ideas become general, by separating from them the circumstances of time and place, and any other ideas that may determine them to this or that particular existence. By this way of abstraction they are made capable of representing more individuals than one; each of which having in it a conformity to that abstract idea, is (as we call it) of that sort.

(From III.ii.7—*Shown by the way we enlarge our complex ideas from infancy*) ... [T]here is nothing more evident, than that the ideas of the persons children converse with (to instance in them alone) are, like the persons themselves, only particular. The ideas of the nurse and the mother are well framed in their minds; and, like pictures of them there, represent only those individuals. The names they first gave to them are confined to these individuals; and the names of **nurse** and **mamma**, the child uses, determine themselves to those persons. Afterwards, when time and a larger acquaintance have made them observe that there are a great many other things in the world, that in some common agreements of shape, and several other qualities, resemble their father and mother, and those persons they have been used to, they frame an idea, which they find those many particulars do partake in; and to that they give, with others, the name **man**, for example. And thus they come to have a general name, and a general idea. Wherein they make nothing new; but only leave out of the complex idea they had of Peter and James, Mary and Jane, that which is peculiar to each, and retain only what is common to them all.

(From III.iii.11–*General and Universal are Creatures of the Understanding, and belong not to the Real Existence of things*) [I]t is plain, by what has been said, that **general** and **universal** belong not to the real existence of things; but are the inventions and creatures of the understanding, made by it for its own use, and concern only signs, whether words or ideas. ... [I]deas are general when they are set up as the representatives of many particular things: but universality belongs not to things themselves, which are all of them particular in their existence, even those words and ideas which in their signification are general. When therefore we quit particulars, the generals that rest are only creatures of our own making; their general nature being nothing but the capacity they are put into, by the understanding, of signifying or representing many particulars. For the signification they have is nothing but a relation that, by the mind of man, is added to them.

(From III.iii.13–*They are the Workmanship of the Understanding, but have their Foundation in the Similitude of Things*) I would not here be thought to forget, much less to deny, that Nature, in the production of things, makes several of them alike: there is nothing more obvious, especially in the races of animals, and all things propagated by seed. But yet I think we may say, **the sorting of them under names is the workmanship of the understanding, taking occasion, from the similitude it observes amongst them, to make abstract general ideas**, and set them up in the mind, with names annexed to them, as patterns or forms, (for, in that sense, the word **form** has a very proper signification,) to which as particular things existing are found to agree, so they come to be of that species, have that denomination, or are put into that **class**.

(From III.iii.15–*Several significations of the word Essence*) But since the essences of things are thought by some (and not without reason) to be wholly unknown, it may not be amiss to consider the several significations of the word **essence**.

1. *Real essences.* First, essence may be taken for the very being of anything, whereby it is what it is. And thus the real internal, but generally (in substances) unknown constitution of things, whereon their discoverable qualities depend, may be called their essence. This is the proper original signification of the word, as is evident from the formation of it; essential in its primary notation, signifying properly, being. And in this sense it is still used, when we speak of the essence of **particular** things, without giving them any name.

2. *Nominal essences.* Secondly, the learning and disputes of the schools having been much busied about genus and species, the word essence has almost lost its primary signification: and, instead of the real constitution of things, has been almost wholly applied to the artificial constitution of genus and species. It is true, there is ordinarily supposed a real constitution of the sorts of things; and it is past doubt there must be some real constitution, on which any collection of

simple ideas co-existing must depend. But, it being evident that things are ranked under names into sorts or species, only as they agree to certain abstract ideas, to which we have annexed those names, the essence of each **genus**, or sort, comes to be nothing but that abstract idea which the general, or sortal (if I may have leave so to call it from sort, as I do general from genus,) name stands for. And this we shall find to be that which the word essence imports in its most familiar use. These two sorts of essences, I suppose, may not unfitly be termed, the one the **real**, the other **nominal essence**.

(From III.iii.17—*Supposition, that Species are distinguished by their real Essences useless*) [The opinion that considers] real essences as a certain number of forms or moulds, wherein all natural things that exist are cast, and do equally partake, has, I imagine, very much perplexed the knowledge of natural things. The frequent productions of monsters, in all the species of animals, and of changelings, and other strange issues of human birth, carry with them difficulties, not possible to consist with this hypothesis; since it is as impossible that two things partaking exactly of the same real essence should have different properties, as that two figures partaking of the same real essence of a circle should have different properties. But were there no other reason against it, yet the supposition of essences that cannot be known; and the making of them, nevertheless, to be that which distinguishes the species of things, is so wholly useless and unserviceable to any part of our knowledge, that that alone were sufficient to make us lay it by ...

(From III.vi.6—*Even the real essences of individual substances imply potential sorts*) It is true, I have often mentioned a **real essence**, distinct in substances from those abstract ideas of them, which I call their nominal essence. By this real essence I mean, that real constitution of anything, which is the foundation of all those properties that are combined in, and are constantly found to co-exist with the nominal essence; that particular constitution which everything has within itself, without any relation to anything without it. But essence, even in this sense, **relates to a sort, and supposes a species**. For, being that real constitution on which the properties depend, it necessarily supposes a sort of things, properties belonging only to species, and not to individuals: e.g., supposing the nominal essence of gold to be a body of such a peculiar colour and weight, with malleability and fusibility, the real essence is that constitution of the parts of matter on which these qualities and their union depend; and is also the foundation of its solubility in *aqua regia* and other properties, accompanying that complex idea. Hre are essences and properties, but all upon supposition of a sort or general abstract idea, which is considered as immutable; but there is no individual parcel of matter to which any of these qualities are so annexed as to be essential to it or inseparable from it.

(From III.vi.50) For, let us consider, when we affirm that 'all gold is fixed,' either it means that fixedness is a part of the definition, i.e., part of the nominal essence the word 'gold' stands for; and so this affirmation, 'all gold is fixed,' contains nothing but the signification of the term 'gold'.

Or else it means, that fixedness, not being a part of the definition of 'gold', is a property of that substance itself: in which case it is plain that the word 'gold' stands in the place of a substance, having the real essence of a species of things made by nature. In which way of substitution it has so confused and uncertain a signification, that, though this proposition—'gold is fixed'—be in that sense an affirmation of something real; yet it is a truth will always fail us in its particular application, and so is of no real use or certainty. For let it be ever so true, that all gold, i.e., all that has the real essence of gold, is fixed, what serves this for, whilst we know not, in this sense, **what is or is not gold?** For if we know not the real essence of gold, it is impossible we should know what parcel of matter has that essence, and so whether it be true gold or no.

1. *In this passage, Locke argues that all general claims about kinds (e.g., 'gold is fixed') are either trivial or uncertain. Using the gold example, explain each of these alternatives. In what way can it be taken as trivial? As uncertain?*

Body

Now that we have some story about how our ideas of substances are constructed, we need to look at the two main kinds of substance we seem to find in the world: mind and body. Notice Locke's argument against Descartes's conflation of body and extension. Locke also replies here to Leibniz's argument against Newtonian space, namely, that it must be either a substance or an accident, and neither makes much sense.

(From II.xiii.17—*Cohesion of solid parts and Impulse, the primary ideas peculiar to Body*) The primary ideas we have **peculiar to body**, as contradistinguished to spirit, are the **cohesion of solid, and consequently separable, parts**, and a **power of communicating motion by impulse**. These, I think, are the original ideas proper and peculiar to body; for figure is but the consequence of finite extension.

(From II.xiii.11—*Extension and Body not the same*) There are some that would persuade us, that body and extension are the same thing ... If, therefore, they mean by body and extension the same that other people do, viz. By **body** something that is solid and extended, whose parts are separable and movable different ways; and by **extension**, only the space that lies between the extremities of those solid coherent parts, and which is possessed by them, [then] they confound very different ideas one with another; for I appeal to every man's own thoughts, whether the idea of space be not as distinct from that of solidity, as it is from the idea of scarlet colour? It is true, solidity cannot exist without extension, neither can scarlet colour exist without extension, but this hinders not, but that they are distinct ideas.

And if it be a reason to prove that spirit is different from body, because thinking includes not the idea of extension in it; the same reason will be as valid, I suppose, to prove that space is not body, because it includes not the idea of solidity in it; **space** and **solidity** being as distinct ideas as **thinking** and **extension**, and as wholly separable in the mind one from another ... Extension includes no solidity, nor resistance to the motion of body, as body does.

(From II.xiii.3—*Space and Extension*) This space, considered barely in length between any two beings, without considering anything else between them, is called **distance**: if considered in length, breadth, and thickness, I think it may be called **capacity**. When considered between the extremities of matter, which fills the capacity of space with something solid, tangible, and moveable, it is properly called **extension**. And so extension is an idea belonging to body only; but space may, as is evident, be considered without it.

(From II.xiii.17—*Substance, which we know not, no proof against space without body*) If it be demanded (as usually it is) whether this space, void of body, be **substance** or **accident**, I shall readily answer I know not; nor shall be ashamed to own my ignorance, till they that ask show me a clear distinct idea of substance.

Mind

Locke here sets out the constituent ideas that make up the complex idea of the mind. He also launches an attack against Descartes's claim that thought is the essence of the soul. Most famously, he denies that we can be sure that what thinks in us in an immaterial substance.

(From II.xxiii.18. *Thinking and motivity*) The ideas we have belonging and **peculiar to spirit**, are **thinking, and will**, or a **power of putting body into motion by thought, and, which is consequent to it, liberty**. For, as body cannot but communicate its motion by impulse to another body, which it meets with at rest, so the mind can put bodies into motion, or forbear to do so, as it pleases. The ideas of **existence, duration**, and **mobility**, are common to them both.

(From II.i.10–*The Soul thinks not always; for this wants Proofs*) ... I confess myself to have one of those dull souls, that doth not perceive itself always to contemplate ideas; nor can conceive it any more necessary for the soul always to think, than for the body always to move: the perception of ideas being (as I conceive) to the soul, what motion is to the body; not its essence, but one of its operations. And therefore, though thinking be supposed never so much the proper action of the soul, yet it is not necessary to suppose that it should be always thinking, always in action. ... To say that actual thinking is essential to the soul, and inseparable from it, is to beg what is in question, and not to prove it by reason; which is necessary to be done, if it be not a self-evident proposition But whether this, "That the soul always thinks," be a self-evident proposition, that everybody assents to at first hearing, I appeal to mankind. It is doubted whether I thought at all last night or no. The question being about a matter of fact, it is begging it to bring, as a proof for it, an hypothesis, which is the very thing in dispute: by which way one may prove anything ...

But men in love with their opinions may not only suppose what is in question, but allege wrong matter of fact. How else could any one make it an inference of mine, that a thing is not, because we are not sensible of it in our sleep? I do not say there is no **soul** in a man, because he is not sensible of it in his sleep; but I do say, he cannot **think** at any time, waking or sleeping, without being sensible of it. Our being sensible of it is not necessary to anything but to our thoughts; and to them it is; and to them it always will be necessary, till we can think without being conscious of it.

---

1. *Locke begins with an argument from experience. How does it work? We can think of it as a* reductio ad absurdum:

    Premise 1: The soul's essence is to think (Descartes's view)
    Premise 2: Given 1, it follows that the soul _____ (since this is part of what it is to be an essential property)
    Premise 3: But experience shows _____.
    Conclusion: _____.

Now, Locke realizes that the Cartesian will not leave things at that; he will insist that minds think even during sleep, though they do not remember it. Locke thinks this move has a heavy price:

(From II.i.11—*It is not always conscious of [thinking]*) I grant that the soul, in a waking man, is never without thought, because it is the condition of being awake. But whether sleeping without dreaming be not an affection of the whole man, mind as well as body, may be worth a waking man's consideration; it being hard to conceive that anything should think and not be conscious of it. If the soul doth think in a sleeping man without being conscious of it, I ask whether, during such thinking, it has any pleasure or pain, or be capable of happiness or misery? I am sure the man is not; no more than the bed or earth he lies on. For to be happy or miserable without being conscious of it, seems to me utterly inconsistent and impossible. Or if it be possible that the **soul** can, whilst the body is sleeping, have its thinking, enjoyments, and concerns, its pleasures or pain, apart, which the **man** is not conscious of nor partakes in—it is certain that Socrates asleep and Socrates awake is not the same person; but his soul when he sleeps, and Socrates the man, consisting of body and soul, when he is waking, are two persons: since waking Socrates has no knowledge of, or concernment for that happiness or misery of his soul, which it enjoys alone by itself whilst he sleeps, without perceiving anything of it; no more than he has for the happiness or misery of a man in the indies, whom he knows not. For, if we take wholly away all consciousness of our actions and sensations, especially of pleasure and pain, and the concernment that accompanies it, it will be hard to know wherein to place personal identity.

1. *What price does Locke think Descartes must pay, in order to hang on to his claim that the soul always thinks?*

(From II.xxiii.5—*As clear an idea of spiritual substance as of corporeal substance*) The same thing happens concerning the operations of the mind, viz. thinking, reasoning, fearing, &c., which we concluding not to subsist of themselves, nor apprehending how they can belong to body, or be produced by it, we are apt to think these the actions of some other **substance**, which we call **spirit**; whereby yet it is evident that, having no other idea or notion of matter, but something wherein those many sensible qualities which affect our senses do subsist; by supposing a substance wherein thinking, knowing, doubting, and a power of moving, &c., do subsist, we have as clear a notion of the substance of spirit, as we have of body; the one being supposed to be (without knowing what it is) the **substratum** to those simple ideas we have from without; and the other supposed (with a like ignorance of what it is) to be the **substratum** to those operations we experiment in ourselves within. It is plain then, that the idea of **corporeal substance** in matter is as remote from our conceptions and apprehensions, as that of **spiritual substance**, or spirit: and therefore, from our not having, any notion of the substance of spirit, we can no more conclude its non-existence, than we can, for the same reason, deny the existence of body ...

(From II.xxiii.16—*No Idea of abstract Substance either in Body or Spirit*) By the complex idea of extended, figured, coloured, and all other sensible qualities, which is all that we know of it, we are as far from the idea of the substance of body, as if we knew nothing at all: nor after all the acquaintance and familiarity which we imagine we have with matter, and the many qualities men assure themselves they perceive and know in bodies, will it perhaps upon examination be found, that they have any more or clearer primary ideas belonging to body, than they have belonging to immaterial spirit.

(From II.xxiii.23—*Cohesion of solid Parts in Body as hard to be conceived as thinking in a Soul*) [I]f [a man] says he knows not how he thinks, I answer, Neither knows he how he is extended, how the solid parts of body are united or cohere together to make extension. For though the pressure of the particles of air may account for the cohesion of several parts of matter that are grosser than the particles of air, and have pores less than the corpuscles of air, yet the weight or pressure of the air will not explain, nor can be a cause of the coherence of the particles of air themselves. And if the pressure of the aether, or any subtiler matter than the air, may unite, and hold fast together, the parts of a particle of air, as well as other bodies, yet it cannot make bonds for **itself**, and hold together the parts that make up every the least corpuscle of that **materia subtilis**.

(From II.xxiii.28—*Communication of Motion by Impulse, or by Thought, equally unintelligible*) Another idea we have of body is, **the power of communication of motion by impulse**; and of our souls, **the power of exciting motion by thought**. These ideas, the one of body, the other of our minds, every day's experience clearly furnishes us with: but if here again we inquire how this is done, we are equally in the dark. For, in the communication of motion by impulse, wherein as much motion is lost to one body as is got to the other, which is the ordinariest case, we can have no other conception, but of the passing of motion out of one body into another; which, I think, is as obscure and inconceivable as how our minds move or stop our bodies by thought, which we every moment find they do. We have by daily experience clear evidence of motion produced both by impulse and by thought; but the manner how, hardly comes within our comprehension: we are equally at a loss in both. So that, however we consider motion, and its communication, either from body or spirit, the idea which belongs to spirit is at least as clear as that which belongs to body. And if we consider the active power of moving, or, as I may call it, motivity, it is much clearer in spirit than body; since two bodies, placed by one another at rest, will never afford us the idea of a power in the one to move the other, but by a borrowed motion. ...

---

1. *Locke is here raising the problem of transference: how can one body give its motion to another? See Aquinas,* Summa Contra Gentiles *Chapter Sixty-nine, Section Seven, and Descartes's* Principles *(Part II, sections xxiv-v). How would each react to what Locke says here?*

(From IV.iii.6—*Our Knowledge, therefore narrower than our Ideas*) From all which it is evident, that the **extent of our knowledge** comes not only short of the reality of things, but even of the extent of our own ideas. Though our knowledge be limited to our ideas, and cannot exceed them either in extent or perfection; ... Yet it would be well with us if our knowledge were but as large as our ideas, and there were not many doubts and inquiries **concerning the ideas** we **have**, whereof we are not, nor I believe ever shall be in this world resolved. Nevertheless, I do not question but that human knowledge, under the present circumstances of our beings and constitutions, may be carried much further than it has hitherto been, if men would sincerely, and with freedom of mind, employ all that industry and labour of thought, in improving the means of discovering truth, which they do for the colouring or support of falsehood, to maintain a system, interest, or party they are once engaged in.

... We have the ideas of a **square**, a **circle**, and **equality**; and yet, perhaps, shall never be able to find a circle equal to a square, and certainly know that it is so. We have the ideas of **matter** and **thinking**, but possibly shall never be able to know whether [any mere material being] thinks or no; it being impossible for us, by the contemplation of our own ideas, without revelation, to discover whether Omnipotency has not given to some systems of matter, fitly disposed, a power to perceive and think, or else joined and fixed to matter, so disposed, a thinking immaterial substance: it being, in respect of our notions, not much more remote from our comprehension to conceive that **God** can, if he pleases, superadd to matter a **faculty of thinking**, than that he should superadd to it **another substance with** a **faculty of thinking**; since we know not wherein thinking consists, nor to what sort of substances the Almighty has been pleased to give that power, which cannot be in any created being, but merely by the good pleasure and bounty of the Creator. For I see no contradiction in it, that the first Eternal thinking Being, or Omnipotent Spirit, should, if he pleased, give to certain systems of created senseless matter, put together as he thinks fit, some degrees of sense, perception, and thought: though, as I think I have proved, lib. iv. Ch. 10, Section 14, &c., it is no less than a contradiction to suppose matter (which is evidently in its own nature void of sense and thought) should be that Eternal first-thinking Being. What certainty of knowledge can any one have, that some perceptions, such as, e.g., pleasure and pain, should not be in some bodies themselves, after a certain manner modified and moved, as well as that they should be in an immaterial substance, upon the motion of the parts of body: Body, as far as we can conceive, being able only to strike and affect body, and motion, according to the utmost reach of our ideas, being able to produce nothing but motion; so that when we allow it to produce pleasure or pain, or the idea of a colour or sound, we are fain to quit our reason, go beyond our ideas, and attribute it wholly to the good pleasure of our Maker. For, since we must allow He has annexed effects to motion which we can no way conceive motion able to produce, what reason have we to conclude that He could not order them as well to be produced in a subject we cannot conceive capable of them, as well as in a subject we cannot conceive the motion of matter can any way operate upon? I say not this, that I would any way lessen the belief of the soul's immateriality: I am not here speaking of probability, but knowledge, and I think not only that it becomes the modesty of philosophy not to pronounce magisterially, where we want that evidence that can produce knowledge; but also, that it is of use to us to discern how far our knowledge does reach; for the state we are at present in, not being that of vision, we must in many things content ourselves with faith and probability: and in the present question, about the Immateriality of the Soul, if our faculties cannot arrive at demonstrative certainty, we need not think it strange. All the great ends of morality and religion are well enough secured, without philosophical proofs of the soul's immateriality ... since it is evident, that he who made us at the beginning to subsist here, sensible intelligent beings, and for several years continued us in such a state, can and will restore us to the like state of sensibility in another world, and make us capable there to receive the retribution he has designed to men, according to their doings in this life.

And therefore it is not of such mighty necessity to determine one way or the other, as some, over-zealous for or against the immateriality of the soul, have been forward to make the world believe. Who, either on the one side, indulging too much their thoughts immersed altogether in matter, can allow no existence to what is not material: or who, on the other side, finding not **cogitation** within the natural powers of matter, examined over and over again by the utmost intention of mind, have the confidence to conclude—that Omnipotency itself cannot give perception and thought to a substance which has the modification of solidity. He that considers how hardly sensation is, in our thoughts, reconcilable to extended matter; or existence to anything that has no extension at all, will confess that he is very far from certainly knowing what his soul is. It is a point which seems to me to be put out of the reach of our knowledge: and he who will give himself leave to consider freely, and look into the dark and intricate part of each hypothesis, will scarce find his reason able to determine him fixedly for or against the soul's materiality. Since, on which side soever he views it, either as an **unextended substance**, or as a **thinking extended matter**, the difficulty to conceive either will, whilst either alone is in his thoughts, still drive him to the contrary side. ...

It is past controversy, that we have in us **something** that thinks; our very doubts about what it is, confirm the certainty of its being, though we must content ourselves in the ignorance of what **kind** of being it is: and it is in vain to go about to be sceptical in this, as it is unreasonable in most other cases to be positive against the being of anything, because we cannot comprehend its nature. For I would fain know what substance exists, that has not something in it which manifestly baffles our understandings ...

Personal Identity

Can Locke make good on his claim that 'all the great ends of religion and morality' can be served, even without a proof of the soul's immortality? Both religion and morality require, Locke thinks, the certainty of post-mortem rewards and harms. But how can we make sense of the self surviving the death of the body, if we cannot show that the self is immaterial?

(From II.xxvii.8–*Idea of identity suited to the idea it is applied to*) It is not therefore unity of substance that comprehends all sorts of identity, or will determine it in every case; but to conceive and judge of it aright, we must consider what idea the word it is applied to stands for: it being one thing to be the same **substance**, another the same **man**, and a third the same **person**, if **person**, **man**, and **substance**, are three names standing for three different ideas;–for such as is the idea belonging to that name, such must be the identity; which, if it had been a little more carefully attended to, would possibly have prevented a great deal of that confusion which often occurs about this matter, with no small seeming difficulties, especially concerning **personal** identity, which therefore we shall in the next place a little consider.

(From II.xxvii.4) [L]et us suppose an atom, i.e., a continued body under one immutable superficies, existing in a determined time and place; it is evident, that, considered in any instant of its existence, it is in that instant the same with itself. For, being at that instant what it is, and nothing else, it is the same, and so must continue as long as its existence is continued; for so long it will be the same, and no other. In like manner, if two or more atoms be joined together into the same mass, every one of those atoms will be the same, by the foregoing rule: and whilst they exist united together, the mass, consisting of the same atoms, must be the same mass, or the same body, let the parts be ever so differently jumbled. But if one of these atoms be taken away, or one new one added, it is no longer the same mass or the same body. In the state of living creatures, their identity depends not on a mass of the same particles, but on something else. For in them the variation of great parcels of matter alters not the identity: an oak growing from a plant to a great tree, and then lopped, is still the same oak; and a colt grown up to a horse, sometimes fat, sometimes lean, is all the while the same horse: though, in both these cases, there may be a manifest change of the parts; so that truly they are not either of them the same masses of matter, though they be truly one of them the same oak, and the other the same horse. The reason whereof is, that, in these two cases–a **mass of matter** and a **living body**–identity is not applied to the same thing.

(From II.xxvii.5–*Identity of Vegetables*) We must therefore consider wherein an oak differs from a mass of matter, and that seems to me to be in this, that the one is only the cohesion of particles of matter any how united, the other such a disposition of them as constitutes the parts of an oak; and such an organization of those parts as is fit to receive and distribute nourishment, so as to continue and frame the wood, bark, and leaves, &c., of an oak, in which consists the vegetable life. That being then one plant which has such an organization of parts in one coherent body, partaking of one common life, it continues to be the same plant as long as it partakes of the same life, though that life be communicated to new particles of matter vitally united to the living plant, in a like continued organization conformable to that sort of plants. For this organization, being at any one instant in any one collection of matter, is in that particular concrete distinguished from all other, and *is* that individual life, which existing constantly from that moment both forwards and backwards, in the same continuity of insensibly succeeding parts united to the living body of the plant, it has that identity which makes the same plant, and all the parts of it, parts of the same plant, during all the time that they exist united in that continued organization, which is fit to convey that common life to all the parts so united.

(From II.xxvii.6–*Identity of Animals*) The case is not so much different in **brutes** but that any one may hence see what makes an animal and continues it the same. Something we have like this in machines, and may serve to illustrate it. For example, what is a watch? it is plain it is nothing but a fit organization or construction of parts to a certain end, which, when a sufficient force is added to it, it is capable to attain. If we would suppose this machine one continued body, all whose organized parts were repaired, increased, or diminished by a constant addition or separation of insensible parts, with one common life, we should have something very much like the body of an animal ...

(From II.xxvii.7–*The Identity of Man*) This also shows wherein the identity of the same **man** consists; viz. in nothing but a participation of the same continued life, by constantly fleeting particles of matter, in succession vitally united to the same organized body.

(From II.xxvii.11–*Personal Identity*) This being premised, to find wherein personal identity consists, we must consider what **person** stands for; which, I think, is a thinking intelligent being, that has reason and reflection, and can consider itself as itself, the same thinking thing, in different times and places; which it does only by that consciousness which is inseparable from thinking, and, as it seems to me, essential to it: it being impossible for any one to perceive without **perceiving** that he does perceive. When we see, hear, smell, taste, feel, meditate, or will anything, we know that we do so. Thus it is always as to our present sensations and perceptions: and by this every one is to himself that which he calls **self**—it not being considered, in this case, whether the same self be continued in the same or divers substances. For, since consciousness always accompanies thinking, and it is that which makes every one to be what he calls self, and thereby distinguishes himself from all other thinking things, in this alone consists personal identity, i.e., the sameness of a rational being: and as far as this consciousness can be extended backwards to any past action or thought, so far reaches the identity of that person; it is the same self now it was then; and it is by the same self with this present one that now reflects on it, that that action was done.

(From II.xxvii.12–*Consciousness makes personal Identity*) But it is further inquired, whether it be the same identical substance. This few would think they had reason to doubt of, if these perceptions, with their consciousness, always remained present in the mind, whereby the same thinking thing would be always consciously present, and, as would be thought, evidently the same to itself. But that which seems to make the difficulty is this, that this consciousness being interrupted always by forgetfulness, there being no moment of our lives wherein we have the whole train of all our past actions before our eyes in one view, but even the best memories losing the sight of one part whilst they are viewing another; and we sometimes, and that the greatest part of our lives, not reflecting on our past selves, being intent on our present thoughts, and in sound sleep having no thoughts at all, or at least none with that consciousness which remarks our waking thoughts—I say, in all these cases, our consciousness being interrupted, and we losing the sight of our past selves, doubts are raised whether we are the same thinking thing, i.e., the same **substance** or no. Which, however reasonable or unreasonable, concerns not **personal** identity at all. ... For as far as any intelligent being *can* repeat the idea of any past action with the same consciousness it had of it at first, and with the same consciousness it has of any present action; so far it is the same personal self. For it is by the consciousness it has of its present thoughts and actions, that it is **self to itself** now, and so will be the same self, as far as the same consciousness can extend to actions past or to come; and would be by distance of time, or change of substance, no more two persons, than a man be two men by wearing other clothes to-day than he did yesterday, with a long or a short sleep between: the same consciousness uniting those distant actions into the same person, whatever substances contributed to their production.

(From II.xxvii.14—*Personality in Change of Substance*) But the question is, Whether if the same substance which thinks be changed, it can be the same person; or, remaining the same, it can be different persons? And to this I answer: First, This can be no question at all to those who place thought in a purely material animal constitution, void of an immaterial substance. For, whether their supposition be true or no, it is plain they conceive personal identity preserved in something else than identity of substance; as animal identity is preserved in identity of life, and not of substance. And therefore those who place thinking in an immaterial substance only, before they can come to deal with these men, must show why personal identity cannot be preserved in the change of immaterial substances, or variety of particular immaterial substances, as well as animal identity is preserved in the change of material substances, or variety of particular bodies ...

(From II.xxvii.15—*Whether in Change of thinking Substances there can be one Person*) [I]t must be allowed, that, if the same consciousness (which, as has been shown, is quite a different thing from the same numerical figure or motion in body) can be transferred from one thinking substance to another, it will be possible that two thinking substances may make but one person. For the same consciousness being preserved, whether in the same or different substances, the personal identity is preserved.

(From II.xxvii.17—*The body, as well as the soul, goes to the making of a Man*) And thus may we be able, without any difficulty, to conceive the same person at the resurrection, though in a body not exactly in make or parts the same which he had here, the same consciousness going along with the soul that inhabits it. But yet the soul alone, in the change of bodies, would scarce to any one but to him that makes the soul the man, be enough to make the same man. For should the soul of a prince, carrying with it the consciousness of the prince's past life, enter and inform the body of a cobbler, as soon as deserted by his own soul, every one sees he would be the same **person** with the prince, accountable only for the prince's actions: but who would say it was the same **man**?

(From II.xxvii.19—*Self depends on Consciousness, not on Substance*) **Self** is that conscious thinking thing—whatever substance made up of (whether spiritual or material, simple or compounded, it matters not)—which is sensible or conscious of pleasure and pain, capable of happiness or misery, and so is concerned for itself, as far as that consciousness extends.

(From II.xxvii.20—*Persons, not Substances, the Objects of Reward and Punishment*) In this personal identity is founded all the right and justice of reward and punishment; happiness and misery being that for which every one is concerned for **himself**, and not mattering what becomes of any **substance**, not joined to, or affected with that consciousness.

(From II.xxvii.21—*Which shows wherein Personal identity consists*) This may show us wherein personal identity consists: not in the identity of substance, but, as I have said, in the identity of consciousness ... if

Socrates waking and sleeping do not partake of the same consciousness, Socrates waking and sleeping is not the same person. And to punish Socrates waking for what sleeping Socrates thought, and waking Socrates was never conscious of, would be no more of right, than to punish one twin for what his brother-twin did, whereof he knew nothing, because their outsides were so like, that they could not be distinguished; for such twins have been seen.

(From II.xxvii.24—*Objection*) But is not a man drunk and sober the same person? Why else is he punished for the fact he commits when drunk, though he be never afterwards conscious of it? Just as much the same person as a man that walks, and does other things in his sleep, is the same person, and is answerable for any mischief he shall do in it. Human laws punish both, with a justice suitable to *their* way of knowledge; because, in these cases, they cannot distinguish certainly what is real, what counterfeit: and so the ignorance in drunkenness or sleep is not admitted as a plea. But in the great day, wherein the secrets of all hearts shall be laid open, it may be reasonable to think, no one shall be made to answer for what he knows nothing of; but shall receive his doom, his conscience accusing or excusing him.

---

1. *What is Locke's sortal relativity thesis?*
2. *Given this, what makes something the same:*

   1. Atom over time?
   2. Mass of atoms?
   3. Plant?
   4. Animal?
   5. Man?
   6. Person?

3. *What does Descartes think accounts for personal identity over time?*
4. *What does Locke think is wrong with Descartes's answer?*

The Limits of Knowledge

It now makes sense to turn to Locke's official discussion of the limits of knowledge. Keep in mind that the two orders of classification Locke introduces (manners or degrees of knowledge and the objects known) cut across each other. I've chosen to frame the discussion in terms of the objects of knowledge: identity (known by intuition), relation (by demonstration), co-existence, and real existence (by sensation).

(From IV.i.1—*Our Knowledge conversant about our Ideas only*) Since the mind, in all its thoughts and reasonings, hath no other immediate object but its own ideas, which it alone does or can contemplate, it is evident that our knowledge is only conversant about them.

(From IV.i.2—*Knowledge is the perception of the agreement or disagreement of two ideas*) **Knowledge** then seems to me to be nothing but **the perception of the connexion of and agreement, or disagreement and repugnancy of any of our ideas**. In this alone it consists. Where this perception is, there is knowledge, and where it is not, there, though we may fancy, guess, or believe, yet we always come short of knowledge. For when we know that white is not black, what do we else but perceive, that these two ideas do not agree? when we possess ourselves with the utmost security of the demonstration, that the three angles of a triangle are equal to two right ones, what do we more but perceive, that equality to two right ones does necessarily agree to, and is inseparable from, the three angles of a triangle?

(From IV.i.3−*This Agreement or Disagreement may be any of four sorts*) But to understand a little more distinctly wherein this agreement or disagreement consists, I think we may reduce it all to these four sorts: i. **identity**, or **diversity**. ii. **relation**. iii. **co-existence**, or **necessary connexion**. iv. **real existence**.

(From IV.i.4−*First, of Identity, or Diversity in ideas*) **First**, as to the first sort of agreement or disagreement, viz. **identity** or **diversity**. It is the first act of the mind, when it has any sentiments or ideas at all, to perceive its ideas; and so far as it perceives them, to know each what it is, and thereby also to perceive their difference, and that one is not another.

(From IV.i.5−*Secondly, of abstract Relations between ideas*) **Secondly**, the next sort of agreement or disagreement the mind perceives in any of its ideas may, I think, be called **relative**, and is nothing but the perception of the **relation** between any two ideas, of what kind soever, whether substances, modes, or any other.

(From IV.i.6−*Thirdly, of their necessary Co-existence in Substances*) The **third** sort of agreement or disagreement to be found in our ideas, which the perception of the mind is employed about, is **co-existence** or **non-co-existence** in the **same subject**; and this belongs particularly to substances. Thus when we pronounce concerning gold, that it is fixed, our knowledge of this truth amounts to no more but this, that fixedness, or a power to remain in the fire unconsumed, is an idea that always accompanies and is joined with that particular sort of yellowness, weight, fusibility, malleableness, and solubility in **aqua regia**, which make our complex idea signified by the word 'gold'.

(From IV.iii.9−*Of their Co-existence, extends only a very little way*) [A]s to the … agreement or disagreement of our ideas in **co-existence**, in this our knowledge is very short; though in this consists the greatest and most material part of our knowledge concerning substances. For our ideas of the species of substances being, as I have showed, nothing but certain collections of simple ideas united in one subject, and so co-existing together; e.g., our idea of flame is a body hot, luminous, and moving upward; of gold, a body heavy to a certain degree, yellow, malleable, and fusible: for these, or some such complex ideas as these, in men's minds, do these two names of the different substances, flame and gold, stand for. When we would know anything further concerning these, or any other sort of substances, what do we inquire, but what other qualities or powers these substances have or have not? which is nothing else but to know what other simple ideas do, or do not co-exist with those that make up that complex idea?

(From IV.iii.10−*Because the Connexion between simple Ideas in substances is for the most part unknown*) This, how weighty and considerable a part soever of human science, is yet very narrow, and scarce any at all. The reason whereof is, that the simple ideas whereof our complex ideas of substances are made up are, for the most part, such as carry with them, in their own nature, no visible necessary connexion or inconsistency with any other simple ideas, whose co-existence with them we would inform ourselves about.

(From IV.iii.25) If a great, nay, far the greatest part of the several ranks of bodies in the universe escape our notice by their remoteness, there are others that are no less concealed from us by their minuteness. These **insensible corpuscles**, being the active parts of matter, and the great instruments of nature, on which depend not only all their secondary qualities, but also most of their natural operations, our want of precise distinct ideas of their primary qualities keeps us in an incurable ignorance of what we desire to know about them.

I doubt not but if we could discover the figure, size, texture, and motion of the minute constituent parts of any two bodies, we should know without trial several of their operations one upon another; as we do now the properties of a square or a triangle. Did we know the mechanical affections of the particles of rhubarb, hemlock, opium, and a man, as a watchmaker does those of a watch, whereby it performs its operations; and of a file, which by rubbing on them will alter the figure of any of the wheels; we should be able to tell beforehand that rhubarb will purge, hemlock kill, and opium make a man sleep: as well as a watchmaker can, that a little piece of paper laid on the balance will keep the watch from going till it be removed; or that, some small part of it being rubbed by a file, the machine would quite lose its motion, and the watch go no more. The dissolving of silver in **aqua fortis**, and gold in **aqua regia**, and not **vice versa**, would be then perhaps no more difficult to know than it is to a smith to understand why the turning of one key will open a lock, and not the turning of another. But whilst we are destitute of senses acute enough to discover the minute particles of bodies, and to give us ideas of their mechanical affections, we must be content to be ignorant of their properties and ways of operation; nor can we be assured about them any further than some few trials we make are able to reach. But whether they will succeed again another time, we cannot be certain. This hinders our certain knowledge of universal truths concerning natural bodies: and our reason carries us herein very little beyond particular matter of fact.

(From IV.vi.9—No *discoverable necessary connexion between nominal essence gold, and other simple ideas*) As there is no discoverable connexion between fixedness and the colour, weight, and other simple ideas of that nominal essence of gold; so, if we make our complex idea of gold, a body yellow, fusable, ductile, weighty, and fixed, we shall be at the same uncertainty concerning solubility in **aqua regia**, and for the same reason. Since we can never, from consideration of the ideas themselves, with certainty affirm or deny of a body whose complex idea is made up of yellow, very weighty, ductile, fusible, and fixed, that it is soluble in **aqua regia**: and so on of the rest of its qualities. I would gladly meet with one general affirmation concerning any will, no doubt, be presently objected, is not this an universal proposition, **"all gold is malleable"**? to which I answer, it is a very complex idea the word 'gold' stands for. But then here is nothing affirmed of gold, but that that sound stands for an idea in which malleableness is contained: and such a sort of truth and certainty as this it is, to say a centaur is four-footed. But if malleableness make not a part of the specific essence the name of 'gold' stands for, it is plain, **"all gold is malleable"**, is not a certain proposition. Because, let the complex idea of *gold* be made up of whichsoever of its other qualities you please, malleableness will not appear to depend on that complex idea, nor follow from any simple one contained in it: the connexion that malleableness has (if it has any) with those other qualities being only by the intervention of the real constitution of its insensible parts; which, since we know not, it is impossible we should perceive that connexion, unless we could discover that which ties them together.

(From IV.i.7—*Fourthly, of real Existence agreeing to any idea*) The fourth and last sort is that of **actual real existence** agreeing to any idea.

(From IV.ii.1—*Of the degrees, or differences in clearness, of our Knowledge*)

1. *Intuitive*: The different clearness of our knowledge seems to me to lie in the different way of perception the mind has of the agreement or disagreement of any of its ideas. For if we will reflect on our own ways of thinking, we will find, that sometimes the mind perceives the agreement or disagreement of two ideas **immediately by themselves**, without the intervention of any other: and this I think we may call **intuitive knowledge**.

(From IV.ii.2)

1. *Demonstrative*: The next degree of knowledge is, where the mind perceives the agreement or disagreement of any ideas, but not immediately. Though wherever the mind perceives the agreement or disagreement of any of its ideas, there be certain knowledge; yet it does not always happen, that the mind sees that agreement or disagreement, which there is between them, even where it is discoverable; and in that case remains in ignorance, and at most gets no further than a probable conjecture. ... In this case then, when the mind cannot so bring its ideas together as by their immediate comparison, and as it were juxta-position or application one to another, to perceive their agreement or disagreement, it is fain, by **the intervention of other ideas**, (one or more, as it happens) to discover the agreement or disagreement which it searches; and this is that which we call **reasoning**. ...

(From IV.ii.14)

1. Sensitive knowledge of the particular existence of finite beings without us. These two, viz. intuition and demonstration, are the degrees of our **knowledge**; whatever comes short of one of these, with what assurance soever embraced, is but **faith** or **opinion**, but not knowledge, at least in all general truths. There is, indeed, another perception of the mind, employed about **the particular existence of finite beings without** us, which, going beyond bare probability, and yet not reaching perfectly to either of the foregoing degrees of certainty, passes under the name of **knowledge**. There can be nothing more certain than that the idea we receive from an external object is in our minds: this is intuitive knowledge. But whether there be anything more than barely that idea in our minds; whether we can thence certainly infer the existence of anything without us, which corresponds to that idea, is that whereof some men think there may be a question made; because men may have such ideas in their minds, when no such thing exists, no such object affects their senses. But yet here I think we are provided with an evidence that puts us past doubting. For I ask any one, whether he be not invincibly conscious to himself of a different perception, when he looks on the sun by day, and thinks on it by night; when he actually tastes wormwood, or smells a rose, or only thinks on that savour or odour? We as plainly find the difference there is between any idea revived in our minds by our own memory, and actually coming into our minds by our senses, as we do between any two distinct ideas. If any one say, a dream may do the same thing, and all these ideas may be produced, in us without any external objects; he may please to dream that I make him this answer:

    1. That it is no great matter, whether I remove his scruple or no: where all is but dream, reasoning and arguments are of no use, truth and knowledge nothing.
    2. That I believe he will allow a very manifest difference between dreaming of being in the fire, and being actually in it. But yet if he be resolved to appear so sceptical as to maintain, that what I call being actually in the fire is nothing but a dream; and that we cannot thereby certainly know, that any such thing as fire actually exists without us: I answer, that we certainly finding that pleasure or pain follows upon the application of certain objects to us, whose existence we perceive, or dream that we perceive, by our senses; this certainty is as great as our happiness or misery, beyond which we have no concernment to know or to be. So that, I think, we may add to the two former sorts of

knowledge this also, of the existence of particular external objects, by that perception and consciousness we have of the actual entrance of ideas from them, and allow these three degrees of knowledge, viz. **intuitive**, **demonstrative**, and **sensitive**; in each of which there are different degrees and ways of evidence and certainty.

(From IV.iv.1—*Objection: "Knowledge placed in our ideas may be all unreal or chimerical"*) I *doubt* not but my reader, by this time, may be apt to think that I have been all this while only building a castle in the air; and be ready to say to me: To what purpose all this stir? knowledge, say you, is only the perception of the agreement or disagreement of our own ideas: but who knows what those ideas may be? Is there anything so extravagant as the imaginations of men's brains? where is the head that has no chimeras in it? ... If it be true, that all knowledge lies only in the perception of the agreement or disagreement of our own ideas, the visions of an enthusiast and the reasonings of a sober man will be equally certain.

(From IV.iv.2—*Answer Not so, where Ideas agree with Things*) To which I answer, That if our knowledge of our ideas terminate in them, and reach no further, where there is something further intended, our most serious thoughts will be of little more use than the reveries of a crazy brain. ... But I hope, before I have done, to make it evident, that this way of certainty, by the knowledge of our own ideas, goes a little further than bare imagination: and I believe it will appear that all the certainty of general truths a man has lies in nothing else.

(From IV.iv.3—*But what shall be the criterion of this agreement?*) It is evident the mind knows not things immediately, but only by the intervention of the ideas it has of them. Our knowledge, therefore, is real only so far as there is a **conformity** between our ideas and the reality of things. But what shall be here the criterion? How shall the mind, when it perceives nothing but its own ideas, know that they agree with things themselves? this, though it seems not to want difficulty, yet, I think, there be two sorts of ideas that we may be assured agree with things.

(From IV.iv.4—*As, first all simple ideas are really conformed to things*) **First**, the first are simple ideas, which since the mind, as has been showed, can by no means make to itself, must necessarily be the product of things operating on the mind, in a natural way, and producing therein those perceptions which by the Wisdom and Will of our Maker they are ordained and adapted to. From whence it follows, that simple ideas are not fictions of our fancies, but the natural and regular productions of things without us, really operating upon us; and so carry with them all the conformity which is intended; or which our state requires: for they represent to us things under those appearances which they are fitted to produce in us: whereby we are enabled to distinguish the sorts of particular substances, to discern the states they are in, and so to take them for our necessities, and apply them to our uses. Thus the idea of whiteness, or bitterness, as it is in the mind, exactly answering that power which is in any body to produce it there, has all the real conformity it can or ought to have, with things without us. And this conformity between our simple ideas and the existence of things, is sufficient for real knowledge.

---

1. *What is the difference between knowledge and 'real' knowledge?*
2. *How can we know whether we have 'real' knowledge or not?*

God

Scholars disagree on just how Locke means to respond to skepticism. But it certainly looks as if he is invoking God at some crucial points in his defense of the reality of knowledge. What follows is Locke's sketch of his argument for God's existence; the details are to be found later in IV.x.

(From IV.x.1–*We are capable of knowing certainly that there is a God*) Though God has given us no innate ideas of himself; though he has stamped no original characters on our minds, wherein we may read his being; yet having furnished us with those faculties our minds are endowed with, he hath not left himself without witness ...

(From IV.x.2–*For Man knows that he himself exists*) I think it is beyond question, that man has a clear idea of his own being; he knows certainly he exists, and that he is something. He that can doubt whether he be anything or no, I speak not to ... This, then, I think I may take for a truth, which every one's certain knowledge assures him of, beyond the liberty of doubting, viz. that he is **something that actually exists**.

(From IV.x.3–*He knows also that Nothing cannot produce a Being; therefore something must have existed from Eternity*) In the next place, man knows, by an intuitive certainty, that bare **nothing can no more produce any real being, than it can be equal to two right angles**. [I]t is [thus] an evident demonstration, that **from eternity there has been something**; since what was not from eternity had a beginning; and what had a beginning must be produced by something else.

(From IV.x.4–*And that eternal being must be most powerful*) Next, it is evident, that what had its being and beginning from another, must also have all that which is in and belongs to its being from another too. All the powers it has must be owing to and received from the same source. This eternal source, then, of all being must also be the source and original of all power; and so **this eternal being must be also the most powerful**.

(From IV.x.5–*And most knowing*) Again, a man finds in **himself** perception and knowledge. We have then got one step further; and we are certain now that there is not only some being, but some knowing, intelligent being in the world. There was a time, then, when there was no knowing being, and when knowledge began to be; or else there has been also a **knowing being from eternity**. If it be said, there was a time when no being had any knowledge, when that eternal being was void of all understanding; I reply, that then it was impossible there should ever have been any knowledge: it being as impossible that things wholly void of knowledge, and operating blindly, and without any perception, should produce a knowing being, as it is impossible that a triangle should make itself three angles bigger than two right ones. For it is as repugnant to the idea of senseless matter, that it should put into itself sense, perception, and knowledge, as it is repugnant to the idea of a triangle, that it should put into itself greater angles than two right ones.

(From IV.x.6–*And therefore God*) Thus, from the consideration of ourselves, and what we infallibly find in our own constitutions, our reason leads us to the knowledge of this certain and evident truth–**that there is an eternal, most powerful, and most knowing being**; which whether any one will please to call God, it matters not.

---

1. *Locke's argument for God's existence, as presented in these passages, looks pretty weak. What's wrong*

with it?

6. George Berkeley (1685–1753)

- A *Treatise Concerning the Principles of Human Knowledge* (1710)
  - Introduction, Section One
  - Introduction, Section Two
  - Introduction, Section Three
  - Introduction, Section Four
  - Introduction, Section Five
  - Introduction, Section Six
  - Introduction, Section Seven
  - Introduction, Section Eight
  - Introduction, Section Nine
  - Introduction, Section Ten
  - Introduction, Section Eleven
  - Introduction, Section Twelve
  - Introduction, Section Sixteen
  - Introduction, Section Eighteen
  - Introduction, Section Nineteen
  - Introduction, Section Twenty
  - Introduction, Section Twenty-one
  - Introduction, Section Twenty-two
  - Part One, Section One
  - Part One, Section Two
  - Part One, Section Three
  - Part One, Section Four
  - Part One, Section Five
  - Part One, Section Six
  - Part One, Section Seven
  - Part One, Section Eight
  - Part One, Section Nine
  - Part One, Section Ten
  - Part One, Section Eleven
  - Part One, Section Twelve
  - Part One, Section Thirteen
  - Part One, Section Fourteen
  - Part One, Section Fifteen
  - Part One, Section Sixteen
  - Part One, Section Seventeen
  - Part One, Section Eighteen
  - Part One, Section Nineteen
  - Part One, Section Twenty

- *De Motu*, Section One
- *De Motu*, Section Two
- *De Motu*, Section Three
- *De Motu*, Section Four
- *De Motu*, Section Five
- *De Motu*, Section Six
- *De Motu*, Section Seven
- *De Motu*, Section Eight
- *De Motu*, Section Eleven
- *De Motu*, Section Seventeen
- *De Motu*, Section Eighteen
- *De Motu*, Section Twenty-eight
- *De Motu*, Section Twenty-nine
- *De Motu*, Section Thirty-four
- *De Motu*, Section Thirty-five
- *De Motu*, Section Thirty-six
- *De Motu*, Section Thirty-seven
- *De Motu*, Section Thirty-eight
- *De Motu*, Section Thirty-nine
- *De Motu*, Section Forty
- *De Motu*, Section Sixty-six
- *De Motu*, Section Sixty-eight

Born in Kilkenny, Ireland, George Berkeley was appointed Bishop of Cloyne (near Cork) in 1734. In 1709, he published An Essay towards a New Theory of Vision, *which lays the groundwork for his attack on the belief in material substance. His* Treatise concerning the Principles of Human Knowledge, *the main work excerpted here, appeared in 1710 and was revised in 1734. His views encountered resistance and sometimes mockery; in 1713, he restated his overall position and arguments again, this time in dialogue form, in* Three Dialogues between Hylas and Philonous. *In 1721, Berkeley published* De Motu (On Motion), *a work that presents the earliest version of instrumentalism in philosophy of science.*

The Introduction to the Principles attacks abstract ideas. As you go, it is worth wondering why Berkeley is spending so much time on this issue, given his ultimate goal of establishing a world of only spirits and ideas. Part One of that work (there is no Part Two—Berkeley claims to have lost the manuscript in Italy) forms the main part of the work. Here is an outline, by section number, of the PHK, Part One.[1]

Sections 1-24: Arguments against material substance
> Sections 25-33 Statement of Berkeley's positive view
> Sections 34-84: Objections and replies
> Sections 85-156: Attractive consequences of Berkeley's view with regard to:

> > Sections 101-117: Natural science
> > Sections 118-132: Mathematics and geometry
> > Sections 135-156: Spirits/Minds, incl. God

(Textual note: The standard edition of Berkeley's Works is that of Luce and Jessop. Modern editions are plentiful; Desmond Clarke's anthology with Cambridge is especially useful. Berkeley's Notebooks (sometimes called the 'Philosophical Commentaries'), probably written in 1707–10, provide a fascinating insight into the development of Berkeley's thought. These are available in Luce and Jessop and in Michael Ayers's anthology of Berkeley's works, though not in Clarke's.)

A Treatise Concerning the Principles of Human Knowledge (1710)

Wherein the chief causes of error and difficulty in the sciences, with the grounds of scepticism, atheism, and irreligion, are inquired into.

Introduction, Section One

Philosophy being nothing else but the study of wisdom and truth, it may with reason be expected that those who have spent most time and pains in it should enjoy a greater calm and serenity of mind, a greater clearness and evidence of knowledge, and be less disturbed with doubts and difficulties than other men. Yet so it is, we see the illiterate bulk of mankind that walk the high-road of plain common sense, and are governed by the dictates of nature, for the most part easy and undisturbed. To them nothing that is familiar appears unaccountable or difficult to comprehend. They complain not of any want of evidence in their senses, and are out of all danger of becoming Sceptics. But no sooner do we depart from sense and instinct to follow the light of a superior principle, to reason, meditate, and reflect on the nature of things, but a thousand scruples spring up in our minds concerning those things which before we seemed fully to comprehend. Prejudices and errors of sense do from all parts discover themselves to our view; and, endeavouring to correct these by reason, we are insensibly drawn into uncouth paradoxes, difficulties, and inconsistencies, which multiply and grow upon us as we advance in speculation, till at length, having wandered through many intricate mazes, we find ourselves just where we were, or, which is worse, sit down in a forlorn Scepticism.

Introduction, Section Two

The cause of this is thought to be the obscurity of things, or the natural weakness and imperfection of our understandings. It is said, the faculties we have are few, and those designed by nature for the support and comfort of life, and not to penetrate into the inward essence and constitution of things. Besides, the mind of man being finite, when it treats of things which partake of infinity, it is not to be wondered at if it run into absurdities and contradictions, out of which it is impossible it should ever extricate itself, it being of the nature of infinite not to be comprehended by that which is finite.

---

1. *The view Berkeley sets out in Section Two is not his, as indicated by the passive voice ('...is thought to be...', 'It is said...') Whose view, then, is he discussing?*

Introduction, Section Three

But, perhaps, we may be too partial to ourselves in placing the fault originally in our faculties, and not rather in the wrong use we make of them. It is a hard thing to suppose that right deductions from true principles should ever end in consequences which cannot be maintained or made consistent. We should believe that God has dealt more bountifully with the sons of men than to give them a strong desire for that knowledge which he had placed quite out of their reach. This were not agreeable to the wonted indulgent methods of Providence, which, whatever appetites it may have implanted in the creatures, doth usually furnish them with such means as, if rightly made use of, will not fail to satisfy them. Upon the whole, I am inclined to think that the far greater part, if not all, of those difficulties which have hitherto amused philosophers, and blocked up the way to knowledge, are entirely owing to ourselves—that we have first raised a dust and then complain we cannot see.

Introduction, Section Four

My purpose therefore is, to try if I can discover what those Principles are which have introduced all that doubtfulness and uncertainty, those absurdities and contradictions, into the several sects of philosophy; insomuch that the wisest men have thought our ignorance incurable, conceiving it to arise from the natural dullness and limitation of our faculties. And surely it is a work well deserving our pains to make a strict inquiry concerning the First Principles of Human Knowledge, to sift and examine them on all sides, especially since there may be some grounds to suspect that those lets and difficulties, which stay and embarrass the mind in its search after truth, do not spring from any darkness and intricacy in the objects, or natural defect in the understanding, so much as from false Principles which have been insisted on, and might have been avoided.

Introduction, Section Five

How difficult and discouraging soever this attempt may seem, when I consider how many great and extraordinary men have gone before me in the like designs, yet I am not without some hopes—upon the consideration that the largest views are not always the clearest, and that he who is short-sighted will be obliged to draw the object nearer, and may, perhaps, by a close and narrow survey, discern that which had escaped far better eyes.

Introduction, Section Six

In order to prepare the mind of the reader for the easier conceiving what follows, it is proper to premise somewhat, by way of Introduction, concerning the nature and abuse of Language. But the unravelling this matter leads me in some measure to anticipate my design, by taking notice of what seems to have had a chief part in rendering speculation intricate and perplexed, and to have occasioned innumerable errors and difficulties in almost all parts of knowledge. And that is the opinion that the mind hath a power of framing abstract ideas or notions of things. He who is not a perfect stranger to the writings and disputes of philosophers must needs acknowledge that no small part of them are spent about abstract ideas. These are in a more especial manner thought to be the object of those sciences which go by the name of Logic and Metaphysics, and of all that which passes under the notion of the most abstracted and sublime learning, in all which one shall scarce find any question handled in such a manner as does not suppose their existence in the mind, and that it is well acquainted with them.

Introduction, Section Seven

It is agreed on all hands that the qualities or modes of things do never really exist each of them apart by itself, and separated from all others, but are mixed, as it were, and blended together, several in the same object. But, we are told, the mind being able to consider each quality singly, or abstracted from those other qualities with which it is united, does by that means frame to itself abstract ideas. For example, there is perceived by sight an object extended, coloured, and moved: this mixed or compound idea the mind resolving into its simple, constituent parts, and viewing each by itself, exclusive of the rest, does frame the abstract ideas of extension, colour, and motion. Not that it is possible for colour or motion to exist without extension; but only that the mind can frame to itself by abstraction the idea of colour exclusive of extension, and of motion exclusive of both colour and extension.

Introduction, Section Eight

Again, the mind having observed that in the particular extensions perceived by sense there is something common and alike in all, and some other things peculiar, as this or that figure or magnitude, which distinguish them one from another; it considers apart or singles out by itself that which is common, making thereof a most abstract idea of extension, which is neither line, surface, nor solid, nor has any figure or magnitude, but is an idea entirely prescinded from all these. So likewise the mind, by leaving out of the particular colours perceived by sense that which distinguishes them one from another, and retaining that only which is common to all, makes an idea of colour in abstract which is neither red, nor blue, nor white, nor any other determinate colour. And, in like manner, by considering motion abstractedly not only from the body moved, but likewise from the figure it describes, and all particular directions and velocities, the abstract idea of motion is framed; which equally corresponds to all particular motions whatsoever that may be perceived by sense.

Introduction, Section Nine

And as the mind frames to itself abstract ideas of qualities or modes, so does it, by the same precision or mental separation, attain abstract ideas of the more compounded beings which include several coexistent qualities. For example, the mind having observed that Peter, James, and John resemble each other in certain common agreements of shape and other qualities, leaves out of the complex or compounded idea it has of Peter, James, and any other particular man, that which is peculiar to each, retaining only what is common to all, and so makes an abstract idea wherein all the particulars equally partake—abstracting entirely from and cutting off all those circumstances and differences which might determine it to any particular existence. And after this manner it is said we come by the abstract idea of man, or, if you please, humanity, or human nature; wherein it is true there is included colour, because there is no man but has some colour, but then it can be neither white, nor black, nor any particular colour, because there is no one particular colour wherein all men partake. So likewise there is included stature, but then it is neither tall stature, nor low stature, nor yet middle stature, but something abstracted from all these. And so of the rest. Moreover, their being a great variety of other creatures that partake in some parts, but not all, of the complex idea of man, the mind, leaving out those parts which are peculiar to men, and retaining those only which are common to all the living creatures, frames the idea of animal, which abstracts not only from all particular men, but also all birds, beasts, fishes, and insects. The constituent parts of the abstract idea of animal are body, life, sense, and spontaneous motion. By body is meant body without any particular shape or figure, there being no one shape or figure common to all animals, without covering, either of hair, or feathers, or scales, &c., nor yet naked: hair, feathers, scales, and nakedness being the distinguishing properties of particular animals, and for that reason left out of the abstract idea. Upon the same account the spontaneous motion must be neither walking, nor flying, nor creeping; it is nevertheless a motion, but what that motion is it is not easy to conceive.

Introduction, Section Ten

Whether others have this wonderful faculty of abstracting their ideas, they best can tell: for myself, I find indeed I have a faculty of imagining, or representing to myself, the ideas of those particular things I have perceived, and of variously compounding and dividing them. I can imagine a man with two heads, or the upper parts of a man joined to the body of a horse. I can consider the hand, the eye, the nose, each by itself abstracted or separated from the rest of the body. But then whatever hand or eye I imagine, it must have some particular shape and colour. Likewise the idea of man that I frame to myself must be either of a white, or a black, or a tawny, a straight, or a crooked, a tall, or a low, or a middle-sized man. I cannot by any effort of thought conceive the abstract idea above described. And it is equally impossible for me to form the abstract idea of motion distinct from the body moving, and which is neither swift nor slow, curvilinear nor rectilinear; and the like may be said of all other abstract general ideas whatsoever. To be plain, I own myself able to abstract in one sense, as when I consider some particular parts or qualities separated from others, with which, though they are united in some object, yet it is possible they may really exist without them. But I deny that I can abstract from one another, or conceive separately, those qualities which it is impossible should exist so separated; or that I can frame a general notion, by abstracting from particulars in the manner aforesaid—which last are the two proper acceptations of abstraction. And there are grounds to think most men will acknowledge themselves to be in my case. The generality of men which are simple and illiterate never pretend to abstract notions. It is said they are difficult and not to be attained without pains and study; we may therefore reasonably conclude that, if such there be, they are confined only to the learned.

Introduction, Section Eleven

I proceed to examine what can be alleged in defence of the doctrine of abstraction, and try if I can discover what it is that inclines the men of speculation to embrace an opinion so remote from common sense as that seems to be. There has been a late deservedly esteemed philosopher who, no doubt, has given it very much countenance, by seeming to think the having abstract general ideas is what puts the widest difference in point of understanding betwixt man and beast. "The having of general ideas," saith he, "is that which puts a perfect distinction betwixt man and brutes, and is an excellency which the faculties of brutes do by no means attain unto. For, it is evident we observe no foot-steps in them of making use of general signs for universal ideas; from which we have reason to imagine that they have not the faculty of abstracting, or making general ideas, since they have no use of words or any other general signs." And a little after: "Therefore, I think, we may suppose that it is in this that the species of brutes are discriminated from men, and it is that proper difference wherein they are wholly separated, and which at last widens to so wide a distance. For, if they have any ideas at all, and are not bare machines (as some would have them), we cannot deny them to have some reason. It seems as evident to me that they do, some of them, in certain instances reason as that they have sense; but it is only in particular ideas, just as they receive them from their senses. They are the best of them tied up within those narrow bounds, and have not (as I think) the faculty to enlarge them by any kind of abstraction" (*Essay on Human Understanding*, II.xi.10 and 11). I readily agree with this learned author, that the faculties of brutes can by no means attain to abstraction. But then if this be made the distinguishing property of that sort of animals, I fear a great many of those that pass for men must be reckoned into their number. The reason that is here assigned why we have no grounds to think brutes have abstract general ideas is, that we observe in them no use of words or any other general signs; which is built on this supposition—that the making use of words implies the having general ideas. From which it follows that men who use language are able to abstract or generalize their ideas. That this is the sense and arguing of the author will further appear by his answering the question he in another place puts: "Since all things that exist are only particulars, how come we by general terms?" His answer is: "Words become general by being made the signs of general ideas" (*Essay on Human Understanding*, IV.iii.6). But it seems that a word becomes general by being made the sign, not of an abstract general idea, but of several particular ideas, any one of which it indifferently suggests to the mind. For example, when it is said "the change of motion is proportional to the impressed force," or that "whatever has extension is divisible," these propositions are to be understood of motion and extension in general; and nevertheless it will not follow that they suggest to my thoughts an idea of motion without a body moved, or any determinate direction and velocity, or that I must conceive an abstract general idea of extension, which is neither line, surface, nor solid, neither great nor small, black, white, nor red, nor of any other determinate colour. It is only implied that whatever particular motion I consider, whether it be swift or slow, perpendicular, horizontal, or oblique, or in whatever object, the axiom concerning it holds equally true. As does the other of every particular extension, it matters not whether line, surface, or solid, whether of this or that magnitude or figure.

Introduction, Section Twelve

By observing how ideas become general we may the better judge how words are made so. And here it is to be noted that I do not deny absolutely there are general ideas, but only that there are any abstract general ideas; for, in the passages we have quoted wherein there is mention of general ideas, it is always supposed that they are formed by abstraction, after the manner set forth in Sections Eight and Nine. Now, if we will annex a meaning to our words, and speak only of what we can conceive, I believe we shall acknowledge that an idea which, considered in itself, is particular, becomes general by being made to represent or stand for all other particular ideas of the same sort. To make this plain by an example, suppose a geometrician is demonstrating the method of cutting a line in two equal parts. He draws, for instance, a black line of an inch in length: this, which in itself is a particular line, is nevertheless with regard to its signification general, since, as it is there used, it represents all particular lines whatsoever; so that what is demonstrated of it is demonstrated of all lines, or, in other words, of a line in general. And, as that particular line becomes general by being made a sign, so the name "line," which taken absolutely is particular, by being a sign is made general. And as the former owes its generality not to its being the sign of an abstract or general line, but of all particular right lines that may possibly exist, so the latter must be thought to derive its generality from the same cause, namely, the various particular lines which it indifferently denotes. ...

Introduction, Section Sixteen

But here it will be demanded, how we can know any proposition to be true of all particular triangles, except we have first seen it demonstrated of the abstract idea of a triangle which equally agrees to all? For, because a property may be demonstrated to agree to some one particular triangle, it will not thence follow that it equally belongs to any other triangle, which in all respects is not the same with it. For example, having demonstrated that the three angles of an isosceles rectangular triangle are equal to two right ones, I cannot therefore conclude this affection agrees to all other triangles which have neither a right angle nor two equal sides. It seems therefore that, to be certain this proposition is universally true, we must either make a particular demonstration for every particular triangle, which is impossible, or once for all demonstrate it of the abstract idea of a triangle, in which all the particulars do indifferently partake and by which they are all equally represented. To which I answer, that, though the idea I have in view whilst I make the demonstration be, for instance, that of an isosceles rectangular triangle whose sides are of a determinate length, I may nevertheless be certain it extends to all other rectilinear triangles, of what sort or bigness soever. And that because neither the right angle, nor the equality, nor determinate length of the sides are at all concerned in the demonstration. It is true the diagram I have in view includes all these particulars, but then there is not the least mention made of them in the proof of the proposition. It is not said the three angles are equal to two right ones, because one of them is a right angle, or because the sides comprehending it are of the same length. Which sufficiently shows that the right angle might have been oblique, and the sides unequal, and for all that the demonstration have held good. And for this reason it is that I conclude that to be true of any obliquangular or scalenon which I had demonstrated of a particular right-angled equicrural triangle, and not because I demonstrated the proposition of the abstract idea of a triangle And here it must be acknowledged that a man may consider a figure merely as triangular, without attending to the particular qualities of the angles, or relations of the sides. So far he may abstract; but this will never prove that he can frame an abstract, general, inconsistent idea of a triangle. In like manner we may consider Peter so far forth as man, or so far forth as animal without framing the fore-mentioned abstract idea, either of man or of animal, inasmuch as all that is perceived is not considered. ...

Introduction, Section Eighteen

I come now to consider the source of this prevailing notion, and that seems to me to be language. And surely nothing of less extent than reason itself could have been the source of an opinion so universally received. The truth of this appears as from other reasons so also from the plain confession of the ablest patrons of abstract ideas, who acknowledge that they are made in order to naming; from which it is a clear consequence that if there had been no such things as speech or universal signs there never had been any thought of abstraction. See III.vi.39, and elsewhere of the *Essay on Human Understanding*. Let us examine the manner wherein words have contributed to the origin of that mistake.

First then, it is thought that every name has, or ought to have, one only precise and settled signification, which inclines men to think there are certain abstract, determinate ideas that constitute the true and only immediate signification of each general name; and that it is by the mediation of these abstract ideas that a general name comes to signify any particular thing. Whereas, in truth, there is no such thing as one precise and definite signification annexed to any general name, they all signifying indifferently a great number of particular ideas. All which doth evidently follow from what has been already said, and will clearly appear to anyone by a little reflexion. To this it will be objected that every name that has a definition is thereby restrained to one certain signification. For example, a triangle is defined to be "a plain surface comprehended by three right lines," by which that name is limited to denote one certain idea and no other. To which I answer, that in the definition it is not said whether the surface be great or small, black or white, nor whether the sides are long or short, equal or unequal, nor with what angles they are inclined to each other; in all which there may be great variety, and consequently there is no one settled idea which limits the signification of the word triangle. It is one thing for to keep a name constantly to the same definition, and another to make it stand everywhere for the same idea; the one is necessary, the other useless and impracticable.

Introduction, Section Nineteen

But, to give a farther account how words came to produce the doctrine of abstract ideas, it must be observed that it is a received opinion that language has no other end but the communicating our ideas, and that every significant name stands for an idea. This being so, and it being withal certain that names which yet are not thought altogether insignificant do not always mark out particular conceivable ideas, it is straightway concluded that they stand for abstract notions. That there are many names in use amongst speculative men which do not always suggest to others determinate, particular ideas, or in truth anything at all, is what nobody will deny. And a little attention will discover that it is not necessary (even in the strictest reasonings) significant names which stand for ideas should, every time they are used, excite in the understanding the ideas they are made to stand for—in reading and discoursing, names being for the most part used as letters are in Algebra, in which, though a particular quantity be marked by each letter, yet to proceed right it is not requisite that in every step each letter suggest to your thoughts that particular quantity it was appointed to stand for.

Introduction, Section Twenty

Besides, the communicating of ideas marked by words is not the chief and only end of language, as is commonly supposed. There are other ends, as the raising of some passion, the exciting to or deterring from an action, the putting the mind in some particular disposition—to which the former is in many cases barely subservient, and sometimes entirely omitted, when these can be obtained without it, as I think does not unfrequently happen in the familiar use of language. I entreat the reader to reflect with himself, and see if it doth not often happen, either in hearing or reading a discourse, that the passions of fear, love, hatred, admiration, disdain, and the like, arise immediately in his mind upon the perception of certain words, without any ideas coming between. At first, indeed, the words might have occasioned ideas that were fitting to produce those emotions; but, if I mistake not, it will be found that, when language is once grown familiar, the hearing of the sounds or sight of the characters is oft immediately attended with those passions which at first were wont to be produced by the intervention of ideas that are now quite omitted. May we not, for example, be affected with the promise of a good thing, though we have not an idea of what it is? Or is not the being threatened with danger sufficient to excite a dread, though we think not of any particular evil likely to befal us, nor yet frame to ourselves an idea of danger in abstract? If any one shall join ever so little reflexion of his own to what has been said, I believe that it will evidently appear to him that general names are often used in the propriety of language without the speaker's designing them for marks of ideas in his own, which he would have them raise in the mind of the hearer.

Even proper names themselves do not seem always spoken with a design to bring into our view the ideas of those individuals that are supposed to be marked by them. For example, when a schoolman tells me "Aristotle hath said it," all I conceive he means by it is to dispose me to embrace his opinion with the deference and submission which custom has annexed to that name. And this effect is often so instantly produced in the minds of those who are accustomed to resign their judgment to authority of that philosopher, as it is impossible any idea either of his person, writings, or reputation should go before. Innumerable examples of this kind may be given, but why should I insist on those things which every one's experience will, I doubt not, plentifully suggest unto him?

Introduction, Section Twenty-one

We have, I think, shewn the impossibility of Abstract Ideas. We have considered what has been said for them by their ablest patrons; and endeavored to show they are of no use for those ends to which they are thought necessary. And lastly, we have traced them to the source from whence they flow, which appears evidently to be language. It cannot be denied that words are of excellent use, in that by their means all that stock of knowledge which has been purchased by the joint labours of inquisitive men in all ages and nations may be drawn into the view and made the possession of one single person. But at the same time it must be owned that most parts of knowledge have been strangely perplexed and darkened by the abuse of words, and general ways of speech wherein they are delivered. Since therefore words are so apt to impose on the understanding, whatever ideas I consider, I shall endeavour to take them bare and naked into my view, keeping out of my thoughts so far as I am able, those names which long and constant use hath so strictly united with them; from which I may expect to derive the following advantages:

Introduction, Section Twenty-two

First, I shall be sure to get clear of all controversies purely verbal—the springing up of which weeds in almost all the sciences has been a main hindrance to the growth of true and sound knowledge.

Secondly, this seems to be a sure way to extricate myself out of that fine and subtle net of abstract ideas which has so miserably perplexed and entangled the minds of men; and that with this peculiar circumstance, that by how much the finer and more curious was the wit of any man, by so much the deeper was he likely to be ensnared and faster held therein.

Thirdly, so long as I confine my thoughts to my own ideas divested of words, I do not see how I can easily be mistaken. The objects I consider, I clearly and adequately know. I cannot be deceived in thinking I have an idea which I have not. It is not possible for me to imagine that any of my own ideas are alike or unlike that are not truly so. To discern the agreements or disagreements there are between my ideas, to see what ideas are included in any compound idea and what not, there is nothing more requisite than an attentive perception of what passes in my own understanding.

---

1. *'We have first raised a dust and then complain that we cannot see.' (Section Three. Who is 'we'? What is the dust?*
2. *What are Berkeley's targets?*

   Abstraction 1: Taking a simple idea (of a determinate shape, for example) and paring it off from the other ideas with which it came into the mind.

   Abstraction 2: Taking a bunch of complex ideas (of extended objects, for example) and isolating what's common to them (extension as a determinable; human being as a kind).

   By contrast, what is Abstraction 3, and why is it fine?
3. *There are two big puzzles posed by the introduction. First, what exactly is the argument against abstract ideas supposed to be? It looks as if Section Ten goes something like this:*

   1. I (Berkeley) cannot abstract in sense 1 and 2.
   2. _ _ _ _ _ _ _ _
   3. _ _ _ _ _ _ _ _
   4. Therefore, no one can abstract in senses 1 and 2.

   What weaknesses do you see in this argument?

   In a later work (Alciphron, or the Minute Philosopher, 1732), Berkeley offers a different argument against abstract ideas. In this dialogue, Euphranor is Berkeley's spokesman; Alciphron is supposed to represent Locke's views:

   Euphranor: Pray, Alciphron, which are those things you would call absolutely impossible?

   Alciphron: Such as include a contradiction.

   Euphranor: Can you frame an idea of what includes a contradiction?

   Alciphron: I cannot.

   Euphranor: Consequently, whatever is absolutely impossible you cannot form an idea of.

   Alciphron: This I grant.

Euphranor: But can a colour or triangle, such as you describe their abstract general ideas, really exist?

Alciphron: It is absolutely impossible such things should exist in nature.

Euphranor: Should it not follow, then, that they cannot exist in your mind, or, in other words, that you cannot conceive or frame an idea of them?[2]

Reconstruct Euphranor's argument:

Premise 1: If x is impossible, then x includes a contradiction.
  Premise 2: If x includes a contradiction, then _____.
  Premise 3: It follows that if x is impossible, x is _____.
  Premise 4: _____
  Conclusion: _____.

4. *The second puzzle: why is Berkeley so worried about abstraction? Keep this question in mind as you read the rest of the* Principles.

Part One, Section One

It is evident to any one who takes a survey of the objects of human knowledge, that they are either ideas actually imprinted on the senses; or else such as are perceived by attending to the passions and operations of the mind; or lastly, ideas formed by help of memory and imagination–either compounding, dividing, or barely representing those originally perceived in the aforesaid ways. By sight I have the ideas of light and colours, with their several degrees and variations. By touch I perceive hard and soft, heat and cold, motion and resistance, and of all these more and less either as to quantity or degree. Smelling furnishes me with odours; the palate with tastes; and hearing conveys sounds to the mind in all their variety of tone and composition. And as several of these are observed to accompany each other, they come to be marked by one name, and so to be reputed as one thing. Thus, for example a certain colour, taste, smell, figure and consistence having been observed to go together, are accounted one distinct thing, signified by the name apple; other collections of ideas constitute a stone, a tree, a book, and the like sensible things–which as they are pleasing or disagreeable excite the passions of love, hatred, joy, grief, and so forth.

Part One, Section Two

But, besides all that endless variety of ideas or objects of knowledge, there is likewise something which knows or perceives them, and exercises divers operations, as willing, imagining, remembering, about them. This perceiving, active being is what I call mind, spirit, soul, or myself. By which words I do not denote any one of my ideas, but a thing entirely distinct from them, wherein, they exist, or, which is the same thing, whereby they are perceived–for the existence of an idea consists in being perceived.

Part One, Section Three

That neither our thoughts, nor passions, nor ideas formed by the imagination, exist without the mind, is what everybody will allow. And it seems no less evident that the various sensations or ideas imprinted on the sense, however blended or combined together (that is, whatever objects they compose), cannot exist otherwise than in a mind perceiving them. I think an intuitive knowledge may be obtained of this by any one that shall attend to what is meant by the term exists, when applied to sensible things. The table I write on I say exists, that is, I see and feel it; and if I were out of my study I should say it existed—meaning thereby that if I was in my study I might perceive it, or that some other spirit actually does perceive it. There was an odour, that is, it was smelt; there was a sound, that is, it was heard; a colour or figure, and it was perceived by sight or touch. This is all that I can understand by these and the like expressions. For as to what is said of the absolute existence of unthinking things without any relation to their being perceived, that seems perfectly unintelligible. Their *esse* is *percepi*, nor is it possible they should have any existence out of the minds or thinking things which perceive them.

Part One, Section Four

It is indeed an opinion strangely prevailing amongst men, that houses, mountains, rivers, and in a word all sensible objects, have an existence, natural or real, distinct from their being perceived by the understanding. But, with how great an assurance and acquiescence soever this principle may be entertained in the world, yet whoever shall find in his heart to call it in question may, if I mistake not, perceive it to involve a manifest contradiction. For, what are the fore-mentioned objects but the things we perceive by sense? And what do we perceive besides our own ideas or sensations? And is it not plainly repugnant that any one of these, or any combination of them, should exist unperceived?

Part One, Section Five

If we thoroughly examine this tenet it will, perhaps, be found at bottom to depend on the doctrine of abstract ideas. For can there be a nicer strain of abstraction than to distinguish the existence of sensible objects from their being perceived, so as to conceive them existing unperceived? Light and colours, heat and cold, extension and figures—in a word, the things we see and feel—what are they but so many sensations, notions, ideas, or impressions on the sense? and is it possible to separate, even in thought, any of these from perception? For my part, I might as easily divide a thing from itself. I may, indeed, divide in my thoughts, or conceive apart from each other, those things which, perhaps I never perceived by sense so divided. Thus, I imagine the trunk of a human body without the limbs, or conceive the smell of a rose without thinking on the rose itself. So far, I will not deny, I can abstract—if that may properly be called abstraction which extends only to the conceiving separately such objects as it is possible may really exist or be actually perceived asunder. But my conceiving or imagining power does not extend beyond the possibility of real existence or perception. Hence, as it is impossible for me to see or feel anything without an actual sensation of that thing, so is it impossible for me to conceive in my thoughts any sensible thing or object distinct from the sensation or perception of it.

Part One, Section Six

Some truths there are so near and obvious to the mind that a man need only open his eyes to see them. Such I take this important one to be, viz., that all the choir of heaven and furniture of the earth, in a word all those bodies which compose the mighty frame of the world, have not any subsistence without a mind, that their being is to be perceived or known; that consequently so long as they are not actually perceived by me, or do not exist in my mind or that of any other created spirit, they must either have no existence at all, or else subsist in the mind of some Eternal Spirit—it being perfectly unintelligible, and involving all the absurdity of abstraction, to attribute to any single part of them an existence independent of a spirit. To be convinced of which, the reader need only reflect, and try to separate in his own thoughts the being of a sensible thing from its being perceived.

Part One, Section Seven

From what has been said it follows there is not any other Substance than Spirit, or that which perceives. But, for the fuller proof of this point, let it be considered the sensible qualities are colour, figure, motion, smell, taste, etc., i.e., the ideas perceived by sense. Now, for an idea to exist in an unperceiving thing is a manifest contradiction, for to have an idea is all one as to perceive; that therefore wherein colour, figure, and the like qualities exist must perceive them; hence it is clear there can be no unthinking substance or substratum of those ideas.

Part One, Section Eight

But, say you, though the ideas themselves do not exist without the mind, yet there may be things like them, whereof they are copies or resemblances, which things exist without the mind in an unthinking substance. I answer, an idea can be like nothing but an idea; a colour or figure can be like nothing but another colour or figure. If we look but never so little into our thoughts, we shall find it impossible for us to conceive a likeness except only between our ideas. Again, I ask whether those supposed originals or external things, of which our ideas are the pictures or representations, be themselves perceivable or no? If they are, then they are ideas and we have gained our point; but if you say they are not, I appeal to any one whether it be sense to assert a colour is like something which is invisible; hard or soft, like something which is intangible; and so of the rest.

Part One, Section Nine

Some there are who make a distinction betwixt primary and secondary qualities. By the former they mean extension, figure, motion, rest, solidity or impenetrability, and number; by the latter they denote all other sensible qualities, as colours, sounds, tastes, and so forth. The ideas we have of these they acknowledge not to be the resemblances of anything existing without the mind, or unperceived, but they will have our ideas of the primary qualities to be patterns or images of things which exist without the mind, in an unthinking substance which they call Matter. By Matter, therefore, we are to understand an inert, senseless substance, in which extension, figure, and motion do actually subsist. But it is evident from what we have already shown, that extension, figure, and motion are only ideas existing in the mind, and that an idea can be like nothing but another idea, and that consequently neither they nor their archetypes can exist in an unperceiving substance. Hence, it is plain that that the very notion of what is called Matter or corporeal substance, involves a contradiction in it.

Part One, Section Ten

They who assert that figure, motion, and the rest of the primary or original qualities do exist without the mind in unthinking substances, do at the same time acknowledge that colours, sounds, heat cold, and suchlike secondary qualities, do not–which they tell us are sensations existing in the mind alone, that depend on and are occasioned by the different size, texture, and motion of the minute particles of matter. This they take for an undoubted truth, which they can demonstrate beyond all exception. Now, if it be certain that those original qualities are inseparably united with the other sensible qualities, and not, even in thought, capable of being abstracted from them, it plainly follows that they exist only in the mind. But I desire any one to reflect and try whether he can, by any abstraction of thought, conceive the extension and motion of a body without all other sensible qualities. For my own part, I see evidently that it is not in my power to frame an idea of a body extended and moving, but I must withal give it some colour or other sensible quality which is acknowledged to exist only in the mind. In short, extension, figure, and motion, abstracted from all other qualities, are inconceivable. Where therefore the other sensible qualities are, there must these be also, to wit, in the mind and nowhere else.

Part One, Section Eleven

Again, great and small, swift and slow, are allowed to exist nowhere without the mind, being entirely relative, and changing as the frame or position of the organs of sense varies. The extension therefore which exists without the mind is neither great nor small, the motion neither swift nor slow, that is, they are nothing at all. But, say you, they are extension in general, and motion in general: thus we see how much the tenet of extended movable substances existing without the mind depends on the strange doctrine of abstract ideas. And here I cannot but remark how nearly the vague and indeterminate description of Matter or corporeal substance, which the modern philosophers are run into by their own principles, resembles that antiquated and so much ridiculed notion of materia prima, to be met with in Aristotle and his followers. Without extension solidity cannot be conceived; since therefore it has been shewn that extension exists not in an unthinking substance, the same must also be true of solidity.

Part One, Section Twelve

That number is entirely the creature of the mind, even though the other qualities be allowed to exist without, will be evident to whoever considers that the same thing bears a different denomination of number as the mind views it with different respects. Thus, the same extension is one, or three, or thirty-six, according as the mind considers it with reference to a yard, a foot, or an inch. Number is so visibly relative, and dependent on men's understanding, that it is strange to think how any one should give it an absolute existence without the mind. We say one book, one page, one line, etc.; all these are equally units, though some contain several of the others. And in each instance, it is plain, the unit relates to some particular combination of ideas arbitrarily put together by the mind.

Part One, Section Thirteen

Unity I know some will have to be a simple or uncompounded idea, accompanying all other ideas into the mind. That I have any such idea answering the word unity I do not find; and if I had, methinks I could not miss finding it: on the contrary, it should be the most familiar to my understanding, since it is said to accompany all other ideas, and to be perceived by all the ways of sensation and reflexion. To say no more, it is an abstract idea.

Part One, Section Fourteen

I shall farther add, that, after the same manner as modern philosophers prove certain sensible qualities to have no existence in Matter, or without the mind, the same thing may be likewise proved of all other sensible qualities whatsoever. Thus, for instance, it is said that heat and cold are affections only of the mind, and not at all patterns of real beings, existing in the corporeal substances which excite them, for that the same body which appears cold to one hand seems warm to another. Now, why may we not as well argue that figure and extension are not patterns or resemblances of qualities existing in Matter, because to the same eye at different stations, or eyes of a different texture at the same station, they appear various, and cannot therefore be the images of anything settled and determinate without the mind? Again, it is proved that sweetness is not really in the sapid thing, because the thing remaining unaltered the sweetness is changed into bitter, as in case of a fever or otherwise vitiated palate. Is it not as reasonable to say that motion is not without the mind, since if the succession of ideas in the mind become swifter, the motion, it is acknowledged, shall appear slower without any alteration in any external object?

Part One, Section Fifteen

In short, let any one consider those arguments which are thought manifestly to prove that colours and taste exist only in the mind, and he shall find they may with equal force be brought to prove the same thing of extension, figure, and motion. Though it must be confessed this method of arguing does not so much prove that there is no extension or colour in an outward object, as that we do not know by sense which is the true extension or colour of the object. But the arguments foregoing plainly shew it to be impossible that any colour or extension at all, or other sensible quality whatsoever, should exist in an unthinking subject without the mind, or in truth, that there should be any such thing as an outward object.

Part One, Section Sixteen

But let us examine a little the received opinion.

It is said extension is a mode or accident of Matter, and that Matter is the substratum that supports it. Now I desire that you would explain to me what is meant by Matter's supporting extension. Say you, I have no idea of Matter and therefore cannot explain it. I answer, though you have no positive, yet, if you have any meaning at all, you must at least have a relative idea of Matter; though you know not what it is, yet you must be supposed to know what relation it bears to accidents, and what is meant by its supporting them. It is evident 'support' cannot here be taken in its usual or literal sense—as when we say that pillars support a building; in what sense therefore must it be taken?

Part One, Section Seventeen

If we inquire into what the most accurate philosophers declare themselves to mean by material substance, we shall find them acknowledge they have no other meaning annexed to those sounds but the idea of Being in general, together with the relative notion of its supporting accidents. The general idea of Being appeareth to me the most abstract and incomprehensible of all other; and as for its supporting accidents, this, as we have just now observed, cannot be understood in the common sense of those words; it must therefore be taken in some other sense, but what that is they do not explain. So that when I consider the two parts or branches which make the signification of the words material substance, I am convinced there is no distinct meaning annexed to them. But why should we trouble ourselves any farther, in discussing this material substratum or support of figure and motion, and other sensible qualities? Does it not suppose they have an existence without the mind? And is not this a direct repugnancy, and altogether inconceivable?

Part One, Section Eighteen

But, though it were possible that solid, figured, movable substances may exist without the mind, corresponding to the ideas we have of bodies, yet how is it possible for us to know this? Either we must know it by sense or by reason. As for our senses, by them we have the knowledge only of our sensations, ideas, or those things that are immediately perceived by sense, call them what you will: but they do not inform us that things exist without the mind, or unperceived, like to those which are perceived. This the materialists themselves acknowledge. It remains therefore that if we have any knowledge at all of external things, it must be by reason, inferring their existence from what is immediately perceived by sense. But what reason can induce us to believe the existence of bodies without the mind, from what we perceive, since the very patrons of Matter themselves do not pretend there is any necessary connexion betwixt them and our ideas? I say it is granted on all hands (and what happens in dreams, phrensies, and the like, puts it beyond dispute) that it is possible we might be affected with all the ideas we have now, though there were no bodies existing without resembling them. Hence, it is evident the supposition of external bodies is not necessary for the producing our ideas; since it is granted they are produced sometimes, and might possibly be produced always in the same order, we see them in at present, without their concurrence.

Part One, Section Nineteen

But, though we might possibly have all our sensations without them, yet perhaps it may be thought easier to conceive and explain the manner of their production, by supposing external bodies in their likeness rather than otherwise; and so it might be at least probable there are such things as bodies that excite their ideas in our minds. But neither can this be said; for, though we give the materialists their external bodies, they by their own confession are never the nearer knowing how our ideas are produced; since they own themselves unable to comprehend in what manner body can act upon spirit, or how it is possible it should imprint any idea in the mind. Hence it is evident the production of ideas or sensations in our minds can be no reason why we should suppose Matter or corporeal substances, since that is acknowledged to remain equally inexplicable with or without this supposition. If therefore it were possible for bodies to exist without the mind, yet to hold they do so, must needs be a very precarious opinion; since it is to suppose, without any reason at all, that God has created innumerable beings that are entirely useless, and serve to no manner of purpose.

Part One, Section Twenty

In short, if there were external bodies, it is impossible we should ever come to know it; and if there were not, we might have the very same reasons to think there were that we have now. Suppose—what no one can deny possible—an intelligence without the help of external bodies, to be affected with the same train of sensations or ideas that you are, imprinted in the same order and with like vividness in his mind. I ask whether that intelligence hath not all the reason to believe the existence of corporeal substances, represented by his ideas, and exciting them in his mind, that you can possibly have for believing the same thing? Of this there can be no question—which one consideration were enough to make any reasonable person suspect the strength of whatever arguments be may think himself to have, for the existence of bodies without the mind.

Part One, Section Twenty-one

Were it necessary to add any farther proof against the existence of Matter after what has been said, I could instance several of those errors and difficulties (not to mention impieties) which have sprung from that tenet. It has occasioned numberless controversies and disputes in philosophy, and not a few of far greater moment in religion. But I shall not enter into the detail of them in this place, as well because I think arguments *a posteriori* are unnecessary for confirming what has been, if I mistake not, sufficiently demonstrated *a priori*, as because I shall hereafter find occasion to speak somewhat of them.

Part One, Section Twenty-two

I am afraid I have given cause to think I am needlessly prolix in handling this subject. For, to what purpose is it to dilate on that which may be demonstrated with the utmost evidence in a line or two, to any one that is capable of the least reflexion? It is but looking into your own thoughts, and so trying whether you can conceive it possible for a sound, or figure, or motion, or colour to exist without the mind or unperceived. This easy trial may perhaps make you see that what you contend for is a downright contradiction. Insomuch that I am content to put the whole upon this issue: If you can but conceive it possible for one extended movable substance, or, in general, for any one idea, or anything like an idea, to exist otherwise than in a mind perceiving it, I shall readily give up the cause. And, as for all that compages of external bodies you contend for, I shall grant you its existence, though you cannot either give me any reason why you believe it exists, or assign any use to it when it is supposed to exist. I say, the bare possibility of your opinions being true shall pass for an argument that it is so.

Part One, Section Twenty-three

But, say you, surely there is nothing easier than for me to imagine trees, for instance, in a park, or books existing in a closet, and nobody by to perceive them. I answer, you may so, there is no difficulty in it; but what is all this, I beseech you, more than framing in your mind certain ideas which you call books and trees, and the same time omitting to frame the idea of any one that may perceive them? But do not you yourself perceive or think of them all the while? This therefore is nothing to the purpose; it only shews you have the power of imagining or forming ideas in your mind: but it does not shew that you can conceive it possible the objects of your thought may exist without the mind. To make out this, it is necessary that you conceive them existing unconceived or unthought of, which is a manifest repugnancy. When we do our utmost to conceive the existence of external bodies, we are all the while only contemplating our own ideas. But the mind taking no notice of itself, is deluded to think it can and does conceive bodies existing unthought of or without the mind, though at the same time they are apprehended by or exist in itself. A little attention will discover to any one the truth and evidence of what is here said, and make it unnecessary to insist on any other proofs against the existence of material substance.

Part One, Section Twenty-four

It is very obvious, upon the least inquiry into our thoughts, to know whether it is possible for us to understand what is meant by the absolute existence of sensible objects in themselves, or without the mind. To me it is evident those words mark out either a direct contradiction, or else nothing at all. And to convince others of this, I know no readier or fairer way than to entreat they would calmly attend to their own thoughts; and if by this attention the emptiness or repugnancy of those expressions does appear, surely nothing more is requisite for the conviction. It is on this therefore that I insist, to wit, that the absolute existence of unthinking things are words without a meaning, or which include a contradiction. This is what I repeat and inculcate, and earnestly recommend to the attentive thoughts of the reader.

---

1. *Berkeley's arguments for immaterialism fall into two classes: (A) those that challenge the intelligibility of materialism, and (B) those that grant its intelligibility but try to show that it is unjustified. Mark each argument below with an 'A' or 'B' as you go.*
2. *Materialists think that objects can exist unperceived. But to say that an object exists is just to say what? (From Part One, Section Three.)*
3. *This argument is from Part One, Section Four; there's a parallel argument in section 7:*
    1. An object is _____.
    2. _____.
    3. Therefore, objects are ideas.
4. *Locke used resemblance to account for the representative powers of ideas of primary qualities. But:*
    1. Likeness Principle: an idea can only be like _____.
    2. The only way an idea can represent anything is by virtue of _____ it.
    3. Therefore, no idea can represent anything but _____. (From Part One, Section Eight.)
5. *Locke restricts resemblance to ideas of primary qualities and says that secondary qualities exist only in the mind. But:*
    1. This means that I must be able to think of an object that has _____.
    2. Given the arguments of the Introduction, we can say that

    _____.
    3. No object denuded of secondary qualities is even_____ _____.

(From Part One, Section Ten.)

6. *Locke says that matter is the substratum that supports the observable qualities of bodies. But in order to think of such a thing, we'd have to first understand what is meant by the word _____ here. And _____. (From Part One, Section Sixteen.)*

7. *Suppose matter exists. How could we be justified in believing in it? Either (1) by sensation (direct experience) or (2) reason (i.e., a demonstration or a logically sound argument).*

Against (1): _____

   Against (2): If we could demonstrate the existence of matter, there would have to be a _____ between our ideas and the objects they represent. But we can see that there is no such _____, simply by noticing that _____. In fact, even the proponents of matter grant that there is no _____ between ideas and their objects.

   Now, a materialist might agree that we cannot prove by demonstration that matter exists. (In fact, this seems to be Descartes's position; see the last paragraph of his Synopsis of the Meditations.) Still, the materialist might argue, we can be justified in believing in matter's existence by means of an inference to the best explanation. The best explanation for our experiences is that they are experiences of a real, mind-independent world. How does Berkeley challenge this move? (From Part One, Sections Eighteen and Nineteen.)

8. *The 'master argument'—Matter is by definition something that can exist even when no mind is thinking about it. What could be easier than conceiving of something that exists unconceived? (To imagine, conceive, and perceive, are all used here by Berkeley pretty much interchangeably—each means having a given idea in the mind.) But:*

   1. I think of *x* existing unperceived. (The materialist's presupposition)
   2. But this is the wrong description of what I have thought of, since _____.
   3. Therefore, no one can think of something that exists unperceived.

Berkeley says in Three Dialogues *that conceiving something unconceived is analogous to 'seeing something unseen.' (From Part One, Sections 22, 23, and 24; see also Section Five.)*

Part One, Section Twenty-five

All our ideas, sensations, notions, or the things which we perceive, by whatsoever names they may be distinguished, are visibly inactive—there is nothing of power or agency included in them. So that one idea or object of thought cannot produce or make any alteration in another. To be satisfied of the truth of this, there is nothing else requisite but a bare observation of our ideas. For, since they and every part of them exist only in the mind, it follows that there is nothing in them but what is perceived: but whoever shall attend to his ideas, whether of sense or reflexion, will not perceive in them any power or activity; there is, therefore, no such thing contained in them. A little attention will discover to us that the very being of an idea implies passiveness and inertness in it, insomuch that it is impossible for an idea to do anything, or, strictly speaking, to be the cause of anything: neither can it be the resemblance or pattern of any active being, as is evident from Section Eight. Whence it plainly follows that extension, figure, and motion cannot be the cause of our sensations. To say, therefore, that these are the effects of powers resulting from the configuration, number, motion, and size of corpuscles, must certainly be false.

Part One, Section Twenty-six

We perceive a continual succession of ideas, some are anew excited, others are changed or totally disappear. There is therefore some cause of these ideas, whereon they depend, and which produces and changes them. That this cause cannot be any quality or idea or combination of ideas, is clear from the preceding section. I must therefore be a substance; but it has been shewn that there is no corporeal or material substance: it remains therefore that the cause of ideas is an incorporeal active substance or Spirit.

Part One, Section Twenty-seven

A spirit is one simple, undivided, active being—as it perceives ideas it is called the understanding, and as it produces or otherwise operates about them it is called the will. Hence there can be no idea formed of a soul or spirit; for all ideas whatever, being passive and inert (see Section Twenty-five), they cannot represent unto us, by way of image or likeness, that which acts. A little attention will make it plain to any one, that to have an idea which shall be like that active principle of motion and change of ideas is absolutely impossible. Such is the nature of spirit, or that which acts, that it cannot be of itself perceived, but only by the effects which it produceth. If any man shall doubt of the truth of what is here delivered, let him but reflect and try if he can frame the idea of any power or active being, and whether he has ideas of two principal powers, marked by the names will and understanding, distinct from each other as well as from a third idea of Substance or Being in general, with a relative notion of its supporting or being the subject of the aforesaid powers—which is signified by the name soul or spirit. This is what some hold; but, so far as I can see, the words will, soul, spirit, do not stand for different ideas, or, in truth, for any idea at all, but for something which is very different from ideas, and which, being an agent, cannot be like unto, or represented by, any idea whatsoever. Though it must be owned at the same time that we have some notion of soul, spirit, and the operations of the mind: such as willing, loving, hating—inasmuch as we know or understand the meaning of these words.

Part One, Section Twenty-eight

I find I can excite ideas in my mind at pleasure, and vary and shift the scene as oft as I think fit. It is no more than willing, and straightway this or that idea arises in my fancy; and by the same power it is obliterated and makes way for another. This making and unmaking of ideas doth very properly denominate the mind active. Thus much is certain and grounded on experience; but when we think of unthinking agents or of exciting ideas exclusive of volition, we only amuse ourselves with words.

Part One, Section Twenty-nine

But, whatever power I may have over my own thoughts, I find the ideas actually perceived by Sense have not a like dependence on my will. When in broad daylight I open my eyes, it is not in my power to choose whether I shall see or no, or to determine what particular objects shall present themselves to my view; and so likewise as to the hearing and other senses; the ideas imprinted on them are not creatures of my will. There is therefore some other Will or Spirit that produces them.

Part One, Section Thirty

The ideas of Sense are more strong, lively, and distinct than those of the imagination; they have likewise a steadiness, order, and coherence, and are not excited at random, as those which are the effects of human wills often are, but in a regular train or series, the admirable connexion whereof sufficiently testifies the wisdom and benevolence of its Author. Now the set rules or established methods wherein the Mind we depend on excites in us the ideas of sense, are called the laws of nature; and these we learn by experience, which teaches us that such and such ideas are attended with such and such other ideas, in the ordinary course of things.

Part One, Section Thirty-one

This gives us a sort of foresight which enables us to regulate our actions for the benefit of life. And without this we should be eternally at a loss; we could not know how to act anything that might procure us the least pleasure, or remove the least pain of sense. That food nourishes, sleep refreshes, and fire warms us; that to sow in the seed-time is the way to reap in the harvest; and in general that to obtain such or such ends, such or such means are conducive—all this we know, not by discovering any necessary connexion between our ideas, but only by the observation of the settled laws of nature, without which we should be all in uncertainty and confusion, and a grown man no more know how to manage himself in the affairs of life than an infant just born.

Part One, Section Thirty-two

And yet this consistent uniform working, which so evidently displays the goodness and wisdom of that Governing Spirit whose Will constitutes the laws of nature, is so far from leading our thoughts to Him, that it rather sends them wandering after second causes. For, when we perceive certain ideas of Sense constantly followed by other ideas and we know this is not of our own doing, we forthwith attribute power and agency to the ideas themselves, and make one the cause of another, than which nothing can be more absurd and unintelligible. Thus, for example, having observed that when we perceive by sight a certain round luminous figure we at the same time perceive by touch the idea or sensation called heat, we do from thence conclude the sun to be the cause of heat. And in like manner perceiving the motion and collision of bodies to be attended with sound, we are inclined to think the latter the effect of the former.

Part One, Section Thirty-three

The ideas imprinted on the Senses by the Author of nature are called real things; and those excited in the imagination being less regular, vivid, and constant, are more properly termed ideas, or images of things, which they copy and represent. But then our sensations, be they never so vivid and distinct, are nevertheless ideas, that is, they exist in the mind, or are perceived by it, as truly as the ideas of its own framing. The ideas of Sense are allowed to have more reality in them, that is, to be more strong, orderly, and coherent than the creatures of the mind; but this is no argument that they exist without the mind. They are also less dependent on the spirit, or thinking substance which perceives them, in that they are excited by the will of another and more powerful spirit; yet still they are ideas, and certainly no idea, whether faint or strong, can exist otherwise than in a mind perceiving it.

Part One, Section Thirty-four

Before we proceed any farther it is necessary we spend some time in answering objections which may probably be made against the principles we have hitherto laid down. In doing of which, if I seem too prolix to those of quick apprehensions, I hope it may be pardoned, since all men do not equally apprehend things of this nature, and I am willing to be understood by everyone.

First, then, it will be objected that by the foregoing principles all that is real and substantial in nature is banished out of the world, and instead thereof a chimerical scheme of ideas takes place. All things that exist, exist only in the mind, that is, they are purely notional. What therefore becomes of the sun, moon and stars? What must we think of houses, rivers, mountains, trees, stones; nay, even of our own bodies? Are all these but so many chimeras and illusions on the fancy? To all which, and whatever else of the same sort may be objected, I answer, that by the principles premised we are not deprived of any one thing in nature. Whatever we see, feel, hear, or anywise conceive or understand remains as secure as ever, and is as real as ever. There is a rerum natura, and the distinction between realities and chimeras retains its full force. This is evident from Sections 29, 30, and 33, where we have shewn what is meant by real things in opposition to chimeras or ideas of our own framing; but then they both equally exist in the mind, and in that sense they are alike ideas.

Part One, Section Thirty-five

I do not argue against the existence of any one thing that we can apprehend either by sense or reflexion. That the things I see with my eyes and touch with my hands do exist, really exist, I make not the least question. The only thing whose existence we deny is that which philosophers call Matter or corporeal substance. And in doing of this there is no damage done to the rest of mankind, who, I dare say, will never miss it. The Atheist indeed will want the colour of an empty name to support his impiety; and the Philosophers may possibly find they have lost a great handle for trifling and disputation.

Part One, Section Thirty-six

If any man thinks this detracts from the existence or reality of things, he is very far from understanding what hath been premised in the plainest terms I could think of. Take here an abstract of what has been said: There are spiritual substances, minds, or human souls, which will or excite ideas in themselves at pleasure; but these are faint, weak, and unsteady in respect of others they perceive by sense—which, being impressed upon them according to certain rules or laws of nature, speak themselves the effects of a mind more powerful and wise than human spirits. These latter are said to have more reality in them than the former: by which is meant that they are more affecting, orderly, and distinct, and that they are not fictions of the mind perceiving them. And in this sense the sun that I see by day is the real sun, and that which I imagine by night is the idea of the former. In the sense here given of reality it is evident that every vegetable, star, mineral, and in general each part of the mundane system, is as much a real being by our principles as by any other. Whether others mean anything by the term reality different from what I do, I entreat them to look into their own thoughts and see.

Part One, Section Thirty-eight

But after all, say you, it sounds very harsh to say we eat and drink ideas, and are clothed with ideas. I acknowledge it does so—the word idea not being used in common discourse to signify the several combinations of sensible qualities which are called things; and it is certain that any expression which varies from the familiar use of language will seem harsh and ridiculous. But this doth not concern the truth of the proposition, which in other words is no more than to say, we are fed and clothed with those things which we perceive immediately by our senses. The hardness or softness, the colour, taste, warmth, figure, or suchlike qualities, which combined together constitute the several sorts of victuals and apparel, have been shewn to exist only in the mind that perceives them; and this is all that is meant by calling them ideas; which word if it was as ordinarily used as thing, would sound no harsher nor more ridiculous than it. I am not for disputing about the propriety, but the truth of the expression. If therefore you agree with me that we eat and drink and are clad with the immediate objects of sense, which cannot exist unperceived or without the mind, I shall readily grant it is more proper or conformable to custom that they should be called things rather than ideas.

Part One, Section Thirty-nine

If it be demanded why I make use of the word idea, and do not rather in compliance with custom call them things; I answer, I do it for two reasons: first, because the term thing in contradistinction to idea, is generally supposed to denote somewhat existing without the mind; secondly, because thing hath a more comprehensive signification than idea, including spirit or thinking things as well as ideas. Since therefore the objects of sense exist only in the mind, and are withal thoughtless and inactive, I chose to mark them by the word idea, which implies those properties.

Part One, Section Forty

But, say what we can, someone perhaps may be apt to reply, he will still believe his senses, and never suffer any arguments, how plausible soever, to prevail over the certainty of them. Be it so; assert the evidence of sense as high as you please, we are willing to do the same. That what I see, hear, and feel doth exist, that is to say, is perceived by me, I no more doubt than I do of my own being. But I do not see how the testimony of sense can be alleged as a proof for the existence of anything which is not perceived by sense. We are not for having any man turn sceptic and disbelieve his senses; on the contrary, we give them all the stress and assurance imaginable; nor are there any principles more opposite to Scepticism than those we have laid down, as shall be hereafter clearly shewn.

Part One, Section Forty-one

Secondly, it will be objected that there is a great difference betwixt real fire for instance, and the idea of fire, betwixt dreaming or imagining oneself burnt, and actually being so: if you suspect it to be only the idea of fire which you see, do but put your hand into it and you will be convinced with a witness. This and the like may be urged in opposition to our tenets. To all which the answer is evident from what hath been already said; and I shall only add in this place, that if real fire be very different from the idea of fire, so also is the real pain that it occasions very different from the idea of the same pain, and yet nobody will pretend that real pain either is, or can possibly be, in an unperceiving thing, or without the mind, any more than its idea.

---

1. *What is the second objection (Section Forty-one) Berkeley entertains? Berkeley says that 'the answer is evident from what hath been already said.' What answer can you construct for him, based on the earlier sections of the Principles?*

Part One, Section Forty-two

Thirdly, it will be objected that we see things actually without or at a distance from us, and which consequently do not exist in the mind; it being absurd that those things which are seen at the distance of several miles should be as near to us as our own thoughts. In answer to this, I desire it may be considered that in a dream we do oft perceive things as existing at a great distance off, and yet for all that, those things are acknowledged to have their existence only in the mind.

Part One, Section Forty-three

But, for the fuller clearing of this point, it may be worth while to consider how it is that we perceive distance and things placed at a distance by sight. For, that we should in truth see external space, and bodies actually existing in it, some nearer, others farther off, seems to carry with it some opposition to what hath been said of their existing nowhere without the mind. The consideration of this difficulty it was that gave birth to my "Essay towards a New Theory of Vision," which was published not long since, wherein it is shewn that distance or outness is neither immediately of itself perceived by sight, nor yet apprehended or judged of by lines and angles, or anything that hath a necessary connexion with it; but that it is only suggested to our thoughts by certain visible ideas and sensations attending vision, which in their own nature have no manner of similitude or relation either with distance or things placed at a distance; but, by a connexion taught us by experience, they come to signify and suggest them to us, after the same manner that words of any language suggest the ideas they are made to stand for; insomuch that a man born blind and afterwards made to see, would not, at first sight, think the things he saw to be without his mind, or at any distance from him. See Section 41 of the forementioned treatise.

Part One, Section Forty-four

The ideas of sight and touch make two species entirely distinct and heterogeneous. The former are marks and prognostics of the latter. That the proper objects of sight neither exist without mind, nor are the images of external things, was shewn even in that treatise. Though throughout the same the contrary be supposed true of tangible objects—not that to suppose that vulgar error was necessary for establishing the notion therein laid down, but because it was beside my purpose to examine and refute it in a discourse concerning Vision. So that in strict truth the ideas of sight, when we apprehend by them distance and things placed at a distance, do not suggest or mark out to us things actually existing at a distance, but only admonish us what ideas of touch will be imprinted in our minds at such and such distances of time, and in consequence of such or such actions. It is, I say, evident from what has been said in the foregoing parts of this Treatise, and in Section 147 and elsewhere of the "Essay Concerning Vision", that visible ideas are the Language whereby the Governing Spirit on whom we depend informs us what tangible ideas he is about to imprint upon us, in case we excite this or that motion in our own bodies.

Part One, Section Forty-five

Fourthly, it will be objected that from the foregoing principles it follows things are every moment annihilated and created anew. The objects of sense exist only when they are perceived; the trees therefore are in the garden, or the chairs in the parlour, no longer than while there is somebody by to perceive them. Upon shutting my eyes all the furniture in the room is reduced to nothing, and barely upon opening them it is again created. In answer to all which, I refer the reader to what has been said in Sections Three, Four, &c., and desire he will consider whether he means anything by the actual existence of an idea distinct from its being perceived. For my part, after the nicest inquiry I could make, I am not able to discover that anything else is meant by those words; and I once more entreat the reader to sound his own thoughts, and not suffer himself to be imposed on by words. If he can conceive it possible either for his ideas or their archetypes to exist without being perceived, then I give up the cause; but if he cannot, he will acknowledge it is unreasonable for him to stand up in defence of he knows not what, and pretend to charge on me as an absurdity the not assenting to those propositions which at bottom have no meaning in them.

Part One, Section Forty-six

It will not be amiss to observe how far the received principles of philosophy are themselves chargeable with those pretended absurdities. It is thought strangely absurd that upon closing my eyelids all the visible objects around me should be reduced to nothing; and yet is not this what philosophers commonly acknowledge, when they agree on all hands that light and colours, which alone are the proper and immediate objects of sight, are mere sensations that exist no longer than they are perceived? Again, it may to some perhaps seem very incredible that things should be every moment creating, yet this very notion is commonly taught in the schools. For the Schoolmen, though they acknowledge the existence of Matter, and that the whole mundane fabric is framed out of it, are nevertheless of opinion that it cannot subsist without the divine conservation, which by them is expounded to be a continual creation.

Part One, Section Forty-seven

Farther, a little thought will discover to us that though we allow the existence of Matter or corporeal substance, yet it will unavoidably follow, from the principles which are now generally admitted, that the particular bodies, of what kind soever, do none of them exist whilst they are not perceived. For, it is evident from Section Two and the following sections, that the Matter philosophers contend for is an incomprehensible somewhat, which hath none of those particular qualities whereby the bodies falling under our senses are distinguished one from another. But, to make this more plain, it must be remarked that the infinite divisibility of Matter is now universally allowed, at least by the most approved and considerable philosophers, who on the received principles demonstrate it beyond all exception. Hence, it follows there is an infinite number of parts in each particle of Matter which are not perceived by sense. The reason therefore that any particular body seems to be of a finite magnitude, or exhibits only a finite number of parts to sense, is, not because it contains no more, since in itself it contains an infinite number of parts, but because the sense is not acute enough to discern them. In proportion therefore as the sense is rendered more acute, it perceives a greater number of parts in the object, that is, the object appears greater, and its figure varies, those parts in its extremities which were before unperceivable appearing now to bound it in very different lines and angles from those perceived by an obtuser sense. And at length, after various changes of size and shape, when the sense becomes infinitely acute the body shall seem infinite. During all which there is no alteration in the body, but only in the sense. Each body therefore, considered in itself, is infinitely extended, and consequently void of all shape or figure. From which it follows that, though we should grant the existence of Matter to be never so certain, yet it is withal as certain, the materialists themselves are by their own principles forced to acknowledge, that neither the particular bodies perceived by sense, nor anything like them, exists without the mind. Matter, I say, and each particle thereof, is according to them infinite and shapeless, and it is the mind that frames all that variety of bodies which compose the visible world, any one whereof does not exist longer than it is perceived.

Part One, Section Forty-eight

If we consider it, the objection proposed in Section Forty-five will not be found reasonably charged on the principles we have premised, so as in truth to make any objection at all against our notions. For, though we hold indeed the objects of sense to be nothing else but ideas which cannot exist unperceived; yet we may not hence conclude they have no existence except only while they are perceived by us, since there may be some other spirit that perceives them though we do not. Wherever bodies are said to have no existence without the mind, I would not be understood to mean this or that particular mind, but all minds whatsoever. It does not therefore follow from the foregoing principles that bodies are annihilated and created every moment, or exist not at all during the intervals between our perception of them.

Part One, Section Forty-nine

Fifthly, it may perhaps be objected that if extension and figure exist only in the mind, it follows that the mind is extended and figured; since extension is a mode or attribute which (to speak with the schools) is predicated of the subject in which it exists. I answer, those qualities are in the mind only as they are perceived by it—that is, not by way of mode or attribute, but only by way of idea; and it no more follows the soul or mind is extended, because extension exists in it alone, than it does that it is red or blue, because those colours are on all hands acknowledged to exist in it, and nowhere else. As to what philosophers say of subject and mode, that seems very groundless and unintelligible. For instance, in this proposition "a die is hard, extended, and square," they will have it that the word die denotes a subject or substance, distinct from the hardness, extension, and figure which are predicated of it, and in which they exist. This I cannot comprehend: to me a die seems to be nothing distinct from those things which are termed its modes or accidents. And, to say a die is hard, extended, and square is not to attribute those qualities to a subject distinct from and supporting them, but only an explication of the meaning of the word die.

Part One, Section Fifty

Sixthly, you will say there have been a great many things explained by matter and motion; take away these and you destroy the whole corpuscular philosophy, and undermine those mechanical principles which have been applied with so much success to account for the phenomena. In short, whatever advances have been made, either by ancient or modern philosophers, in the study of nature do all proceed on the supposition that corporeal substance or Matter doth really exist. To this I answer that there is not any one phenomenon explained on that supposition which may not as well be explained without it, as might easily be made appear by an induction of particulars. To explain the phenomena, is all one as to shew why, upon such and such occasions, we are affected with such and such ideas. But how Matter should operate on a Spirit, or produce any idea in it, is what no philosopher will pretend to explain; it is therefore evident there can be no use of Matter in natural philosophy. Besides, they who attempt to account for things do it not by corporeal substance, but by figure, motion, and other qualities, which are in truth no more than mere ideas, and, therefore, cannot be the cause of anything, as hath been already shewn. See Section Twenty-five.

Part One, Section Fifty-one

Seventhly, it will upon this be demanded whether it does not seem absurd to take away natural causes, and ascribe everything to the immediate operation of Spirits? We must no longer say upon these principles that fire heats, or water cools, but that a Spirit heats, and so forth. Would not a man be deservedly laughed at, who should talk after this manner? I answer, he would so; in such things we ought to "think with the learned, and speak with the vulgar." They who to demonstration are convinced of the truth of the Copernican system do nevertheless say "the sun rises," "the sun sets," or "comes to the meridian"; and if they affected a contrary style in common talk it would without doubt appear very ridiculous. A little reflexion on what is here said will make it manifest that the common use of language would receive no manner of alteration or disturbance from the admission of our tenets.

Part One, Section Fifty-two

In the ordinary affairs of life, any phrases may be retained, so long as they excite in us proper sentiments, or dispositions to act in such a manner as is necessary for our well-being, how false soever they may be if taken in a strict and speculative sense. Nay, this is unavoidable, since, propriety being regulated by custom, language is suited to the received opinions, which are not always the truest. Hence it is impossible, even in the most rigid, philosophic reasonings, so far to alter the bent and genius of the tongue we speak, as never to give a handle for cavillers to pretend difficulties and inconsistencies. But, a fair and ingenuous reader will collect the sense from the scope and tenor and connexion of a discourse, making allowances for those inaccurate modes of speech which use has made inevitable.

Part One, Section Fifty-three

As to the opinion that there are no Corporeal Causes, this has been heretofore maintained by some of the Schoolmen, as it is of late by others among the modern philosophers, who though they allow Matter to exist, yet will have God alone to be the immediate efficient cause of all things. These men saw that amongst all the objects of sense there was none which had any power or activity included in it; and that by consequence this was likewise true of whatever bodies they supposed to exist without the mind, like unto the immediate objects of sense. But then, that they should suppose an innumerable multitude of created beings, which they acknowledge are not capable of producing any one effect in nature, and which therefore are made to no manner of purpose, since God might have done everything as well without them: this I say, though we should allow it possible, must yet be a very unaccountable and extravagant supposition.

Part One, Section Fifty-four

In the **eighth** place, the universal concurrent assent of mankind may be thought by some an invincible argument in behalf of Matter, or the existence of external things. Must we suppose the whole world to be mistaken? And if so, what cause can be assigned of so widespread and predominant an error? I answer, *first*, that, upon a narrow inquiry, it will not perhaps be found so many as is imagined do really believe the existence of Matter or things without the mind. Strictly speaking, to believe that which involves a contradiction, or has no meaning in it, is impossible; and whether the foregoing expressions are not of that sort, I refer it to the impartial examination of the reader. In one sense, indeed, men may be said to believe that Matter exists, that is, they act as if the immediate cause of their sensations, which affects them every moment, and is so nearly present to them, were some senseless unthinking being. But, that they should clearly apprehend any meaning marked by those words, and form thereof a settled speculative opinion, is what I am not able to conceive. This is not the only instance wherein men impose upon themselves, by imagining they believe those propositions which they have often heard, though at bottom they have no meaning in them.

Part One, Section Fifty-five

But *secondly*, though we should grant a notion to be never so universally and steadfastly adhered to, yet this is weak argument of its truth to whoever considers what a vast number of prejudices and false opinions are everywhere embraced with the utmost tenaciousness, by the unreflecting (which are the far greater) part of mankind. There was a time when the antipodes and motion of the earth were looked upon as monstrous absurdities even by men of learning: and if it be considered what a small proportion they bear to the rest of mankind, we shall find that at this day those notions have gained but a very inconsiderable footing in the world.

Part One, Section Fifty-six

But it is demanded that we assign a cause of this prejudice, and account for its obtaining in the world. To this I answer, that men knowing they perceived several ideas, whereof they themselves were not the authors—as not being excited from within nor depending on the operation of their wills—this made them maintain those ideas, or objects of perception had an existence independent of and without the mind, without ever dreaming that a contradiction was involved in those words. But, philosophers having plainly seen that the immediate objects of perception do not exist without the mind, they in some degree corrected the mistake of the vulgar; but at the same time run into another which seems no less absurd, to wit, that there are certain objects really existing without the mind, or having a subsistence distinct from being perceived, of which our ideas are only images or resemblances, imprinted by those objects on the mind. And this notion of the philosophers owes its origin to the same cause with the former, namely, their being conscious that they were not the authors of their own sensations, which they evidently knew were imprinted from without, and which therefore must have some cause distinct from the minds on which they are imprinted.

Part One, Section Fifty-seven

But why they should suppose the ideas of sense to be excited in us by things in their likeness, and not rather have recourse to Spirit which alone can act, may be accounted for, *first*, because they were not aware of the repugnancy there is, as well in supposing things like unto our ideas existing without, as in attributing to them power or activity. *Secondly*, because the Supreme Spirit which excites those ideas in our minds, is not marked out and limited to our view by any particular finite collection of sensible ideas, as human agents are by their size, complexion, limbs, and motions. And *thirdly*, because His operations are regular and uniform. Whenever the course of nature is interrupted by a miracle, men are ready to own the presence of a superior agent. But, when we see things go on in the ordinary course they do not excite in us any reflexion; their order and concatenation, though it be an argument of the greatest wisdom, power, and goodness in their creator, is yet so constant and familiar to us that we do not think them the immediate effects of a Free Spirit; especially since inconsistency and mutability in acting, though it be an imperfection, is looked on as a mark of freedom.

Part One, Section Fifty-eight

Tenthly, it will be objected that the notions we advance are inconsistent with several sound truths in philosophy and mathematics. For example, the motion of the earth is now universally admitted by astronomers as a truth grounded on the clearest and most convincing reasons. But, on the foregoing principles, there can be no such thing. For, motion being only an idea, it follows that if it be not perceived it exists not; but the motion of the earth is not perceived by sense. I answer, that tenet, if rightly understood, will be found to agree with the principles we have premised; for, the question whether the earth moves or no amounts in reality to no more than this, to wit, whether we have reason to conclude, from what has been observed by astronomers, that if we were placed in such and such circumstances, and such or such a position and distance both from the earth and sun, we should perceive the former to move among the choir of the planets, and appearing in all respects like one of them; and this, by the established rules of nature which we have no reason to mistrust, is reasonably collected from the phenomena.

Part One, Section Fifty-nine

We may, from the experience we have had of the train and succession of ideas in our minds, often make, I will not say uncertain conjectures, but sure and well-grounded predictions concerning the ideas we shall be affected with pursuant to a great train of actions, and be enabled to pass a right judgment of what would have appeared to us, in case we were placed in circumstances very different from those we are in at present. Herein consists the knowledge of nature, which may preserve its use and certainty very consistently with what hath been said. It will be easy to apply this to whatever objections of the like sort may be drawn from the magnitude of the stars, or any other discoveries in astronomy or nature.

Part One, Section Sixty

In the **eleventh** place, it will be demanded to what purpose serves that curious organization of plants, and the animal mechanism in the parts of animals; might not vegetables grow, and shoot forth leaves of blossoms, and animals perform all their motions as well without as with all that variety of internal parts so elegantly contrived and put together; which, being ideas, have nothing powerful or operative in them, nor have any necessary connexion with the effects ascribed to them? If it be a Spirit that immediately produces every effect by a fiat or act of his will, we must think all that is fine and artificial in the works, whether of man or nature, to be made in vain. By this doctrine, though an artist hath made the spring and wheels, and every movement of a watch, and adjusted them in such a manner as he knew would produce the motions he designed, yet he must think all this done to no purpose, and that it is an Intelligence which directs the index, and points to the hour of the day. If so, why may not the Intelligence do it, without his being at the pains of making the movements and putting them together? Why does not an empty case serve as well as another? And how comes it to pass that whenever there is any fault in the going of a watch, there is some corresponding disorder to be found in the movements, which being mended by a skilful hand all is right again? The like may be said of all the clockwork of nature, great part whereof is so wonderfully fine and subtle as scarce to be discerned by the best microscope. In short, it will be asked, how, upon our principles, any tolerable account can be given, or any final cause assigned of an innumerable multitude of bodies and machines, framed with the most exquisite art, which in the common philosophy have very apposite uses assigned them, and serve to explain abundance of phenomena?

Part One, Section Sixty-one

To all which I answer, *first*, that though there were some difficulties relating to the administration of Providence, and the uses by it assigned to the several parts of nature, which I could not solve by the foregoing principles, yet this objection could be of small weight against the truth and certainty of those things which may be proved *a priori*, with the utmost evidence and rigor of demonstration. Secondly, but neither are the received principles free from the like difficulties; for, it may still be demanded to what end God should take those roundabout methods of effecting things by instruments and machines, which no one can deny might have been effected by the mere command of His will without all that apparatus; nay, if we narrowly consider it, we shall find the objection may be retorted with greater force on those who hold the existence of those machines without of mind; for it has been made evident that solidity, bulk, figure, motion, and the like have no activity or efficacy in them, so as to be capable of producing any one effect in nature. See Section Twenty-five. Whoever therefore supposes them to exist (allowing the supposition possible) when they are not perceived does it manifestly to no purpose; since the only use that is assigned to them, as they exist unperceived, is that they produce those perceivable effects which in truth cannot be ascribed to anything but Spirit.

Part One, Section Sixty-two

But, to come nigher the difficulty, it must be observed that though the fabrication of all those parts and organs be not absolutely necessary to the producing any effect, yet it is necessary to the producing of things in a constant regular way according to the laws of nature. There are certain general laws that run through the whole chain of natural effects; these are learned by the observation and study of nature, and are by men applied as well to the framing artificial things for the use and ornament of life as to the explaining various phenomena—which explication consists only in shewing the conformity any particular phenomenon hath to the general laws of nature, or, which is the same thing, in discovering the uniformity there is in the production of natural effects; as will be evident to whoever shall attend to the several instances wherein philosophers pretend to account for appearances. That there is a great and conspicuous use in these regular constant methods of working observed by the Supreme Agent hath been shewn in Section Thirty-one. And it is no less visible that a particular size, figure, motion, and disposition of parts are necessary, though not absolutely to the producing any effect, yet to the producing it according to the standing mechanical laws of nature. Thus, for instance, it cannot be denied that God, or the Intelligence that sustains and rules the ordinary course of things, might if He were minded to produce a miracle, cause all the motions on the dial-plate of a watch, though nobody had ever made the movements and put them in it: but yet, if He will act agreeably to the rules of mechanism, by Him for wise ends established and maintained in the creation, it is necessary that those actions of the watchmaker, whereby he makes the movements and rightly adjusts them, precede the production of the aforesaid motions; as also that any disorder in them be attended with the perception of some corresponding disorder in the movements, which being once corrected all is right again.

Part One, Section Sixty-three

It may indeed on some occasions be necessary that the Author of nature display His overruling power in producing some appearance out of the ordinary series of things. Such exceptions from the general rules of nature are proper to surprise and awe men into an acknowledgement of the Divine Being; but then they are to be used but seldom, otherwise there is a plain reason why they should fail of that effect. Besides, God seems to choose the convincing our reason of His attributes by the works of nature, which discover so much harmony and contrivance in their make, and are such plain indications of wisdom and beneficence in their Author, rather than to astonish us into a belief of His Being by anomalous and surprising events.

Part One, Section Sixty-four

To set this matter in a yet clearer light, I shall observe that what has been objected in Section Sixty amounts in reality to no more than this: ideas are not anyhow and at random produced, there being a certain order and connexion between them, like to that of cause and effect; there are also several combinations of them made in a very regular and artificial manner, which seem like so many instruments in the hand of nature that, being hid as it were behind the scenes, have a secret operation in producing those appearances which are seen on the theatre of the world, being themselves discernible only to the curious eye of the philosopher. But, since one idea cannot be the cause of another, to what purpose is that connexion? And, since those instruments, being barely inefficacious perceptions in the mind, are not subservient to the production of natural effects, it is demanded why they are made; or, in other words, what reason can be assigned why God should make us, upon a close inspection into His works, behold so great variety of ideas so artfully laid together, and so much according to rule; it not being credible that He would be at the expense (if one may so speak) of all that art and regularity to no purpose.

Part One, Section Sixty-five

To all which my answer is, *first*, that the connexion of ideas does not imply the relation of cause and effect, but only of a mark or sign with the thing signified. The fire which I see is not the cause of the pain I suffer upon my approaching it, but the mark that forewarns me of it. In like manner the noise that I hear is not the effect of this or that motion or collision of the ambient bodies, but the sign thereof. *Secondly*, the reason why ideas are formed into machines, that is, artificial and regular combinations, is the same with that for combining letters into words. That a few original ideas may be made to signify a great number of effects and actions, it is necessary they be variously combined together. And, to the end their use be permanent and universal, these combinations must be made by rule, and with wise contrivance. By this means abundance of information is conveyed unto us, concerning what we are to expect from such and such actions and what methods are proper to be taken for the exciting such and such ideas; which in effect is all that I conceive to be distinctly meant when it is said that, by discerning a figure, texture, and mechanism of the inward parts of bodies, whether natural or artificial, we may attain to know the several uses and properties depending thereon, or the nature of the thing.

Part One, Section Sixty-six

Hence, it is evident that those things which, under the notion of a cause co-operating or concurring to the production of effects, are altogether inexplicable, and run us into great absurdities, may be very naturally explained, and have a proper and obvious use assigned to them, when they are considered only as marks or signs for our information. And it is the searching after and endeavouring to understand those signs instituted by the Author of Nature, that ought to be the employment of the natural philosopher; and not the pretending to explain things by corporeal causes, which doctrine seems to have too much estranged the minds of men from that active principle, that supreme and wise Spirit "in whom we live, move, and have our being." ...

Having covered Berkeley's arguments for immaterialism and his replies to objections, we can now look at the following selections from later in the Principles, *which bring out important features of his positive view.*

Part One, Section Ninety-eight

For my own part, whenever I attempt to frame a simple idea of time, abstracted from the succession of ideas in my mind, which flows uniformly and is participated by all beings, I am lost and embrangled in inextricable difficulties. I have no notion of it at all, only I hear others say it is infinitely divisible, and speak of it in such a manner as leads me to entertain odd thoughts of my existence; since that doctrine lays one under an absolute necessity of thinking, either that he passes away innumerable ages without a thought, or else that he is annihilated every moment of his life, both which seem equally absurd. Time therefore being nothing, abstracted from the succession of ideas in our minds, it follows that the duration of any finite spirit must be estimated by the number of ideas or actions succeeding each other in that same spirit or mind. Hence, it is a plain consequence that the soul always thinks; and in truth whoever shall go about to divide in his thoughts, or abstract the existence of a spirit from its cogitation, will, I believe, find it no easy task.

---

1. *Berkeley seems to agree with Descartes in at least one respect: both think that spirit/mind _____ (Section Ninety-eight. But how do their arguments for this claim differ?*

Part One, Section Ninety-nine

So likewise when we attempt to abstract extension and motion from all other qualities, and consider them by themselves, we presently lose sight of them, and run into great extravagances. All which depend on a twofold abstraction; first, it is supposed that extension, for example, may be abstracted from all other sensible qualities; and secondly, that the entity of extension may be abstracted from its being perceived. But, whoever shall reflect, and take care to understand what he says, will, if I mistake not, acknowledge that all sensible qualities are alike sensations and alike real; that where the extension is, there is the colour, too, i.e., in his mind, and that their archetypes can exist only in some other mind; and that the objects of sense are nothing but those sensations combined, blended, or (if one may so speak) concreted together; none of all which can be supposed to exist unperceived.

Part One, Section One Hundred and Seven

After what has been premised, I think we may lay down the following conclusions. *First*, it is plain philosophers amuse themselves in vain, when they inquire for any natural efficient cause, distinct from a mind or spirit. *Secondly*, considering the whole creation is the workmanship of a wise and good Agent, it should seem to become philosophers to employ their thoughts (contrary to what some hold) about the final causes of things; and I confess I see no reason why pointing out the various ends to which natural things are adapted, and for which they were originally with unspeakable wisdom contrived, should not be thought one good way of accounting for them, and altogether worthy a philosopher. *Thirdly*, from what has been premised no reason can be drawn why the history of nature should not still be studied, and observations and experiments made, which, that they are of use to mankind, and enable us to draw any general conclusions, is not the result of any immutable habitudes or relations between things themselves, but only of God's goodness and kindness to men in the administration of the world. See Sections Thirty and Thirty-one above. *Fourthly*, by a diligent observation of the phenomena within our view, we may discover the general laws of nature, and from them deduce the other phenomena; I do not say demonstrate, for all deductions of that kind depend on a supposition that the Author of nature always operates uniformly, and in a constant observance of those rules we take for principles: which we cannot evidently know.

---

1. Recall Aquinas's argument in *Summa Contra Gentiles*, *Chapter Sixty-nine. How would he react to Berkeley's view about nature? (See especially Section Seven)*
2. *How does Berkeley reply to this argument (see Section 107)?*

Part One, Section One Hundred and Thirty-nine

But it will be objected that, if there is no idea signified by the terms soul, spirit, and substance, they are wholly insignificant, or have no meaning in them. I answer, those words do mean or signify a real thing, which is neither an idea nor like an idea, but that which perceives ideas, and wills, and reasons about them. What I am myself, that which I denote by the term I, is the same with what is meant by soul or spiritual substance. If it be said that this is only quarreling at a word, and that, since the immediately significations of other names are by common consent called ideas, no reason can be assigned why that which is signified by the name spirit or soul may not partake in the same appellation. I answer, all the unthinking objects of the mind agree in that they are entirely passive, and their existence consists only inbeing perceived; whereas a soul or spirit is an active being, whose existence consists, not in being perceived, but in perceiving ideas and thinking. It is therefore necessary, in order to prevent equivocation and confounding natures perfectly disagreeing and unlike, that we distinguish between spirit and idea. See Section Twenty-seven.

Part One, Section One Hundred and Forty

Our idea of spirit—in a large sense, indeed, we may be said to have an idea or rather a notion of spirit; that is, we understand the meaning of the word, otherwise we could not affirm or deny anything of it. Moreover, as we conceive the ideas that are in the minds of other spirits by means of our own, which we suppose to be resemblances of them; so we know other spirits by means of our own soul—which in that sense is the image or idea of them; it having like respect to other spirits that blueness or heat by me perceived has to those ideas perceived by another.

Part One, Section One Hundred and Forty-six

But, though there be some things which convince us human agents are concerned in producing them; yet it is evident to every one that those things which are called the Works of Nature, that is, the far greater part of the ideas or sensations perceived by us, are not produced by, or dependent on, the wills of men. There is therefore some other Spirit that causes them; since it is repugnant that they should subsist by themselves. See Section Twenty-nine. But, if we attentively consider the constant regularity, order, and concatenation of natural things, the surprising magnificence, beauty, and perfection of the larger, and the exquisite contrivance of the smaller parts of creation, together with the exact harmony and correspondence of the whole, but above all the never–enough-admired laws of pain and pleasure, and the instincts or natural inclinations, appetites, and passions of animals; I say if we consider all these things, and at the same time attend to the meaning and import of the attributes One, Eternal, Infinitely Wise, Good, and Perfect, we shall clearly perceive that they belong to the aforesaid Spirit, "who works all in all," and "by whom all things consist."

Hence, it is evident that God is known as certainly and immediately as any other mind or spirit whatsoever distinct from ourselves. We may even assert that the existence of God is far more evidently perceived than the existence of men; because the effects of nature are infinitely more numerous and considerable than those ascribed to human agents. There is not any one mark that denotes a man, or effect produced by him, which does not more strongly evince the being of that Spirit who is the Author of Nature. For, it is evident that in affecting other persons the will of man has no other object than barely the motion of the limbs of his body; but that such a motion should be attended by, or excite any idea in the mind of another, depends wholly on the will of the Creator.

---

1. *Why can't we have an idea of spirit/mind, according to Berkeley? Remember his 'likeness principle' from the opening argument of Part One.*
2. *The big picture: Berkeley sets out to undermine 'materialism': what is materialism?*
3. *Berkeley's positive view is captured by the slogan 'esse est percipi aut percipere'; what does this mean?*
4. *What, according to Berkeley, is the only substance?*
5. *Why does Berkeley attack the doctrine of abstract ideas?*

De Motu, Section One

In the pursuit of truth we must beware of being misled by terms which we do not rightly understand. That is the chief point. Almost all philosophers utter the caution; few observe it. Yet it is not so difficult to observe where sense, experience, and geometrical reasoning obtain, as is especially the case in physics. Laying aside, then, as far as possible, all prejudice, whether rooted in linguistic usage or in philosophical authority, let us fix our gaze on the very nature of things. For no one's authority ought to rank so high as to set a value on his words and terms unless they are found to be based on clear and certain fact.

De Motu, Section Two

The consideration of motion greatly troubled the minds of the ancient philosophers, giving rise to various exceedingly difficult opinions (not to say absurd) which have almost entirely gone out of fashion, and not being worth a detailed discussion need not delay us long. In works on motion by the more recent and sober thinkers of our age, not a few terms of somewhat abstract and obscure signification are used, such as solicitation of gravity, urge, dead forces, etc., terms which darken writings in other respects very learned, and beget opinions at variance with truth and the common sense of men. These terms must be examined with great care, not from a desire to prove other people wrong, but in the interest of truth.

De Motu, Section Three

Solicitation and effort or conation belong properly to animate beings alone. When they are attributed to other things, they must be taken in a metaphorical sense; but a philosopher should abstain from metaphor.

Besides, anyone who has seriously considered the matter will agree that those terms have no clear and distinct meaning apart from all affection of the mind and motion of the body.

De Motu, Section Four

While we support heavy bodies we feel in ourselves effort, fatigue, and discomfort. We perceive also in heavy bodies falling an accelerated motion towards the centre of the earth; and that is all the senses tell us. By reason, however, we infer that there is some cause or principle of these phenomena, and that is popularly called gravity. But since the cause of the fall of heavy bodies is unseen and unknown, gravity in that usage cannot properly be styled a sensible quality. It is, therefore, an occult quality. But what an occult quality is, or how any quality can act or do anything, we can scarcely conceive—indeed, we cannot conceive. And so men would do better to let the occult quality go and attend only to the sensible effects. Abstract terms (however useful they may be in argument) should be discarded in meditation, and the mind should be fixed on the particular and the concrete, that is, on the things themselves.

De Motu, Section Five

Force likewise is attributed to bodies; and that word is used as if it meant a known quality, and one distinct from motion, figure, and every other sensible thing and also from every affection of the living thing. But examine the matter more carefully and you will agree that such force is nothing but an occult quality. Animal effort and corporeal motion are commonly regarded as symptoms and measures of this occult quality.

De Motu, Section Six

Obviously then it is idle to lay down gravity or force as the principle of motion; for how could that principle be known more clearly by being styled an occult quality? What is itself occult explains nothing. And I need not say that an unknown acting cause could be more correctly styled substance than quality. Again, force, gravity, and terms of that sort are more often used in the concrete (and rightly so) so as to connote the body in motion, the effort of resisting, etc. But when they are used by philosophers to signify certain natures carved out and abstracted from all these things, natures which are not objects of sense, nor can be grasped by any force of intellect, nor pictured by the imagination, then indeed they breed errors and confusion.

De Motu, Section Seven

About general and abstract terms many men make mistakes; they see their value in argument, but they do not appreciate their purpose. In part the terms have been invented by common habit to abbreviate speech, and in part they have been thought out by philosophers for instructional purposes, not that they are adapted to the natures of things which are in fact singulars and concrete, but they come in useful for handing on received opinions by making the notions or at least the propositions universal.

De Motu, Section Eight

We generally suppose that corporeal force is something easy to conceive. Those, however, who have studied the matter more carefully are of a different opinion, as appears from the strange obscurity of their language when they try to explain it. Torricelli says that force and impetus are abstract and subtle things and quintessences which are included in corporeal substance as in the magic vase of Circe ... Leibniz likewise in explaining the nature of force has this: 'Active primitive force which is *entelechia prote* corresponds to the soul or substantial form.' See *Acta Erudit.Lips.* Thus even the greatest men when they give way to abstractions are bound to pursue terms which have no certain significance and are mere shadows of scholastic things. Other passages in plenty from the writings of the younger men could be produced which give abundant proof that metaphysical abstractions have not in all quarters given place to mechanical science and experiment, but still make useless trouble for philosophers.

De Motu, Section Eleven

The force of gravitation is not to be separated from momentum; but there is no momentum without velocity, since it is mass multiplied by velocity; again, velocity cannot be understood without motion, and the same holds therefore of the force of gravitation. Then no force makes itself known except through action, and through action it is measured; but we are not able to separate the action of a body from its motion; therefore as long as a heavy body changes the shape of a piece of lead put under it, or of a cord, so long is it moved; but when it is at rest, it does nothing, or (which is the same thing) it is prevented from acting. In brief, those terms dead force and gravitation by the aid of metaphysical abstraction are supposed to mean something different from moving, moved, motion, and rest, but, in point of fact, the supposed difference in meaning amounts to nothing at all.

De Motu, Section Seventeen

Force, gravity, attraction, and terms of this sort are useful for reasonings and reckonings about motion and bodies in motion, but not for understanding the simple nature of motion itself or for indicating so many distinct qualities. As for attraction, it was certainly introduced by Newton, not as a true, physical quality, but only as a mathematical hypothesis. ...

De Motu, Section Eighteen

A similar account must be given of the composition and resolution of any direct forces into any oblique ones by means of the diagonal and sides of the parallelogram. They serve the purpose of mechanical science and reckoning; but to be of service to reckoning and mathematical demonstrations is one thing, to set for the nature of things is another.

De Motu, Section Twenty-eight

Action and reaction are said to be in bodies, and that way of speaking suits the purposes of mechanical demonstrations; but we must not on that account suppose that there is some real virtue in them which is the cause or principle of motion. For those terms are to be understood in the same way as the term attraction; and just as attraction is only a mathematical hypothesis, and not a physical quality, the same must be understood also about action and reaction, and for the same reason. For in mechanical philosophy the truth and the use of theorems about the mutual attraction of bodies remain firm, as founded solely in the motion of bodies, whether that motion be supposed to be caused by the action of bodies mutually attracting each other, or by the action of some agent different from the bodies, impelling and controlling them. Similarly the traditional formulations of rules and laws of motions, along with the theorems thence deduced remain unshaken, provided that sensible effects and the reasonings grounded in them are granted, whether we suppose the action itself or the force that causes these effects to be in the body or in the incorporeal agent.

De Motu, Section Twenty-nine

Take away from the idea of body extension, solidity, and figure, and nothing will remain. But those qualities are indifferent to motion, nor do they contain anything which could be called the principle of motion. This is clear from our very ideas. If therefore by the term body be meant that which we conceive, obviously the principle of motion cannot be sought therein, that is, no part or attribute thereof is the true, efficient cause of the production of motion. But to employ a term, and conceive nothing by it is quite unworthy of a philosopher.

De Motu, Section Thirty-four

Modern thinkers consider motion and rest in bodies as two states of existence in either of which every body, without pressure from external force, would naturally remain passive; whence one might gather that the cause of the existence of bodies is also the cause of their motion and rest. For no other cause of the successive existence of the body in different parts of space should be sought, it would seem, than that cause whence is derived the successive existence of the same body in different parts of time. But to treat of the good, and great God, creator and preserver of all things, and to show how all things depend on supreme and true being, although it is the most excellent part of human knowledge, is however rather the province of first philosophy or metaphysics and the theology than of natural philosophy which to–day is almost entirely confined to experiments and mechanics. And so natural philosophy either presupposes the knowledge of God or borrows it from some superior science. ...

De Motu, Section Thirty-five

The imperfect understanding of this situation has caused some to make the mistake of rejecting the mathematical principles of physics on the ground that they do not assign the efficient causes of things. It is not, however, in fact the business of physics or mechanics to establish efficient causes, but only the rules of the impulsions or attractions and, in a word, the laws of motions, and from the established laws to assign the solution, not the efficient cause, of particular phenomena.

De Motu, Section Thirty-six

It will be of great importance to consider what properly a principle is, and how that term is to be understood by philosophers. The true, efficient and conserving cause of an things by supreme right is called their fount and principle. Yet it is proper to describe as the 'principles' of experimental philosophy the foundations upon which it rests, the springs from which flows, not the existence, but our knowledge of corporeal things; I mean, the senses and experience. Similarly in mechanical philosophy those are to be called principles, in which the whole discipline is grounded and contained, those primary laws of motions which have been proved by experiments, elaborated by reason and rendered universal. These laws of motion are conveniently called principles, since from them are derived both general mechanical theorems and particular explanations of the phenomena.

De Motu, Section Thirty-seven

A thing can be said to be explained mechanically then indeed when it is reduced to those most simple and universal principles, and shown by accurate reasoning to be in agreement and connection with them. For once the laws of nature have been found out, then it is the philosopher's task to show that each phenomenon is in constant conformity with those laws, that is, necessarily follows from those principles. In that consist the explanation and solution of phenomena and the assigning their cause, i.e., the reason why they take place.

De Motu, Section Thirty-eight

The human mind delights in extending and expanding its knowledge; and for this purpose general notions and propositions have to be formed in which particular propositions and cognitions are in some way comprised, which then, and not till then, are believed to be understood. Geometers know this well. In mechanics also notions are premised, i.e., definitions and first and general statements about motion from which afterwards by mathematical method conclusions more remote and less general are deduced. And just as by the application of geometrical theorems, the sizes of particular bodies are measured, so also by the application of the universal theorems of mechanics, the movements of any parts of the mundane system, and the phenomena thereon depending, become known and are determined. And that is the sole mark at which the physicist must aim.

De Motu, Section Thirty-nine

And just as geometers for the sake of their art make use of many devices which they themselves cannot describe nor find in the nature of things, even so the mechanician makes use of certain abstract and general terms, imagining in bodies force, action, attraction, solicitation, etc., which are of first utility for theories and formulations, as also for computations about motion, even if in the truth of things, and in bodies actually existing, they would be looked for in vain, just like the geometers' fictions made by mathematical abstraction.

De Motu, Section Forty

We actually perceive by the aid of the senses nothing except the effects or sensible qualities and corporeal things entirely passive, whether in motion or at rest; and reason and experience advise us that there is nothing active except mind or soul. Whatever else is imagined must be considered to be of a kind with other hypotheses and mathematical abstractions. This ought to be laid to heart; otherwise we are in danger of sliding back into the obscure subtlety of the Schoolmen, which for so many ages like some dread plague, has corrupted philosophy.

De Motu, Section Sixty-six

From the foregoing it is clear that the following rules will be of great service in determining the true nature of motion:

1. To distinguish mathematical hypotheses from the natures of things;
2. To beware of abstractions;
3. To consider motion as something sensible, or at least imaginable; and to be content with relative measures.

If we do so, all the famous theorems of the mechanical philosophy by which the secrets of nature are unlocked, and by which the system of the world is reduced to human calculation, will remain untouched; and the study of motion will be freed from a thousand minutiae, subtleties, and abstract ideas. And let these words suffice about the nature of motion.

De Motu, Section Sixty-eight

Let us lay down that the new motion in the body struck is conserved either by the natural force by reason of which any body persists in its own uniform state of motion or of rest, or by the impressed force, received (while the percussion lasts) into the body struck, and there remaining; it will be the same in fact, the difference existing only in name. Similarly when the striking moveable body loses motion, and the struck body acquires it, it is not worth disputing whether the acquired motion is numerically the same as the motion lost; the discussion would lead into metaphysical and even verbal minutiae about identity. And so it comes to the same thing, whether we say that motion passes from the striker to the struck, or that motion is generated de novo (anew) in the struck, and is destroyed in the striker. In either cases it is understood that one body loses motion, the other acquires it, and besides that, nothing.

---

1. *According to Section Thirty-five, what is the true business of natural science? Of philosophy?*
2. *What is gravity? Is there a sense in which even asking this question is a mistake?*
3. *What problem is Berkeley discussing in Section Sixty-eight? How does his handling of it differ from Locke's?*

---

1. In this outline, I mainly follow Jonathan Dancy's introduction to the Oxford edition of the *Principles* (OUP, 1998).↵
2. *Works*, Volume Three, 333–334.↵

7. David Hume's (1711–1776) Enquiry Concerning Human Understanding

- Section Two: Of the Origin of Ideas
- Section Three: Of the Association of Ideas
- Section Four: Sceptical Doubts Concerning the Operations of the Understanding, Part One
- Section Four: Sceptical Doubts Concerning the Operations of the Understanding, Part Two
- Section Five: Sceptical Solution of these Doubts, Part One
- Section Five: Sceptical Solution of these Doubts, Part One
- Section Six: Of Probability
- Section Seven: Of the Idea of Necessary Connexion, Part One
- Section Seven: Of the Idea of Necessary Connexion, Part Two
- Section Nine: Of the Reason of Animals
- Section Eight: Of Liberty and Necessity, Part One
- Section Eight: Of Liberty and Necessity, Part Two
- Section Ten: Of Miracles, Part One
- Section Ten: Of Miracles, Part One
- Section Eleven: Of a Particular Providence and of a Future State
- Section Twelve: Of the Academical or Sceptical Philosophy, Part One
- Section Twelve: Of the Academical or Sceptical Philosophy, Part Two
- Section Twelve: Of the Academical or Sceptical Philosophy, Part Three
- A *Treatise of Human Nature* (1739), Appendix

Born in Edinburgh, David Hume published his A Treatise of Human Nature *in 1739–40. Recognizing that it 'fell dead-born from the press,' he started from scratch, repudiating the youthful* Treatise *and asking to be judged on the basis of his Enquiries instead. The first of these enquiries, from 1748, is the* Enquiry Concerning Human Understanding. *The contents:*

1. Of the different Species of Philosophy
2. Of the Origin of Ideas
3. Of the Association of Ideas
4. Sceptical Doubts Concerning the Operations of the Understanding
5. Sceptical Solution of these Doubts
6. Of Probability
7. Of the Idea of Necessary Connexion
8. Of Liberty and Necessity
9. Of the Reason of Animals
10. Of Miracles
11. Of a Particular Providence and of a Future State
12. Of the Academical or Sceptical Philosophy

In these selections, I have omitted Section One. Section Nine makes much more sense if it is read immediately after Section Seven.

(Textual note: the best recent editions of Hume's works are in the Oxford series (the Treatise, edited by Norton & Norton; Enquiry, edited by T. Beauchamp.)

Section Two: Of the Origin of Ideas

Every one will readily allow, that there is a considerable difference between the perceptions of the mind, when a man feels the pain of excessive heat, or the pleasure of moderate warmth, and when he afterwards recalls to his memory this sensation, or anticipates it by his imagination. These faculties may mimic or copy the perceptions of the senses; but they never can entirely reach the force and vivacity of the original sentiment. The utmost we say of them, even when they operate with greatest vigour, is, that they represent their object in so lively a manner, that we could almost say we feel or see it: but, except the mind be disordered by disease or madness, they never can arrive at such a pitch of vivacity, as to render these perceptions altogether undistinguishable. All the colours of poetry, however splendid, can never paint natural objects in such a manner as to make the description be taken for a real landscape. The most lively thought is still inferior to the dullest sensation.

We may observe a like distinction to run through all the other perceptions of the mind. A man in a fit of anger, is actuated in a very different manner from one who only thinks of that emotion. If you tell me, that any person is in love, I easily understand your meaning, and form a just conception of his situation; but never can mistake that conception for the real disorders and agitations of the passion. When we reflect on our past sentiments and affections, our thought is a faithful mirror, and copies its objects truly; but the colours which it employs are faint and dull, in comparison of those in which our original perceptions were clothed. It requires no nice discernment or metaphysical head to mark the distinction between them.

Here therefore we may divide all the perceptions of the mind into two classes or species, which are distinguished by their different degrees of force and vivacity. The less forcible and lively are commonly denominated Thoughts or Ideas. The other species want a name in our language, and in most others; I suppose, because it was not requisite for any, but philosophical purposes, to rank them under a general term or appellation. Let us, therefore, use a little freedom, and call them Impressions; employing that word in a sense somewhat different from the usual. By the term impression, then, I mean all our more lively perceptions, when we hear, or see, or feel, or love, or hate, or desire, or will. And impressions are distinguished from ideas, which are the less lively perceptions, of which we are conscious, when we reflect on any of those sensations or movements above mentioned.

Nothing, at first view, may seem more unbounded than the thought of man, which not only escapes all human power and authority, but is not even restrained within the limits of nature and reality. To form monsters, and join incongruous shapes and appearances, costs the imagination no more trouble than to conceive the most natural and familiar objects. And while the body is confined to one planet, along which it creeps with pain and difficulty; the thought can in an instant transport us into the most distant regions of the universe; or even beyond the universe, into the unbounded chaos, where nature is supposed to lie in total confusion. What never was seen, or heard of, may yet be conceived; nor is any thing beyond the power of thought, except what implies an absolute contradiction.

But though our thought seems to possess this unbounded liberty, we shall find, upon a nearer examination, that it is really confined within very narrow limits, and that all this creative power of the mind amounts to no more than the faculty of compounding, transposing, augmenting, or diminishing the materials afforded us by the senses and experience. When we think of a golden mountain, we only join two consistent ideas, gold, and mountain, with which we were formerly acquainted. A virtuous horse we can conceive; because, from our own feeling, we can conceive virtue; and this we may unite to the figure and shape of a horse, which is an animal familiar to us. In short, all the materials of thinking are derived either from our outward or inward sentiment: the mixture and composition of these belongs alone to the mind and will. Or, to express myself in philosophical language, all our ideas or more feeble perceptions are copies of our impressions or more lively ones.

To prove this, the two following arguments will, I hope, be sufficient. **First**, when we analyze our thoughts or ideas, however compounded or sublime, we always find that they resolve themselves into such simple ideas as were copied from a precedent feeling or sentiment. Even those ideas, which, at first view, seem the most wide of this origin, are found, upon a nearer scrutiny, to be derived from it. The idea of God, as meaning an infinitely intelligent, wise, and good Being, arises from reflecting on the operations of our own mind, and augmenting, without limit, those qualities of goodness and wisdom. We may prosecute this enquiry to what length we please; where we shall always find, that every idea which we examine is copied from a similar impression. Those who would assert that this position is not universally true nor without exception, have only one, and that an easy method of refuting it; by producing that idea, which, in their opinion, is not derived from this source. It will then be incumbent on us, if we would maintain our doctrine, to produce the impression, or lively perception, which corresponds to it.

Secondly. If it happen, from a defect of the organ, that a man is not susceptible of any species of sensation, we always find that he is as little susceptible of the correspondent ideas. A blind man can form no notion of colours; a deaf man of sounds. Restore either of them that sense in which he is deficient; by opening this new inlet for his sensations, you also open an inlet for the ideas; and he finds no difficulty in conceiving these objects. The case is the same, if the object, proper for exciting any sensation, has never been applied to the organ. A Laplander or Negro has no notion of the relish of wine. And though there are few or no instances of a like deficiency in the mind, where a person has never felt or is wholly incapable of a sentiment or passion that belongs to his species; yet we find the same observation to take place in a less degree. A man of mild manners can form no idea of inveterate revenge or cruelty; nor can a selfish heart easily conceive the heights of friendship and generosity. It is readily allowed, that other beings may possess many senses of which we can have no conception; because the ideas of them have never been introduced to us in the only manner by which an idea can have access to the mind, to wit, by the actual feeling and sensation.

There is, however, one contradictory phenomenon, which may prove that it is not absolutely impossible for ideas to arise, independent of their correspondent impressions. I believe it will readily be allowed, that the several distinct ideas of colour, which enter by the eye, or those of sound, which are conveyed by the ear, are really different from each other; though, at the same time, resembling. Now if this be true of different colours, it must be no less so of the different shades of the same colour; and each shade produces a distinct idea, independent of the rest. For if this should be denied, it is possible, by the continual gradation of shades, to run a colour insensibly into what is most remote from it; and if you will not allow any of the means to be different, you cannot, without absurdity, deny the extremes to be the same. Suppose, therefore, a person to have enjoyed his sight for thirty years, and to have become perfectly acquainted with colours of all kinds except one particular shade of blue, for instance, which it never has been his fortune to meet with. Let all the different shades of that colour, except that single one, be placed before him, descending gradually from the deepest to the lightest; it is plain that he will perceive a blank, where that shade is wanting, and will be sensible that there is a greater distance in that place between the contiguous colour than in any other. Now I ask, whether it be possible for him, from his own imagination, to supply this deficiency, and raise up to himself the idea of that particular shade, though it had never been conveyed to him by his senses? I believe there are few but will be of opinion that he can: and this may serve as a proof that the simple ideas are not always, in every instance, derived from the correspondent impressions; though this instance is so singular, that it is scarcely worth our observing, and does not merit that for it alone we should alter our general maxim.

Here, therefore, is a proposition, which not only seems, in itself, simple and intelligible; but, if a proper use were made of it, might render every dispute equally intelligible, and banish all that jargon, which has so long taken possession of metaphysical reasonings, and drawn disgrace upon them. All ideas, especially abstract ones, are naturally faint and obscure: the mind has but a slender hold of them: they are apt to be confounded with other resembling ideas; and when we have often employed any term, though without a distinct meaning, we are apt to imagine it has a determinate idea annexed to it. On the contrary, all impressions, that is, all sensations, either outward or inward, are strong and vivid: the limits between them are more exactly determined: nor is it easy to fall into any error or mistake with regard to them. When we entertain, therefore, any suspicion that a philosophical term is employed without any meaning or idea (as is but too frequent), we need but enquire, from what impression is that supposed idea derived? And if it be impossible to assign any, this will serve to confirm our suspicion. By bringing ideas into so clear a light we may reasonably hope to remove all dispute, which may arise, concerning their nature and reality.

---

1. *What does Hume's* **Copy Principle** *(CPY) assert about every idea?*
2. *Hume gives two arguments for the Copy Principle. What are they? Are they any good?*
3. *Why does the missing shade of blue seem to be a counterexample to the CPY? Why isn't Hume bothered by it? Why doesn't he just give up the CPY?*
4. *In Section Seven, Hume likens the CPY to 'a new microscope' that will bring as much benefit to philosophy as its counterpart did to natural science. Why does he think this?*

Section Three: Of the Association of Ideas

It is evident that there is a principle of connexion between the different thoughts or ideas of the mind, and that in their appearance to the memory or imagination, they introduce each other with a certain degree of method and regularity. In our more serious thinking or discourse this is so observable that any particular thought, which breaks in upon the regular tract or chain of ideas, is immediately remarked and rejected. And even in our wildest and most wandering reveries, nay in our very dreams, we shall find, if we reflect, that the imagination ran not altogether at adventures, but that there was still a connexion upheld among the different ideas, which succeeded each other. Were the loosest and freest conversation to be transcribed, there would immediately be observed something which connected it in all its transitions. Or where this is wanting, the person who broke the thread of discourse might still inform you, that there had secretly revolved in his mind a succession of thought, which had gradually led him from the subject of conversation. Among different languages, even where we cannot suspect the least connexion or communication, it is found, that the words, expressive of ideas, the most compounded, do yet nearly correspond to each other:

a certain proof that the simple ideas, comprehended in the compound ones, were bound together by some universal principle, which had an equal influence on all mankind.

Though it be too obvious to escape observation, that different ideas are connected together; I do not find that any philosopher has attempted to enumerate or class all the principles of association; a subject, however, that seems worthy of curiosity. To me, there appear to be only three principles of connexion among ideas, namely, Resemblance, Contiguity in time or place, and Cause or Effect.

That these principles serve to connect ideas will not, I believe, be much doubted. A picture naturally leads our thoughts to the original: the mention of one apartment in a building naturally introduces an enquiry or discourse concerning the others: and if we think of a wound, we can scarcely forbear reflecting on the pain which follows it. But that this enumeration is complete, and that there are no other principles of association except these, may be difficult to prove to the satisfaction of the reader, or even to a man's own satisfaction. All we can do, in such cases, is to run over several instances, and examine carefully the principle which binds the different thoughts to each other, never stopping till we render the principle as general as possible. The more instances we examine, and the more care we employ, the more assurance shall we acquire, that the enumeration, which we form from the whole, is complete and entire.

Section Four introduces a new distinction. Just as there are two kinds of perceptions, there are two kinds of 'objects of human reason' or propositions.

1. *What are the two kinds of perceptions?*

Some propositions (or declarative sentences, for our purposes) are relations of ideas (ROIs) and some are matters of fact (MOFs). These are objects of human reason or inquiry; not all of them are true. The distinction is based not on whether the proposition is true or not, but rather on what it would take to make the proposition true.

Section Four also makes use of two other principles, in addition to the Copy Principle (CPY).

The **Separability Principle** *(SP) says that any two distinct perceptions can, in thought, be separated. No matter how many times the taste of an apple accompanies the sight of an apple, I can still think of the one perception without the other.*

The **Conceivability Principle** *(CP) is familiar from Descartes's Sixth Meditation. and from Berkeley's work. If a state of affairs is conceivable, what follows, according to the CP?*

As you read, note where Hume is employing CP, SP, and CPY. This will help you keep track of his argument.

Section Four: Sceptical Doubts Concerning the Operations of the Understanding, Part One

All the objects of human reason or enquiry may naturally be divided into two kinds, to wit, **Relations of Ideas**, and **Matters of Fact**. Of the first kind are the sciences of Geometry, Algebra, and Arithmetic; and in short, every affirmation which is either intuitively or demonstratively certain. That the square of the hypotenuse is equal to the square of the two sides, is a proposition which expresses a relation between these figures. That three times five is equal to the half of thirty, expresses a relation between these numbers. Propositions of this kind are discoverable by the mere operation of thought, without dependence on what is anywhere existent in the universe. Though there never were a circle or triangle in nature, the truths demonstrated by Euclid would for ever retain their certainty and evidence.

Matters of fact, which are the second objects of human reason, are not ascertained in the same manner; nor is our evidence of their truth, however great, of a like nature with the foregoing. The contrary of every matter of fact is still possible; because it can never imply a contradiction, and is conceived by the mind with the same facility and distinctness, as if ever so conformable to reality. That the sun will not rise to-morrow is no less intelligible a proposition, and implies no more contradiction than the affirmation, that it will rise. We should in vain, therefore, attempt to demonstrate its falsehood. Were it demonstratively false, it would imply a contradiction, and could never be distinctly conceived by the mind. ...

All reasonings concerning matter of fact seem to be founded on the relation of Cause and Effect. By means of that relation alone we can go beyond the evidence of our memory and senses. If you were to ask a man, why he believes any matter of fact, which is absent; for instance, that his friend is in the country, or in France; he would give you a reason; and this reason would be some other fact; as a letter received from him, or the knowledge of his former resolutions and promises. A man finding a watch or any other machine in a desert island, would conclude that there had once been men in that island. All our reasonings concerning fact are of the same nature. And here it is constantly supposed that there is a connexion between the present fact and that which is inferred from it. Were there nothing to bind them together, the inference would be entirely precarious. The hearing of an articulate voice and rational discourse in the dark assures us of the presence of some person: Why? because these are the effects of the human make and fabric, and closely connected with it. If we anatomize all the other reasonings of this nature, we shall find that they are founded on the relation of cause and effect, and that this relation is either near or remote, direct or collateral. Heat and light are collateral effects of fire, and the one effect may justly be inferred from the other.

If we would satisfy ourselves, therefore, concerning the nature of that evidence, which assures us of matters of fact, we must enquire how we arrive at the knowledge of cause and effect.

I shall venture to affirm, as a general proposition, which admits of no exception, that the knowledge of this relation is not, in any instance, attained by reasonings *a priori*; but arises entirely from experience, when we find that any particular objects are constantly conjoined with each other. Let an object be presented to a man of ever so strong natural reason and abilities; if that object be entirely new to him, he will not be able, by the most accurate examination of its sensible qualities, to discover any of its causes or effects. Adam, though his rational faculties be supposed, at the very first, entirely perfect, could not have inferred from the fluidity and transparency of water that it would suffocate him, or from the light and warmth of fire that it would consume him. No object ever discovers, by the qualities which appear to the senses, either the causes which produced it, or the effects which will arise from it; nor can our reason, unassisted by experience, ever draw any inference concerning real existence and matter of fact.

This proposition, that causes and effects are discoverable, not by reason but by experience, will readily be admitted with regard to such objects, as we remember to have once been altogether unknown to us; since we must be conscious of the utter inability, which we then lay under, of foretelling what would arise from them. Present two smooth pieces of marble to a man who has no tincture of natural philosophy; he will never discover that they will adhere together in such a manner as to require great force to separate them in a direct line, while they make so small a resistance to a lateral pressure. Such events, as bear little analogy to the common course of nature, are also readily confessed to be known only by experience; nor does any man imagine that the explosion of gunpowder, or the attraction of a loadstone, could ever be discovered by arguments *a priori*. In like manner, when an effect is supposed to depend upon an intricate machinery or secret structure of parts, we make no difficulty in attributing all our knowledge of it to experience. Who will assert that he can give the ultimate reason, why milk or bread is proper nourishment for a man, not for a lion or a tiger?

But the same truth may not appear, at first sight, to have the same evidence with regard to events, which have become familiar to us from our first appearance in the world, which bear a close analogy to the whole course of nature, and which are supposed to depend on the simple qualities of objects, without any secret structure of parts. We are apt to imagine that we could discover these effects by the mere operation of our reason, without experience. We fancy, that were we brought on a sudden into this world, we could at first have inferred that one Billiard-ball would communicate motion to another upon impulse; and that we needed not to have waited for the event, in order to pronounce with certainty concerning it. Such is the influence of custom, that, where it is strongest, it not only covers our natural ignorance, but even conceals itself, and seems not to take place, merely because it is found in the highest degree.

But to convince us that all the laws of nature, and all the operations of bodies without exception, are known only by experience, the following reflections may, perhaps, suffice. Were any object presented to us, and were we required to pronounce concerning the effect, which will result from it, without consulting past observation; after what manner, I beseech you, must the mind proceed in this operation? It must invent or imagine some event, which it ascribes to the object as its effect; and it is plain that this invention must be entirely arbitrary. The mind can never possibly find the effect in the supposed cause, by the most accurate scrutiny and examination. For the effect is totally different from the cause, and consequently can never be discovered in it. Motion in the second Billiard-ball is a quite distinct event from motion in the first; nor is there anything in the one to suggest the smallest hint of the other. A stone or piece of metal raised into the air, and left without any support, immediately falls: but to consider the matter *a priori*, is there anything we discover in this situation which can beget the idea of a downward, rather than an upward, or any other motion, in the stone or metal?

And as the first imagination or invention of a particular effect, in all natural operations, is arbitrary, where we consult not experience; so must we also esteem the supposed tie or connexion between the cause and effect, which binds them together, and renders it impossible that any other effect could result from the operation of that cause. When I see, for instance, a Billiard-ball moving in a straight line towards another; even suppose motion in the second ball should by accident be suggested to me, as the result of their contact or impulse; may I not conceive, that a hundred different events might as well follow from that cause? May not both these balls remain at absolute rest? May not the first ball return in a straight line, or leap off from the second in any line or direction? All these suppositions are consistent and conceivable. Why then should we give the preference to one, which is no more consistent or conceivable than the rest? All our reasonings *a priori* will never be able to show us any foundation for this preference.

In a word, then, every effect is a distinct event from its cause. It could not, therefore, be discovered in the cause, and the first invention or conception of it, *a priori*, must be entirely arbitrary. And even after it is suggested, the conjunction of it with the cause must appear equally arbitrary; since there are always many other effects, which, to reason, must seem fully as consistent and natural. In vain, therefore, should we pretend to determine any single event, or infer any cause or effect, without the assistance of observation and experience.

Hence we may discover the reason why no philosopher, who is rational and modest, has ever pretended to assign the ultimate cause of any natural operation, or to show distinctly the action of that power, which produces any single effect in the universe. It is confessed, that the utmost effort of human reason is to reduce the principles, productive of natural phenomena, to a greater simplicity, and to resolve the many particular effects into a few general causes, by means of reasonings from analogy, experience, and observation. But as to the causes of these general causes, we should in vain attempt their discovery; nor shall we ever be able to satisfy ourselves, by any particular explication of them. These ultimate springs and principles are totally shut up from human curiosity and enquiry. Elasticity, gravity, cohesion of parts, communication of motion by impulse; these are probably the ultimate causes and principles which we shall ever discover in nature; and we may esteem ourselves sufficiently happy, if, by accurate enquiry and reasoning, we can trace up the particular phenomena to, or near to, these general principles. The most perfect philosophy of the natural kind only staves off our ignorance a little longer: as perhaps the most perfect philosophy of the moral or metaphysical kind serves only to discover larger portions of it. Thus the observation of human blindness and weakness is the result of all philosophy, and meets us at every turn, in spite of our endeavours to elude or avoid it.

---

1. *What is the difference between MOFs and ROIs? For each kind of proposition, say whether it is* **analytic** *or* **synthetic**; **contingent** *or* **necessary**; *justified by demonstration or by appeal to experience.*
2. *In which category does a proposition like 'fire causes heat' fall? What is Hume's argument for this? use CP, SP, and CPY, if applicable.*

Section Four: Sceptical Doubts Concerning the Operations of the Understanding, Part Two

But we have not yet attained any tolerable satisfaction with regard to the question first proposed. Each solution still gives rise to a new question as difficult as the foregoing, and leads us on to farther enquiries. When it is asked, *What is the nature of all our reasonings concerning matter of fact?* the proper answer seems to be, that they are founded on the relation of cause and effect. When again it is asked, *What is the foundation of all our reasonings and conclusions concerning that relation?* it may be replied in one word, Experience. But if we still carry on our sifting humour, and ask, *What is the foundation of all conclusions from experience?* this implies a new question, which may be of more difficult solution and explication. ...

I shall content myself, in this section, with an easy task, and shall pretend only to give a negative answer to the question here proposed. I say then, that, even after we have experience of the operations of cause and effect, our conclusions from that experience are not founded on reasoning, or any process of the understanding. This answer we must endeavour both to explain and to defend.

It must certainly be allowed, that nature has kept us at a great distance from all her secrets, and has afforded us only the knowledge of a few superficial qualities of objects; while she conceals from us those powers and principles on which the influence of those objects entirely depends. Our senses inform us of the colour, weight, and consistence of bread; but neither sense nor reason can ever inform us of those qualities which fit it for the nourishment and support of a human body. Sight or feeling conveys an idea of the actual motion of bodies; but as to that wonderful force or power, which would carry on a moving body for ever in a continued change of place, and which bodies never lose but by communicating it to others; of this we cannot form the most distant conception.

But notwithstanding this ignorance of natural powers and principles, we always presume, when we see like sensible qualities, that they have like secret powers, and expect that effects, similar to those which we have experienced, will follow from them. If a body of like colour and consistence with that bread, which we have formerly eat, be presented to us, we make no scruple of repeating the experiment, and foresee, with certainty, like nourishment and support. Now this is a process of the mind or thought, of which I would willingly know the foundation. It is allowed on all hands that there is no known connexion between the sensible qualities and the secret powers; and consequently, that the mind is not led to form such a conclusion concerning their constant and regular conjunction, by anything which it knows of their nature. As to past Experience, it can be allowed to give direct and certain information of those precise objects only, and that precise period of time, which fell under its cognizance: but why this experience should be extended to future times, and to other objects, which for aught we know, may be only in appearance similar; this is the main question on which I would insist. The bread, which I formerly eat, nourished me; that is, a body of such sensible qualities was, at that time, endued with such secret powers: but does it follow, that other bread must also nourish me at another time, and that like sensible qualities must always be attended with like secret powers? The consequence seems nowise necessary. At least, it must be acknowledged that there is here a consequence drawn by the mind; that there is a certain step taken; a process of thought, and an inference, which wants to be explained. These two propositions are far from being the same. I have found that such an object has always been attended with such an effect, and I foresee, that other objects, which are, in appearance, similar, will be attended with similar effects. I shall allow, if you please, that the one proposition may justly be inferred from the other: I know, in fact, that it always is inferred. But if you insist that the inference is made by a chain of reasoning, I desire you to produce that reasoning. The connexion between these propositions is not intuitive. There is required a medium, which may enable the mind to draw such an inference, if indeed it be drawn by reasoning and argument. What that medium is, I must confess, passes my comprehension; and it is incumbent on those to produce it, who assert that it really exists, and is the origin of all our conclusions concerning matter of fact.

This negative argument must certainly, in process of time, become altogether convincing, if many penetrating and able philosophers shall turn their enquiries this way and no one be ever able to discover any connecting proposition or intermediate step, which supports the understanding in this conclusion. But as the question is yet new, every reader may not trust so far to his own penetration, as to conclude, because an argument escapes his enquiry, that therefore it does not really exist. For this reason it may be requisite to venture upon a more difficult task; and enumerating all the branches of human knowledge, endeavour to show that none of them can afford such an argument.

All reasonings may be divided into two kinds, namely, demonstrative reasoning, or that concerning relations of ideas, and moral reasoning, or that concerning matter of fact and existence. That there are no demonstrative arguments in the case seems evident; since it implies no contradiction that the course of nature may change, and that an object, seemingly like those which we have experienced, may be attended with different or contrary effects. May I not clearly and distinctly conceive that a body, falling from the clouds, and which, in all other respects, resembles snow, has yet the taste of salt or feeling of fire? Is there any more intelligible proposition than to affirm, that all the trees will flourish in December and January, and decay in May and June? Now whatever is intelligible, and can be distinctly conceived, implies no contradiction, and can never be proved false by any demonstrative argument or abstract reasoning *a priori*.

If we be, therefore, engaged by arguments to put trust in past experience, and make it the standard of our future judgment, these arguments must be probable only, or such as regard matter of fact and real existence according to the division above mentioned. But that there is no argument of this kind, must appear, if our explication of that species of reasoning be admitted as solid and satisfactory. We have said that all arguments concerning existence are founded on the relation of cause and effect; that our knowledge of that relation is derived entirely from experience; and that all our experimental conclusions proceed upon the supposition that the future will be conformable to the past. To endeavour, therefore, the proof of this last supposition by probable arguments, or arguments regarding experience, must be evidently going in a circle, and taking that for granted, which is the very point in question.

In reality, all arguments from experience are founded on the similarity which we discover among natural objects, and by which we are induced to expect effects similar to those which we have found to follow from such objects. And though none but a fool or madman will ever pretend to dispute the authority of experience, or to reject that great guide of human life, it may surely be allowed a philosopher to have so much curiosity at least as to examine the principle of human nature, which gives this mighty authority to experience, and makes us draw advantage from that similarity which nature has placed among different objects. From causes which appear similar we expect similar effects. This is the sum of all our experimental conclusions. ...

When a man says, I have found, in all past instances, such sensible qualities conjoined with such secret powers: And when he says, Similar sensible qualities will always be conjoined with similar secret powers, he is not guilty of a tautology, nor are these propositions in any respect the same. You say that the one proposition is an inference from the other. But you must confess that the inference is not intuitive; neither is it demonstrative: Of what nature is it, then? To say it is experimental, is begging the question. For all inferences from experience suppose, as their foundation, that the future will resemble the past, and that similar powers will be conjoined with similar sensible qualities. If there be any suspicion that the course of nature may change, and that the past may be no rule for the future, all experience becomes useless, and can give rise to no inference or conclusion. It is impossible, therefore, that any arguments from experience can prove this resemblance of the past to the future; since all these arguments are founded on the supposition of that resemblance. Let the course of things be allowed hitherto ever so regular; that alone, without some new argument or inference, proves not that, for the future, it will continue so. In vain do you pretend to have learned the nature of bodies from your past experience. Their secret nature, and consequently all their effects and influence, may change, without any change in their sensible qualities. This happens sometimes, and with regard to some objects: Why may it not happen always, and with regard to all objects? What logic, what process or argument secures you against this supposition? My practice, you say, refutes my doubts. But you mistake the purport of my question. As an agent, I am quite satisfied in the point; but as a philosopher, who has some share of curiosity, I will not say scepticism, I want to learn the foundation of this inference. No reading, no enquiry has yet been able to remove my difficulty, or give me satisfaction in a matter of such importance. Can I do better than propose the difficulty to the public, even though, perhaps, I have small hopes of obtaining a solution? We shall at least, by this means, be sensible of our ignorance, if we do not augment our knowledge.

I must confess that a man is guilty of unpardonable arrogance who concludes, because an argument has escaped his own investigation, that therefore it does not really exist. ... But with regard to the present subject, there are some considerations which seem to remove all this accusation of arrogance or suspicion of mistake.

It is certain that the most ignorant and stupid peasants—nay infants, nay even brute beasts—improve by experience, and learn the qualities of natural objects, by observing the effects which result from them. When a child has felt the sensation of pain from touching the flame of a candle, he will be careful not to put his hand near any candle; but will expect a similar effect from a cause which is similar in its sensible qualities and appearance. If you assert, therefore, that the understanding of the child is led into this conclusion by any process of argument or ratiocination, I may justly require you to produce that argument; nor have you any pretence to refuse so equitable a demand. You cannot say that the argument is abstruse, and may possibly escape your enquiry; since you confess that it is obvious to the capacity of a mere infant. If you hesitate, therefore, a moment, or if, after reflection, you produce any intricate or profound argument, you, in a manner, give up the question, and confess that it is not reasoning which engages us to suppose the past resembling the future, and to expect similar effects from causes which are, to appearance, similar. This is the proposition which I intended to enforce in the present section. If I be right, I pretend not to have made any mighty discovery. And if I be wrong, I must acknowledge myself to be indeed a very backward scholar; since I cannot now discover an argument which, it seems, was perfectly familiar to me long before I was out of my cradle.

---

1. *Only one of the principles of the association of ideas can tell us about any matter of fact. Which is it?*
2. *How do we make the transition from the impression of a _____ to an idea of its _____? Or vice versa?*
3. *Hume says he will content himself with proving a negative proposition in Part Two (see the second paragraph). What is this negative proposition?Here's one way to represent the inference/transition:*

   1. I have found in the past that all instances of A (say, fire) have been followed by instances of B (say, heat).
   2. I predict that future A's will be followed by B's.

   If the move from 1 to 2 is a rational, justified inference, it would have to be either demonstrative reasoning or reasoning from experience.

   1. Why can't it be demonstrative reasoning?
   2. Why can't it be reasoning from experience?

   Objection: *What's missing here is a further premise, viz., Premise 1.5 The future will be like the past. What is the problem with adding this premise?*

   Objection: *Why can't I conclude at least that it's probable that the sun will rise tomorrow? (To answer this, you might try re-writing the mini-argument above, with the conclusion restricted to probability. Does the inference become justified, once its conclusion is qualified?)*

Section Five: Sceptical Solution of these Doubts, Part One

[We are in danger of reasoning ourselves into skepticism. But we need not] fear that this philosophy, while it endeavours to limit our enquiries to common life, should ever undermine the reasonings of common life, and carry its doubts so far as to destroy all action, as well as speculation. Nature will always maintain her rights, and prevail in the end over any abstract reasoning whatsoever. Though we should conclude, for instance, as in the foregoing section, that, in all reasonings from experience, there is a step taken by the mind which is not supported by any argument or process of the understanding; there is no danger that these reasonings, on which almost all knowledge depends, will ever be affected by such a discovery. If the mind be not engaged by argument to make this step, it must be induced by some other principle of equal weight and authority; and that principle will preserve its influence as long as human nature remains the same. What that principle is may well be worth the pains of enquiry.

Suppose a person, though endowed with the strongest faculties of reason and reflection, to be brought on a sudden into this world; he would, indeed, immediately observe a continual succession of objects, and one event following another; but he would not be able to discover anything farther. He would not, at first, by any reasoning, be able to reach the idea of cause and effect; since the particular powers, by which all natural operations are performed, never appear to the senses; nor is it reasonable to conclude, merely because one event, in one instance, precedes another, that therefore the one is the cause, the other the effect. Their conjunction may be arbitrary and casual. There may be no reason to infer the existence of one from the appearance of the other. And in a word, such a person, without more experience, could never employ his conjecture or reasoning concerning any matter of fact, or be assured of anything beyond what was immediately present to his memory and senses.

Suppose, again, that he has acquired more experience, and has lived so long in the world as to have observed familiar objects or events to be constantly conjoined together; what is the consequence of this experience? He immediately infers the existence of one object from the appearance of the other. Yet he has not, by all his experience, acquired any idea or knowledge of the secret power by which the one object produces the other; nor is it by any process of reasoning, he is engaged to draw this inference. But still he finds himself determined to draw it: and though he should be convinced that his understanding has no part in the operation, he would nevertheless continue in the same course of thinking. There is some other principle which determines him to form such a conclusion.

This principle is Custom or Habit. For wherever the repetition of any particular act or operation produces a propensity to renew the same act or operation, without being impelled by any reasoning or process of the understanding, we always say, that this propensity is the effect of Custom. By employing that word, we pretend not to have given the ultimate reason of such a propensity. We only point out a principle of human nature, which is universally acknowledged, and which is well known by its effects. Perhaps we can push our enquiries no farther, or pretend to give the cause of this cause; but must rest contented with it as the ultimate principle, which we can assign, of all our conclusions from experience. It is sufficient satisfaction, that we can go so far, without repining at the narrowness of our faculties because they will carry us no farther. And it is certain we here advance a very intelligible proposition at least, if not a true one, when we assert that, after the constant conjunction of two objects—heat and flame, for instance, weight and solidity—we are determined by custom alone to expect the one from the appearance of the other. This hypothesis seems even the only one which explains the difficulty, why we draw, from a thousand instances, an inference which we are not able to draw from one instance, that is, in no respect, different from them. Reason is incapable of any such variation. The conclusions which it draws from considering one circle are the same which it would form upon surveying all the circles in the universe. But no man, having seen only one body move after being impelled by another, could infer that every other body will move after a like impulse. All inferences from experience, therefore, are effects of custom, not of reasoning.

Custom, then, is the great guide of human life. It is that principle alone which renders our experience useful to us, and makes us expect, for the future, a similar train of events with those which have appeared in the past. Without the influence of custom, we should be entirely ignorant of every matter of fact beyond what is immediately present to the memory and senses. We should never know how to adjust means to ends, or to employ our natural powers in the production of any effect. There would be an end at once of all action, as well as of the chief part of speculation. ...

What, then, is the conclusion of the whole matter? A simple one; though, it must be confessed, pretty remote from the common theories of philosophy. All belief of matter of fact or real existence is derived merely from some object, present to the memory or senses, and a customary conjunction between that and some other object. Or in other words; having found, in many instances, that any two kinds of objects—flame and heat, snow and cold—have always been conjoined together; if flame or snow be presented anew to the senses, the mind is carried by custom to expect heat or cold, and to believe that such a quality does exist, and will discover itself upon a nearer approach. This belief is the necessary result of placing the mind in such circumstances. It is an operation of the soul, when we are so situated, as unavoidable as to feel the passion of love, when we receive benefits; or hatred, when we meet with injuries. All these operations are a species of natural instincts, which no reasoning or process of the thought and understanding is able either to produce or to prevent.

At this point, it would be very allowable for us to stop our philosophical researches. In most questions we can never make a single step farther; and in all questions we must terminate here at last, after our most restless and curious enquiries. But still our curiosity will be pardonable, perhaps commendable, if it carry us on to still farther researches, and make us examine more accurately the nature of this belief, and of the customary conjunction, whence it is derived.

Recall the transition set out in (125) above. Hume wants to explain how we make the transition. But no process of reasoning—neither demonstrative reasoning nor reasoning from experience—is up to the task. So how do we do it?

Hume takes his clue from the thought experiment of Adam. Just by looking at water, Adam is unable to figure out that it will quench his thirst. But after he's experienced the constant conjunction of drinking water and having his thirst quenched, he makes the transition from the perception of one to the other very readily. If we can figure out what makes the difference, we'll be able to figure out what mechanism is responsible for the transition.

1. *When (and only when) do we in fact make causal connections between two events? There must be some connecting principle that explains our practice of taking past constant conjunctions to be a good guide to the future. What is it?*
2. *How is this a 'skeptical' solution, rather than a plain old solution?*
3. *What is the price to be paid for accepting Hume's skeptical solution?*
4. *How would Berkeley respond to Hume's skepticism about the transition? (See PHK, Part One, Sections Thirty and Thirty-one.)*
5. *Why can't Hume use this response?*

In Part Two and in the following section on probability, Hume examines the nature of belief. He shows how his principles of association—cause and effect, resemblance, and contiguity in time and place—can be used to explain how our ideas become so enlivened as to qualify as beliefs.

Nothing is more free than the imagination of man; and though it cannot exceed that original stock of ideas furnished by the internal and external senses, it has unlimited power of mixing, compounding, separating, and dividing these ideas, in all the varieties of fiction and vision. It can feign a train of events, with all the appearance of reality, ascribe to them a particular time and place, conceive them as existent, and paint them out to itself with every circumstance, that belongs to any historical fact, which it believes with the greatest certainty.

Wherein, therefore, consists the difference between such a fiction and belief? It lies not merely in any peculiar idea, which is annexed to such a conception as commands our assent, and which is wanting to every known fiction. For as the mind has authority over all its ideas, it could voluntarily annex this particular idea to any fiction, and consequently be able to believe whatever it pleases; contrary to what we find by daily experience. We can, in our conception, join the head of a man to the body of a horse; but it is not in our power to believe that such an animal has ever really existed.

It follows, therefore, that the difference between fiction and belief lies in some sentiment or feeling, which is annexed to the latter, not to the former, and which depends not on the will, nor can be commanded at pleasure. It must be excited by nature, like all other sentiments; and must arise from the particular situation, in which the mind is placed at any particular juncture. Whenever any object is presented to the memory or senses, it immediately, by the force of custom, carries the imagination to conceive that object, which is usually conjoined to it; and this conception is attended with a feeling or sentiment, different from the loose reveries of the fancy. In this consists the whole nature of belief. For as there is no matter of fact which we believe so firmly that we cannot conceive the contrary, there would be no difference between the conception assented to and that which is rejected, were it not for some sentiment which distinguishes the one from the other. If I see a billiard-ball moving toward another, on a smooth table, I can easily conceive it to stop upon contact. This conception implies no contradiction; but still it feels very differently from that conception by which I represent to myself the impulse and the communication of motion from one ball to another. ...

Let us, then, take in the whole compass of this doctrine, and allow, that the sentiment of belief is nothing but a conception more intense and steady than what attends the mere fictions of the imagination, and that this manner of conception arises from a customary conjunction of the object with something present to the memory or senses: I believe that it will not be difficult, upon these suppositions, to find other operations of the mind analogous to it, and to trace up these phenomena to principles still more general.

We have already observed that nature has established connexions among particular ideas, and that no sooner one idea occurs to our thoughts than it introduces its correlative, and carries our attention towards it, by a gentle and insensible movement. These principles of connexion or association we have reduced to three, namely, **Resemblance**, **Contiguity** and **Causation**; which are the only bonds that unite our thoughts together, and beget that regular train of reflection or discourse, which, in a greater or less degree, takes place among all mankind. Now here arises a question, on which the solution of the present difficulty will depend. Does it happen, in all these relations, that, when one of the objects is presented to the senses or memory, the mind is not only carried to the conception of the correlative, but reaches a steadier and stronger conception of it than what otherwise it would have been able to attain? This seems to be the case with that belief which arises from the relation of cause and effect. And if the case be the same with the other relations or principles of associations, this may be established as a general law, which takes place in all the operations of the mind.

... The transition from a present object does in all cases [Contiguity, Resemblance, and Cause and Effect] give strength and solidity to the related idea.

Here, then, is a kind of pre-established harmony between the course of nature and the succession of our ideas; and though the powers and forces, by which the former is governed, be wholly unknown to us; yet our thoughts and conceptions have still, we find, gone on in the same train with the other works of nature. Custom is that principle, by which this correspondence has been effected; so necessary to the subsistence of our species, and the regulation of our conduct, in every circumstance and occurrence of human life. Had not the presence of an object, instantly excited the idea of those objects, commonly conjoined with it, all our knowledge must have been limited to the narrow sphere of our memory and senses; and we should never have been able to adjust means to ends, or employ our natural powers, either to the producing of good, or avoiding of evil. Those, who delight in the discovery and contemplation of final causes, have here ample subject to employ their wonder and admiration.

I shall add, for a further confirmation of the foregoing theory, that, as this operation of the mind, by which we infer like effects from like causes, and vice versa, is so essential to the subsistence of all human creatures, it is not probable, that it could be trusted to the fallacious deductions of our reason, which is slow in its operations; appears not, in any degree, during the first years of infancy; and at best is, in every age and period of human life, extremely liable to error and mistake. It is more conformable to the ordinary wisdom of nature to secure so necessary an act of the mind, by some instinct or mechanical tendency, which may be infallible in its operations, may discover itself at the first appearance of life and thought, and may be independent of all the laboured deductions of the understanding. As nature has taught us the use of our limbs, without giving us the knowledge of the muscles and nerves, by which they are actuated; so has she implanted in us an instinct, which carries forward the thought in a correspondent course to that which she has established among external objects; though we are ignorant of those powers and forces, on which this regular course and succession of objects totally depends.

Section Six: Of Probability

Though there be no such thing as Chance in the world; our ignorance of the real cause of any event has the same influence on the understanding, and begets a like species of belief or opinion.

There is certainly a probability, which arises from a superiority of chances on any side; and according as this superiority increases, and surpasses the opposite chances, the probability receives a proportionable increase, and begets still a higher degree of belief or assent to that side, in which we discover the superiority. If a dye were marked with one figure or number of spots on four sides, and with another figure or number of spots on the two remaining sides, it would be more probable, that the former would turn up than the latter; though, if it had a thousand sides marked in the same manner, and only one side different, the probability would be much higher, and our belief or expectation of the event more steady and secure. This process of the thought or reasoning may seem trivial and obvious; but to those who consider it more narrowly, it may, perhaps, afford matter for curious speculation.

It seems evident, that, when the mind looks forward to discover the event, which may result from the throw of such a dye, it considers the turning up of each particular side as alike probable; and this is the very nature of chance, to render all the particular events, comprehended in it, entirely equal. But finding a greater number of sides concur in the one event than in the other, the mind is carried more frequently to that event, and meets it oftener, in revolving the various possibilities or chances, on which the ultimate result depends. This concurrence of several views in one particular event begets immediately, by an inexplicable contrivance of nature, the sentiment of belief, and gives that event the advantage over its antagonist, which is supported by a smaller number of views, and recurs less frequently to the mind. If we allow, that belief is nothing but a firmer and stronger conception of an object than what attends the mere fictions of the imagination, this operation may, perhaps, in some measure, be accounted for. The concurrence of these several views or glimpses imprints the idea more strongly on the imagination; gives it superior force and vigour; renders its influence on the passions and affections more sensible; and in a word, begets that reliance or security, which constitutes the nature of belief and opinion.

The case is the same with the probability of causes, as with that of chance. There are some causes, which are entirely uniform and constant in producing a particular effect; and no instance has ever yet been found of any failure or irregularity in their operation. Fire has always burned, and water suffocated every human creature: the production of motion by impulse and gravity is an universal law, which has hitherto admitted of no exception. But there are other causes, which have been found more irregular and uncertain; nor has rhubarb always proved a purge, or opium a soporific to every one, who has taken these medicines. It is true, when any cause fails of producing its usual effect, philosophers ascribe not this to any irregularity in nature; but suppose, that some secret causes, in the particular structure of parts, have prevented the operation. Our reasonings, however, and conclusions concerning the event are the same as if this principle had no place. Being determined by custom to transfer the past to the future, in all our inferences; where the past has been entirely regular and uniform, we expect the event with the greatest assurance, and leave no room for any contrary supposition. But where different effects have been found to follow from causes, which are to appearance exactly similar, all these various effects must occur to the mind in transferring the past to the future, and enter into our consideration, when we determine the probability of the event. Though we give the preference to that which has been found most usual, and believe that this effect will exist, we must not overlook the other effects, but must assign to each of them a particular weight and authority, in proportion as we have found it to be more or less frequent. It is more probable, in almost every country of Europe, that there will be frost sometime in January, than that the weather will continue open through out that whole month ... Here then it seems evident, that, when we transfer the past to the future, in order to determine the effect, which will result from any cause, we transfer all the different events, in the same proportion as they have appeared in the past, and conceive one to have existed a hundred times, for instance, another ten times, and another once. As a great number of views do here concur in one event, they fortify and confirm it to the imagination, beget that sentiment which we call belief, and give its object the preference above the contrary event, which is not supported by an equal number of experiments, and recurs not so frequently to the thought in transferring the past to the future. Let any one try to account for this operation of the mind upon any of the received systems of philosophy, and he will be sensible of the difficulty. For my part, I shall think it sufficient, if the present hints excite the curiosity of philosophers, and make them sensible how defective all common theories are in treating of such curious and such sublime subjects.

---

1. *Hume points out that we don't always experience a constant conjunction of any two events; perhaps more often, they go together only sometimes (like frost in January). How does the human mind react to*

such experiences? Why?

Section Seven: Of the Idea of Necessary Connexion, Part One

If Hume has given us the right story about the transition, he has explained how human minds move from past experience to predictions about the future. But none of the philosophers we've read would be satisfied by this. However human minds make the transition, isn't it still the case that there is cause and effect out there in the world? Don't some objects have the power to bring about their effects? When I say that 'fire causes heat' I don't just mean 'whenever I see fire, I expect to feel heat'; I mean that fire brings about or produces heat. In this section, then, Hume gives an account of what 'power' and 'cause' really amount to.

Pay special attention to Hume's footnote argument against Locke.

... There are no ideas, which occur in metaphysics, more obscure and uncertain, than those of power, force, energy or necessary connexion, of which it is every moment necessary for us to treat in all our disquisitions. We shall, therefore, endeavour, in this section, to fix, if possible, the precise meaning of these terms, and thereby remove some part of that obscurity, which is so much complained of in this species of philosophy.

It seems a proposition, which will not admit of much dispute, that all our ideas are nothing but copies of our impressions, or, in other words, that it is impossible for us to think of anything, which we have not antecedently felt, either by our external or internal senses. I have endeavoured to explain and prove this proposition, and have expressed my hopes, that, by a proper application of it, men may reach a greater clearness and precision in philosophical reasonings, than what they have hitherto been able to attain. Complex ideas, may, perhaps, be well known by definition, which is nothing but an enumeration of those parts or simple ideas, that compose them. But when we have pushed up definitions to the most simple ideas, and find still more ambiguity and obscurity; what resource are we then possessed of? By what invention can we throw light upon these ideas, and render them altogether precise and determinate to our intellectual view? Produce the impressions or original sentiments, from which the ideas are copied. These impressions are all strong and sensible. They admit not of ambiguity. They are not only placed in a full light themselves, but may throw light on their correspondent ideas, which lie in obscurity. And by this means, we may, perhaps, attain a new microscope or species of optics, by which, in the moral sciences, the most minute, and most simple ideas may be so enlarged as to fall readily under our apprehension, and be equally known with the grossest and most sensible ideas, that can be the object of our enquiry.

To be fully acquainted, therefore, with the idea of power or necessary connexion, let us examine its impression; and in order to find the impression with greater certainty, let us search for it in all the sources, from which it may possibly be derived.

When we look about us towards external objects, and consider the operation of causes, we are never able, in a single instance, to discover any power or necessary connexion; any quality, which binds the effect to the cause, and renders the one an infallible consequence of the other. We only find, that the one does actually, in fact, follow the other. The impulse of one billiard-ball is attended with motion in the second. This is the whole that appears to the outward senses. The mind feels no sentiment or inward impression from this succession of objects: consequently, there is not, in any single, particular instance of cause and effect, any thing which can suggest the idea of power or necessary connexion.

From the first appearance of an object, we never can conjecture what effect will result from it. But were the power or energy of any cause discoverable by the mind, we could foresee the effect, even without experience; and might, at first, pronounce with certainty concerning it, by mere dint of thought and reasoning.

In reality, there is no part of matter, that does ever, by its sensible qualities, discover any power or energy, or give us ground to imagine, that it could produce any thing, or be followed by any other object, which we could denominate its effect. Solidity, extension, motion; these qualities are all complete in themselves, and never point out any other event which may result from them. The scenes of the universe are continually shifting, and one object follows another in an uninterrupted succession; but the power of force, which actuates the whole machine, is entirely concealed from us, and never discovers itself in any of the sensible qualities of body. We know that, in fact, heat is a constant attendant of flame; but what is the connexion between them, we have no room so much as to conjecture or imagine. It is impossible, therefore, that the idea of power can be derived from the contemplation of bodies, in single instances of their operation; because no bodies ever discover any power, which can be the original of this idea.

[*Hume's footnote*: Mr. Locke, in his chapter of power, says that, finding from experience, that there are several new productions in matter, and concluding that there must somewhere be a power capable of producing them, we arrive at last by this reasoning at the idea of power. But no reasoning can ever give us a new, original, simple idea; as this philosopher himself confesses. This, therefore, can never be the origin of that idea.]

Since, therefore, external objects as they appear to the senses, give us no idea of power or necessary connexion, by their operation in particular instances, let us see, whether this idea be derived from reflection on the operations of our own minds, and be copied from any internal impression. It may be said, that we are every moment conscious of internal power; while we feel, that, by the simple command of our will, we can move the organs of our body, or direct the faculties of our mind. An act of volition produces motion in our limbs, or raises a new idea in our imagination. This influence of the will we know by consciousness. Hence we acquire the idea of power or energy; and are certain, that we ourselves and all other intelligent beings are possessed of power. This idea, then, is an idea of reflection, since it arises from reflecting on the operations of our own mind, and on the command which is exercised by will, both over the organs of the body and faculties of the soul.

We shall proceed to examine this pretension; and first with regard to the influence of volition over the organs of the body. This influence, we may observe, is a fact, which, like all other natural events, can be known only by experience, and can never be foreseen from any apparent energy or power in the cause, which connects it with the effect, and renders the one an infallible consequence of the other. The motion of our body follows upon the command of our will. Of this we are every moment conscious. But the means, by which this is effected; the energy, by which the will performs so extraordinary an operation; of this we are so far from being immediately conscious, that it must for ever escape our most diligent enquiry.

For **first**: Is there any principle in all nature more mysterious than the union of soul with body; by which a supposed spiritual substance acquires such an influence over a material one, that the most refined thought is able to actuate the grossest matter? Were we empowered, by a secret wish, to remove mountains, or control the planets in their orbit; this extensive authority would not be more extraordinary, nor more beyond our comprehension. But if by consciousness we perceived any power or energy in the will, we must know this power; we must know its connexion with the effect; we must know the secret union of soul and body, and the nature of both these substances; by which the one is able to operate, in so many instances, upon the other.

Secondly, We are not able to move all the organs of the body with a like authority; though we cannot assign any reason besides experience, for so remarkable a difference between one and the other. Why has the will an influence over the tongue and fingers, not over the heart or liver? This question would never embarrass us, were we conscious of a power in the former case, not in the latter. We should then perceive, independent of experience, why the authority of will over the organs of the body is circumscribed within such particular limits. Being in that case fully acquainted with the power or force, by which it operates, we should also know, why its influence reaches precisely to such boundaries, and no farther.

A man, suddenly struck with palsy in the leg or arm, or who had newly lost those members, frequently endeavours, at first to move them, and employ them, in their usual offices. Here he is as much conscious of power to command such limbs, as a man in perfect health is conscious of power to actuate any member which remains in its natural state and condition. But consciousness never deceives. Consequently, neither in the one case nor in the other, are we ever conscious of any power. We learn the influence of our will from experience alone. And experience only teaches us, how one event constantly follows another; without instructing us in the secret connexion, which binds them together, and renders them inseparable.

Thirdly, We learn from anatomy, that the immediate object of power in voluntary motion, is not the member itself which is moved, but certain muscles, and nerves, and animal spirits, and, perhaps, something still more minute and more unknown, through which the motion is successively propagated, ere it reach the member itself whose motion is the immediate object of volition. Can there be a more certain proof, that the power, by which this whole operation is performed, so far from being directly and fully known by an inward sentiment or consciousness is, to the last degree, mysterious and unintelligible? Here the mind wills a certain event. Immediately another event, unknown to ourselves, and totally different from the one intended, is produced: This event produces another, equally unknown: till at last, through a long succession, the desired event is produced. But if the original power were felt, it must be known: were it known, its effect also must be known; since all power is relative to its effect. And vice versa, if the effect be not known, the power cannot be known nor felt. How indeed can we be conscious of a power to move our limbs, when we have no such power; but only that to move certain animal spirits, which, though they produce at last the motion of our limbs, yet operate in such a manner as is wholly beyond our comprehension?

We may, therefore, conclude from the whole, I hope, without any temerity, though with assurance; that our idea of power is not copied from any sentiment or consciousness of power within ourselves, when we give rise to animal motion, or apply our limbs to their proper use and office. That their motion follows the command of the will is a matter of common experience, like other natural events: But the power or energy by which this is effected, like that in other natural events, is unknown and inconceivable.

Shall we then assert, that we are conscious of a power or energy in our own minds, when, by an act or command of our will, we raise up a new idea, fix the mind to the contemplation of it, turn it on all sides, and at last dismiss it for some other idea, when we think that we have surveyed it with sufficient accuracy? I believe the same arguments will prove, that even this command of the will gives us no real idea of force or energy.

First, It must be allowed, that, when we know a power, we know that very circumstance in the cause, by which it is enabled to produce the effect: for these are supposed to be synonymous. We must, therefore, know both the cause and effect, and the relation between them. But do we pretend to be acquainted with the nature of the human soul and the nature of an idea, or the aptitude of the one to produce the other?

This is a real creation; a production of something out of nothing: which implies a power so great, that it may seem, at first sight, beyond the reach of any being, less than infinite. At least it must be owned, that such a power is not felt, nor known, nor even conceivable by the mind. We only feel the event, namely, the existence of an idea, consequent to a command of the will: but the manner, in which this operation is performed, the power by which it is produced, is entirely beyond our comprehension.

Secondly, The command of the mind over itself is limited, as well as its command over the body; and these limits are not known by reason, or any acquaintance with the nature of cause and effect, but only by experience and observation, as in all other natural events and in the operation of external objects. Our authority over our sentiments and passions is much weaker than that over our ideas; and even the latter authority is circumscribed within very narrow boundaries. Will any one pretend to assign the ultimate reason of these boundaries, or show why the power is deficient in one case, not in another.

Thirdly, This self-command is very different at different times. A man in health possesses more of it than one languishing with sickness. We are more master of our thoughts in the morning than in the evening: fasting, than after a full meal. Can we give any reason for these variations, except experience? Where then is the power, of which we pretend to be conscious? Is there not here, either in a spiritual or material substance, or both, some secret mechanism or structure of parts, upon which the effect depends, and which, being entirely unknown to us, renders the power or energy of the will equally unknown and incomprehensible?

Volition is surely an act of the mind, with which we are sufficiently acquainted. Reflect upon it. Consider it on all sides. Do you find anything in it like this creative power, by which it raises from nothing a new idea, and with a kind of Fiat, imitates the omnipotence of its Maker, if I may be allowed so to speak, who called forth into existence all the various scenes of nature? So far from being conscious of this energy in the will, it requires as certain experience as that of which we are possessed, to convince us that such extraordinary effects do ever result from a simple act of volition.

The generality of mankind never find any difficulty in accounting for the more common and familiar operations of nature—such as the descent of heavy bodies, the growth of plants, the generation of animals, or the nourishment of bodies by food: but suppose that, in all these cases, they perceive the very force or energy of the cause, by which it is connected with its effect, and is for ever infallible in its operation. They acquire, by long habit, such a turn of mind, that, upon the appearance of the cause, they immediately expect with assurance its usual attendant, and hardly conceive it possible that any other event could result from it. It is only on the discovery of extraordinary phaenomena, such as earthquakes, pestilence, and prodigies of any kind, that they find themselves at a loss to assign a proper cause, and to explain the manner in which the effect is produced by it. It is usual for men, in such difficulties, to have recourse to some invisible intelligent principle as the immediate cause of that event which surprises them, and which, they think, cannot be accounted for from the common powers of nature. But philosophers, who carry their scrutiny a little farther, immediately perceive that, even in the most familiar events, the energy of the cause is as unintelligible as in the most unusual, and that we only learn by experience the frequent Conjunction of objects, without being ever able to comprehend anything like Connexion between them.

Here, then, many philosophers think themselves obliged by reason to have recourse, on all occasions, to the same principle, which the vulgar never appeal to but in cases that appear miraculous and supernatural. They acknowledge mind and intelligence to be, not only the ultimate and original cause of all things, but the immediate and sole cause of every event which appears in nature. They pretend that those objects which are commonly denominated causes, are in reality nothing but occasions; and that the true and direct principle of every effect is not any power or force in nature, but a volition of the Supreme Being, who wills that such particular objects should for ever be conjoined with each other. Instead of saying that one billiard-ball moves another by a force which it has derived from the author of nature, it is the Deity himself, they say, who, by a particular volition, moves the second ball, being determined to this operation by the impulse of the first ball, in consequence of those general laws which he has laid down to himself in the government of the universe. But philosophers advancing still in their inquiries, discover that, as we are totally ignorant of the power on which depends the mutual operation of bodies, we are no less ignorant of that power on which depends the operation of mind on body, or of body on mind, nor are we able, either from our senses or consciousness, to assign the ultimate principle in one case more than in the other. The same ignorance, therefore, reduces them to the same conclusion. They assert that the Deity is the immediate cause of the union between soul and body; and that they are not the organs of sense, which, being agitated by external objects, produce sensations in the mind; but that it is a particular volition of our omnipotent Maker, which excites such a sensation, in consequence of such a motion in the organ. In like manner, it is not any energy in the will that produces local motion in our members: it is God himself, who is pleased to second our will, in itself impotent, and to command that motion which we erroneously attribute to our own power and efficacy. Nor do philosophers stop at this conclusion. They sometimes extend the same inference to the mind itself, in its internal operations. Our mental vision or conception of ideas is nothing but a revelation made to us by our Maker. When we voluntarily turn our thoughts to any object, and raise up its image in the fancy, it is not the will which creates that idea: it is the universal Creator, who discovers it to the mind, and renders it present to us.

Thus, according to these philosophers, every thing is full of God. Not content with the principle, that nothing exists but by his will, that nothing possesses any power but by his concession: they rob nature, and all created beings, of every power, in order to render their dependence on the Deity still more sensible and immediate. They consider not that, by this theory, they diminish, instead of magnifying, the grandeur of those attributes, which they affect so much to celebrate. It argues surely more power in the Deity to delegate a certain degree of power to inferior creatures than to produce every thing by his own immediate volition. It argues more wisdom to contrive at first the fabric of the world with such perfect foresight that, of itself, and by its proper operation, it may serve all the purposes of providence, than if the great Creator were obliged every moment to adjust its parts, and animate by his breath all the wheels of that stupendous machine.

But if we would have a more philosophical confutation of this theory, perhaps the two following reflections may suffice:

> First, it seems to me that this theory of the universal energy and operation of the Supreme Being is too bold ever to carry conviction with it to a man, sufficiently apprized of the weakness of human reason, and the narrow limits to which it is confined in all its operations. Though the chain of arguments which conduct to it were ever so logical, there must arise a strong suspicion, if not an absolute assurance, that it has carried us quite beyond the reach of our faculties, when it leads to conclusions so extraordinary, and so remote from common life and experience. We are got into fairy land, long ere we have reached the last steps of our theory; and there we have no reason to trust our common methods of argument, or to think that our usual analogies and probabilities have any authority. Our line is too short to fathom such immense abysses. And however we may flatter ourselves that we are guided, in every step which we take, by a kind of verisimilitude and experience, we may be assured that this fancied experience has no authority when we thus apply it

to subjects that lie entirely out of the sphere of experience. But on this we shall have occasion to touch afterwards.

Secondly, I cannot perceive any force in the arguments on which this theory is founded. We are ignorant, it is true, of the manner in which bodies operate on each other: their force or energy is entirely incomprehensible: but are we not equally ignorant of the manner or force by which a mind, even the supreme mind, operates either on itself or on body? Whence, I beseech you, do we acquire any idea of it? We have no sentiment or consciousness of this power in ourselves. We have no idea of the Supreme Being but what we learn from reflection on our own faculties. Were our ignorance, therefore, a good reason for rejecting any thing, we should be led into that principle of denying all energy in the Supreme Being as much as in the grossest matter. We surely comprehend as little the operations of one as of the other. Is it more difficult to conceive that motion may arise from impulse than that it may arise from volition? All we know is our profound ignorance in both cases.

---

1. *How does Hume think Locke accounts for the origin of the idea of power? How does he critique (his version of) Locke?*
2. *How might Locke respond?*
3. *Hume says that 'Solidity, extension, motion; these qualities are all complete in themselves, and never point out any other event which may result from them.' Would Aquinas agree? Would Locke?*

Section Seven: Of the Idea of Necessary Connexion, Part Two

[W]e have sought in vain for an idea of power or necessary connexion in all the sources from which we could suppose it to be derived. It appears that, in single instances of the operation of bodies, we never can, by our utmost scrutiny, discover any thing but one event following another, without being able to comprehend any force or power by which the cause operates, or any connexion between it and its supposed effect. The same difficulty occurs in contemplating the operations of mind on body—where we observe the motion of the latter to follow upon the volition of the former, but are not able to observe or conceive the tie which binds together the motion and volition, or the energy by which the mind produces this effect. The authority of the will over its own faculties and ideas is not a whit more comprehensible: so that, upon the whole, there appears not, throughout all nature, any one instance of connexion which is conceivable by us. All events seem entirely loose and separate. One event follows another; but we never can observe any tie between them. They seem conjoined, but never connected. And as we can have no idea of any thing which never appeared to our outward sense or inward sentiment, the necessary conclusion seems to be that we have no idea of connexion or power at all, and that these words are absolutely, without any meaning, when employed either in philosophical reasonings or common life.

But there still remains one method of avoiding this conclusion, and one source which we have not yet examined. When any natural object or event is presented, it is impossible for us, by any sagacity or penetration, to discover, or even conjecture, without experience, what event will result from it, or to carry our foresight beyond that object which is immediately present to the memory and senses. Even after one instance or experiment where we have observed a particular event to follow upon another, we are not entitled to form a general rule, or foretell what will happen in like cases; it being justly esteemed an unpardonable temerity to judge of the whole course of nature from one single experiment, however accurate or certain. But when one particular species of event has always, in all instances, been conjoined with another, we make no longer any scruple of foretelling one upon the appearance of the other, and of employing that reasoning, which can alone assure us of any matter of fact or existence. We then call the one object, Cause; the other, Effect. We suppose that there is some connexion between them; some power in the one, by which it infallibly produces the other, and operates with the greatest certainty and strongest necessity.

It appears, then, that this idea of a necessary connexion among events arises from a number of similar instances which occur of the constant conjunction of these events; nor can that idea ever be suggested by any one of these instances, surveyed in all possible lights and positions. But there is nothing in a number of instances, different from every single instance, which is supposed to be exactly similar; except only, that after a repetition of similar instances, the mind is carried by habit, upon the appearance of one event, to expect its usual attendant, and to believe that it will exist. This connexion, therefore, which we feel in the mind, this customary transition of the imagination from one object to its usual attendant, is the sentiment or impression from which we form the idea of power or necessary connexion. Nothing farther is in the case. Contemplate the subject on all sides; you will never find any other origin of that idea. This is the sole difference between one instance, from which we can never receive the idea of connexion, and a number of similar instances, by which it is suggested. The first time a man saw the communication of motion by impulse, as by the shock of two billiard balls, he could not pronounce that the one event was connected: but only that it was conjoined with the other. After he has observed several instances of this nature, he then pronounces them to be connected. What alteration has happened to give rise to this new idea of connexion? Nothing but that he now feels these events to be connected in his imagination, and can readily foretell the existence of one from the appearance of the other. When we say, therefore, that one object is connected with another, we mean only that they have acquired a connexion in our thought, and give rise to this inference, by which they become proofs of each other's existence: A conclusion which is somewhat extraordinary, but which seems founded on sufficient evidence. Nor will its evidence be weakened by any general diffidence of the understanding, or sceptical suspicion concerning every conclusion which is new and extraordinary. No conclusions can be more agreeable to scepticism than such as make discoveries concerning the weakness and narrow limits of human reason and capacity.

And what stronger instance can be produced of the surprising ignorance and weakness of the understanding than the present. For surely, if there be any relation among objects which it imports to us to know perfectly, it is that of cause and effect. On this are founded all our reasonings concerning matter of fact or existence. By means of it alone we attain any assurance concerning objects which are removed from the present testimony of our memory and senses. The only immediate utility of all sciences, is to teach us, how to control and regulate future events by their causes. Our thoughts and enquiries are, therefore, every moment, employed about this relation: yet so imperfect are the ideas which we form concerning it, that it is impossible to give any just definition of cause, except what is drawn from something extraneous and foreign to it. Similar objects are always conjoined with similar. Of this we have experience.

Suitably to this experience, therefore, we may define a cause to be an object, followed by another, and where all the objects similar to the first are followed by objects similar to the second. Or in other words where, if the first object had not been, the second never had existed. The appearance of a cause always conveys the mind, by a customary transition, to the idea of the effect. Of this also we have experience. We may, therefore, suitably to this experience, form another definition of cause, and call it, an object followed by another, and whose appearance always conveys the thought to that other. But though both these definitions be drawn from circumstances foreign to the cause, we cannot remedy this inconvenience, or attain any more perfect definition, which may point out that circumstance in the cause, which gives it a connexion with its effect. We have no idea of this connexion, nor even any distant notion what it is we desire to know, when we endeavour at a conception of it. We say, for instance, that the vibration of this string is the cause of this particular sound. But what do we mean by that affirmation? We either mean that this vibration is followed by this sound, and that all similar vibrations have been followed by similar sounds; or, that this vibration is followed by this sound, and that upon the appearance of one the mind anticipates the senses, and forms immediately an idea of the other. We may consider the relation of cause and effect in either of these two lights; but beyond these, we have no idea of it.

To recapitulate, therefore, the reasonings of this section: Every idea is copied from some preceding impression or sentiment; and where we cannot find any impression, we may be certain that there is no idea. In all single instances of the operation of bodies or minds, there is nothing that produces any impression, nor consequently can suggest any idea of power or necessary connexion. But when many uniform instances appear, and the same object is always followed by the same event; we then begin to entertain the notion of cause and connexion. We then feel a new sentiment or impression, to wit, a customary connexion in the thought or imagination between one object and its usual attendant; and this sentiment is the original of that idea which we seek for. For as this idea arises from a number of similar instances, and not from any single instance, it must arise from that circumstance, in which the number of instances differ from every individual instance. But this customary connexion or transition of the imagination is the only circumstance in which they differ. In every other particular they are alike. The first instance which we saw of motion communicated by the shock of two billiard balls (to return to this obvious illustration) is exactly similar to any instance that may, at present, occur to us; except only, that we could not, at first, infer one event from the other; which we are enabled to do at present, after so long a course of uniform experience. ...

---

1. *One way to think about Hume is to see that he is not so much denying that something exists, or that a concept useful, as replacing that thing or concept with something else. What is his replacement for the traditional concept of necessary connexion, or power?*
2. *Hume offers two definitions of 'cause.' What are they? Put them in your own words. To think about: Why are there two definitions here? Are they co-extensive? In other words, is every possible state of affairs that counts as a cause and effect relation according to Definition 1 also going to count as such a relation on Definition 2, and vice versa?*

Section Nine: Of the Reason of Animals

I have inserted section Nine here, because it directly concerns the picture of belief and reasoning Hume has been developing. The section placed immediately after it—Section Eight—applies his views on causation to the question of freedom of the will.

All our reasonings concerning matter of fact are founded on a species of Analogy, which leads us to expect from any cause the same events, which we have observed to result from similar causes. Where the causes are entirely similar, the analogy is perfect, and the inference, drawn from it, is regarded as certain and conclusive: nor does any man ever entertain a doubt, where he sees a piece of iron, that it will have weight and cohesion of parts; as in all other instances, which have ever fallen under his observation. But where the objects have not so exact a similarity, the analogy is less perfect, and the inference is less conclusive; though still it has some force, in proportion to the degree of similarity and resemblance. The anatomical observations, formed upon one animal, are, by this species of reasoning, extended to all animals; and it is certain, that when the circulation of the blood, for instance, is clearly proved to have place in one creature, as a frog, or fish, it forms a strong presumption, that the same principle has place in all. These analogical observations may be carried farther, even to this science, of which we are now treating; and any theory, by which we explain the operations of the understanding, or the origin and connexion of the passions in man, will acquire additional authority, if we find, that the same theory is requisite to explain the same phenomena in all other animals. We shall make trial of this, with regard to the hypothesis, by which we have, in the foregoing discourse, endeavoured to account for all experimental reasonings; and it is hoped, that this new point of view will serve to confirm all our former observations.

First, It seems evident, that animals as well as men learn many things from experience, and infer, that the same events will always follow from the same causes. By this principle they become acquainted with the more obvious properties of external objects, and gradually, from their birth, treasure up a knowledge of the nature of fire, water, earth, stones, heights, depths, &c., and of the effects which result from their operation. The ignorance and inexperience of the young are here plainly distinguishable from the cunning and sagacity of the old, who have learned, by long observation, to avoid what hurt them, and to pursue what gave ease or pleasure. ...

This is still more evident from the effects of discipline and education on animals, who, by the proper application of rewards and punishments, may be taught any course of action, and most contrary to their natural instincts and propensities. Is it not experience, which renders a dog apprehensive of pain, when you menace him, or lift up the whip to beat him? Is it not even experience, which makes him answer to his name, and infer, from such an arbitrary sound, that you mean him rather than any of his fellows, and intend to call him, when you pronounce it in a certain manner, and with a certain tone and accent?

In all these cases, we may observe, that the animal infers some fact beyond what immediately strikes his senses; and that this inference is altogether founded on past experience, while the creature expects from the present object the same consequences, which it has always found in its observation to result from similar objects.

Secondly, It is impossible, that this inference of the animal can be founded on any process of argument or reasoning, by which he concludes, that like events must follow like objects, and that the course of nature will always be regular in its operations. For if there be in reality any arguments of this nature, they surely lie too abstruse for the observation of such imperfect understandings; since it may well employ the utmost care and attention of a philosophic genius to discover and observe them. Animals, therefore are not guided in these inferences by reasoning: neither are children; neither are the generality of mankind, in their ordinary actions and conclusions: neither are philosophers themselves, who, in all the active parts of life, are, in the main, the same with the vulgar, and are governed by the same maxims. Nature must have provided some other principle, of more ready, and more general use and application; nor can an operation of such immense consequence in life, as that of inferring effects from causes, be trusted to the uncertain process of reasoning and argumentation. ...

But though animals learn many parts of their knowledge from observation, there are also many parts of it, which they derive from the original hand of nature; which much exceed the share of capacity they possess on ordinary occasions; and in which they improve, little or nothing, by the longest practice and experience. These we denominate Instincts, and are so apt to admire as something very extraordinary, and inexplicable by all the disquisitions of human understanding. But our wonder will, perhaps, cease or diminish, when we consider, that the experimental reasoning itself, which we possess in common with beasts, and on which the whole conduct of life depends, is nothing but a species of instinct or mechanical power, that acts in us unknown to ourselves; and in its chief operations, is not directed by any such relations or comparisons of ideas, as are the proper objects of our intellectual faculties. Though the instinct be different, yet still it is an instinct, which teaches a man to avoid the fire; as much as that, which teaches a bird, with such exactness, the art of incubation, and the whole economy and order of its nursery. ...

---

1. *How does Hume's attitude towards animals differ from that of Descartes? What does this attitude suggest about human beings and their place in the universe?*

Section Eight: Of Liberty and Necessity, Part One

It might reasonably be expected in questions which have been canvassed and disputed with great eagerness, since the first origin of science, and philosophy, that the meaning of all the terms, at least, should have been agreed upon among the disputants; and our enquiries, in the course of two thousand years, been able to pass from words to the true and real subject of the controversy. For how easy may it seem to give exact definitions of the terms employed in reasoning, and make these definitions, not the mere sound of words, the object of future scrutiny and examination? But if we consider the matter more narrowly, we shall be apt to draw a quite opposite conclusion. From this circumstance alone, that a controversy has been long kept on foot, and remains still undecided, we may presume that there is some ambiguity in the expression, and that the disputants affix different ideas to the terms employed in the controversy. For as the faculties of the mind are supposed to be naturally alike in every individual; otherwise nothing could be more fruitless than to reason or dispute together; it were impossible, if men affix the same ideas to their terms, that they could so long form different opinions of the same subject; especially when they communicate their views, and each party turn themselves on all sides, in search of arguments which may give them the victory over their antagonists. It is true, if men attempt the discussion of questions which lie entirely beyond the reach of human capacity, such as those concerning the origin of worlds, or the economy of the intellectual system or region of spirits, they may long beat the air in their fruitless contests, and never arrive at any determinate conclusion. But if the question regard any subject of common life and experience, nothing, one would think, could preserve the dispute so long undecided but some ambiguous expressions, which keep the antagonists still at a distance, and hinder them from grappling with each other.

This has been the case in the long disputed question concerning liberty and necessity; and to so remarkable a degree that, if I be not much mistaken, we shall find, that all mankind, both learned and ignorant, have always been of the same opinion with regard to this subject, and that a few intelligible definitions would immediately have put an end to the whole controversy. I own that this dispute has been so much canvassed on all hands, and has led philosophers into such a labyrinth of obscure sophistry, that it is no wonder, if a sensible reader indulge his ease so far as to turn a deaf ear to the proposal of such a question, from which he can expect neither instruction or entertainment. But the state of the argument here proposed may, perhaps, serve to renew his attention; as it has more novelty, promises at least some decision of the controversy, and will not much disturb his ease by any intricate or obscure reasoning.

I hope, therefore, to make it appear that all men have ever agreed in the doctrine both of necessity and of liberty, according to any reasonable sense, which can be put on these terms; and that the whole controversy, has hitherto turned merely upon words.

---

1. *Why has the dispute over freedom of the will not yet been resolved?*

We shall begin with examining the doctrine of necessity.

It is universally allowed that matter, in all its operations, is actuated by a necessary force, and that every natural effect is so precisely determined by the energy of its cause that no other effect, in such particular circumstances, could possibly have resulted from it. The degree and direction of every motion is, by the laws of nature, prescribed with such exactness that a living creature may as soon arise from the shock of two bodies as motion in any other degree or direction than what is actually produced by it. Would we, therefore, form a just and precise idea of necessity, we must consider whence that idea arises when we apply it to the operation of bodies.

It seems evident that, if all the scenes of nature were continually shifted in such a manner that no two events bore any resemblance to each other, but every object was entirely new, without any similitude to whatever had been seen before, we should never, in that case, have attained the least idea of necessity, or of a connexion among these objects. We might say, upon such a supposition, that one object or event has followed another; not that one was produced by the other. The relation of cause and effect must be utterly unknown to mankind. Inference and reasoning concerning the operations of nature would, from that moment, be at an end; and the memory and senses remain the only canals, by which the knowledge of any real existence could possibly have access to the mind. Our idea, therefore, of necessity and causation arises entirely from the uniformity observable in the operations of nature, where similar objects are constantly conjoined together, and the mind is determined by custom to infer the one from the appearance of the other. These two circumstances form the whole of that necessity, which we ascribe to matter. Beyond the constant conjunction of similar objects, and the consequent inference from one to the other, we have no notion of any necessity or connexion.

If it appear, therefore, that all mankind have ever allowed, without any doubt or hesitation, that these two circumstances take place in the voluntary actions of men, and in the operations of mind; it must follow, that all mankind have ever agreed in the doctrine of necessity, and that they have hitherto disputed, merely for not understanding each other.

As to the first circumstance, the constant and regular conjunction of similar events, we may possibly satisfy ourselves by the following considerations: It is universally acknowledged that there is a great uniformity among the actions of men, in all nations and ages, and that human nature remains still the same, in its principles and operations. The same motives always produce the same actions: the same events follow from the same causes. Ambition, avarice, self-love, vanity, friendship, generosity, public spirit: these passions, mixed in various degrees, and distributed through society, have been, from the beginning of the world, and still are, the source of all the actions and enterprises, which have ever been observed among mankind. Would you know the sentiments, inclinations, and course of life of the Greeks and Romans? Study well the temper and actions of the French and English: You cannot be much mistaken in transferring to the former most of the observations which you have made with regard to the latter. Mankind are so much the same, in all times and places, that history informs us of nothing new or strange in this particular. Its chief use is only to discover the constant and universal principles of human nature, by showing men in all varieties of circumstances and situations, and furnishing us with materials from which we may form our observations and become acquainted with the regular springs of human action and behaviour. These records of wars, intrigues, factions, and revolutions, are so many collections of experiments, by which the politician or moral philosopher fixes the principles of his science, in the same manner as the physician or natural philosopher becomes acquainted with the nature of plants, minerals, and other external objects, by the experiments which he forms concerning them. Nor are the earth, water, and other elements, examined by Aristotle, and Hippocrates, more like to those which at present lie under our observation than the men described by Polybius and Tacitus are to those who now govern the world.

Should a traveller, returning from a far country, bring us an account of men, wholly different from any with whom we were ever acquainted; men, who were entirely divested of avarice, ambition, or revenge; who knew no pleasure but friendship, generosity, and public spirit; we should immediately, from these circumstances, detect the falsehood, and prove him a liar, with the same certainty as if he had stuffed his narration with stories of centaurs and dragons, miracles and prodigies. And if we would explode any forgery in history, we cannot make use of a more convincing argument, than to prove, that the actions ascribed to any person are directly contrary to the course of nature, and that no human motives, in such circumstances, could ever induce him to such a conduct. The veracity of Quintus Curtius is as much to be suspected, when he describes the supernatural courage of Alexander, by which he was hurried on singly to attack multitudes, as when he describes his supernatural force and activity, by which he was able to resist them. So readily and universally do we acknowledge a uniformity in human motives and actions as well as in the operations of body. ...

We must not, however, expect that this uniformity of human actions should be carried to such a length as that all men, in the same circumstances, will always act precisely in the same manner, without making any allowance for the diversity of characters, prejudices, and opinions. Such a uniformity in every particular, is found in no part of nature. On the contrary, from observing the variety of conduct in different men, we are enabled to form a greater variety of maxims, which still suppose a degree of uniformity and regularity.

Are the manners of men different in different ages and countries? We learn thence the great force of custom and education, which mould the human mind from its infancy and form it into a fixed and established character. ... I grant it possible to find some actions, which seem to have no regular connexion with any known motives, and are exceptions to all the measures of conduct which have ever been established for the government of men. But if we would willingly know what judgment should be formed of such irregular and extraordinary actions, we may consider the sentiments commonly entertained with regard to those irregular events which appear in the course of nature, and the operations of external objects. All causes are not conjoined to their usual effects with like uniformity. An artificer, who handles only dead matter, may be disappointed of his aim, as well as the politician, who directs the conduct of sensible and intelligent agents.

The vulgar, who take things according to their first appearance, attribute the uncertainty of events to such an uncertainty in the causes as makes the latter often fail of their usual influence; though they meet with no impediment in their operation. But philosophers, observing that, almost in every part of nature, there is contained a vast variety of springs and principles, which are hid, by reason of their minuteness or remoteness, find, that it is at least possible the contrariety of events may not proceed from any contingency in the cause, but from the secret operation of contrary causes. This possibility is converted into certainty by farther observation, when they remark that, upon an exact scrutiny, a contrariety of effects always betrays a contrariety of causes, and proceeds from their mutual opposition. A peasant can give no better reason for the stopping of any clock or watch than to say that it does not commonly go right: But an artist easily perceives that the same force in the spring or pendulum has always the same influence on the wheels; but fails of its usual effects, perhaps by reason of a grain of dust, which puts a stop to the whole movement. From the observation of several parallel instances, philosophers form a maxim that the connexion between all causes and effects is equally necessary, and that its seeming uncertainty in some instances proceeds from the secret opposition of contrary causes.

Thus, for instance, in the human body, when the usual symptoms of health or sickness disappoint our expectation; when medicines operate not with their wonted powers; when irregular events follow from any particular cause; the philosopher and physician are not surprised at the matter, nor are ever tempted to deny, in general, the necessity and uniformity of those principles by which the animal economy is conducted. They know that a human body is a mighty complicated machine: That many secret powers lurk in it, which are altogether beyond our comprehension: That to us it must often appear very uncertain in its operations: And that therefore the irregular events, which outwardly discover themselves, can be no proof that the laws of nature are not observed with the greatest regularity in its internal operations and government.

The philosopher, if he be consistent, must apply the same reasoning to the actions and volitions of intelligent agents. The most irregular and unexpected resolutions of men may frequently be accounted for by those who know every particular circumstance of their character and situation. A person of an obliging disposition gives a peevish answer: But he has the toothache, or has not dined. A stupid fellow discovers an uncommon alacrity in his carriage: But he has met with a sudden piece of good fortune. Or even when an action, as sometimes happens, cannot be particularly accounted for, either by the person himself or by others; we know, in general, that the characters of men are, to a certain degree, inconstant and irregular. This is, in a manner, the constant character of human nature; though it be applicable, in a more particular manner, to some persons who have no fixed rule for their conduct, but proceed in a continued course of caprice and inconstancy. The internal principles and motives may operate in a uniform manner, notwithstanding these seeming irregularities; in the same manner as the winds, rain, cloud, and other variations of the weather are supposed to be governed by steady principles; though not easily discoverable by human sagacity and enquiry.

Thus it appears, not only that the conjunction between motives and voluntary actions is as regular and uniform as that between the cause and effect in any part of nature; but also that this regular conjunction has been universally acknowledged among mankind, and has never been the subject of dispute, either in philosophy or common life. Now, as it is from past experience that we draw all inferences concerning the future, and as we conclude that objects will always be conjoined together which we find to have always been conjoined; it may seem superfluous to prove that this experienced uniformity in human actions is a source whence we draw inferences concerning them. But in order to throw the argument into a greater variety of lights we shall also insist, though briefly, on this latter topic.

The mutual dependence of men is so great in all societies that scarce any human action is entirely complete in itself, or is performed without some reference to the actions of others, which are requisite to make it answer fully the intention of the agent. The poorest artificer, who labours alone, expects at least the protection of the magistrate, to ensure him the enjoyment of the fruits of his labour. He also expects that, when he carries his goods to market, and offers them at a reasonable price, he shall find purchasers, and shall be able, by the money he acquires, to engage others to supply him with those commodities which are requisite for his subsistence. In proportion as men extend their dealings, and render their intercourse with others more complicated, they always comprehend, in their schemes of life, a greater variety of voluntary actions, which they expect, from the proper motives, to co-operate with their own. In all these conclusions they take their measures from past experience, in the same manner as in their reasonings concerning external objects; and firmly believe that men, as well as all the elements, are to continue, in their operations, the same that they have ever found them. A manufacturer reckons upon the labour of his servants for the execution of any work as much as upon the tools which he employs, and would be equally surprised were his expectations disappointed. In short, this experimental inference and reasoning concerning the actions of others enters so much into human life that no man, while awake, is ever a moment without employing it. Have we not reason, therefore, to affirm that all mankind have always agreed in the doctrine of necessity according to the foregoing definition and explication of it?

Nor have philosophers even entertained a different opinion from the people in this particular. For, not to mention that almost every action of their life supposes that opinion, there are even few of the speculative parts of learning to which it is not essential. What would become of history, had we not a dependence on the veracity of the historian according to the experience which we have had of mankind? How could politics be a science, if laws and forms of government had not a uniform influence upon society? Where would be the foundation of morals, if particular characters had no certain or determinate power to produce particular sentiments, and if these sentiments had no constant operation on actions? And with what pretence could we employ our criticism upon any poet or polite author, if we could not pronounce the conduct and sentiments of his actors either natural or unnatural to such characters, and in such circumstances? It seems almost impossible, therefore, to engage either in science or action of any kind without acknowledging the doctrine of necessity, and this inference from motive to voluntary actions, from characters to conduct.

And indeed, when we consider how aptly natural and moral evidence link together, and form only one chain of argument, we shall make no scruple to allow that they are of the same nature, and derived from the same principles. A prisoner who has neither money nor interest, discovers the impossibility of his escape, as well when he considers the obstinacy of the gaoler, as the walls and bars with which he is surrounded; and, in all attempts for his freedom, chooses rather to work upon the stone and iron of the one, than upon the inflexible nature of the other. The same prisoner, when conducted to the scaffold, foresees his death as certainly from the constancy and fidelity of his guards, as from the operation of the axe or wheel. His mind runs along a certain train of ideas: the refusal of the soldiers to consent to his escape; the action of the executioner; the separation of the head and body; bleeding, convulsive motions, and death. Here is a connected chain of natural causes and voluntary actions; but the mind feels no difference between them in passing from one link to another: Nor is it less certain of the future event than if it were connected with the objects present to the memory or senses, by a train of causes, cemented together by what we are pleased to call a physical necessity. The same experienced union has the same effect on the mind, whether the united objects be motives, volition, and actions; or figure and motion. We may change the name of things; but their nature and their operation on the understanding never change.

Were a man, whom I know to be honest and opulent, and with whom I live in intimate friendship, to come into my house, where I am surrounded with my servants, I rest assured that he is not to stab me before he leaves it in order to rob me of my silver standish; and I no more suspect this event than the falling of the house itself, which is new, and solidly built and founded—*But he may have been seized with a sudden and unknown frenzy*—So may a sudden earthquake arise, and shake and tumble my house about my ears. I shall therefore change the suppositions. I shall say that I know with certainty that he is not to put his hand into the fire and hold it there till it be consumed: and this event, I think I can foretell with the same assurance, as that, if he throw himself out at the window, and meet with no obstruction, he will not remain a moment suspended in the air. No suspicion of an unknown frenzy can give the least possibility to the former event, which is so contrary to all the known principles of human nature. A man who at noon leaves his purse full of gold on the pavement at Charing-Cross, may as well expect that it will fly away like a feather, as that he will find it untouched an hour after. Above one half of human reasonings contain inferences of a similar nature, attended with more or less degrees of certainty proportioned to our experience of the usual conduct of mankind in such particular situations.

---

1. *What is the doctrine of necessity? Why does Hume think that everyone holds this doctrine?*

I have frequently considered, what could possibly be the reason why all mankind, though they have ever, without hesitation, acknowledged the doctrine of necessity in their whole practice and reasoning, have yet discovered such a reluctance to acknowledge it in words, and have rather shown a propensity, in all ages, to profess the contrary opinion. The matter, I think, may be accounted for after the following manner. If we examine the operations of body, and the production of effects from their causes, we shall find that all our faculties can never carry us farther in our knowledge of this relation than barely to observe that particular objects are constantly conjoined together, and that the mind is carried, by a customary transition, from the appearance of one to the belief of the other. But though this conclusion concerning human ignorance be the result of the strictest scrutiny of this subject, men still entertain a strong propensity to believe that they penetrate farther into the powers of nature, and perceive something like a necessary connexion between the cause and the effect. When again they turn their reflections towards the operations of their own minds, and feel no such connexion of the motive and the action; they are thence apt to suppose, that there is a difference between the effects which result from material force, and those which arise from thought and intelligence. But being once convinced that we know nothing farther of causation of any kind than merely the constant conjunction of objects, and the consequent inference of the mind from one to another, and finding that these two circumstances are universally allowed to have place in voluntary actions; we may be more easily led to own the same necessity common to all causes. And though this reasoning may contradict the systems of many philosophers, in ascribing necessity to the determinations of the will, we shall find, upon reflection, that they dissent from it in words only, not in their real sentiment. Necessity, according to the sense in which it is here taken, has never yet been rejected, nor can ever, I think, be rejected by any philosopher. It may only, perhaps, be pretended that the mind can perceive, in the operations of matter, some farther connexion between the cause and effect; and connexion that has not place in voluntary actions of intelligent beings. Now whether it be so or not, can only appear upon examination; and it is incumbent on these philosophers to make good their assertion, by defining or describing that necessity, and pointing it out to us in the operations of material causes.

It would seem, indeed, that men begin at the wrong end of this question concerning liberty and necessity, when they enter upon it by examining the faculties of the soul, the influence of the understanding, and the operations of the will. Let them first discuss a more simple question, namely, the operations of body and of brute unintelligent matter; and try whether they can there form any idea of causation and necessity, except that of a constant conjunction of objects, and subsequent inference of the mind from one to another. If these circumstances form, in reality, the whole of that necessity, which we conceive in matter, and if these circumstances be also universally acknowledged to take place in the operations of the mind, the dispute is at an end; at least, must be owned to be thenceforth merely verbal. But as long as we will rashly suppose, that we have some farther idea of necessity and causation in the operations of external objects; at the same time, that we can find nothing farther in the voluntary actions of the mind; there is no possibility of bringing the question to any determinate issue, while we proceed upon so erroneous a supposition. The only method of undeceiving us is to mount up higher; to examine the narrow extent of science when applied to material causes; and to convince ourselves that all we know of them is the constant conjunction and inference above mentioned. We may, perhaps, find that it is with difficulty we are induced to fix such narrow limits to human understanding: but we can afterwards find no difficulty when we come to apply this doctrine to the actions of the will. For as it is evident that these have a regular conjunction with motives and circumstances and characters, and as we always draw inferences from one to the other, we must be obliged to acknowledge in words that necessity, which we have already avowed, in every deliberation of our lives, and in every step of our conduct and behaviour.

But to proceed in this reconciling project with regard to the question of liberty and necessity; the most contentious question of metaphysics, the most contentious science; it will not require many words to prove, that all mankind have ever agreed in the doctrine of liberty as well as in that of necessity, and that the whole dispute, in this respect also, has been hitherto merely verbal. For what is meant by liberty, when applied to voluntary actions? We cannot surely mean that actions have so little connexion with motives, inclinations, and circumstances, that one does not follow with a certain degree of uniformity from the other, and that one affords no inference by which we can conclude the existence of the other. For these are plain and acknowledged matters of fact. By liberty, then, we can only mean a power of acting or not acting, according to the determinations of the will; this is, if we choose to remain at rest, we may; if we choose to move, we also may. Now this hypothetical liberty is universally allowed to belong to every one who is not a prisoner and in chains. Here, then, is no subject of dispute.

Whatever definition we may give of liberty, we should be careful to observe two requisite circumstances; First, that it be consistent with plain matter of fact; secondly, that it be consistent with itself. If we observe these circumstances, and render our definition intelligible, I am persuaded that all mankind will be found of one opinion with regard to it.

1. *How does Hume propose to make the doctrines of necessity and liberty (here, the claim that human beings are usually free) consistent? How does his definition of liberty differ from the definition used by both hard determinists and libertarians?*

In Part Two, Hume defends his view of liberty against the objection that it is dangerous to religion and to morality. (This is also a theme of Section Eleven below).

Section Eight: Of Liberty and Necessity, Part Two

There is no method of reasoning more common, and yet none more blameable, than, in philosophical disputes, to endeavour the refutation of any hypothesis, by a pretence of its dangerous consequences to religion and morality. When any opinion leads to absurdities, it is certainly false; but it is not certain that an opinion is false, because it is of dangerous consequence. Such topics, therefore, ought entirely to be forborne; as serving nothing to the discovery of truth, but only to make the person of an antagonist odious. This I observe in general, without pretending to draw any advantage from it. I frankly submit to an examination of this kind, and shall venture to affirm that the doctrines, both of necessity and of liberty, as above explained, are not only consistent with morality, but are absolutely essential to its support.

Necessity may be defined two ways, conformably to the two definitions of cause, of which it makes an essential part. It consists either in the constant conjunction of like objects, or in the inference of the understanding from one object to another. Now necessity, in both these senses, (which, indeed, are at bottom the same) has universally, though tacitly, in the schools, in the pulpit, and in common life, been allowed to belong to the will of man; and no one has ever pretended to deny that we can draw inferences concerning human actions, and that those inferences are founded on the experienced union of like actions, with like motives, inclinations, and circumstances. The only particular in which any one can differ, is, that either, perhaps, he will refuse to give the name of necessity to this property of human actions: but as long as the meaning is understood, I hope the word can do no harm: or that he will maintain it possible to discover something farther in the operations of matter. But this, it must be acknowledged, can be of no consequence to morality or religion, whatever it may be to natural philosophy or metaphysics. We may here be mistaken in asserting that there is no idea of any other necessity or connexion in the actions of body: But surely we ascribe nothing to the actions of the mind, but what everyone does, and must readily allow of. We change no circumstance in the received orthodox system with regard to the will, but only in that with regard to material objects and causes. Nothing, therefore, can be more innocent, at least, than this doctrine.

All laws being founded on rewards and punishments, it is supposed as a fundamental principle, that these motives have a regular and uniform influence on the mind, and both produce the good and prevent the evil actions. We may give to this influence what name we please; but, as it is usually conjoined with the action, it must be esteemed a cause, and be looked upon as an instance of that necessity, which we would here establish.

The only proper object of hatred or vengeance is a person or creature, endowed with thought and consciousness; and when any criminal or injurious actions excite that passion, it is only by their relation to the person, or connexion with him. Actions are, by their very nature, temporary and perishing; and where they proceed not from some cause in the character and disposition of the person who performed them, they can neither redound to his honour, if good; nor infamy, if evil. The actions themselves may be blameable; they may be contrary to all the rules of morality and religion: but the person is not answerable for them;

and as they proceeded from nothing in him that is durable and constant, and leave nothing of that nature behind them, it is impossible he can, upon their account, become the object of punishment or vengeance. According to the principle, therefore, which denies necessity, and consequently causes, a man is as pure and untainted, after having committed the most horrid crime, as at the first moment of his birth, nor is his character anywise concerned in his actions, since they are not derived from it, and the wickedness of the one can never be used as a proof of the depravity of the other.

Men are not blamed for such actions as they perform ignorantly and casually, whatever may be the consequences. Why? but because the principles of these actions are only momentary, and terminate in them alone. Men are less blamed for such actions as they perform hastily and unpremeditatedly than for such as proceed from deliberation. For what reason? but because a hasty temper, though a constant cause or principle in the mind, operates only by intervals, and infects not the whole character. Again, repentance wipes off every crime, if attended with a reformation of life and manners. How is this to be accounted for? but by asserting that actions render a person criminal merely as they are proofs of criminal principles in the mind; and when, by an alteration of these principles, they cease to be just proofs, they likewise cease to be criminal. But, except upon the doctrine of necessity, they never were just proofs, and consequently never were criminal.

It will be equally easy to prove, and from the same arguments, that liberty, according to that definition above mentioned, in which all men agree, is also essential to morality, and that no human actions, where it is wanting, are susceptible of any moral qualities, or can be the objects either of approbation or dislike. For as actions are objects of our moral sentiment, so far only as they are indications of the internal character, passions, and affections; it is impossible that they can give rise either to praise or blame, where they proceed not from these principles, but are derived altogether from external violence.

I pretend not to have obviated or removed all objections to this theory, with regard to necessity and liberty. I can foresee other objections, derived from topics which have not here been treated of. It may be said, for instance, that, if voluntary actions be subjected to the same laws of necessity with the operations of matter, there is a continued chain of necessary causes, pre-ordained and pre-determined, reaching from the original cause of all to every single volition of every human creature. No contingency anywhere in the universe; no indifference; no liberty. While we act, we are, at the same time, acted upon. The ultimate Author of all our volitions is the Creator of the world, who first bestowed motion on this immense machine, and placed all beings in that particular position, whence every subsequent event, by an inevitable necessity, must result. Human actions, therefore, either can have no moral turpitude at all, as proceeding from so good a cause; or if they have any turpitude, they must involve our Creator in the same guilt, while he is acknowledged to be their ultimate cause and author. For as a man, who fired a mine, is answerable for all the consequences whether the train he employed be long or short; so wherever a continued chain of necessary causes is fixed, that Being, either finite or infinite, who produces the first, is likewise the author of all the rest, and must both bear the blame and acquire the praise which belong to them. Our clear and unalterable ideas of morality establish this rule, upon unquestionable reasons, when we examine the consequences of any human action; and these reasons must still have greater force when applied to the volitions and intentions of a Being infinitely wise and powerful. Ignorance or impotence may be pleaded for so limited a creature as man; but those imperfections have no place in our Creator. He foresaw, he ordained, he intended all those actions of men, which we so rashly pronounce criminal. And we must therefore conclude, either that they are not criminal, or that the Deity, not man, is accountable for them. But as either of these positions is absurd and impious, it follows, that the doctrine from which they are deduced cannot possibly be true, as being liable to all the same objections. An absurd consequence, if necessary, proves the original doctrine to be absurd; in the same manner as criminal actions render criminal the original cause, if the connexion between them be necessary and inevitable.

This objection consists of two parts, which we shall examine separately;

1. First, that, if human actions can be traced up, by a necessary chain, to the Deity, they can never be criminal; on account of the infinite perfection of that Being from whom they are derived, and who can intend nothing but what is altogether good and laudable. Or,

2. Secondly, if they be criminal, we must retract the attribute of perfection, which we ascribe to the Deity, and must acknowledge him to be the ultimate author of guilt and moral turpitude in all his creatures.

The answer to the **first objection** seems obvious and convincing. There are many philosophers who, after an exact scrutiny of all the phenomena of nature, conclude, that the **whole**, considered as one system, is, in every period of its existence, ordered with perfect benevolence; and that the utmost possible happiness will, in the end, result to all created beings, without any mixture of positive or absolute ill or misery. Every physical ill, say they, makes an essential part of this benevolent system, and could not possibly be removed, even by the deity himself, considered as a wise agent, without giving entrance to greater ill, or excluding greater good, which will result from it. From this theory, some philosophers, and the ancient stoics among the rest, derived a topic of consolation under all afflictions, while they taught their pupils that those ills under which they laboured were, in reality, goods to the universe; and that to an enlarged view, which could comprehend the whole system of nature, every event became an object of joy and exultation. But though this topic be specious and sublime, it was soon found in practice weak and ineffectual. You would surely more irritate than appease a man lying under the racking pains of the gout by preaching up to him the rectitude of those general laws, which produced the malignant humours in his body, and led them through the proper canals, to the sinews and nerves, where they now excite such acute torments. These enlarged views may, for a moment, please the imagination of a speculative man, who is placed in ease and security; but neither can they dwell with constancy on his mind, even though undisturbed by the emotions of pain or passion; much less can they maintain their ground when attacked by such powerful antagonists. The affections take a narrower and more natural survey of their object; and by an economy, more suitable to the infirmity of human minds, regard alone the beings around us, and are actuated by such events as appear good or ill to the private system.

The case is the same with moral as with physical ill. It cannot reasonably be supposed, that those remote considerations, which are found of so little efficacy with regard to one, will have a more powerful influence with regard to the other. The mind of man is so formed by nature that, upon the appearance of certain characters, dispositions, and actions, it immediately feels the sentiment of approbation or blame; nor are there any emotions more essential to its frame and constitution. The characters which engage our approbation are chiefly such as contribute to the peace and security of human society; as the characters which excite blame are chiefly such as tend to public detriment and disturbance: whence it may reasonably be presumed, that the moral sentiments arise, either mediately or immediately, from a reflection of these opposite interests. What though philosophical meditations establish a different opinion or conjecture; that everything is right with regard to the **whole**, and that the qualities, which disturb society, are, in the main, as beneficial, and are as suitable to the primary intention of nature as those which more directly promote its happiness and welfare? are such remote and uncertain speculations able to counterbalance the sentiments which arise from the natural and immediate view of the objects? a man who is robbed of a considerable sum; does he find his vexation for the loss anywise diminished by these sublime reflections? why then should his moral resentment against the crime be supposed incompatible with them? or why should not the acknowledgment of a real distinction between vice and virtue be reconcilable to all speculative systems of philosophy, as well as that of a real distinction between personal beauty and deformity? Both these distinctions are founded in the natural sentiments of the human mind: And these sentiments are not to be controuled or altered by any philosophical theory or speculation whatsoever.

The **second objection** admits not of so easy and satisfactory an answer; nor is it possible to explain distinctly, how the Deity can be the mediate cause of all the actions of men, without being the author of sin and moral turpitude. These are mysteries, which mere natural and unassisted reason is very unfit to handle; and whatever system she embraces, she must find herself involved in inextricable difficulties, and even contradictions, at every step which she takes with regard to such subjects. To reconcile the indifference and contingency of human actions with prescience; or to defend absolute decrees, and yet free the Deity from being the author of sin, has been found hitherto to exceed all the power of philosophy. Happy, if she be thence sensible of her temerity, when she pries into these sublime mysteries; and leaving a scene so full of obscurities and perplexities, return, with suitable modesty, to her true and proper province, the examination of common life; where she will find difficulties enough to employ her enquiries, without launching into so boundless an ocean of doubt, uncertainty, and contradiction!

---

1. *Give each of the two objections Hume examines, and his reply to them.*

Section Ten: Of Miracles, Part One

... Though experience be our only guide in reasoning concerning matters of fact; it must be acknowledged, that this guide is not altogether infallible, but in some cases is apt to lead us into errors. One, who in our climate, should expect better weather in any week of June than in one of December, would reason justly, and conformably to experience; but it is certain, that he may happen, in the event, to find himself mistaken. However, we may observe, that, in such a case, he would have no cause to complain of experience; because it commonly informs us beforehand of the uncertainty, by that contrariety of events, which we may learn from a diligent observation. All effects follow not with like certainty from their supposed causes. Some events are found, in all countries and all ages, to have been constantly conjoined together: Others are found to have been more variable, and sometimes to disappoint our expectations; so that, in our reasonings concerning matter of fact, there are all imaginable degrees of assurance, from the highest certainty to the lowest species of moral evidence.

A wise man, therefore, proportions his belief to the evidence. In such conclusions as are founded on an infallible experience, he expects the event with the last degree of assurance, and regards his past experience as a full proof of the future existence of that event. In other cases, he proceeds with more caution: he weighs the opposite experiments: he considers which side is supported by the greater number of experiments: to that side he inclines, with doubt and hesitation; and when at last he fixes his judgment, the evidence exceeds not what we properly call probability. All probability, then, supposes an opposition of experiments and observations, where the one side is found to overbalance the other, and to produce a degree of evidence, proportioned to the superiority. A hundred instances or experiments on one side, and fifty on another, afford a doubtful expectation of any event; though a hundred uniform experiments, with only one that is contradictory, reasonably beget a pretty strong degree of assurance. In all cases, we must balance the opposite experiments, where they are opposite, and deduct the smaller number from the greater, in order to know the exact force of the superior evidence.

To apply these principles to a particular instance; we may observe, that there is no species of reasoning more common, more useful, and even necessary to human life, than that which is derived from the testimony of men, and the reports of eye-witnesses and spectators. This species of reasoning, perhaps, one may deny to be founded on the relation of cause and effect. I shall not dispute about a word. It will be sufficient to observe that our assurance in any argument of this kind is derived from no other principle than our observation of the veracity of human testimony, and of the usual conformity of facts to the reports of witnesses. It being a general maxim, that no objects have any discoverable connexion together, and that all the inferences, which we can draw from one to another, are founded merely on our experience of their constant and regular conjunction; it is evident, that we ought not to make an exception to this maxim in favour of human testimony, whose connexion with any event seems, in itself, as little necessary as any other. Were not the memory tenacious to a certain degree; had not men commonly an inclination to truth and a principle of probity; were they not sensible to shame, when detected in a falsehood: were not these, I say, discovered by experience to be qualities, inherent in human nature, we should never repose the least confidence in human testimony. A man delirious, or noted for falsehood and villainy, has no manner of authority with us.

And as the evidence, derived from witnesses and human testimony, is founded on past experience, so it varies with the experience, and is regarded either as a proof or a probability, according as the conjunction between any particular kind of report and any kind of object has been found to be constant or variable. There are a number of circumstances to be taken into consideration in all judgments of this kind; and the ultimate standard, by which we determine all disputes, that may arise concerning them, is always derived from experience and observation. Where this experience is not entirely uniform on any side, it is attended with an unavoidable contrariety in our judgments, and with the same opposition and mutual destruction of argument as in every other kind of evidence. We frequently hesitate concerning the reports of others. We balance the opposite circumstances, which cause any doubt or uncertainty; and when we discover a superiority on any side, we incline to it; but still with a diminution of assurance, in proportion to the force of its antagonist.

This contrariety of evidence, in the present case, may be derived from several different causes; from the opposition of contrary testimony; from the character or number of the witnesses; from the manner of their delivering their testimony; or from the union of all these circumstances. We entertain a suspicion concerning any matter of fact, when the witnesses contradict each other; when they are but few, or of a doubtful character; when they have an interest in what they affirm; when they deliver their testimony with hesitation, or on the contrary, with too violent asseverations. There are many other particulars of the same kind, which may diminish or destroy the force of any argument, derived from human testimony.

Suppose, for instance, that the fact, which the testimony endeavours to establish, partakes of the extraordinary and the marvellous; in that case, the evidence, resulting from the testimony, admits of a diminution, greater or less, in proportion as the fact is more or less unusual. The reason why we place any credit in witnesses and historians, is not derived from any connexion, which we perceive *a priori*, between testimony and reality, but because we are accustomed to find a conformity between them. But when the fact attested is such a one as has seldom fallen under our observation, here is a contest of two opposite experiences; of which the one destroys the other, as far as its force goes, and the superior can only operate on the mind by the force, which remains. The very same principle of experience, which gives us a certain degree of assurance in the testimony of witnesses, gives us also, in this case, another degree of assurance against the fact, which they endeavour to establish; from which contradiction there necessarily arises a counterpoize, and mutual destruction of belief and authority.

I should not believe such a story were it told me by Cato, was a proverbial saying in Rome, even during the lifetime of that philosophical patriot. The incredibility of a fact, it was allowed, might invalidate so great an authority.

The Indian prince, who refused to believe the first relations concerning the effects of frost, reasoned justly; and it naturally required very strong testimony to engage his assent to facts, that arose from a state of nature, with which he was unacquainted, and which bore so little analogy to those events, of which he had had constant and uniform experience. Though they were not contrary to his experience, they were not conformable to it.

But in order to encrease the probability against the testimony of witnesses, let us suppose, that the fact, which they affirm, instead of being only marvellous, is really miraculous; and suppose also, that the testimony considered apart and in itself, amounts to an entire proof; in that case, there is proof against proof, of which the strongest must prevail, but still with a diminution of its force, in proportion to that of its antagonist.

A **miracle is a violation of the laws of nature**; and as a firm and unalterable experience has established these laws, the proof against a miracle, from the very nature of the fact, is as entire as any argument from experience can possibly be imagined. Why is it more than probable, that all men must die; that lead cannot, of itself, remain suspended in the air; that fire consumes wood, and is extinguished by water; unless it be, that these events are found agreeable to the laws of nature, and there is required a violation of these laws, or in other words, a miracle to prevent them? Nothing is esteemed a miracle, if it ever happen in the common course of nature. It is no miracle that a man, seemingly in good health, should die on a sudden: because such a kind of death, though more unusual than any other, has yet been frequently observed to happen. But it is a miracle, that a dead man should come to life; because that has never been observed in any age or country. There must, therefore, be a uniform experience against every miraculous event, otherwise the event would not merit that appellation. And as a uniform experience amounts to a proof, there is here a direct and full proof, from the nature of the fact, against the existence of any miracle; nor can such a proof be destroyed, or the miracle rendered credible, but by an opposite proof, which is superior.

The plain consequence is (and it is a general maxim worthy of our attention), 'that no testimony is sufficient to establish a miracle, unless the testimony be of such a kind, that its falsehood would be more miraculous, than the fact, which it endeavors to establish; and even in that case there is a mutual destruction of arguments, and the superior only gives us an assurance suitable to that degree of force, which remains, after deducting the inferior.' When anyone tells me, that he saw a dead man restored to life, I immediately consider with myself, whether it be more probable, that this person should either deceive or be deceived, or that the fact, which he relates, should really have happened. I weigh the one miracle against the other; and according to the superiority, which I discover, I pronounce my decision, and always reject the greater miracle. If the falsehood of his testimony would be more miraculous, than the event which he relates; then, and not till then, can he pretend to command my belief or opinion.

1. *Define 'miracle'.*
2. *We seem to learn of miracles only through what means? By definition, then, a miracle pits our belief in the laws of nature against what?*

Which belief wins, and why?

Section Ten: Of Miracles, Part One

In the foregoing reasoning we have supposed, that the testimony, upon which a miracle is founded, may possibly amount to an entire proof, and that the falsehood of that testimony would be a real prodigy: but it is easy to shew, that we have been a great deal too liberal in our concession, and that there never was a miraculous event established on so full an evidence. For **first**, there is not to be found, in all history, any miracle attested by a sufficient number of men, of such unquestioned good-sense, education, and learning, as to secure us against all delusion in themselves; of such undoubted integrity, as to place them beyond all suspicion of any design to deceive others; of such credit and reputation in the eyes of mankind, as to have a great deal to lose in case of their being detected in any falsehood; and at the same time, attesting facts performed in such a public manner and in so celebrated a part of the world, as to render the detection unavoidable: all which circumstances are requisite to give us a full assurance in the testimony of men.

Secondly. We may observe in human nature a principle which, if strictly examined, will be found to diminish extremely the assurance, which we might, from human testimony, have in any kind of prodigy. ... The passion of surprise and wonder, arising from miracles, being an agreeable emotion, gives a sensible tendency towards the belief of those events, from which it is derived. And this goes so far, that even those who cannot enjoy this pleasure immediately, nor can believe those miraculous events, of which they are informed, yet love to partake of the satisfaction at second-hand or by rebound, and place a pride and delight in exciting the admiration of others.

With what greediness are the miraculous accounts of travellers received, their descriptions of sea and land monsters, their relations of wonderful adventures, strange men, and uncouth manners? But if the spirit of religion join itself to the love of wonder, there is an end of common sense; and human testimony, in these circumstances, loses all pretensions to authority.

Thirdly. It forms a strong presumption against all supernatural and miraculous relations, that they are observed chiefly to abound among ignorant and barbarous nations; or if a civilized people has ever given admission to any of them, that people will be found to have received them from ignorant and barbarous ancestors, who transmitted them with that inviolable sanction and authority, which always attend received opinions. When we peruse the first histories of all nations, we are apt to imagine ourselves transported into some new world; where the whole frame of nature is disjointed, and every element performs its operations in a different manner, from what it does at present. Battles, revolutions, pestilence, famine and death, are never the effect of those natural causes, which we experience. Prodigies, omens, oracles, judgements, quite obscure the few natural events, that are intermingled with them. But as the former grow thinner every page, in proportion as we advance nearer the enlightened ages, we soon learn, that there is nothing mysterious or supernatural in the case, but that all proceeds from the usual propensity of mankind towards the marvellous, and that, though this inclination may at intervals receive a check from sense and learning, it can never be thoroughly extirpated from human nature.

It is strange, a judicious reader is apt to say, upon the perusal of these wonderful historians, that such prodigious events never happen in our days. But it is nothing strange, I hope, that men should lie in all ages. You must surely have seen instances enough of that frailty. You have yourself heard many such marvellous relations started, which, being treated with scorn by all the wise and judicious, have at last been abandoned even by the vulgar. Be assured, that those renowned lies, which have spread and flourished to such a monstrous height, arose from like beginnings; but being sown in a more proper soil, shot up at last into prodigies almost equal to those which they relate. ...

Fourthly. I may add as a fourth reason, which diminishes the authority of prodigies, that there is no testimony for any, even those which have not been expressly detected, that is not opposed by an infinite number of witnesses; so that not only the miracle destroys the credit of testimony, but the testimony destroys itself. To make this the better understood, let us consider, that, in matters of religion, whatever is different is contrary; and that it is impossible the religions of ancient Rome, of Turkey, of Siam, and of China should, all of them, be established on any solid foundation. Every miracle, therefore, pretended to have been wrought in any of these religions (and all of them abound in miracles), as its direct scope is to establish the particular system to which it is attributed; so has it the same force, though more indirectly, to overthrow every other system. In destroying a rival system, it likewise destroys the credit of those miracles, on which that system was established; so that all the prodigies of different religions are to be regarded as contrary facts, and the evidences of these prodigies, whether weak or strong, as opposite to each other. According to this method of reasoning, when we believe any miracle of Mahomet or his successors, we have for our warrant the testimony of a few barbarous Arabians: and on the other hand, we are to regard the authority of Titus Livius, Plutarch, Tacitus, and, in short, of all the authors and witnesses, Grecian, Chinese, and Roman Catholic, who have related any miracle in their particular religion; I say, we are to regard their testimony in the same light as if they had mentioned that Mahometan miracle, and had in express terms contradicted it, with the same certainty as they have for the miracle they relate. This argument may appear over subtile and refined; but is not in reality different from the reasoning of a judge, who supposes, that the credit of two witnesses, maintaining a crime against any one, is destroyed by the testimony of two others, who affirm him to have been two hundred leagues distant, at the same instant when the crime is said to have been committed. ...

Upon the whole, then, it appears, that no testimony for any kind of miracle has ever amounted to a probability, much less to a proof; and that, even supposing it amounted to a proof, it would be opposed by another proof; derived from the very nature of the fact, which it would endeavour to establish. It is experience only, which gives authority to human testimony; and it is the same experience, which assures us of the laws of nature. When, therefore, these two kinds of experience are contrary, we have nothing to do but subtract the one from the other, and embrace an opinion, either on one side or the other, with that assurance which arises from the remainder. But according to the principle here explained, this subtraction, with regard to all popular religions, amounts to an entire annihilation; and therefore we may establish it as a maxim, that no human testimony can have such force as to prove a miracle, and make it a just foundation for any such system of religion. ...

I am the better pleased with the method of reasoning here delivered, as I think it may serve to confound those dangerous friends or disguised enemies to the Christian Religion, who have undertaken to defend it by the principles of human reason. Our most holy religion is founded on Faith, not on reason; and it is a sure method of exposing it to put it to such a trial as it is, by no means, fitted to endure. To make this more evident, let us examine those miracles, related in scripture; and not to lose ourselves in too wide a field, let us confine ourselves to such as we find in the Pentateuch, which we shall examine, according to the principles of these pretended Christians, not as the word or testimony of God himself, but as the production of a mere human writer and historian. Here then we are first to consider a book, presented to us by a barbarous and ignorant people, written in an age when they were still more barbarous, and in all probability long after the facts which it relates, corroborated by no concurring testimony, and resembling those fabulous accounts, which every nation gives of its origin. Upon reading this book, we find it full of prodigies and miracles. It gives an account of a state of the world and of human nature entirely different from the present: of our fall from that state: of the age of man, extended to near a thousand years: of the destruction of the world by a deluge: of the arbitrary choice of one people, as the favourites of heaven; and that people the countrymen of the author: of their deliverance from bondage by prodigies the most astonishing imaginable: I desire any one to lay his hand upon his heart, and after a serious consideration declare, whether he thinks that the falsehood of such a book, supported by such a testimony, would be more extraordinary and miraculous than all the miracles it relates; which is, however, necessary to make it be received, according to the measures of probability above established.

What we have said of miracles may be applied, without any variation, to prophecies; and indeed, all prophecies are real miracles, and as such only, can be admitted as proofs of any revelation. If it did not exceed the capacity of human nature to foretell future events, it would be absurd to employ any prophecy as an argument for a divine mission or authority from heaven. So that, upon the whole, we may conclude, that the Christian Religion not only was at first attended with miracles, but even at this day cannot be believed by any reasonable person without one. Mere reason is insufficient to convince us of its veracity: and whoever is moved by Faith to assent to it, is conscious of a continued miracle in his own person, which subverts all the principles of his understanding, and gives him a determination to believe what is most contrary to custom and experience.

---

1. *In this Part Two, Hume gives four reasons why testimony of miracles should be doubted. Give at least two of these reasons.*
2. *Why does Hume think that the Christian religion 'cannot be believed by a reasonable person' without a miracle?*
3. *Hume is sometimes read as defending 'fideism': the view that religious belief neither needs nor can summon rational support. Do you think this reading is plausible?*

Section Eleven: Of a Particular Providence and of a Future State

I was lately engaged in conversation with a friend who loves sceptical paradoxes; where, though he advanced many principles, of which I can by no means approve, yet as they seem to be curious, and to bear some relation to the chain of reasoning carried on throughout this enquiry, I shall here copy them from my memory as accurately as I can, in order to submit them to the judgement of the reader.

Our conversation began with my admiring the singular good fortune of philosophy, which, as it requires entire liberty above all other privileges, and chiefly flourishes from the free opposition of sentiments and argumentation, received its first birth in an age and country of freedom and toleration, and was never cramped, even in its most extravagant principles, by any creeds, concessions, or penal statutes. For, except the banishment of Protagoras, and the death of Socrates, which last event proceeded partly from other motives, there are scarcely any instances to be met with, in ancient history, of this bigoted jealousy, with which the present age is so much infested. Epicurus lived at Athens to an advanced age, in peace and tranquillity: Epicureans were even admitted to receive the sacerdotal character, and to officiate at the altar, in the most sacred rites of the established religion: and the public encouragement of pensions and salaries was afforded equally, by the wisest of all the Roman emperors, to the professors of every sect of philosophy. How requisite such kind of treatment was to philosophy, in her early youth, will easily be conceived, if we reflect, that, even at present, when she may be supposed more hardy and robust, she bears with much difficulty the inclemency of the seasons, and those harsh winds of calumny and persecution, which blow upon her.

You admire, says my friend, as the singular good fortune of philosophy, what seems to result from the natural course of things, and to be unavoidable in every age and nation. This pertinacious bigotry, of which you complain, as so fatal to philosophy, is really her offspring, who, after allying with superstition, separates himself entirely from the interest of his parent, and becomes her most inveterate enemy and persecutor. Speculative dogmas of religion, the present occasions of such furious dispute, could not possibly be conceived or admitted in the early ages of the world; when mankind, being wholly illiterate, formed an idea of religion more suitable to their weak apprehension, and composed their sacred tenets of such tales chiefly as were the objects of traditional belief, more than of argument or disputation. After the first alarm, therefore, was over, which arose from the new paradoxes and principles of the philosophers; these teachers seem ever after, during the ages of antiquity, to have lived in great harmony with the established superstition, and to have made a fair partition of mankind between them; the former claiming all the learned and wise, the latter possessing all the vulgar and illiterate.

It seems then, say I, that you leave politics entirely out of the question, and never suppose, that a wise magistrate can justly be jealous of certain tenets of philosophy, such as those of Epicurus, which, denying a divine existence, and consequently a providence and a future state, seem to loosen, in a great measure the ties of morality, and may be supposed, for that reason, pernicious to the peace of civil society.

I know, replied he, that in fact these persecutions never, in any age, proceeded from calm reason, or from experience of the pernicious consequences of philosophy; but arose entirely from passion and prejudice. But what if I should advance farther, and assert, that if Epicurus had been accused before the people, by any of the sycophants or informers of those days, he could easily have defended his cause, and proved his principles of philosophy to be as salutary as those of his adversaries, who endeavoured, with such zeal, to expose him to the public hatred and jealousy?

I wish, said I, you would try your eloquence upon so extraordinary a topic, and make a speech for Epicurus, which might satisfy, not the mob of Athens, if you will allow that ancient and polite city to have contained any mob, but the more philosophical part of his audience, such as might be supposed capable of comprehending his arguments.

The matter would not be difficult, upon such conditions, replied he: and if you please, I shall suppose myself Epicurus for a moment, and make you stand for the Athenian people, and shall deliver you such an harangue as will fill all the urn with white beans, and leave not a black one to gratify the malice of my adversaries.

Very well [said I]: pray proceed upon these suppositions.

1. *Why is this speech is a speech of Epicurus to the Athenians? What were Epicurus and the Athenians known for?*

I come hither, O ye Athenians, to justify in your assembly what I maintain in my school, and I find myself impeached by furious antagonists, instead of reasoning with calm and dispassionate enquirers. Your deliberations, which of right should be directed to questions of public good, and the interest of the commonwealth, are diverted to the disquisitions of speculative philosophy; and these magnificent, but perhaps fruitless enquiries, take place of your more familiar but more useful occupations. But so far as in me lies, I will prevent this abuse. We shall not here dispute concerning the origin and government of worlds. We shall only enquire how far such questions concern the public interest. And if I can persuade you, that they are entirely indifferent to the peace of society and security of government, I hope that you will presently send us back to our schools, there to examine, at leisure, the question the most sublime, but, at the same time, the most speculative of all philosophy.

The religious philosophers, not satisfied with the tradition of your forefathers, and doctrine of your priests (in which I willingly acquiesce), indulge a rash curiosity, in trying how far they can establish religion upon the principles of reason; and they thereby excite, instead of satisfying, the doubts, which naturally arise from a diligent and scrutinous enquiry. They paint, in the most magnificent colours, the order, beauty, and wise arrangement of the universe; and then ask, if such a glorious display of intelligence could proceed from the fortuitous concourse of atoms, or if chance could produce what the greatest genius can never sufficiently admire. I shall not examine the justness of this argument. I shall allow it to be as solid as my antagonists and accusers can desire. It is sufficient, if I can prove, from this very reasoning, that the question is entirely speculative, and that, when, in my philosophical disquisitions, I deny a providence and a future state, I undermine not the foundations of society, but advance principles, which they themselves, upon their own topics, if they argue consistently, must allow to be solid and satisfactory.

You then, who are my accusers, have acknowledged, that the chief or sole argument for a divine existence (which I never questioned) is derived from the order of nature; where there appear such marks of intelligence and design, that you think it extravagant to assign for its cause, either chance, or the blind and unguided force of matter. You allow, that this is an argument drawn from effects to causes. From the order of the work, you infer, that there must have been project and forethought in the workman. If you cannot make out this point, you allow, that your conclusion fails; and you pretend not to establish the conclusion in a greater latitude than the phenomena of nature will justify. These are your concessions. I desire you to mark the consequences.

When we infer any particular cause from an effect, we must proportion the one to the other, and can never be allowed to ascribe to the cause any qualities, but what are exactly sufficient to produce the effect. A body of ten ounces raised in any scale may serve as a proof, that the counterbalancing weight exceeds ten ounces; but can never afford a reason that it exceeds a hundred. If the cause, assigned for any effect, be not sufficient to produce it, we must either reject that cause, or add to it such qualities as will give it a just proportion to the effect. But if we ascribe to it farther qualities, or affirm it capable of producing other effects, we can only indulge the licence of conjecture, and arbitrarily suppose the existence of qualities and energies, without reason or authority.

The same rule holds, whether the cause assigned be brute unconscious matter, or a rational intelligent being. If the cause be known only by the effect, we never ought to ascribe to it any qualities, beyond what are precisely requisite to produce the effect: nor can we, by any rules of just reasoning, return back from the cause, and infer other effects from it, beyond those by which alone it is known to us. No one, merely from the sight of one of Zeuxis's pictures, could know, that he was also a statuary or architect, and was an artist no less skilful in stone and marble than in colours. The talents and taste, displayed in the particular work before us; these we may safely conclude the workman to be possessed of. The cause must be proportioned to the effect; and if we exactly and precisely proportion it, we shall never find in it any qualities, that point farther, or afford an inference concerning any other design or performance. Such qualities must be somewhat beyond what is merely requisite for producing the effect, which we examine.

Allowing, therefore, the gods to be the authors of the existence or order of the universe; it follows, that they possess that precise degree of power, intelligence, and benevolence, which appears in their workmanship; but nothing farther can ever be proved, except we call in the assistance of exaggeration and flattery to supply the defects of argument and reasoning. So far as the traces of any attributes, at present, appear, so far may we conclude these attributes to exist. The supposition of farther attributes is mere hypothesis; much more the supposition, that, in distant regions of space or periods of time, there has been, or will be, a more magnificent display of these attributes, and a scheme of administration more suitable to such imaginary virtues. We can never be allowed to mount up from the universe, the effect, to Jupiter, the cause; and then descend downwards, to infer any new effect from that cause; as if the present effects alone were not entirely worthy of the glorious attributes, which we ascribe to that deity. The knowledge of the cause being derived solely from the effect, they must be exactly adjusted to each other; and the one can never refer to anything farther, or be the foundation of any new inference and conclusion.

You find certain phenomena in nature. You seek a cause or author. You imagine that you have found him. You afterwards become so enamoured of this offspring of your brain, that you imagine it impossible, but he must produce something greater and more perfect than the present scene of things, which is so full of ill and disorder. You forget, that this superlative intelligence and benevolence are entirely imaginary, or, at least, without any foundation in reason; and that you have no ground to ascribe to him any qualities, but what you see he has actually exerted and displayed in his productions. Let your gods, therefore, O philosophers, be suited to the present appearances of nature: and presume not to alter these appearances by arbitrary suppositions, in order to suit them to the attributes, which you so fondly ascribe to your deities.

When priests and poets, supported by your authority, O Athenians, talk of a golden or silver age, which preceded the present state of vice and misery, I hear them with attention and with reverence. But when philosophers, who pretend to neglect authority, and to cultivate reason, hold the same discourse, I pay them not, I own, the same obsequious submission and pious deference. I ask; who carried them into the celestial regions, who admitted them into the councils of the gods, who opened to them the book of fate, that they thus rashly affirm, that their deities have executed, or will execute, any purpose beyond what has actually appeared? If they tell me, that they have mounted on the steps or by the gradual ascent of reason, and by drawing inferences from effects to causes, I still insist, that they have aided the ascent of reason by the wings of imagination; otherwise they could not thus change their manner of inference, and argue from causes to effects; presuming, that a more perfect production than the present world would be more suitable to such perfect beings as the gods, and forgetting that they have no reason to ascribe to these celestial beings any perfection or any attribute, but what can be found in the present world.

Hence all the fruitless industry to account for the ill appearances of nature, and save the honour of the gods; while we must acknowledge the reality of that evil and disorder, with which the world so much abounds. The obstinate and intractable qualities of matter, we are told, or the observance of general laws, or some such reason, is the sole cause, which controlled the power and benevolence of Jupiter, and obliged him to create mankind and every sensible creature so imperfect and so unhappy. These attributes then, are, it seems, beforehand, taken for granted, in their greatest latitude. And upon that supposition, I own that such conjectures may, perhaps, be admitted as plausible solutions of the ill phenomena. But still I ask; Why take these attributes for granted, or why ascribe to the cause any qualities but what actually appear in the effect? Why torture your brain to justify the course of nature upon suppositions, which, for aught you know, may be entirely imaginary, and of which there are to be found no traces in the course of nature?

The religious hypothesis, therefore, must be considered only as a particular method of accounting for the visible phenomena of the universe: but no just reasoner will ever presume to infer from it any single fact, and alter or add to the phenomena, in any single particular. If you think, that the appearances of things prove such causes, it is allowable for you to draw an inference concerning the existence of these causes. In such complicated and sublime subjects, every one should be indulged in the liberty of conjecture and argument. But here you ought to rest. If you come backward, and arguing from your inferred causes, conclude, that any other fact has existed, or will exist, in the course of nature, which may serve as a fuller display of particular attributes; I must admonish you, that you have departed from the method of reasoning, attached to the present subject, and have certainly added something to the attributes of the cause, beyond what appears in the effect; otherwise you could never, with tolerable sense or propriety, add anything to the effect, in order to render it more worthy of the cause.

Where, then, is the odiousness of that doctrine, which I teach in my school, or rather, which I examine in my gardens? Or what do you find in this whole question, wherein the security of good morals, or the peace and order of society, is in the least concerned?

I deny a providence, you say, and supreme governor of the world, who guides the course of events, and punishes the vicious with infamy and disappointment, and rewards the virtuous with honour and success, in all their undertakings. But surely, I deny not the course itself of events, which lies open to every one's inquiry and examination. I acknowledge, that, in the present order of things, virtue is attended with more peace of mind than vice, and meets with a more favourable reception from the world. I am sensible, that, according to the past experience of mankind, friendship is the chief joy of human life, and moderation the only source of tranquillity and happiness. I never balance between the virtuous and the vicious course of life; but am sensible, that, to a well-disposed mind, every advantage is on the side of the former. And what can you say more, allowing all your suppositions and reasonings? You tell me, indeed, that this disposition of things proceeds from intelligence and design. But whatever it proceeds from, the disposition itself, on which depends our happiness or misery, and consequently our conduct and deportment in life is still the same. It is still open for me, as well as you, to regulate my behaviour, by my experience of past events. And if you affirm, that, while a divine providence is allowed and a supreme distributive justice in the universe, I ought to expect some more particular reward of the good, and punishment of the bad, beyond the ordinary course of events; I here find the same fallacy, which I have before endeavoured to detect. You persist in imagining, that, if we grant that divine existence, for which you so earnestly contend, you may safely infer consequences from it, and add something to the experienced order of nature, by arguing from the attributes which you ascribe to your gods. You seem not to remember, that all your reasonings on this subject can only be drawn from effects to causes; and that every argument, deducted from causes to effects, must of necessity be a gross sophism; since it is impossible for you to know anything of the cause, but what you have antecedently, not inferred, but discovered to the full, in the effect.

But what must a philosopher think of those vain reasoners, who instead of regarding the present scene of things as the sole object of their contemplation, so far reverse the whole course of nature, as to render this life merely a passage to something farther; a porch, which leads to a greater, and vastly different building; a prologue, which serves only to introduce the piece, and give it more grace and propriety? Whence, do you think, can such philosophers derive their idea of the gods? From their own conceit and imagination surely. For if they derived it from the present phenomena, it would never point to anything farther, but must be exactly adjusted to them. That the divinity may possibly be endowed with attributes, which we have never seen exerted; may be governed by principles of action, which we cannot discover to be satisfied: all this will freely be allowed. But still this is mere possibility and hypothesis. We never can have reason to infer any attributes, or any principles of action in him, but so far as we know them to have been exerted and satisfied.

Are there any marks of a distributive justice in the world? If you answer in the affirmative, I conclude, that, since justice here exerts itself, it is satisfied. If you reply in the negative, I conclude, that you have then no reason to ascribe justice, in our sense of it, to the gods. If you hold a medium between affirmation and negation, by saying, that the justice of the gods, at present, exerts itself in part, but not in its full extent; I answer, that you have no reason to give it any particular extent, but only so far as you see it, at present, exert itself.

Thus I bring the dispute, O Athenians, to a short issue with my antagonists. The course of nature lies open to my contemplation as well as to theirs. The experienced train of events is the great standard, by which we all regulate our conduct. Nothing else can be appealed to in the field, or in the senate. Nothing else ought ever to be heard of in the school, or in the closet. In vain would our limited understanding break through those boundaries, which are too narrow for our fond imagination. While we argue from the course of nature, and infer a particular intelligent cause, which first bestowed, and still preserves order in the universe, we embrace a principle, which is both uncertain and useless. It is uncertain; because the subject lies entirely beyond the reach of human experience. It is useless; because our knowledge of this cause being derived entirely from the course of nature, we can never, according to the rules of just reasoning, return back from the cause with any new inference, or making additions to the common and experienced course of nature, establish any new principles of conduct and behaviour.

I observe (said I, finding he had finished his harangue) that you neglect not the artifice of the demagogues of old; and as you were pleased to make me stand for the people, you insinuate yourself into my favour by embracing those principles, to which, you know, I have always expressed a particular attachment. But allowing you to make experience (as indeed I think you ought) the only standard of our judgment concerning this, and all other questions of fact; I doubt not but, from the very same experience, to which you appeal, it may be possible to refute this reasoning, which you have put into the mouth of Epicurus. If you saw, for instance, a half-finished building, surrounded with heaps of brick and stone and mortar, and all the instruments of masonry; could you not infer from the effect, that it was a work of design and contrivance? And could you not return again, from this inferred cause, to infer new additions to the effect, and conclude, that the building would soon be finished, and receive all the further improvements, which art could bestow upon it? If you saw upon the sea-shore the print of one human foot, you would conclude, that a man had passed that way, and that he had also left the traces of the other foot, though effaced by the rolling of the sands or inundation of the waters. Why then do you refuse to admit the same method of reasoning with regard to the order of nature? Consider the world and the present life only as an imperfect building, from which you can infer a superior intelligence; and arguing from that superior intelligence, which can leave nothing imperfect; why may you not infer a more finished scheme or plan, which will receive its completion in some distant point of space or time? Are not these methods of reasoning exactly similar? And under what pretence can you embrace the one, while you reject the other?

The infinite difference of the subjects, replied he, is a sufficient foundation for this difference in my conclusions. In works of human art and contrivance, it is allowable to advance from the effect to the cause, and returning back from the cause, to form new inferences concerning the effect, and examine the alterations, which it has probably undergone, or may still undergo. But what is the foundation of this method of reasoning? Plainly this; that man is a being, whom we know by experience, whose motives and designs we are acquainted with, and whose projects and inclinations have a certain connexion and coherence, according to the laws which nature has established for the government of such a creature. When, therefore, we find, that any work has proceeded from the skill and industry of man; as we are otherwise acquainted with the nature of the animal, we can draw a hundred inferences concerning what may be expected from him; and these inferences will all be founded in experience and observation. But did we know man only from the single work or production which we examine, it were impossible for us to argue in this manner; because our knowledge of all the qualities, which we ascribe to him, being in that case derived from the production, it is impossible they could point to anything farther, or be the foundation of any new inference. The print of a foot in the sand can only prove, when considered alone, that there was some figure adapted to it, by which it was produced: but the print of a human foot proves likewise, from our other experience, that there was probably another foot, which also left its impression, though effaced by time or other accidents. Here we mount from the effect to the cause; and descending again from the cause, infer alterations in the effect; but this is not a continuation of the same simple chain of reasoning. We comprehend in this case a hundred other experiences and observations, concerning the usual figure and members of that species of animal, without which this method of argument must be considered as fallacious and sophistical.

The case is not the same with our reasonings from the works of nature. The Deity is known to us only by his productions, and is a single being in the universe, not comprehended under any species or genus, from whose experienced attributes or qualities, we can, by analogy, infer any attribute or quality in him. As the universe shews wisdom and goodness, we infer wisdom and goodness. As it shews a particular degree of these perfections, we infer a particular degree of them, precisely adapted to the effect which we examine. But farther attributes or farther degrees of the same attributes, we can never be authorised to infer or suppose, by any rules of just reasoning. Now, without some such licence of supposition, it is impossible for us to argue from the cause, or infer any alteration in the effect, beyond what has immediately fallen under our observation. Greater good produced by this Being must still prove a greater degree of goodness: a more impartial distribution of rewards and punishments must proceed from a greater regard to justice and equity. Every supposed addition to the works of nature makes an addition to the attributes of the Author of nature; and consequently, being entirely unsupported by any reason or argument, can never be admitted but as mere conjecture and hypothesis.

The great source of our mistake in this subject, and of the unbounded licence of conjecture, which we indulge, is, that we tacitly consider ourselves, as in the place of the Supreme Being, and conclude, that he will, on every occasion, observe the same conduct, which we ourselves, in his situation, would have embraced as reasonable and eligible. But, besides that the ordinary course of nature may convince us, that almost everything is regulated by principles and maxims very different from ours; besides this, I say, it must evidently appear contrary to all rules of analogy to reason, from the intentions and projects of men, to those of a Being so different, and so much superior. In human nature, there is a certain experienced coherence of designs and inclinations; so that when, from any fact, we have discovered one intention of any man, it may often be reasonable, from experience, to infer another, and draw a long chain of conclusions concerning his past or future conduct. But this method of reasoning can never have place with regard to a Being, so remote and incomprehensible, who bears much less analogy to any other being in the universe than the sun to a waxen taper, and who discovers himself only by some faint traces or outlines, beyond which we have no authority to ascribe to him any attribute or perfection. What we imagine to be a superior perfection, may really be a defect. Or were it ever so much a perfection, the ascribing of it to the Supreme Being, where it appears not to have been really exerted, to the full, in his works, savours more of flattery and panegyric, than of just reasoning and sound philosophy. All the philosophy, therefore, in the world, and all the religion, which is nothing but a species of philosophy, will never be able to carry us beyond the usual course of experience, or give us measures of conduct and behaviour different from those which are furnished by reflections on common life. No new fact can ever be inferred from the religious hypothesis; no event foreseen or foretold; no reward or punishment expected or dreaded, beyond what is already known by practice and observation. So that my apology for Epicurus will still appear solid and satisfactory; nor have the political interests of society any connexion with the philosophical disputes concerning metaphysics and religion.

There is still one circumstance, replied I, which you seem to have overlooked. Though I should allow your premises, I must deny your conclusion. You conclude, that religious doctrines and reasonings can have no influence on life, because they ought to have no influence; never considering, that men reason not in the same manner you do, but draw many consequences from the belief of a divine Existence, and suppose that the Deity will inflict punishments on vice, and bestow rewards on virtue, beyond what appear in the ordinary course of nature. Whether this reasoning of theirs be just or not, is no matter. Its influence on their life and conduct must still be the same. And those, who attempt to disabuse them of such prejudices, may, for aught I know, be good reasoners, but I cannot allow them to be good citizens and politicians; since they free men from one restraint upon their passions, and make the infringement of the laws of society, in one respect, more easy and secure.

After all, I may, perhaps, agree to your general conclusion in favour of liberty, though upon different premises from those, on which you endeavour to found it. I think, that the state ought to tolerate every principle of philosophy; nor is there an instance, that any government has suffered in its political interests by such indulgence. There is no enthusiasm among philosophers; their doctrines are not very alluring to the people; and no restraint can be put upon their reasonings, but what must be of dangerous consequence to the sciences, and even to the state, by paving the way for persecution and oppression in points, where the generality of mankind are more deeply interested and concerned.

But there occurs to me (continued I) with regard to your main topic, a difficulty, which I shall just propose to you without insisting on it; lest it lead into reasonings of too nice and delicate a nature. In a word, I much doubt whether it be possible for a cause to be known only by its effect (as you have all along supposed) or to be of so singular and particular a nature as to have no parallel and no similarity with any other cause or object, that has ever fallen under our observation. It is only when two species of objects are found to be constantly conjoined, that we can infer the one from the other; and were an effect presented, which was entirely singular, and could not be comprehended under any known species, I do not see, that we could form any conjecture or inference at all concerning its cause. If experience and observation and analogy be, indeed, the only guides which we can reasonably follow in inferences of this nature; both the effect and cause must bear a similarity and resemblance to other effects and causes, which we know, and which we have found, in many instances, to be conjoined with each other. I leave it to your own reflection to pursue the consequences of this principle. I shall just observe, that, as the antagonists of Epicurus always suppose the universe, an effect quite singular and unparalleled, to be the proof of a Deity, a cause no less singular and unparalleled; your reasonings, upon that supposition, seem, at least, to merit our attention. There is, I own, some difficulty, how we can ever return from the cause to the effect, and, reasoning from our ideas of the former, infer any alteration on the latter, or any, addition to it.

---

1. *Hume sets out two principles of causal reasoning above:*
    1. 'When we infer any particular cause from an effect, we must proportion the one to the other...' Put this in your own words.
    2. If you infer from an effect to a cause, you cannot then turn around and conclude that whatever caused the effect will _____.
2. *Explain how (i) and (ii) undermine the argument for design.*
3. *At the end of this section, Hume applies his own theory of causation to the design argument. Briefly explain what he means by 'cause' and then explain how this notion of cause makes trouble for the design argument.*

Section Twelve: Of the Academical or Sceptical Philosophy, Part One

There is not a greater number of philosophical reasonings, displayed upon any subject, than those, which prove the existence of a Deity, and refute the fallacies of Atheists; and yet the most religious philosophers still dispute whether any man can be so blinded as to be a speculative atheist. How shall we reconcile these contradictions? The knights errant, who wandered about to clear the world of dragons and giants, never entertained the least doubt with regard to the existence of these monsters.

The Sceptic is another enemy of religion, who naturally provokes the indignation of all divines and graver philosophers; though it is certain, that no man ever met with any such absurd creature, or conversed with a man, who had no opinion or principle concerning any subject, either of action or speculation. This begets a very natural question; What is meant by a sceptic? And how far it is possible to push these philosophical principles of doubt and uncertainty?

There is a species of scepticism, antecedent to all study and philosophy, which is much inculcated by Descartes and others, as a sovereign preservative against error and precipitate judgement. It recommends an universal doubt, not only of all our former opinions and principles, but also of our very faculties; of whose veracity, say they, we must assure ourselves, by a chain of reasoning, deduced from some original principle, which cannot possibly be fallacious or deceitful. But neither is there any such original principle, which has a prerogative above others, that are self-evident and convincing: or if there were, could we advance a step beyond it, but by the use of those very faculties, of which we are supposed to be already diffident. The Cartesian doubt, therefore, were it ever possible to be attained by any human creature (as it plainly is not) would be entirely incurable; and no reasoning could ever bring us to a state of assurance and conviction upon any subject.

It must, however, be confessed, that this species of scepticism, when more moderate, may be understood in a very reasonable sense, and is a necessary preparative to the study of philosophy, by preserving a proper impartiality in our judgments, and weaning our mind from all those prejudices, which we may have imbibed from education or rash opinion. To begin with clear and self-evident principles, to advance by timorous and sure steps, to review frequently our conclusions, and examine accurately all their consequences; though by these means we shall make both a slow and a short progress in our systems; are the only methods, by which we can ever hope to reach truth, and attain a proper stability and certainty in our determinations.

There is another species of scepticism, consequent to science and enquiry, when men are supposed to have discovered, either the absolute fallaciousness of their mental faculties, or their unfitness to reach any fixed determination in all those curious subjects of speculation, about which they are commonly employed. Even our very senses are brought into dispute, by a certain species of philosophers; and the maxims of common life are subjected to the same doubt as the most profound principles or conclusions of metaphysics and theology. As these paradoxical tenets (if they may be called tenets) are to be met with in some philosophers, and the refutation of them in several, they naturally excite our curiosity, and make us enquire into the arguments, on which they may be founded.

I need not insist upon the more trite topics, employed by the sceptics in all ages, against the evidence of sense; such as those which are derived from the imperfection and fallaciousness of our organs, on numberless occasions; the crooked appearance of an oar in water; the various aspects of objects, according to their different distances; the double images which arise from the pressing one eye; with many other appearances of a like nature. These sceptical topics, indeed, are only sufficient to prove, that the senses alone are not implicitly to be depended on; but that we must correct their evidence by reason, and by considerations, derived from the nature of the medium, the distance of the object, and the disposition of the organ, in order to render them, within their sphere, the proper criteria of truth and falsehood. There are other more profound arguments against the senses, which admit not of so easy a solution.

It seems evident, that men are carried, by a natural instinct or prepossession, to repose faith in their senses; and that, without any reasoning, or even almost before the use of reason, we always suppose an external universe, which depends not on our perception, but would exist, though we and every sensible creature were absent or annihilated. Even the animal creation are governed by a like opinion, and preserve this belief of external objects, in all their thoughts, designs, and actions.

It seems also evident, that, when men follow this blind and powerful instinct of nature, they always suppose the very images, presented by the senses, to be the external objects, and never entertain any suspicion, that the one are nothing but representations of the other. This very table, which we see white, and which we feel hard, is believed to exist, independent of our perception, and to be something external to our mind, which perceives it. Our presence bestows not being on it: our absence does not annihilate it. It preserves its existence uniform and entire, independent of the situation of intelligent beings, who perceive or contemplate it.

But this universal and primary opinion of all men is soon destroyed by the slightest philosophy, which teaches us, that nothing can ever be present to the mind but an image or perception, and that the senses are only the inlets, through which these images are conveyed, without being able to produce any immediate intercourse between the mind and the object. The table, which we see, seems to diminish, as we remove farther from it: but the real table, which exists independent of us, suffers no alteration: it was, therefore, nothing but its image, which was present to the mind. These are the obvious dictates of reason; and no man, who reflects, ever doubted, that the existences, which we consider, when we say, this house and that tree, are nothing but perceptions in the mind, and fleeting copies or representations of other existences, which remain uniform and independent.

So far, then, are we necessitated by reasoning to contradict or depart from the primary instincts of nature, and to embrace a new system with regard to the evidence of our senses. But here philosophy finds herself extremely embarrassed, when she would justify this new system, and obviate the cavils and objections of the sceptics. She can no longer plead the infallible and irresistible instinct of nature: for that led us to a quite different system, which is acknowledged fallible and even erroneous. And to justify this pretended philosophical system, by a chain of clear and convincing argument, or even any appearance of argument, exceeds the power of all human capacity.

By what argument can it be proved, that the perceptions of the mind must be caused by external objects, entirely different from them, though resembling them (if that be possible) and could not arise either from the energy of the mind itself, or from the suggestion of some invisible and unknown spirit, or from some other cause still more unknown to us? It is acknowledged, that, in fact, many of these perceptions arise not from anything external, as in dreams, madness, and other diseases. And nothing can be more inexplicable than the manner, in which body should so operate upon mind as ever to convey an image of itself to a substance, supposed of so different, and even contrary a nature.

It is a question of fact, whether the perceptions of the senses be produced by external objects, resembling them: how shall this question be determined? By experience surely; as all other questions of a like nature. But here experience is, and must be entirely silent. The mind has never anything present to it but the perceptions, and cannot possibly reach any experience of their connexion with objects. The supposition of such a connexion is, therefore, without any foundation in reasoning.

To have recourse to the veracity of the supreme Being, in order to prove the veracity of our senses, is surely making a very unexpected circuit. If his veracity were at all concerned in this matter, our senses would be entirely infallible; because it is not possible that he can ever deceive. Not to mention, that, if the external world be once called in question, we shall be at a loss to find arguments, by which we may prove the existence of that Being or any of his attributes.

This is a topic, therefore, in which the profounder and more philosophical sceptics will always triumph, when they endeavour to introduce an universal doubt into all subjects of human knowledge and enquiry. Do you follow the instincts and propensities of nature, may they say, in assenting to the veracity of sense? But these lead you to believe that the very perception or sensible image is the external object. Do you disclaim this principle, in order to embrace a more rational opinion, that the perceptions are only representations of something external? You here depart from your natural propensities and more obvious sentiments; and yet are not able to satisfy your reason, which can never find any convincing argument from experience to prove, that the perceptions are connected with any external objects.

There is another sceptical topic of a like nature, derived from the most profound philosophy; which might merit our attention, were it requisite to dive so deep, in order to discover arguments and reasonings, which can so little serve to any serious purpose. It is universally allowed by modern enquirers, that all the sensible qualities of objects, such as hard, soft, hot, cold, white, black, &c. Are merely secondary, and exist not in the objects themselves, but are perceptions of the mind, without any external archetype or model, which they represent. If this be allowed, with regard to secondary qualities, it must also follow, with regard to the supposed primary qualities of extension and solidity; nor can the latter be any more entitled to that denomination than the former. The idea of extension is entirely acquired from the senses of sight and feeling; and if all the qualities, perceived by the senses, be in the mind, not in the object, the same conclusion must reach the idea of extension, which is wholly dependent on the sensible ideas or the ideas of secondary qualities. Nothing can save us from this conclusion, but the asserting, that the ideas of those primary qualities are attained by Abstraction, an opinion, which, if we examine it accurately, we shall find to be unintelligible, and even absurd. An extension, that is neither tangible nor visible, cannot possibly be conceived: and a tangible or visible extension, which is neither hard nor soft, black nor white, is equally beyond the reach of human conception. Let any man try to conceive a triangle in general, which is neither Isosceles nor Scalenum, nor has any particular length or proportion of sides; and he will soon perceive the absurdity of all the scholastic notions with regard to abstraction and general ideas.

[*Hume's footnote*: This argument is drawn from Dr. Berkeley; and indeed most of the writings of that very ingenious author form the best lessons of scepticism, which are to be found either among the ancient or modern philosophers, Bayle not excepted. He professes, however, in his title-page (and undoubtedly with great truth) to have composed his book against the sceptics as well as against the atheists and free-thinkers. But that all his arguments, though otherwise intended, are, in reality, merely sceptical, appears from this, that they admit of no answer and produce no conviction. Their only effect is to cause that momentary amazement and irresolution and confusion, which is the result of scepticism.]

Thus the first philosophical objection to the evidence of sense or to the opinion of external existence consists in this, that such an opinion, if rested on natural instinct, is contrary to reason, and if referred to reason, is contrary to natural instinct, and at the same time carries no rational evidence with it, to convince an impartial enquirer. The second objection goes farther, and represents this opinion as contrary to reason: at least, if it be a principle of reason, that all sensible qualities are in the mind, not in the object. Bereave matter of all its intelligible qualities, both primary and secondary, you in a manner annihilate it, and leave only a certain unknown, inexplicable something, as the cause of our perceptions; a notion so imperfect, that no sceptic will think it worth while to contend against it.

---

1. *There are two claims Hume might be making here:*
    1. We have no good reason to believe in the external world;
    2. We cannot even conceive of anything other than perceptions, and thus cannot conceive of an external world.

    Is he making one of these, or both?
      How would the Copy Principle affect your answer?
2. *What is the 'universal and primary opinion of all men' that is 'destroyed by the slightest philosophy'? How does philosophy destroy it?*
3. *Use the distinction between* **matters of fact** *and* **relations of ideas** *to reconstruct Hume's argument (starting in the paragraph that begins 'by what argument').*
4. *How would Descartes's Meditator answer Hume? How does Hume object to Descartes's view?*

Section Twelve: Of the Academical or Sceptical Philosophy, Part Two

It may seem a very extravagant attempt of the sceptics to destroy reason by argument and ratiocination; yet is this the grand scope of all their enquiries and disputes. They endeavour to find objections, both to our abstract reasonings, and to those which regard matter of fact and existence.

The chief objection against all abstract reasonings is derived from the ideas of space and time; ideas, which, in common life and to a careless view, are very clear and intelligible, but when they pass through the scrutiny of the profound sciences (and they are the chief object of these sciences) afford principles, which seem full of absurdity and contradiction. No priestly dogmas, invented on purpose to tame and subdue the rebellious reason of mankind, ever shocked common sense more than the doctrine of the infinitive divisibility of extension, with its consequences; as they are pompously displayed by all geometricians and metaphysicians, with a kind of triumph and exultation. A real quantity, infinitely less than any finite quantity, containing quantities infinitely less than itself, and so on in infinitum; this is an edifice so bold and prodigious, that it is too weighty for any pretended demonstration to support, because it shocks the clearest and most natural principles of human reason.

But what renders the matter more extraordinary, is, that these seemingly absurd opinions are supported by a chain of reasoning, the clearest and most natural; nor is it possible for us to allow the premises without admitting the consequences. Nothing can be more convincing and satisfactory than all the conclusions concerning the properties of circles and triangles; and yet, when these are once received, how can we deny, that the angle of contact between a circle and its tangent is infinitely less than any rectilineal angle, that as you may increase the diameter of the circle *ad infinitum*, this angle of contact becomes still less, even *ad infinitum*, and that the angle of contact between other curves and their tangents may be infinitely less than those between any circle and its tangent, and so on, *ad infinitum*? The demonstration of these principles seems as unexceptionable as that which proves the three angles of a triangle to be equal to two right ones, though the latter opinion be natural and easy, and the former big with contradiction and absurdity. Reason here seems to be thrown into a kind of amazement and suspence, which, without the suggestions of any sceptic, gives her a diffidence of herself, and of the ground on which she treads. She sees a full light, which illuminates certain places; but that light borders upon the most profound darkness. And between these she is so dazzled and confounded, that she scarcely can pronounce with certainty and assurance concerning any one object.

The absurdity of these bold determinations of the abstract sciences seems to become, if possible, still more palpable with regard to time than extension. An infinite number of real parts of time, passing in succession, and exhausted one after another, appears so evident a contradiction, that no man, one should think, whose judgment is not corrupted, instead of being improved, by the sciences, would ever be able to admit of it.

Yet still reason must remain restless, and unquiet, even with regard to that scepticism, to which she is driven by these seeming absurdities and contradictions. How any clear, distinct idea can contain circumstances, contradictory to itself, or to any other clear, distinct idea, is absolutely incomprehensible; and is, perhaps, as absurd as any proposition, which can be formed. So that nothing can be more sceptical, or more full of doubt and hesitation, than this scepticism itself, which arises from some of the paradoxical conclusions of geometry or the science of quantity.

The sceptical objections to moral evidence, or to the reasonings concerning matter of fact, are either popular or philosophical. The popular objections are derived from the natural weakness of human understanding; the contradictory opinions, which have been entertained in different ages and nations; the variations of our judgment in sickness and health, youth and old age, prosperity and adversity; the perpetual contradiction of each particular man's opinions and sentiments; with many other topics of that kind. It is needless to insist farther on this head. These objections are but weak. For as, in common life, we reason every moment concerning fact and existence, and cannot possibly subsist, without continually employing this species of argument, any popular objections, derived from thence, must be insufficient to destroy that evidence. The great subverter of Pyrrhonism or the excessive principles of scepticism is action, and employment, and the occupations of common life. These principles may flourish and triumph in the schools;

where it is, indeed, difficult, if not impossible, to refute them. But as soon as they leave the shade, and by the presence of the real objects, which actuate our passions and sentiments, are put in opposition to the more powerful principles of our nature, they vanish like smoke, and leave the most determined sceptic in the same condition as other mortals.

The sceptic, therefore, had better keep within his proper sphere, and display those philosophical objections, which arise from more profound researches. Here he seems to have ample matter of triumph; while he justly insists, that all our evidence for any matter of fact, which lies beyond the testimony of sense or memory, is derived entirely from the relation of cause and effect; that we have no other idea of this relation than that of two objects, which have been frequently conjoined together; that we have no argument to convince us, that objects, which have, in our experience, been frequently conjoined, will likewise, in other instances, be conjoined in the same manner; and that nothing leads us to this inference but custom or a certain instinct of our nature; which it is indeed difficult to resist, but which, like other instincts, may be fallacious and deceitful. While the sceptic insists upon these topics, he shows his force, or rather, indeed, his own and our weakness; and seems, for the time at least, to destroy all assurance and conviction. These arguments might be displayed at greater length, if any durable good or benefit to society could ever be expected to result from them.

For here is the chief and most confounding objection to excessive scepticism, that no durable good can ever result from it; while it remains in its full force and vigour. We need only ask such a sceptic, What his meaning is? And what he proposes by all these curious researches? He is immediately at a loss, and knows not what to answer. A Copernican or Ptolemaic, who supports each his different system of astronomy, may hope to produce a conviction, which will remain constant and durable, with his audience. A Stoic or Epicurean displays principles, which may not be durable, but which have an effect on conduct and behaviour. But a Pyrrhonian cannot expect, that his philosophy will have any constant influence on the mind: or if it had, that its influence would be beneficial to society. On the contrary, he must acknowledge, if he will acknowledge anything, that all human life must perish, were his principles universally and steadily to prevail. All discourse, all action would immediately cease; and men remain in a total lethargy, till the necessities of nature, unsatisfied, put an end to their miserable existence. It is true; so fatal an event is very little to be dreaded. Nature is always too strong for principle. And though a Pyrrhonian may throw himself or others into a momentary amazement and confusion by his profound reasonings; the first and most trivial event in life will put to flight all his doubts and scruples, and leave him the same, in every point of action and speculation, with the philosophers of every other sect, or with those who never concerned themselves in any philosophical researches. When he awakes from his dream, he will be the first to join in the laugh against himself, and to confess, that all his objections are mere amusement, and can have no other tendency than to show the whimsical condition of mankind, who must act and reason and believe; though they are not able, by their most diligent enquiry, to satisfy themselves concerning the foundation of these operations, or to remove the objections, which may be raised against them.

---

1. *In the case of induction, Hume offered a 'skeptical solution' to the problem. Does his position on the external world amount to a skeptical or a straightforward solution? Why?*

There is, indeed, a more mitigated scepticism or academical philosophy, which may be both durable and useful, and which may, in part, be the result of this pyrrhonism, or excessive scepticism, when its undistinguished doubts are, in some measure, corrected by common sense and reflection. The greater part of mankind are naturally apt to be affirmative and dogmatical in their opinions; and while they see objects only on one side, and have no idea of any counterpoising argument, they throw themselves precipitately into the principles, to which they are inclined; nor have they any indulgence for those who entertain opposite sentiments. To hesitate or balance perplexes their understanding, checks their passion, and suspends their action. They are, therefore, impatient till they escape from a state, which to them is so uneasy: and they think, that they could never remove themselves far enough from it, by the violence of their affirmations and obstinacy of their belief. But could such dogmatical reasoners become sensible of the strange infirmities of human understanding, even in its most perfect state, and when most accurate and cautious in its determinations; such a reflection would naturally inspire them with more modesty and reserve, and diminish their fond opinion of themselves, and their prejudice against antagonists. The illiterate may reflect on the disposition of the learned, who, amidst all the advantages of study and reflection, are commonly still diffident in their determinations: and if any of the learned be inclined, from their natural temper, to haughtiness and obstinacy, a small tincture of Pyrrhonism might abate their pride, by showing them, that the few advantages, which they may have attained over their fellows, are but inconsiderable, if compared with the universal perplexity and confusion, which is inherent in human nature. In general, there is a degree of doubt, and caution, and modesty, which, in all kinds of scrutiny and decision, ought for ever to accompany a just reasoner.

Another species of mitigated scepticism which may be of advantage to mankind, and which may be the natural result of the Pyrrhonian doubts and scruples, is the limitation of our enquiries to such subjects as are best adapted to the narrow capacity of human understanding. The imagination of man is naturally sublime, delighted with whatever is remote and extraordinary, and running, without control, into the most distant parts of space and time in order to avoid the objects, which custom has rendered too familiar to it. A correct Judgement observes a contrary method, and avoiding all distant and high enquiries, confines itself to common life, and to such subjects as fall under daily practice and experience; leaving the more sublime topics to the embellishment of poets and orators, or to the arts of priests and politicians. To bring us to so salutary a determination, nothing can be more serviceable, than to be once thoroughly convinced of the force of the Pyrrhonian doubt, and of the impossibility, that anything, but the strong power of natural instinct, could free us from it. Those who have a propensity to philosophy, will still continue their researches; because they reflect, that, besides the immediate pleasure attending such an occupation, philosophical decisions are nothing but the reflections of common life, methodized and corrected. But they will never be tempted to go beyond common life, so long as they consider the imperfection of those faculties which they employ, their narrow reach, and their inaccurate operations. While we cannot give a satisfactory reason, why we believe, after a thousand experiments, that a stone will fall, or fire burn; can we ever satisfy ourselves concerning any determination, which we may form, with regard to the origin of worlds, and the situation of nature, from, and to eternity?

This narrow limitation, indeed, of our enquiries, is, in every respect, so reasonable, that it suffices to make the slightest examination into the natural powers of the human mind and to compare them with their objects, in order to recommend it to us. We shall then find what are the proper subjects of science and enquiry.

It seems to me, that the only objects of the abstract science or of demonstration are quantity and number, and that all attempts to extend this more perfect species of knowledge beyond these bounds are mere sophistry and illusion. As the component parts of quantity and number are entirely similar, their relations become intricate and involved; and nothing can be more curious, as well as useful, than to trace, by a variety of mediums, their equality or inequality, through their different appearances. But as all other ideas are clearly distinct and different from each other, we can never advance farther, by our utmost scrutiny, than to observe this diversity, and, by an obvious reflection, pronounce one thing not to be another. Or if there be any difficulty in these decisions, it proceeds entirely from the undeterminate meaning of words, which is corrected by juster definitions. That the square of the hypotenuse is equal to the squares of the other two sides, cannot be known, let the terms be ever so exactly defined, without a train of reasoning and enquiry. But to convince us of this proposition, that where there is no property, there can be no injustice, it is only necessary to define the terms, and explain injustice to be a violation of property. This proposition is, indeed, nothing but a more imperfect definition. It is the same case with all those pretended syllogistical reasonings, which may be found in every other branch of learning, except the sciences of quantity and number; and these may safely, I think, be pronounced the only proper objects of knowledge and demonstration.

All other enquiries of men regard only matter of fact and existence; and these are evidently incapable of demonstration. Whatever is may not be. No negation of a fact can involve a contradiction. The non-existence of any being, without exception, is as clear and distinct an idea as its existence. The proposition, which affirms it not to be, however false, is no less conceivable and intelligible, than that which affirms it to be. The case is different with the sciences, properly so called. Every proposition, which is not true, is there confused and unintelligible. That the cube root of 64 is equal to the half of 10, is a false proposition, and can never be distinctly conceived. But that Caesar, or the angel Gabriel, or any being never existed, may be a false proposition, but still is perfectly conceivable, and implies no contradiction.

The existence, therefore, of any being can only be proved by arguments from its cause or its effect; and these arguments are founded entirely on experience. If we reason *a priori*, anything may appear able to produce anything. The falling of a pebble may, for aught we know, extinguish the sun; or the wish of a man control the planets in their orbits. It is only experience, which teaches us the nature and bounds of cause and effect, and enables us to infer the existence of one object from that of another. Such is the foundation of moral reasoning, which forms the greater part of human knowledge, and is the source of all human action and behaviour.

Moral reasonings are either concerning particular or general facts. All deliberations in life regard the former; as also all disquisitions in history, chronology, geography, and astronomy.

The sciences, which treat of general facts, are politics, natural philosophy, physic, chemistry, &c. Where the qualities, causes and effects of a whole species of objects are enquired into.

Divinity or Theology, as it proves the existence of a Deity, and the immortality of souls, is composed partly of reasonings concerning particular, partly concerning general facts. It has a foundation in reason, so far as it is supported by experience. But its best and most solid foundation is faith and divine revelation.

Morals and criticism are not so properly objects of the understanding as of taste and sentiment. Beauty, whether moral or natural, is felt, more properly than perceived. Or if we reason concerning it, and endeavour to fix its standard, we regard a new fact, to wit, the general tastes of mankind, or some such fact, which may be the object of reasoning and enquiry.

When we run over libraries, persuaded of these principles, what havoc must we make? If we take in our hand any volume; of divinity or school metaphysics, for instance; let us ask, Does it contain any abstract reasoning concerning quantity or number? No. Does it contain any experimental reasoning concerning matter of fact and existence? No. Commit it then to the flames: for it can contain nothing but sophistry and illusion.

---

1. *To think about: is Hume's* Enquiry *just a re-writing of the* Meditations, *without God?*

A Treatise of Human Nature (1739), Appendix

In the Enquiry, *we've seen Hume use his three main principles (CP, SP, and CPY), and deploy his two main distinctions (**impressions** vs. **ideas**; **matters of fact** vs. **relations of ideas**). We've seen Hume's application of these principles to the external world, God, and causation/induction. Hume is, rather remarkably, silent on the question of the self. Is the self a substance? If so, is it material, or immaterial? We have to turn to the much earlier* Treatise *to find out Hume's views. The appendix gives us some indication of why Hume chose not to discuss the topic of the self in the* Enquiry.

I had entertain'd some hopes, that however deficient our theory of the intellectual world might be, it wou'd be free from those contradictions, and absurdities, which seem to attend every explication, that human reason can give of the material world. But upon a more strict review of the section concerning personal identity, I find myself involv'd in such a labyrinth, that, I must confess, I neither know how to correct my former opinions, nor how to render them consistent. If this be not a good general reason for scepticism, 'tis at least a sufficient one (if I were not already abundantly supplied) for me to entertain a diffidence and modesty in all my decisions. I shall propose the arguments on both sides, beginning with those that induc'd me to deny the strict and proper identity and simplicity of a self or thinking being.

When we talk of self or substance, we must have an idea annex'd to these terms, otherwise they are altogether unintelligible. Every idea is deriv'd from preceding impressions; and we have no impression of self or substance, as something simple and individual. We have, therefore, no idea of them in that sense.

Whatever is distinct, is distinguishable; and whatever is distinguishable, is separable by the thought or imagination. All perceptions are distinct. They are, therefore, distinguishable, and separable, and may be conceiv'd as separately existent, and may exist separately, without any contradiction or absurdity. When I view this table and that chimney, nothing is present to me but particular perceptions, which are of a like nature with all the other perceptions. This is the doctrine of philosophers. But this table, which is present to me, and the chimney, may and do exist separately. This is the doctrine of the vulgar, and implies no contradiction. There is no contradiction, therefore, in extending the same doctrine to all the perceptions.

In general, the following reasoning seems satisfactory. All ideas are borrow'd from preceding perceptions. Our ideas of objects, therefore, are deriv'd from that source. Consequently no proposition can be intelligible or consistent with regard to objects, which is not so with regard to perceptions. But 'tis intelligible and consistent to say, that objects exist distinct and independent, without any common simple substance or subject of inhesion. This proposition, therefore, can never be absurd with regard to perceptions.

When I turn my reflection on myself, I never can perceive this self without some one or more perceptions; nor can I ever perceive any thing but the perceptions. Tis the composition of these, therefore, which forms the self. We can conceive a thinking being to have either many or few perceptions. Suppose the mind to be reduc'd even below the life of an oyster. Suppose it to have only one perception, as of thirst or hunger. Consider it in that situation. Do you conceive any thing but merely that perception? Have you any notion of self or substance? If not, the addition of other perceptions can never give you that notion.

The annihilation, which some people suppose to follow upon death, and which entirely destroys this self, is nothing but an extinction of all particular perceptions; love and hatred, pain and pleasure, thought and sensation. These therefore must be the same with self; since the one cannot survive the other. Is self the same with substance? If it be, how can that question have place, concerning the subsistence of self, under a change of substance? If they be distinct, what is the difference betwixt them? For my part, I have a notion of neither, when conceiv'd distinct from particular perceptions.

Philosophers begin to be reconcil'd to the principle, that we have no idea of external substance, distinct from the ideas of particular qualities. This must pave the way for a like principle with regard to the mind, that we have no notion of it, distinct from the particular perceptions.

So far I seem to be attended with sufficient evidence. But having thus loosen'd all our particular perceptions, when I proceed to explain the principle of connexion, which binds them together, and makes us attribute to them a real simplicity and identity; I am sensible, that my account is very defective, and that nothing but the seeming evidence of the precedent reasonings cou'd have induc'd me to receive it. If perceptions are distinct existences, they form a whole only by being connected together. But no connexions among distinct existences are ever discoverable by human understanding. We only feel a connexion or determination of the thought, to pass from one object to another. It follows, therefore, that the thought alone finds personal identity, when reflecting on the train of past perceptions, that compose a mind, the ideas of them are felt to be connected together, and naturally introduce each other. However extraordinary this conclusion may seem, it need not surprize us. Most philosophers seem inclin'd to think, that personal identity arises from consciousness; and consciousness is nothing but a reflected thought or perception. The present philosophy, therefore, has so far a promising aspect. But all my hopes vanish, when I come to explain the principles, that unite our successive perceptions in our thought or consciousness. I cannot discover any theory, which gives me satisfaction on this head.

In short there are two principles, which I cannot render consistent; nor is it in my power to renounce either of them, viz., [**first**] that all our distinct perceptions are distinct existences, and [**second**] that the mind never perceives any real connexion among distinct existences. Did our perceptions either inhere in something simple and individual, or did the mind perceive some real connexion among them, there wou'd be no difficulty in the case. For my part, I must plead the privilege of a sceptic, and confess, that this difficulty is too hard for my understanding. I pretend not, however, to pronounce it absolutely insuperable. Others, perhaps, or myself, upon more mature reflections, may discover some hypothesis, that will reconcile those contradictions.

8. Immanuel Kant (1724–1804)

- *Prolegomena to Every Future System of Metaphysics Which Can Claim to Rank as Science*, Introduction
- *Prolegomena*, Introductory Remarks on the Speciality of All Metaphysical Knowledge
  - Section One: Of the Source of Metaphysics
  - Section Two: Of the Mode of Cognition that can Alone be Termed Metaphysical
  - Section Three: Observation on the Universal Division of Judgments into Analytic and Synthetic
  - Section Four: The General Question of the Prolegomena: Is Metaphysics possible at all?
  - Section Five: General Question: How is Knowledge from Pure Reason possible?
  - Section Six: The Main Transcendental Question—First Part: How is pure Mathematics possible?
  - Section Seven: The First Part, Continued
  - Section Eight: The First Part, Continued
  - Section Nine: The First Part, Continued
  - Section Ten: The First Part, Continued
  - Section Eleven: The First Part, Continued
  - Section Twelve: The First Part, Continued
  - Section Thirteen: The First Part, Continued
- The CPR: "The Transcendental Aesthetic", Section One, "Of Space"
- The *Prolegomena*, Remark One
- The *Prolegomena*, Remark Two
- The *Prolegomena*, Remark Three
- The *Prolegomena*, Section Fourteen: The Main Transcendental Question—Second Part: How is pure Natural Science possible?
- Section Fifteen: The Second Part, Continued
- Section Sixteen: The Second Part, Continued
- Section Seventeen: The Second Part, Continued
- Section Eighteen: The Second Part, Continued
- Section Nineteen: The Second Part, Continued
- Section Twenty: The Second Part, Continued
- Section Twenty-one: The Second Part, Continued
- Logical Table of the Judgements
- Transcendental Table of the Concepts of the Understanding
- Section Twenty-one (A): The Second Part, Continued
- Section Twenty-two: The Second Part, Continued
- Section Twenty-three: The Second Part, Continued
- Section Twenty-five: The Second Part, Continued
- Section Twenty-six: The Second Part, Continued
- Section Twenty-seven: The Second Part, Continued
- Section Twenty-eight: The Second Part, Continued
- Section Twenty-nine: The Second Part, Continued
- Section Thirty: The Second Part, Continued

Born in Königsberg, Prussia, Immanuel Kant is the only writer included in this book to have been a philosophy professor. Kant published his massive Critique of Pure Reason (CPR) in 1781, which he revised in 1787. In between, he wrote the Prolegomena (1783). As you'll see, Kant was stung by the critical reception of the Critique; the Prolegomena is intended to serve as a kind of introduction to the Critique. I've interspersed relevant parts of the Critique within the text of the Prolegomena below.

Here, by section number, is an outline of the Prolegomena, using Kant's own headings. I've also indicated where i've introduced material from the CPR.

- Introduction
- Sections 6–13: How is pure mathematics possible?
- From the CPR: The Transcendental Aesthetic (Space)
- Sections 14–30: How is pure natural science possible?
- From the CPR: The Second Analogy
- Sections 31–39

From the CPR: Transcendental Deduction

- Sections 40–49: How is metaphysics possible at all?
- From CPR: The Paralogisms
- Sections 50–60: Conclusion

(*Textual note: the standard translations of Kant's work are in the Cambridge Edition of the* Works of Immanuel Kant in Translation. *Norman Kemp Smith's translation of the* Critique of Pure Reason *is still very useful, however.*)

Prolegomena to Every Future System of Metaphysics Which Can Claim to Rank as Science, Introduction

… My purpose is to convince all those who care to trouble themselves with metaphysics that it is indispensably necessary for the present to suspend their work, to look upon all that is gone before as non-existent, and, above all things, first to propose the question "Whether such a thing as metaphysics be even possible at all?"

If it be a science, how comes it that it cannot like other sciences win for itself a universal and lasting recognition? If it be not one, how is it that under the semblance of a science it is ceaselessly boasting and holding out to the human understanding hopes that are never extinguished and never fulfilled? Something must be definitely decided respecting the nature of this assumed science, whether it be to demonstrate our knowledge or our ignorance; for it is impossible that it should remain longer on the same footing as heretofore. It seems nearly ridiculous, while every other science ceaselessly progresses, that this which is supposed to be wisdom itself, whose oracle every one interrogates, is continually turning round on the same spot, without moving a step in advance. Its votaries have also much decreased, and we do not see those who feel themselves strong enough to shine in other sciences, willing to risk their fame in this, where every one, ignorant though he be in all else, ventures upon a decided opinion, because in this sphere there is no certain weight and measure at hand by which to distinguish profundity from worthless jargon.

It is, however, not unheard of, after lengthened treatment of a science, when wonders are thought as to the progress made in it, that some one lets fall the question: Whether and how such a science is possible at all? For the human Reason is so fond of building, that it has many times reared up a lofty tower and afterwards pulled it down again, to see how its foundation was laid. It is never too late to become reasonable and wise; but it is always more difficult when the knowledge comes late to bring it into working order.

To ask, whether a science is possible presupposes a doubt as to its reality. But such a doubt must offend all those whose whole fortune, perhaps, consists in this supposed treasure; any one who starts such a doubt may always make up his mind then for resistance on all sides. Some, in the proud consciousness of their old and therefore, as they think, legitimate possession, with their metaphysical compendiums in their hands, will look down upon it with contempt. Others, who never see anything anywhere that does not coincide with what they have elsewhere previously seen, will not understand it, and everything will remain for some time as though nothing at all had happened to prepare or to admit the hope of a near change.

At the same time, I may confidently predict that the open-minded reader of these *Prolegomena* will not merely doubt his previous science, but in the end will be quite convinced, that there cannot exist such a science without the demands here made being satisfied, upon which its possibility rests, and that inasmuch as this has never happened, that there is as yet no such thing as metaphysics at all. But as notwithstanding the search after it can never lose its interest, because the interests of the universal human Reason are so intimately bound up with it, he will confess that a complete reform, or rather a new birth according to a plan hitherto quite unknown, is inevitable, however much it may be striven against for a time.

Since the attempts of Locke and Leibniz, or rather since the first rise of metaphysics as far as its history will reach, no event has occurred that in view of the fortunes of the science could be more decisive than the attack made upon it by David Hume. He threw no light upon this order of knowledge, but he struck a spark by which a light might have been kindled, had it touched a receptive substance, to have preserved and enlarged its glimmer.

Hume took for his starting-point, mainly, a single but important conception of metaphysics, namely, that of the *connection of Cause and Effect* (together with the derivative conceptions of Force and Action, &c.) and required of the Reason which professes to have given it birth a rigid justification of its right, to think, that something is so constructed that on its being posited something else is therewith necessarily also posited; for so much is contained in the conception of Cause. He proved irrefutably that it is quite impossible for Reason *a priori*, out of mere conceptions, to cogitate this connection, since it involves necessity; but the problem nevertheless was not to be overlooked, how that, because something exists, something else must necessarily also exist, and thus how the conception of such a connection can be regarded as *a priori*. Hence he concluded that Reason completely deceived itself with this conception, that it falsely claimed it as its own child, while it was nothing more than a bastard of the imagination, which, impregnated by experience, had brought certain presentations under the law of association, and had substituted a subjective necessity arising thence, i.e., from habit, for an objective one founded on insight. From this he concluded that Reason possessed no faculty of cogitating such connections even in general, because its conceptions would then be mere inventions, and all its pretended *a priori* cognitions nothing but common experiences mislabelled; which is as much as to say, no such thing as metaphysics exists at all, and there is no possibility of its ever existing.

However hasty and incorrect his conclusion may have been, it was at least based on investigation, and it would have been well worth while if the good heads of his time had united to solve the problem in the sense in which he had stated it, if as far as possible with happier results; the consequence of which must have been a speedy and complete reform of the science.

But the always unfavourable fate of metaphysics, willed that he should be understood by no one. It is positively painful to see how completely his opponents, Reid, Oswald, Beattie, and, lastly, Priestley, missed the point of his problem in taking that for granted which was precisely what he doubted, and on the other hand in proving with warmth, and in most cases great immodesty, what it had never entered his head to question, and as a result in so completely mistaking his reforming hint that everything remained in the same state as though nothing had happened. It was not the question whether the conception of Cause was correct and useful, and in view of the whole knowledge of Nature, indispensable, for upon this Hume had never cast a doubt, but whether it could be cogitated *a priori* by Reason in such a manner as to constitute an inward truth independent of all experience, and therefore of a more extended use than that of being solely applied to the objects of experience; it was upon this that Hume desired enlightenment. The question was as to the origin of the idea, not as to its practical necessity in use; were the former ascertained, the conditions of its use and the extent in which it is valid would have been sufficiently obvious.

The opponents of this celebrated man, to have done the problem full justice, must have penetrated deeply into the nature of Reason, in so far as it is occupied solely with pure thought, a thing which was inconvenient for them. They invented therefore a more convenient means, by which, without any insight, they might defy him, namely, the appeal to the *common sense* of mankind. It is indeed a great natural gift to possess, straightforward (or, as it has been recently called, plain) common sense. But it must be proved by deeds, by the thoughtfulness and rationality of what one thinks and says, and not by appealing to it as an oracle, when one has nothing wise to adduce in one's justification. When insight and science are at a low ebb, then and not before to appeal to common sense is one of the subtle inventions of modern times, by which the emptiest talker may coolly confront the profoundest thinker and hold out against him. But so long as there is a small remnant of insight left, one will be cautious of clutching at this straw. And seen in its true light, the argument is nothing better than an appeal to the verdict of the multitude; a clamour before which the philosopher blushes, and the popular witling scornfully triumphs. But I should think that Hume can make as good claim to the possession of common sense as Beattie, and in addition, to something the latter certainly did not possess, namely, a critical Reason, to hold common sense within bounds in order not to let it overreach itself in speculations; or if we are merely concerned with the latter, not to require it to decide, seeing that it is incompetent to deal with matters outside its own axioms; for only in this way will it remain a healthy common sense. Chisel and hammer are quite sufficient to shape a piece of deal, but for copper-engraving an etching-needle is necessary. In the same way, common, no less than speculative understanding, is useful in its kind; the former when we have to do with judgments having an immediate bearing on experience, but the latter, where we have to judge, universally, out of mere conceptions, as for instance in metaphysics, where the self-styling (though often *per antiphrasin*) healthy understanding is capable of no judgment at all.

I readily confess, the reminder of David Hume was what many years ago first broke my dogmatic slumber, and gave my researches in the field of speculative philosophy quite a different direction. I was far enough removed from giving him an ear so far as his consequences were concerned, the latter resulting merely from his not having placed his problem fully before him, but only attacking a part of it, which, without taking the whole into consideration, could not possibly afford a solution. When one starts from a well-founded, though undeveloped, idea that a predecessor has left, one may well hope, by increased reflection, to bring it further than was possible for the acute man one has to thank for the original sparks of its light.

First of all, I tried whether Hume's observation could not be made general, and soon found that the conception of the connection of cause and effect was not by a long way the only one by which the understanding cogitates *a priori* the connections of things, but that metaphysics consists entirely of such. I endeavoured to ascertain their number, and as I succeeded in doing this to my satisfaction, namely, out of a single principle, I proceeded to the deduction of these conceptions, which I was now assured could not, as Hume had pretended, be derived from experience but must have originated in the pure understanding. This deduction, that seemed impossible to my acute predecessor, that had not even occurred to any one except him, although every one unconcernedly used the conception (without asking on what its objective validity rested); this, I say, was the most difficult problem that could ever be undertaken in the interests of metaphysics, and the worst of it was, that metaphysics, so far as it anywhere exists at present, could not afford me the least help, because the above deduction had in the first place to make metaphysics possible.

Having now succeeded in the solution of Hume's problem, not in one particular case only, but in respect of the whole capacity of pure Reason, I could at least more surely, though still only by slow steps, determine the whole range of pure Reason, in its limits as well as in its content, completely according to universal principles, which was what metaphysics required, in order to construct its system on an assured plan.

I am afraid, however, lest the carrying out of the problem of Hume in its greatest possible development (namely, in the *Critique of Pure Reason*) should fare as the problem itself fared when it was first stated. It will be falsely judged, because it is misunderstood; it will be misunderstood, because people, though they may care to turn over the leaves of the book, will not care to think it out; and they will be unwilling to expend this trouble upon it because the work is dry, obscure, and opposed to all accustomed conceptions, besides being diffuse. But I must confess, it was quite unexpected for me to hear from a philosopher complaints as to its want of popularity, entertainingness, and agreeable arrangement, when the question was of a branch of knowledge highly prized and indispensable to humanity, and which cannot be treated otherwise than according to the most strict rules of scholastic precision; whereby popularity may indeed follow in time, but can never be expected at the commencement. As regards a certain obscurity, however, arising partly from the diffuseness of the plan, in consequence of which the main points of the investigation are not so readily grasped, the grievance must be admitted, and this it is the task of the present *Prolegomena* to remove.

The above work, which presents the capacity of pure Reason in its whole range and boundaries, always remains the foundation to which the *Prolegomena* are only preparatory; for the *Critique* must, as science, stand complete and systematic even down to the smallest detail, before we can so much as think of the rise of metaphysics, or even allow ourselves the most distant hope in this direction.

We have been long accustomed to see old and worn-out branches of knowledge receive a new support, by being taken out of their former coverings, and suited with a systematic garment according to our own approved style, but under new titles; and the great majority of readers will expect nothing different from our *Critique*. But these *Prolegomena* will convince him that it is quite a new science, of which no one previously had had the smallest conception, of which even the idea was unknown, and with reference to which all hitherto received knowledge was unavailable, with the exception of the hint afforded by Hume's doubt. But Hume never dreamt of a possible formal science of this nature, and in order to land his ship in safety, ran it aground on the shore of scepticism, where it might lie and rot; instead of which, it is my purpose to furnish a pilot, who, according to certain principles of seamanship, derived from a knowledge of the globe, and supplied with a complete map and compass, may steer the ship with safety wherever it seems good to him.
...

---

1. As Kant reads him, what exactly was Hume calling into question?
2. Is Hume's problem merely about causation, or does it extend to other concepts? Why, or why not?

Prolegomena, Introductory Remarks on the Speciality of All Metaphysical Knowledge

Section One: Of the Source of Metaphysics

In presenting a branch of knowledge as *science*, it is necessary to be able to define with precision its distinguishing characteristic, that which it possesses in common with no other branch, and which is therefore *special* to itself; when this is not the case the boundaries of all sciences run into one another, and no one of them can be thoroughly treated of, according to its own nature.

Now this speciality may consist in the distinction of its *object*, of its *sources of cognition*, of its *mode of cognition*, or lastly, of several if not all these points taken together, on which the idea of a possible science and of its territory primarily rests.

Firstly, as regards the *sources* of metaphysical knowledge, the very conception of the latter shows that these cannot be empirical. Its principles (under which not merely its axioms, but also its fundamental conceptions are included) must consequently never be derived from experience; since it is not *physical* but *metaphysical* knowledge, i.e., knowledge beyond experience, that is wanted. Thus neither external experience, the source of physical science proper, nor internal experience, the groundwork of empirical psychology, will suffice for its foundation. It consists, then, in knowledge *a priori*, that is, knowledge derived from pure understanding and pure reason. ...

Section Two: Of the Mode of Cognition that can Alone be Termed Metaphysical

a. *Of the distinction between synthetic and analytic judgments generally.*

Metaphysical knowledge must contain simply judgments *a priori*, so much is demanded by the speciality of its sources. But judgments, let them have what origin they may, or let them even as regards logical form be constituted as they may, possess a distinction according to their content, by virtue of which they are either simply *explanatory* and contribute nothing to the content of a cognition, or they are *extensive*, and enlarge the given cognition; the first may be termed *analytic*, and the second *synthetic* judgments.

Analytic judgments say nothing in the predicate, but what was already cogitated in the conception of the subject, though perhaps not so clearly, or with the same degree of consciousness. When I say, all bodies are extended, I do not thereby enlarge my conception of a body in the least, but simply analyse it, inasmuch as extension, although not expressly stated, was already cogitated in that conception; the judgment is, in other words, analytic. On the other hand, the proposition, some bodies are heavy, contains something in the predicate which was not already cogitated in the general conception of a body; it enlarges, that is to say, my knowledge, in so far as it adds something to my conception; and must therefore be termed a synthetic judgment.

b. *The common principle of all analytic judgments is the principle of contradiction.*

All analytic judgments are based entirely on the principle of contradiction, and are by their nature cognitions *a priori*, whether the conceptions serving as their matter be empirical or not. For inasmuch as the predicate of an affirmative analytic judgment is previously cogitated in the conception of the subject, it cannot without contradiction be denied of it; in the same way, its contrary, in a negative analytic judgment, must necessarily be denied of the subject, likewise in accordance with the principle of contradiction. It is thus with the propositions—every body is extended; no body is unextended (simple). For this reason all analytic propositions are judgments *a priori*, although their conceptions may be empirical. Let us take as an instance the proposition, gold is a yellow metal. Now, to know this, I require no further experience beyond my conception of gold, which contains the propositions that this body is yellow and a metal; for this constitutes precisely my conception, and therefore I have only to dissect it, without needing to look around for anything elsewhere.

c. *Synthetic judgments demand a principle other than that of contradiction.*

There are synthetic judgments *a posteriori* whose origin is empirical; but there are also others of an *a priori* certainty, that spring from the Understanding and Reason. But both are alike in this, that they can never have their source solely in the axiom of analysis, viz., the principle of contradiction; they require an altogether different principle, notwithstanding that whatever principle they may be deduced from, they must always *conform to the principle of contradiction*, for nothing can be opposed to this principle, although not everything can be deduced from it. I will first of all bring synthetic judgments under certain classes.

1. *Judgments of experience* are always synthetic. It would be absurd to found an analytic judgment on experience, as it is unnecessary to go beyond my own conception in order to construct the judgment, and therefore the confirmation of experience is unnecessary to it. That a body is extended is a proposition possessing *a priori* certainty, and no judgment of experience. For before I go to experience I have all the conditions of my judgment already present in the conception, out of which I simply draw the predicate in accordance with the principle of contradiction, and thereby at the same time the *necessity* of the judgment may be known, a point which experience could never teach me.

2. *Mathematical judgments* are in their entirety synthetic. This truth seems hitherto to have altogether escaped the analysts of human Reason; indeed, to be directly opposed to all their suppositions, although it is indisputably certain and very important in its consequences. For, because it was found that the conclusions of mathematicians all proceed according to the principle of contradiction (which the nature of every apodictic certainty demands), it was concluded that the axioms were also known through the principle of contradiction, which was a great error; for though a synthetic proposition can be viewed in the light of the above principle, it can only be so by presupposing another synthetic proposition from which it is derived, but never by itself.

It must be first of all remarked that essentially mathematical propositions are always *a priori*, and never empirical, because they involve necessity, which cannot be inferred from experience. Should any one be unwilling to admit this, I will limit my assertion to *pure mathematics*, the very conception of which itself brings with it the fact that it contains nothing empirical, but simply pure knowledge *a priori*.

At first sight, one might be disposed to think the proposition $7+5=12$ merely analytic, resulting from the conception of a sum of seven and five, according to the principle of contradiction. But more closely considered it will be found that the conception of the sum of 7 and 5 comprises nothing beyond the union of two numbers in a single one, and that therein nothing whatever is cogitated as to what this single number is, that comprehends both the others. The conception of twelve is by no means already cogitated, when I think merely of the union of seven and five, and I may dissect my conception of such a possible sum as long as I please, without discovering therein the number twelve. One must leave these conceptions, and call to one's aid an intuition corresponding to one or other of them, as for instance one's five fingers (or, like Segner in his Arithmetic, five points), and so gradually add the units of the five given in intuition to the conception of the seven. One's conception is therefore really enlarged by the proposition $7+5=12$;

to the first a new one being added, that was in nowise cogitated in the former; in other words, arithmetical propositions are always synthetic, a truth which is more apparent when we take rather larger numbers, for we must then be clearly convinced, that turn and twist our conceptions as we may, without calling intuition to our aid, we shall never find the sum required, by the mere dissection of them.

Just as little is any axiom of pure geometry analytic. That a *straight* line is the shortest between two points, is a synthetic proposition. For my conception of *straight*, has no reference to size, but only to quality. The conception of the "shortest" therefore is quite additional, and cannot be drawn from any analysis of the conception of a straight line. Intuition must therefore again be taken to our aid, by means of which alone the synthesis is possible.

Certain other axioms, postulated by geometricians, are indeed really analytic and rest on the principle of contradiction, but they only serve, like identical propositions, as links in the chain of method, and not themselves as principles; as for instance a=a, the whole is equal to itself, or (a+b) > a, i.e., the whole is greater than its part. But even these, although they are contained in mere conceptions, are only admitted in mathematics because they can be presented in intuition. What produces the common belief that the predicate of such apodictic judgments lies already in our conception, and that the judgment is therefore analytic, is merely the ambiguity of expression. We *ought*, namely, to cogitate a certain predicate to a given conception, and this necessity adheres even to the conceptions themselves. But the question is not what we *ought* to, but what we actually *do*, although obscurely, cogitate in them; this shows us that the predicate of those conceptions is dependent indeed necessarily, though not immediately (but by means of an added intuition), upon its subject.

Section Three: Observation on the Universal Division of Judgments into Analytic and Synthetic

This division is in view of the Critique of human understanding indispensable, and deserves therefore to be classic in this department; though I am not aware of any other in which it has any important use. And here I also find the cause why dogmatic philosophers who looked for the sources of metaphysical judgments in metaphysics itself (rather than outside of it, in the laws of pure Reason in general), have always neglected this division, that seems so naturally to offer itself, and like the celebrated Wolff, or the acute Baumgarten, who followed in his steps, have sought the proof of the principle of sufficient reason, which is obviously synthetic, in that of contradiction. On the other hand, I can trace already in Locke's *Essay Concerning Human Understanding* a notion of this division. For in the third chapter of the fourth book, (Chapter Three, Section Nine, *et seq.*,) after he has spoken of the connection of different presentations in judgments, and of their sources, one of which he places in identity or contradiction (analytic judgments), and the other in the existence of presentations in a subject (synthetic judgments), he confesses (Section Ten) that our knowledge (*a priori*) of the last is very limited, amounting almost to nothing. But there is so little that is definite and reduced to rule in what he says respecting this kind of knowledge, that one cannot wonder that nobody, strange to say, not excepting hume, was induced thereby to institute investigations into the class of propositions in question. For universal yet definite principles like these, are not easily learnt from other men, to whom they have been only dimly discernible. One must, first of all, have come upon them through one's own reflection, and one will then find them elsewhere, in places where otherwise they would certainly not have been discovered; since not even the authors knew that such an idea lay at the foundation of their own remarks. ...

Section Four: The General Question of the Prolegomena: Is Metaphysics possible at all?

Were metaphysics actually present as a science, one might say: Here is metaphysics, you only require to learn it, and it will convince you permanently and irresistibly of its truth. In that case the present question would be unnecessary, and there would only remain one which would more concern a testing of our acuteness, than a proof of the existence of the thing itself; namely, the question, How is it possible, and how is Reason to set about attaining it? Unfortunately, in this case, human Reason is not in such a happy position. There is no single book that can be shown, like for instance Euclid, of which it can be said: This is metaphysics, herein is to be found the chief end of the science, the knowledge of a Supreme Being and of a future world, demonstrated upon principles of pure Reason. It is possible, doubtless, to bring forward many propositions that are apodictically certain, and that have never been contested; but these are in their entirety analytic, and concern more the materials and the elements of construction, than the extension of knowledge, which is our special object in the present case. But even when synthetic propositions are produced (such as the principle of sufficient Reason), which though they have never been proved from mere Reason, that is, *a priori*, as they ought to have been, are willingly admitted; even then, whenever it is attempted to make use of them for the main purpose, one is landed in such unstable and doubtful assertions, that it has always happened that one system of metaphysics has contradicted another, either in respect of the assertions themselves or their proofs, and has thus destroyed all claim to a lasting recognition. The very attempts made to establish the science have without doubt been the primary cause of the scepticism that so early arose, a mode of thought in which Reason treats itself with such violence, that it would never have arisen but from the latter's utter despair of satisfying its chief aspirations. For long before man began methodically to question Nature, he interrogated his own isolated Reason, already practised, in a measure by common experience; because Reason is always present, while the laws of Nature generally require to be laboriously sought out. And so metaphysics floated to the surface like foam, and like foam, too, no sooner was it gathered up than it dissolved, while another mass of it appeared upon the scene which some were always found eager to grasp; while others, instead of seeking to penetrate the cause of the phenomenon in question, thought themselves wise in laughing at the futile exertions of the former.

The essential feature distinguishing pure mathematical knowledge from all other knowledge *a priori*, is that it does not proceed from conceptions themselves, but always through the construction of conceptions. (*Critique*, p. 435.) Since, therefore, in its propositions it must pass out of the conception to that containing the corresponding intuition, these can and ought never to arise from the dissection of conceptions, that is, analytically; in other words, they are, in their entirety, synthetic.

I cannot refrain from remarking on the disadvantage resulting to philosophy from a neglect of this simple and apparently insignificant observation. Hume, indeed, feeling it a task worthy of a philosopher, cast his eye over the whole field of pure knowledge *a priori* in which the human understanding claims such extensive possession. He, however, inconsiderately severed from it an entire, and indeed the most important, province, namely, that of pure mathematics, under the impression that its nature, and, so to speak, its constitution, rested on totally different principles, that is, solely on the principle of contradiction; and although he did not make such a formal and universal division of propositions as is here done by me, or under the same name, yet it was as good as saying, pure mathematics contains simply analytic judgments, but metaphysics, synthetic judgments *a priori*. Now in this he made a great mistake, and this mistake had decidedly injurious consequences on his whole conception. For if he had not made it, he would have extended his question respecting the origin of our synthetic judgments far beyond his metaphysical conception of causality, and comprehended therein the possibility of mathematics a priori; for he must have regarded this as equally synthetic. But in the latter case he could, under no circumstances, have based his metaphysical propositions on mere experience, as he would then have been obliged to have subordinated the axioms of pure mathematics themselves to experience, a proceeding for which he was much too penetrating.

The good company into which metaphysics would then have been brought must have ensured it against contemptuous treatment; for the strokes aimed at the latter must have also hit the former, and this neither was nor could have been his intention. The result must have been to lead the acute man to considerations similar to those with which we are now occupied, but which must have gained infinitely by his inimitable style.

Essentially metaphysical judgments are, in their entirety, synthetic. We must distinguish between judgments belonging to metaphysics from metaphysical judgments proper. Among the former are comprised many that are analytic, but they only furnish the means for metaphysical judgments, these forming the entire purpose of the science, and being all synthetic. For when conceptions belong to metaphysics, as, for instance, that of substance, the judgments arising from their dissection belong also to metaphysics; e.g., substance is that which only exists as subject, &c., and many more similar analytic judgments, by means of which an endeavour is made to approach the definition of the conception. Since, however, the analysis of a pure conception of the understanding (such as those metaphysics contains) cannot proceed differently from the analysis of any other conception (even an empirical one) not belonging to metaphysics (e.g., air is an elastic fluid, the elasticity of which is not destroyed by any known degree of cold), it follows that the conception but not the analytic judgment, is properly metaphysical. The science in question has something special and peculiar in the production of its cognitions *a priori*, which must be distinguished from what it has in common with all other cognitions of the understanding; so, for instance, the proposition, "all that is substance in things is permanent," is a synthetic and properly metaphysical judgment.

When the conceptions *a priori* constituting the materials of metaphysics have been previously collected according to fixed principles, the dissection of these conceptions is of great value. They can be then presented as a special department (as it were a *philosophia definitiva*), containing solely analytic propositions relating to metaphysics, though quite distinct from the synthetic, which constitute metaphysics itself. For, indeed, these analyses have nowhere any important use, except in metaphysics, that is, in reference to the synthetic propositions, to be generated from these dissected conceptions.

The conclusion drawn in this section is then, that metaphysics is properly concerned with synthetic propositions *a priori*, and that these alone constitute its purpose, but that, in addition to this, it requires frequent dissections of its conceptions, or analytic judgments, the procedure in this respect being only the same as in other departments of knowledge, where conceptions are sought to be made plain by analysis. But the *generation* of knowledge *a priori*, as much in intuition as in conceptions, in fine, synthetic propositions *a priori* in philosophical cognitions, make up the essential content of metaphysics.

Wearied, then, of the dogmatism that teaches us nothing, as well as of the scepticism that promises us nothing, not even the rest of a permissible ignorance, led on by the importance of the knowledge we need, rendered mistrustful by a long experience, of all we believe ourselves to possess, or that offers itself in the name of pure Reason, there only remains one critical question, the answer to which must regulate our future procedure—Is *metaphysics possible at all?* But this question must not be answered by sceptical objections to particular assertions of any actual system of metaphysics (for we do not admit any at present), but from the, as yet, only problematical conception of such a science.

In the *Critique of Pure Reason*, I went synthetically to work in respect of this question, in instituting researches into pure Reason itself, and in this source endeavoured to determine the elements, as well as the laws of its pure use, according to principles. The task is difficult, and demands a resolute reader, gradually to think out a system, having no datum other than Reason itself, and which, therefore, without supporting itself on any fact, seeks to unfold knowledge from its original germs. Prolegomena should, on the contrary, be preparatory exercises, designed more to show what has to be done, to realise a science as far as is possible, than to expound one. They must, therefore, rely on something known as trustworthy, from which we may with confidence proceed, and ascend to its sources, as yet unknown to us, and the discovery of which will not only explain what we already knew, but at the same time exhibit to us a range of many cognitions, all arising from these same sources. The methodical procedure of Prolegomena, especially of those destined to prepare a future system of metaphysics, will therefore be analytic.

Now it fortunately happens that, although we cannot accept metaphysics as a real science, we may assert with confidence that certain pure synthetic cognitions are really given *a priori*, namely, pure mathematics and pure natural science, for both contain propositions, partly apodictically certain through mere Reason, and partly recognised by universal consent as coming from experience, and yet as completely independent of it.

We have, then, at least some uncontested, synthetic knowledge *a priori*, and do not require to ask whether this is possible, since it is actual, but only—*How it is possible*, in order to be able to deduce from the principle, rendering possible what is already given, the possibility of all the rest.

1. *Kant's 'regressive' method in the* Prolegomena *can be called a defense of metaphysics by means of a 'companions in virtue' strategy. Kant first identifies a key feature of metaphysical claims—they are synthetic and* a priori—*and then looks to see whether some more established sciences, whose existence and legitimacy we take for granted, share this feature. What other sciences fall into this category?*

Section Five: General Question: How is Knowledge from Pure Reason possible?

We have already seen the important distinction between analytic and synthetic judgments. The possibility of analytic propositions can be very easily conceived, for they are based simply on the principle of contradiction. The possibility of synthetic propositions *a posteriori*, i.e., of such as are derived from experience, requires no particular explanation, for experience is nothing more than a continual adding together (synthesis) of perceptions. There remains, then, only synthetic propositions *a priori*, the possibility of which has yet to be sought for, or examined, because it must rest on other principles than that of contradiction.

But we do not require to search out the possibility of such propositions, that is, to ask whether they are possible, for there are enough of them, actually given, and with unquestionable certainty; and as the method we are here following is analytic, we shall assume at the outset that such synthetic but pure knowledge from Reason, is real; but thereupon we must investigate the ground of this possibility and proceed to ask—*How is this knowledge possible?* in order that, from the principles of its possibility, we may be in a position to determine the conditions, the scope, and limits of its use. The proper problem, on which everything turns, when expressed with scholastic precision, will accordingly stand thus—*How are synthetic propositions* a priori *possible?*

In the above, for the sake of popularity, I have expressed the question somewhat differently, namely, as an inquiry after knowledge from pure Reason, which I could do on this occasion without detriment to the desired insight. For as we are here simply concerned with metaphysics and its sources, I hope, after the above remarks, readers will constantly bear in mind that, when we here speak of knowledge from pure Reason, we invariably refer to synthetic and never to analytic knowledge. Upon the solution of this problem, the standing or falling of metaphysics, in other words, its very existence, entirely depends. Let any one lay down assertions, however plausible, with regard to it, pile up conclusions upon conclusions to the point of overwhelming, if he has not been able first to answer satisfactorily the above question, I have a right to say: It is all vain, baseless philosophy, and false wisdom. You speak through pure Reason, and claim to create *a priori* cognitions, inasmuch as you pretend not merely to dissect given conceptions but new connections which do not rest on the principle of contradiction, and which you think you conceive quite independently of all experience. How do you arrive at them, and how will you justify yourself in such pretensions? To appeal to the concurrence of the general common sense of mankind you cannot be allowed, for that is a witness whose reputation rests only on vulgar report.

But indispensable as is the answer to this question, it is at the same time no less difficult, and although the chief cause why men have not long ago endeavoured to answer it, lies in the fact of its never having occurred to them that anything of the kind could be asked; there is a second cause, in that the satisfactory answer to this one question demands a more persistent, a deeper and more laborious reflection than the most diffuse work, on metaphysics, the first appearance of which has given promise of immortal fame to its author. And every thoughtful reader, on attentively considering the requirement of this problem, frightened at the outset by its difficulty, would regard it as insoluble; and indeed, were it not for the actual existence of such pure synthetic cognitions *a priori*, as altogether impossible. This happened in the case of David Hume, although he did not place the problem before him in such generality by far as is here done, and as must be done if the answer is to be decisive for the whole of metaphysics. For how is it possible, said the acute man, that when a conception is given me, I can pass out of it, and connect it with another, which is not contained in the former, and indeed in such a manner as if it necessarily belonged to it? Only experience can present us with such connections (this he concluded from the difficulty which he mistook for an impossibility), and all this imagined necessity, or, what is the same thing, knowledge assumed to be *a priori*, is nothing but a long habit of finding something true, and thence of holding the subjective necessity for objective. If the reader complains of the difficulty and trouble I shall give him in the solution of this problem, let him only set about the attempt to solve it in an easier way. He will then perhaps feel obliged to one who has undertaken for him the labour of such deep research, and rather show some surprise at the facility with which the solution has been able to be given, when the nature of the subject is taken into account. It has cost years of trouble to solve this problem in its whole universality (in the sense in which mathematicians use this word, namely, as sufficient for all cases), and to be able finally to present it in analytic form, such as the reader will here find.

All metaphysicians are therefore solemnly and lawfully suspended from their occupations, till they shall have adequately answered the question—*How are synthetic cognitions* a priori *possible?* for in their answer alone consists the credentials they must produce, if they have aught to bring us in the name of pure Reason;

in default of this, they can expect nothing else, than to be rejected, without any further inquiry as to their productions, by sensible people who have been so often deceived.

If, on the other hand, they carry on their business not as a *science*, but as an art of wholesome persuasion, suitable to the general common sense of mankind, this calling cannot in fairness be denied them. In that case they will only use the modest language of a rational belief; they will admit that it is not allowed them even to *conjecture*, much less to *know*, anything, respecting that which lies beyond the boundaries of all possible experience, but merely to *assume* (not indeed for speculative use, for this they must renounce, but for purely practical purposes) what is possible and even indispensable for the direction of the understanding and will, in life. In this way alone can they possibly carry the reputation of wise and useful men, and they will do so the more in proportion as they renounce that of metaphysicians. For the object of the latter is to be speculative philosophers, and inasmuch as when we are concerned with judgments *a priori*, bare probabilities are not to be relied on (for what on its assumption is known *a priori*, is thereby announced as necessary), it cannot be allowed them to play with conjectures, but their assertions must be either *science*, or they are nothing at all.

It may be said that the whole transcendental philosophy which necessarily precedes all metaphysics is itself nothing more than the full solution in systematic order and completeness of the question here propounded, and that therefore as yet we have no transcendental philosophy. For what bears its name is properly a part of metaphysics, but the former science must first constitute the possibility of the latter, and must therefore precede all metaphysics. Considering, then, that a complete and in itself entirely new science, and one respecting which no aid is to be derived from other sciences, is necessary before a single question can be adequately answered, it is not to be wondered at if the solution of the same is attended with trouble and difficulty, and even perhaps with some degree of obscurity.

As we now proceed to this solution according to analytic method, in which we presuppose that such cognitions from pure Reason are real, we can only call to our aid two sciences of theoretic knowledge (with which alone we are here concerned), namely, *pure mathematics* and *pure natural science*, for only these can present to us objects in intuition, and therefore (if a cognition *a priori* should occur in them) show their truth or agreement with the object *in concreto*, i.e., their reality; from which to the ground of their possibility we can proceed on the analytic road. This facilitates the matter very much, as the universal considerations are not merely applied to facts but even start from them, rather than as in synthetic procedure, being obliged to be derived, wholly *in abstracto*, from conceptions.

But from these real and at the same time well-grounded pure cognitions *a priori*, to rise to a possible one such as we are seeking, namely, to metaphysics as a science, we must needs embrace under our main question that which occasions it, to wit, the naturally given, though as regards its truth not unsuspicious, knowledge *a priori* lying at its foundation, and the working out of which, without any critical examination of its possibility, is now usually called metaphysics—in a word, the natural tendency to such a science; and thus the transcendental main question, divided into four other questions, will be answered step by step:

1. How is pure mathematics possible?
2. How is pure natural science possible?
3. How is metaphysics in general possible?
4. How is metaphysics as a science possible?

It will be seen, that although the solution of these problems is chiefly meant to illustrate the essential contents of the *Critique*, it has nevertheless something special, which is of itself worthy of attention, namely, to seek the sources of given sciences in Reason, in order to investigate and measure this, their faculty of knowing something *a priori*, by means of the act itself. In this way the particular science itself must gain, if not in respect of its content, at least as regards its right employment, and while it throws light on the higher question of its common origin, at the same time give occasion to better elucidating its own nature.

Section Six: The Main Transcendental Question—First Part: How is pure Mathematics possible?

Here is a great and established branch of knowledge, already of remarkable compass, and promising unbounded extension in the future, carrying with it a thorough apodictic certainty, i.e., absolute necessity, and thus resting on no empirical grounds, but being a pure product of Reason, besides thoroughly synthetic. "How is it possible for the human Reason to bring about such a branch of knowledge entirely a priori?" Does not this capacity, as it does not and cannot stand on experience, presuppose some ground of knowledge *a priori*, lying deep-hidden, but which might reveal itself through these its effects, if their first beginnings were only diligently searched for?

Section Seven: The First Part, Continued

But we find that all mathematical knowledge has this speciality, that it must present its conception previously in *intuition*, and indeed *a priori*, that is, in an intuition that is not empirical but pure, without which means it cannot make a single step; its judgments therefore are always intuitive, whereas philosophy must be satisfied with *discursive* judgments out of mere conceptions; for though it can explain its apodictic doctrines by intuition, these can never be derived from such a source. This observation respecting the nature of mathematics, itself furnishes us with a guide as to the first and foremost condition of its possibility, namely, that *some pure intuition* must be at its foundation, wherein it can present all its conceptions *in concreto* and *a priori* at the same time, or as it is termed, construct them. If we can find out this pure intuition together with its possibility, it will be readily explicable how synthetic propositions *a priori* are possible in pure mathematics, and therefore, also, how this science is itself possible. For just as empirical intuition enables us, without difficulty, to extend synthetically in experience the conception we form of an object of intuition, by new predicates, themselves afforded us by intuition, so will the pure intuition, only with this difference: that in the last case the synthetic judgment *a priori* is certain and apodictic, while in the first case it is no more than *a posteriori* and empirically certain, because the latter only contains what is met with in chance empirical intuition, but the former what is necessarily met with in the pure intuition, inasmuch as being intuition *a priori*, it is indissolubly bound up with the conception before all experience or perception of individual things.

Section Eight: The First Part, Continued

But the difficulty seems rather to increase than to diminish by this step. For the question is now: How is it possible to intuit anything *a priori*? Intuition is a presentation, as it would immediately depend on the presence of the object. It seems therefore impossible to intuit originally *a priori*, because the intuition must then take place without either a previous or present object to which it could refer, and hence could not be intuition. Conceptions are indeed of a nature that some of them, namely, those containing only the thought of an object in general, may be very well formed *a priori*, without our being in immediate relation to the object (e.g., the conceptions of quantity, of cause, &c.), but even these require a certain use *in concreto*, i.e., an application to some intuition, if they are to acquire sense and meaning, whereby an object of them is to be given us. But how can intuition of an object precede the object itself?

Section Nine: The First Part, Continued

Were our intuition of such a nature as to present *things as they are in themselves*, no intuition *a priori* would take place at all, but it would always be empirical. For what is contained in the object in itself, I can only know when it is given and present to me. It is surely then inconceivable how the intuition of a present thing should enable me to know it as it is in itself, seeing that its properties cannot pass over into my presentative faculty. But granting the possibility of this, the said intuition would not take place *a priori*, that is, before the object was presented to me, for without it no ground of connection between my presentation and the object could be imagined; in which case it must rest on inspiration (*Eingebung*). Hence there is only one way possible, by which my intuition can precede the reality of the object and take place as knowledge *a priori*, and that is, if it contain nothing else but that form of sensibility which precedes in my subject all real impressions, by which I am affected by objects. For, that objects of sense can only be intuited in accordance with this form of sensibility, is a fact I can know *a priori*. From this it follows, that propositions merely concerning the form of sensible intuition, will be valid and possible for all objects of sense; and conversely, that intuitions possible *a priori*, can never concern other things than objects of our sense.

---

1. *What would go wrong if the objects of synthetic* a priori *knowledge (propositions like 'the shortest distance between two points is a straight line') were supposed to tell us about things as they are in themselves?*
2. *What then do such propositions tell us about?*

Section Ten: The First Part, Continued

Hence, it is only by means of the form of sensuous intuition that we can intuit things *a priori*, but in this way we intuit the objects only as they appear to our senses, not as they may be in themselves; an assumption absolutely necessary if synthetic propositions *a priori* are to be admitted as possible, or in the event of their being actually met with, if their possibility is to be conceived and defined beforehand.

Now, such intuitions are space and time, and these lie at the basis of all the cognitions and judgments of pure mathematics, exhibiting themselves at once as apodictic and necessary. For mathematics must present all its conceptions primarily in intuition, and pure mathematics in pure intuition, i.e., it must construct them. For without this it is impossible to make a single step, so long, that is to say, as a pure intuition is wanting, in which alone the matter of synthetic judgments *a priori* can be given; because it cannot proceed analytically, that is, by the dissection of conceptions, but is obliged to proceed synthetically. The pure intuition of space constitutes the basis of geometry—even arithmetic brings about its numerical conceptions by the successive addition of units in time; but above all, pure mechanics can evolve its conception of motion solely with the aid of the presentation of time. Both presentations, however, are mere intuitions; for when all that is empirical, namely, that belongs to feeling, is left out of the empirical intuitions of bodies and their changes (motion), space and time still remain over, and are therefore pure intuitions, lying *a priori* at the foundation of the former. For this reason, they can never be left out, but being pure intuitions *a priori*, prove that they are the bare forms of our sensibility, which must precede all empirical intuition, i.e., the perception of real objects, and in accordance with which objects can be known *a priori*, though only as they appear to us.

Section Eleven: The First Part, Continued

The problem of the present section is therefore solved. Pure mathematics is only possible as synthetic knowledge *a priori*, in so far as it refers simply to objects of sense, whose empirical intuition has for its foundation a pure intuition *a priori* (that of time and space), which intuition is able to serve as a foundation, because it is nothing more than the pure form of sensibility itself, that precedes the real appearance of objects, in that it makes them in the first place possible. Yet this faculty of intuiting *a priori* does not concern the matter of the phenomenon, i.e., that which is feeling (*Empfindung*) in the latter, for this constitutes the empirical element therein; but only its form, space and time. Should anybody cast the least doubt on the fact that neither of them are conditions of things in themselves, but only dependent on their relation to sensibility. I should be glad to be informed how he deems it possible to know *a priori*, and therefore before all acquaintance with the things, that is, before they are given us, how their intuition must be constructed, as is here the case with space and time. Yet this is quite conceivable, as soon as they both count for nothing more than formal determinations of our sensibility, and the objects merely as phenomena, for in that case the form of the phenomenon, that is, the pure intuition, can be conceived as coming from ourselves, in other words, as *a priori*.

---

1. *What makes mathematics possible? How can we anticipate geometrical features of all objects of possible experience* before *we experience them?*

Section Twelve: The First Part, Continued

To contribute something to the explanation and confirmation of the above, we have only to consider the ordinary and necessary procedure of geometricians. All the proofs of complete likeness between two given figures, turn at last upon the fact of their covering each other; in other words, of the possibility of substituting one, in every point, for the other, which is obviously nothing else but a synthetic proposition resting on immediate intuition. Now this intuition must be given pure and *a priori*, for otherwise the proposition in question could not count as apodictically certain, but would possess only empirical certainty. We could only say in that case, it has been always so observed, or it is valid so far as our perception has hitherto extended. That complete space, itself no boundary of a further space, has three dimensions, and that no space can have more than this number, is founded on the proposition that not more than three lines can bisect each other at right angles in a single point. But this proposition cannot be presented from conceptions, but rests immediately on intuition, and indeed on pure *a priori* intuition, because it is apodictically certain that we can require a line to be drawn out to infinity (*in indefinitum*), or that a series of changes (e.g., spaces passed through by motion) shall be continued to infinity, and this presupposes a presentation of space and time, merely dependent on intuition, namely, so far as in itself, it is bounded by nothing, for from conceptions it could never be concluded. Pure intuitions *a priori*, then, really lie at the foundation of mathematics, and these make its synthetic and apodictically valid propositions possible, and hence our transcendental deduction of conceptions in space and time explains at the same time the possibility of pure mathematics, which without such a deduction, and without our assuming that "all which can be given to our senses (the outer in space, the inner in time) is only intuited by us, as it appears to us, and not as it is in itself," might indeed be conceded, but could in nowise be understood.

Section Thirteen: The First Part, Continued

Those who are unable to free themselves from the notion, that space and time are real qualities (*Beschaffenheiten*) appertaining to the things in themselves, may exercise their wits on the following paradoxes, and when they have in vain attempted their solution, may suppose, being freed from their prejudices at least for a few moments, that perhaps the degradation of space and time to the position of mere forms of our sensible intuition, may have some foundation.

When two things are exactly alike [equal] in all points that can be cognised in each by itself (i.e., in all respecting quantity or quality), it must follow, that one can in all cases and relations be put in the place of the other, without this substitution occasioning the least cognisable difference. This indeed applies to plane figures in geometry; but there are many spherical figures, which in spite of this complete internal agreement exhibit in their external relations an agreement falling short of admitting one to be put in the place of the other.

For instance, two spherical triangles on opposite hemispheres, having an arc of the equator as a common base, are perfectly equal both in respect of their sides and their angles, so that in neither of them, if separately and at the same time completely described, would anything be found which was not equally present in the other; and yet notwithstanding this, one cannot be put in the place of the other, i.e., on the opposite hemisphere, and herein consists the internal difference of both triangles, that no understanding can indicate as internal, but which reveals itself only by means of the external relation in space. I will now adduce some more ordinary cases taken from common life.

What can more resemble my hand or my ear, and be in all points more like, than its image in the looking-glass? And yet I cannot put such a hand as I see in the glass in the place of its original; for when the latter is a right hand, the one in the glass is a left hand, and the image of the right ear is a left one, which can never take the place of the former. Now, here there are no internal differences that could be imagined by any understanding. And yet the differences are internal, so far as the senses teach us, for the left hand cannot, despite all equality and similarity, be enclosed within the same bounds as the right (they are not congruent); the glove of one hand cannot be used for the other. What then is the solution? These objects are not presentations of things as they are in themselves, and as the pure understanding would cognise them, but they are sensuous intuitions, i.e., phenomena, the possibility of which rests on the relations of certain unknown *things in themselves* to something else, namely, to our sensibility. Now, space is the form of the outward intuition of these, and the inward determination of every space is only possible through the determination of outward relations to the whole space, of which each [separate] space is a part (i.e., by its relation to the outward sense); in other words, the part is only possible through the whole, which though it could never be the case with things in themselves, namely, with objects of the mere understanding, can very well be so with mere phenomena. Hence we can render the difference of similar and equal, though incongruent things (e.g., spirals winding opposite ways) intelligible by no single conception, but only by the relation of the right and left hands, which refers immediately to intuition.

---

1. *Kant here appeals to 'incongruent counterparts'—objects that are qualitatively identical in all their internal relations (in the case of the hands, the relation between thumb and forefinger, say) and yet cannot be substituted one for another. Can you think of other pairs of incongruent counterparts?*

Kant goes on in the Prolegomena *to answer some objections (see his three 'Remarks' below). But before turning to objections, we should look at Kant's arguments for his position from the* Critique. *In this selection, from the 'Transcendental Aesthetic' of the CPR, Kant lays out four arguments about space.*

The *CPR*: "The Transcendental Aesthetic", Section One, "Of Space"

1. Space[1] is not a conception which has been derived from outward experiences. For, in order that certain sensations may relate to something without me (that is, to something which occupies a different part of space from that in which I am); in like manner, in order that I may represent them not merely as without, of, and near to each other, but also in separate places, the representation of space must already exist as a foundation. Consequently, the representation of space cannot be borrowed from the relations of external phenomena through experience; but, on the contrary, this external experience is itself only possible through the said antecedent representation.
2. Space then is a necessary representation *a priori*, which serves for the foundation of all external intuitions. We never can imagine or make a representation to ourselves of the non-existence of space, though we may easily enough think that no objects are found in it. It must, therefore, be considered as the condition of the possibility of phenomena, and by no means as a determination dependent on them, and is a representation *a priori*, which necessarily supplies the basis for external phenomena.
3. Space is no discursive, or as we say, general conception of the relations of things, but a pure intuition. For, in the first place, we can only represent to ourselves one space, and, when we talk of divers spaces, we mean only parts of one and the same space. Moreover, these parts cannot antecede this one all-embracing space, as the component parts from which the aggregate can be made up, but can be cogitated only as existing in it. Space is essentially one, and multiplicity in it, consequently the general notion of spaces, of this or that space, depends solely upon limitations. Hence it follows that an *a priori* intuition (which is not empirical) lies at the root of all our conceptions of space. Thus, moreover, the principles of geometry—for example, that "in a triangle, two sides together are greater than the third," are never deduced from general conceptions of line and triangle, but from intuition, and this *a priori*, with apodictic certainty.
4. Space is represented as an infinite given quantity. Now every conception must indeed be considered as a representation which is contained in an infinite multitude of different possible representations, which, therefore, comprises these under itself; but no conception, as such, can be so conceived, as if it contained within itself an infinite multitude of representations. Nevertheless, space is so conceived of, for all parts of space are equally capable of being produced to infinity. Consequently, the original representation of space is an intuition *a priori*, and not a conception.

1. *Kant thinks you can mount exactly parallel arguments for time. Choose one of the four arguments above and re-cast it as an argument about the nature of time.*

The *Prolegomena*, Remark One

Pure mathematics, and especially pure geometry, can only possess objective reality under the condition that they merely refer to objects of sense, in view of which, however, the axiom holds good that our sensuous presentation is in nowise a presentation of things in themselves, but only of the manner wherein they appear to us. Hence it follows that the propositions of geometry are not the mere determinations of a creation of our poetic fancy, which therefore cannot be referred with confidence to real objects, but that they are necessarily valid of space, and consequently of everything that may be found in space; because space is nothing more than the form of all external phenomena, under which alone objects of sense can be given us. Sensibility, the form of which lies at the foundation of geometry, is that whereon the possibility of external phenomena rests; so these can never contain anything but what geometry prescribes for them. It would be quite different if the senses had to present the objects as they are in themselves. For in that case it would by no means follow from the presentation of space (which the geometrician posits with all its properties as an *a priori* basis), that all this, together with what is deduced therefrom, is exactly so constituted in Nature. The space of the geometrician would be regarded as a mere fiction, and no objective validity ascribed to it, because we do not see why things must necessarily conform to the image that we make of them spontaneously and beforehand. But when this image, or rather this formal intuition, is the essential property of our sensibility by means of which alone objects are presented to us; and yet this sensibility presents not things in themselves, but only their appearances, it is quite easy to conceive, and at the same time incontrovertibly proved, that all the external objects of our sense-world must necessarily conform with the most complete accuracy to the propositions of geometry. For sensibility, by its form of external intuition (space) with which the geometrician is occupied, makes those objects themselves (though as mere appearances) primarily possible. It will always remain a remarkable phenomenon in the history of philosophy that there has been a time when even mathematicians who were also philosophers began to doubt, not indeed of the correctness of their propositions in so far as they concerned space, but of the objective validity and application of this conception, with all its geometrical determinations, to Nature. They were concerned lest a line in Nature might consist of physical points, and the true space in the object, accordingly of simple parts, whereas the space the geometrician has in his mind can never consist of such. They did not recognise that this space in thought makes the physical space, i.e., the extension of matter, itself possible; that the latter is no quality of things in themselves, but only a form of our sensible faculty of presentation; that all objects in space are mere phenomena, i.e., are not things in themselves, but presentations of our sensuous intuition; and hence that space, as the geometrician thinks it, is exactly the form of sensuous intuition we find *a priori* in ourselves, containing the ground of possibility of all external phenomena (as regards their form); and that these must necessarily and in the most exact manner agree with the propositions of the geometrician, which he draws from no fictitious conception, but from the subjective foundation of all external phenomena, namely, the sensibility itself. In such and no other manner can the geometrician be ensured as to the indubitable objective reality of his propositions against all the cavils of an arid metaphysics, however strange it may seem to him, owing to his not having reverted to the sources of his conceptions.

All that is given us as object, must be given us in intuition. But all our intuition takes place by means of the senses alone; the understanding intuits nothing, but only reflects. Inasmuch then as the senses, according to what is above observed, never enable us to cognise, not even in one single point, the things in themselves, but only their phenomena, while these are mere presentations of sensibility, "all bodies, together with the space in which they are found, must be held to be nothing but mere presentations, existing nowhere but in our thoughts." Now is this not the plainest idealism?

Idealism consists in the assertion that there exist none but thinking entities; the other things we think we perceive in intuition, being only presentations of the thinking entity, to which no object outside the latter can be found to correspond. I say, on the contrary, things are given as objects discoverable by our senses, external to us, but of what they may be in themselves we know nothing; we know only their phenomena, i.e., the presentations they produce in us as they affect our senses. I therefore certainly admit that there are bodies outside us, that is, things, which although they are wholly unknown to us, as to what they may be in themselves, we cognise through presentations, obtained by means of their influence on our sensibility. To these we give the designation of body, a word signifying merely the phenomenon of that to us unknown, but not the less real, object. Can this be termed idealism? It is indeed rather the contrary thereof.

That without calling in question the existence of external things, it may be said of a number of their predicates that they do not belong to the things in themselves, but only to their phenomena, and have no self-existence outside our presentation, is what had been generally accepted and admitted long before Locke's time, but more than ever since then. To these belong heat, colour, taste, &c. No one can adduce the least ground for saying that it is inadmissible on my part, when for important reasons I count in addition the remaining qualities of bodies called *primarias*, such as extension, place, and more especially space, together with what is dependent thereon (impenetrability or materiality, figure, &c.) amongst the number of these phenomena. And just as little as the man who will not admit colours to be properties of the object in itself, but only to pertain as modifications to the sense of sight, is on that account called an idealist, so little can my conception be termed idealistic because I find in addition that *all properties which make up the intuition of a body* belong merely to its appearance. For the existence of a thing, which appears, is not thereby abolished as with real idealism, but it is only shown that we cannot cognise it, as it is in itself, through the senses.

I should like to know how my assertions must be fashioned, if they are not to contain an idealism. I should doubtless have to say, that the presentation of space is not alone completely in accordance with the relation of our sensibility to objects, for that I have already said, but that it is exactly similar to the object itself; an assertion to which no sense can be attached, just as little as that the feeling of red has a similarity with the cinnabar producing this feeling in me.

---

1. *One of the early criticisms of the CPR was that Kant's view is really just a complicated version of immaterialism; Kant was called 'a Teutonic Berkeley.' why is Kant so sure that his view about space and time—that they are empirically real (i.e., characteristics of all possible objects of experience) but transcendentally ideal (i.e., they do not characterize things as they are in themselves)—does not amount to Berkeleyan idealism?*

Hence we may readily set aside an easily foreseen but pointless objection: namely, that through the ideality of space and time, the whole sense-world would be changed to sheer illusion. All philosophical insight into the nature of sensuous cognition was ruined from the first by making sensibility to consist simply in a confused mode of presentation, by which we cognise the things as they are, without having the capacity to bring everything in this, our cognition, to clear consciousness. On the other hand, it has been proved by us that sensibility does not consist in this logical distinction of clearness and obscurity, but in the genetic distinction of the origin of knowledge itself, since sensuous cognition does not present the things as they are, but only the manner in which they affect our senses; and that therefore through them mere phenomena, and not the things themselves, are given to the understanding for reflection. After this necessary correction, a consideration presents itself, arising from an inexcusable and almost purposeless misapplication, as though my doctrine changed all the objects of sense into mere illusion.

When an appearance is given us we are quite free as to what we thence infer with regard to the matter. The former, namely, the appearance, rests on the senses, but the judgment on the understanding; and the only question is, whether or not there is truth in the determination of the object. But the distinction between truth and dream is not decided by the construction of the presentations, which are referred to objects, for they are alike in both, but by the connection of the same according to the rules determining the coherence of presentations in the conception of an object, and by whether they can stand together in an experience or not. Hence the fault does not lie with the phenomena, if our cognition takes the illusion for truth, i.e., if an intuition, whereby an object is given, is held to be the conception of the object or its existence, which the understanding alone can cogitate. The senses present to us the course of the planets as first forwards and then backwards, and in this there is neither falsehood nor truth, because so long as it is considered as an appearance only, no judgment is yet formed as to the objective character of their motion. But inasmuch as when the understanding does not take great care lest this subjective mode of presentation be held for objective, a false judgment may easily arise; it is said, they *seem* to go back; the illusion, however, is not to be laid to the account of the senses, but of the understanding, whose province alone it is to form an objective judgment on the phenomenon.

In this manner, even if we did not reflect on the origin of our presentations, and let our intuitions of sense contain what they may, if it be but connected according to the coherence of all knowledge in an experience, [we shall find that] deceptive illusion or truth will arise according as we are negligent or careful; for it concerns solely the use of sensuous presentations in the understanding, and not their origin. In the same way, if I hold all presentations of sense together with their form, namely, space and time, to be nothing but phenomena, and the latter to be a mere form of sensibility not present in the objects external to it, and I make use of these presentations only in reference to a possible experience, there is not therein the least temptation to error, neither is there an illusion implied in my regarding them as mere appearances; for in spite of this they can rightly cohere according to the rules of truth in an experience. In such wise all the propositions of geometry respecting space are valid just as much of all the objects of sense, and therefore in respect of all possible experience, whether I regard space as a mere form of sensibility or as something inhering in the things themselves. But in the first case alone can I conceive *how* it is possible to know *a priori* the above propositions concerning objects of external intuition. Otherwise everything remains in respect to all merely possible experience just as though I had never undertaken this departure from the popular judgment.

But, let me only venture with my conceptions of space and time beyond all possible experience, which is unavoidable if I give them out as qualities appertaining to the things in themselves (for what should prevent me from assuming them as valid of these same things, even though my senses were differently constructed, and whether they were suited to them or not?) then a serious error may arise, resting on an illusion giving out as universally valid what is a mere condition of the intuition of things pertaining to my subject (certain for all the objects of sense, and thereby for all possible experience), because I refer them to things in themselves and fail to limit them to the conditions of experience.

So far, then, from my doctrine of the ideality of space and time reducing the whole sense-world to mere illusion, it is rather the only means of ensuring the application of some of the most important cognitions, namely, those propounded *a priori* by mathematics, to real objects, and of guarding them from being held as illusion. For without this observation it would be quite impossible to ascertain whether the intuitions of space and time we borrow from no experience, but which nevertheless lie *a priori* in our faculty of presentation, were not mere self-made cobwebs of the brain, to which no object, or at least no adequate object, corresponded, and geometry itself therefore a mere illusion; instead of which, its incontestable validity in respect of all objects of the sense-world, owing to these being simply phenomena, has been able to be demonstrated by us.

Secondly, so far from my principles, because they reduce the presentations of the senses to phenomena, turning the truth of experience into illusion, they are rather the only means of guarding against the transcendental illusion, whereby metaphysics has always been deceived and misled into childish endeavours to grasp at soap-bubbles, by taking phenomena, which are mere presentations, for things in themselves; whence have resulted the remarkable assumptions of the antinomy of Reason, of which I shall make mention farther on, and which are abolished by the single observation that appearance, as long as it is used simply in experience, produces truth, but as soon as it passes beyond the bounds of the latter and becomes transcendent, nothing but pure illusion.

Inasmuch, then, as I leave their reality to the things we intuit to ourselves through the senses, and only limit our sensuous intuition of those things in that they in no particular, not even in the pure intuitions of space and time, represent more than the appearance of the above things, and never their constitution as they are in themselves; this is no thorough-going illusion of my own invention [applied to] Nature. My protestation against all supposition of an idealism is so decisive and clear, that it might seem superfluous were it not for incompetent judges, who like to have an old name for every departure from their distorted although common opinion, and who never judge of the spirit of philosophical terminology, but cling simply to the letter, being ready to put their own delusion in the place of well-defined perceptions, and so to distort and deform them. For the fact of my having myself given my theory the name of transcendental idealism, can justify no one in confounding it with the idealism of Descartes (though this was only a problem, on account of whose insolubility every one was free, in the opinion of Descartes, to deny the existence of the bodily world, because it could never be satisfactorily solved), or with the mystical and visionary idealism of Berkeley, against which and other similar cobwebs of the brain our *Critique* rather contains the best specific. For what is by me termed idealism, does not touch the existence of things (the doubt of the same being what properly constitutes idealism in the opposite sense), for to doubt them has never entered my head, but simply concerns the sensuous presentation of things, to which space and time chiefly belong; and of these and of all phenomena I have only shown that they are neither things (but only modes of presentation), nor determinations belonging to things in themselves. But the word 'transcendental', which with me never implies a reference to our *knowledge* of things, but only to our *faculty of knowledge* (*Erkenntnissvermogen*) should guard against this misconception. Rather, however, than occasion its further continuance, I prefer to withdraw the expression, and let it be known as critical (idealism). If it be indeed an objectionable idealism, to change into mere presentations real things (not phenomena), what name shall be applied to that which conversely turns mere presentations into things? I think we may term it the *dreaming* idealism, in contradistinction to the foregoing, that may be termed the *visionary*, but both of which ought to have been obviated by my elsewhere so-called transcendental, but better, *critical*, idealism.

---

1. *One way previous philosophers (like Locke and Descartes) made sense of the appearance/reality distinction was in terms of those representations that correspond to things in themselves and those that don't. Why isn't Kant entitled to make the distinction in this way?*
2. *How, then, does he propose to make the distinction?*

The *Prolegomena*, Section Fourteen: The Main Transcendental Question—Second Part: How is pure Natural Science possible?

Nature is the existence of things, in so far as it is determined according to universal laws. If Nature signified the existence of *things in themselves*, we could never know it either *a priori* or *a posteriori*. Not *a priori*, for how shall we know what applies to things in themselves? since this can never be done by the dissection of our conceptions (analytic propositions). For what I want to know, is not what is contained in my conception of a thing (for that concerns its logical nature), but what in the reality of the thing is superadded to this conception, by which the thing itself is determined outside my conception. My understanding and the conditions under which alone it can connect the determination of things in their existence, prescribes no rules for the things in themselves; these do not conform themselves to my understanding, but my understanding conforms itself to them. They must therefore be previously given me, in order for these determinations to be discovered in them; and in this case they would not be known *a priori*.

But *a posteriori* such a knowledge of the nature of things in themselves would be equally impossible. For if experience is to teach me laws to which the existence of things is subordinated, these must, in so far as they concern things in themselves, of necessity also apply to them outside my experience. Now experience teaches me, indeed, what exists and how it exists, but never that it exists necessarily in such a manner and no other. It can never, therefore, teach the nature of things in themselves.

Section Fifteen: The Second Part, Continued

We are nevertheless really in possession of a pure natural science, which *a priori* and with all the necessity requisite to apodictic propositions, puts forward laws to which Nature is subordinated. I only require here to call to witness that propaedeutic, which, under the title of universal natural science, precedes all physical science based on empirical principles. Therein we find mathematics applied to phenomena, also those discursive principles (from conceptions) constituting the philosophical part of pure natural knowledge. But the latter also contains much that is not pure, and independent of the sources of experience, as the conception of motion, of impenetrability (on which the empirical conception of matter rests), of inertia and others, which prevent its being called a perfectly pure natural science. Besides, it is only concerned with the objects of the external sense, and thus furnishes no example of a pure natural science in its strictest meaning; for this would have to bring Nature generally under universal laws, irrespective of whether it concerned the object of the outer or of the inner sense of physical science, or of psychology. But among the principles of the above universal physical science are to be found some that really possess the universality we require, as the proposition that *substance continues and is permanent*, and that all which happens is at all times previously *determined by a cause*, according to fixed laws. These are really universal natural laws, existing completely *a priori*. There is then in fact a pure natural science, and now the question arises—*how is it possible?*

Section Sixteen: The Second Part, Continued

The word Nature further assumes another meaning, which defines the object, whereas in the above meaning the mere regularity of the existence of the determinations of things generally, is denoted. Nature considered *materialiter* is *the sum-total of all the objects of experience*. With this we are alone concerned at present, for things which could never be objects of an experience were they to be known according to their nature, would necessitate us to form conceptions, to which meaning could never be given *in concreto* (in any example from a possible experience), and of the nature of which we should be obliged to make conceptions alone, whose reality, that is, whether they really referred to objects or were mere figments of thought, could never be decided. With that which cannot be an object of experience, the knowledge of which would be hyperphysical, or anything like it, we have here nothing at all to do, but only with the natural knowledge whose reality can be confirmed by experience, notwithstanding its being *a priori* possible, and preceding all experience.

Section Seventeen: The Second Part, Continued

The *formal* in Nature, in this narrower signification, is then the regularity of all the objects of experience, and in so far as they are known *a priori*, their *necessary* regularity. But it has been just demonstrated that the laws of Nature can never be known *a priori* in objects, in so far as they are considered not as the objects of a possible experience but as things in themselves. We are not here concerned with things in themselves (the qualities of which we put on one side), but merely with things as the objects of a possible experience, and the sum-total of which is properly what we call Nature. And I now ask, whether, if the question be as to the possibility of a cognition of Nature *a priori*, it would be better to formulate the problem, as follows: How is it possible to cognise *a priori* the necessary regularity of things as objects of experience? or, How is the necessary regularity of experience itself in respect of all its objects, generally [possible to be cognised *a priori*]?

Seen in its true light, the solution of the problem, whether presented in the one or in the other form, in respect of the pure cognition of Nature (which constitutes the real point of the question) is in the end altogether the same. For the subjective laws under which alone an experiential cognition of things is possible, are valid also of those things as objects of a possible experience (though not indeed as things in themselves; but the latter we are not here considering). It is quite the same, then, whether I say: Without the law—that on an event being perceived, it must invariably be referred to something preceding it, upon which it follows according to a universal rule—a judgment of perception can never avail as experience; or whether I express myself thus: Everything that experience teaches us, happens, must have a cause.

It is, however, advisable to choose the first formula. For as we can have a knowledge *a priori* and before all given objects, of those conditions under which alone an experience in respect of them is possible, but never of what laws, they, without reference, to a possible experience, are subordinated to, in themselves; we shall not be able to study the nature of things *a priori*, otherwise than by investigating the conditions and universal (although subjective) laws, under which such a knowledge is alone possible (in respect of mere form), as experience, and in accordance therewith determine the possibility of things as objects of experience. Were I to choose the second mode of expression and seek the conditions *a priori* under which Nature is possible as an object of experience, I should easily be led into misunderstanding, and fancy I had to explain Nature as a thing in itself, and I should then be fruitlessly involved in endless endeavours to seek laws for things of which nothing is given me.

We shall here, therefore, be simply concerned with experience, and the universal and *a priori* given conditions of its possibility, and thence determine Nature as the complete object of all possible experience. I think it will be understood, that I do not refer to the rules for the observation of a nature already given, which presuppose experience, or how through experience we can arrive at the laws of Nature, for these would not then be laws *a priori*, and would give no pure science of Nature; but how the conditions *a priori* of the possibility of experience are at the same time the sources from which all the universal laws of Nature must be derived.

Section Eighteen: The Second Part, Continued

We must first of all observe then, that, although all the judgments of experience are empirical, i.e., have their ground in the immediate perception of sense, yet on the other hand all empirical judgments are not judgments of experience, but that beyond the empirical, and beyond the given sensuous intuition generally, special conceptions must be superadded, having their origin entirely *a priori* in the pure understanding, under which every perception is primarily subsumed, and by means of which only it can be transformed into experience.

Empirical judgments, in so far as they have objective validity, are judgments of experience; but those which are merely *subjectively valid* I call judgments of perception. The last require no pure conception of the understanding; but only the logical connection of perception in a thinking subject. But the first demand, above the presentations of sensuous intuition, *special conceptions originally generated in the understanding*, which make the judgment of experience objectively valid.

All our judgments are at first mere judgments of perception; they are valid simply for us, namely, for our subject. It is only subsequently that we give them a new reference, namely, to an object, and insist that they shall be valid for us always, as well as for every one else. For when a judgment coincides with an object, all judgments must both coincide with the same object and with one another, and thus the objective validity of the judgment of experience implies nothing more than the necessary universal validity of the same. But, on the other hand, when we see reason to hold a judgment of necessity universally valid (which never hinges on the perception itself, but on the pure conception of the understanding under which the perception is subsumed), we are obliged to regard it as objective, i.e., as expressing not merely the reference of the perception to a subject but a quality of the object; for there would be no reason why the judgments of other persons must necessarily coincide with mine, if it were not that the unity of the object to which they all refer, and with which they coincide, necessitates them all agreeing with one another.

Objective validity and necessary universality (for every one) are therefore exchangeable notions, and although we do not know the object in itself, yet when we regard a judgment as at once universal and necessary, objective validity is therewith understood. We cognise in this judgment the object (though it remain unknown what it is in itself) by the universal and necessary connection of given perceptions, and as this is the case with all objects of sense, judgments of experience owe their objective validity not to the immediate cognition of the object (for this is impossible), but merely to the condition of universality in the empirical judgment, which, as has been said, never rests on empirical, or on any sensuous conditions, but on a pure conception of the understanding. The object in itself always remains unknown; but when through the conception of the understanding, the connection of the presentations given to our sensibility by the latter is determined as universally valid, the object is determined by this relation, and the judgment is objective.

That the room is warm, the sugar sweet, the wormwood bitter, are merely subjectively valid judgments. I do not expect that I shall always, or that every other person, will find them as I do now. They only express a reference of two sensations to the same subject, namely, myself, and that only in my present state of perception, and are not therefore valid of objects. I call these judgments of perception. With judgments of experience the case is altogether different. What experience teaches me under certain circumstances, it must teach me at all times, and every other person as well; its validity is not limited to the subject or to the state of the latter at a particular time. I pronounce, therefore, all such judgments to be objectively valid. For instance when I say "the air is elastic", this judgment is immediately a judgment of perception, since I only refer the feelings in my senses to one another. If I insist it shall be called a judgment of experience, I expect this connection to stand under a condition making it universally valid. I insist, that is, that I at all times and every other person, shall necessarily so combine the same perceptions, under the same circumstances.

---

1. *A key distinction is between judgments of perception (JOPs) and judgments of experience (JOEs). Judgments are propositions in which the mind unites intuitions according to a rule (see below). What is the distinction between JOPs and JOEs? what transforms a mere JOP into a JOE?*

Section Twenty: The Second Part, Continued

We must therefore dissect experience, in order to see what is contained in this product of sense and understanding, and how the judgment of experience itself is possible. The intuition of which I am conscious, namely, perception, which merely belongs to the senses, lies at its foundation. But secondly, judgment (which pertains solely to the understanding) also belongs to it. This [act of] judgment may be twofold; firstly, I may simply compare the perceptions in a particular state of my own consciousness; or secondly, I may combine them in a consciousness in general. The first judgment is a simple judgment of perception, and has therefore only subjective validity, being the mere connection of perceptions in my mental state, without reference to the object. Hence it is not sufficient for experience, as is commonly imagined, to compare perceptions and to connect them in a consciousness by means of the judgment. No universality and necessity in the judgment can arise therefrom, by means of which alone it can be objectively valid, and experience.

There is another and quite a different judgment presupposed, before perception can become experience. The given intuition must be subsumed under a conception determining the form of the judgment generally in respect of the intuition, connecting the empirical consciousness of the last in a consciousness in general, and thereby obtaining universality for the empirical judgment; such a conception is a pure *a priori* conception of the understanding, that does nothing but determine for an intuition the general manner in which it can serve for judgment. Should the conception be that of cause, it determines the intuition subsumed under it in respect of judgment generally; for instance, in the case of air, that in respect of expansion, it stands in the relation of antecedent to consequent, in a hypothetical judgment. The conception of cause is then a pure conception of the understanding, entirely distinct from all possible perception, and only serves to determine that presentation contained under it, in respect of judgment generally, in short, to make a universally valid judgment possible.

Now, before a judgment of perception can become a judgment of experience, it is first of all necessary that the perception be subsumed under these conceptions of the understanding. For instance, air belongs to the conception of causes, which determines the judgment regarding its extension, as hypothetical. In this way, the extension is represented not merely as belonging to my perception of air in my particular state, or in many of my states, or in a particular state of the perception of others, but as *necessarily* belonging thereto; and the judgment, "the air is elastic", becomes universally valid, and therefore a judgment of experience, preceded by certain judgments, which subsume the intuition of air under the conception of cause and effect, and thereby the perceptions, not merely with respect to one another in my subject, but relatively to the form of judgment generally (here the hypothetical), and thus make the empirical judgment universally valid. ...

Section Twenty-one: The Second Part, Continued

In order to demonstrate the possibility of experience, in so far as it rests on pure *a priori* conceptions of the understanding, we must first present what belongs to judgment generally, and the various momenta of the understanding in the same, in a complete table, for the pure conceptions of the understanding, which are nothing more than conceptions of intuitions in general, in so far as these are determined in themselves by one or other of these momenta of judgment, that is, are necessarily and universally valid, must run exactly parallel to them [viz., these *momenta*]. In this way, the axioms *a priori* of the possibility of all experience as an objectively valid empirical cognition, are precisely determined. For they are nothing but propositions, subsuming all perception (in accordance with certain universal conditions of perception), under the above pure conceptions of the understanding.

Logical Table of the Judgements

Quantity	Quality	Relation	Modality
Universal	Affirmative	Categorical	Problematical
Particular	Negative	Hypothetical	Assertorical
Singular	Infinite	Disjunctive	Apodictic

Transcendental Table of the Concepts of the Understanding

Quantity	Quality	Relation	Modality
Unity (the measure)	Reality	Substance	Possibility
Plurality (the amount)	Negation	Cause	Actuality
Totality (the whole)	Limitation	Reciprocity	Necessity

Section Twenty-one (A): The Second Part, Continued

In order to grasp the preceding in a single notion, it is necessary to remind the reader that we are not here speaking of the origin of experience, but of that which lies within it. The first belongs to empirical psychology, and would exist without the second, which belongs to the critique of cognition, and especially to that of the understanding, and can never be sufficiently developed.

Experience consists of intuitions, belonging to sensibility, and of judgments which are entirely the work of the understanding. But the judgments the understanding constructs merely out of sensuous intuitions, are not, by far, judgments of experience. For in the one case the judgment simply connects the perceptions, as they are given in sensuous intuition; but in the other, the judgments must say what experience generally contains, and not what the mere perception, the validity of which is purely subjective, contains. The judgment of experience must add something to a judgment, over and above the sensuous intuition, and the logical connection of the same (after it has been made universal by comparison), something that determines the synthetic judgment, as at once necessary and thereby universally valid; and this can be nothing else but that conception which presents the intuition as determined in itself, in respect to one form of judgment rather than another, i.e., a conception of that synthetic unity of intuitions, which can only be presented through a given logical function of the judgment.

Section Twenty-two: The Second Part, Continued

The sum of the above is this: the business of the senses is to intuit, that of the understanding to think. But to think is to unite presentations in a consciousness. This union is either merely relative to the subject, and is contingent and subjective, or is given unconditionally, and is necessary or objective. The union of presentations in a consciousness is judgment. Thinking, then, is the same as judging, or referring presentations to judgments in general. Hence judgments are either entirely subjective when presentations are solely referred to a consciousness in one subject, and are therein united, or they are objective when they are united in a consciousness in general, that is, are necessarily united therein. The logical momenta of all judgments are so many possible modes of uniting presentations in a consciousness. But if they serve as conceptions, they are conceptions of the necessary union of the same in a consciousness, and therefore principles of objectively valid judgments. This union in a consciousness is either analytic by identity, or synthetic by the combination and addition of different presentations to one another. Experience consists in the synthetic connection of phenomena (perceptions) in a consciousness, in so far as this is necessary. Hence pure conceptions of the understanding are those under which all perceptions must be previously subsumed, before they can serve as judgments of experience, in which the synthetic unity of perceptions is presented as necessary and universal.

Before going forward, it's important to make sure we have the basic terminology in hand:

Sensibility

The faculty of the mind that 'receives' intuitions

Intuition (Anschauung)

A bit of sensory awareness. This can refer to any kind of sensory awareness, from any sense modality whatsoever, as well as those bits of awareness that are also called up by the memory.

All intuitions are in time (as objects of thought, they always occur in temporal positions relative to each other); some of these are also in space (that is, they represent their objects as having spatial location). Time is the form of inner intuition; space, outer intuition.

*The **matter** of an intuition is its purely sensory element—in visual images, for example, this would include color. Its **form** is the spatial or temporal structure the sensibility imposes on this 'matter.' So even in sensation the mind is not purely passive—it is actively structuring its perceptions.*

Understanding

The faculty that unites intuitions into thoughts

Sensibility generates intuitions; the understanding generates concepts. But how can we bring these together? Intuitions without concepts are blind; concepts without intuitions are empty. How are the two going to be united?

Judgment

The basic unit of thought, in which the mind unites distinct intuitions into a coherent whole. All judgments are judgments of perception; some judgments are also judgments of experience. The basic unit of thought, as opposed to sensibility, then, is the proposition: a claim that things are thus-and-so.

*A **judgment of perception** unites intuitions merely according to the logical forms of judgment (page 600, Section 21). These judgments only have **subjective validity**; that is, they make a claim only about the perceptions of the person doing the judging. In a JOP, I "merely compare perceptions and connect them in a consciousness of my state" (599).*

Example: when I say, 'if I perceive gold being immersed in aqua regia, I then perceive its dissolution,' I have not said anything about whether this must happen, will happen in all cases, or, most importantly, why it happens. I have only made a report about my own perceptions. Or: suppose I conjure up an image of a dagger. I can unite these intuitions according to the mere form of judgment and bring together the perceptions of the handle and the blade. But I don't think of the dagger as a real object that others would see if they were here and could use to open their mail.

*A **judgment of experience**, by contrast, unites intuitions according to the logical forms of judgment and the pure concepts of the understanding, the categories. When I say that putting gold in aqua regia causes it to dissolve, I am not merely saying that the one perception follows the other. I am saying that this happens necessarily, i.e., that it happens according to a law of nature. My claim is **objectively valid**: that is, I am claiming that anyone similarly situated will observe exactly what I observe when I dropped the gold into the solution. (Objective validity is a necessary, but not sufficient, condition for truth. An objectively valid judgment is a candidate for being true; it is not automatically so. See the CPR, A58/B83).*

"Experience consists in the synthetic connection of appearances in consciousness, so far as this connection is

necessary." Thinking of this connection as necessary and as holding for all similarly situated cognitive beings requires the **categories**, **pure concepts of the understanding** *that structure our intuitions into experience. Concepts of any kind are always rules for making judgments. The concept dog, for example, is a rule that tells you which of your intuitions to unite so you can come to think of those intuitions as a single thing, viz., a dog. So the categories are the maximally general rules we use to generate experience. (Imagine what your 'experience' would be like if you lacked these pure concepts.)*

Sensibility imposes a form on the material element of sensation and generates an intuition; in parallel fashion, the understanding imposes a form on intuitions and generates experience.

Section 22 above presents a clear summary of Kant's argument so far. Here is one way to sketch it; I encourage you to try your own.

1. We have experience (in the weighty sense), not just a flood of intuitions (what sensibility provides) and not just a set of thoughts about our mental states (JOPs).
2. Experience is possible only if we unite intuitions in propositions.
3. Only judgment can unite these intuitions.
4. To do more than think about our own mental states (JOPs), we have to use certain concepts.
5. These concepts allow us to unite our intuitions in propositions that, if true at all, are true for all possible subjects of experience. They involve a necessary connection between the objects of my intuitions, not merely the connection of intuitions in my own private experience.
6. These concepts must be synthetic and *a priori*.

Section Twenty-three: The Second Part, Continued

Judgments, considered merely as the union of given presentations in a consciousness, are rules. These rules, in so far as they present the union as necessary, are rules *a priori*, and in so far as there are none beyond them from which they can be derived, they are axioms. Since, then, in respect of the possibility of all experience, when viewed as the mere form of thought, there are no conditions of the judgments of experience beyond those which bring the phenomena in the various forms of their intuition under the pure conceptions of the understanding which make the empirical judgment objectively valid, these must be the *a priori* axioms of all possible experience.

The axioms of possible experience are at the same time the universal laws of Nature as known *a priori*. And thus the problem contained in our present second question—*How is pure natural science possible?* is solved. For the systematic character required by the form of a science is met with here in completeness, since beyond the above-named formal conditions of all judgments in general, that is, of all the general rules to be found in logic, there are none possible, and these constitute a logical system; while the conceptions founded upon them, containing the conditions *a priori* of all synthetic and necessary judgments, [constitute] in the same way a transcendental system, and finally the axioms, by means of which all phenomena are subsumed under these conceptions, [constitute] a physiological system, i.e., a system of nature, preceding all empirical knowledge of nature, rendering this in the first place possible, and therefore to be properly termed the universal and pure natural science. ...

As regards the relation of phenomena, and indeed simply as to their existence, the determination of this relation is not mathematic but dynamic, and can never be valid objectively, and therefore adequate to an experience, if it be not subordinated to principles *a priori* rendering the cognition of experience regarding them in the first place possible. Hence phenomena must be subsumed under the conception of substance, which lies at the foundation of all determination of existence as a conception of the thing itself; or secondly, in so far as a succession, that is, an event, is met with among the phenomena, under the conception of an effect in reference to cause; or in so far as co-existence is to be cognised objectively, that is, through a judgment of experience, under the conception of community (reciprocal action); and these principles *a priori* lie at the foundation of objectively valid although empirical judgments, that is, the possibility of experience in so far as it is to connect the existence of objects in Nature. These principles are the particular laws of Nature, which may be termed dynamic.

There belongs, finally, to the judgments of experience the cognition of the agreement and connection, not so much of phenomena among one another in experience, as of their relation to experience generally, which unites either their agreement with the formal conditions cognised by the understanding or their coherence with the material of sense and of perception, or both, in one conception, and consequently contains possibility, reality and necessity, according to universal natural laws, thereby constituting the physiological doctrine of method, the distinction between truth and hypotheses, and the limits of the reliability of the latter.

Section Twenty-six: The Second Part, Continued

Although the third table of the principles drawn from the nature of the understanding on the critical method, shows a completeness in itself, which raises it far above every other that has been vainly attempted or may be attempted in the future [to be drawn] from the nature of the thing itself, in a dogmatic way, inasmuch as therein all synthetic axioms *a priori* have been produced in accordance with a principle, that is, the possibility of judgment in general, which constitutes the essence of experience, in reference to the understanding, in such a manner that one may be certain there are no more such axioms (a satisfaction never to be obtained from the dogmatic method)—yet this is by far not its greatest service.

Attention must be paid to the ground of proof, which discovers the possibility of this knowledge *a priori*, and limits at the same time all such axioms by a condition, that must never be overlooked, if they are not to be misunderstood, and extended farther in use than the original sense attached to them by the understanding will admit of: namely, that they only contain the conditions of possible experience in general, in so far as it is subordinated to laws *a priori*. Thus I do not say that *things in themselves* contain a quantity, their reality, a degree, their existence, connection of accidents in a substance, &c.; for this no one can prove, because such a synthetic connection is simply impossible out of mere conceptions, where all reference to sensuous intuition on the one hand, and all connection of the same in a possible experience on the other, is wanting. The essential limitation of conceptions in these axioms is, therefore, that all things only stand under the above-mentioned conditions *a priori* as *objects of experience*.

From this there follows, in the second place, a special and peculiar mode of proof of the foregoing: that the axioms in question do not refer directly to phenomena and their relation, but to the possibility of experience of which phenomena constitute the matter but not the form, i.e., to objective and universally valid synthetic propositions, wherein judgments of experience are distinguished from mere judgments of perception. This happens in that the phenomena as mere intuitions, taking in a portion of space and time, are subordinated to the conception of quantity, which unites the manifold in the same synthetically in accordance with *a priori* rules; and that in so far as the perception contains feeling as well as intuition, between which and zero, namely, its total disappearance, a progression by diminution always takes place, the real of the phenomena must have a basis, seeing that in itself it takes in no portion of space or time. But this progression towards it [viz., reality] from empty time or space, is only possible in time. Consequently, although feeling as the quality of empirical intuition can never be known *a priori* in respect of that wherein it is specifically distinguished from other feelings, it can nevertheless be distinguished in a possible experience generally, as quantity of perception intensively [distinct] from every other of the same kind; which means the application of mathematics to Nature in respect of the sensuous intuition, by which the former is given us, and by which it becomes in the first place possible and definite.

But the reader must give the greatest attention to the mode of proof of the principles coming under the name of analogies of experience. For inasmuch as these do not, like the principles of the application of mathematics to natural science generally, concern the generation of intuitions, but the connection of their existence in an experience, this can be nothing but the determination of existence in time according to necessary laws, under which alone they are objectively valid, and therefore experience. Thus the proof of synthetic unity does not turn on the connection of things in themselves, but of perceptions, and even of these, not in respect of their content but of their determination in time, and of the relation of existence thereto, according to universal laws. These universal laws contain, therefore, the necessity of the determination of existence in time generally (consequently, according to a rule of the understanding, a priori) when the empirical determination in the relative time is to be objectively valid, that is, experience. ...

Section Twenty-seven: The Second Part, Continued

It is here the place to raze Hume's doubt from its foundation. He maintained justly that we can in nowise discern through Reason the possibility of causation, namely, the reference of the existence of one thing to the existence of some other thing posited by the former. I may add to this, that we can just as little discern the conception of subsistence, i.e., the necessity contained therein, that a subject must lie at the basis of the existence of a thing, and itself be no predicate of any other thing. [I would say even] that we can form no conception of the possibility of such a thing (though we can point out examples of its use in experience). In the same way this inconceivability attaches even to the community of things, since it is not discernible how, from the state of one thing, a consequence can be drawn as to the state of some totally different thing, external to it, and vice versa; and how substances of which each has its own separate existence, are necessarily dependent on one another. At the same time, I am far from regarding these conceptions as merely borrowed from experience, and the necessity, that is presented in them, as fictitious and mere illusion, induced in us by long custom. I have, rather, sufficiently shown that both they and the axioms deduced from them, subsist *a priori* before all experience, and possess indubitable objective correctness, though unquestionably only in respect of experiences.

Section Twenty-eight: The Second Part, Continued

Although I cannot have the slightest notion of such a connection of things in themselves as of their existing as substances, working as causes, or being able to stand in community with other [substances] as parts of a real whole, I can still less conceive such properties in phenomena as phenomena, because these conceptions contain nothing that lies in the phenomena, but something the understanding alone can conceive. We have, then, from such a connection of presentations in our understanding, and, indeed, in judgments generally, a similar conception, namely, that presentations cohere in one kind of judgments, as subject with reference to predicate, in another as cause with reference to effect, in a third as parts together making up a complete possible cognition. Further, we cognise *a priori*, that without the presentation of an object, in respect of one or the other of these momenta, to be considered as something definite, we could have no cognition that could be valid of objects, and if we occupied ourselves with the object in itself, there would be no single mark possible, by which I could cognise whether it was determined in respect of one or of another cogitated moment, i.e., whether it cohered under the conception of substance, or of cause, or (in relation to other substances) of reciprocity, for of the possibility of such a connection of existence I should have no conception. But it is not the question, how things in themselves, but how cognition of experience of things in respect of cogitated momenta of judgments generally, is defined, that is, how things as objects of experience can and should be subsumed under the above conceptions of the understanding. And hence it is clear, that I fully recognise not only the possibility, but also the necessity, of subsuming all phenomena under these conceptions, namely, of using them as axioms of the possibility of experience.

Section Twenty-nine: The Second Part, Continued

Let us now attempt a solution of Hume's problematical conception, namely, the conception of Cause. Firstly, there is given me, *a priori*, by means of Logic, the form of a conditioned judgment generally, one cognition as antecedent and another as consequent. But it is possible that in the perception, a rule of the relation may be met with, which will say, that on [the occurrence of a] given phenomenon another always follows (though not conversely), and this would be a case in which to make use of the hypothetical judgment, and to say, for instance, if a body be illumined long enough by the sun, it will become warm. There is certainly no necessity of connection here, in other words, no conception of cause. But I continue: if the above proposition, which is a mere subjective connection of perception, is to be a proposition of experience, it must be regarded as necessary and universally valid; but such a proposition would run: Sun is through its light the cause of heat. The above empirical rule is now looked upon as law, and indeed, not alone as valid of phenomena, but valid of them in relation to a possible experience, which requires thoroughly, and therefore necessarily, valid rules. I perfectly understand, then, the conception of Cause, as a conception necessarily belonging to the mere form of experience, and its possibility as a synthetic union of perceptions, in a consciousness in general; but the possibility of a thing in general as a cause I do not understand, because the conception of cause does not refer at all to things, but only indicates the condition attaching to experience, namely, that this can be only an objectively valid knowledge of phenomena, and their sequence in time, in so far as the antecedent can be united to the consequent according to the rule of hypothetical judgments.

---

1. *What is Kant's solution to Hume's doubts about the concept of cause?*
2. *In the terms we used to describe Hume's own solution to this nexus of problems, is Kant's solution a straightforward solution, a skeptical solution, or something else? Why?*

Hence the pure conceptions of the understanding have no meaning whatever, when they quit the objects of experience and refer to things in themselves (*noumena*). They serve, as it were, to spell out phenomena, that these may be able to be read as experience. The axioms arising from their relation to the world of sense, only serve our understanding for use in experience. Beyond this, are only arbitrary combinations, destitute of objective reality, and the possibility of which can neither be known *a priori*, nor their reference to objects be confirmed, or even made intelligible by an example, because all examples are borrowed from some possible experience, and consequently the objects of those conceptions are nothing but what may be met with in a possible experience.

This complete solution of Hume's problem, although it turns out to be contrary to the opinion of its originator, preserves for the pure conceptions of the understanding their origin *a priori*, and for the universal laws of Nature their validity as laws of the understanding, but in such a manner that their use is limited to experience, because their possibility has its basis, solely, in the reference of the understanding to experience; not because they are derived from experience, but because experience is derived from them, which completely reversed mode of connection never occurred to Hume.

The following result of all previous researches follows from the above investigations: "All synthetic axioms *a priori* are nothing more than principles of possible experience," and can never be referred to things in themselves, but only to phenomena as objects of experience. Hence pure mathematics no less than pure natural science can never refer to anything more than mere phenomena, and only present that which either makes experience in general possible, or which, inasmuch as it is derived from these principles, must always be able to be presented in some possible experience.

---

1. *What constraint does Kant put on the application of the categories?*

Since Kant's reply to Hume is at the heart of his work, we should look at the argument he mounts against Hume in the CPR.

The *CPR*: "The Second Analogy"

Principle of the Succession of Time According to the Law of Causality: All changes take place according to the law of the connection of Cause and Effect.[2]

Proof ... I perceive that phenomena succeed one another, that is to say, a state of things exists at one time, the opposite of which existed in a former state. In this case, then, I really connect together two perceptions in time. Now connection is not an operation of mere sense and intuition, but is the product of a synthetical faculty of imagination, which determines the internal sense in respect of a relation of time. But imagination can connect these two states in two ways, so that either the one or the other may antecede in time; for time in itself cannot be an object of perception, and what in an object precedes and what follows cannot be empirically determined in relation to it. I am only conscious, then, that my imagination places one state before and the other after; not that the one state antecedes the other in the object. In other words, the objective relation of the successive phenomena remains quite undetermined by means of mere perception.

Now in order that this relation may be cognized as determined, the relation between the two states must be so cogitated that it is thereby determined as necessary, which of them must be placed before and which after, and not conversely. But the conception which carries with it a necessity of synthetical unity, can be none other than a pure conception of the understanding which does not lie in mere perception; and in this case it is the conception of "the relation of cause and effect," the former of which determines the latter in time, as its necessary consequence, and not as something which might possibly antecede (or which might in some cases not be perceived to follow). It follows that it is only because we subject the sequence of phenomena, and consequently all change, to the law of causality, that experience itself, that is, empirical cognition of phenomena, becomes possible; and consequently, that phenomena themselves, as objects of experience, are possible only by virtue of this law.

Our apprehension of the manifold of phenomena is always successive. The representations of parts succeed one another. Whether they succeed one another in the object also, is a second point for reflection, which was not contained in the former. Now we may certainly give the name of object to everything, even to every representation, so far as we are conscious thereof; but what this word may mean in the case of phenomena, not merely in so far as they (as representations) are objects, but only in so far as they indicate an object, is a question requiring deeper consideration. In so far as they, regarded merely as representations, are at the same time objects of consciousness, they are not to be distinguished from apprehension, that is, reception into the synthesis of imagination, and we must therefore say: "The manifold of phenomena is always produced successively in the mind." If phenomena were things in themselves, no man would be able to conjecture from the succession of our representations how this manifold is connected in the object; for we have to do only with our representations. How things may be in themselves, without regard to the representations through which they affect us, is utterly beyond the sphere of our cognition. Now although phenomena are not things in themselves, and are nevertheless the only thing given to us to be cognized, it is my duty to show what sort of connection in time belongs to the manifold in phenomena themselves, while the representation of this manifold in apprehension is always successive. For example, the apprehension of the manifold in the phenomenon of a house which stands before me, is successive. Now comes the question whether the manifold of this house is in itself successive—which no one will be at all willing to grant. But, so soon as I raise my conception of an object to the transcendental signification thereof, I find that the house is not a thing in itself, but only a phenomenon, that is, a representation, the transcendental object of which remains utterly unknown. What then am I to understand by the question: "How can the manifold be connected in the phenomenon itself—not considered as a thing in itself, but merely as a phenomenon?" Here that which lies in my successive apprehension is regarded as representation, whilst the phenomenon which is given me, notwithstanding that it is nothing more than a complex of these representations, is regarded as the object thereof, with which my conception, drawn from the representations of apprehension, must harmonize. It is very soon seen that, as accordance of the cognition with its object constitutes truth, the question now before us can only relate to the formal conditions of empirical truth; and that the phenomenon, in opposition to the representations of apprehension, can only be distinguished therefrom as the object of them, if it is subject to a rule which distinguishes it from every other apprehension, and which renders necessary a mode of connection of the manifold. That in the phenomenon which contains the condition of this necessary rule of apprehension, is the object.

Let us now proceed to our task. That something happens, that is to say, that something or some state exists which before was not, cannot be empirically perceived, unless a phenomenon precedes, which does not contain in itself this state. For a reality which should follow upon a void time, in other words, a beginning, which no state of things precedes, can just as little be apprehended as the void time itself. Every apprehension of an event is therefore a perception which follows upon another perception. But as this is the case with all synthesis of apprehension, as I have shown above in the example of a house, my apprehension of an event is not yet sufficiently distinguished from other apprehensions. But I remark also that if in a phenomenon which contains an occurrence, I call the antecedent state of my perception, A, and the following state, B, the perception B can only follow A in apprehension, and the perception A cannot follow B, but only precede it. For example, I see a ship float down the stream of a river. My perception of its place lower down follows upon my perception of its place higher up the course of the river, and it is impossible that, in the apprehension of this phenomenon, the vessel should be perceived first below and afterwards higher up the stream. Here, therefore, the order in the sequence of perceptions in apprehension is determined; and by this order apprehension is regulated. In the former example, my perceptions in the apprehension of a house might begin at the roof and end at the foundation, or vice versa; or I might apprehend the manifold in this empirical intuition, by going from left to right, and from right to left. Accordingly, in the series of these perceptions, there was no determined order, which necessitated my beginning at a certain point, in order empirically to connect the manifold. But this rule is always to be met with in the perception of that which happens, and it makes the order of the successive perceptions in the apprehension of such a phenomenon necessary.

I must, therefore, in the present case, deduce the subjective sequence of apprehension from the objective sequence of phenomena, for otherwise the former is quite undetermined, and one phenomenon is not distinguishable from another. The former alone proves nothing as to the connection of the manifold in an object, for it is quite arbitrary. The latter must consist in the order of the manifold in a phenomenon, according to which order the apprehension of one thing (that which happens) follows that of another thing (which precedes), in conformity with a rule. In this way alone can I be authorized to say of the phenomenon itself, and not merely of my own apprehension, that a certain order or sequence is to be found therein. That is, in other words, I cannot arrange my apprehension otherwise than in this order.

In conformity with this rule, then, it is necessary that in that which antecedes an event there be found the condition of a rule, according to which in this event follows always and necessarily; but I cannot reverse this and go back from the event, and determine (by apprehension) that which antecedes it. For no phenomenon goes back from the succeeding point of time to the preceding point, although it does certainly relate to a preceding point of time; from a given time, on the other hand, there is always a necessary progression to the determined succeeding time. Therefore, because there certainly is something that follows, I must of necessity connect it with something else, which antecedes, and upon which it follows, in conformity with a rule, that is necessarily, so that the event, as conditioned, affords certain indication of a condition, and this condition determines the event.

Let us suppose that nothing precedes an event, upon which this event must follow in conformity with a rule. All sequence of perception would then exist only in apprehension, that is to say, would be merely subjective, and it could not thereby be objectively determined what thing ought to precede, and what ought to follow in perception. In such a case, we should have nothing but a play of representations, which would possess no application to any object. That is to say, it would not be possible through perception to distinguish one phenomenon from another, as regards relations of time; because the succession in the act of apprehension would always be of the same sort, and therefore there would be nothing in the phenomenon to determine the succession, and to render a certain sequence objectively necessary. And, in this case, I cannot say that two states in a phenomenon follow one upon the other, but only that one apprehension follows upon another. But this is merely subjective, and does not determine an object, and consequently cannot be held to be cognition of an object—not even in the phenomenal world.

Accordingly, when we know in experience that something happens, we always presuppose that something precedes, whereupon it follows in conformity with a rule. For otherwise I could not say of the object that it follows; because the mere succession in my apprehension, if it be not determined by a rule in relation to something preceding, does not authorize succession in the object. Only, therefore, in reference to a rule, according to which phenomena are determined in their sequence, that is, as they happen, by the preceding state, can I make my subjective synthesis (of apprehension) objective, and it is only under this presupposition that even the experience of an event is possible.

There are two alternatives to consider: rationalism and empiricism. But the rationalist picture is hard to take seriously, since it amounts to a deus ex machina. Let's look at empiricism.

Recall Locke on power (Essay, II.xxi). For Locke, we first notice changes in the world and then infer that bodies have powers that bring them about. (Cp. Locke on space: we experience space and derive our idea from that experience.) So for Locke, there's a primitive difference in experience between objects and events, between things and the changes we observe. Let's see if this makes any sense.

Consider two sets of appearances: (O) those that we take to be of a house, and (E) those we take to be of a log being consumed by fire. Is the difference between these something we, as it were, just see? Is it there to be discovered in experience?

What will Kant say? Why? (See 689.)

Moral: a succession of appearances is not necessarily an appearance of succession.

So: the difference between O and E cannot lie in the appearances themselves. In imagination, I can order the successive appearances of the house (O) any way I want to, and still have a representation of a house. I don't think of parts of the house happening one after another. But I do think that the successive appearances of the log in (E) must be ordered in exactly one way. Another way to put this: in O, I don't think that anyone observing the house has to have exactly the same order of appearances. But in E, I do: I think that anyone observing the event fire has to see the appearances in the same order I do. Where does this must come from?

It can only derive from the fact that I am subjecting the appearances in (E) to a rule, which I am not applying to (O).

1. *This rule cannot be derived from experience; in order to have the experience of (E), I first have to deploy the rule. What is that rule?*

So again: where Locke thought we have observation, Kant thinks we have invention.

We can now say that every event must have a cause. But notice that we've proved it only for _____.

We now return to the Prolegomena. Having established the necessary application of the Categories to experience, Kant goes on to discuss the origin of metaphysical illusion. Why are we not content to admit that the Categories apply only to objects as we must experience them, not to things in themselves?

And thus we have at last something definite to hold by in all metaphysical undertakings, which hitherto, bold enough, but always blind, have pursued all things without distinction. Dogmatic thinkers have never let it occur to them, that the goal of their endeavours should be extended such a short way from them, and even those most confident in their imagined common sense have started with conceptions and principles of mere Reason, legitimate and natural, it is true, but intended merely for use in experience, [in search of] spheres of knowledge, for which they neither knew nor could know of any definite boundaries, because they had neither reflected nor could reflect on the nature or even the possibility of any such pure understanding.

Many a naturalist of pure Reason (by which I understand he who ventures to decide in questions of metaphysics, without any science) might well profess that what has been here put forward with so much preparation, or if he will have it so, with tediously pedantic pomp, he has long ago not merely conjectured but known and penetrated, by the prophetic spirit of his common sense, namely, "that with all our Reason, we can never pass beyond the field of experiences." But he must confess, notwithstanding, when questioned *seriatim* as to his principles of Reason, that amongst these there are many to be found not drawn from experience, and therefore valid, independently thereof, and *a priori*. How then, and on what grounds, will he hold the dogmatist and himself in limits, who use these conceptions and principles outside all possible experience, simply because they are recognised as independent of it? And even this adept of common sense, in spite of all his pretended, cheaply acquired, wisdom, is not proof against wandering, unobserved, beyond the objects of experience into the field of chimeras. He is, indeed, in the ordinary way, deeply enough involved therein, although by the use of popular language, by putting everything forward as probability, reasonable supposition or analogy, he gives some colour to his groundless assumptions.

Section Thirty-two: The Second Part, Continued

From the earliest ages of philosophy, investigators of pure Reason have postulated, beyond the sensible essences (*phenomena*) which constitute the world of sense, special essences of the understanding (*noumena*) which are supposed to constitute a world of understanding; and since they held appearance and illusion [*Erscheinung und Schein*] for the same thing, which in an undeveloped epoch is to be excused, ascribed reality to the intelligible essence alone.

In fact, when we regard the objects of sense, as is correct, as mere appearances, we thereby at the same time confess that a thing in itself lies at their foundation, although we do not know it, as it is constituted in itself, but only its appearance, that is, the manner in which our senses are affected by this unknown something. The understanding then, by accepting appearances, admits also the existence of things in themselves, and we may even say that the presentation of such essences as lie at the basis of appearances, in short, mere essences of the understanding, is not only admissible, but unavoidable.

Our critical deduction does not by any means exclude such things (*noumena*), but rather limits the principles of æsthetic, in so far that these should not be extended to all things, whereby everything would be changed into mere appearance, but that they should only be valid of objects of a possible experience. Essences of the understanding are hereby admitted only by the emphasising of this rule, which admits of no exception, that we know nothing definite whatever of these pure essences of the understanding, neither can we know anything of them, because our pure conceptions of the understanding no less than our pure intuitions, concern nothing but objects of a possible experience, in short, mere essences of sense, and as soon as we leave these, the above conceptions have not the least significance remaining.

Section Thirty-three: The Second Part, Continued

There is indeed something seductive about our pure conceptions of the understanding, as regards temptation to a transcendent use; for so I name that which transcends all possible experience. Not only do our conceptions of substance, force, action, reality, &c., which are entirely independent of experience containing no phenomenon of sense, really seem to concern things in themselves (*noumena*); but what strengthens this supposition is, that they contain a necessity of determination in themselves, to which experience can never approach. The conception of cause contains a rule, according to which from one state another follows in a necessary manner; but experience only teaches us that often, or at most usually, one state of a thing follows upon another, and can therefore acquire neither strict universality nor necessity.

Hence these conceptions of the understanding seem to have far too much significance and content for mere use in experience to exhaust their entire determination, and the understanding builds in consequence, unobserved, by the side of the house of experience, a much more imposing wing, which it fills with sheer essences of thought, without even noticing that it has overstepped the legitimate bounds of its otherwise correct conceptions.

Section Thirty-four: The Second Part, Continued

There were two important, and indeed altogether indispensable, although exceedingly dry investigations necessary, that have been undertaken in the *Critique*, in the first of which it was shown that the senses do not furnish the pure conceptions of the understanding *in concreto*, but only the *schema* for their use, and that the object which conforms to it is only to be met with in experience as the [common] product of the understanding, and the materials of sense. In the second investigation it is shown, that—notwithstanding the independence of our pure conceptions of the understanding and principles of experience, even to the apparently greater range of their use—nothing whatever could be conceived through them outside the field of experience, because they can do nothing but determine the merely logical form of judgment in respect of given intuitions. But since, beyond the field of sensibility, no intuition is given, these pure conceptions become totally void of meaning, in as much as they can in no way be presented *in concreto*. Consequently, all these *noumena* together with their sum-total, an intelligible world, are nothing but presentations of a problem, the subject of which in itself is indeed possible, but the solution of which is, by the nature of our understanding, utterly impossible, since our understanding is no faculty of intuition, but is merely the connection of given intuitions in an experience, and must comprise therefore all objects for our conceptions; but apart from these, all conceptions which cannot be supported by an intuition, must be without meaning.

Section Thirty-five: The Second Part, Continued

The imagination may perhaps be forgiven, if it sometimes dreams, and fails to keep itself carefully within the limits of experience; for certainly it is invigorated and strengthened by a free flight like this, and it is always easier to moderate its boldness than to stimulate its languor. But for the understanding, which ought to think, to dream instead, can never be forgiven, as it is our only support in setting bounds to the fantasies of the imagination, where this is necessary.

It begins, however, very innocently and modestly. First of all, it reduces the elementary cognitions inhering in it before all experience, but having their application, notwithstanding, in experience, to their pure state. Gradually it lets fall these limits; and what is there then to hinder it, seeing that the understanding has taken its principles quite freely from itself? First of all, it is led to newly invented powers in Nature, soon after to essences outside Nature, in a word, to a world for whose fitting-up we can never fail in material, because by a fruitful imagination this will always be richly procured, and although not substantiated by experience, will yet never be confuted by it. This is the reason why young thinkers are so fond of metaphysics, treated in a genuinely dogmatic manner, and sacrifice to it their time and talents which might be otherwise useful.

But it is of no avail attempting to moderate these fruitless attempts of pure Reason, by all manner of cautions as to the difficulty of the solution of such deeply-hidden questions, lamentations over the limits of our Reason, and by lowering assertions to mere conjectures. For if their *impossibility* be not clearly shown, and the *self-knowledge* of Reason be not [raised to] a true science, in which the field of its right use is separated from that of its nugatory and fruitless use, so to speak, with geometrical certainty, these vain endeavours will never be completely laid aside.

Section Thirty-six: How is Nature itself possible?

This question, which is the highest point the transcendental philosophy can ever touch, and to which it must also, as its boundary and completion, be directed, properly comprises two questions.

Firstly: How is Nature, in its material signification, namely, as intuition, as the sum-total of *phenomena*—how is space, time, and that which fills them both, namely, the object of feeling in general—possible? The answer is, by means of the construction of our sensibility, in accordance with which, it is affected in a special manner by objects, in themselves unknown and entirely distinct from these appearances. This answer has been given in the book itself in the Transcendental Æsthetic, but in these *Prolegomena* in the solution of the first general question.

Secondly: How is Nature in its *formal* signification—as the sum-total of the rules to which all *phenomena* must be subordinated, if they are to be thought of as connected in an experience—possible? The answer can only be: It is only possible by means of the construction of our understanding, in accordance with which all the above presentations of sensibility are necessarily referred to a consciousness, and whereby the special manner of our thought (namely, by rules), and by means of these, experience (which is to be wholly distinguished from a knowledge of things in themselves) is possible. ...

But how this special property of our sensibility itself, or of our understanding together with the necessary apperception lying at its basis, and at that of all thought, is possible, will not admit of any further solution or answer, because we invariably require it for all answers and for all thought of objects.

There are many laws of Nature that we can only know by means of experience, but regularity in the connection of phenomena, i.e., Nature in general, we can never learn through experience, because experience itself requires such laws, and these lie at the foundation of its possibility *a priori*. The possibility of experience in general is at once the universal law of Nature, and the axioms of the one are at the same time the laws of the other. For we know nothing of Nature otherwise than as the sum-total of *phenomena*, namely, of presentations in us, and hence can derive the law of their connection in no other way than from the principles of the same connection in ourselves; in other words, from the conditions of necessary union in a consciousness, which constitutes the possibility of experience.

Even the main proposition, worked out through the whole of this section, that universal natural laws are to be known *a priori*, of itself leads to the further proposition, that the highest legislation of Nature must lie in ourselves, namely, in our understanding, and that we must seek its universal laws, not in Nature, by means of experience; but conversely, must seek Nature, as to its universal regularity, solely in the conditions of the possibility of experience lying in our sensibility and understanding. For how would it otherwise be possible to know these laws *a priori* if they be not rules of analytic knowledge, but actually synthetic extensions of the same? Such a necessary agreement of the principles of possible experience with the laws of the possibility of Nature can only occur from one of two causes; either the laws are borrowed from Nature by means of experience, or conversely, Nature is derived from the laws of the possibility of experience generally, and is entirely the same thing as the purely formal regularity of the latter. The first supposition contradicts itself, for the universal laws of Nature can and must be known *a priori* (i.e., independently of all experience), and be posited as the basis of the empirical use of the understanding; so that only the second [hypothesis] remains to us.

But we must distinguish the empirical laws of Nature, which always presuppose particular perceptions, from the pure or universal natural laws, which without any particular perceptions at their foundation, merely contain the conditions of their necessary union in an experience; and in respect of the last, Nature and possible experience are the same thing. Hence, as in this, the legitimacy rests on the necessary connection of phenomena in an experience, in other words, on the original laws of the understanding (without which we could cognise no object of the sensuous world whatever), it sounds at first singular, but is none the less certain, when I say in respect of the latter: The understanding draws its laws (*a priori*) not from Nature, but prescribes them to it. ...

How is Natural Science possible?

1. *Step One: Clarifying the problem*

   Natural science, despite appearances, includes a 'pure' (i.e., non-empirical) element. Every science makes two assumptions. What are they?
   These assumptions are pre-conditions for even engaging in science in the first place.
   Two main competitors: rationalism and (Lockean) empiricism. Neither works. So we need to start over and find a third way. Turn now to JOEs. What makes them possible?
   But these just are the universal laws of nature (602). That is, the principles upon which all sciences depend also lie at the bottom of all _____, and make it possible.
   So we've really got just one problem here: how can we justify claims that involve the pure concepts of the understanding, claims like cause, effect, substance, etc.?
2. *Step Two: What did Hume teach us?*

   1. These claims cannot be empirical. Why?
   2. But nor can they be analytic. Why?

*These are the prongs of Hume's fork; for him, every proposition is either a **matter of fact** or a **relation of ideas**. Hume concludes that these principles have only _____ necessity; they are the 'bastard offspring' of _____ impregnated by _____.*

3. Step Three: Putting it all together:

Hume is right to claim that experience can't justify _____. But he's wrong to think that this means that _____. Instead, the concept of cause and effect is a pure _____. That is, it is not something we read off from experience, but something we use to construct experience in the first place. There's no room for skepticism about causation, since to have any experiences at all, I must be uniting _____ in judgments according to the concept of a cause. Like geometry, pure natural science depends on _____.

4. Step Four: What are the consequences?

But just as with geometry, this means that the categories can be applied _____. Is Kant saying that things as they are in themselves must be connected by cause and effect, or that they are things at all, in the way a tree is a thing? _____, because _____.

5. *Another way to see the same point: remember, all judgments require _____. Applied to things in themselves, the categories have _____. (See Sections Thirty and Thirty-four). When we try to apply the categories to things in themselves, we leave out _____, and so generate only empty logical forms, structure without stuffing.*

So far, we've seen Kant explain how metaphysics' companions in guilt—pure natural science and mathematics—are entitled to use synthetic a priori reasoning. Before we see Kant close the circle and return to metaphysics proper, we should take a look at an important passage from the CPR that tells us a great deal about the limitations Kant is imposing on the application of the categories, and on the kinds of questions we can and cannot ask.

The *CPR*, "Deduction of the Pure Concepts of the Understanding"

This cognition,[3] which is limited to objects of experience, is not for that reason derived entirely *from* experience. There are, unquestionably, elements of cognition, which exist in the mind *a priori* [e.g., the Categories and the pure forms of intuition]. Now there are only two ways in which a necessary harmony of experience with the conceptions of its objects can be cogitated. Either experience makes these conceptions possible, or the conceptions make experience possible. The former of these statements will not hold good with respect to the categories (nor in regard to pure sensuous intuition), for they are *a priori* conceptions, and therefore independent of experience. ...

Consequently, nothing remains but to adopt the second alternative, namely, that on the part of the understanding the categories do contain the grounds of the possibility of all experience. But with respect to the questions how they make experience possible, and what are the principles of the possibility thereof with which they present us in their application to phenomena, the following section on the transcendental exercise of the faculty of judgement will inform the reader.

It is quite possible that someone may propose a species of preformation-system of pure reason—a middle way between the two—to wit, that the categories are neither innate and first *a priori* principles of cognition, nor derived from experience, but are merely subjective aptitudes for thought implanted in us contemporaneously with our existence, which were so ordered and disposed by our Creator, that their exercise perfectly harmonizes with the laws of nature which regulate experience. Now, not to mention that with such an hypothesis it is impossible to say at what point we must stop in the employment of predetermined aptitudes, the fact that the categories would in this case entirely lose that character of necessity which is essentially involved in the very conception of them, is a conclusive objection to it. The conception of cause, for example, which expresses the necessity of an effect under a presupposed condition, would be false, if it rested only upon such an arbitrary subjective necessity of uniting certain empirical representations according to such a rule of relation. I could not then say, "The effect is connected with its cause in the object (that is, necessarily)," but only, "I am so constituted that I can think this representation as so connected, and not otherwise." Now this is just what the sceptic wants. For in this case, all our knowledge, depending on the supposed objective validity of our judgement, is nothing but mere illusion; nor would there be wanting people who would deny any such subjective necessity in respect to themselves, though they must feel it. At all events, we could not dispute with any one on that which merely depends on the manner in which his subject is organized.

---

1. *The problem Kant confronts here is this: why is it that our concepts match experience? Kant says, it's because we construct our experiences. One alternative is empiricism (experience gives us the concepts). What's wrong with this view?*
2. *What is the third alternative here? Does it remind you of any view we've encountered before?*

Now we return to the Prolegomena, and Kant's answer to the main question of that work.

The *Prolegomena*, Section Forty: The Main Transcendental Question—Third Part: How is Metaphysics possible at all?

Pure mathematics and pure natural science would not require *for their own security* and certainty a deduction such as we have just concluded with respect to them both; for the former rests upon its own evidence, while the latter, although arising from the pure sources of the understanding, is dependent upon the complete substantiation of experience, a witness it is unable altogether to repudiate and do without, seeing that with all its certainty, as philosophy, it can never compete with mathematics. Both these sciences required the foregoing investigation, not for their own sake, but for the sake of another science, namely, metaphysics.

Metaphysics is concerned not merely with natural conceptions, having invariably an application in experience, but, in addition to these, with pure conceptions of Reason, which can never be given in any possible experience; that is, with conceptions whose objective reality (as distinguished from simple cobwebs of the brain), and with assumptions whose truth or falsity can be confirmed or discovered by no experience. This part of metaphysics is precisely that which constitutes its essential purpose, all else being merely a means thereto, and hence this science requires such a deduction *for its own sake*. The third problem, now before us, concerns, as it were, the essence and speciality of metaphysics, namely, the occupation of Reason with itself alone, inasmuch as it broods over its own conceptions and the knowledge of objects supposed to arise immediately from them, without having need of the mediation of experience, or indeed without the possibility of being able to attain thereto by its means. Without a satisfactory solution of this problem, Reason can never be just to itself. The empirical use to which Reason limits the understanding, does not exhaust its own function. Each special experience is but a portion of the whole sphere of its domain. But the *absolute totality of all possible experience*, though in itself no experience, constitutes nevertheless for Reason a necessary problem, to the mere presentation of which it demands quite different conceptions from the pure conceptions of the understanding, the use of which is only *immanent*, i.e., referable to experience, so far as it can be given; whereas the conceptions of Reason extend to the completeness, i.e., the collective unity of all possible experience, thereby passing beyond any given experience and becoming *transcendent*.

As, then, the understanding required the Categories for experience, so Reason contains in itself the ground of Ideas, by which I understand necessary conceptions the subject of which cannot be given in any experience. The latter are as inherent in the nature of Reason as the former in the nature of the Understanding, and if they carry with them an illusion that may easily mislead, this illusion is unavoidable, although we may very well guard ourselves from being misled by it.

As all illusion consists in the subjective ground of judgment being taken for objective, the self-knowledge of pure Reason, in its transcendent (exaggerated) use, is the only preservative against the aberrations into which Reason falls when it misapplies its function, and refers its transcendent character, concerning only its own subject and its direction in all immanent uses, to the object itself.

Section Forty-one: The Third Part, Continued

The distinction between the ideas, or pure conceptions of Reason, and the categories or pure conceptions of the understanding as being cognitions of quite another order, origin, and use, is so important a point in the foundation of a science, destined to contain the system of all these cognitions *a priori*, that without a division of this kind metaphysics would be simply impossible, or at best an incoherent, clumsy attempt at building a house of cards, without a knowledge of the materials handled, and of their capacity for this or that purpose. If the *Critique of Pure Reason* had only accomplished the direction of attention to the distinction for the first time, it would have thereby contributed more to the explanation of our conceptions and to the guidance of investigation in the field of metaphysics, than all the fruitless endeavours at solving the transcendental problems of pure Reason that have ever been undertaken, in which the suspicion has never occurred that the field was quite other than that of the pure understanding, and where consequently the conceptions of the understanding and Reason have been classed together as though they were of the same kind.

Section Forty-two: The Third Part, Continued

All pure cognitions of the understanding have the peculiarity that their conceptions are given in experience, and their axioms can be confirmed by experience; whereas the transcendent cognitions of Reason are neither given as concerns their ideas in experience, nor can their axioms be confirmed or refuted by experience. Hence the error possibly arising can be detected by nothing else but pure Reason itself, and this is very difficult, because Reason by means of its ideas is naturally dialectic, and this unavoidable illusion can be held in check by no objective and dogmatic investigations of the matter, but solely by the subjectivity of Reason itself as a source of ideas.

Section Forty-three: The Third Part, Continued

It has always been my greatest aim in the *Critique*, not alone to distinguish carefully the modes of cognition, but also to derive from their common source all the conceptions pertaining to them severally, so that I should not only be informed whence they come and hence be able to determine their use with certainty, but also that I should have the altogether unexpected, but priceless, advantage of knowing the numeration, classification, and specification of the conceptions *a priori*, and, therefore, according to principles. Without this, everything in metaphysics is mere rhapsody, in which one never knows whether what one possesses is sufficient, or whether there may not be something wanting in it; and if so, where. We can certainly only have this advantage in pure philosophy, but of this latter it constitutes the essence.

As I had found the origin of the categories in the four logical functions of all judgments of the understanding, it was only natural to seek the origin of the ideas in the three functions of the conclusions of Reason. For if such pure conceptions of Reason (transcendental ideas) be once given, they could not, unless they were regarded as innate, be found elsewhere than in the same act of Reason, which, as far as form is concerned, constitutes the logical element of the conclusions of Reason, but so far as it presents the judgments of the understanding as determined with respect, either to one or the other form *a priori*, [constitutes] the transcendental conceptions of pure Reason.

The formal distinction of the conclusions of Reason, renders their division into categorical, hypothetical and disjunctive, necessary. The conceptions of Reason based thereon, contain, *firstly*, the idea of the complete subject (substantial); *secondly*, the idea of the complete series of conditions; *thirdly*, the determination of all conceptions in the idea of a complete content of the possible. The first idea is psychological, the second cosmological, and the third theological; and as all three give occasion to a dialectic, each of its own kind, the division of the whole dialectic of pure Reason founded thereupon, is into the Paralogism, the Antinomy, and finally the Ideal of the same. By this division we are fully assured that all demands of pure Reason are here presented, in their completeness; that no single one can fail, because the capacity of Reason itself, as that from which they all take their origin, is thereby completely surveyed.

Section Forty-four: The Third Part, Continued

In this general consideration it is noteworthy, that the ideas of Reason, unlike the categories, are not of any service whatever in the use of the understanding in experience, but can be wholly dispensed with in this connection; indeed, they are impediments to the maxims of the understanding's knowledge of nature, notwithstanding their necessity for another purpose, yet to be determined. Whether the soul be, or be not, a simple substance, can be quite indifferent to us, so far as the explanation of its phenomena is concerned, for we cannot render the conception of a simple essence comprehensible, sensuously or *in concreto*, by any possible experience; and hence it is quite barren as to the hoped-for insight into the cause of the phenomena; and cannot serve as any principle of explanation for what is afforded, either by internal or external experience. Just as little can the cosmological ideas of the beginning of the world or of the eternity of the world (*a parte ante*) avail us to explain an occurrence in the world itself. Finally, we must, in accordance with a just maxim of the philosophy of Nature, refrain from all explanation of the order of Nature, which is derived from the will of a Supreme Being, because this is no longer a philosophy of Nature, but a confession that we have finished with the latter. Hence these ideas have quite a different determination of their use from the categories, by means of which, and of the principles based upon them, experience itself is first possible. But our laborious analytic of the understanding would be quite superfluous, if our aim were nothing else but mere knowledge of Nature, such as can be given in experience; for Reason accomplishes its work both in mathematics and natural science, certainly and well, without any of this subtle deduction. Thus our Critique of the understanding combines with the ideas of pure Reason, in an aim placed beyond the empirical use of the understanding, of which we have above said that, in this respect, it is quite impossible, and destitute alike of object and meaning. But there must, nevertheless, be an agreement between that which belongs to the nature of Reason and of the understanding, and the former must contribute to the completion of the latter, and cannot possibly confuse it.

The solution of this problem is as follows: pure Reason has no particular objects denoted by its ideas which lie outside the field of experience in view, but merely requires completeness of the use of the understanding within the system of experience. This completeness, however, can only be a completeness of principles, but not of intuitions and objects. But in order to represent the former definitely, it regards them as the cognition of an object, a cognition completely determined as regards these rules, but the object of which is only an idea, designed to bring the cognition of the understanding as near as possible to the completeness indicated by that idea.

---

1. *What is the difference between an Idea of Reason and a Category of the Understanding? How are they similar?*

Section Forty-five: Preliminary Observation on the Dialectic of pure Reason

We have above (Sections Thirty-three and Thirty-four) shown, that the purity of the categories, from all admixture of sensuous determinations, may mislead Reason into extending its use entirely beyond the range of all experience, to things in themselves; for although they can find no intuition that could lend them meaning and sense *in concreto*, yet as mere logical functions they may represent a thing in general, notwithstanding that, independently, they are unable to give a definite conception of anything whatever. Such hyperbolical objects are what are termed *noumena*, or pure essences of the Understanding (better essences of thought), as, for instance, *substance*, when considered as *without permanence* in time, or a *cause*, which does not *operate in time*, &c., inasmuch as predicates are then attached to them, which serve merely to make the conformability of experience to law possible, and at the same time all the conditions of intuition—under which experience is alone possible—are taken away from them, whereby these conceptions lose all significance. There is, however, no danger of the understanding of itself, unimpressed by laws foreign to it, branching out so rashly into the field of mere essences of thought. But when Reason, which cannot be completely satisfied with an empirical use of the rules of the understanding, requires the completion of this chain of conditions, the understanding is driven out of its own sphere, partly to present objects of experience in a series extended so far that no experience can grasp it, and partly (in order to complete this series) to search for *noumena*, wholly outside the same, to which it may attach the above chain, and thereby, being at last independent of experience, render its attitude once for all complete. These are the transcendental ideas, which, in accordance with the true but hidden ends of the natural determination of our Reason, are designed not for extravagant conceptions, but merely for the unlimited extension of empirical use; but which, however, by an unavoidable illusion seduce the understanding into a *transcendent* use, that although deceitful, cannot be kept within the bounds of experience by any resolution, but can only be restrained within [due] limits with pains, and by means of scientific instruction.

Section Forty-six: "Psychological Idea"

It has long been observed that the subject proper, in all substances, namely, that which remains over after all accidents (as predicates) have been abstracted, that is, the *substantial* itself, is unknown, and oft-repeated complaints have been made of these limitations of our insight. But it is to be observed as regards this, that the human understanding is not to be taken to task for not knowing the substantial of things, that is, for not being able to determine it by itself, but rather for expecting to know it definitely, like a given object, when it is a mere idea. Pure Reason requires of every predicate of a thing the subject belonging to it, but to this, which is again necessarily only predicate, it requires a further subject, and so on *ad infinitum* (or as far as we can reach). But it follows from the above, that nothing to which we can attain is to be taken for an ultimate subject, and that the substantial itself can never be thought by our understanding, however deeply penetrating it may be, not even if the whole of Nature were unveiled before it; because the specific nature of our understanding consists in that it thinks all things discursively, i.e., through conceptions, and hence solely by means of predicates, to which the absolute subject must always be wanting. For this reason all real qualities whereby we cognise bodies, even to impenetrability, which must always present itself as the effect of a force, are simply accidents, the subject of which eludes us.

Now it seems as though in our own consciousness (the thinking subject) we have this substantial, and indeed in an immediate intuition; for all predicates of the internal sense refer to the *ego*, the subject, and this cannot be thought of as predicate of any other subject whatever. Here, then, the completeness in the connection of the given conceptions as predicates of a subject, not merely an idea, but an existence, namely, the *absolute subject* itself, seem to be given in experience. But this experience is vain, for the *ego* is no conception at all, but merely a designation of the object of the internal sense, so far as we can cognise it by no further predicate, and hence in itself it can indeed be no predicate of another thing, and just as little a definite conception of an absolute subject, but only, as in all other cases, the reference of the internal phenomena to their unknown subject. At the same time, this idea (which serves well enough, as regulative principle, completely to annihilate all materialistic explanations of the internal phenomena of our soul) occasions, owing to a perfectly natural misunderstanding, a very plausible argument, by inferring from this supposed cognition of the substantial in our thinking entity, its nature, in so far as the knowledge of the same falls entirely outside the content of experience.

Section Forty-seven: "Psychological Idea", Continued

This thinking self (the soul) may however, as the ultimate subject of thought, which cannot be conceived as the predicate of another thing, be called substance; but this conception remains wholly barren, and void of all results, if permanence, which makes the conception of substances in experience fruitful, cannot be proved of it.

But permanence can never be proved from the conception of a substance, as a thing in itself, but only for the purposes of experience. The above has been fully explained in the first analogy of experience (in the CPR), and, if this demonstration be not accepted, the attempt need only be made as to whether it is possible to prove, from the conception of a subject, not existing as the predicate of some other thing, that its existence is thoroughly permanent, and that neither in itself, nor through any natural cause, can it arise or pass away. Such synthetic propositions *a priori* can never be proved in themselves, but only with reference to things as objects of possible experience.

Section Forty-eight: "Psychological Idea", Continued

When from the conception of the soul as substance we infer its permanence, this can be only valid of it as an object of possible experience, and not as a thing in itself, outside all possible experience. Now the subjective condition of all our possible experience is life; consequently, the permanence of the soul can only be inferred in life, for the death of man is the end of all experience, of which the soul is an object, unless the contrary be proved, and this is precisely the question. Hence, the permanence of the soul can only be proved in the life of man (the proof of which will not be required of us), but not after death, which is the real point at issue, for the general reason that the conception of substance, viewed as necessarily conjoined with the conception of permanence, is only [based on] an axiom of possible experience, and therefore only serviceable for the purposes of the latter.

Section Forty-nine: "Psychological Idea", Continued

That something real not merely corresponds but must correspond to our external perceptions, can be proved as concerns experience, but not as a connection of things in themselves. This is as much as to say, that something of an empirical kind, as phenomenon in space, exists outside us, can be proved; for with objects, other than those belonging to a possible experience, we have nothing to do, because, inasmuch as they can be given in no experience, they are to us nothing. That is empirically outside me which can be intuited in space, and as the latter, together with all the phenomena it contains, belongs to the presentations, whose connection according to the laws of experience proves their objective reality, just as much as the connection of the phenomena of the internal sense proves the reality of my soul, as an object of the internal sense; so, by means of external experience, I am just as conscious of the reality of bodies as external phenomena in space, as I am of the existence of my soul in time by means of the internal experience, which I also cognise only through phenomena, as an object of the internal sense, [that is, as] constituting an internal condition, of which the essence in itself, lying at the foundation of these phenomena, is unknown to me. The Cartesian idealism only distinguishes external experience from dream; its regularity being the criterion of the truth of the one as against the irregularity and false illusion of the other. It presupposes, in both of them, space and time as conditions of the reality of the objects, and only asks whether the objects of our external sense, which when awake we meet with in space, are really to be found therein, and in the same way whether the object of the internal sense, the soul, really exists in time; in other words, whether experience can afford certain criteria for the distinction between truth and imagination. Now this doubt may be easily decided, and we always do decide it in common life, in that we investigate the connection of the phenomena in both according to universal laws of experience, and we cannot doubt, when the presentation of external things thoroughly agrees with these, that they constitute reliable experience. Material idealism may accordingly be refuted very easily, inasmuch as phenomena *qua* phenomena are only considered as to their connection in experience; and it is just as certain an experience that bodies exist *outside ourselves* (in space), as that I myself according to the presentation of the internal sense exist (in time); for the conception of outside ourselves, denotes simply existence in space. But as the I in the proposition *I am*, signifies not merely the object of internal intuition (in time) but the subject of consciousness, so in the same way *body* signifies not merely the external intuition (in space), but also the thing *in itself* at the basis of this phenomenon, and hence the question as to whether bodies (as phenomena of the external sense) exist *apart from my thoughts* as bodies, may, in the nature of things, be denied without hesitation. But there is no difference as to the question, whether I myself as phenomenon of the *internal sense* (soul, according to the empirical psychology) exist in time, apart from my power of presentation, for this must be just as much denied. In the same way, everything when reduced to its true meaning is decided and certain. Formal idealism (otherwise called transcendental by me) really refutes the material or Cartesian [idealism]. For if space be nothing but a form of my sensibility, it is just as real as a presentation in me as I am myself, and the question only turns on the empirical truth of phenomena in the same. If this, however, be not the case, but space and the phenomena [contained] therein are something existing outside ourselves, all criteria of experience, apart from our perception, can never prove the reality of the objects external to us.

Kant mounts a different attack on the "Psychological Idea" in the Critique. *What follows is an excerpt from the B edition of the "Paralogisms [fallacies] of Pure Reason".*

The *CPR*, "The Paralogisms of Pure Reason"

Now,[4] as the proposition "I think" (in the problematical sense) contains the form of every judgement in general and is the constant accompaniment of all the categories, it is manifest that conclusions are drawn from it only by a transcendental employment of the understanding. This use of the understanding excludes all empirical elements; and we cannot, as has been shown above, have any favourable conception beforehand of its procedure. We shall therefore follow with a critical eye this proposition through all the predicaments of pure psychology ...

Before entering on this task, however, the following general remark may help to quicken our attention to this mode of argument. It is not merely through my thinking that I cognize an object, but only through my determining a given intuition in relation to the unity of consciousness in which all thinking consists. It follows that I cognize myself, not through my being conscious of myself as thinking, but only when I am conscious of the intuition of myself as determined in relation to the function of thought. All the modes of self-consciousness in thought are hence not conceptions of objects (conceptions of the understanding—categories); they are mere logical functions, which do not present to thought an object to be cognized, and cannot therefore present my Self as an object. Not the consciousness of the determining, but only that of the determinable self, that is, of my internal intuition (in so far as the manifold contained in it can be connected conformably with the general condition of the unity of apperception in thought), is the object.

1. [*On the inference from 'I think' to 'I exist as a substance*]—In all judgements I am the determining subject

of that relation which constitutes a judgement. But that the I which thinks, must be considered as in thought always a subject, and as a thing which cannot be a predicate to thought, is an apodeictic and identical proposition. But this proposition does not signify that I, as an object, am, for myself, a self-subsistent being or substance. This latter statement—an ambitious one—requires to be supported by data which are not to be discovered in thought; and are perhaps (in so far as I consider the thinking self merely as such) not to be discovered in the thinking self at all.

---

1. *'It is raining outside; therefore, there is an It that rains.' How is Descartes's cogito inference analogous?*

---

1. [*On the inference from 'I think' to 'I exist as a simple substance*]—That the I or *ego* of apperception, and consequently in all thought, is singular or simple, and cannot be resolved into a plurality of subjects, and therefore indicates a logically simple subject—this is self-evident from the very conception of an *ego*, and is consequently an analytical proposition. But this is not tantamount to declaring that the thinking *ego* is a simple substance—for this would be a synthetical proposition. The conception of substance always relates to intuitions, which with me cannot be other than sensuous, and which consequently lie completely out of the sphere of the understanding and its thought: but to this sphere belongs the affirmation that the *ego* is simple in thought. It would indeed be surprising, if the conception of "substance," which in other cases requires so much labour to distinguish from the other elements presented by intuition—so much trouble, too, to discover whether it can be simple (as in the case of the parts of matter)—should be presented immediately to me, as if by revelation, in the poorest mental representation of all.

2. [*On the inference from 'I think' to 'I am the same thinking substance over time*]—The proposition of the identity of my Self amidst all the manifold representations of which I am conscious, is likewise a proposition lying in the conceptions themselves, and is consequently analytical. But this identity of the subject, of which I am conscious in all its representations, does not relate to or concern the intuition of the subject, by which it is given as an object. This proposition cannot therefore enounce the identity of the person, by which is understood the consciousness of the identity of its own substance as a thinking being in all change and variation of circumstances. To prove this, we should require not a mere analysis of the proposition, but synthetical judgements based upon a given intuition.

3. [*On the inference from 'I think' to 'I exist as a thinking substance distinct from any material substance*]—I distinguish my own existence, as that of a thinking being, from that of other things external to me—among which my body also is reckoned. This is also an analytical proposition, for other things are exactly those which I think as different or distinguished from myself. But whether this consciousness of myself is possible without things external to me; and whether therefore I can exist merely as a thinking being (without being man)—cannot be known or inferred from this proposition.

Thus we have gained nothing as regards the cognition of myself as object, by the analysis of the consciousness of my Self in thought. The logical exposition of thought in general is mistaken for a metaphysical determination of the object.

Our *Critique* would be an investigation utterly superfluous, if there existed a possibility of proving *a priori*, that all thinking beings are in themselves simple substances, as such, therefore, possess the inseparable attribute of personality, and are conscious of their existence apart from and unconnected with matter. For we should thus have taken a step beyond the world of sense, and have penetrated into the sphere of noumena; and in this case the right could not be denied us of extending our knowledge in this sphere, of establishing ourselves, and, under a favouring star, appropriating to ourselves possessions in it. For the proposition: "Every thinking being, as such, is simple substance," is an *a priori* synthetical proposition; because in the first place it goes beyond the conception which is the subject of it, and adds to the mere notion of a thinking being the mode of its existence, and in the second place annexes a predicate (that of simplicity) to the latter conception—a predicate which it could not have discovered in the sphere of experience. It would follow that *a priori* synthetical propositions are possible and legitimate, not only, as we have maintained, in relation to objects of possible experience, and as principles of the possibility of this experience itself, but are applicable to things in themselves—an inference which makes an end of the whole of this Critique, and obliges us to fall back on the old mode of metaphysical procedure. But indeed the danger is not so great, if we look a little closer into the question.

There lurks in the procedure of rational Psychology a paralogism, which is represented in the following syllogism:

1. That which cannot be cogitated otherwise than as subject, does not exist otherwise than as subject, and is therefore substance.
2. A thinking being, considered merely as such, cannot be cogitated otherwise than as subject. Therefore,
3. It exists also as such, that is, as substance.

In the major premise [i] we speak of a being that can be cogitated generally and in every relation, consequently as it may be given in intuition. But in the minor premise [ii] we speak of the same being only in so far as it regards itself as subject, relatively to thought and the unity of consciousness, but not in relation to intuition, by which it is presented as an object to thought. Thus the conclusion is here arrived at by equivocation.

That this famous argument is a mere paralogism, will be plain to any one who will consider the general remark which precedes our exposition of the principles of the pure understanding, and the section on noumena. For it was there proved that the conception of a thing, which can exist per se—only as a subject and never as a predicate, possesses no objective reality; that is to say, we can never know whether there exists any object to correspond to the conception; consequently, the conception is nothing more than a conception, and from it we derive no proper knowledge. If this conception is to indicate by the term substance, an object that can be given, if it is to become a cognition, we must have at the foundation of the cognition a permanent intuition, as the indispensable condition of its objective reality. For through intuition alone can an object be given. But in internal intuition there is nothing permanent, for the *ego* is but the consciousness of my thought. If then, we appeal merely to thought, we cannot discover the necessary condition of the application of the conception of substance—that is, of a subject existing per se—to the subject as a thinking being. And thus the conception of the simple nature of substance, which is connected with the objective reality of this conception, is shown to be also invalid, and to be, in fact, nothing more than the logical qualitative unity of self-consciousness in thought; whilst we remain perfectly ignorant whether the subject is composite or not.

1. *What would Kant make of the argument (in Descartes's Sixth Meditation) for the real distinction between mind and body?*

We now return to the Prolegomena. Having finished with the Idea of the self as substance, Kant moves on to the Idea of the world of experience as a whole.

The *Prolegomena*, Section Fifty: "The Cosmological Idea"

This product of pure Reason in its transcendent use is its most remarkable phenomenon, and is moreover the one most powerful in awakening philosophy out of its dogmatic slumber, and in urging it on, to the heavy tasks of the *Critique of Reason*.

I term this idea cosmological, because it always takes its object from the world of sense, and only requires those [conceptions] whose object is an object of sense, being therefore native [immanent] and not transcendent, and consequently, thus far, no idea; while, on the other hand, to conceive the soul as a simple substance, is equivalent to conceiving an object (the simple) which cannot be presented to the senses. But notwithstanding this, the cosmological idea extends the connection of the conditioned with its condition (whether mathematical or dynamical) so far, that experience can never reach it, and hence remains, as regards this point, always an idea, the object of which can never be adequately given in any experience whatever.

1. *In what way does the "Cosmological Idea" remain within the bounds of possible experience? In what way does it go beyond these bounds?*

Section Fifty-one: "The Cosmological Idea", Continued

It is here that the usefulness of a system of categories shows itself so plainly and unmistakably, that, even were there not several other proofs of it, this alone would quite sufficiently demonstrate its indispensableness in the system of pure Reason. There are not more than four of these transcendent ideas, as many as there are classes of categories; but each of them is only concerned with the absolute completion of a series of conditions to a given conditioned. In accordance with these cosmological ideas there are four dialectical assertions of pure Reason, which, inasmuch as they are dialectical, show that to each one is opposed a contradictory assumption, on equally plausible principles of pure Reason; and this is a conflict no metaphysical art of the subtlest distinction can avoid, but which compels philosophers to go back to the primary sources of pure Reason. The above antinomy, which is not arbitrarily invented, but has its basis in the nature of human Reason, and is hence unavoidable and never-ending, contains the following four theses together with their antitheses:

	Thesis
1	The world has a *beginning* in time and space
2	Everything in the world consists of *simple* [parts].
3	There are in the world causes through *freedom.*
4	In the series of world-causes there exists a *necessary* being.

	Antithesis
1	The world is *infinite* in time and space
2	There is nothing simple, but everything is *composite.*
3	There is no freedom, but all is *Nature*
4	There is nothing necessary, but in this series *all is contingent.*

Section Fifty-two: "The Cosmological Idea", Continued

The above is the most remarkable phenomenon of the human Reason, of which no instance can be shown in any other sphere. If, as generally happens, we regard the phenomena of the world of sense as things in themselves; if we assume the principles of their connection as universal of things in themselves and not merely as principles valid of experience, as is usual and indeed unavoidable without our Critique; then an unexpected conflict arises, never to be quelled in the ordinary dogmatic way, because both theses and antitheses can be demonstrated by equally evident, clear and irresistible proofs—for I pledge myself as to the correctness of all these proofs—and Reason thus sees itself at issue with itself, a state over which the sceptic rejoices, but which must plunge the critical philosopher into reflection and disquiet.

Section Fifty-two (B): "The Cosmological Idea", Continued

One may bungle in metaphysics in many ways, without any danger of being detected in fallacy. For if we only do not contradict ourselves, which is quite possible in synthetic propositions, even though they may be purely invented, we can never in such cases (the conceptions we connect, being mere ideas, which as to their whole content can never be given in experience) be refuted by experience. For how should we decide by experience whether the world exists from eternity, or has a beginning? or whether matter is infinitely divisible, or consists of simple parts? Such conceptions cannot be given in any, even the largest possible experience, and therefore the fallacy of the propositions maintained or denied cannot be discovered by that test.

The only possible case in which Reason could reveal against its will its secret dialectic, fallaciously given out by it as dogmatic, would be, if it grounded an assertion on a universally admitted axiom, and from another, equally conceded, drew a precisely opposite conclusion, with the greatest logical accuracy. This case is here realised, and indeed in respect of four natural ideas of Reason whence four assertions on the one hand, and just as many counter-assertions on the other, arise, each as a correct consequence from universally admitted premises, and thereby reveal the dialectical illusion of pure Reason in the use of these principles, which must otherwise have been for ever hidden.

Here then is a decisive attempt, which must necessarily disclose to us the fallacy lying hidden in the assumptions of Reason. Of two mutually contradictory propositions, both cannot be false, unless the conception at their basis be itself contradictory. For instance, two propositions, a square circle is round and a square circle is not round, are both false. For as regards the first, it is false that the [figure] mentioned is round, because it is square, but it is also false that it is not round, or that it is square, because it is a circle. For in this consists the logical mark of the impossibility of a conception, that under the same assumption two contradictory propositions would be equally false; in other words, because no middle can be conceived between them, *nothing at all* is cogitated by that conception.

Section Fifty-two (C): "The Cosmological Idea", Continued

Now, a contradictory conception like the foregoing lies at the basis of the two first antinomies, which I call mathematical, because they are concerned with the addition or division of things similar in Nature; and thence I explain how it happens that thesis and antithesis are alike false.

When I speak of objects in time and space, I do not speak of things in themselves, because of these I know nothing, but only of things in the phenomenon, in other words, of experience, as the special mode of the cognition of objects, which is alone vouchsafed to man. I must not say that what I think in space or in time exists in itself in space and time apart from this my thought; for I should then contradict myself, because space and time, together with the phenomena in them, are nothing existing in themselves and apart from my presentations, but are themselves only modes of presentations, and it is obviously contradictory to say that a mere mode of our presentation exists outside our presentation. The objects of sense exist then only in experience; and to give them a special substantive existence for themselves, apart from or before the latter, is equivalent to imagining that experience can be present without or before experience.

Now, when I inquire as to the size of the world in space and time, it is for all my conceptions just as impossible to say, it is infinite, as it is finite. For neither of them can be contained in experience, because experience is neither possible respecting an *infinite* space, or an infinite time, or the boundary of the world by an empty space or a previous empty time; these [things] are only ideas. Hence as regards either one or the other kind of determinate quantity, it must lie in the world itself, separate from all experience. But this contradicts the conception of a world of sense, which is only a content of experience, whose reality and connection takes place in presentation, namely, in experience, because it is not a thing in itself, but is itself nothing but a mode of presentation. It follows from the above, that, as the conception of a self-existent world is in itself contradictory, the solution of the problem as to its size will be always fallacious, no matter whether it be affirmatively or negatively attempted.

The same applies to the second antinomy, which concerns the division of phenomena. For these are mere presentations, and the parts exist merely in their presentation, and therefore in their division; in other words, in a possible experience in which they are given, and they only extend as far as the latter reaches. To assume that a phenomenon, for instance, that of body, contains all parts in itself, before all experience, to which nought but possible experience can ever attain, is equal to giving to a mere appearance, which can exist only in experience, a special existence preceding experience, or to say that mere presentations are there before they are met with in the faculty of presentation, which contradicts itself; and so, consequently, does every solution of this misunderstood problem, whether it be maintained that bodies consist of infinitely many parts, or of a finite number of simple parts.

Thesis—Causality according to the laws of nature, is not the only causality operating to originate the phenomena of the world. A causality of freedom is also necessary to account fully for these phenomena.

Antithesis—There is no such thing as freedom, but everything in the world happens solely according to the laws of nature.

The *Prolegomena*, Section Fifty-three: "The Cosmological Idea", Continued

In the first class of antinomy (the mathematical), the fallacy of the assumption consisted in that what is self-contradictory (namely, phenomenon and thing in itself) was represented as capable of union in one idea. But as regards the second, or dynamical class of antinomy, the fallacy of the assumption consists in that what is capable of union is represented as contradictory, and consequently, as in the first case, both contradictory assertions were false; so here, where they are opposed to one another merely through misunderstanding, both may be true.

The mathematical connection necessarily presupposes homogeneity in the connected (in the conception of quantity), while the dynamical by no means requires this. Where the quantity of the extended is concerned, all the parts must be homogeneous, both with each other and with the whole; whereas in the connection of cause and effect, although homogeneity may also be met with, it is not necessary. For the conception of causality, by means of which a thing is posited by something quite distinct therefrom, at least does not require it. If the objects of the sense-world were taken for things in themselves, and the above-cited laws of Nature for laws of things in themselves, the contradiction would be un avoidable. In the same way, if the subject of freedom were presented like other objects as mere appearance, the contradiction would be equally unavoidable; for the same thing would be at once affirmed and denied of the same kind of object in the same sense. But if natural necessity be referred merely to phenomena, and freedom merely to things in themselves, no contradiction arises, in assuming or admitting both kinds of causality, however difficult or impossible it may be to render the latter kind comprehensible.

In the phenomenon, every effect is an event, or something that happens in time; a determination of the causality of its cause (a state of the same), must precede it, upon which it follows according to a uniform law. But this determination of the cause to causality must also be something that takes place, or happens. The cause must have begun to act, otherwise between it and the effect, no succession in time could be conceived. The effect would always have existed, as well as the causality of the cause. Thus, among phenomena, the *determination* of the cause *to the effect* must also have arisen, and therefore be just as much as its effect, an event which, in its turn, must have a cause, and so on; and consequently, necessity must be the condition according to which the efficient causes are determined. If, on the other hand, freedom be a characteristic of certain causes of phenomena, it must, as regards the latter as events, be a faculty of beginning them *from itself* (*sponte*), i.e., without the causality of the causes themselves having begun, and hence another ground would be necessary to determine its beginning. In that case, however, the cause, as to its causality, must not be subject to time determinations of its state; that is, it must *not* be *phenomenon*, but it must be regarded as a thing in itself, and its effects only, as phenomena. If one can conceive such an influence of the essences of the understanding on phenomena without contradiction, though necessity would attach to all connection of cause and effect in the sense-world, yet of the cause which is itself no phenomenon, although it lies at the foundation of the latter, freedom would be admitted. Thus Nature and

Freedom can be attributed without contradiction to the same thing, at one time as phenomenon, at another, as thing in itself.

We have a faculty within us, not only standing in connection with its subjective determining grounds, which are the natural causes of its actions, and in so far the faculty of a being, belonging to phenomena, but also referable to objective grounds, though these are merely ideas, in so far as they can determine this faculty; and this connection is expressed by *ought*. The above faculty is termed *Reason*, and when we contemplate a being (man) simply according to this subjectively determining Reason, it cannot be regarded as an essence of sense, but the quality thought of is the quality of a thing in itself, of the possibility of which, namely, the *ought* of that which has never happened, and yet the activity of which can be the determination and cause of actions, whose effect is phenomenal in the sense-world, of this we can form no conception whatever. At the same time, the causality of Reason as concerns its effects in the sense-world would be freedom, so far as *objective grounds*, which are themselves ideas, are regarded as determining these effects. For its action would then depend not on subjective, and therefore on time-conditions, nor on natural laws, serving to determine these, since grounds of Reason in general would furnish the rule for actions according to principles, without the influence of circumstances, time, or place.

What I adduce here, is merely meant as an instance for the sake of intelligibility, and does not necessarily belong to our question, which must be decided from mere conceptions, independently of the qualities we meet with in the real world.

I can say now without contradiction, that all actions of rational beings, inasmuch as they are phenomena, met with in any experience, are subject to necessity; but precisely the same actions, with reference to the rational subject, and its capacity of acting according to mere Reason, are free. For what is demanded by necessity? Nothing more than the determinability of every event in the sense-world according to uniform laws; in other words, a reference to Cause in the phenomenon, whereby the thing in itself, lying at its foundation, and its causality, remains unknown. But I say: the natural law subsists alike, whether the rational being [acting] from Reason, and hence through freedom, be the cause of the effects in the sense-world, or whether these are determined by other grounds than those of Reason. For in the first case, the action happens according to maxims, whose effect in the phenomenon will be always in accordance with uniform laws; in the second case, if the action does not happen according to principles of Reason, it is subordinated to the empirical laws of the sensibility, and in both cases the effects are connected according to uniform laws; more than this we do not require to [constitute] natural necessity, nay, more we do not know respecting it. But in the first case, Reason is the cause of these natural laws, and is hence free; in the second case, the effects follow the mere natural laws of the sensibility, because Reason exercises no influence upon them; Reason, however, is not on this account itself determined by the sensibility (which is impossible), and is consequently in this case also free. The freedom does not hinder the natural law of the phenomena, any more than the latter interferes with the freedom of the practical use of Reason, which stands in connection with things in themselves as determining grounds.

In this way, the practical freedom, namely, that by which Reason has causality, according to objective determining grounds, is saved, without natural necessity being curtailed in the least, in respect of the same effects as phenomena. The above may also be serviceable as an explanation of what we had to say regarding transcendental freedom, and its union with natural necessity (in the same subject, but not taken in the same connection). For as to this, every beginning of the action of a being, from objective causes, so far as its determining grounds are concerned, is always a *first beginning*, although the same action in the series of phenomena is only a *subaltern beginning*, necessarily preceded by a state of the cause determining it, and itself determined by a [state] immediately preceding; so that without falling into contradiction with the laws of Nature, we may conceive of a faculty in rational beings, or in beings generally, in so far as their causality is determined in them, as things in themselves, by which a series of states is begun of themselves. For the relation of the action to objective grounds of Reason is no relation in time; here, what determines the causality does not precede the action according to time, because such determining grounds [as these] do not present a reference of the objects to sense, or, in other words, to causes in the phenomenon, but to determining causes, as things in themselves, which are not subordinated to time-conditions. Hence, the action may be viewed with regard to the causality of Reason as a first beginning, but at the same time, as regards the series of the phenomena, as a merely subordinate beginning, and without contradiction, in the former aspect as free, and in the latter, inasmuch as it is merely phenomenon, as subordinate to natural necessity.

As concerns the *fourth* antinomy, it is solved in the same manner as is the conflict of Reason with itself, in the third. For if *the cause in the phenomenon* be only distinguished from *the cause of the phenomena*, so far as they can be considered as *things in themselves*, both propositions can subsist beside one another, namely, that no cause takes place anywhere in the sense-world (according to similar laws of causality) whose existence is absolutely necessary; while, on the other hand, this world may be connected with a necessary being as its cause, though of another kind, and according to other laws; the incompatibility of the above two propositions simply resting on the misunderstanding by which what is merely valid of phenomena is extended to things in themselves, both being mixed up in one conception.

---

1. *In the case of the third and fourth antinomies, the mistake lies in thinking that the propositions are incompatible, when in fact they are. How does Kant make sense of this? How can both propositions in each pair be true?*

Section Fifty-four: "The Cosmological Idea", Continued

This is the arrangement and solution of the whole antinomy, in which Reason finds itself involved, in the application of its principles to the sense-world, and of which even this (the mere arrangement) would be itself a considerable service to the knowledge of the human Reason, even though the solution of the conflict should not fully satisfy the reader, who has here a natural illusion to combat, which has only recently been presented to him as such, and which he has previously regarded as true. For one consequence of this is inevitable, namely, that seeing it is quite impossible to get free of this conflict of Reason with itself, so long as the objects of the sense-world are taken for things in themselves, and not for what they are in reality, namely, mere phenomena, the reader is necessitated thereby again to undertake the deduction of all our knowledge a priori, and its examination as given by me, in order to come to a decision in the matter. I do not require more [than this] at present; for if he has but first penetrated deeply enough into the nature of pure Reason, the conceptions by which the solution of this conflict of Reason is alone possible, will be already familiar to him, without which circumstance I cannot expect full credit even from the most attentive reader.

To think about: in some sense, Kant can be called a 'compatibilist': he thinks it's at least possible that determinism and free will should co-exist. Is this any different from Hume's compatibilism? If so, how?

Section Fifty-five: "The Theological Idea"

The third transcendental idea, which furnishes material to the most important, but, when merely conducted speculatively, to the exaggerated (transcendent) and thereby dialectical use of Reason, is the ideal of pure Reason. Reason does not here, as with the psychological and cosmological ideas, start from experience, and is not, by a [progressive] raising (*Steigerung*) of the grounds, misled into an endeavour to contemplate the series in absolute completeness, but wholly breaks therewith, and from mere conceptions of what would constitute the absolute completeness of a thing in general, and consequently by means of the idea of a most perfect original being, descends to the determination of the possibility, and thereby also to the reality, of all other things. For this reason, the mere assumption of a being, which although not given in the series of experience, is nevertheless conceived for the sake of experience, to render comprehensible the connection, order, and unity of the latter, that is, the *Idea* is more easily distinguishable from the conceptions of experience [in the present] than in the foregoing cases. The dialectical illusion therefore arising from our holding the subjective conditions of our thought for the objective conditions of things themselves, and a necessary hypothesis for the satisfaction of our Reason for a dogma, may be easily exposed to view; and hence I have nothing further to recall on the assumptions of the transcendental theology, for what the Critique has said on this point is comprehensible, clear, and decisive.

Section Fifty-six: General Remark on the Transcendental Ideas.

The objects given us through experience are in many respects incomprehensible, and there are many problems to which the natural law leads us, when it is carried to a certain height, (though always in accordance with these laws,) which can never be solved; as for instance, how it is that substances attract one another. But, if we entirely leave Nature, or in the progress of its connection overstep all possible experience, and thereby immerse ourselves in mere ideas, we cannot then say that the object is incomprehensible, and that the nature of things places insoluble problems before us; for we have in that case, nothing whatever to do with Nature or with given objects, but merely with conceptions, having their origin simply in our Reason, and with mere essences of thought, in respect of which all problems arising from the conception of the same, can be solved, because Reason can and must certainly give a complete account of its own procedure. As the psychological, cosmological, and theological ideas, are simply conceptions of Reason, not capable of being given in any experience, so the problems which Reason in respect thereof places before us, are not propounded by the objects, but by mere maxims of Reason for its own satisfaction, and must be capable of being adequately answered in their totality, which is effected by showing them to be principles [designed] to bring the use of our understanding to thorough agreement, completeness and synthetic unity, and which are in so far valid merely of experience, but of the *whole* of the latter.

Now, although an absolute whole of experience is impossible, the idea of a whole of knowledge according to principles in general, is what alone can procure a particular kind of unity, namely, that of a system, without which our knowledge is nothing but a patchwork, and cannot be used for the highest end (which is always the system of all ends); by this I understand not merely the practical, but also the highest end of the speculative use of Reason.

The transcendental ideas express, then, the specific destiny of Reason, namely, as being a principle of the systematic unity of the use of the understanding. But when this unity of the mode of cognition be viewed as though it depended upon the object of cognition; when we hold that which is merely *regulative* for *constitutive*, and persuade ourselves that we can extend our cognition by means of these ideas, far beyond all possible experience in a transcendent manner, notwithstanding that they merely serve to bring experience as nearly as possible to completeness, i.e., to limit its progress by nothing which cannot belong to experience—then this is a simple misunderstanding in judging the special destiny of our Reason and its principles, and a dialectic, partly confusing the use of Reason in experience, and partly making Reason to be at issue with itself.

Section Fifty-seven: Conclusion: On the determination of the boundary of pure Reason

After all the very clear proofs we have above given, it would be absurd for us to expect to cognise more in any object than what belongs to its possible experience, or to lay claim to the least knowledge of anything whatever which would determine its constitution in itself, unless we assume it to be an object of possible experience. For wherewith shall we effect this determination, inasmuch as time, space, and all the conceptions of the understanding, and still more the conceptions derived from empirical intuition or *perception* in the sense-world would neither have nor could have any other use than merely to make experience possible, and when if we leave out this condition from the pure conceptions of the understanding, they determine no object whatever, and have no significance anywhere.

But it would be a still greater absurdity for us not to admit things in themselves at all, or to wish to give out our experience for the only possible mode of the cognition of objects, in other words, our intuition in space and time for the only possible intuition, and our discursive understanding for the model of every possible understanding, thereby wishing principles of the possibility of experience to be held for the universal conditions of things in themselves.

Our principles, which limit the use of Reason to possible experience, might accordingly become *transcendent*, and the limits of our Reason be given out for the limits of things themselves, ... if a careful Critique of the boundaries of our Reason did not keep watch on its empirical use, and set a limit to its pretensions. Scepticism originally arose from metaphysics and its anarchical (*Polizeilosen*) dialectic. At first, to favour the empirical use of the understanding, it might well give out for nugatory and deceptive all that exceeded this; but gradually, as it became evident that the very same principles which we make use of in experience are *a priori*, and that they led unobserved, and as it seemed with the same right, still farther than experience reaches, a doubt began to be thrown on the principles of experience themselves. Now as to these there is no danger, for herein a healthy understanding will always assert its rights; but there arose a special confusion in science, which could not determine how far, and why only thus far and no farther, Reason is to be trusted; but this confusion can only be got rid of, and any future relapse prevented, by a formal limitation of the use of our Reason, derived from principles. It is true we cannot form any definite conception of what things in themselves, beyond all possible experience, may be. But we are nevertheless not free to withdraw ourselves wholly from the inquiry as to these; for experience never fully suffices for Reason; it thrusts us ever farther and farther back for the answer to this question, and leaves us as regards its complete solution dissatisfied; as any one can see from the dialectic of pure Reason, which on this account has its valid subjective ground. Who can tolerate [the circumstance] that by the nature of our soul we can attain to the clear consciousness of the subject, and to the conviction that its phenomena cannot be explained *materialistically* without asking what the soul really is, and if no empirical conception suffices [to explain] this, at least assuming a conception of Reason (of a simple immaterial essence) merely for the above purpose, although we cannot demonstrate its objective reality in any way? Who can satisfy himself in all cosmological questions, as to the size and duration of the world, of freedom or natural necessity, with mere empirical knowledge, since, begin it as we will, every answer given according to the fundamental laws of experience, gives birth to a new question, just as much requiring an answer, and thereby clearly exposing the inadequacy of all physical modes of explanation for the satisfaction of Reason? Finally, who in the face of the thoroughgoing contingency and dependence of all that he can assume and think according to empirical principles, does not see the impossibility of taking his stand on these, and does not feel himself necessarily impelled, in spite of all prohibition against losing himself in transcendent ideas, to seek rest and satisfaction beyond all conceptions he can verify by experience, in that of a Being, of whom the possibility of the idea in itself cannot indeed be apprehended, but which cannot be refuted, because it is a mere being [essence] of the understanding, and without which Reason must remain for ever unsatisfied.

Boundaries (with extended beings) always presuppose a space, met with, outside a certain definite place, and enclosing it. Limits do not require this, being mere negations affecting a quantity, so far as it has no absolute completeness. Our Reason, however, sees around it as it were a space for the cognition of things in themselves, although it can never have definite conceptions of them, being limited to phenomena.

As long as the cognition of Reason is homogeneous, no definite boundaries can be conceived therein. In mathematics and natural science the human Reason recognises indeed limits but no boundaries, i.e., [it recognises] that something exists outside itself, to which it can never attain, but not that it can itself be anywhere terminated in its inner progress. The extension of our views in mathematics and the possibility of new inventions reaches to infinity; and the same can be said of the discovery of new qualities in Nature, and of new forces and laws, through continued experience and the union of the same by Reason. But, at the same time, it cannot be mistaken that there are limits here, for mathematics refers only to *phenomena*, and what cannot be an object of sensuous intuition, such as the conceptions of metaphysics and morals, lies wholly outside its sphere, [in a region] to which it can never lead, and which does not at all require it. There is, then, a continuous progress and approach to these sciences, and as it were a point or line of contact. Natural science will never discover for us the inner [nature] of things, namely, that which is not phenomenon, but which can still serve as the highest ground of the explanation of phenomena. But it does not require this for its physical explanations; nay, if such were offered it from another source (e.g., the influence of immaterial beings), it ought to reject it, and on no account to bring it into the course of its explanations, but invariably to base these on that which pertains to experience as object of sense, and which can be brought into connection with our real perceptions, and empirical laws.

But metaphysics leads us to boundaries in the dialectical attempts of pure Reason (which are not commenced arbitrarily or rashly, but to which the nature of Reason itself urges us), and the transcendental ideas, as we cannot have intercourse with them, and as they will never allow themselves to be realised, serve, not only to show us the actual boundaries of the use of pure Reason, but also the way to determine them. And this is also the end and use of this natural disposition of our Reason, which has given birth to metaphysics as its pet child, whose generation, like that of everything else in the world, is not to be ascribed to chance, but to an original germ, wisely organised for great ends. For metaphysics is, perhaps more than any other science, rooted in us in its fundamental features by Nature herself, and can by no means be regarded as the product of a voluntary choice or as chance extension in the progress of experiences (from which it is wholly divided).

Reason, though all its conceptions and laws of the understanding are adequate in the sense-world, does not find any satisfaction for itself in them, for it is deprived of all hope of a complete solution by questions recurring *ad infinitum*. The transcendental ideas which have this completion for an object are such problems of Reason. It sees clearly that the sense-world cannot contain the completeness [required], and therefore just as little can those conceptions which serve simply to the understanding of the same, namely, space and time, and all that we have adduced under the name of pure conceptions of the understanding. The sense-world is nothing but a chain of phenomena, connected according to universal laws, and has therefore no subsistence for itself, being not properly the thing in itself, and only being necessarily referable to that which contains the ground of this phenomenon, to essences that cannot be cognised merely as phenomena but as things in themselves. Only in the cognition of these can Reason hope to see its desire for completeness in the progress from the conditioned to its conditions, once for all satisfied.

We have above (Sections Thirty-three and Thirty-four) assigned the limits of Reason in respect of all cognition of mere beings of thought. Now, as the transcendental ideas make the progress up to these necessary, and have thus led us, as it were, to the contact of the full space (of experience) with the void of which we know nothing (to the *noumena*), we can determine the boundaries of pure Reason. For in all boundaries there is something positive (for instance surface is the boundary of corporeal space and yet is itself a space; line, a space which is the boundary of the surface; point, the boundary of the line, but still [occupying] a position in space), while, on the other hand, limits contain mere negations. The limits assigned in the paragraph cited, are not sufficient, after we have found that something lies beyond them (although we can never know what this may be in itself). For the question is now, what is the attitude of our Reason in this connection of that which we know, with that which we do not know, and never can know? Here is a real connection of the known with a wholly unknown (and something that will always remain unknown), and even if in this the unknown should not become in the least [degree] more known–which is indeed not to be expected–the conception of this connection must be able, notwithstanding, to be determined and reduced to distinctness.

We are obliged, then, to think of an immaterial essence, an intelligible world, and a highest of all beings (mere *noumena*), because only in these, as things in themselves, does Reason meet with the completeness and satisfaction it can never hope for from the derivation of phenomena from their homogeneous ground, because they really refer to something distinct from the latter (and therefore wholly heterogeneous), inasmuch as phenomena always presuppose a thing in itself, and indicate this, [it matters not] whether we may know it more closely or not.

---

1. *If Ideas of Reason cannot be used constitutively–that is, they cannot be taken as showing us the nature of things as they are in themselves–what good are they? Pick one of the Ideas (God, the World, or the Soul), and try to explain how it might be worthwhile, before looking below to see what Kant himself says.*

But as we can never know these beings of the understanding as to what they may be in themselves, that is, determinately, but are obliged nevertheless to assume such in relation to the sense-world, and to connect them with it through Reason, we shall be at least able to cogitate this connection by means of such conceptions as express its relation to the sense-world. For if we cogitate the essence of the understanding, through nothing but pure conceptions of the understanding, we really cogitate thereby nothing definite, and our conception is consequently without meaning; if we cogitate it through qualities borrowed from the sense-world, then it is no longer an essence of the understanding, but is conceived as one of the phenomena, and belongs to the sense-world. We will take an instance from the conception of the Supreme Being.

The *deistic* conception is an entirely pure conception of Reason, which, however, only represents a thing containing all reality, without our being able to determine a single one of its [qualities], because for this an instance would have to be borrowed from the sense-world, in which case I should always have to do with an object of sense, and not with something completely heterogeneous, and which cannot be an object of sense. For instance, I attribute understanding to it; but I have no conception whatever of any understanding but of one like my own, namely, of one to which intuitions must be given through the senses, and which occupies itself with reducing these under rules of the unity of the consciousness. But then the elements of my conception would always lie in the phenomenon; yet I was necessitated by the inadequacy of the phenomena to pass beyond this, to the conception of a being in no way dependent on phenomena, or bound up with them, as conditions of its determination. If, however, I sever the understanding from the sensibility in order to have a pure understanding, nothing remains over but the mere form of thought without intuition, by means of which I can cognise nothing determinate as object. For this purpose I should have to conceive another understanding which intuited objects, but of which I have not the least conception, because the human understanding is discursive and can only cognise through universal conceptions. But I am also involved in contradiction if I attribute will to the Supreme Being. For I have this conception only in so far as I derive it from my inner experience, and thereby from the dependence of my satisfaction from objects whose existence we require; but at the foundation of this lies sensibility, which wholly contradicts the pure conception of the Supreme Being. The objections of Hume to Deism are weak, touching no more than the proofs, and never the proposition of the deistic assertion itself. But as regards Theism, which must be arrived at by a closer determination of our, there [viz., in Deism], merely transcendent conception of the Supreme Being, they are very strong, and, according as the conception is constructed, in certain (indeed in all ordinary) cases are irrefragable. Hume always insists, that through the mere conception of an original being, to whom we can attribute none but ontological predicates (eternity, omnipresence, omnipotence) we really think nothing definite, but that qualities expressing an object *in concreto* must be superadded. It is not enough to say it is Cause, but [we must also say] what is the nature of its causality, as, whether [it operates] through understanding and will; and at this point his attacks on the thing itself, namely, on Theism, commence, whereas before he had only stormed the grounds of proof of Deism, which does not carry any especial danger with it. His dangerous arguments refer entirely to anthropomorphism, which he holds to be inseparable from Theism, and to make it contradictory in itself; while if this be left out, [Theism itself] would also fall, and nothing would remain but a Deism wherewith nothing could be done, which could not avail us for anything, and could not serve as a foundation for religion and morals. If this inevitability of anthropomorphism were certain, the proofs of the existence of a Supreme Being might be what one liked, and all conceded, yet the conception of this Being would never be able to be determined by us, without involving ourselves in contradictions.

But if with the injunction to avoid all transcendent judgments of pure Reason, we connect the apparently contradictory injunction to proceed to conceptions lying outside the field of its immanent (empirical) use, we shall be aware that both may subsist together, but only on the exact *boundary* of all admissible use of Reason; for this belongs as much to the field of experience as to that of essences of thought, and we shall be taught thereby, at the same time, how the above remarkable ideas serve simply, for the determination of the boundaries of the human Reason; namely, on the one hand not to extend cognition of experience in an unbounded manner, so that nothing but mere world remains for us to cognise, and on the other hand not to pass beyond the boundaries of experience, or to seek to judge of things outside the latter as things in themselves.

But we keep to this boundary when we limit our judgment to the relation the world may have to a Being, whose conception itself lies outside all the cognition of which we are capable within the world. For in this case, we do not attribute to the Supreme Being any of the qualities *in themselves* by which we cogitate objects of experience, and thereby avoid the *dogmatic* anthropomorphism; but we apply the relations of the same to the world, and thereby allow ourselves a *symbolical* anthropomorphism, which as a matter of fact only concerns the language and not the object.

When I say we are obliged to regard the world *as though* it were the work of a supreme understanding and will, I do not really say more than—as a watch, a ship, a regiment is related to the artisan, shipbuilder or general, so is the sense-world (or all that which constitutes the foundation of this sum-total of phenomena) [related] to the unknown, that I cognise, not indeed according to what it is in itself, but according to what it is for me, namely, in respect of the world, of which I am a part. ...

Section Fifty-nine: Conclusion, Continued

[O]ur original proposition remains, which is the result of the whole Critique: "that our Reason can never teach more by its principles *a priori* than simply objects of possible experience, and even of these no more than what can be cognised in experience." But this limitation does not prevent it from leading us to the objective *boundary* of experience, namely, the reference to something which is not itself object of experience, but is nevertheless the highest ground of all experience, without however teaching us anything respecting this in itself, but only with reference to its [viz., Reason's] own complete use as directed to its highest end, within the field of possible experience. But this is also all the use that can be reasonably expected or even wished, as concerns it, and with this we have cause to be content.

Section Sixty: Conclusion, Continued

Thus we have fully exhibited metaphysics according to its subjective necessity, as it is really given *in the natural disposition* of the human Reason, and indeed in what constitutes its essential purpose. We have found in the course of this investigation, that such a *merely natural* use of such a disposition of our Reason involves us in extravagant dialectical conclusions, partly apparently, and partly really, conflicting [with one another], if no discipline bridles it and keeps it within limits, which is only possible by means of scientific criticism. And, in addition, [we have found] this fallacious metaphysics to be dispensable to the promotion of the knowledge of Nature, and even prejudicial to it. It always remains, notwithstanding, a task worthy of research, to find out the *natural ends* aimed at by this disposition in our Reason to transcendent conceptions, since everything in Nature must have been originally designed for some useful purpose.

Such an investigation is here out of place; I confess, moreover, that all I here say respecting the primary ends of Nature is only conjecture, but which may be permitted me in this case, as the question does not concern the objective validity of metaphysical judgments, but refers merely to the natural disposition to the latter, and thus lies outside the system of metaphysics, in that of anthropology.

When I compare all transcendental ideas whose content constitutes the special problem of the natural, pure Reason, compelling it to leave the mere contemplation of Nature and to pass beyond all possible experience, and in this endeavour to produce the thing (be it knowledge or nonsense) called metaphysics, I believe myself to have discovered that this natural disposition is intended to free our conceptions from the chains of experience and the limits of the mere contemplation of Nature, in so far that it may at least see a field opened before it, containing mere objects for pure Reason, which cannot be arrived at by any sensibility. The purpose is not, indeed, to occupy ourselves speculatively with these objects, (because we can find no firm ground for our feet), but because practical principles, without finding such a space before them for their necessary expectation and hope, could not expand themselves to the universality, Reason indispensably requires, from a moral point of view.

Now, I find that the *psychological* idea, however little may be the insight I obtain by its means into the pure nature of the human soul, which is raised above all conceptions of experience, at least sufficiently shows me the inadequacy of the latter, and thereby preserves me from materialism as being a psychological conception of no avail for the explanation of Nature, and besides, as narrowing Reason in its practical aspect. In the same way the *cosmological* ideas, by the obvious inadequacy of all possible knowledge of Nature to satisfy Reason in its justifiable inquiries, serve to keep us from the Naturalism which proclaims Nature for self-sufficing. Finally, as all natural necessity in the sense-world is invariably conditioned, inasmuch as it always presupposes dependence of things on one another, and, as unconditioned necessity must be sought for in the unity of a Cause separate from the sense-world, (but the causality of which, if it were mere Nature, could yet never render comprehensible the existence of the contingent as its consequence;) [this being so,] Reason frees itself by means of the *theological idea* from fatalism, as well from that of a blind natural necessity in the coherence of Nature, without a first principle, as in the causality of this principle itself, and leads to the conception of a cause through freedom, in other words, a supreme intelligence. Thus the transcendental ideas serve, if not to instruct us positively, at least to do away with the audacious assertions of *materialism*, *naturalism*, and *fatalism*, which narrow the field of Reason, and thereby to procure a place for moral ideas outside the region of speculation; and this, as it seems to me, will in some measure explain the above natural disposition.

The practical utility a merely speculative science may have, lies outside the boundaries of this science, and hence can be merely viewed as a scholium, and, like all scholia, not as forming a part of the science itself. At the same time, this reference lies at least within the boundaries of philosophy, especially of that which draws from the sources of pure Reason, where the speculative use of Reason in metaphysics must have a necessary unity with its practical use in morals. Hence the unavoidable dialectic of pure Reason in metaphysics must be considered as natural disposition–not merely as an illusion requiring to be resolved, but as a natural institution, as concerns its end–deserving, if possible, to be explained, although this task, being supererogatory, cannot in justice be claimed of metaphysics proper. ...

And thus I conclude the analytical solution of the problem I had myself proposed–*How is metaphysics at all possible?* having proceeded from that in which its use is really given, at least in its consequences, to the grounds of its possibility.

1. *Kant insists on the thinkability—though not on the actuality—of God, of the soul, and of causality through freedom. Is he entitled to this? Think back to the limitations Kant imposed on the use of the Categories earlier in the* Prolegomena.

Solution of the General Problem of the *Prolegomena*: How is Metaphysics Possible as Science?

Metaphysics, as a natural disposition of Reason, is real, but it is also, in itself, dialectical and deceptive (as was proved in the analytical solution of the third main problem). Hence to attempt to draw our principles from it, and in their employment to follow this natural but none the less fallacious illusion, can never produce science, but only an empty dialectical art, in which one school may indeed outdo the other, but none can ever attain a justifiable and lasting success. In order that, as science, it may lay claim not merely to deceptive persuasion, but to insight and conviction, a Critique of Reason must exhibit in a complete system the whole stock of conceptions *a priori*, arranged according to their different sources—the Sensibility, the Understanding, and Reason; it must present a complete table of these conceptions, together with their analysis and all that can be deduced from them, but more especially the possibility of synthetic knowledge *a priori* by means of their deduction, the principles of its use, and finally, its boundaries. Thus criticism contains, and it alone contains, the whole plan well tested and approved, indeed all the means whereby metaphysics may be perfected as a science; by other ways and means this is impossible. The question now is not, however, how this business is possible, but only how we are to set about it; how good heads are to be turned from their previous mistaken and fruitless path to a non-deceptive treatment, and how such a combination may be best directed towards the common end.

This much is certain: he who has once tried criticism will be sickened for ever of all the dogmatic trash he was compelled to content himself with before, because his Reason, requiring something, could find nothing better for its occupation. Criticism stands to the ordinary school-metaphysics exactly in the same relation as *chemistry* to *alchemy*, or as *astronomy* to fortune-telling *astrology*. I guarantee that no one who has comprehended and thought out the conclusions of criticism, even in these Prolegomena, will ever return to the old sophistical pseudo-science. He will rather look forward with a kind of pleasure to a metaphysics, certainly now within his power, which requires no more preparatory discoveries, and which alone can procure for Reason permanent satisfaction. For this is an advantage upon which metaphysics alone can reckon with confidence, among all possible sciences; namely, that it can be brought to completion and to a durable position, as it cannot change any further, nor is it susceptible of any increase through new discoveries. Since Reason does not here find the sources of its knowledge in objects and in their intuition (which cannot teach it anything), but in itself; so that when the principles of its possibility are presented completely, and without any misunderstanding, nothing remains for pure Reason to know *a priori*, or even with justice to ask. The certain prospect of so definite and perfect a knowledge has a special attraction about it, even if all its uses (of which I shall hereafter speak) be set aside.

All false art, all empty wisdom, lasts its time; but it destroys itself in the end, and its highest cultivation is at the same time the moment of its decline. That as regards metaphysics this time has now come, is proved by the state to which it has declined among all cultivated nations, notwithstanding the zeal with which every other kind of science is being worked out. The old arrangement of the university studies preserves its outlines still, a single academy of sciences bestirs itself now and then, by holding out prizes to induce another attempt to be made therein; but it is no longer counted among fundamental sciences, and any one may judge for himself how an intellectually-gifted man, to whom the term great metaphysician were applied, would take this well-meant, but scarcely by any one, coveted, compliment.

But although the period of the decline of all dogmatic metaphysics is undoubtedly come, there are many things wanting to enable us to say that the time of its re-birth by means of a thorough and complete Critique of Reason, has already appeared. All transitional phases from one tendency to its opposite pass through the state of indifference, and this moment is the most dangerous for an author, but, as it seems to me, the most favourable for the science. For when, through the complete dissolution of previous combinations, party spirit is extinguished, men's minds are in the best mood for listening gradually to proposals for a combination on another plan. If I say that I hope that these *Prolegomena* will perhaps make research in the field of criticism more active, and will offer to the general spirit of philosophy, which seems to be wanting in nourishment on its speculative side, a new and very promising field for its occupation, I can already foresee that every one who has trodden unwillingly and with vexation the thorny way I have led him in the Critique, will ask me on what I ground this hope. I answer—*on the irresistible law of necessity.*

That the spirit of man will ever wholly give up metaphysical investigations is just as little to be expected, as that in order not always to be breathing bad air we should stop breathing altogether. Metaphysics will always exist in the world then, and what is more, [exist] with every one, but more especially with reflecting men, who in default of a public standard will each fashion it in his own way. Now, what has hitherto been termed metaphysics, can satisfy no acute mind; but to renounce it entirely is impossible; hence a Critique of pure Reason itself must be at last *attempted*, and when obtained must be *investigated* and subjected to a universal test, because otherwise there are no means of relieving this pressing requirement, which means something more than mere thirst for knowledge. ...

Should any one feel himself offended by what is here said, he can very easily refute the accusation if he will only adduce a single synthetic proposition belonging to metaphysics which admits of being demonstrated in a dogmatic manner *a priori*; for only when he has achieved this shall I allow that he has really advanced the science, even though the proposition in question may be sufficiently confirmed by common experience. No demand can be more moderate, and more fair, and in the event (unquestionably certain) of non-accomplishment, no statement can be juster than that metaphysics as science has not hitherto existed at all.

I must only forbid two things, in case the challenge be accepted: first, the apparatus of *probability* and conjecture, which just as ill becomes metaphysics as geometry; and secondly, a decision by means of the magic wand of so-called *sound common sense*, which every one does not wave, but which regulates itself according to personal characteristics. For *as regards the first*, nothing can be more absurd than in a system of metaphysics, a philosophy of pure Reason, to attempt to base judgments on probability and conjecture. All that can be known *a priori* is thereby given out as apodictically certain, and must be proved as such. A geometry or arithmetic might just as well be attempted to be founded on conjectures; (for as concerns the *calculus probabilium* of the latter, it does not contain probable but perfectly certain judgments, on the degree of possibility in certain cases, under given similar conditions, which in the sum of all possible cases must infallibly follow in accordance with the rule—although in respect of any single instance this is not sufficiently determined). Even in empirical natural science conjectures (by means of induction and analogy) can only be permitted, in such a manner that at least the possibility of what I assume must be quite certain.

With the *appeal to sound common sense* we are still worse off, if possible, when we have to do with conceptions and principles, not so far as they are valid in respect of experience, but when they would be given out as valid outside the conditions of experience. For what is sound sense? It is the *common understanding* rightly used. And what is the common understanding? It is the faculty of the cognition and employment of rules *in concreto* in contradistinction to the *speculative understanding*, which is a faculty for the cognition of rules *in abstracto*. Thus, the common understanding will hardly comprehend the rule that all which happens is determined by means of its cause, and never be able to view this rule in its universal bearing. Hence it requires an example from experience, and when it hears that it points to nothing else but what it had always thought, when a window-pane was broken or a household utensil lost, it understands the axiom and admits it. Common understanding has no farther use, then, than to be able to see its rules confirmed in experience (although they really pertain to it *a priori*), and therefore to regard them *a priori* and independently of experience belongs to the speculative understanding, and lies wholly outside the horizon of the common understanding. But metaphysics is exclusively occupied with the latter kind of knowledge, and it is certainly a bad sign of a sound understanding to appeal to a protector, having no right of judgment here, and which one otherwise only looks at askance, except when one sees oneself pressed, and does not know how to advise or help oneself in a speculation.

A usual resource employed by these false friends of the common human understanding (who sometimes honour it highly, though they generally despise it) is to say: there must be some propositions, immediately certain, and of which one not only requires to give no proof, but no account whatever, as otherwise we should never come to an end of the grounds of our judgments; but in proof of this assertion they can never bring forward anything undoubted, and which they can attribute immediately to the common human understanding (except the axiom of contradiction, which is inadequate to demonstrate the truth of synthetic judgments) and mathematical propositions; as, for instance, that twice two make four, that between two points there is only one straight line, &c. But these are judgments from which those of metaphysics are totally distinct. For in mathematics I can make (construct) all this by my own thinking, representing it to myself as possible through a conception; I gradually add to the one two, the other two, and myself make the number four; or drawing in thought all sorts of lines from one point to another, can only draw one that is similar in all its parts, equal no less than unequal. But I cannot with my whole power of thought bring out from the conception of one thing the conception of something else, the existence of which is necessarily connected with the first, but must call experience to my aid; and although my understanding *a priori* offers me such a conception, [viz.] causality (though only in reference to possible experience), I cannot present it *a priori* in intuition, like the conceptions of mathematics, and thus exhibit its possibility *a priori*, but the conception together with the principles of its use, if it is to be valid *a priori* (as is required in metaphysics), demands a demonstration and deduction of its possibility, since otherwise we do not know how far it is valid, and whether it can only be used in experience or [may be used] outside [experience]. Hence, in metaphysics as a speculative science of pure Reason, we can never appeal to the common human understanding, but when we are obliged to leave it, and to renounce all pure speculative cognition, which must be always a branch of knowledge, and therefore under certain circumstances metaphysics itself and its teaching, a reasonable faith will be found alone possible, and indeed sufficient to our needs, and perhaps even better for us than knowledge itself. Then the aspect of the matter is quite altered. Metaphysics must be a science, not alone as a whole, but in all its parts, else it is nothing; because in speculation of pure Reason, nothing has a standing but universal notions. But, apart from this, probability and healthy human understanding, have their useful and justifiable employment, but on their own special principles, whose validity always depends on their relation to the practical.

It is this which I hold myself justified in demanding of a system of metaphysics, as science.

1. The first *Critique* was issued in two editions, 1781 and 1787. Standard translations combine the two editions, giving 'A' for pages in the first edition, and 'B' for those in the second, separated by a '/' when the two editions overlap. The present selection is A 23/B 38–A 25/B 40.↩
2. A189/B233–A195/B240↩
3. B167–8↩
4. B406–B413↩